MACHINE INTELLIGENCE 9

Machine Expertise and the Human Interface

Machine Intelligence
Editor-in-Chief. Donald Michie

Volumes 1 – 7 are published by
Edinburgh University Press
and in the United States by
Halsted Press (a subsidiary of John Wiley & Sons, Inc.)

Volumes 8 – 9 are published by
Ellis Horwood Ltd., Publishers, Chichester
and in the United States by
Halsted Press (a subsidiary of John Wiley & Sons, Inc.)

MACHINE INTELLIGENCE 9

edited by

J. E. HAYES
Research Associate
University of Edinburgh

DONALD MICHIE
Professor of Machine Intelligence
University of Edinburgh

and

L. I. MIKULICH
Artificial Intelligence Council of
the USSR Academy of Sciences

ELLIS HORWOOD LIMITED
Publishers Chichester

Halsted Press: a division of
JOHN WILEY & SONS
New York - Chichester - Brisbane - Toronto

First published in 1979 by

ELLIS HORWOOD LIMITED

Market Cross House, Cooper Street, Chichester, West Sussex, PO19 1EB, England

The publisher's colophon is reproduced from James Gillison's drawing of the ancient Market Cross, Chichester

Distributors:

Australia, New Zealand, South-east Asia:
Jacaranda-Wiley Ltd., Jacaranda Press,
JOHN WILEY & SONS INC.,
G.P.O. Box 859, Brisbane, Queensland 40001, Australia.

Canada:
JOHN WILEY & SONS CANADA LIMITED
22 Worcester Road, Rexdale, Ontario, Canada.

Europe, Africa:
JOHN WILEY & SONS LIMITED
Baffins Lane, Chichester, West Sussex, England.

North and South America and the rest of the world:
HALSTED PRESS, a division of
JOHN WILEY & SONS
605 Third Avenue, New York, N.Y. 10016, U.S.A.

British Library Cataloguing in Publication Data

Machine intelligence. –
(Ellis Horwood series in computers and their applications).
9: Machine expertise and the human interface
1. Artificial intelligence
I. Hayes, Jean Elizabeth II. Michie, Donald III. Mikulich, L. I.
001.53'5 Q335 79-40785

ISBN 0-85312-112-5 (Ellis Horwood Ltd., Publishers)
ISBN 0-470-26714-3 (Halsted Press)

Typeset in Press Roman by Ellis Horwood Ltd.
Printed in Great Britain by Biddles of Guildford

PREFACE

One intelligent approach to prefaces – is to have the empty preface. The well prepared reader will form a good idea of the technical programme just from looking at the table of contents; together with the names of the authors, this gives him a good idea of what happened at the symposium. I could try to assess the talks and direct the reader's attention to the more interesting communications. But I fear this would be too subjective and unfair to the remaining authors – all of them equally represented in this book.

However, recalling that Spring week in Repino, a resort 20 kilometres from Leningrad on the Bay of Finland and unpopulated at that time of year, I have come to the definite conclusion that the scientific meeting was in its own way unique. What circumstances gave this symposium its special character?

First, it was not a regular IJCAI-type conference for which there is advance preparation, taking into account previous conferences of the series and knowing that others will follow. The technical programme was more spontaneous than preplanned; there was neither selection of papers nor restrictions on the subjects. This element of improvisation gave the meeting a more free and varied character. The fresh audience and the absence of prehistory encouraged the authors not to restrict themselves to presenting their results, but to pay more attention to analysing the premises and motivation of their research. This gave some of the presentations greater depth and scope, much to the satisfaction of the audience.

Of course, it was important that the conference was an occasion for a "meeting of East and West". The mass media often play up such meetings, but I must admit that this meeting did not provide an occasion for such dramatizations. At the same time, the direct and friendly contacts between scientists with common interests, recognizing their common problems and diverse approaches to their solution – all that made the conference a kind of "festival of thought", greatly amplifying the creative motivation of the participants.

On the other hand, it did not turn out that the forum character made the symposium superficial. Not at all. It can be said that the theme of the conference was "AI at work", and this is readily confirmed by the programme. At the same time, this obvious desire to do "real work" in artificial intelligence forced us to restate the question: Has there emerged a stable paradigm for research and development in AI? Is there a single paradigm or are these several of them – or is it possible to do successful work in AI without conscious use of any particular paradigm? Even though many authorities in the field were present, no-one tried to give a final answer to these questions. However, the participants at the final panel discussion unanimously agreed that AI had got its "second wind" in recent years and was again on the upswing.

It seems reasonable to conclude that the business-like programme combined with the atmosphere of enthusiastic exchange of ideas thoroughly justifies optimistic expectations.

ANDREI ERSHOV
December 1978

CONTENTS

PERCEPTION AND WORLD MODELS

ROBOT AND CONTROL SYSTEMS

MACHINE ANALYSIS OF CHESS

KNOWLEDGE ENGINEERING

NATURAL LANGUAGE

This volume in the Machine Intelligence series is based on the Ninth International Machine Intelligence Workshop held at Repino, near Leningrad, in April, 1977.

ABSTRACT MODELS FOR COMPUTATION

1

Relational Programming

R. J. Popplestone
Department of Artificial Intelligence
University of Edinburgh, UK

1. INTRODUCTION

A programming language needs simple and well defined semantics. The two favoured theoretical bases for languages have been lambda calculus as advocated by Landin and others, and predicate calculus as advocated by Kowalski (see Landin (1966) and Kowalski (1973)). In this paper I adopt an approach based on predicate calculus, but in a manner that differs from the existing PROLOG language (Warren 1975 and Battani & Meloni 1973) in that I adopt a "forward inference" approach – inferring conclusions from premises, rather than the "backward inference" approach of PROLOG, which starts with a desired conclusion and tries to find ways of inferring it. This difference is reflected in the internal structure of the associated implementations, that of PROLOG being a "backtrack search" kind of implementation, while the most obvious implementation of the system proposed here involves a kind of mass operation on tables of data, reminiscent of APL (Iverson 1962) but in fact identical in many respects with the work of Codd (Codd 1970) on relational data bases. Indeed, from one perspective this paper can be seen as an extension of Codd's work into the realm of general purpose computing.

As in the case of PROLOG it is necessary for the user of the relational programming system to make statements which are not associated with the logical structure of the problem, but reflect the need to control the computation. In PROLOG these are effected by the use of extra-logical control primitives, but in our system control is exercised by the introduction of predicates for that purpose, which have exactly the same semantics as the predicates relevant to the logical structure of the problem.

In later sections I deal with the problem of introducing equality into the system, in a way that reflects the normal mathematical usage of equality. In this I am attempting something that programming systems normally do not try, although the ABSYS system (Elcock et. al. 1971) was built with equality as a central concept, and the unification algorithms of PROLOG provide a limited treatment.

When we come to consider the question of implementation, the relational system seems to open a number of avenues of possibility, and it certainly raises a number of problems. The most interesting developments compared with other Artificial Intelligence languages are the possibility of making efficient use of the address space of a modest size computer, or of handling much bigger problems on a larger machine, and of exploiting parallelism. The major problem raised by the system is that the most natural implementation involves repeating computations unnecessarily.

2. AN EXAMPLE

Figure 1A shows a simple "blocks world" in which we have five blocks denoted by the numbers 1, 2, 3, 4, 5. In this example we use numbers to denote the entities in the world as a matter of convenience, since we are going to express the relations holding between entities in the form of tables, and numbers are the most convenient symbols to use. In later sections of the paper we shall use the numbers "as numbers", that is as entities that can be operated on by the normal functions of arithmetic, and will want to distinguish them from non-numeric entities like blocks.

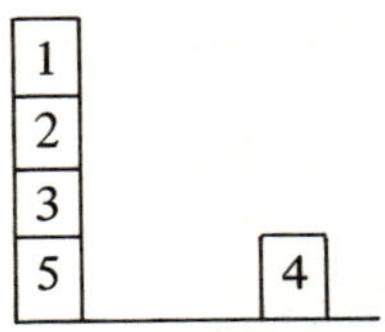

Fig. 1A – A simple "blocks world".

ON	
1	2
2	3
3	5

Fig. 1B – The table for the ON relation.

Suppose that the state of this world is specified by stating which blocks are on others. This relationship, which we shall call ON, can be expressed in tabular form as in Fig. 1B. This can be regarded as an association of the name ON, which we shall call a predicate name, or just a predicate, with a binary relation, that is the set of pairs {(1,2) (2,3) (3,5)}. Now suppose we want to define a new relation, called ABOVE, in terms of ON. This can be done by using the following two clauses

$$\mathrm{ON}\,(X,Y) \Rightarrow \mathrm{ABOVE}(X,Y) \qquad \text{(C1)}$$
$$\mathrm{ON}\,(X,Y)\ \&\ \mathrm{ABOVE}(Y,Z) \Rightarrow \mathrm{ABOVE}(X,Z) \qquad \text{(C2)}$$

That is if *X* is ON *Y*, then *X* is ABOVE *Y*, and if *X* is ON *Y*, and *Y* is ABOVE *Z*, then *X* is ABOVE *Z*.

It is possible to find a value for ABOVE, while keeping the same value for ON, by applying a process illustrated in Fig. 2. In this process we cycle round the clauses C1 and C2 and at each stage we form a table whose columns are labelled with the names of the variables of the clause currently being examined, and whose rows tabulate the possible values of the variables of the left side of each clause. We then use this table to produce new rows to be added into the table which is the current value of ABOVE. In this way we create a sequence *r*1 . . . . *r*4 of tables which specify possible approximations to the ABOVE relationship. If we carry on with the process beyond *r*4 no new rows are added to in producing *r*5 . . . . , and we say we have reached a fixed point. At this point ON = {(1,2) (2,3) (3,5)} and ABOVE = {(1,2) (1,3) (1,5) (2,3) (2,5) (3,5)} and with these values (1) and (2) are satisfied according to the usual laws of logic.

In a more general case, where the values of a number of predicates are being built up, each step in the approximation will be represented by a sequence of tables, each table specifying a possible value for one of the predicates, and in

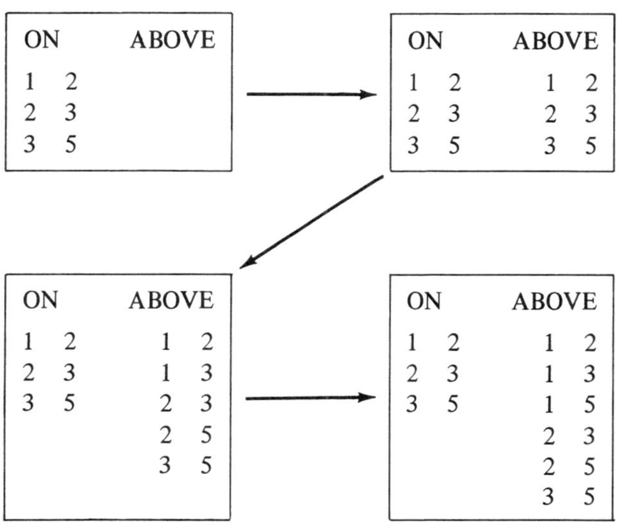

Fig. 2 – Computing the ABOVE relation.

the next two sections we shall give a formal definition of the process illustrated by the example above, and prove that it gives rise to a sequence of relations which form an interpretation of a given set of logic clauses.

3. A FORMAL SPECIFICATION OF THE SYSTEM

Let us now develop a precise mathematical specification of systems of the type outlined above.

3.1 The basic sets

We need a set E of entities, which form the universe of discourse. Thus in the above example $E = \{1, 2, 3, 4, 5\}$.

We also need a set P of "predicate symbols" and a set V of "variable symbols". Thus in our example $P = \{$"ON", "ABOVE"$\}$, and $V = \{$"X", "Y", "Z"$\}$, where the quotes denote that the symbol itself is being referred to. We insist that E and V are disjoint sets.

3.2 Finite sequences

For many purposes we will need to make use of finite sequences of elements, usually of entities and variables. We shall use bold lower case letters to denote sequences. If **a** is a sequence, then a_k denotes the kth element of **a**. (a_k) is occasionally used to denote the sequence **a**. By $|\mathbf{a}|$ we mean the set $\{\mathrm{a}_k\}$ of elements of the sequence **a**. The length of a sequence **a**; denoted by length (**a**) is the number of elements in it (counting repetitions). It is convenient to use a sequence without repetitions as a way of referring to the members of another sequence of the same length. Let **v** be a sequence without repeated members, and let **a** be a sequence. Let ν_k be a member of $|\mathbf{v}|$. Then we use the notation

$$\nu_k \text{ of } \mathbf{a} \text{ wrt } \mathbf{v} = \mathrm{a}_k \quad .$$

For example, let $\mathbf{v} = (\text{"}X\text{"}, \text{"}Y\text{"})$ then

$$\text{"}Y\text{" of } (5,6) \text{ wrt } (\text{"}X\text{"}, \text{"}Y\text{"}) = 6 \quad ,$$

and

$$\text{"}Y\text{" of } (5,7) \text{ wrt } (\text{"}Y\text{"}, \text{"}X\text{"}) = 5 \quad .$$

The empty sequence, which we shall denote by (), is a sequence of no elements. If **x** is a sequence, and x is an element, then conseq(x,**x**) = **t**, where $t_1 = x$, and $t_k = x_{k-1}$. We shall use a form of structural induction (Burstall 1969) on sequences, whereby to prove a result for all sequences, it is sufficient to prove it for the empty sequence, and to prove that if a result holds for a sequence **x**, then it holds for conseq(x,**x**).

We will often need to extend a mapping defined on elements to apply to a sequence. If σ is a mapping and **x** is a sequence then $\sigma(\mathbf{x}) = (\sigma(x_j))$.

3.3 Horn clauses

The logical sentences which we shall use will consist of conjunctions of Horn clauses. A Horn clause has the form L_1 & L_2 & ...... L_n => L where the L_j and L are literals, that is they simply take the form of a predicate applied to arguments. More formally, a clause is a pair $(\mathbf{L},L')$ consisting of a sequence $\mathbf{L}$ of literals which we shall call the negative literals of the clause, and a literal L' which we shall call the positive literal of the clause. Each literal itself is a pair $(p,\mathbf{a})$ where p is a predicate in P, and $\mathbf{a}$ is a sequence of "arguments" drawn from $V \cup E$.

3.3.1 *A restriction on clauses*

An additional constraint which we place on the clauses allowed in our system is that if $(\mathbf{L}, L')$ is a clause then all variables occurring in L' must occur in some L in $|\mathbf{L}|$.

Thus from our example, ("ON"("X", "X")), and ("ON",("X",1)) are literals, as well as ("ON",("X", "Y")). In the sequel, we shall use the normal notation (for example ON(X,Y)) when referring to particular literals of the object language. We are not of course restricted to binary predicates, for example one might have BETWEEN, which is ternary, as in BETWEEN(X,Y,Z). However, we suppose that with each predicate symbol p there is associated a positive integer arity(p) which specifies the length of any argument sequence which is associated with it in forming a literal.

3.4 Relations

Our clauses will be interpreted in terms of relations on E. By a k-ary relation on E we mean a subset r of the cartesian product E^k. We denote the set of all k-ary relations on E by Rel(E,k) which is of course the power set of E^k. Thus in our example the tables, without column headings, represent relations, with the rows being the "tuples" taken from E^k.

We will interpret a sequence of clauses $\mathbf{C}$ by associating a relation with each predicate occurring in $\mathbf{C}$. In fact, let $\mathbf{p}$ be a sequence, without repetitions of the predicates of $\mathbf{C}$. Then a sequence of relations $\mathbf{r}$, with length $(\mathbf{r})$ = length $(\mathbf{p})$ can be considered as a possible interpretation if arity (r_k) = arity (p_k) $1 \leqslant k \leqslant$ length $(\mathbf{p})$. We denote the set of all such relation sequences by $\mathcal{R}$ and call it the domain of interpretation of $\mathbf{C}$. $\mathcal{R}$ is then the cartesian product

$$\mathcal{R} = \Pi_k \text{ Rel}(E, \text{arity } (p_k)) \tag{3.4.1}$$

In our example, $\mathbf{C}$ can be the sequence (C1, C2) and $\mathbf{p}$ the sequence ("ON", "ABOVE").

$\mathcal{R}$ is the product Rel$(E,2)$ $\times$ Rel$(E,2)$, so that if $(r1,r2)$ in $\mathcal{R}$ then $r1$ is a possible value for ON, and $r2$ is a possible value for ABOVE.

Now, for any k, Rel(E,k) is a complete lattice under the normal set theory operations of union and intersection. It follows that $\mathcal{R}$ is also a complete lattice, since it is the direct product of such lattices. We need to make use of the following "fix point" theorem about completing lattices.

3.4.2 *Theorem*

If $\mathcal{L}$ is a complete lattice, and $\theta : \mathcal{L} \to \mathcal{L}$ has the property that $\theta(1) \geqslant 1$, for each 1 in $\mathcal{L}$, then there is an element u in $\mathcal{L}$ with the property that $\theta(u) = u$.

Proof

Let $\nu = \cup\{1 | \text{theta}(1) > 1\}$. Then either $\theta(\nu) = \nu$, in which case the required result holds, or $\theta(\nu) > \nu$, (where $\cup$ denotes the lattice operation). Let us suppose that $\theta(\nu) > \nu$. Then either $\theta(\theta\ (\nu)) = \theta(\nu)$, in which case $\theta(\nu)$ is the required "fixed point" or $\theta(\ \theta(\nu)) > (\nu)$. But $\nu = \cup\{1 | \theta(1) > 1\}$, and $\theta(\nu) > \nu$, a contradiction.

That $\theta(\nu)$ is in fact sometimes the fixed point can be shown by the following example. Let $\mathcal{L}$ = [0,1] union {2}, with the standard ordering on the reals. Let $\theta(x) = x + (1-x)2$, $x < 1$, $\theta(x) = 2$ otherwise. Then $\nu = 1$ in the above proof, but $\theta(\nu) = 2$ is the fixed point.

We shall also have need of a more constructive form of the fixed point theorem.

3.4.3 *Theorem*

Let $\mathcal{L}$ be a complete lattice. Let $\theta : \mathcal{L} \to \mathcal{L}$ have the properties (i) $\theta(1) \geqslant 1$, and (ii) If $\{1_\alpha\} \subset \mathcal{L}$ is an ascending chain of members of $\mathcal{L}$, then $\theta(\cup\{1_\alpha\}) = \cup\{\theta(1_\alpha)\}$. Let 1_α be any element of $\mathcal{L}$. Then if $1_\alpha = \bigcup_i \theta^i(1_\alpha)$, $\theta(1_\alpha) = 1_\alpha$.

Proof

$\theta(1_\alpha) = \theta(\bigcup_{i \geqslant 0} \theta^i(1_\alpha)) = \bigcup_{i>0} \theta(1_\alpha) = \bigcup_{i \geqslant 0} \theta^i(1_\alpha)$ since $\theta^i(1_\alpha) \geqslant \theta^0(1_\alpha) = 1_\alpha$.

In the theory of computation, it is customary to refer to a function satisfying the preconditions of (3.4.3) as being continuous.

3.5 Labelled relations

To simplify some of the definitions we shall make later, and to clarify the processes involved, we need to introduce the notion of a labelled relation, which is a pair, (**v**,r) where **v** is a sequence of variables without repetition, and r is a relation having the property that arity(r) = length (**v**). The main benefit of this device is to be found in the definitions of attach, detach, and join, to be found below. In Fig. 2, the labelled relations are represented by tables with column labels, the row of column labels corresponding to the sequence of variables. In the first development of the theory we used unlabelled relations, which necessitated permuting columns in a way that was difficult to follow. It should be noted that the relational data base work of Codd and others makes use of labelled relations, but the necessity of attaching and detaching labels seems not to be generally recognised.

We shall denote labelled relations by q, q', q'', etc. In particular, $q_0 = ((), \{()\})$ will be called the null labelled relation.

If $\{q_\alpha\} = \{(\mathbf{v}, r_\alpha)\}$ is a family of labelled relations with the same label sequence, then we write $\cup_\alpha q_\alpha$ for $(\mathbf{v}, \underset{\alpha}{\cup} r_\alpha)$. We will not require a union operation over labelled relations having different $\mathbf{v}$'s.

3.6 The rho function

In this section we define a function ρ, which has the property that if $\mathbf{C}$ is a sequence of clauses: $\rho(\mathbf{C}) : \mathcal{R} \to \mathcal{R}$, and $\rho(\mathbf{C})$ satisfies the conditions specified for θ in (3.4.2) and (3.4.3). In Sec. 4 we shall show that any fixed point of $\rho(\mathbf{C})$ is an interpretation of $\mathbf{C}$.

ρ is defined for clause sequences by building up a definition via predicates, literals, and literal-sequences and clauses. The definition involves a number of auxiliary functions which we shall define, namely inject, project, attach, detach, and join (this last is written $*$). Let $\mathbf{C}$ be a clause sequence, $C = (\mathbf{L}, (p', \mathbf{a}'))$ be a clause, where $\mathbf{L}$ is a literal sequence. Let $L = (p, \mathbf{a})$ be a literal. Then

$$\rho(\,(\mathrm{C})\,) = \rho\,(\mathrm{C}) \qquad \rho 1$$
$$\rho(\mathrm{consseq}(\mathrm{C}, \mathbf{C})) = \rho\,(\mathrm{C}) \circ \rho\,(\mathbf{C}) \qquad \rho 2$$
$$\rho(\,(\mathbf{L}, (p', \mathbf{a}')\,)(\mathbf{r}) = \mathbf{r} \cup \mathrm{inject}\,(p', \mathbf{p})(\mathrm{detach}(\mathbf{a}, \rho'(\mathbf{L})(\mathbf{r}))) \qquad \rho 3$$
$$\rho'((\,))(\mathbf{r}) = q_0 \qquad \rho 4$$
$$\rho'(\mathrm{consseq}((L\,, \mathbf{L}))(\mathbf{r}) = \rho(L)(\mathbf{r}) * \rho'(\mathbf{L})(\mathbf{r}) \qquad \rho 5$$
$$\rho((p, \mathbf{a}))(\mathbf{r}) = \mathrm{attach}\,(\mathbf{a}, \rho(p)(\mathbf{r})) \qquad \rho 6$$
$$\rho(p)(\mathbf{r}) = \mathrm{project}\,(p, \mathbf{p})(\mathbf{r}) \qquad \rho 7$$

where $\circ$ is the functional composition operation defined by $(f \circ g)(x) = g(f(x))$.

Before we go on to complete the formal details of the definition of ρ, let us consider its meaning in our example. $\rho(\mathrm{C}1)$ is a function which takes a pair, $(r1, r2)$, where $r1$ is a possible value for the ON relation, and $r2$ is a possible value for the ABOVE relation, and produces $(r1', r2')$, which are again possible values for ON, and ABOVE respectively, according to the procedure sketched out in Sect. 2. Note that the value of ON will not in fact change, since it does not occur positively in any clause, nevertheless it is convenient to include it in the considerations.

3.7 The auxiliary functions

Returning to the definition of $\rho 1$–$\rho 7$, the inject and project mappings simply serve to access components of members of the cartesian product, $\mathcal{R}$. In fact

$$\mathrm{inject}(p, \mathbf{p})(r) = (r_k) \text{ where } r_k = r \text{ if } p_k = p, \text{ and } r_k = \emptyset \text{ otherwise.} \qquad \rho 8$$
$$\mathrm{project}(p, \mathbf{p})(\mathbf{r}) = p \text{ of } \mathbf{r} \text{ wrt } \mathbf{p} \qquad \rho 9$$

Thus in our example,

$$\text{project (ON, (ON,ABOVE))}(\{(1,2),(2,3),(3,5)\}, \{\ \}) = \{(1,2),(2,3),(3,5)\}$$

and selects the value of the ON relation. Likewise,

$$\text{inject(ABOVE, (ON,ABOVE)}\ (\{(1,3),(2,5)\}) = (\{\ \}, \{(1,3),(2,5)\})$$

and is used in the creation of a new value for the ABOVE relation.

While unlabelled relations are associated with predicates, labelled relations are associated with literals, and sequences of literals. If L is a literal, with associated labelled relation $(\mathbf{v}, r)$ then $\mathbf{v}$ is the sequence of variables of L, without repetitions. The same is true for literal sequences. The attach function is used to go from unlabelled relations associated with predicates to labelled relations associated with literals, and the detach function makes the opposite transition. detach $(\mathbf{a},(\mathbf{v},r))$ takes an argument sequence $\mathbf{a}$, $|\mathbf{a}| \subset E \cup V$ and a labelled relation $(\mathbf{v},r)$, and produces an unlabelled relation r' for which arity(r') = length$(\mathbf{a})$. Our clauses are restricted by (3.3.1) so that the condition $|\mathbf{a}| \cap V \subset |\mathbf{v}|$ is always satisfied.

$$\begin{aligned}&\text{detach}\ (\mathbf{a}(\mathbf{v},r)) = \\ &\{\mathbf{t}' \mid \exists \mathbf{t} \in r \\ &\quad a_k \in |\mathbf{v}| = \mathbf{t}'_k = a_k \text{ of } \mathbf{t} \text{ wrt } \mathbf{v} \\ &\quad a_k \in E => t'_k = a_k\}.\end{aligned} \qquad \rho 10$$

In our example, for C2, when we are forming a new value of ABOVE, we use detach with arguments ("X","Z") and (("X","Y","Z"), (1,2,3),(2,3,5)) to obtain the relation $\{(1,3),(2,5)\}$ to be added into ABOVE.

Suppose now that $\mathbf{a}$ is a sequence for which $|\mathbf{a}| \subset \mathrm{E} \cup \mathrm{V}$ and r is a relation, such that arity(r) = length$(\mathbf{a})$. Then attach $(\mathbf{a},r)$ is a labelled relation $(\mathbf{v},r')$, where $|\mathbf{v}| = |\mathbf{a}| \cap V$ and

$$\begin{aligned}&r' = \{\mathbf{t}' \mid \exists \mathbf{t} \in r \\ &\forall k,k' v_{k'} = a_k => v_{k'} \text{ of } \mathbf{t}' \text{ wrt } \mathbf{v} = \mathrm{t}_k \\ &\forall k\ a_k \in |E| => t_k = a_k\}.\end{aligned} \qquad \rho 11$$

In our example, if L = ABOVE(Y,Z), then we have to perform

$$\text{attach}((\text{"}Y\text{"},\text{"}Z\text{"}), \{(1,2),(2,3),(3,5)\}) = ((\text{"}Y\text{"},\text{"}Z\text{"}), \{(1,2),(2,3),(3,5)\})$$

a trivial example in fact. If, however, we attach ("X","X") to the above relation, then we get the labelled relation (("X"), {}), since nothing is above itself. If we attach ("X",5), we get (("X"), {(3)}).

The next operation we have to consider is the join operation. This is involved in combining the labelled relations derived from two different literals. Let $(\mathbf{v}, r)$ and $(\mathbf{v}', r')$ be two labelled relations, then

$$
\begin{aligned}
&(\mathbf{v}'', r'') = (\mathbf{v}, r) * (\mathbf{v}', r') <=> \\
&|\mathbf{v}''| = |\mathbf{v}| \cup |\mathbf{v}'|). \\
&r'' = \{\mathbf{t}'' \mid \exists \mathbf{t}, \mathbf{t}' \\
&\qquad \nu \in |\mathbf{v}| => \nu \text{ of } \mathbf{t}'' \text{ wrt } \mathbf{v}'' = \nu \text{ of } \mathbf{t} \text{ wrt } \mathbf{v} \\
&\qquad \nu' \in |\mathbf{v}'| => \mathbf{v}' \text{ of } \mathbf{t}'' \text{ wrt } \mathbf{v}'' = \nu' \text{ of } \mathbf{t}' \text{ wrt } \mathbf{v}' \}. \qquad \rho 12
\end{aligned}
$$

For example, in processing C2 we have to compute the join

$$
\begin{aligned}
&((\text{“}X\text{”},\text{“}Y\text{”}), \{(1,2),(2,3),(3,5)\}) * ((\text{“}Y\text{”},\text{“}Z\text{”}), \{(1,2),(2,3),(3,5)\}) \\
&= ((\text{“}X\text{”},\text{“}Y\text{”},\text{“}Z\text{”}), \{(1,2,3),(2,3,5)\}).
\end{aligned}
$$

Note that $q0 = ((), \{()\})$ is an identity for $*$, and that $*$ is commutative and associative.

3.8 Summary of section 3

We have now completed the definition of ρ. Note that $\rho 3$ implies that $\rho(C)(\mathbf{r}) \geqslant \mathbf{r}$ and so, from $\rho 1$ and $\rho 2$, $\rho(\mathbf{C})(\mathbf{r}) \geqslant \mathbf{r}$. Thus $\rho(\mathbf{C})$ has at least one fixed point by 3.4.2, $\mathbf{r}_1$, say, and moreover, $\mathbf{r}_1$ must also be a fixed point for $\rho(\mathbf{C})$ or all C in $|\mathbf{C}|$, by the definition of $\rho(\mathbf{C})$. It follows that $\mathbf{r}_1$ is a fixed point for any clause sequence $\mathbf{C}'$ st $|\mathbf{C}'| = |\mathbf{C}|$ so that the fixed point depends only on the set of clauses, not on their order. Before we investigate the properties of ρ further in Sec. 4, let us work through an example of the application of ((C1,C2)).

Let us consider the initial state of our example, represented by $\mathbf{r}_0 =$ ({(1,2),(2,3),(3,5)}, {}), $\mathbf{p}$ = ("ON", "ABOVE") so that "ON" is associated with the first relation in the pair $\mathbf{r}_0$, and ABOVE with the second (null) relation. Then by $\rho 1$ & $\rho 2$

$$
\begin{aligned}
&\rho((\text{C1},\text{C2}))(\mathbf{r}_0) = \rho(\text{C2})(\rho(\text{C1})(\mathbf{r}_0)) && (3.8.1) \\
&\rho(\text{C1})(\mathbf{r}_0) = \mathbf{r}_0 \cup \text{inject}(\text{“ABOVE”}, \mathbf{p})(\text{detach}((\text{“}X\text{”},\text{“}Y\text{”}), \rho'(\mathbf{L})(\mathbf{r}_0)) \\
&\quad \text{where } \mathbf{L} = (\text{“ON”},(\text{“}X\text{”},\text{“}Y\text{”}))) && (3.8.2) \\
&\rho'(\mathbf{L})(\mathbf{r}_0) = q_0 * \rho((\text{“ON”},(\text{“}X\text{”},\text{“}Y\text{”})))(\mathbf{r}_0) && (3.8.3) \\
&\rho((\text{“ON”},(\text{“}X\text{”},\text{“}Y\text{”})))(\mathbf{r}_0) = \text{attach}((\text{“}X\text{”},\text{“}Y\text{”}), \rho(\text{“ON”})(\mathbf{r}_0)) \\
&= \text{attach}((\text{“}X\text{”},\text{“}Y\text{”}), \text{project}((\text{“ON”}(\text{“ON”},\text{“ABOVE”})))(\mathbf{r}_0)) \\
&= \text{attach}((\text{“}X\text{”},\text{“}Y\text{”}), \{(1,2),(2,3),(3,5)\}) \\
&= ((\text{“}X\text{”},\text{“}Y\text{”}), \{(1,2),(2,3),(3,5)\}) = \rho'(\mathbf{L})(\mathbf{r}_0)
\end{aligned}
$$

since q_0 is an identity for $*$.

Thus, applying (3.8.2) we get that

$$\rho(\mathbf{C}1)(\mathbf{r}_0) = \mathbf{r}_0 \cup \text{inject}(\text{"ABOVE"},\mathbf{p})\,(\text{detach}((\text{"}X\text{"},\text{"}Y\text{"}),\ ((\text{"}X\text{"},\text{"}Y\text{"}),\{(1,2),(2,3),(3,5)\})))$$
$$= \mathbf{r}_0 \cup \text{inject}(\text{"ABOVE"},\mathbf{p})(\{(1,2),(2,3),(3,5)\})$$
$$= \mathbf{r}_0 \cup (\{\},\{(1,2),(2,3),(3,5)\}$$
$$= (\{(1,2),(2,3),(3,5)\},\{(1,2),(2,3),(3,5)\}).$$

We shall not compute $\rho(\mathbf{C}2)(\mathbf{r}_0)$ in detail, but note that the join operation involved is the one given as an example after the definition of join.

4. FIXED POINTS ARE INTERPRETATIONS

In this section we prove two theorems. The first states that the fixed point of $\rho(\mathbf{C})$ gives rise to an interpretation of **C**, that is a correspondence between predicates of **C** and relations in which the clauses of **C** are satisfied.

The second theorem shows that $\rho(\mathbf{C})$ is continuous, and thus provides a basis for finding fixed points by repeated applications of $\rho(\mathbf{C})$ to an initial relation sequence.

4.1 *Theorem*

Let **C** be a sequence of clauses. Let **r** be a fixed point of $\rho(\mathbf{C})$. Let $C \in |\mathbf{C}|$. Let $\sigma : V \cup E \rightarrow E$ be a function for which $\sigma(\ell) = \ell$ for $\ell \in E$. Suppose that for each literal $(p,\mathbf{a})$ occurring negatively in C, $\sigma(\mathbf{a}) \in$ project $(p,\mathbf{p})(\mathbf{r})$. Let $(p',\mathbf{a}')$ be the positive literal of C. Then $\sigma(\mathbf{a}') \in$ project $(p',\mathbf{p})(\mathbf{r})$.

Comment on the meaning of this theorem.

With each predicate p occurring in **C** we associate a relation, project $(p,\mathbf{p})(\mathbf{r}_0)$. We can regard this association relation as an interpretation of the predicate. The theorem states that however we substitute constants for variables in C, if we regard $p(e_1, e_2 \text{ -- } e_k)$ as being satisfied when $(e_1, e_2 \ldots\ldots)$ in r, where r is the associated relation with p, then if all the literals on the left of a clause are satisfied, then that on the right must be satisfied.

Thus in our example, let us consider C2, and let

$$\sigma(\text{"}X\text{"}) = 2, \sigma(\text{"}Y\text{"}) = 3 \text{ and } \sigma(\text{"}Z\text{"}) = 5$$

and let

$$\mathbf{r} = (\{(1,2),(2,3),(3,5)\}, \{(1,2),(2,3),(3,5),(1,3),(2,5),(1,5)\}).$$

Then

$$\sigma((\text{"}X\text{"},\text{"}Y\text{"})) = (2,3) \in \text{project }(\text{"ON"}, (\text{"ON"}, \text{"ABOVE"}))$$
$$= \{(1,2),(2,3),(3,5)\}$$

and likewise sigma$((\text{"}Y\text{"},\text{"}Z\text{"})) \in$ project$(\text{"ABOVE"},(\text{"ON"},\text{"ABOVE"}))(\mathbf{r}_0)$ thus the left-hand side of C2 is satisfied, and we find that the right-hand side is satisfied, since

$$\sigma(\text{"}X\text{"},\text{"}Z\text{"}) = (2,5) \in \text{project}(\text{"ABOVE"},(\text{"ON"},\text{"ABOVE"}))(\mathbf{r}_0)\,.$$

Before we can prove (4.1) we need the following two lemmas.

4.2 Lemma

Let a be a sequence with $|\mathbf{a}| \subset E \cup V$. Let r be a relation. Let $(\mathbf{v}, r') = \text{attach}(\mathbf{a}, r)$.

Then for any $\sigma : V \cup E \to E$ for which $e \epsilon E \Rightarrow \sigma(e) = e$

$$\sigma(\mathbf{a}) \epsilon r \Rightarrow \sigma(\mathbf{v}) \epsilon r'.$$

Proof

Suppose $\sigma(\mathbf{a}) \epsilon r$

Let $v_{k'} = a_k$ for some k,k'

$$v_{k'} \text{ of } \sigma(\mathbf{v}) \text{wrt } \mathbf{v} = \sigma(\mathbf{v})_{k'} = \sigma(v_{k'}) = \sigma(\mathbf{a}_k) = \sigma(\mathbf{a})_k .$$

Moreover if $a_k \epsilon E$ then $\sigma(\mathbf{a})_k = a_k$.

Hence $\sigma(\mathbf{a}) \epsilon r'$ from the definition of attach (ρ11).

4.3 Lemma

Let $\mathbf{v}, \mathbf{v}', \mathbf{v}''$ be sequences of variables, and let r, r', r'' be relations for which

$$(\mathbf{v}'', r'') = (\mathbf{v}, r) * (\mathbf{v}', r')$$

then if $\sigma : V \cup E \to E$

$$\sigma(\mathbf{v}) \epsilon r \,\&\, \sigma(\mathbf{v}') \epsilon r' \Rightarrow \sigma(\mathbf{v}'') \epsilon r''.$$

Proof

Let $v \epsilon |\mathbf{v}|$ and let $v' \epsilon |\mathbf{v}'|$.

$$v \text{ of } \sigma(\mathbf{v}'') \text{ wrt } \mathbf{v}'' = \sigma(\mathbf{v}) = v \text{ of } \sigma(\mathbf{v}) \text{wrt } \mathbf{v}$$
$$v' \text{ of } \sigma(\mathbf{v}'') \text{ wrt } \mathbf{v}'' = \sigma(\mathbf{v}') = v' \text{ of } \sigma(\mathbf{v}') \text{ wrt } \mathbf{v}'.$$

Thus $\sigma(\mathbf{v})$ & $\sigma(\mathbf{v}')$ satisfy the requirements to be the **t** & **t**′ in the definition of $*$, and so we conclude $\sigma(\mathbf{v}'') \epsilon r''$.

4.4 The proof of theorem 4.1

It follows from Sec. 3.8 that **r** must be a fixed point for $\rho(C)$ for each $C \epsilon |\mathbf{C}|$.

Now let $(p, \mathbf{a})$ be a literal occurring negatively in C. Then from Lemma 4.2 and ρ7

$$\sigma(\mathbf{a}) \epsilon \text{ project}(p, \mathbf{p})(\mathbf{r}_0) \Rightarrow \sigma(\mathbf{a}) \epsilon \rho(p)(\mathbf{r}_0)$$
$$\Rightarrow \sigma(\mathbf{v}) \epsilon r' \text{ where } (\mathbf{v}, r') = \rho((p, \mathbf{a}))(\mathbf{r}_0)$$

Thus if σ satisfies the preconditions of our theorem (4.1), then for each literal $(p,\mathbf{a})$ occurring negatively in C

$$(v,r') = \rho((p\ \mathbf{a}))(\mathbf{r}_0) \Rightarrow \sigma(\mathbf{v}) \in r' \qquad (4.4.1)$$

Let $\mathbf{L}''$ be a sequence of these literals. We shall show, by structural induction (Burstall, 1969), that if $(\mathbf{v}'',r'') = \rho'(\mathbf{L}'')$ then $\sigma(\mathbf{v}) \in r''$.

Suppose $L'' = ()$. Then $(\mathbf{v}'',r'') = q_0 = ((),\{()\})$, by $\rho 4$. Thus $\sigma(\mathbf{v}'') = \sigma(()) = \sigma(()) = () \in \{()\}$, so founding our induction. Suppose $\mathbf{L}'' = \text{consseq}(\mathbf{L},\mathbf{L}')$, and suppose that $\sigma(\mathbf{v}') \in r'$, where $\rho(\mathbf{L}')(\mathbf{r}_0) = (\mathbf{v}',\mathbf{r}')$.

Now by $\rho 5$,

$$\sigma'(\mathbf{L}'')(\mathbf{r}_0) = \rho(L)(\mathbf{r}_0) * \rho'(\mathbf{L}')(\mathbf{r}_0) = (\mathbf{v}'',r''), \text{ say}$$

Let $\rho(L)(\mathbf{r}_0) = (\mathbf{v},r)$, so that $\sigma(\mathbf{v}) \in r$ by (4.4.1).
We can conclude from Lemma 4.3 that $\sigma(v'') \in r''$.
Thus if $\mathrm{C} = (\mathbf{L},L')$ and $\rho'(\mathbf{L})(\mathbf{r}_0) = (\mathbf{v},r)$ then $\sigma(\mathbf{v}) \in r$.
Now $\mathbf{r}_0$ is a fixed point of $\rho(C)$, and from $\rho 3$ we see that this implies that

$$\text{inject}\ (p',\mathbf{p})\ (\text{detach}(\mathbf{a}',(\mathbf{v},r))) \subset \mathbf{r}_0 .$$

Thus

$$\begin{aligned}&\text{project}(p',\mathbf{p})\text{inject}(p',\mathbf{p})\ \text{detach}(\mathbf{a}',(\mathbf{v},r)))\\ &= \text{detach}(\mathbf{a}',(\mathbf{v},r)) \subset \text{project}(p',\mathbf{p})(\mathbf{r}))\ .\end{aligned}$$

Consider $\sigma(\mathbf{a}')$

If $a'_k \in E$ then $\sigma(\mathbf{a}')_k = a'_k$

If $a'_k \in V$ then a'_k of $\sigma(\mathbf{v})$wrt $\mathbf{v} = \sigma(a'_k) = \sigma(\mathbf{a}')_k$.

Hence, by the definition of detach with $\sigma(\mathbf{v})$ playing the part of $\mathbf{t}$, and $\sigma(\mathbf{a}')$ playing the part of $\mathbf{t}'$, we conclude that $\sigma(\mathbf{a}') \in \text{detach}(\mathbf{a}',(\mathbf{v},r))$, and so $\sigma(\mathbf{a}') \in \text{project}(p',\mathbf{p})(\mathbf{r}_0)$.

This concludes the proof.

Let us now return to the proof that $\rho(\mathbf{C})$ is chain continuous. We begin with lemmas showing that attach, detach and join are continuous, the latter in both its arguments, and then prove the chain-continuity of $\rho(\mathbf{C})$ by building up the definitions $\rho 1$–7.

4.5 *Lemma*

If $\{r_\alpha\}$ is a set of relations, and $\mathbf{a}$ sequence for which $|\mathbf{a}| \subset E \cup V$, then

$$\text{attach}\ (\mathbf{a}, \bigcup_\alpha r_\alpha) = \bigcup_\alpha (\text{attach}(\mathbf{a},r_\alpha)).$$

Proof

Let $(\mathbf{v}, r') = \text{attach}(\mathbf{a}, \bigcup_\alpha r_\alpha)$

$$(\mathbf{v}, r'') = \bigcup_\alpha \text{attach}(\mathbf{a}\ r_\alpha)$$

Then $r'' = \bigcup_\alpha r''_\alpha$ where $(\mathbf{v}\ r''_\alpha) = \text{attach}(\mathbf{a}\ r_\alpha)$

Let $\mathbf{t}' \in r'$. Then

$$\exists t, t \in \bigcup_\alpha r_\alpha \ \&\ a_k = v_{k'} \Rightarrow a_k \text{ of } \mathbf{t}' \text{wrt } \mathbf{a} = v_k \text{ of } \mathbf{t} \text{ wrt } \mathbf{v}$$
$$\&\ a_k \in E \Rightarrow t_k = a_k\ .$$

Suppose $\mathbf{t} \in r_\beta$, for some β. Then $\mathbf{t}' \in r''_\beta$ and hence $\mathbf{t}' \in \bigcup_a r_\alpha$. The converse proof is similar.

4.6 *Lemma*

If $\{(\mathbf{v}, r_\alpha)\}$ is a set of labelled relations, with identical labels, and $\mathbf{a}$ is an argument sequence, then

$$\text{detach}\ (\mathbf{a}, \bigcup_\alpha (\mathbf{v}, r_\alpha)) = \bigcup_\alpha \text{detach}\ (\mathbf{a}, (\mathbf{v}, r_\alpha))\ .$$

The proof is straightforward, and is not included in this paper.

4.7 *Lemma*

If $(\mathbf{v}, r)$ is a labelled relation, and $\{(\mathbf{v}', r'_\alpha)\}$ is a set of labelled relations, then

$$(\mathbf{v}, r) * \bigcup_\alpha (\mathbf{v}', r_\alpha) = \bigcup_\alpha ((\mathbf{v}, r) * (\mathbf{v}', r'_\alpha))\ .$$

Proof

Let $(\mathbf{v}'', r'') = (\mathbf{v}', r) * (\bigcup_\alpha (\mathbf{v}', r'_\alpha))$

Then $|\mathbf{v}''| = |\mathbf{v}| \cup |\mathbf{v}'|$

Let $\mathbf{t}'' \in r''$. Then

$$\exists \mathbf{t}, \mathbf{t}', \mathbf{t} \in r\ \&\ \mathbf{t}' \in \bigcup_\alpha r'_\alpha\ \&\ \forall \nu \in \mathbf{v}, \forall \nu' \in \mathbf{v}'$$
$$\nu \text{ of } \mathbf{t}'' \text{ wrt } \mathbf{v}'' = \nu \text{ of } \mathbf{t} \text{ wrt } \mathbf{v}$$
$$\nu' \text{ of } \mathbf{t}'' \text{ wrt } \mathbf{v}'' = \nu \text{ of } \mathbf{t}' \text{ wrt } \mathbf{v}'\ .$$

Suppose $\mathbf{t}' \in r'_\beta$ for some β. Then

$$\mathbf{t} \in (\mathbf{v}, r) * (\mathbf{v}', r'_\beta)$$
and so $\mathbf{t} \in \bigcup_\alpha ((\mathbf{v}, r) * (\mathbf{v}', r'_\alpha))$

and similarly conversely.

We also need the following two results, for which the proof is sufficiently straightforward to be omitted.

4.8 *Lemma*

If $\{r_\alpha\}$ is a set of relation sequences, and p is a predicate, then

$$\text{project}\,(p,\mathbf{p})\,(\bigcup_\alpha r_\alpha) = \bigcup_\alpha (\text{project}(p,\mathbf{p})(r_\alpha)).$$

4.9 *Lemma*

If $\{r_\alpha\}$ is a set of relations, and p is a predicate, then

$$\text{inject}\,(p,\mathbf{p})\,(\bigcup_\alpha r_\alpha) = \bigcup_\alpha (\text{inject}(p,\mathbf{p})(r_\alpha)).$$

We are now able to prove the following.

4.10 *Theorem*

$\rho(x)$ is a chain-continuous, from $\mathcal{R}$ to $\mathcal{R}$, whether x be a predicate, literal, clause or clause sequence, and if $\mathbf{L}$ is a literal sequence, then $\rho'(\mathbf{L})$ is chain-continuous.

Proof

Let r_α be an ascending chain of members of $\mathcal{R}$, indexed by α in some totally ordered set A.

(i) Let p be a predicate. Then

$$\begin{aligned}
&\rho(p)\,(\bigcup_\alpha r_\alpha) = \text{project}\,(p,\mathbf{p})\,(\bigcup_\alpha \mathbf{r}_\alpha) \\
&= \bigcup_\alpha \text{project}(p,\mathbf{p})(r_\alpha) && \text{(by 4.8)} \\
&= \bigcup_\alpha \rho(p)\mathbf{r}_\alpha. && \text{(by } \rho 7\text{)}
\end{aligned}$$

(ii) Let (p,**a**) be a literal. Then

$$\begin{aligned}
&\rho(p,\mathbf{a})(\bigcup_\alpha \mathbf{r}_\alpha) = \text{attach}(\mathbf{a}\ \rho(\mathrm{p})(\bigcup_\alpha \mathbf{r}_\alpha)) \\
&= \text{attach}\,(\mathbf{a},\bigcup_\alpha \rho(p)(\mathbf{r}_\alpha)) && \text{(by (i))} \\
&= \bigcup_\alpha \text{attach}\,(\mathrm{a},\rho(p)(\mathbf{r}_\alpha)) && \text{(by 4.5)} \\
&= \bigcup_\alpha \rho(p,\mathbf{a})(\mathbf{r}_\alpha). && \text{(by } \rho 6\text{)}
\end{aligned}$$

(iii) This section of the proof, which lifts continuity over the join operation, is the root of the restriction to chain-continuity, which arises essentially from the cross-terms generated by join. So, we shall prove, by structural induction, that

$$\rho'(\mathbf{L})(\bigcup_\alpha \mathbf{r}_\alpha) = \bigcup_\alpha (\rho'(\mathbf{L})(\mathbf{r}_\alpha))\ .$$

To found the induction we observe that

$$\rho'(())(\underset{\alpha}{\cup}\mathbf{r}_\alpha) = q_0 = \underset{\alpha}{\cup}\rho'(())(\mathbf{r}_\alpha).$$

Now suppose that for some **L**

$$\rho'(\mathbf{L})(\cup\mathbf{r}_\alpha) = \cup\,\rho'(\mathbf{L})(\mathbf{r}_\alpha)\,.$$

Then, by $\rho 5$

$$\rho'(\text{consseq}(\mathrm{L},\mathbf{L})(\underset{\alpha}{\cup}\mathbf{r}_\alpha) = \rho(\mathrm{L})(\underset{\alpha}{\cup}\mathbf{r}_\alpha) * \rho'(\mathbf{L})(\underset{\alpha}{\cup}\mathbf{r}_\alpha)$$

$$= \underset{\alpha}{\cup}\,\rho(L)(\mathbf{r}_\alpha) * \underset{\beta}{\cup}\rho'(\mathbf{L})(\mathbf{r}_\beta) \qquad \text{(by (ii) and inductive hypothesis, where } \rho \in \mathrm{A})$$

$$= \underset{\beta}{\cup}(\underset{\alpha}{\cup}\,\rho\,(L)(\mathbf{r}_\alpha) * \rho'(\mathbf{L})(\mathbf{r}_\beta)) \qquad \text{(by 4.7)}$$

$$= \underset{\beta}{\cup}\,\underset{\alpha}{\cup}(\rho(L)(\mathbf{r}_\alpha) * \rho'(\mathbf{L})(\mathbf{r}_\beta)) \qquad \text{(by 4.7 and commutativity of } *)$$

$$= \underset{\alpha}{\cup}(\rho'(\text{consseq}(L,\mathrm{L}))(\mathbf{r}_\alpha)\,) \qquad \text{(by } \rho 5\text{, and the properties of } \cup)$$

Since for any α and β in A, either $\alpha \leqslant \beta$ or $\beta \leqslant \alpha$ and so

$$\rho(L)(\mathbf{r}_\alpha) * \rho'(\mathbf{L})(\mathbf{r}_\beta) \leqslant \rho(L)(\mathbf{r}_\alpha) * \rho'(\mathbf{L})(\mathbf{r}_\alpha)$$

or

$$\rho(L)(\mathbf{r}_\alpha) * \rho'(\mathbf{L})(\mathbf{r}_\beta) \leqslant \rho(L)(\mathbf{r}_\beta) * \rho'(\mathbf{L})(\mathbf{r}_\beta)\,.$$

(iv) Let (**L**, (**p**′,**a**′)) be a clause

$$\rho(\mathbf{L}(\mathbf{p}',\,\mathbf{a}'))(\underset{\alpha}{\cup}\,\mathbf{r}_\alpha) =$$

$$\underset{\alpha}{\cup}\,\mathbf{r}_\alpha\,\underset{\alpha}{\cup}\,\text{inject}(p',\mathbf{p})(\text{detach}(\mathbf{a}',\rho'(\mathbf{L})(\underset{\alpha}{\cup}\mathbf{r}_\alpha)))$$

$$= \underset{\alpha}{\cup}\mathbf{r}_\alpha \cup \underset{\alpha}{\cup}(\text{inject}(p',\mathbf{p})(\text{detach}(\mathbf{a}',\rho'(\mathbf{L})(\mathbf{r}_\alpha))) \qquad \text{(by (iii), 4.6, 4.9)}$$

$$= \underset{\alpha}{\cup}(\mathbf{r}_\alpha \cup \text{inject}(p',\mathbf{p})(\text{detach}(\mathbf{a}',\rho'(\mathbf{L})(\mathbf{r}_\alpha))).$$

(v) Finally we prove, by structural induction, that ρ(**C**) is chain-continuous for the clause-sequence **C**.

$$\rho((C))(\cup\,\mathbf{r}_\alpha) = \rho(C)(\cup\mathbf{r}_\alpha) \qquad \text{(by } \rho 1)$$

$$= \underset{\alpha}{\cup}\,\rho(C)(\mathbf{r}_\alpha) \qquad \text{(by (iv))}$$

$$= \underset{\alpha}{\cup}\rho((C))(\mathbf{r}_\alpha) \qquad \text{(by } \rho 1)$$

Suppose now for some **C** that $\rho(\mathbf{C})(\cup\mathbf{r}'_\alpha) = \cup\,\rho(\mathbf{C})(\mathbf{r}'_\alpha)$ for any ascending chain $\mathbf{r}'_\alpha$.

Then

$$\rho(\text{consseq}(C,\mathbf{C}))(\bigcup_\alpha \mathbf{r}_\alpha)$$
$$= \rho(C)(\rho(\mathbf{C})(\bigcup_\alpha \mathbf{r}_\alpha) \qquad \text{(by } \rho 2)$$
$$= \rho(C)(\bigcup_\alpha \rho(\mathbf{C})(\mathbf{r}_\alpha)) \qquad \text{(by (iv)}$$
$$= \bigcup_\alpha \rho(C)(\rho(\mathbf{C})(\mathbf{r}_\alpha))$$

by inductive hypothesis, since $\rho(\mathbf{C})(\mathbf{r}_\alpha)$ is an ascending sequence

$$= \bigcup_\alpha \rho(\text{consseq}(C,\mathbf{C}))(\mathbf{r}_\alpha) \qquad \text{(by } \rho 2)$$

which concludes the proof.

5. APPLICATION OF THE THEORY

The conclusion that we can draw from Secs. 3 and 4, is that given a sequence of clauses, $\mathbf{C}$ and an initial sequence of relations $\mathbf{r}_0$, that there exists a relation sequence $\mathbf{r}$ which is defined by

$$r_\infty = \bigcup_n{}^n (\mathbf{C})(\mathbf{r}_0)$$

and which provides an interpretation of $\mathbf{C}$ in the sense that for any substitution of constants for variables in a clause C of $\mathbf{C}$ if the left-hand side of C is satisfied then the right-hand side must be.

Now if we are dealing only with finite relations, the sequence $(\rho^n(\mathbf{C})(\mathbf{r}_0))$ must reach its least upper bound after a finite number of steps, so that, for some $n, r_\infty = \rho^n(C)(r_0)$.

The interesting problems arise when some of the relations concerned are infinite. We are not proposing a treatment of the general case, but shall restrict ourselves to consideration of the case where infinite relations only occur negatively in clauses, and where join only produces finite results.

In order to be able to perform arithmetic computations within our relational system, we need some representation specifying that the set E contains the reals, and that the arithmetic operations, $+ - * /$, are represented as relations on E (there need be no confusion between the use of $*$ at the meta-level for join, and at the object-level for multiplication). It is also convenient to add the distinguished set $\{T,F\}$ for "true", "false", to E.

We shall use R to denote the set of real numbers.

The technical device used to incorporate the real number operations into the relational system is based on the following definition.

5.1 ***Definition***

Let $E' \subset E$. Let $f : E'^n \to E'$. Then $\mu(f)$ is the relation

$$\{t \mid t_{n+1} = f(t, \ldots t_n), t, \ldots t_n \in E'\} .$$

Thus it is possible to incorporate arithmetic into the system by insisting that P contain the set {"+", "—", "*", "/"} and by associating with each an operator applied to the corresponding function. It is also clear that the arithmetic relations, $<, >, \leqslant, \geqslant$, can be extended to apply to E.

5.2 Implementation of infinite relations

The introduction of infinite relations into the system can only be bought at a cost. The representation of finite relations in a computer raises no problems of principle, although there may be practical difficulties in handling large relations economically. On the other hand there are difficulties involved in representing infinite relations in a way that is effective computationally, and of course there is no guarantee that any clause sequence will give rise to a fixed point in a finite number of iterations. This second difficulty is unavoidable if the system is to have full computational power – it is equivalent to the halting problem.

There are conventionally two methods of representing infinite objects in a computer – as a program or symbolically. (These two are not necessarily distinct; LISP program can be treated as symbolic, although this is seldom done in practice). We propose to restrict the system and to deal only with finite relations, apart from the basic arithmetic ones defined above. This is possible on account of the following.

5.2.1 *Theorem*

Let $(\mathbf{v}, r)$ be a finite labelled relation. Let $f : E'^n \rightarrow E'$, $E' \subset E$. Let a be an argument sequence of length $n + 1$, for which

$$i < n + 1 => a_i \subset |\mathbf{v}| \cup E$$

then

$$(\mathbf{v}, r) * \text{attach}(\mathbf{a}, \mu(f))$$

is finite.

Proof

Let $(\mathbf{v}', r') = \text{attach}(\mathbf{a}, \mu(f))$

Let $(\mathbf{v}'', r'') = (\mathbf{v}, r) * (\mathbf{v}', r')$

Let $\theta : r'' \rightarrow r$ be defined by

If $\mathbf{t}'' \epsilon\, r''$, choose $\theta(\mathbf{t}'') \epsilon\, r$ s.t.
$\nu \epsilon\, |\mathbf{v}| => \nu$ of $\mathbf{t}''$ wrt $\mathbf{v}'' = \nu$ of $\theta(\mathbf{t}'')$ wrt $\mathbf{v}$

We shall show that θ is $1 - 1$.

Suppose $\theta(\mathbf{t}'') = \theta(s'') = \mathbf{t}$, say, for some s'', t'' ϵ r''
There are two cases to consider.

Case 1

$a_{n+1} \epsilon E \cup \{a, \ldots . a_n\}$. Then $|\mathbf{v}'| \subset |\mathbf{v}|$
therefore $\nu'' \epsilon |\mathbf{v}''| => \nu'' \epsilon |\nu|$ since $|\mathbf{v}''| = |\mathbf{v}| \cup |\mathbf{v}'|$
therefore $\forall \mathrm{v}'' \epsilon |\mathbf{v}''| =>$
ν'' of $\mathbf{t}''$ wrt $\mathbf{v}'' = \nu''$ of $\theta(\mathbf{t}'')$ wrt $\mathbf{v} = \nu''$ of $\theta(\mathrm{s}'')$ wrt $\mathbf{v}$
$= \nu''$ of s'' wrt v''
therefore s'' = t'' .

Case 2

$a_{n+2} \epsilon V, a_{n+1} \neq a_i \; i \leqslant n.$
Let $\nu_k' = a_{n+1}$
Let $\mathbf{t}^0 \; \mathrm{s}^0 \; \epsilon \; \mu(f)$ for which

$$\nu_{k'} = a_k => \nu_{k'} \text{ of } \mathbf{t}' \text{ wrt } \mathbf{v}' = t_k^0$$
$$\nu_{k'} \text{ of } \mathrm{s}' \text{ wrt } \mathbf{v}' = s_k^0$$
$$a_k \epsilon E => t_k^0 = a_k = s_k^0 \; .$$

Then for $k \leqslant n$, let $a_k = \nu_{k'}$. Then $\nu_{k'} \epsilon |\nu|$.
$t_k'' = \nu_{k'}$ of $\mathbf{t}'$ wrt $\mathbf{v}' = \nu_{k'}$ of $\mathbf{t}''$ wrt $\mathbf{v}''$
$= \nu_{k'}$ of $\mathbf{t}$, wrt $\mathbf{v} = \nu_{k'}$ of s wrt $\mathbf{v}$
$= \nu_{k'}$ of s'' wrt $\mathbf{v}'' = \nu_{k'}$ of s' wrt $\mathbf{v}' = s_k^0$.
Thus $t_k^0 = s_k^0 \; k \leqslant n.$
But $t_{k+1}^0 = f(t_,^0 \ldots t_n^0) = f(s_1^0, - s_n^0) = s_{n+1}^0$
therefore ν_k' of $\mathbf{t}''$ wrt $\mathbf{v}'' = \nu_k'$ of $\mathbf{t}'$ wrt $\mathbf{v}' = t_{n+1}^0$
$= \mathrm{s}_{n+1}^0 = \nu_k'$ of s' wrt $\mathbf{v}' = \nu_k'$ of s'' wrt $\mathbf{v}''$
and, for $\nu'' \neq \nu_k, \nu'' \epsilon |\mathbf{v}|$
so ν'' of $\mathbf{t}''$ wrt $\mathbf{v}'' = \nu''$ of $\theta(\mathbf{t}'')$ wrt $\mathbf{v} = \nu''$ of $\theta(\mathrm{s}'')$ wrt $\mathbf{v}$
$= \nu''$ of s'' wrt v''
therefore $\mathbf{t}'' = \mathrm{s}''$
Thus θ is $1-1$, hence r'' is finite, since r is finite.

5.2.2 *Theorem*
Let (**v**, *r*) be a finite labelled relation. Let *r'* be relation. Let **a** be an argument sequence, length(**a**) = arity(*r'*). Then

$$(\mathbf{v}, r) * \text{attach}(\mathbf{a}, r')$$

is finite.

The proof is similar to the preceding theorem, and is omitted.

The import of the above two theorems is that the relations involved in the computation of $\rho(C)$, for some clause C, will be finite if for every literal (p,a) where p is associated with an infinite relation $\mu(f), a, \ldots a_n$ are either constants, or are variables which have already occurred in earlier literals in the clause (arity(p) = $n+1$). Moreover, every literal (p,a) for which p is associated with a non-functional, infinite relation of arity n, then $a, \ldots. a_n$ must either be constant, or have occurred earlier in the clause.

5.3 Free functions

In order to provide some equivalent facility to the data structures of conventional programming languages, let us suppose that there is a set $\{f_{mn}\}$ of functions, $f_{mn} : E^m \rightarrow E$, for which

$$f_{mn}(x, \ldots x_m) = f_{m'n'}(x', \ldots x'_{m'})$$
$$\Rightarrow m = m', n = n', x_i = x'_i .$$

The f_{mn} are called free functions on E.

We can associate free functions with predicate symbols, as in the last section. It should be noted that in addition to the uses of these permitted by Theorems 5.2.1 and 5.2.2, it is possible to have a literal $(p$,a), for which p is associated with f_{mn}, where a_{m+1} is a variable which has occurred earlier in the clause, while a_i, $i \leqslant n$ have not necessarily occurred earlier. This observation does not carry through to the quotient interpretations discussed in the next section.

6. THE TREATMENT OF EQUALITY

Most mechanised logic systems have problems in their treatment of equality. The basic intuitive notion that if entities are equal then they should behave identically when acted on by functions can be expressed by axioms of the sort

$$x = y \Rightarrow f(x) = f(y)$$

which have to be written out for every function named in the system. It is possible to ensure that this substitutivity property of equality is automatically provided by adding the predicate "=" to the set P of predicates, and by modifying the definition of $p(\mathbf{C})$, for some sequence of clauses $\mathbf{C}$ to

$$\rho_{\text{eq}}(\mathbf{C}) = \rho(\mathbf{C}) \circ \eta(\mathbf{r})$$

where $\eta(\mathbf{r})$ is defined as follows:

Let r_{eq} = "=" of $\mathbf{r}$ wrt $\mathbf{p}$
Let r'_{eq} be the reflexive symmetric and transitive closure of r_{eq}.

Then $\eta(\mathbf{r})$ is $\mathbf{r}'$ where

(i) "=" of $\mathbf{r}'$ wrt $\mathbf{p} = r'_{eq}$
(ii) If $p \in |\mathbf{p}|, p \neq$ "=" and let
$r = p$ of $\mathbf{r}$ wrt $\mathbf{p}$. Then
$r' = p$ of $\mathbf{r}'$ wrt $\mathbf{p}$ is defined to be
$r' = \{t' \mid \exists t \in r, \forall i (t'_i, t_i) \in r'_{eq}\}$.

The effect of the above definition can be stated simply by saying that in each cycle of the interactive process of interpreting clauses, we take the equalities that have been deduced, apply the rules of reflexivity, symmetry and transitivity to produce an extended equality relation, and then use this to infer that if two entities are equal, and one is related to some further, then the other must also be related to these entities.

4.6.1 Introducing η is equivalent to introducing equality axioms

In this section we show that if $\mathbf{C}$ is a clause sequence, then any fixed point of $\rho_{eq}(\mathbf{C})$ is a fixed point of $\mathbf{C}'$ where $\mathbf{C}'$ is formed from $\mathbf{C}$ by adjoining equality axioms.

Let $\mathbf{r}_1$ be a fixed point of $\rho_{eq}(\mathbf{C})$, and let us note that for all $\mathbf{r}$, $\eta(\mathbf{r}) \geqslant \mathbf{r}$, from the reflexivity of r'_{eq} in the definition of η.

We can easily see that $\mathbf{r}_1$ is a fixed point of $\rho(\mathbf{C})$ for

$$\rho(\mathbf{C})(\mathbf{r}_1) \leqslant \eta(\rho(\mathbf{C})(\mathbf{r}_1)) = \rho_{eq}(\mathbf{C})(\mathbf{r}_1) = \mathbf{r}_1.$$

But from the definition of ρ

$$\rho(\mathbf{C})(\mathbf{r}_1) \geqslant r_1.$$

Similarly, we can show that $\eta(\mathbf{r}_1) = \mathbf{r}_1$.

6.1.1 *Theorem*

If $\mathbf{C}$ is a clause sequence, and $\mathbf{r}$ is a fixed point of $\rho_{eq}(\mathbf{C})$ then

(i) $\mathbf{r}_1$ is a fixed point of
$\rho(x = y => y = x)$

(ii) $\mathbf{r}_1$ is a fixed point of
$\rho(x = y \,\&\, y = z => x = z)$

(iii) for any $p \in |\mathbf{p}|$, r_1 is a fixed point of
$$\rho(x = y \,\&\, p(x_1 \ldots x \ldots x_n) => p(x_1 \ldots y \ldots x_n)).$$

We shall omit the proof of (i) and (ii) and only give the proof of (iii). Since q_0 is an identity of $*$, we need to consider

$$t \in \text{detach}((x_1 \ldots y \ldots x_n), \text{attach}((x,y), r_{eq}) * \text{attach}((x_1 \ldots x \ldots x_n), r_p))$$
where $r_{eq} = "=" \text{ of } \mathbf{r}_1 \text{ wrt } \mathbf{p}$ and $r_p = p \text{ of } \mathbf{r}_1 \text{ wrt } \mathbf{p}$.

We need to show that $\mathbf{t} \in r_p$
Now from the definition of detach (ρ10),

$$\exists \mathbf{t}' \in \text{attach}((x,y), r_{eq}) * \text{attach}((x, \ldots x \ldots x_n) r_p)$$

for which

$$\nu \in |\mathbf{v}'| => \nu \text{ of } \mathbf{t} \text{ wrt } (x_1 \ldots y \ldots x_n) = \nu \text{ of } \mathbf{t}' \text{ wrt } \mathbf{v}' \qquad \text{(I)}$$

where $\mathbf{v}'$ is a sequence without repetitions and $|\mathbf{v}'| = \{x_1 \ldots x_n, x, y\}$.
Now, form the definition of $*$ and attach, ρ11 & ρ12,

$$\exists \mathbf{t}'', \mathbf{t}''', \mathbf{t}'' \in r_{eq} \;\&\; \mathbf{t}''' \in r_p \quad st.$$
$$\text{v}'' \in \{\text{x,y}\} =>$$
$$\nu'' \text{ of } \mathbf{t}' \text{ wrt } \mathbf{v}' = \nu'' \text{ of } \mathbf{t}'' \text{ wrt } (x,y) \qquad \text{(II)}$$
$$\nu''' \{x, \ldots x \ldots x_n\} =>$$
$$\nu''' \text{ of } \mathbf{t}' \text{ wrt } \mathbf{v}' = \nu''' \text{ of } \mathbf{t}''' \text{ wrt } (x_1 \ldots x \ldots x_n). \qquad \text{(III)}$$

Let $\nu \in \{x_1 \ldots \ldots x_n\}$. Then

$$\nu \text{ of } \mathbf{t} \text{ wrt } (x \ldots y \ldots x_n) = \nu \text{ of } \mathbf{t}' \text{ wrt } \mathbf{v}' \qquad \text{from (I).}$$
$$= \nu \text{ of } \mathbf{t}''' \text{ wrt } (x_1 \ldots x \ldots x_n) \qquad \text{from (III).}$$

and

$$y \text{ of } \mathbf{t} \text{ wrt } (x_1 \ldots y \ldots x_n) = y \text{ of } \mathbf{t}' \text{ wrt } \mathbf{v}' \qquad \text{from (I)}$$
$$= y \text{ of } \mathbf{t}'' \text{ wrt } (x,y). \qquad \text{from (II)}$$

Now $\eta(r_1) = r_1$ so that r_{eq} is its own reflexive symmetric & transitive closure, so that it is itself reflexive symmetric and transitive. Thus

$$\nu \in \{x_1 \ldots x_n\} => (\nu \text{ of } \mathbf{t} \text{ wrt}(x_1 \ldots y \ldots x_n),$$
$$\nu \text{ of } \mathbf{t}''' \text{ wrt}(x_1 \ldots x \ldots x_n)) \in r_{eq}$$

by the reflexivity of r_{eq} and

$$(y \text{ of } \mathbf{t} \text{ wrt } (x_1 \ldots y \ldots x_n), x \text{ of } \mathbf{t}''' \text{ wrt } (x_1 \ldots x, \ldots x_n)) \in r_{eq}$$

since

$$(y \text{ of } \mathbf{t} \text{ wrt}(x_1 \ldots y \ldots x_n), x \text{ of } \mathbf{t}''' \text{ wrt } (x_1 \ldots x \ldots x_n))$$
$$= (y \text{ of } \mathbf{t}'' \text{ wrt}(x,y), x \text{ of } \mathbf{t}' \text{ wrt } \mathbf{v}) = (y \text{ of } \mathbf{t}'' \text{ wrt}(x,y), x \text{ of } t'' \text{ wrt } (x)$$
$$= (t_\alpha t_\beta) \text{ say, from the definition of } *. \; (\rho 12)$$

Now since r_{eq} is symmetric and

$$\mathbf{t}'' = (x \text{ of } \mathbf{t}'' \text{ wrt}(x,y), y \text{ of } \mathbf{t}'' \text{wrt}(x\ y))$$

it follows that $(t_\alpha t_\beta) \in r_{eq}$
But $\mathbf{t}''' \in r_p$, and we have shown that for each i, $(t_i\ t_i''') \in r_{eq}$.
Therefore, from the definition of η, and the fact that $\eta(\mathbf{r}_1) = \mathbf{r}_1$ it follows that $\mathbf{t} \in r_p$.

6.2 A discussion of equality

Theorem 6.1.1 shows that it is possible to make the interpretation system behave as though the equality axioms were explicitly present.

From a practical point of view this method of treating equality suffers from a major disadvantage in that the application of the equality rules results in a large expansion of the relations. It seems likely that the obvious ploy of using r_{eq} to define equivalence classes of entities, and only recording relationships between canonical members of these classes, would be theoretically sound, but I have not completed a proof that this is so.

7. DISCUSSION

In this paper we have shown how it is possible to use certain combinators on relations to produce an interpretation of a class of clauses (Horn Clauses) in predicate logic. The work was inspired by a particular view of the task of writing certain kinds of program, but has not yet given rise to a system implemented on a digital computer, although some initial studies have been made. The mathematical apparatus used is hardly novel – perhaps my most direct debt is to D. Park (1969).

REFERENCES

Batani, G. and Meloni, H. (1973). *Interpreteur du Language de Programmation* PROLOG. Marseille: Université d'Aix-Marseille.

Burstall, R. M. (1969). Proving properties of programs by structural induction. *Computer Journal*, **12**, 41–48.

Codd, E. F. (1970). A relational model of data for large shared data banks. *Comm. Ass. Comp. Mach.*, **13**, 377–387.

Elcock, E. W., Foster, J. M., Gray, P. M. D., McGregor, J. J. and Murray, A. M. (1971). ABSET: A programming language based on sets; motivation and examples. *Machine Intelligence 6*, pp. 467–492 (eds. Meltzer, B. and Michie, D.). Edinburgh: Edinburgh University Press.

Iverson, K. E. (1962). *A Programming Language.* New York: Wiley.

Kowalski, R. (1973). Predicate logic as a programming language. *DCL Memo No. 70.* Edinburgh: Dept. of Artificial Intelligence, University of Edinburgh.

Landin, P. J. (1966). The next 700 programming languages. *Comm. Ass. Comp. Mach.*, **9**, 157–166.

Park, D. (1969). Fixpoint induction and proofs of program properties. In *Machine Intelligence 5*, pp. 59–77 (eds. Meltzer, B. and Michie, D.). Edinburgh: Edinburgh University Press.

Warren, D. (1975). Users guide to DEC System 10 PROLOG. *DAI Internal Memo.* Edinburgh: Dept. of Artificial Intelligence, University of Edinburgh.

2

The use of a graph representation in optimization of variable replacement in LISP in the presence of side effects

V. L. Stefanuk

Institute for Information Transmission Problems
USSR Academy of Sciences, Moscow, USSR

Abstract

A certain canonical representation for a directed graph is found to be useful in reduction of search in some problems. In this report it is applied to the solution of a problem of optimization of evaluation order in the arguments of LISP recursive code in the light of recursion removal. The program, given the sequence requiring the minimal number of intermediate precautionary measures, is described. The main feature of the approach is an attempt to take side-effects into account. For this reason, the problem of side-effects in a LISP system is also looked into. The program is implemented in BNN-INTERLISP system.

1. THE CANONICAL REPRESENTATION OF DIRECTED GRAPHS

Let G be a directed graph without loops. The following couple of representations of G are of interest for some applications. The TD (Top-Down) representation is constructed by the following process, called Canon (G):

Set S', the set of all unsubordinated nodes of G. If S' is empty, set S' to be the set of all unsubordinated pairs of nodes of G. If this S' is empty, set S' to be the set of all unsubordinated triples of nodes, etc. (a group of nodes is called unsubordinated if and only if there are no links pointing to the group from the rest of the graph).

For non-empty S' let G' be the remainder of the graph G, provided that all of the links from S' are discarded,

$$\text{Canon}\ (G) = \text{Append}\ (S'\ \text{Canon}\ (G'))$$

Fig. 1.1.

The TD representation for the graph shown at Fig. 1.2 is shown below, at Fig. 1.3.

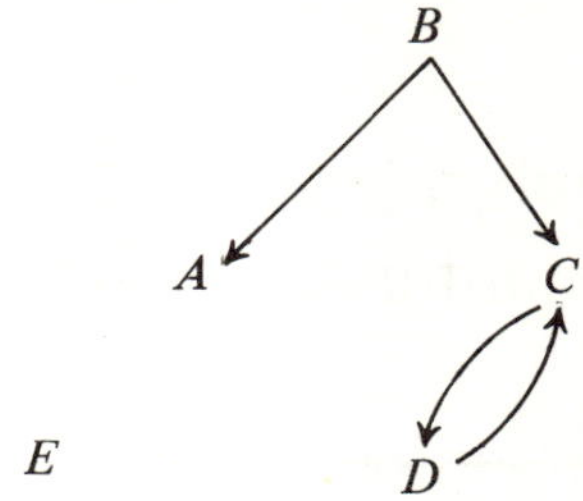

Fig. 1.2.

$$((E)\ (B))\ ((A))\ ((G\,D))$$

Fig. 1.3.

Equivalently it is possible to build the BU (Bottom-Up) representation if one sets S' to be nodes or groups of them, which do not influence the remainder of the graph G. The BU for the same graph is

$$((E)\ (A))\quad ((C\,D))\ ((B))$$

Fig. 1.4.

The TD representation is of interest when one would like to find first the least dependable part of a system, then work on it, and afterwards proceed with the rest of the system. In Stefanuk [1975], the TD representation was actually used to demonstrate that local control in systems without mutual interaction is always stable.

The BU representation is of interest in the problem considered below of the optimization of the order of evaluation of LISP functions, taking into consideration possible side-effects.

However, these representations have the following properties:

1. For a given graph G the set-representations TD and BU are unique, as we are not ordering elements within S' and within subgroups of S'.
2. TD (G) is identical with BU (G'), where G' is the reverse of G (all arrows pointing in backward directions).
3. If G is a graph without cycles, then TD (G) is identical with the reverse of BU (G).
4. Each subgroup of S' has at least one simple cycle of the order k, where k is the number of its elements.

Property 2 shows that the algorithm for construction of BU and TD is essentially the same.

Property 4 suggests a deeper sorting algorithm for the graph G, in which after the failure to find unsubordinated nodes, one tries to find a non-zero set S' of nodes, each of which has not more than one link pointing to it. The LISP function for such a process is given below:

```
(CANONC
    [LAMBDA (G V)
                    (* "CANONC '(F1 F2 F3) NIL" produces a representation
                     taking away elements with no links to the rest, with
                     one link, with two, etc.)
      (COND
        ((NULL G)
        NIL)
       (T (CONS (SETQ V (CANONB G O))
                (CANONC (REMOVE V G]) 

(CANONB
   [LAMBDA (G S)
     (COND
       ((NULL G)
       NIL)
       ((CANONA G G S))
       (T (CANONA G G (ADD1 S])

(CANONA
   [LAMBDA (G U S)
     (COND
       ((NULL G)
       NIL)
       ((EQ S (TEST (LIST (CAR G))
                    (REMOVE (CAR G)
                    U)))
        (CAR G))
       (T (CANONA (CDR G)
                  U S])
```

In Fig. 1.5 we show another example of a graph, together with the representations TD, BU, TD*, BU*, the latter corresponding to "Top-Down" and "Bottom-Up" in the last mentioned algorithm.

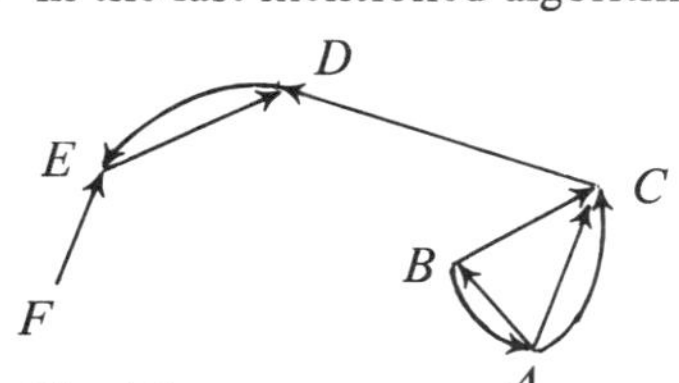

Fig. 1.5.

TD : [(*F*)] [(*A B*)] [(*C*)] [(*E D*)]
BU : [(*E D*)] [(*F*) (*C*)] [(*A B*)]
TD* : [(*F*)] [(*E*) (*B*) (*A*)] [(*C*)) ((*D*)]
BU* : [(*F*) (*E*) (*C*)] [(*D*)] [(*A*)] [(*B*)]

We will not use this new algorithm here, because the BU representation is all that we need: one can work on the elements of the representation (on subgroups of S') one at a time, from left to right, and be sure that nothing wrong will happen to the rest of the graph.

However, we are planning to have a full search within a group in the hope that, in practice, these groups will not contain very many elements, so the total time will be reasonable.

2. VARIABLE REPLACEMENT IN RECURSIVE CODES

The following problem was formulated by J. Urmi and A. Haraldson. Suppose one is given the list of functions:

$$G\colon (F1(X1, \ldots, XN)\ F2(X1, \ldots, XN)\ \ldots\ F3(X1, \ldots, XN))$$

Fig. 2.1.

and the corresponding list of "new variables":

$$(X1\ X2\ \ldots\ XN)$$

Fig. 2.2.

such that the value of $X1$ is to be set equal to the value of $F1$, the value of $X2$ to the value of $F2$, etc.

In the general case, these functions will interfere with each other in the sense that if previous evaluation results are put in some of the variables, the value of the next processed function might change (we assume that the functions in G are always evaluated in the order left to right). One would therefore have to introduce a number of temporaries to save intermediate results and the corresponding number of intermediate operations of SETQ type.

The problem is to find an optimal order of evaluation of elements G to minimize the numbers mentioned. In the following, by $F1$, $F2$,. . . we will assume any functional forms, though sometimes it is more convenient to refer to them as functions, having certain lists of lambda-variables, etc.

This optimization problem shows up most clearly in the case of recursion removal. Let us consider a rather artificial example of a recursive code:

```
(FOO
    [LAMBDA (X Y Z)
        (COND
            ((NULL (AND X Y Z)) NIL)
            (T (CONS(QUOTE *)
                    (FOO (CDR X)
                         (CONS(CAR X)
                              (CDR Y))
                         (CONS (CAR X)
                               (CONS(CAR Y)
                                    (CDR Z])
```

Fig. 2.3.

where

> $F1$ is (CDR X)
> $F2$ is (CONS(CAR X) (CDR Y))
> $F3$ is (CONS(CAR X) (CONS (CAR Y) (CDR Z)))

Fig. 2.4.

Now, trying to compute FOO iteratively, we will see that it would be wrong to evaluate the arguments of a call of FOO in their natural order $F1$ $F2$ $F3$: in that case, one would need to introduce two temporaries to save the results of evaluating $F1$ $F2$, or "spoil" the original values of $X1$ $X2$ now needed for evaluation of $F3$. The best order is, of course, $F3$ $F2$ $F1$, in which case no temporary is needed.

This type of optimization is embedded in the program REMREC of T. Risch, at least for the seven types of recursion which this program is able to handle, provided that there are no additional side-effects, induced by the forms $F1$, $F2$, $F3$, themselves.

It is important to note here that today we do not have a recursion removal which is in some sense universal, and existing programs might well be inefficient when side-effects are allowed for because then they are bound to follow a "worst possible case" approach (as REMREC does).

We feel that an optimization program (let us call it REMREM), being separated from recursion removal, is an efficient tool for introducing into the system some additional knowledge about the functions in question, particularly about side-effects.

3. PROPOSED REMMEM ORGANIZATION AND ITS USE

The program REMMEM can be considered as an extra program to be applied before a recursion removal (REMREC).

The program REMMEM has to provide for the following. For a given order of evaluation of forms, it should be able to find the cost of the number of necessary temporaries, find the optimal order and the optimal cost, and, if necessary, rearrange the original evaluation order of recursive code. Below we will give a brief description of those supporting REMMEM functions that were first written for the simulated INTERLISP on the PDP-10 system in Stockholm and now are transferred to the BBN-INTERLISP on the DEC-20 system of the Datalogy Department, Linkoeping University. A fuller description is given later.

The function (EXPRISI ($F1$ $F2$ . . . FN)) gives a list, the head being the optimal cost, the tail being the optimal evaluation order. For example, for the collection of functions

($F1$ X) ($F2$ X Y) ($F3$ X Y Z)

with (*X Y Z*) as a list of the new variables, this function gives

(0 (*F*3 *F*2 *F*1)).

(We assume no side-effects in forms *F*1 *F*2 *F*3 in this example).

The function (SEMPROG '(*F*1 *F*2 . . . *F*N)) gives a so-called semantic program of function evaluation, that in our example (SEMPROG '(*F*1 *F*2 *F*3)) will look as follows:

((SAVE *F*1 *X*) (SAVE *F*2 *Y*) *F*3 (RETURN *X F*1 *X*)

((SAVE *F*1 *X*) (SAVE *F*2 *Y*) *F*3 (RETURN *X F*1 *X*) (RETURN *Y F*2 *Y*))

This by REMMEM is to be converted to

((SETQ *T*__1 (*F*1 *X*)) (SETQ *T*__2 (*F*2 *X*)) (SETQ *Z F*3)

(SETQ *X T*__1) (SETQ *Y T*__2))

4. TAKING SIDE-EFFECTS INTO ACCOUNT

To the best of our knowledge there is no attempt to incorporate knowledge of side-effects in forms and optimize the evaluation order using it [Risch; Burstall & Darlington]. On the other hand, we did not find a suitable classification of side-effects in the INTERLISP system. In what follows we are trying, through a discussion of different examples, to construct a definition of side-effect and relative side-effect that can serve our purpose. Experienced LISP users are advised to skip the following section.

In "pure" LISP any legitimate expression is constructed from a number of primitives: NIL, lists, atoms, and functions, among which are CAR, CDR, CONS, COND, EQUAL. In Boyer and Moore [1975] one can find an example of such a "pure" system. The interpreter has initial information consisting of numbers of atoms (names and their values, properties) as well as a number of lists. The interpreter takes one expression at a time and returns its value. It is a property of the "pure" system that after the evaluation the LISP system "restarts" in its initial state. There is no obvious trace in the system showing that some expression has been evaluated. (CONS does create a new list, but there will be no pointer to it.) The only way to change the result of evaluation of a given expression is to change the initially chosen sets of atoms (values, properties) and lists. One might say that the system has no memory for such an expression.

However, for the sake of convenience, efficiency etc., a number of functions of quite a different nature were introduced into the LISP system.

The most commonly used is an assignment, SETQ. For example

(SETQ V 'LISP)

has a value, but it is not of primary interest. The most useful and essential property is that in addition to this expression obtaining a value, a new atom, v, with value lisp has been constructed. This expression will be remembered by the system. And this is a side-effect.

The expression

(DE FOO(L) (MEMB 'L '(A B V C)))

also has a side-effect: now the system knows how to calculate a new function.

The functions (print (x, file)) and (read (file)) have both side-effects in this sense – the LISP system will be changed as a result of their evaluation, if one includes the input-output media into the system.

Last we will mention a group of structure destroying functions, like RPLACA. This function may or may not produce a side-effect in the system, depending on its use. For instance, if the function FEE is defined as follows:

```
(FEE
   [LAMBDA (X)
           (RPLACA X (QUOTE E])
```

then (FEE '(*A B C*) will have value (*E B C*). This is an example of a function producing a side-effect on its lambda-variable: we will refer to it as "lambda side-effect".

We say the a LISP expression produces a side-effect on the system if and only if the evaluation of this expression will change the system state to the extent that some other expressions being evaluated before and after this event will get different values. (It is interesting to note that in more "ordinary" computer languages it is only the side-effects that matter, when we enter with a program. However, the complete program if it terminates normally and no errors occur, should not have a side-effect on the system, as the computer system restarts in its initial state.)

Now returning to our optimization problem, we need a definition of a relative side-effect, relevant to pairs of expressions, evaluated sequentially. These are special cases of side-effects as defined above.

Definition. We say that the form $F1$ produces a relative side-effect on the form $F2$ if and only if the evaluation of the form $F1$ might change the result of evaluation of $F2$.

Note that the last definition includes, for example, the case of PRINT. Indeed, if both $F1$, $F2$ are PRINT, the user will normally be interested in having the printing done in a specific order (otherwise a result will be lost). In other words, the evaluation $F2$ will be "of value" only if $F1$ has been evaluated (that is PRINT has been performed). So one can say that it is also a relative side-effect when a certain order of evaluation is prescribed.

In case of a recursion removal, one comes across two categories of side-effect. Suppose that in a recursive call of function FOO (X1 X2 ... XN)) we have FOO (*F*1 *F*2 ... *F*N). Then in an iterative code we have to assign:

```
(SETQ X1 F1)
(SETQ X2 F2)

(SETQ XN FN)
```

Thus the iterative pattern will introduce some side-effects, even if the forms *F*1 ... *F*N have no side-effects. We will call these side-effects *negative* (as one does not normally want the value of some *F*3 to be changed by previous assignments). It is this kind of side-effect that is taken care of in the program REMREC [Risch (1973)].

However, the forms *F*1 ... *F*N themselves might produce side-effects. We believe that both types of side-effects should be treated within the same formalism, and we illustrate this approach below.

We have a file DIMA–P that takes care of restrictions on the order of evaluation. This seems to be the most frequent type of relative side-effect in practice.

The file DIMANP concerns a somewhat wider type of relative side-effect, namely a side-effect through a variable. In this program it is reasonably assumed that this kind of side-effect can be desirable or undesirable (we refer to them as "positive" or "negative" side-effects).

5. DESCRIPTION OF DIMA–P, DIMANP AND EXAMPLES

One should not be surprised to see that the use of an automatic program taking side-effects into account, requests a certain number of declarative statements to be made. Eventually we intend to work in the prompt mode, when these declarations are not made before the system itself requests them.

Normally, these declarations are a source of additional inconvenience for the user, and he will probably prefer "the worst case" approach, when no optimization is allowed. However, if efficiency of computation is essential, then these declarations become necessary (and they should not be a problem for the user, because they exist in his brain at the time of function design, if he intentionally introduced some kind of relative side-effect).

In the program DIMA–P the only declaration is a list PSEFLIST, which contains pairs of forms, whose evaluation order must not be changed. Given PSEFLIST, the program DIMA–P will find an optimal evaluation sequence under this constraint.

In the program DIMANP the declarations may be of a more sophisticated type. This program takes care of relative side-effects through a variable, and the user is asked to declare for each of the forms in question, which variables are influenced by side-effects (if any). This information is stored under the property SIDEF for each form. Then the relative side-effects are treated separately whether the corresponding pair of forms is in the list PSEFLIST or not. Only in the last case is the side-effect treated as a negative one, and the system will introduce a temporary if necessary to save the corresponding function from "harm".

We conclude this paragraph with an example, covering the questions discussed above. Before this we note that some authors (Burstall and Darlington) have mentioned that the loss of efficiency in a recursive program is sometimes due to the fact that the same forms are evaluated many times.

Suppose one has to give an iterative form for the computation of a recursive given function:

(FOO *X Y Z U*)

Fig. 5.1.

where in the recursive call to FOO we have to evaluate

```
[FOO
        (CDR X)
        (CONS (CAR X)
              (CDR Z))
        (CONS (CAR X)
              (CDR Z))
        (CDR Y]
```

Fig. 5.2.

Here we have four forms $F1$ $F2$ $F3$ $F4$, and in a normal run, the form $F2$ will be evaluated twice, because it constitutes a part of the form $F3$.

If the recursion is deep, then for the sake of speed of computation one may replace the code Fig. 5.2 with the following:

```
[FOO
        (CDR X)
        (SETQ T__1 (CONS (CAR X)
                         (CDR Z)))
        (CONS (CAR X)
              T__1)
        (CDR Y]
```

Fig. 5.3.

and in the iterative form we will find assignments:

```
(SETQ X (CDR X))
(SETQ T__1 (CONS(CAR X) (CDR Z)))
(SETQ U(CDR Y))
```

The forms *F*2 *F*3 now have been replaced with *F*2! *F*3!. The form *F*2! has a relative side-effect on *F*3! through the variable *T*__1. This is a positive side-effect, as we introduced it intentionally.

Given the code Fig. 5.3 and ((*F*2! *F*3!)) as the value of PSEDLIST, the program DIMA-P will preserve the order, and at the same time it will save *Y* for (CDR *Y*). (Actually, in this example DIMA-P will instead evaluate *F*4 before *F*2!).

Without the declaration of the PSEFLIST value the program might give an error. There will be no error if we use the slightly different function FEE:

```
[FEE
        (CDR X)
        (SETQ T__1 (CONS (CAR Y)
                         (CDR Z)))
        (CONS (CAR Y)
              T__1)
        (CDR Y]
```

Fig. 5.4.

In this case DIMA-P will save *Y* for the form *F*3! (and for *F*4).

Returning back to codes for FOO, we see that there will be an error if one takes instead of Fig. 5.3 the following:

```
[FOO
        (CDR X)
        (SETQ Y (CONS(CAR X)
                     (CDR Z)))
        (CONS (CAR X)
              Y)
        (CDR Y]
```

Fig. 5.5.

Here we have also a negative (undesirable) side-effect of form *F*2! to the form *F*4.

Now let us consider the following iterative pattern:

```
(SETQ X (CDR X))
(SETQ Y (CAR X) (CDR Z))
(SETQ Z (CAR X)  Y)
(SETQ U (CDR Y))
```

Fig. 5.6A.

This will give the same result if now the second assignment is considered to be positive for the third form but negative for the fourth, and this information should be supplied. A user might wish to avoid this complication, by putting the fourth form in front of the second. However, he would be better off supplying the information; otherwise a correct optimization will be excluded.

```
[FOO
        (CDR X)
        (CONS (CAR X)
              (CDR Z)))
        (CONS (CAR Y)
                    Y)
        (CDR Y]
```

Fig. 5.6B.

In the case of Fig. 5.5 the program DIMANP, given the value of PSEFLIST as ((*F*2! *F*3! *Y*)), will understand the difference between the two relative side-effects and will either save the variable *Y* itself for use in *F*4, or will evaluate *F*4 prior to *F*2!

Finally in the case of Fig. 5.6, the program DIMA-P will give a different result from what we wanted: it will save the value of *Y* for the form *F*3! or even reverse the order. Even declaring the value PSEFLIST as ((*F*2! *F*3!)) will not help.

This side-effect will be treated by DIMANP correctly, even in the case of Fig. 5.6 if supplied with the information ((*F*2! *F*3! *Y*)). Indeed this case looks the most effective in gain of computation speed. If the value of PSEFLIST is given here as ((*F*2! *F*3!)), the program will consider this "generalized" side-effect as negative for all the forms involved and will save *Y*.

Thus, we would assert that previous programs like REMREC are able to deal only with negative side-effects of a certain type with NIL as the value of PSEFLIST.

We conclude with an example where nothing can be done to achieve the goal as the use of side-effects there is inherently contradictory, as in the following code for function FEE mentioned above:

```
[FEE
        (CDR X)
        (CONS (CAR Y)
              (CDR Z)))
        (CONS (CAR Y)
                    Y)
        (CDR Y]
```

Fig. 5.7.

This expression will never give the same result as Fig. 5.4.

In summary, we can see through our analysis that three cases can appear while converting a recursive code into an iterative form in the presence of side-effects:

(1) No side-effects in forms *F*1 *F*2 . . . *F*N themselves, then the side effects that appear in the assignment process are to be considered as negative.

(2) A relative side-effect, requiring a certain order of evaluation of the forms, these side-effects (mentioned above) are to be considered as negative.

(3) A "positive" side-effect through a variable such that some of these assignment side-effects now are to be treated as desirable as in the example of Fig. 5.7.

(4) A combination of these cases.

In the INTERLISP compiler (Teitelman *et al.*) the basic frame for a function changes the pointers to a new value of a variable after all the forms have been evaluated. This arrangement takes care of cases (1) and (2), but not case (3). The following adjustment will allow the possibility of full use of the side-effects idea: in case (3) the result of evaluation of the form producing this "positive" side-effect should be pointed as the new value of the corresponding variable immediately upon the evaluation of the form. Then, provided that a certain declaration is available, the code of Fig. 5.6 will produce the same result as the code of Fig. 5.2, but more efficiently.

However, this reorganization will require an additional check in the compiler, and the overall efficiency might be reduced.

6. OUTLINE AND DETAILED DESCRIPTION OF PROGRAMS

Below we give a description of the program DIMANP. DIMA-P is a shorter and simplified version of this. However, we would like to represent the main file DIMANP because it can solve a wider class of problems, and it has certain possibilities for extension.

The general approach in this program is based on search of optimal sequencing of form evaluation starting with the pairwise description of relations among the forms in question.

The following is the list of possible "conflicts" of *F*1 and *F*2 on the variable *X*, provided that these forms are evaluated in the order *F*1 *F*2:

$F1>X>F2$	(*F*1 has s-e on *X*; *X* used by *F*2)
$F1>X*>F2$	(*F*1 has s-e on *X*; *X* used by *F*2, value *F*2 to *X*)
$F1>*X>F2$	(*F*1 has s-e on *X*, value *F*1 to *X*; *X* used by *F*2)
$F1-*X<F2$	(value *F*1 to *X*; *F*2 has s-e on *X*)
$F1<*X<F2$	(*X* used by *F*1, value *F*1 to *X*; *F*2 has s-e on *X*)
$F1>*X>F2$	(*F*1 has s-e on *X*, value *F*1 to *X*; *F*2 has s-e on *X*)
$F1-*X>F2$	(value *F*1 to *X*; *X* used by *F*2)
$F1<*X>F2$	(*X* used by *F*1, value *F*1 to *X*; *X* used by *F*2)

Fig. 6.1 – s-e means "side-effect".

Here we have included only cases where the introduction of a temporary is obligatory. We have not included cases where lambda side-effects in the forms occur, because these cases are not studied completely yet.

Note that for the program DIMA-P, where no side-effects via variable of negative nature are assumed, one need take into account only the two last cases in Fig. 6.1. On the other hand this list can be extended, and we are planning to do it to include the lambda-variable side-effects.

In DIMANP so-called semantic programs are heavily used to represent programs of evaluation. This semantic program is a list containing four primitives:

*F*1 – formname
(SAVE *X*) – a temporary is introduced for *X*
(SAVE *F*1 *X*) – a temporary is used to store the result of evaluation of *F*1
(RETURN *X F*1 *X*) – stored in a temporary value of *F*1 to be returned back to *X*

Fig. 6.2A.

We have found this language rather convenient for use, as it makes the logic of a program very transparent at the stage of design of DIMANP.

The marginal semantic subprograms for collisions of Fig. 6.1 are given below:

For the codes F1>X>F2, F1>X*>F2, F1<*X>F2:
((SAVE *X*) (*F*1) (*F*2)

For the codes F1—*X<F2, F1>*X<F2:
((SAVE *F*1 —) (*F*2) (RETURN *X F*1 —))

For the code F1<*X<F2:
((SAVE *F*1 *X*) (*F*2) (RETURN *X F*1 *X*))

For the code F1—*X>F2:
((SAVE *X*) (*F*1) (*F*2))
or ((SAVE *F*1 —) (*F*2) (RETURN *X F*1 —))

For the code F1<*X>F2:
((SAVE *X*) (*F*1) (*F*2))
or ((SAVE *F*1 *X*) (*F*2) (RETURN *X F*1 *X*))

Fig. 6.2B.

These are stored in the program and used by the function PEPROG to build a semantic program for evaluation of forms *F*1 *F*2 . . . in the given order for one of the variables involved.

The function SEMPROG5 gives the final semantic program of evaluation of the forms in their order for all "conflict" variables. It is done step by step by using PEPROG, taking care of the proper place of all the primitives, in particular, trying to put a RETURN primitive as early as possible, that makes it possible to arrange "the garbage collection of temporaries" at run time [Burstall and Darlington].

Finally, given a semantic program as an input, NORMPROG produces a list representing a program in ordinary terms, using SETQ's and temporaries.

The function FCOST is used to estimate the number of temporaries needed for a variable, that might be 0, 1 or 2. Afterwards the EXPRIS1 calculates the total cost in the number of extra SETQ's needed to evaluate *F*1 *F*2 . . . *F*N in a given order.

Finally, the optimal sequence is discovered with the help of a full search process, which of course is not very efficient as the time of the search grows very rapidly with the number of forms.

However, as in rather general cases treated by DIMANP, we do not see now a more regular procedure to do it, and to save time we are heuristically applying the canonical representation of a graph, described in the first part of the present paper. The function CANON1 gives a partition of the collection of forms into a number of subgroups, having the property that the evaluation of a left group in the list representing this partition has no effect on the result of evaluation of a right group. This property lets the program of the order optimization and the program construction run independently on these groups. Besides, it appears that the same temporaries can be used several times. We believe that in practical cases, even if the collection of forms is large, not all of them are heavily interrelated.

REFERENCES

Boyer, R. S. and Moore, J. S. (1973). Proving theorems about LISP functions. *Proc. 3rd Int. Joint Conf. on Art. Int. (IJCAI-73)* pp. 486–493. Menlo Park: Stanford Research Institute.

Darlington, J. and Burstall, R. M. (1973). A system which automatically improves programs. *Proc. 3rd Int. Joint Conf. on Art. Int. (IJCAI-73)*, pp. 419–485. Menlo Park: Stanford Research Institute.

Risch, T. (1973). REMREC – a program for automatic recursion removal in LISP, *DLU 73/24*. Uppsala: Datalogilaboratoriet, Uppsala University.

Stefanuk, V. L. (1975). On interaction under local control. *Automation and Remote Control*.

Teitelman, W. (1974). *INTERSLIP Reference Manual*. Palo Alto: Xerox Palo Alto Research Center.

3

Modelling Distributed Systems

A. Yonezawa† and C. Hewitt
Artificial Intelligence Laboratory
Massachusetts Institute of Technology, USA

1. INTRODUCTION

Distributed systems are multi-processor information processing systems which do not rely on the central shared memory for communication. The importance of distributed systems has been growing with the advent of "computer networks" of a wide spectrum: networks of geographically distributed computers at one end, and tightly coupled systems built with a large number of inexpensive physical processors at the other end. Both kinds of distributed system are made available by the rapid progress in the technology of large-scale integrated circuits. Yet little has been done in the research on semantics and programming methodologies for distributed information processing systems.

Our main research goal is to understand and describe the behaviour of such distributed systems in seeking the maximum benefit of employing multi-processor computation schemata.

The contribution of such research to Artificial Intelligence is manifold. We advocate an approach to modelling intelligence in terms of cooperation and communication among knowledge-based problem-solving experts. In this approach, we present a coherent methodology for the distribution of active knowledge as a knowledge representation theory. Also this methodology provides flexible control structures which we believe are well suited to organizing distributed active knowledge. Furthermore, we hope to make technical contributions to the central issues of problem solving, such as parallel versus serial processing, centralization versus decentralization of control and information storage, and the "declarative-procedural" controversy.

This paper presents ideas and techniques in modelling distributed systems and their application to Artificial Intelligence. In Secs. 2 and 3, we discuss a

†Now with the Department of Information Science, Tokyo Institute of Technology (Tokyo Kogyo Diagaku), Oh-Okayama, Meguro, Tokyo, Japan.

model of distributed systems and its specification and proof techniques. In Sec. 4 we introduce the simple example of an air line reservation system and illustrate our specification and proof techniques by this example in the subsequent sections. Then we discuss our further work.

2. A MODEL OF DISTRIBUTED SYSTEMS

The actor model of computation (Grief and Hewitt 1975, Grief 1975, Hewitt and Baker 1977) has been developed as a model of communicating parallel processes. The fundamental objects in the model of computation are *actors*. An actor is a potentially active piece of knowledge (procedure) which becomes active when it is sent a message which is also an actor. Actors interact by sending messages to other actors. More than one transmission of messages may take place concurrently. Two events will be said to be *concurrent* if they can possibly occur at the same time. Each actor decides how to respond to messages sent to it. An actor is defined by its two parts, a *script* and a set of *acquaintances*. Its script is a description of how it should behave when it is sent a message. Its acquaintances are a finite set of actors that it directly *knows about*. If an actor A knows about another actor B, A can send a message to B directly. The concept of an *event* is fundamental in the actor model of computation. An event is an *arrival* of a message from actor M at a target actor T and is denoted by the expression ⟦T <= M⟧. A computation is expressed as a partially ordered set of events. We call this partial order the *precedes* ordering. Events which are unordered in the computation are concurrent. Thus the partial order of events naturally generalizes the notion of serial computation (which is a sequence of events) to that of parallel computation.

A collection of actors which communicate and cooperate with each other in a goal-oriented fashion can be implemented as a single actor. In essence, actors are procedural objects which may or may not have local storage. Some may behave like procedures, and some may behave like data structures. Modules in distributed systems are modelled by actors and systems of actors. In this regard, IC (integrated circuit) chips can be viewed as actors.

Knowledge and intelligence can be embedded as actors in a modular and distributed fashion. For example, *frames* (Minsky 1975), (Kuipers 1975), *units* (Bobrow and Winograd 1976), *beings* (Lenat 1975), *stereotypes* (Hewitt 1975) etc. which represent modular knowledge with procedural attachments, are modelled and implemented as actors. In the context of electronic mail systems and business information systems, objects such as forms, documents, customers, mail collecting stations, and mail distributing stations are easily modelled and implemented as actors.

Messages which are sent to target actors usually contain *continuation* actors to indicate where the replies to the messages should be sent. By virtue of continuations in messages, the message-passing in the actor model of computation realizes a universal, yet flexible control structure without using implicit mechanisms such as push-down stacks. Various forms of control structure such as go-to's, procedure calls, and co-routines can be viewed as particular patterns of message passing (Hewitt 1977).

This model of computation has been implemented as a programming language, PLASMA (Hewitt 1977). The script of an actor can be written as a PLASMA program. We believe that message-passing semantics provide a basis for programming languages for distributed systems. In Sec. 5, an example of a PLASMA program is given as a script of a flight-data actor in the model of a simple air line reservation system.

3. TECHNIQUES FOR SPECIFICATION AND VERIFICATION

In designing and implementing a distributed (message-passing) system, it is desirable to have a precise specification of the intended behaviour of the distributed system. Also we need sound techniques for demonstrating that implementations of the system meet its specifications. Below, we give some of the central ideas of our specification and proof techniques based on the model introduced in the previous section. More detailed work will be found in Yonezawa (1977).

In specifying the behaviour of a distributed system, it is not only practically infeasible, but also irrelevant to use global states of the entire system or the global time axis which governs the uniform time reference throughout the system. We are concerned with states of modular components of a distributed system which interact with each other by sending messages. Thus we are interested in the states of actors participating in an event at the instance at which the message is received.

In our specification language, *conceptual representations* are used to express local states of actors (modules). Conceptual representations were originally developed to specify the behaviour of actors which behave like data structures (Yonezawa and Hewitt 1976). We have found them very useful to express states of modules in distributed systems at varying levels of abstraction and from various view-points. The basic motivation of conceptual representations is as an aid in the provision of a specification language which serves as a good interface between programmers and the computer, and also between users and implementers. Conceptual representations are intuitively clear and easy to understand, yet their rigorous interpretations are provided. Instead of going into the details of syntactic constructs of conceptual representations, we shall give a few examples. Below !⟨exp⟩ is the unpack operation on ⟨exp⟩, that is individually writing out all the elements denoted by ⟨exp⟩.

(*CELL* (*contents:* A)) ;*a cell containing* A *as its contents.*
(*QUEUE* (*elements:* [A B C])) ;*a queue with elements* A B C.
(*NODE* (*car:* A)(*cdr:* B)) ;*a LISP node containing* A *and* B.
(*CUSTOMER* (*letters:* {!m})(*#-of-stamps-needed:* n))
;*a customer visiting a post office*
;*who carries letters* !m *and wants* n *stamps.*
(*POST-OFFICE* (*customers:* {!c}) (*collectors:* {!cl}))
;*a post office which contains customers* !c *and mail collectors* !cl.

It should be noted that a conceptual representation does not represent the identity of an actor. It only provides a description of the local state of an actor. Thus to say that an actor Q is in the state expressed by a conceptual representation (*QUEUE* (*elements:* [A B C])), an assertion of the following form is used:

(Q *is-a* (*QUEUE* (*elements:* [A B C])))

Some examples of specification using conceptual representation are given in the later sections.

Symbolic evaluation is a process which interprets a module on abstract data to demonstrate that the module satisfies its specification. Symbolic evaluation differs from ordinary evaluation in that (1) the only properties of input that can be used are the ones specified in the pre-requisites, and (2) if the symbolic evaluation of a module M encounters an invocation of some module N, the specification of N is used to continue the symbolic evaluation. The implementation of N is not used. The technique of symbolic evaluation has been studied by a number of researchers, for example Boyer and Moore (1975), Burstall and Darlington (1975), Hewitt and Smith (1975), Yonezawa (1975), King (1976).

Our method for symbolic evaluation of distributed systems is an extension of the one developed for symbolic evaluation of programs written in SIMULA-like languages (Yonezawa and Hewitt 1976). One of the main techniques we employ in symbolic evaluation is the introduction of a notion of **situations** (McCarthy and Hayes 1969). A situation is the *local* state of an actor system at a given moment. The precise definition of locality in the actor model of computation is found in Hewitt and Baker (1977). By relativizing assertions with situations, relations and assertions about states of modules in different situations can be expressed. Explicit uses of situational tags seems to be very powerful in symbolic evaluation of distributed systems. A simple example is given in Sec. 7.

Another technique we employ in symbolic evaluation is the use of *actor induction* to prove properties holding in a computation. Actor induction is a computational induction based on the *precedes* ordering (cf. Sec. 2) among events. It can be stated intuitively as follows:

> "For each event E in a computation C, if *preconditions* for E imply *preconditions* for each event E′ which is immediately caused by E, then the computation C is carried out according to the overall specification."

The precedes ordering has two kinds of suborderings, (1) the activation ordering, "*activates*", which is the causal relation among events, and (2) the arrival ordering, "*arrives-before*", which expresses ordering among events which have the same target actor. Thus there are two kinds of actor induction according to these suborderings. An example of the induction based on arrival ordering is used in Sec. 7.

4. MODELLING AN AIR-LINE RESERVATION SYSTEM

A specification of an air line reservation system

As an example of distributed systems, let us consider a very simple air-line reservation system. Suppose we have just one flight which has a non-negative number of seats†. A number of travel agencies (parallel processes) independently try to reserve or cancel seats for this flight, possibly concurrently. We model the air-line reservation system as a flight actor F which behaves as follows. The flight actor F accepts two kinds of message, (*reserve-a-seat:*) and (*cancel-a-seat:*). When F receives (*reserve-a-seat:*), if the number of free seats is zero, a message (*no-more-seats:*) is returned. Otherwise a message (*ok-its-reserved:*) is returned and the number of free seats is decreased by one. When F receives (*cancel-a-seat:*), if the number of free seats is less than the maximum number of seats of the flight, a message (*ok-its-cancelled:*) is returned and the number of free seats is increased by one, otherwise (*too-many-cancels:*) is returned. Furthermore, requests by (*reserve-a-seat:*) and (*cancel-a-seat:*) are served on a first-come-first-served basis.

To write a formal specification of the air-line reservation system, we need to describe the states of the flight actor. For this purpose, we use the following conceptual representation:

(*FLIGHT* (*seats-free:* ⟨*m*⟩) (*size:* ⟨*s*⟩))

The number of free seats is ⟨*m*⟩, and ⟨*s*⟩ is the size of the flight in terms of the total number of seats. The formal specification of the air-line reservation system using this conceptual representation is depicted in Fig. 1.

The first ⟨*event:*...⟩-clause states that a new flight actor F is created by an event where the create-flight actor receives a positive number S. ⟨Actor⟩* means that ⟨actor⟩ is newly created. The second ⟨*event:*...⟩-clause has two cases according to the number of free seats at the moment when the flight actor F receives (*reserve-a-seat:*). When the number of free seats is zero (*Case-1*), the state of F does not change. When it is positive (*Case-2*), the number of free seats decreases by one as stated by the assertion in the ⟨*next-cond:*... ⟩1-clause. The notation in Fig. 1:

```
⟨event: ⟦T ⟨= M⟧
  ⟨pre-cond: ... ⟩
  ⟨next-cond: ... ⟨assertion⟩ ... ⟩
  ⟨return: ⟨actor⟩ ⟩ ⟩
```

means that when an event ⟦T ⟨= M⟧ takes place, if the preconditions are satisfied, ⟨assertion⟩s in the ⟨*next-cond:*...⟩-clause hold immediately after the event

†A model of air-line reservation systems which deal with more than one flight is discussed in Yonezawa (1977).

until the next message arrives at T. ⟨Actor⟩ in the ⟨*return:*...⟩-clause is returned as a result of the event. A ⟨*next-cond:*...⟩-clause differs from a ⟨*post-cond:*...⟩-clause in that assertions in a ⟨*post-cond:*...⟩-clause hold at the time ⟨actor⟩ is returned, whereas assertions in a ⟨*next-cond:*...⟩-clause hold at the time the next message arrives. The next message may arrive at T before or after a reply for the previous message is returned. The third ⟨*event:*...⟩-clause is for the cancelling event, which is interpreted in a similar way.

```
⟨event: ⟦create-flight ⟨= S⟧
    ⟨pre-cond: (S ⟩ 0) ⟩
    ⟨return: F*⟩
    ⟨post-cond: (F is-a (FLIGHT (seats-free: S) (size: S))) ⟩⟩

⟨event: ⟦F ⟨= (reserve-a-seat:)⟧
  (case-1:
    ⟨pre-cond: (F is-a (FLIGHT (seats-free: 0) (size: S))) ⟩
    ⟨next-cond: (F is-a (FLIGHT (seats-free: 0) (size: S))) ⟩
    ⟨return: (no-more-seats:) ⟩)
  (case-2:
    ⟨pre-cond:
      (F is-a (FLIGHT (seats-free: N) (size: S)))
      (N ⟩ 0) ⟩
    ⟨next-cond: (F is-a (FLIGHT (seats-free: N − 1) (size: S))) ⟩
    ⟨return: (ok-its-reserved:) ⟩)⟩

⟨event: ⟦F ⟨= (cancel-a-seat:)⟧
  (case-1:
    ⟨pre-cond: (F is-a (FLIGHT (seats-free: S) (size: S))) ⟩
    ⟨next-cond: (F is-a (FLIGHT (seats-free: S) (size: S))) ⟩
    ⟨return: (too-many-cancels:) ⟩)
  (case-2:
    ⟨pre-cond:
      (F is-a (FLIGHT (seats-free: N) (size: S)))
      (N ⟨ S) ⟩
    ⟨next-cond: (F is-a (FLIGHT (seats-free: N + 1) (size: S))) ⟩
    ⟨return: (ok-its-cancelled:) ⟩ ) ⟩
```

Fig. 1 – A specification of the air line reservation system (a specification for the flight actor).

5. IMPLEMENTING THE AIR LINE RESERVATION SYSTEM

Our strategy for implementing the air line reservation system (specified in the previous section) is as follows. First, we implement a flight-data actor which satisfies the specification in Fig. 1.

In Fig. 2 we give an implementation of the flight-data actor in PLASMA.

```
(create-flight-data =s) ≡                 ;create-flight-data receives a size s of flight.
  (create-serialised-actor (size initially s)          ;a variable size is set to s.
      (seats-free initially s)            ;a variable seats-free is set to s.
    then                                            ;the following cases-clause is
                                  ;returned as an actor which behaves as a flight-data.
    (receivers
      (≡〉(reserve-a-seat:)                     ;when a (reserve-...) message is received,
        (rules seats-free
          (≡〉0                                              ;if seats-free is zero,
            (no-more-seats:))                         ;(no-...) message is returned.
          (≡〉(> 0)                                                   ;otherwise
            (seats-free ← (seats-free − 1))           ;seats-free is decreased by one.
            (ok-its-reserved:))))                     ;(ok-...) message is returned.
      (≡〉(cancel-a-seat:)                       ;when a (cancel-...) message is received,
        (rules seats-free
          (≡〉size                                 ;if seats-free is equal to size,
            (too-many-cancels:))                            ;(too-...) is returned,
          (≡〉(< size)                                                 ;otherwise
            (seats-free ← (seats-free + 1))           ;seats-free is increased by one.
            (ok-its-cancelled:)))) ))                           ;(ok-...) is returned.
```

Fig. 2 – An implementation of a flight actor.

It is fairly straightforward to write a specification for this flight F by using a conceptual representation:

(FLIGHT (seats-free: ⟨m⟩) (size: ⟨s⟩))

which describes the state of a flight actor. The number of free seats is ⟨*m*⟩ and ⟨*s*⟩ is the size of the flight in terms of the number of seats. Note that if F were sent more than one message concurrently, anomalous results would be caused unless we take precautions. For example, in the implementation in Fig. 2 if (*reserve-a-seat:*) and (*cancel-a-seat:*) messages are sent concurrently, a (*no-more-seats:*) message might be returned even if there are vacant seats. Therefore in order to model the air line reservation system by using the above implementation of a flight-data actor, the way it is used must be restricted so that inference between different activations may not take place. As suggested in the beginning of this section, the restriction we impose is that F must be *used serially* in the sense that F is not allowed to receive a message until the activation by the previous message is completed. Now the flight actor can be used to implement the air line reservation system under this restriction.

7. SYMBOLIC EVALUATION OF THE AIR LINE RESERVATION SYSTEM

Our implementation of the air line reservation system is expressed by the following simple PLASMA code:

(create-a-flight S)

which creates a flight which initially has the following conceptual representation:

(*FLIGHT* (*seats-free:* S)(*size:* S))

This establishes the first clause of the specification of the air line reservation system. The other clauses are established in the same way using symbolic evaluation.

8. FURTHER WORK

We are currently working to establish a coherent methodology for demonstrating that a distributed message-passing system will meet its task specifications. As an example, an actor model of a simple post office is studied in Yonezawa (1977). It is shown that the overall task specifications of the post office are implied by specifications of the individual behaviour and mutual interaction of actors in the model.

By using the technique of symbolic evaluation, we would like to analyse the relationships and dependencies between modules in a distributed system. This approach will be instrumental in assisting us with the evolutionary development of distributed systems.

We are also working on the application of procedural objects (such as actors) to the area of business automation. In order to replace paper forms and paper documents, we use "active" forms and "active" documents which are displayed on the TV terminal as images accompanied by procedures. Active forms and documents are sent from one site to another whereby clerks are requested to provide necessary information with the guidance of the accompanying procedures. Such procedures may also check the consistency of filled items and point out errors and inconsistencies to persons who are processing forms. Thus active forms and documents accompanied by procedures enormously increase the flexibility and security of message and document systems. Furthermore, we propose to use the "language" of forms and documents as the basis for the user to communicate with the information processing system. One of the ultimate objectives of our research is to develop a methodology for the construction of real-time distributed systems which can be efficiently and effectively used by non-programmers.

Note added in proof

Since this paper was written the message-passing semantics group has continued to develop the preliminary ideas in this paper. Recent results are reported in

Hewitt, C. (1978). Concurrent systems need *both* sequences and serialisers, *Working Paper 179*, Cambridge, Mass: Artificial Intelligence Laboratory, Massachusetts Institute of Technology; Hewitt, C., Attardi, G. and Liebermann, H. (1978), *Working Paper 172*, Cambridge, Mass: Artificial Intelligence Laboratory, Massachusetts Institute of Technology; Hewitt, C., Attardi, G. and Liebermann, H. (1978), *Working Paper 180*, Cambridge, Mass: Artificial Intelligence Laboratory, Massachusetts Institute of Technology.

Acknowledgements

Conversations with Jeff Rulifson have been helpful in further developing the notion of an "active" document. This research was conducted at the Artificial Intelligence Laboratory and Laboratory for Computer Science (formerly Project MAC), Massachusetts Institute of Technology, under the sponsorship of the Office of Naval Research, contract number N00014-75C0522.

BIBLIOGRAPHY

Atkinson, R. and Hewitt, C. (1977). Synchronisation in actor systems. Paper given at 4th ACM (SIGPLAN-SIGACT) Symposium on Principles of Programming Languages, Los Angeles. New York: Association for Computing Machinery (in press).

Birtwhistle, G., Dahl, O.-J., Myrhang, B. and Nygaard, K. (1973). *SIMULA Begin*. Philadelphia: Auerbach.

Bobrow, D. G. and Winograd, T. (1976). An overview of KRL, a knowledge representation language. *Cognitive Science,* **1,** No. 1, 3–46.

Boyer, R. S. and Moore, J. S. (1975). Proving theorems about LISP functions. *JACM.* 22, 129–144.

Burstall, R. M. and Darlington, J. (1975). Some transformations for developing recursive programs. *Proc. of 1975 International Conference on Reliable Software,* Los Angeles. pp. 456–472. Also (1977) *JACM,* **24,** 44–67.

Greif, I. and Hewitt, C (1975). Actor semantics of PLANNER-73. *Proc. of 2nd ACM (SIGPLAN-SIGACT) Symposium on Principles of Programming Languages,* pp. 67–77. New York: Association for Computing Machinery.

Hewitt, C. (1975). How to use what you know. *Advance Papers Fourth International Joint Conference on Artificial Intelligence* (*IJCAI*-**75**) Tbilisi, USSR, pp. 189–198. Cambridge, Mass: Artificial Intelligence Laboratory, MIT.

Hewitt, C. (1977). Viewing control structures as patterns of passing messages. *Artificial Intelligence,* **8,** 323–64. Also *AI-Memo* No. 410. Cambridge, Mass: Artificial Intelligence Laboratory, Massachusetts Institute of Technology.

Hewitt, C. and Baker, H. (1977). Laws for communicating parallel processes. *Proc. of IFIP-***77.** Toronto. Also *Working Paper* 134. Cambridge, Mass: Artificial Intelligence Laboratory, Massachusetts Institute of Technology.

Hewitt, C. and Smith, B. C. (1975). Towards a programming apprentice. *IEEE Transactions on Software Engineering,* **SE-1,** No. 1, pp. 26–45.

Hoare, C. A. R. (1972). Proof of correctness of data representation. *Acta Informatica,* **2,** 271–81.

King, J. (1976). Symbolic execution and program testing. *CACM,* **19,** No. 7, 385–394.

Kuipers, B. J. (1976). A frame for frames: representing knowledge for recognition. In *Representation and Understanding* (eds. Bobrow, D. G. and Collins, A. M.), New York: Academic Press.

Learning Research Group (1976). Personal dynamic media. *SSL*–76–1. Palo Alto: Xerox Palo Alto Research Center.

Lenat, D. B. (1975). Beings: Knowledge as interacting experts. *Advance Papers of Fourth International Joint Conference on Artificial Intelligence* (*IJCAI-75*) Tbilisi, pp. 126–133. Cambridge, Mass: Artificial Intelligence Laboratory, Massachusetts Institute of Technology.

McCarthy, J. and Hayes, P. J. (1969). Some philosophical problems from the standpoint of artificial intelligence. In *Machine Intelligence* **4**, pp. 463-501 (eds. Meltzer, B. and Michie, D.). Edinburgh: Edinburgh University Press.

Minsky, M. (1975). A framework for representing knowledge. In *The Psychology of Computer Vision* (ed. Winston, P. H.) pp. 211–277. New York: McGraw Hill.

Rich, C. and Shrobe, H. E. (1975). Understanding LISP programs: towards a programmers apprentice. *AI-TR No. 354.* Cambridge, Mass: Artificial Intelligence Laboratory, Massachusetts Institute of Technology.

Steiger, R. (1974). Actor machine architecture. M.Sc. Thesis. Cambridge, Mass: Department of Electrical Engineering and Computer Science, Massachusetts Institute of Technology.

Yonezawa, A. (1975). Meta-evaluation of actors with side-effects. *Working Paper 101*, Cambridge, Mass: Artificial Intelligence Laboratory, Massachusetts Institute of Technology.

Yonezawa, A. (1977). Specification and verification of programs based on message-passing semantics. Ph.D thesis, Cambridge, Mass: Department of Electrical Engineering and Computer Science, Massachusetts Institute of Technology.

Yonezawa, A. and Hewitt, C. (1976). Symbolic evaluation using conceptual representations for programs with side-effects. *AI-Memo No. 399*. Cambridge, Mass: Artificial Intelligence Laboratory, Massachusetts Institute of Technology.

REPRESENTATIONS FOR ABSTRACT REASONING

4

A Maximal Method for Set Variables in Automatic Theorem-proving

W. W. Bledsoe
Departments of Mathematics and Computer Science
The University of Texas at Austin, USA

Abstract

A procedure is described which gives values to set variables in automatic theorem proving. The result is that a theorem is thereby reduced to first order logic, which is often much easier to prove. This procedure handles a part of higher order logic, a small but important part. It is not as general as the methods of Huet, Andrews, Pietrzykowski, and Haynes and Henschen, but it seems to be much faster when it applies. It is more in the spirit of J. L. Darlington's F-matching. This procedure is not domain specific: results have been obtained in intermediate analysis (the intermediate value theorem), topology, logic, and program verification (finding internal assertions).

This method is a "maximal method" in that a largest (or maximal) set is usually produced if there is one.

A preliminary version has been programmed for the computer and run to prove several theorems. Some completeness results are given.

1. INTRODUCTION

For many theorems the main difficulty in the proof is in *defining a particular set*. Once that is done the proof often proceeds rather easily. For example, in

Theorem.[1] $\exists A\, \forall x (x \in A \longrightarrow x \leqslant 0)$,

if we let $A = \{x \colon x \leqslant 0\}$, then we are left with the trivial subgoal:

$$(x \leqslant 0 \longrightarrow x \leqslant 0).$$

[1]Refer to Appendix I for the definition of such symbols as $\exists$, $\forall$, $\{x \colon P(x)\}$.

Or, if we are proving the intermediate value theorem,

Theorem. If f is continuous for $a \leqslant x \leqslant b$, $f(a) \leqslant 0$, and $f(b) \geqslant 0$, then $f(x) = 0$ for some x between a and b (See Fig. 1).

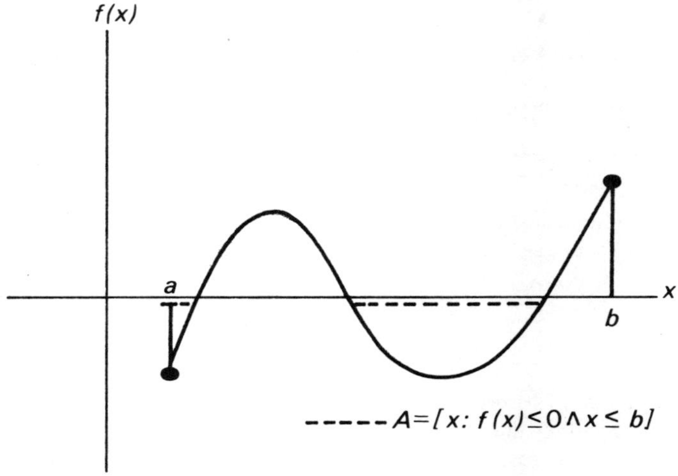

Fig. 1 – The intermediate value theorem.

Using the least upper bound axiom,

LUB Axiom. Each non-empty bounded set A of real numbers has a least upper bound,

and if we let

$$A = \{x: f(x) \leqslant 0 \wedge x \leqslant b\},$$

then again the proof is rather straightforward (but harder than the last example). The question, of course, is how to select A?

There are several other theorems in analysis, such as the Heine-Borel Theorem where the chief difficulty lies in defining a particular set. Also a similar situation comes up again and again in other parts of mathematics, and in application areas such as program verification and program synthesis.

The problem of finding a value for a set variable A, is of course equivalent to the problem of giving a value to a one place predicate variable P. For example, in the threorem

Theorem. $x \geqslant 0 \wedge y \geqslant 0 \longrightarrow \exists P[P(0,x) \wedge \forall A(P(A,0) \longrightarrow A = x \cdot y)$
$\wedge \forall A \; \forall K(P(A,K) \wedge K > 0 \longrightarrow P(A+y, K-1))]$

(which arises from the field of program verification; see Ex. 15, Sec. 5), if we give the predicate P the value

$$P(A,K) \equiv (A = (x - K) \cdot y)$$

then the theorem is reduced to a trivial subgoal.

Of course, this is a part of higher order logic, and as such can be attacked by the systems and ideas of Huet [3], Pieterzykowski [10], Haynes and Henschen [7], Andrews [11], etc. But these are very slow for many simple proofs. For example, Huet's beautiful system [3] is forced into double splitting on the rather easy theorem given in Ex. 4 below. (Even a human has trouble applying his procedure to this example.)

In this paper we describe a procedure which attempts to overcome this difficulty. It is less general than those referenced above; it usually applies only to a part of second order logic (but an important part); and it seems to be much faster when it applies. Ours is more in the spirit of J. L. Darlington's "F-matching", but different in method and scope.

Our methods are neither domain specific, nor just a collection of heuristics for finding sets in a particular area like analysis. They can be used to prove theorems (such as the intermediate value theorem) in analysis where the set A is a set of real numbers, as well as theorems in topology where the set A is a family of sets, and theorems from program verification, or from other areas where set variables are to be instantiated.

In Sec. 2 we give some preliminary examples, and in Sec. 3 we describe our rules for generating the desired set A. They consist of *basic rules* which apply to simple formulas, and *combining rules* for combining the results from the basic rules.

One of our goals in this work is to avoid indiscriminate matches (or attempts at matches) between formulas such as $(t \in A)$ and P, (where P is first order), but rather to allow such a match *only* when $(t \in A)$ and P are somehow "connected". In this way the search is drastically reduced. Our basic rules (see Fig. 2) are a partial attainment of this goal.

Our methods are "maximal" in that they usually generate the largest set with the desired properties (if there is one). Of course some theorems such as,

$$\exists A [A \text{ is dense in } R) \wedge ((R-A) \text{ is dense in } R)]$$

have no maximal (or minimal) solution for A. Also in some cases there is more than one maximal solution (see Ex. 5, Sec. 3), even infinitely many solutions. However, we believe there is a wide class of interesting cases that have a unique maximal solution, or at most one or two maximal solutions.

Our procedure utilizes the automatic prover described in [1] as a "control" (see Sec. 4) for generating the desired sets. But one can follow this presentation without full knowledge of that paper.

In actual practice the prover makes two passes on a theorem: first to define the set A; second to prove the resulting theorem, after the set A has been instantiated. Thus the procedure is sound, that is, there is no danger of it producing a false solution since the solution is always verified.

But the emphasis in this paper will be on the first pass, wherein the desired sets are generated, and not on the second where the proof is completed.

In Sec. 5 we describe some major examples, in Sec. 6 we discuss the induction axiom and difficulties with it, and in Sec. 7 we make several comments.

In Appendix I we list a glossary of terms and symbols, and in Appendix II we give some completeness proofs. Appendix III gives some further details of examples from Sec. 5, and Appendix IV gives some example theorems about general inequalities which might be of interest.

2. SOME PRELIMINARY EXAMPLES

We are concerned here only with cases of the form

$$\exists A\ P(A)$$

or

$$(\forall\ A\ P(A)) \longrightarrow C$$

where the variable A is to be found (that is, given a value). Since $((\forall\ A\ P(A)) \longrightarrow C)$ is equivalent to $\exists A(P(A) \longrightarrow C)$, we will usually act as if our theorem is already in the form $\exists A(P(A)$. Theorems where A is a constant can usually be handled as first order logic.

We will treat only the case where there is but *one* such set variable A. However, our methods will often work for theorems with many such variables.

Once the set A has been found, the theorem becomes *first order,* and, we hope, not too difficult. That will often be the case. However, it is well known that automatic theorem proving for first order logic is a most challenging and unresolved task.

But as was stated earlier, there are many theorems where the first order part is only moderately difficult once a set variable has been properly defined (instantiated).

It is our objective here to automatically define such variables.

Let us look at some examples before giving the rules. These fragments help illuminate the procedure. More substantial theorems will be given later in Sec. 5.

Example 1. $\exists A\ \forall x\ (x \in A \longrightarrow x \leqslant 0)$.

Solution: $A \equiv \{x\colon x \leqslant 0\}$.

This is the simple theorem which states that "there is a set A all of whose members are non-positive". Clearly, one such A is the set of all non-positive reals, and that is exactly what is returned by our program. When this value is substituted for A the theorem reduces to the trivial subgoal

$$(x \leqslant 0 \longrightarrow x \leqslant 0)$$

which our program quickly verifies as true.

Example 2. $\exists G \, \forall A \, (A \in G \longrightarrow \exists B \, (B \in F \wedge A \subseteq B))$.

Solution: $G \equiv \{A\colon \exists B \, (B \in F \wedge A \subseteq B\}$.

This example is very much like the previous one, except that G plays the role of A, A plays the role of x, and $\exists B \, (B \in F \wedge A \subseteq B)$ plays the role of $x \leqslant 0$. Notice that the variable G is a "family" variable rather than a "set" variable. Thus we have (technically) proved a theorem in third order logic, although it is for all practical purposes a theorem in second order. It is desirable, we believe, to keep formulas like $\exists B \, (B \in F \wedge A \subseteq B)$ together during the processing, and this is what our program usually does.

Next we consider a theorem of a little more substance.

Example 3. $(P(a) \longrightarrow \exists A \, [\forall x \, (\underset{\text{ODD}}{x \in A} \longrightarrow P(x)) \wedge \exists y \, (\underset{\text{EVEN}}{y \in A})])$

Solution: $A \equiv \{x\colon P(x)\}$.

It is now time to note that $A \equiv \emptyset$ is a perfectly good solution to Ex. 1. However, $A \equiv \emptyset$ will *not* work for Ex. 3; here we must include in A *at least* the point a. We prefer to put *all we can* in A, thus getting a *maximal* solution.

In Ex. 3 there are two types of occurrences of A: the "EVEN" occurrence $y \in A$, and the "ODD" occurrence $(x \in A \longrightarrow P(x))$[2]. The ODD occurrences are used to determine A, (according to the rules in Sec. 3), and the EVEN occurrences are just checked after A has been defined[3]. Accordingly when the solution given is put in for A we get

$$(P(a) \longrightarrow [\forall x \, (P(x) \longrightarrow P(x)) \wedge \exists y \, (P(y))])$$

in which the ODD part is now trivial and the EVEN part is yet to be checked (but can be).

The next example will illuminate that point.

[2]Note that $(x \in A \longrightarrow P(x))$ is equivalent to $(x \notin A \vee P(x))$. If A does not occur in B (except possibly as a skolem argument -- see footnote 4) then A is in an EVEN position of $A \wedge B$, $A \vee B$, $(B \longrightarrow A)$, B, and A itself; and A is in an ODD position of $(A \longrightarrow B)$, $(\sim A)$, and B. Also an EVEN position of an EVEN position is EVEN, ODD of ODD is EVEN, ODD of EVEN is ODD, and EVEN of ODD is ODD.

[3]This is equivalent to putting the universal set U for A for the EVEN occurrence and intersecting it with the set $\{x\colon P(x)\}$ gotten for the ODD occurrence.

Example 4. $(a < b < c \longrightarrow \exists A\ (a \notin A \wedge b \in A \wedge c \notin A))$
ODD EVEN ODD

Solution: $\{x\colon x \neq a \wedge x \neq c\}$.

The two ODD occurences give respectively $\{x\colon x \neq a\}$ and $\{x\colon x \neq c\}$, and the EVEN occurrence gives U(using the rules of Sec. 3) which are combined (by the "combining rules" of Sec. 3) into the given solution.

Notice that this is not the only solution. There are many others such as

$\{x\colon a < x < c\}$,
$\{x\colon a < x \leqslant b\}$,
$\{b\}$,

but none of these is maximal. Our method gives the maximal solution if there is one.

We could have developed a *minimal* theory, getting the smallest sets, by using the EVEN occurrences of A instead of the ODD, but we have a slight preference for maximal. *Intermediate* sets would be difficult to produce automatically. Only when we work against the extremes do we reduce the complexity of the problem.

3. SET BUILDING RULES

3.1 Basic rules

Our rules for generating maximal sets are of two kinds: (i) basic rules and (ii) combining rules. The basic rules give solutions to certain subformulas of the form: $(x \in A)$, $(x \notin A)$, $(x \in A \longrightarrow P(x))$, and the combining rules consolidate these basic solutions into one general solution, depending on the placement of these subformulas in the theorem. For instance, in Ex. 4 above, the subformulas $(a \notin A)$, $(b \in A)$, and $(c \notin A)$ were connected by "$\wedge$", (and in EVEN positions) so the corresponding solutions $\{x\colon x \neq a\}$, U, and $\{x\colon x \neq c\}$ were intersected to obtain the general solution $\{x\colon x \neq a \wedge x \neq c\}$.

Fig. 2 gives our first set of basic rules. More are added later. In Fig. 2 the subformulas shown are expected to be in an EVEN[2] position of the theorem being proved, and the theorem itself is to be in skolemized form[4].

Also it should be noted that these rules cannot handle an expression in A until it is reduced to the form $(x \in A)$. (This includes the cases $x \notin A$ and $(x \in A \longrightarrow C)$.) This reduction may require the use of hypotheses, definitions, and lemmas.

The rules of Fig. 2 operate under the restrictions listed in Table 1. In Rules B1 and B2, "x" is required to be a skolem[4] function of A, and not appear in the rest of the theorem. That is to say the subformula

$$\forall x\ (x \in A \longrightarrow P(x))$$

[4]See [2], footnote 12, or [1], App. 1 for a complete description of skolemization. Here this means, essentially, that $\forall x\ (x \in A \longrightarrow P(x))$ etc. occurs in an EVEN position of the theorem within the scope of A.

occurs in an EVEN position of the theorem within the scope of A. See Sec. 7 for a further discussion of this and some means of easing these restrictions on x. Similarly for x and y in B2′.

	Subformula	Solution
B1.	$(x \in A \longrightarrow P(x))$	$\{z: P(z)\}$
B2.	$(f(x) \in A \longrightarrow P(x))$	$\{z: \forall s\ (z = f(s) \longrightarrow P(s))\}$
B2′.	$(f(x,y) \in A \longrightarrow P(x,y))$	$\{z: \forall r\ \forall s\ (z = f(r,s) \longrightarrow P(r,s))\}$
B3.	$(t \in A \longrightarrow P)$	$\{z: z = t \longrightarrow P\}$
B4.	$(t \notin A)$	$\{z: z \neq t\}$
B5.	P (does not contain A)	U (universal set) (IGNORED in case of conjunctions)
B6.	$(t \in A)$	U
B7.	E ($t \in A$ is even in E)	U
BQ	If B1-B4 yield $\{z: P(z)\}$, and s is a variable in $P(z)$	$\{z: \exists s\ P(z)\}$
BE	ELSE	U

Fig. 2 – Basic rules.

Table 1

Restrictions on the basic rules of Fig. 2

0. The rules B1-BE apply to subformulas in EVEN positions of the theorem. A is a set variable to be instantiated. It is the only set variable (indeed the only higher order variable) in the theorem. A occurs only in the form $(t \in A)$, or as a skolem function argument.
1. In B1 x is a skolem function[4] of A, A does not occur otherwise in $P(x)$, x does not occur elsewhere in the theorem, and no other variable occurs in x (that is, x is a skolem function of no other variable but A).
2. In B2, B2′, x and y are skolem functions of A, A does not occur otherwise in $P(x)$ or $P(x,y)$, x and y do not occur elsewhere in the theorem, and no other variable occurs in x, y, $f(x)$, or $f(x,y)$.
3. In B3, A does not occur in t or P.
4. In B4, A does not occur in t.
5. In B5, A does not occur in P.
6. In B6, A does not occur in t.
7. In B7, every occurrence of an expression of the form $(t \in A)$ in E, is in an EVEN position of E; A does not occur in t. A cannot occur in E except in one of these subformulas $(t \in A)$.
8. In BQ, s is a variable in $P(z)$, but does not occur elsewhere in the theorem.
9. In BE, the subformulas have the form of B1-B7 or BQ, but the restrictions 1-8 are not satisfied.

Note that when the term "t" is not quantified within the scope of the quantification of A, as in

$$\forall b \; \exists A \; (t \in A \longrightarrow P(t))$$

then by Rule B3, we do *not* derive the solution $\{z\colon P(z)\}$ as was done in Rule B1, because it is not the *maximal* solution. Rather the maximal solution is $\{z\colon z = t \longrightarrow P(t)\}$ as given by Rule B3. Rule B4 acts similarly.

Rules B5-B7 give the universal set U as a solution for expressions of the form $(t \in A)$ and for EVEN combinations of these. Since $(U \cap A_0) = A_0$, the effect is to *ignore* expressions that give the solution U whenever they are conjoined (connected by "$\wedge$") to other expressions.

In BQ, s is allowed to appear only in $P(z)$. (These rules might be changed later so that we delay the quantification of s (in $\{z\colon \exists s\, P(z)\}$) until the entire solution of the whole theorem is obtained, and in that way be able to handle the case when s occurs elsewhere in the theorem.)

These rules and those in Secs. 3.2-3.6 are supported to some degree by the proofs in Appendix II. Our objective is to find maximal sets for a few basic forms, and to give combining rules that retain that maximality.

3.2 Combining rules for conjunctions

We will first give, in Fig. 3, three combining rules for conjunctions before giving others. These three rules, with the basic rules of Fig. 2, have been sufficient to prove a number of interesting theorems. Even our extended list of combining rules is by no means complete; we are now trying to validate and extend both the basic and combining rules.

If

(i) A_1 is the (only)[5] maximal solution for $P(A)$, and

(ii) A_2 is the (only) maximal solution for $Q(A)$, and

(iii) both A_1 and A_2 are obtained from the basic rules of Fig. 2, or from combining rules C1-C3, or if

(iii′) $P(A)$ and $Q(A)$ have the *intermediate property* (see below), then

C1. $(A_1 \cap A_2)$ is a maximal solution of $(P(A) \wedge Q(A))$, if it has a solution, and

C2. $(A_1 \cap A_2)$ is a maximal solution of $(H \longrightarrow P(A) \wedge Q(A))$, if it has a solution, provided that "A" does not occur in H, and

C3. $(A_1 \cap A_2)$ is a maximal solution of $((R \vee P(A)) \wedge Q(A))$ if it has a solution, provided that "A" does not occur in R.

Fig. 3 – Three combining rules for conjunctions.

[5]If $P(A)$ or $Q(A)$ has more than one maximal solution (see Ex. 5 and Fig. 5 below), this rule still applies to at least one of the solutions A_1 of $P(A)$ and one of the solutions A_2 of $Q(A)$.

Definition. We say that a formula P has the *subset property* (*superset property*) if for each B and C, if B is a solution of P, and C is a subset (superset) of B, then C is a solution of P.

Definition. We say that a formula P has the *intermediate property* if for each B, C, and D, if B and D are solutions of P and $B \subseteq C \subseteq D$, then C is a solution of P.

It is easily seen that if P has the subset property or the superset property, then P has the intermediate property, because $\emptyset$ is a solution of a formula with the subset property (if it has any solution), and U is a solution of a formula with the superset property (if it has any solution).

It is easily shown that the subformulas in Rules B1-B5, and BQ, have the sub-set property, and those of Rules B5-B7 have the superset property. See Theorems 7-11 and the accompanying Remark of Appendix II.

Also if P_1 and Q_1 have the subset property and if P_2 and Q_2 have the superset property, and if P_3 and Q_3 have the intermediate property, then

$P_1 \wedge Q_1$ has the subset property
$P_2 \wedge Q_2$ has the superset property
$P_3 \wedge Q_3$ has the intermediate property
$P_1 \wedge Q_2$ has the intermediate property.

This is shown graphically in Fig. 4. (See Appendix II.)

		Q		
	$\wedge$	subset	intermediate	superset
	subset	subset	intermediate	intermediate
P	intermediate	intermediate	intermediate	intermediate
	superset	intermediate	intermediate	superset

Fig. 4 – The status of $(P \wedge Q)$ when P and Q individually have the subset, superset or intermediate property.

Corresponding results hold for

$(H \longrightarrow P_1 \wedge Q_1)$,
$(H \longrightarrow P_2 \wedge Q_2)$,
$((R \vee P_1) \wedge Q_1)$, etc.,

where A does not occur in H or R, and hence the combining rules of Fig. 3 are valid under condition (iii′) as well as (iii), by Theorem 12-13 of Appendix II.

(The reader might wish to skip to Sec. 4 and Exs. 8–12 of Sec. 5 which apply only the rules of Figs. 2 and 3, before continuing this section.)

3.3 Combining rules for disjunctions

Often there can be *more than one* maximal solution or even infinitely many[6]. For example the theorem

$$\exists A[\forall x (x \in A \longrightarrow P(x)) \vee \forall y (y \in A \longrightarrow Q(y))]$$

has two maximal solutions

$$\{z: P(z)\} \text{ and } \{z: Q(z)\}$$

(But

$$\{z: P(z) \vee Q(z)\}$$

is *not* a solution!)

When there is more than one maximal solution we will indicate the "maximal solution" as a family $\mathcal{F}$ of sets. For example,

Example 5. $P(a) \longrightarrow \exists A([\forall (x \in A \longrightarrow P(x)) \wedge \exists y (y \in A)] \vee [\forall x (x \in A \longrightarrow Q(x)) \wedge \exists y (y \in A)])$.

Solution: $\mathcal{F} \equiv \{\{z: P(z)\}, \{z: Q(z)\}\}$.

Then we must verify that some member of $\mathcal{F}$ does indeed satisfy the theorem. In this example only $\{z: P(z)\}$ satisfies.†

This brings us to combining rules C4–C6 in Fig. 5.

It should be noted that the basic Rule B3 is really a special case of rules B4, B6, and C4, because $(x \in b \longrightarrow P)$ is equivalent to $(x \notin b \vee P)$ which yield the solution $\mathcal{F} = \{\{z: z \neq b\}, U\}$, and the solution $\{z: z = b \longrightarrow P\}$ is also either U or $\{z: z \neq b\}$, depending on whether P is, or is not, true.

3.4 Further basic and combining rules

Each of the subformulas in the basic rules of Fig. 2, except Rule BE, have the *intermediate* property (see above). This allowed us to use the rather simple combining rules of Fig. 3 for conjunctions. We will now consider some cases where the subformulas do not have the intermediate property, and we give two rules in Fig. 6 which are combinations of basic and combining rules. ω is the set of non-negative integers.

[6] See Sec. 3.5.

†It is somewhat misleading to call a family like $\mathcal{F}$ the "solution" of a theorem like Ex. 5, because some members of $\mathcal{F}$ may not satisfy the given theorem. A more appropriate term might be "family of candidate solutions", in that this family must contain all maximal sets A which can satisfy the given theorem.

If (i), (ii), (iii′) of Fig. 3, then

C4. $\mathcal{F} = \{A_1, A_2\}$ is the maximal solution of $(P(A) \vee Q(A))$.

Also if

(iv) $P(A)$ has a maximal solution $\mathcal{F}_1$, and

(v) $Q(A)$ has a maximal solution $\mathcal{F}_2$, where

(vi) $\mathcal{F}_1$ and $\mathcal{F}_2$ are gotten from C4, C5, or C6, or are gotten from B1-BQ where the output there is treated as a singleton $\{A_0\}$, then

C5. $(\mathcal{F}_1 \cup \mathcal{F}_2)$ is a maximal solution of $(P(A) \vee Q(A)$, and

C6. $(\mathcal{F}_1 \cap\cap \mathcal{F}_2)$[7] includes a maximal solution of $(P(A) \wedge Q(A))$.

Fig. 5 – Two combining rules for disjunctions.

[7]$(\mathcal{F}_1 \cap\cap \mathcal{F}_2)$ is the family of sets $(D_1 \cap D_2)$ with $D_1 \in \mathcal{F}_1$ and $D_2 \in \mathcal{F}_2$.

If $P(A)$ has the (only)[5] maximal solution

$\{z: p(z)\}$,

and $P(A)$ has the subset property, and $Q(A)$ is

$(x \in A \wedge q(x) \longrightarrow f(x) \in A)$

where x is a skolem function of A, A does not occur otherwise in x, $q(x)$, or $f(x)$, and x does not occur in $P(A)$, and if

$(P(A) \wedge Q(A))$

has a solution, then it has the maximal solution,

BC1 $\{z: p(z) \wedge [\forall n\, (n \in \omega \longrightarrow p\, f^n(z))$
$\vee \exists N\, (N \in \omega \wedge {\sim} q\, f^N(z) \wedge \forall n\, (n \in \omega \wedge n \leqslant N \longrightarrow p\, f^N(z)))]\}$.

The set

BC2 $\{z: p(z) \wedge \forall n\, (n \in \omega \wedge q\, f^n(z) \longrightarrow p\, f^{n+1}(z))\}$

is also a solution of $(P(A) \wedge Q(A))$ provided it is a solution of $Q(A)$, but it may not be maximal.

Fig. 6 – Further combination rules.

The rule BC1 gives a set A_0 which is maximal (see Theorems 14-15, App. II) but often unwieldly. A suggested strategy is to try BC2 and if that fails (because it may not be a solution)then try BC1. (See Exs. 13-15 in Sec. 5.)

The rules of Fig. 6 can be extended to non-monadic cases where x is replaced by (x,y), or (x,y,z), etc. (See, for example, Rules BC1′ and BC2′ of Fig. 7.) Also the quantification Rule BQ can be applied here too.

If $P(A)$ has the (only)[5] maximal solution

$$\{z: p(z)\}$$

and $P(A)$ has the subset property, and $Q(A)$ is

$$((x,y) \in A \wedge q(x,y) \longrightarrow f(x,y) \in A)$$

where x and y are skolem functions of A, A does not occur otherwise in $x, y, q(x,y)$ or $f(x,y)$ and x and y do not occur in $P(A)$, and if

$$(P(A) \wedge Q(A))$$

has a solution, then it has the maximal solution

BC1′ $\{z: p(z) \wedge [\forall n\,(n \in \omega \longrightarrow p\, f^n\,(\Pi_1(z), \Pi_2(z))^{\dagger}$
$\vee\ \exists N\,(N \in \omega \wedge \sim q\ f^N(\Pi_1(z), \Pi_2(z))$
$\wedge\ \forall\, n\,(n \in \omega \wedge n \leqslant N \longrightarrow p\ f^n\,(\Pi_1(z), \Pi_2(z)))]\}$

BC2′ $\{z: p(z) \wedge \forall\, n\,(n \in \omega \wedge q\, f^n(\Pi_1(z), \Pi_2(z)) \longrightarrow p\, f^{n+1}(\Pi_1(z), \Pi_2(z)))\}$

is also a solution of $(P(A) \wedge Q(A))$ provided that it is a solution of $Q(A)$, but it may not be maximal.

† If z is the ordered pair, (a,b) then $\Pi_1(z) = a$, and $\Pi_2(z) = b$.

Fig. 7 – Further combining rules.

3.5 Infinitely many maximal solutions

We saw in Sec. 3.3 an example which has two maximal solutions. Others have more, even infinitely many. For example

Example 5A. $\exists A\ \forall\, x\ \forall\, y\ (x \in A \wedge y \in A \longrightarrow P(x,y))$.
If $P(x,y)$ can be "separated", the solution is easy. For example if $P(x,y) \equiv p(x) \wedge q(y)$, then the maximal solution is $\{z: p(z) \wedge q(z)\}$.

However, if $P(x,y) \equiv (0 \leqslant \frac{x}{2} \leqslant y \leqslant 2x)$, then the maximal solutions consist of the infinite family of sets of the form

$$\{x: a \leqslant x \leqslant 2a\}$$

for $a \geqslant 0$. This is the family of bases of the squares shown in Fig. 8. Notice that these maximal solutions may overlap.

Clearly one could not try all of these solutions in order, as could be done in Ex. 5. However, as we shall see shortly, our rules can be very effective *even when there are infinitely many solutions.*

Example 5B. $\exists A\ \forall L\ \exists y\ \forall z\ [(z \in A \longrightarrow p(z,y)) \wedge q(L,y)]$

This is equivalent to (successively):

$$\exists A\ \exists g\ \forall L\ \forall z\ [(z \in A \longrightarrow p(z,g(L))) \wedge q(L,g(L))]$$
$$\exists g\ \exists A\ [\forall z\ (z \in A \longrightarrow \forall L\ p(z,g(L))) \wedge \forall L\ q(L,g(L))]\,.$$

(1) $$\exists g \exists A\ [\forall z\ (z \in A \longrightarrow P(z,g)) \wedge Q(g)]\,.$$

Now if g_0 is a solution for $Q(g)$ then

$$\{z\colon P(z,g_0)\}$$

is a maximal solution (1). At first blush this would seem of little value, since finding such a g_0 is itself a search problem in *second order logic*, (and since indeed the complete maximal solution of (1) is the possibly infinite family of all such $\{z\colon P(z,g_0)\}$). However, in many applications the family of maximal solutions is *reduced to a family of one* by matches during the proof of other parts of the theorem. This is exactly what happens in the use of the Least Upper Bound Axiom, (LUB), to prove theorems like Ex. 11 of Sec. 5. In such cases we are proving some conclusion C from LUB:

$$(\text{LUB} \longrightarrow \text{C}).$$

This is equivalent to

$$(\sim \text{C} \longrightarrow \sim \text{LUB})$$

which is equivalent to (see Ex. 11 for the statement of LUB)

$$(\sim \text{C} \longrightarrow \exists A\ (\ldots \wedge \forall l[\exists x\ (\ldots) \vee \exists y\ (\forall z\ (z \in A \longrightarrow \ldots) \wedge \ldots)])),$$

which has (partly) the form

$$\exists A\ \forall l \exists y\ \forall z[\ (z \in A \longrightarrow p(z,y)) \wedge q(l,y)]$$

which is like Ex. 5B above. In the proof of Ex. 11 below, we are able to instantiate the variable y (with, say, y_0) and get the corresponding maximal solution

$$\{z: p(z,y_0)\},$$

in a satisfying way.

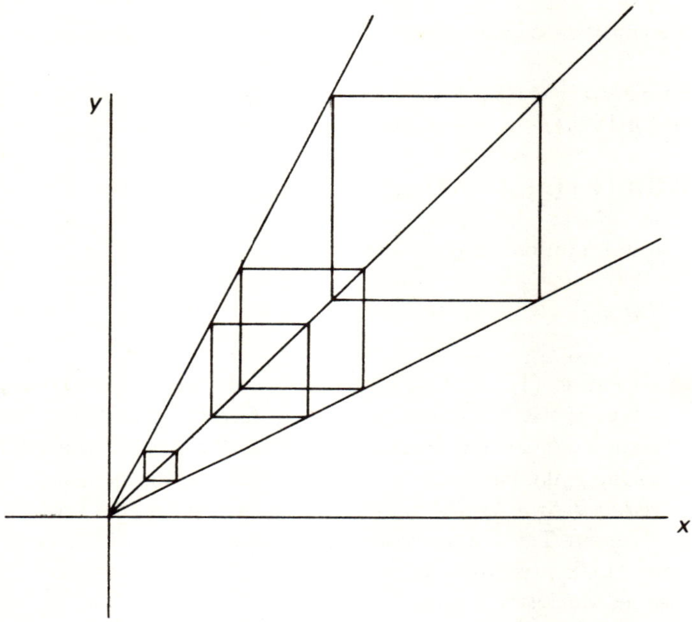

Fig 8 – Infinitely many maximal solutions of $\exists A \, \forall x \, \forall y \, (x \in A \wedge y \in A \longrightarrow P(x,y))$

3.6 Other monadic cases†

In Sec. 3.5 we are given

$$\{z: P(z,z)\}$$

as the maximal solution of

Example 5A. $\exists A \, \forall x \, \forall y \, (x \in A \wedge y \in A \longrightarrow P(x,y))$

in the case when $P(x,y)$ could be expressed as a conjunction of the two monadic predicates $p(x)$ and $q(y)$.

We now give a few other such results.

† This work has a definite relation to that of Behmann. See Sec. 7.4.

Example 5C. $\exists A\ \forall x\ \forall y\ (x \in A \wedge y \in A \longrightarrow p(x) \vee q(y))$.

Solution: $\mathcal{F} = \{A_1, A_2\}$, where $A_1 = \{x\colon p(x)\}, A_2 = \{y\colon q(y)\}$.

Example 5D. $\exists A\ \forall x\ \forall y\ (x \in A \vee y \in A \longrightarrow p(x) \wedge q(y))$.

Solution: $\{z\colon \forall s\ (p(z) \wedge q(s) \wedge p(s) \wedge q(z))\}$.

This is a special case of the following where $P(x,y)$ is not necessarily monadic.

Example 5E. $\exists A\ \forall x\ \forall y\ (x \in A \vee y \in A \longrightarrow P(x,y))$.
Solution: $\{z\colon \forall s\ (p(z,s) \wedge p(s,z))\}$.

Example 5F. $\exists A\ \forall x\ \forall y\ \forall z\ [(x \in A \vee (y \in A \wedge z \in A)) \longrightarrow (p(x) \wedge R(y)) \vee (q(x) \wedge T(z))]$.

Solution: $\mathcal{F} = \{A_1 \cap A_2, A_1 \cap A_3\}$, where
$A_1 = \{x\colon \forall y\ \forall z\ ((p(x) \wedge R(y)) \vee (q(x) \wedge T(z))\}$
$A_2 = \{t\colon \forall x\ (p(x) \wedge R(t))\}$,
$A_3 = \{t\colon \forall x\ (q(x) \wedge T(t))\}$.

It appears that for the monadic case, maximal solutions of the kind given for Ex. 5F can be determined by the pattern of occurrences of $x \in A$, $y \in A$, etc., $p(x)$, $q(y)$, etc. in the conjunctive normal form of the theorem. Such a procedure if worked out and validated may or may not contribute much to *practical* automatic theorem proving, though it should have theoretical interest.

Obviously this is related to Behmann's decision procedure for monadic second order logic [13].

4. CONTROL

4.1 The prover as a control

As mentioned above, the set-building rules of Sec. 3 are used to propose a value for a set variable A and then IMPLY, our automatic prover [1] is used to prove the resulting theorem.

It turns out that the prover is *also* a convenient vehicle for controlling the use of the set-building rules. In doing so it proceeds in its normal way to prove the theorem, applying a list of production rules: to manipulate the theorem, to propose subgoals, to manipulate the data base, to match, etc.[8] The set building rules are added to these production rules.

[8]The reader is referred to [1] for details and examples. For our purposes here the prover described in [1] has been augmented by a data base for handling our set variables and interval types (see Sec. 4.2). These data base manipulations are in the spirit of those mentioned in [9] and applied in [5, 6] and [8].

For example, in proving the theorem,

Example 6. $\exists A\ (P(a) \wedge a \neq b \longrightarrow \forall x\ (x \in A \longrightarrow P(x)) \wedge \exists y\ (y \in A) \wedge b \notin A)$, it first skolemizes and sets up the goal

$$(P(a) \wedge a \neq b \longrightarrow (x_A \in A \longrightarrow P(x_A)) \wedge (y \in A) \wedge b \notin A)\ , \qquad (\ )$$

and then splits it up into subgoals (1), (2), (3).

$$(P(a) \wedge a \neq b \longrightarrow (x_A \in A \longrightarrow P(x_A))). \qquad (1)$$

Rule B1 is applied to this subgoal to yield the solution $\{z: P(z)\}$ for A. This value of A is *not* substituted for A in the remainder of the theorem, but rather is placed in the data base, to be combined with other values gotten later.

$$(P(a) \wedge a \neq b \longrightarrow y \in A). \qquad (2)$$

This subgoal is ignored by Rule B6. (Actually it yields the universal set U, which will be intersected with other sets and therefore "ignored".)

$$(P(a) \wedge a \neq b \longrightarrow b \notin A). \qquad (3)$$

Rule B4 is applied to this subgoal to yield the solution $\{z: z \neq b\}$ for A. This too is placed in the data base, and combined with the earlier solution, yielding

$$\{z: P(z) \wedge z \neq b\} \qquad (*)$$

as the current solution for A.

Since (3) is the last subgoal, the final solution (*) is substituted for A in the original theorem, getting the new goal:

$$(P(a) \wedge a \neq b \longrightarrow (P(x_0) \wedge x_0 \neq b \longrightarrow P(x_0)) \wedge (P(y) \wedge y \neq b)$$
$$\wedge \sim (P(b) \wedge b \neq b)). \qquad (\ )$$

Now this, which is a first order theorem, is proved as a series of subgoals.

Our intention here is to emphasize the part of the process that builds the set A using the set-building rules, and to de-emphasize the proof of the resulting first order theorem.

4.2 Interval types and inequalities

Before describing other examples in Sec. 5 we will describe another part of our data base which is called "Interval types" in [1] and "Typelists" in [5-6] which plays a crucial part in proofs of theorems in real analysis. This is best illustrated with examples.

Example 7. $(P(1) \longrightarrow \exists x\,(0 \leqslant x \leqslant 2 \wedge P(x)))$.

The skolemized goal is

$$(P(1) \longrightarrow (0 \leqslant x \leqslant 2 \wedge P(x))). \qquad (\;)$$

The prover handles the first subgoal

$$(P(1) \longrightarrow 0 \leqslant x \leqslant 2) \qquad (1)$$

not by giving some particular value to x, such as 0 or 2 or 1, but rather by storing the entry $\{x\colon 0\ 2\}$ in the data base, indicating that the variable x is now restricted to the interval $0 \leqslant x \leqslant 2$. The entry $\{x\colon 0\ 2\}$ is called a *restriction interval* for x. The prover then goes to the second subgoal.

$$(P(1) \longrightarrow P(x)) \qquad (2)$$

with x *still a variable*. When this goal is solved, with $1/x$, then it must verify that this substitution is consistent with its data base entry, that is, that

$$0 \leqslant 1 \leqslant 2.$$

Such data base mechanisms are used in the proof of the intermediate value theorem in Ex. 11 below, and other like proofs in real analysis. These concepts which were used in [2], have literally made the undoable doable. Otherwise one is involved in the use of the axioms for the real numbers and for inequalities which tend to choke automatic provers not using special mechanisms like this.

5. SOME MAJOR EXAMPLES

We describe here the proof of some theorems,† following the steps taken by the prover, but omitting much of the detail in order to emphasize the set-building rules of Sec. 3. We will give examples from topology, real analysis (the intermediate value theorem), logic, and program verification.

The non-mathematically-oriented reader can follow these examples to some extent and get the main ideas without studying continuity and topology.

Example 8. If a set B contains an open neighbourhood of each of its points, then B is open.[9]

Or symbolically

$$(\forall\, x\,(x \in B \longrightarrow \exists D\,(\text{Open}\, D \wedge x \in D \wedge D \subseteq B\,)) \longrightarrow \text{Open}\, B).$$

†See Sec. 7.6 for a discussion of what was actually proved by the computer on these examples.

[9] An open neighbourhood of a point x is just an open set containing x. We will use the capitalized OPEN to represent the family of all Open sets. (Union G) is defined to be the set of points contained in some member of G.

We shall use the following lemma:

L: The union of a family of open sets is Open. That is,

$$(\exists G\,(G \subseteq \text{OPEN} \wedge D = (\text{Union } G)) \longrightarrow \text{Open } D).^{9}$$

Our object will be to find this family G.

Using L as a hypothesis, our skolemized goal becomes

$$(\overbrace{[G \subseteq \text{OPEN} \wedge D = (\text{Union } G) \longrightarrow \text{Open } D]}^{\text{L}} \qquad (\;)$$
$$\wedge\; \overbrace{[x \in B_0 \longrightarrow (\text{Open } D_x \wedge x \in D_x \wedge D_x \subseteq B_0)]}^{\beta} \longrightarrow \text{Open } B_0).$$

Using the lemma L (first hypothesis) with B_0/D we obtain the subgoal,

$$(L \wedge \beta \longrightarrow G \subseteq \text{OPEN} \wedge B_0 = (\text{Union } G))\,. \qquad (\;)$$

The first subgoal

$$(\text{L} \wedge \beta \longrightarrow G \subseteq \text{OPEN}) \qquad (1)^{\dagger}$$

becomes, upon definition of $\subseteq$ and OPEN, and skolemization,

$$(\text{L} \wedge \beta \longrightarrow \forall A\,(A \in G \longrightarrow \text{Open } A))\,, \qquad (1)$$
$$(\text{L} \wedge \beta \longrightarrow (A_G \in G \longrightarrow \text{Open } A_G))\,.$$

Rule B1 is applied to obtain the solution $\{z\colon \text{Open } z\}$ for G. This is stored in the data base and G remains a variable.

In the second subgoal

$$(\text{L} \wedge \beta \longrightarrow B_0 = (\text{Union } G)) \qquad (2)$$

the program defines "=", and splits to get subgoals (2 1) and (2 2), in which "$\subseteq$" and "union" are defined, and skolemized.

$$(\text{L} \wedge \beta \longrightarrow B_0 \subseteq (\text{Union } G)) \qquad (2.1)$$
$$(\text{L} \wedge \beta \longrightarrow \forall x\,(x \in B_0 \longrightarrow \exists D\,(D \in G \wedge x \in D)))$$
$$(\text{L} \wedge \beta \longrightarrow (x_0 \in B_0 \longrightarrow (D \in G \wedge x_0 \in D)))$$

IGNORED by Rule B7.

†See footnote 12.

$$(\mathrm{L} \wedge \beta \longrightarrow (\text{Union } G) \subseteq B_0) \qquad (2.2)$$
$$(\mathrm{L} \wedge \beta \longrightarrow \forall D\,(D \in G \longrightarrow D \subseteq B_0))$$
$$(\mathrm{L} \wedge \beta \longrightarrow (D_G \in G \longrightarrow D_G \subseteq B_0)).$$

Rule B1 is applied to obtain the solution $\{z\colon z \subseteq B_0\}$.

Combining Rules C1–C3 are applied to produce the general solution

$$G_0 = \{z\colon \text{open } z \wedge z \subseteq B_0\}$$

for G. When G_0 is substituted for G in the lemma L our goal ( ) p. 70, becomes

$$(\mathrm{L} \wedge \beta \longrightarrow G_0 \subseteq \mathrm{OPEN} \wedge B_0 = (\text{Union } G_0)), \qquad (\ )$$

or

$$(\mathrm{L} \wedge \beta \longrightarrow G_0 \subseteq \mathrm{OPEN} \wedge B_0 \subseteq (\text{Union } G_0) \wedge (\text{Union } G_0) \subseteq B).$$

The first and third subgoals are immediate consequences of the definition of G_0, and the second is a consequence of the hypothesis β. Indeed, we note the general principle that usually the only subgoals that need to be verified are the ones which are IGNORED earlier.

Example 9. If F is a family of open sets covering the regular topological space X, then there exists a family G of open sets which covers X and for which $\bar{G} \subseteq\subseteq F$.[10]

Our object is to find this family G.

We will use the definitions

Regular: $\forall A\, \forall x\, (\text{Open } A \wedge x \in A \longrightarrow \exists B\, (\text{Open } B \wedge x \in B \wedge \bar{B} \subseteq A)$

OC F: $F \subseteq \mathrm{OPEN} \wedge \text{Cover } F$

Cover F: $\forall x\, \exists A\, (A \in F \wedge x \in A)$.

Thus our theorem becomes

$$(\text{Regular} \wedge \text{OC } F \longrightarrow \exists G\, (\text{OC } G \wedge \bar{G} \subseteq\subseteq F)),$$

$$(\text{Regular} \wedge \text{OC } F_0 \longrightarrow (\text{OC } G \wedge \bar{G} \subseteq\subseteq F_0)), \qquad (\ )$$

in skolemized form. This is split into subgoals (1), (2), (1 1), (1 2), using the definition above as appropriate.

$$(\text{Regular} \wedge \text{OC } F_0 \longrightarrow \text{OC } G). \qquad (1)$$

[10] We will denote by $\bar{A}$ the "closure" of a set A, and by $\bar{G}$ the family of closures of members of G, that is, $\bar{G} = \{\bar{A}\colon A \in G\}$. Furthermore $(H \subseteq\subseteq F)$ means that H is a refinement of F, that is, each member of H is a subset of a member of F, or $(\forall A\, (A \in H \longrightarrow \exists B\, (B \in F \wedge \subseteq B))$. Thus $(\bar{G} \subseteq\subseteq F)$ means $\forall A\, (A \in G \longrightarrow \exists B\, (B \in F \wedge \bar{A} \subseteq B))$.

The solution F_0 for G would work for this subgoal but would eventually fail for subgoal (2), and be rejected.

$$(\text{Regular} \wedge \text{OC } F_0 \longrightarrow G \subseteq \text{OPEN} \wedge \text{Cover } G)\,. \tag{1}$$

$$(\text{Regular} \wedge \text{OC } F_0 \longrightarrow G \subseteq \text{OPEN}) \tag{1 1}$$
$$(\text{Regular} \wedge \text{OC } F_0 \longrightarrow \forall\,(A \in G \longrightarrow \text{Open } A))\,.$$

After skolemizing, Rule B1 yields $\{z\colon \text{Open } z\}$ for G.

$$(\text{Regular} \wedge \text{OC } F_0 \longrightarrow \text{Cover } G)\,. \tag{1 2}$$

This is IGNORED by Rule B7, using the definition of "Cover".

$$(\text{Regular} \wedge \text{OC } F_0 \longrightarrow \bar{G} \subseteq \subseteq F_0) \tag{2}$$
$$(\text{Regular} \wedge \text{OC } F_0 \longrightarrow \forall A\;(A \in G \longrightarrow \exists B\,(B \in F_0 \wedge \bar{A} \subseteq B)))$$
$$(\text{Regular} \wedge \text{OC } F_0 \longrightarrow (A_G \in G \longrightarrow (B \in F_0 \wedge \bar{A}_G \subseteq B))).$$

Rules B1 and BQ yield $\{z\colon \exists B\,(B \in F_0 \wedge \bar{Z} \subseteq B)\}$

Combining Rules C1-C3, give the general solution

$$\{Z\colon \text{Open } Z \wedge \exists B\,(B \in F_0 \wedge \bar{Z} \subseteq B)\}$$

which satisfies the theorem.

The next (rather simple) example is given to show *the effect of lemmas* on the maximal solution. Let R represent the real numbers and **Q** the rationals.

Example 10. $\exists A$ (A is dense in $R \wedge (R\text{-}A)$ is dense in R).
This of course has no maximal solution for A. However, if we employ the lemma,

L: $\forall B\,(\mathbf{Q} \subseteq B \longrightarrow B$ is dense in $R)$
$\wedge\, \forall D\,(D \subseteq \mathbf{Q} \longrightarrow (R\text{-}D$ is dense in $R)$.

then we do get a maximal solution.

$$(\mathbf{Q} \subseteq B \overset{\alpha}{\longrightarrow} \text{dense } B) \wedge (D \subseteq \mathbf{Q} \overset{\beta}{\longrightarrow} \text{dense } (R\text{-}D)) \tag{ }$$
$$\longrightarrow \text{dense } A \wedge \text{dense } (R\text{-}A).$$

$$(\alpha \wedge \beta \longrightarrow \text{dense } A).\ \text{Use } \alpha \text{ with } A/B\,. \tag{1}$$

$$(\alpha \wedge \beta \longrightarrow \mathbf{Q} \subseteq A) \tag{1 BC}$$
$$(\alpha \wedge \beta \wedge x_A \in \mathbf{Q} \longrightarrow x_A \in A)\,.$$

IGNORE by Rule B5.

$(\alpha \wedge \beta \longrightarrow \text{dense } (R\text{-}A))$ Use β with A/D. (2)

$(\alpha \wedge \beta \longrightarrow A \subseteq \mathbf{Q})$ (2 BC)
$(\alpha \wedge \beta \longrightarrow (x_A \in A \longrightarrow x_A \in \mathbf{Q}))$.
Rule B1 gives the solution $\{z: z \in \mathbf{Q}\}$ for A.

Here a theorem with no maximal solution was given one by the use of the lemma. In other theorems, the maximal solution is often changed (decreased) by the use of lemmas. Indeed, that is the case in Ex. 11 below where a non-maximal (but adequate) solution

$$\{z: z \leqslant b \wedge f(z) \leqslant 0\}$$

is given instead of the actual maximal solution

$$\{z: \exists x (z \leqslant x \leqslant b \wedge f(x) \leqslant 0)\}.$$

Example 11. (Intermediate Value Theorem)
If f is continuous for $a \leqslant x \leqslant b$, $a \leqslant b$, $f(a) \leqslant 0$, and $f(b) \geqslant 0$, then $f(x) = 0$ for some x between a and b. (See Fig. 1).

The proof of this will require the least upper bound axiom.

LUB. Each non-empty bounded set A has a least upper bound.

The object here is to find the set A required by the least upper bound axiom. The definition of the set needed is not at all obvious (even for humans). We believe that the use of a *natural deduction prover*, such as ours, as a control, is the key to this kind of problem, whereby the prover explores its various subgoals in a natural way and uses the basic set-building Rules B1–BQ as they become applicable. Only combining Rules C1–C3 are applicable in this example, so the basic solutions are intersected to obtain the general solution

$$\{z: z \leqslant b \wedge f(z) \leqslant 0\}$$

for A.

The theorem and axiom (in symbols) are:

Th. $\forall y\, (a \leqslant y \leqslant b \longrightarrow \text{Cont}\, f\, y) \wedge a \leqslant b \wedge f(a) \leqslant 0 \wedge f(b) \geqslant 0$
$\longrightarrow \exists x\, (f(x) = 0)$.

LUB. $\forall A\, (\exists u\, \forall t\, (t \in A \longrightarrow t \leqslant u) \wedge \exists r\, (r \in A) \longrightarrow$
$\exists l\, [\forall x\, (x \in A \longrightarrow x \leqslant l)$
$\wedge \forall y\, (\forall z\, (z \in A \longrightarrow z \leqslant y) \longrightarrow l \leqslant y)])$.

Instead of the definition of continuity we use the two lemmas

L1. $(\mathrm{Cont}\, f\, x \longrightarrow$
$\forall a\, (a < f(x) \longrightarrow \exists t\, (t < x \wedge \forall s\, (t < s \leqslant x \longrightarrow a < f(s))))$

L2. $(\mathrm{Cont}\, f\, x \longrightarrow$
$\forall a\, (f(x) < a \longrightarrow \exists t\, (x < t \wedge \forall s\, (x \leqslant s < t \longrightarrow f(s) < a))))$.

Our skolemized[11] goal is therefore

$$(\mathrm{L1} \wedge \mathrm{L2} \wedge \mathrm{LUB} \wedge H_1 \wedge a \leqslant b \wedge f(a) \leqslant 0 \wedge 0 \leqslant f(b) \longrightarrow f(x) = 0) \quad (\ )$$

where (rearranged and skolemized)

$$\mathrm{L1} \equiv (\mathrm{Cont}\, f\, x' \wedge ((f(s) \leqslant a' \wedge s \leqslant x' \longrightarrow s \leqslant t_1) \longrightarrow x' \leqslant t_1) \longrightarrow f(x') \leqslant a').$$

$$\mathrm{L2} \equiv (\mathrm{Cont}\, f\, x'' \wedge ((a' \leqslant f(s) \wedge x'' \leqslant s \longrightarrow t_2 \leqslant s) \longrightarrow t_2 \leqslant x'') \longrightarrow a' \leqslant f(x'')).$$

$$\mathrm{LUB} \equiv [(t_{Au} \in A \longrightarrow t_{Au} \leqslant u) \wedge r \in A \longrightarrow (x' \in A \longrightarrow x' \leqslant l_0) \wedge ((z_A \in A \longrightarrow z_A \leqslant y) \longrightarrow l_0 \leqslant y)]$$

$$H_1 \equiv (a \leqslant y' \leqslant b \longrightarrow \mathrm{Cont}\, f\, y').$$

We shall denote all of the hypotheses by H in the following.

$$(H \longrightarrow f(x) = 0) \quad (\ )$$

The conclusion is defined, getting

$$(H \longrightarrow f(x) \leqslant 0 \wedge 0 \leqslant f(x))$$

which is split into subgoals (1) and (2) below.

$$(H \longrightarrow f(x) \leqslant 0). \quad (1)$$

Since $f(a) \leqslant 0$ is a hypothesis this goal is satisfied by the substitution a/x, but this value for x will eventually fail on subgoal (2). So it instead uses L1 with $0/a', x/x'$, getting

$$(H \longrightarrow \mathrm{Cont}\, f\, x \wedge ((f(s) \leqslant 0 \wedge s \leqslant x \longrightarrow s \leqslant t_1) \longrightarrow x \leqslant t_1)) \quad (1\ \mathrm{L1})^{12}$$

[11] In some cases here, to simplify the presentation, we have shortened the skolem expressions, with l_0 instead of l_A, t_1 instead of $t_{1x'}$, t_2 instead of $t_{2x''}$, etc.

$(H \longrightarrow \text{Cont} f\, x)$. Use H_1 with x/y'. (1 L1 1)

$(H \longrightarrow a \leqslant x \leqslant b)$. (1 L1 1 L1)

The entry $\{x\colon a\ b\}$ is placed in the data (see Sec. 4.2); x remains a variable.

$$(H \longrightarrow ((f(s) \leqslant 0 \wedge s \leqslant x \longrightarrow s \leqslant t_1) \longrightarrow x \leqslant t_1)) \qquad (1\ \text{L1}\ 2)$$

$$\alpha$$

$$(H \wedge (f(s) \leqslant 0 \wedge s \leqslant x \longrightarrow s \leqslant t_1) \longrightarrow x \leqslant t_1).$$

Use LUB with l_0/x, t_1/y.

$$(H \wedge \alpha \longrightarrow (t_{Au} \in A \longrightarrow t_{Au} \leqslant u) \wedge r \in A \wedge (z_A \in A \longrightarrow z_A \leqslant t_1)).$$
(1 L1 2 LUB)

Before the program can proceed with this subgoal it must check (see Sec. 4.2) that the value l_0 just given x is consistent with the data base entry $\{x\colon a\ b\}$, which was placed there in goal (1 L1 1 H_1), that is, that $a \leqslant l_0 \leqslant b$. The prover calls itself to do this

$(H \longrightarrow a \leqslant l_0 \leqslant b)$ (CHECK)

$(H \longrightarrow a \leqslant l_0)$. Use LUB with a/x'. (CHECK 1)

$(H \longrightarrow (t_{Au} \in A \longrightarrow t_{Au} \leqslant u) \wedge r \in A \wedge a \in A)$. (CHECK 1 LUB)

Again it must check that the substitution a/x is consistent with the data base, that is, that $a \leqslant a \leqslant b$. But this is immediate, so it proceeds.

$(H \longrightarrow (t_{Au} \in A \longrightarrow t_{Au} \leqslant u)$ (CHECK 1 LUB 1)

IGNORED by Rule BE since the variable u is a skolem argument of t_{Au}. (See Restriction 8, Table I).

$(H \longrightarrow r \in A)$. IGNORED by Rule B6. (CHECK 1 LUB 2)

$(H \longrightarrow a \in A)$. IGNORED by Rule B6. (CHECK 1 LUB 3)

$(H \longrightarrow l_0 \leqslant b)$. Use LUB with b/y. (CHECK 2)

$$(H \longrightarrow (t_{Au} \in A \longrightarrow t_{Au} \leqslant u) \wedge r \in A \wedge (z_A \in A \longrightarrow z_A \leqslant b))$$
(CHECK 2 LUB)

[12] The parenthesized list in the right margin represents a "theorem label" or "goal label" which is used by the computer to let the reader know what part of the proof is being attempted. If a goal (λ) is split, its two subgoals are labelled (λ 1) and (λ 2). "L1" means backchaining on lemma L1, etc.

$(H \longrightarrow (t_{Au} \in A \longrightarrow t_{Au} \leqslant u))$ (CHECK 2 LUB 1)

IGNORED by Rule BE

$(H \longrightarrow r \in A)$ (CHECK 2 LUB 2)

IGNORED by Rule B6.

$(H \longrightarrow (z_A \in A \longrightarrow z_A \leqslant b))$ (CHECK 2 LUB 3)

Rule B1 gives $\{z: z \leqslant b\}$ for A which is placed in the data base.

This finishes the subgoal (CHECK), that $(a \leqslant l_0 \leqslant b)$, so the program returns to

(1 L1 2 LUB)

$(H \wedge \alpha \longrightarrow (t_{Au} \in A \longrightarrow t_{Au} \leqslant u) \wedge r \in A \wedge (z_A \in A \longrightarrow z_A \leqslant t_1))$

$(H \wedge \alpha \longrightarrow (t_{Au} \in A \longrightarrow t_{Au} \leqslant u))$. (1 L1 2 LUB 1)

The current value $\{z: z \leqslant b\}$ of A satisfies this goal, with b/u.

$(H \wedge \alpha \longrightarrow r \in A)$. IGNORED by Rule B6. (1 L1 2 LUB 2)

$(H \wedge \alpha \longrightarrow (z_A \in A \longrightarrow z_A \leqslant t_1))$[13] (1 L1 2 LUB 3)

$(H \wedge \alpha \wedge z_A \in A \longrightarrow z_A \leqslant t_1)$. Use α with z_A/s.

$\alpha \equiv (f(s) \leqslant 0 \wedge s \leqslant x \longrightarrow s \leqslant t_1)$

$(H \wedge \alpha \wedge z_A \in A \longrightarrow f(z_A) \leqslant 0 \wedge z_A \leqslant x)$ (1 L1 2 LUB 3 α)

$(H \wedge \alpha \wedge z_A \in A \longrightarrow f(z_A) \leqslant 0)$. (1 L1 2 LUB 3 α 1)

Rule B1 gives the solution $\{z: f(z) \leqslant 0\}$ for A. This is combined with the current value to get $\{z: z \leqslant b \wedge f(z) \leqslant 0\}$ which is placed in the data base.

(1 L1 2 LUB 3 α 2)

$(H \wedge \alpha \wedge z_A \in A \longrightarrow z_A \leqslant x)$. Use LUB, with $z_A/x', l_0/x$.

(1 L1 2 LUB 3 α 2 LUB)

$(H \wedge \alpha \wedge z_A \in A \longrightarrow (t_{Au} \in A \longrightarrow t_{Au} \leqslant u) \wedge r \in A \wedge z_A \in A)$.

These are verified as before.

This finishes subgoal (1). As we shall see, subgoal (2) will produce no more solutions for A, so we will then only be left to check that

$\{z: z \leqslant b \wedge f(z) \leqslant 0\}$ is indeed a solution for A.

[13]Rule B1 cannot be used here because of condition 1, Table I: t_1 is really a skolem function of x' x' is replaced by x, l_0, is a skolem function of A, x is replaced by l_0, so t_1 is a skolem function of A and hence A occurs in t_1. The program easily detects this because its current representation of t_1 shows it as a skolem function of A.

$$(H \longrightarrow 0 \leqslant f(l_0)). \tag{2}$$

Note that the substitution l_A/x gotten from subgoal (1) is used in subgoal (2).

Use L2 with l_0/x'', $0/a'$.

$$(H \longrightarrow \text{Cont}\, f\, l_0 \wedge ((0 \leqslant f(s) \wedge l_0 \leqslant s \longrightarrow t_2 \leqslant s) \longrightarrow t_2 \leqslant l_0)) \quad \text{(2 L2)}$$

$$(H \longrightarrow \text{Cont}\, f\, l_0). \text{ Use } H_1 \quad \text{(2 L2 1)}$$

$$(H \longrightarrow a \leqslant l_0 \leqslant b). \text{ Proved as before.} \quad \text{(2 L2 1 H}_1\text{)}$$

$$(H \longrightarrow ((0 \leqslant f(s) \wedge l_0 \leqslant s \longrightarrow t_2 \leqslant s) \longrightarrow t_2 \leqslant l_0)) \quad \text{(2 L2 2)}$$

$$(H \wedge (0 \leqslant f(s) \wedge l_0 \leqslant s^{\gamma,} \longrightarrow t_2 \leqslant s) \longrightarrow t_2 \leqslant l_0).$$

Use LUB with t_2/x'.

$$(H \wedge \gamma \longrightarrow (t_{Au} \in A \longrightarrow t_{Au} \leqslant u) \wedge r \in A \wedge t_2 \in A). \quad \text{(2 L2 2 LUB)}$$

Subgoals (2 BC 2 BC 1) and (2 BC 2 BC 2) are proved as before.

$$(H \wedge \gamma \longrightarrow t_2 \in A). \text{ IGNORED by Rule B6.} \quad \text{(2 L2 2 LUB 3)}$$

This completes subgoal (2). The solution $\{z: z \leqslant b \wedge f(z) \leqslant 0\}$ is now substituted for A in LUB, and the whole theorem (which is now first order) is proved again. See Appendix IV for this and othed related example theorems.

Example 12. $\forall F\, (\{x\} \in F \longrightarrow \{y\} \in F) \longrightarrow \forall A\, (x \in A \longrightarrow y \in A)$.

This example which was suggested by Peter Andrews[14] is just the theorem

$$(\{x\} = \{y\} \longrightarrow x = y)$$

where $(\alpha = \beta)$ has been characterized by $\forall D\, (\alpha \in D \longrightarrow \beta \in D)$, (with the proper typing on D).

Here we need to find a maximal solution for F.

$$((\{x_0\} \in F \longrightarrow \{y_0\} \in F) \longrightarrow (x_0 \in A_0 \longrightarrow y_0 \in A_0)) \quad (\;)$$

$$((\{x_0\} \in F \longrightarrow \{y_0\} \in F) \wedge x_0 \in A_0 \longrightarrow y_0 \in A_0).$$

When attempting to backchain on the first hypothesis, the subgoal

$$(\{y_0\} \in F \longrightarrow y_0 \in A_0)$$

is attempted which yield, by Rule B3, the solution $\{z: z = \{y_0\} \longrightarrow y_0 \in A_0\}$ for F.

[14]Private communication.

When this is substituted for F in the theorem it becomes first order,

$$([(\{x_0\} = \{y_0\} \longrightarrow y_0 \in A_0) \longrightarrow (\{y_0\} = \{y_0\} \longrightarrow y_0 \in A_0))] \wedge x_0 \in A_0 \longrightarrow y_0 \in A_0) \qquad (\ )$$

which is simplified to

$$([(\{x_0\} = \{y_0\} \longrightarrow \overset{H_1}{y_0} \in A_0) \longrightarrow y_0 \in A_0] \wedge x_0 \in A_0 \longrightarrow y_0 \in A_0)$$

because $\{y_0\} = \{y_0\}$ is recognized as true.

Backchaining on the first hypothesis H_1 gives the subgoal

$$(H_1 \wedge x_0 \in A_0 \longrightarrow (\{x_0\} = \{y_0\} \longrightarrow y_0 \in A_0)) \qquad (H_1)$$
$$(H_1 \wedge x_0 \in A_0 \wedge \{x_0\} = \{y_0\} \longrightarrow y_0 \in A_0).$$

By defining the set equality, "=" (that is, $D = E$ is replaced by $D \subseteq E \wedge E \subseteq D$)), and "$\subseteq$" (that is, $D \subseteq E$ is replaced by $\forall t\ (t \in D \longrightarrow t \in E)$), and reducing $t \in \{x\}$ to $t = x$, this is transformed to the goal

$$(H_1 \wedge x_0 \in A_0 \wedge (t = x_0 \longrightarrow t = y_0) \longrightarrow y_0 \in A_0),$$

which is true with x_0/t by backchaining and equality substitution.

Example 13. $\exists A\ [\forall x\ (x \in A \longrightarrow x \geqslant 0) \wedge \forall x\ (x \in A \wedge x \neq 0 \longrightarrow x - 2 \in A)]$.

(The reader might want to take a minute to obtain the maximal set A himself before seeing the solution given by Rule BC1.)

$$[(x_A \in A \longrightarrow x_A \geqslant 0) \wedge (x_A \in A \wedge x_A \neq 0 \longrightarrow x_A - 2 \in A)]. \qquad (\ )$$

The first subgoal

$$(x_A \in A \longrightarrow x \geqslant 0) \qquad (1)$$

yields by Rule B1,

$$A_1 = \{z\colon z \geqslant 0\}$$

Since subgoal (1) has the subset property[15], it follows that Rule BC1 of Fig. 6 applies to the second subgoal

$$(x_A \in A \wedge x_A \neq 0 \longrightarrow x_A - 2 \in A) \qquad (2)$$

[15] See Sec. 3.2.

to obtain the maximal solution,

$$A_2 = \{z: z \geqslant 0 \wedge [\ \forall n\ (n \in \omega \longrightarrow z - 2n \geqslant 0) \\ \vee \exists N\ (N \in \omega \wedge z - 2N = 0 \wedge \forall n\ (n \in \omega \wedge n \leqslant N \longrightarrow z - 2n \geqslant 0))]\}$$

Since $\forall n\ (n \in \omega \longrightarrow z - 2n \geqslant 0)$ is false, this becomes

$$A_2 = \{z: z \geqslant 0 \wedge \exists N\ (N \in \omega \wedge z = 2N \wedge \forall n\ (n \in \omega \wedge n \leqslant N \longrightarrow \\ z \geqslant 2n))\}$$

This description of A_2 is now simplified (by the author) to obtain

$$A_2 = \{z: z \geqslant 0 \wedge\ \exists N\ (N \in \omega \wedge z = 2N)\} \\ = \text{the non-negative even integers,}$$

because

$$\forall n\ (n \in \omega \wedge n \leqslant N \longrightarrow z \geqslant 2n) \wedge z = 2N \\ \longleftrightarrow \forall n\ (n \in \omega \wedge n \leqslant N \longrightarrow 2N \geqslant 2n) \wedge z = 2N \\ \longleftrightarrow \text{TRUE} \wedge z = 2N \\ \longleftrightarrow z = 2N.$$

Example 14

$$\exists A\ \forall x\ \forall y [(g(x,y) \in A \longrightarrow P(x,y)) \wedge ((x,y) \in A \wedge q(x,y) \longrightarrow \\ f(x,y) \in A)]$$

$$[(g(x_A,y_A) \in A \longrightarrow P(x_A,y_A)) \wedge ((x_A,y_A) \in A \wedge q(x_A,y_A) \longrightarrow \\ f(x_A,y_A) \in A)]. \qquad (\ )$$

The first subgoal

$$(g(x_A,y_A) \in A \longrightarrow P(x_A,y_A)) \qquad (1)$$

yields by Rule B2′,

$$A_1 = \{z: \forall s\ \forall t\ (z = g(s, t) \longrightarrow P(s, t))\}.$$

Since goal (1) has the subset property[15], it follows that Rule BC2′ applies to the second subgoal (with $p(z) \equiv \forall s\ \forall t\ (z = g(s, t) \longrightarrow P(s, t))$),

$$((x_A,y_A) \in A \wedge q(x_A,y_A) \longrightarrow f(x_A,y_A) \in A) \qquad (2)$$

to obtain the solution

$$A_2 = \{z: \forall s\ \forall t\ (z = g(s, t) \longrightarrow P(s, t)) \\ \wedge \forall n\ [n \in \omega \wedge q(f^n(\Pi_1(z), \Pi_2(z))) \longrightarrow \forall s\ \forall t\ (f^{n+1}(\Pi_1(z), \Pi_2(z)) \\ = g(s, t) \longrightarrow P(s, t))]\}.$$

To verify that this is a solution we note first that it clearly satisfies subgoal (1) because $A_2 \subseteq A_1$ and goal (1) has the subset property. Thus we need only verify the second subgoal (2) with A replaced by A_2. This is done in Appendix III. Also we show there that it may not be maximal, but that for the special case of Ex. 14 given in Ex. 15 below, the solution A_2 is maximal.

Example 15.

$$\exists P \, \forall A \, \forall K \, [P(0,x) \wedge (P(A,0) \longrightarrow A = x \cdot y) \wedge (P(A,K) \wedge K \neq 0 \longrightarrow P(A+y,K-1))] .$$

This theorem arises from the field of program verification, in a case where the internal assertion P is *not* given but must be found by the prover. The theorem represents the verification conditions for a simple program which multiplies integers x and y. (See Fig. 9). No attempt is made here to prove that the program halts.

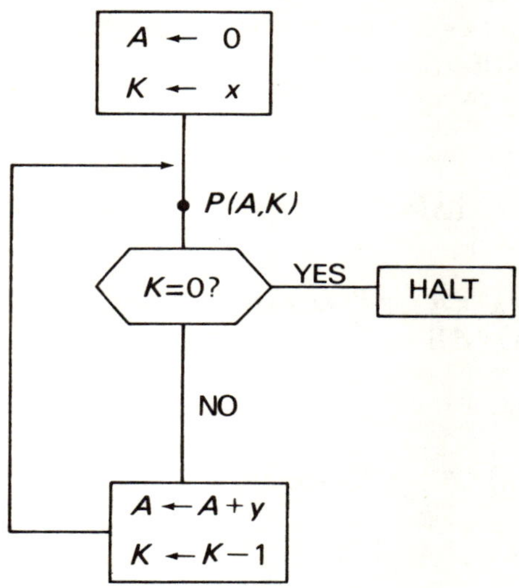

Fig. 9. – Flow chart for a simple multiply program.

We will suppress the input assertions $x \geqslant 0$, $y \geqslant 0$, x,y integers, and will (for consistency of notation only) replace the two-place predicate P by a set B of ordered pairs. Our rules of Sec. 3 were not meant for sets of ordered pairs but appear to work on this example, provided that several facts about ordered pairs and integers are built into the program. This example is included here only to show the kind of examples that might be handled with some more work.

The skolemized theorem is

$$[(0,x_0) \in B \wedge ((A_B,0) \in B \longrightarrow A_B = x_0 \cdot y_0) \wedge ((A_B,K_B) \in B \wedge K_B \neq 0 \longrightarrow (A_B + y_0, K_B - 1) \in B)] . \quad (\ )$$

The first subgoal

$$(0, x_0) \in B \tag{1}$$

is IGNORED by Rule B6.

The second and third subgoals are exactly in the form of Ex. 14 with B/A, A/x, K/y, $\lambda st(s, 0)/g$, $\lambda st(s = x_0 \cdot y_0)/P$, $\lambda st(t \neq 0)/q$, $\lambda st(s + y_0, t-1)/f$. Thus we get, similarly to Ex. 14, a solution

$$\{z: \forall s \forall t (z = (s,0) \longrightarrow s = x_0 \cdot y_0) \\ \wedge \forall n [n \in \omega \wedge \Pi_2 (\lambda st(s + y_0, t-1)^n (\Pi_1(z), \Pi_2(z)) \neq 0 \\ \longrightarrow \forall s_1 (\lambda st(s + y_0, t-1)^{n+1} (\Pi_1(z), \Pi_2(z)) = (s_1, 0) \longrightarrow s_1 = x_0 \cdot y_0)] \}.$$

This solution will work but needs considerable simplification for clarity and ease of use. Much of this simplification, but probably not all, which is done here by the author, can be done by the program, by storing additional entries in the REDUCE table and PAIRS table of the program (see [1]).

The variable Z which represents an ordered pair is replaced by the variable pair (z_1, z_2). The solution is then successively simplified as follows:

$$\{(z_1, z_2): (z_2 = 0 \longrightarrow z_1 = x_0 \cdot y_0) \\ \wedge \forall n [n \in \omega \wedge z_2 - n \neq 0 \\ \longrightarrow \forall s \quad ((z_1 + (n+1) \cdot y_0, z_2 - n - 1) = (s, 0) \longrightarrow s = x_0 \cdot y_0)] \}$$

$$= \{(A,K): (K = 0 \longrightarrow A = x_0 \cdot y_0) \\ \wedge \forall n \forall s \quad [n \in \omega \wedge K \neq n \wedge A + (n+1) \cdot y_0 = s \wedge K = n + 1) \\ \longrightarrow s = x_0 \cdot y_0] \}$$

$$= \{(A,K): (K = 0 \longrightarrow A = x_0 \cdot y_0) \\ \wedge \forall n \forall s \quad [n \in \omega \wedge K = n + 1 \longrightarrow A + (n + 1) y_0 = x_0 \cdot y_0] \}$$

$$= \{(A,K): (K = 0 \longrightarrow A = x_0 \cdot y_0) \\ \wedge \forall n \quad [n \in \omega \wedge K = n + 1 \longrightarrow A = (x_0 - K) y_0]\}$$

$$= \{(A,K): (K \in \omega \longrightarrow A = (x_0 - K) \cdot y_0)\}.$$

This corresponds to the predicate;

$$P(A,K) \equiv (K \in \omega \longrightarrow A = (x_0 - K) \cdot y_0)$$

which is the internal assertion usually given by humans for the program depicted in Fig. 9.

6. THE INDUCTION AXIOM

One of the most used concepts from higher order logic is the induction axiom:

IA: $\forall A\, (0 \in A \wedge \forall x\, (x \in A \longrightarrow x{+}1 \in A\,) \longrightarrow \forall y\, (y \in A))$[16] .

For example in proving

Example 16

$$\sum_{i=1}^{n} i = n(n+1)/2\ ,$$

if we let

$$A = \{n\colon \sum_{i=1}^{n} i = n(n+1)/2\}$$

then we can easily show that $0 \in A$ and $\forall x\, (x \in A \longrightarrow x{+}1 \in A)$ and hence conclude from IA that A contains all non-negative integers.

It was therefore a great disappointment to find that the procedure of this paper would *not* "work" for the induction axiom. Nor is it possible to wait for the instantiation of other variables, as we did so successfully with the Least Upper Bound Axiom (see Sec. 3.5 and Ex. 11, Sec. 5), to unlock our procedures. The following simple example serves to show why.

Example 17.

$$\text{IA} \wedge P(0) \wedge \forall x\, (P(x) \longrightarrow P(x{+}1)) \longrightarrow \forall y\, P(y)\ .$$

When IA is defined we get

$$\begin{aligned}\forall A\ [0 \in A \wedge \forall x\, (x \in A \longrightarrow x{+}1 \in A) \longrightarrow \forall y\, (y \in A)]\\ \wedge P(0) \wedge \forall x\, (P(x) \longrightarrow P(x{+}1)) \longrightarrow \forall y\, P(y)\ ,\end{aligned}$$

which, when skolemized, becomes

$$\begin{aligned}[0 \in A \wedge (x_A \in A \longrightarrow x_A{+}1 \in A) \longrightarrow y \in A)]\\ \wedge P(0) \wedge (P(x) \longrightarrow P(x{+}1)) \longrightarrow P(y_0)\ .\end{aligned}$$

The set variable A occurs only in IA, and no *connection* between IA and the rest of the theorem can be made except by matching a term like $(y \in A)$ against a term like $P(y_0)$. *But this is exactly what we do not want* (and our rules forbid it); we do not want the *indiscriminate* matching of expressions of the form $(y \in A)$ against arbitrary subformulas in the theorem, because this leads to a greatly exploded search. In our rules we match *only when* there is a "con-

[16]Of course this could have been expressed in terms of a predicate P, with $P(x)$ replacing $x \in A$.

nection" between the things being matched. This causes us to fail here, but the saving on other examples is our compensation.

This axiom or its equivalent[16] has been used extensively in automatic theorem proving [17-20] especially in cases where the theorem to be proved can be used as the induction hypothesis. Boyer and Moore [17] have been able in some cases to "generalize" the induction hypothesis and thereby prove (automatically) some theorems not amenable to the simpler techniques.

We can of course add an additional induction-procedure to our prover and use it for induction proofs without compromising the set-building rules of this paper.

7. COMMENTS, QUESTIONS, AND FUTURE PLANS

7.1 Maximal method

We have set ourselves the task of finding a maximal set A_0 satisfying a given condition $Q(A)$, and have given some rules for doing this in certain cases. These have been applied to a number of theorems to obtain successful results, although there are many we cannot handle. Of course there are cases such as Ex. 10 which have no maximal solution. But some of these may become "maximizable" during the proof when a particular lemma is used (as did Ex. 10).

7.2 Delaying

In our procedure we have employed a concept of *delaying*, whereby we delay the final determination of a set A until all parts of the theorem have been processed. Early subgoals place restrictions of the form $\{z: P(z)\}$ on A, but leave A itself as a *variable* to be further considered later. Later subgoals may further restrict A, or may force A to take a particular value A_0 (for example, by matching). In this last eventuality the program must check that A_0 is consistent with the earlier restriction $\{z: P(z)\}$. This kind of delaying has the marked advantage of not closing off the determination of A by assuming early values for it; but rather keeping it "as general as possible," putting on restrictions only as they are forced. Thus we see that the notions of "maximality" and "delaying" are somewhat analogous.

This concept of delaying is an important one in other parts of automatic theorem proving. Huet's Constrained Resolution [3] is an example of it where he delays the higher order unifications until resolution matches have been made. The most general unifier [16] is another example, in that it lets resolution (or whatever prover that uses it) delay as long as possible the assignment of constant values to variables.

Also our use of delaying for set variables is entirely analogous to the concept of interval types [2, 5, 6] explained in Sec. 4.2, when a variable x is restricted to an interval $[a \leqslant x \leqslant b]$ to satisfy an earlier subgoal, but left a variable to be instantiated or further restricted later. This technique has greatly simplified our proofs in analysis, and we expect other such "delaying" methods to be developed.

7.3 Holding formulas together

As mentioned earlier, we try to avoid indiscriminate matching of formulas of the form $t \in A$ (where A is a variable) against all other subformulas P in the theorem. This prevents an "explosion" in the number of search paths.

Also we believe it important to hold formulas together during the proof, and retain, as far as possible, the original quantification (see Ex. 2). Thus we try to avoid procedures which convert the theorem into clausal form or other normal forms.

7.4 Relation to the work of others

Darlington's program [12, 14] has proved Ex. 8 and other examples using his F-matching. Our procedure has a similarity to F-matching and was partly inspired by talks with Darlington. But it is different especially in its use of the maximality concept which is an outgrowth of the ideas in [15, Sec. 10], and in other ways.

This work is of course related to Behmann's decision procedure for monadic first and second order logic [13, 13a, 22] [17]. A cursory look at [13] indicates that our solutions are often the same as Behmann's. His methods might be extended to also handle a number of non-monadic cases (as ours do). So it seems that an extensive study of papers on monadic logic is very much in order.

The procedures of [3, 4, 7, 10, 11] are more general than ours, and their research provides a necessary base for this type of research; we only feel that our work can be more effective on a limited, but important part, of higher order logic.

7.5 Completeness

All of our rules are *sound* because no matter what value we get for the set variable A, we always verify it with another pass through the prover. The only question, then, is one of completeness.

There are three kinds of incompletness encountered here. First, there are cases, as mentioned above, which have no maximal solutions. Secondly, there are cases which have maximal solutions but for which we have as yet no rule. And thirdly, there are cases where the rules we give are not complete. Our basic rules B1–B7 (Fig. 1 with restrictions in Table I), and BC1 (Fig. 4) are complete. Proofs of this are given in Appendix II. And completeness is retained when we combine the basic solution according to the combining rules C1–C5 (Figs. 2, 3). However, we propose using these basic solutions and combining them even in cases where the conditions of Table I, and Figs. 1–4, are not satisfied, and in these cases the results will not always be maximal. Also in cases like Rule BC1 where the maximal set is rather complex we suggest trying first a simplified version, which often gives the maximal solution but may not.

Maximal or not, they still offer in many cases a good (quick) guess for A, a heuristic for generating a candidate for A.

[17] J. A. Robinson first pointed this out to me.

We have used these rules to generate certain *family* variables (for instance Exs. 2, 8, 9) instead of set variables. Much work needs to be done in extending these rules and in investigating their completeness.

We propose using them in cases where *several* set variables are to be instantiated instead of just one, and see no reason why good results cannot be obtained, even though the process is probably not complete.

In many cases the restrictions in Table I will disappear during the proof of a theorem, when a certain variable is instantiated. For example, in trying to prove

$$\forall x\ (f(x,y) \in A \longrightarrow P(x,y))$$

where y is a variable (and therefore not a skolem function of A), Restriction 2 of Table I prevents us from applying Rule B2 (because the variable y appears in $f(x,y)$). But once y is instantiated, by say a_0, then Rule B2 applies and we obtain the solution

$$\{Z\colon \forall t\ (Z = f(t,a_0) \longrightarrow P(t,a_0))\}\ .$$

Another way of overcoming these restrictions is by using an equivalent form of an expression. For example, Rules B1 and B2 cannot be used on

$$\forall x [(x \in A \longrightarrow P(x)) \wedge (f(x) \in A \longrightarrow Q(x))]$$

because in each subgoal "x occurs elsewhere in the theorem," but this can be (automatically) changed to the equivalent form

$$\forall x\ (x \in A \longrightarrow P(x)) \wedge \forall y (f(y) \in A \longrightarrow Q(y))]$$

where that restriction has been eliminated. (This was implicitly assumed in Exs. 13-15).

Also formulas of the form

$$\forall x (q(x) \vee (x \in A \longrightarrow p(x)))$$

can be transformed to

$$\forall x (x \in A \longrightarrow p(x) \vee q(x))\ ;$$

and $\forall x (q(x) \wedge (x \in A \longrightarrow p(x)))$

to $\forall y\ q(y) \vee \forall x (x \in A \longrightarrow p(x))$;

and $\forall x\ \forall y\ (f(x) \in A \vee y \in A \longrightarrow p(x,y))$

to $\forall x (f(x) \in A \longrightarrow p(x,y))$
$\wedge\ \forall y (y \in A \longrightarrow p(x,y))$;

etc.

It should be noted that the "solution" U derived from Rule BE appears to be useless. However, Rule BE has been placed there to prevent the program from failing in some subformulas where the solution U (from those subformulas) can be combined with solutions from other parts of the theorem.

7.6 Implementation

An augmented version of the prover described in [1] has been used to prove some example theorems. This augmented version, which is called "the set variable prover," is designed to proceed in the machine-alone mode (that is, not man-machine), but not all of Exs. 1-15 of this paper were actually proved completely by the computer. Some were proved outright; some could have been proved by minor changes in the program which we are in the process of making; and some require more extensive changes.

Recall, from Sec. 4, that two passes are made by the program in proving a theorem: a first pass to determine a value for the set variable A; and a second pass to prove the resulting theorem, after the new value is substituted for A.

Examples 1-4, 6-10, 12, were run completely by the computer (with no human intervention). Exs. 5, 5C-5F, 11, 13-15, have been done by hand using the procedures of this paper. Exs. 5A, 5B, 16, 17 are for illustrative purposes only.

The first pass of Ex. 11, in which the set

$$A = \{z\colon z \leqslant b \wedge f(z) \leqslant 0\}$$

is defined, using the Rules of Fig. 2, has been run by computer alone. This is the crucial pass for satisfying the aims of this paper. However, after this value is substituted for A in the least upper bound axiom, an interesting and truly challenging theorem about general inequalities results:

Ex. 11′. $H_1 \wedge L_1 \wedge L_2 \wedge \text{LUB}' \longrightarrow \exists x(f(x) \leqslant 0 \wedge 0 \leqslant f(x)),$

where $H_1, L_1,$ and L_2 are given on page 74, and LUB′ is

$$\begin{aligned}&\exists u\, \forall t(t \leqslant b \wedge f(t) \leqslant 0 \longrightarrow t \leqslant u) \wedge \exists r(r \leqslant b \wedge f(r) \leqslant 0) \longrightarrow\\ &\quad \exists l\,[\forall x(x \leqslant b \wedge f(x) \leqslant 0 \longrightarrow x \leqslant l)\\ &\qquad \wedge \forall y(\forall z(z \leqslant b \wedge f(z) \leqslant 0 \longrightarrow z \leqslant y) \longrightarrow l \leqslant y)]\,.\end{aligned}$$

In theory, our program can prove Ex. 11′, but in actual practice it cannot now because of time and space limitations.

These proofs have utilized a newly installed, heuristically controlled, backup mechanism (in the spirit of CONNIVER) which prevents trapping[18]. The remaining difficulty with Ex. 11 might be eliminated by further changes to our backup mechanism.

[18]Trapping occurs in proving a conjunction $(P(x) \wedge Q(x)$, when a value x_0 given to satisfy $P(x)$ later fails on $Q(x)$, and when another value x_1 would have satisfied both.

7.7 Open questions

The rules here are given for only one set variable. What happens when we try to use them for more than one set variable, or for a combination of set variables and family variables (and/or higher order variables)? Hand proofs seem to indicate that these rules can still be applied, with minor alterations, but much needs to be done to determine their completeness. If more than one set variable (or family variable) is present, how many passes are needed by the prover?

Can these methods be extended for instantiating simple function variables (that is, sets of ordered pairs)? Ex. 15 is actually such a case. How about sequences? If one uses the Bolzano-Weierstrass theorem instead of the (equivalent) least upper bound axiom to prove theorems in intermediate analysis (like Ex 11), then instead of instantiating a set variable A, we would be required to instantiate a sequence variable. Is that just as easy?

7.8 Future plans

Try more examples.

Provide for a heuristic backup.

Heuristic control of the use of lemmas and hypotheses.

More basic and combining rules to handle other cases that we now know and that may arise.

Procedures for instantiating simple function variables.

Procedures for handling many set and higher order variables at once. (Obviously this can have only limited success because of theoretical limits on completeness in higher order logic.)

Acknowledgement

This work has benefited from conversations with Mike Ballantyne, Mabry Tyson, Peter Bruell, Alan Robinson, Ernie Sibert, Peter Andrews, and Gerard Huet. Also, Peter Bruell has helped develop and implement the computer program.

This work was supported by NSF Grant DCR74-12866.

REFERENCES

[1] W. W. Bledsoe and M. Tyson. (1975). The UT Interactive Theorem Prover. *Memo ATP-17.* Austin, Texas: Department of Mathematics, University of Austin at Texas.

[2] W. W. Bledsoe, R. S. Boyer and W. H. Henneman. (1972). Computer proofs of limit theorems. *Artificial Intelligence* **3**, 27–60.

[3] G. P. Huet. (1972). Constrained Resolution: a complete method for higher order logic. Ph.D. thesis. *Jennings Computer Center Report 1117.* Cleveland: Jennings Computer Center, Case, Western Reserve University.

[4] G. P. Huet. (1975). A unification algorithm for typed λ-calculus. *Theoretical Computer Science* **1**, 27–57.

[5] D. I. Good, R. L. London and W. W. Bledsoe. (1975). An interactive verification system. *Proc. of the 1975 International Conf. on Reliable Software,* Los Angeles, 482–492. Also *AIEE Trans. on Software Engineering* **1**, 59–67.

[6] W. W. Bledsoe and M. Tyson. (1977). Typing and proof by cases in program verification. *Machine Intelligence 8,* pp. 30–51. (eds. Elcock, E. W. and Michie, D.). Chichester: Ellis Horwood Limited.

[7] G. A. Haynes and L. J. Henschen. (1976). A refutation procedure for omega-order logic. Informal memo. Evanston, Illinois: Dept. of Computer Science, Northwestern University.

[8] A. M. Ballantyne and W. W. Bledsoe. (1977). Automatic proofs of theorems in analysis using non-standard techniques. *J. ACM,* **24**, 353–374.

[9] W. W. Bledsoe. (1977). Non-resolution theorem proving. *Artificial Intelligence* **9**, 1–35.

[10] T. Pietrzykowski. (1973). A complete mechanization of second order type theory. *J. ACM,* **20**, 333–364.

[11] P. B. Andrews. (1971). Resolution in type theory. *Jour. of Symbolic Logic,* **36**, 414–432.

[12] J. L. Darlington. (1972). Deductive plan formation in higher order logic. *Machine Intelligence 7,* pp. 129–137 (eds. Meltzer, B. and Michie, D.), Edinburgh: Edinburgh University Press.

[13] H. Behmann. (1922). Beiträge Zur Algebra Der Logik: Insbesondere Zum Entscheidungsproblem. *Mathematische Annalen,* **86**, 163–229.

[13a] J. R. Buchi. (1960). On a decision method in restricted second order arithmetic. *Proc. Int'l. Congress on Logic Methodology and Philos. Sci.,* (eds. Nagel, E., Suppes, P. and Tarski, A.), 1–11. Stanford: Stanford University Press.

[14] J. L. Darlington. (1976). Talk at Oberwolfach Conference on Automatic Theorem Proving. Oberwolfach, Germany.

[15] W. W. Bledsoe. (1973). Some ideas on automatic theorem proving. *Memo ATP-9.* Austin, Texas: Dept. of Mathematics, University of Texas at Austin.

[16] J. A. Robinson. (1965). A machine-oriented logic based on the resolution principle. *J. ACM* **12**, 23–41.

[17] R. S. Boyer and J S. Moore. (1975). Proving theorems about LISP functions. *J. ACM* **22**, 129–144.

[18] J. L. Darlington. (1968). Automatic theorem proving with equality substitution and mathematical induction. *Machine Intelligence 3,* pp. 113–127 (ed. Michie, D.) University of Edinburgh Press.

[19] C. Chang and R. C. Lee. (1973). *Symbolic Logic and Mechanical Theorem Proving.* Section 11–10. New York: Academic Press.

[20] W. W. Bledsoe. (1971). Splitting and reduction heuristics in automatic theorem proving. *Artificial Intelligence,* **2**, 55–77.

[21] J. L. Darlington. (1977). Improving the efficiency of higher-order unification. *Proc. 5th Int. Jnt. Conf. on Art. Int.* (IJCAI-77). pp. 520–526. Pittsburgh: Dept. of Computer Science, Carnegie-Mellon University.

[22] D. Hilbert and W. Ackerman. (1950). *Principles of Mathematical Logic.* New York: Chelsea Pub. (First Published 1928).

APPENDIX I

Glossary of terms

$x \in A$	x is a member or element of the set A
$\{a\}$	The set whose only member is a
$\{x: P(x)\}$	The set of those x's for which $P(x)$ is true
$P \longrightarrow Q$	$P \longrightarrow Q$; that is, if P then Q
$P \wedge Q$	P and Q
$P \vee Q$	P or Q
$\sim P$	not P
$\exists x\, P(x)$	for some x, $P(x)$; that is, there exists an x such that $P(x)$
$\forall x\, P(x)$	For all x $P(x)$; that is, $P(x)$ is true for each x
R	the set of all real numbers
$\mathbf{Q}$	the set of all rational numbers

A is dense in R — for each two numbers x and y in R there is a number z in A with $x < z < y$

See a calculus book for the definition of "continuous".

See a topology book (for example, J. L. Kelly, *General Topology*, Van Nostrand), for definitions of terms such as: topology, open, closed, neighbourhood, union, regular topological space, cover, refinement.

APPENDIX II

Some completeness results

The purpose of this Appendix is to show that the rules of Sec. 3 do indeed give the maximal solution for the cases considered.

Theorems 1-7 below establish this for the basic Rules B1-B7 of Fig. 2, and Theorems 12-13, for combining Rules C1-C3 of Fig. 3. Theorem 8Q relates to Basic Rule BQ, Fig. 2, and Theorems 14-15 to Figs. 6 and 7.

In this Appendix we will consider formulas Q which contain only one set variable A, and such that A occurs only in the form $x \in A$, or as arguments of skolem functions.

We will say that a subformula S of Q is in an EVEN position of Q if Q has one of the forms:

$$(S \wedge R), (R \wedge S), (S \vee R), (R \vee S), (R \longrightarrow S), \forall x\, S,\ \exists x\, S,$$

and if A does not occur in R except as a skolem argument, and S is in an ODD position of Q if Q has the one of the forms:

$$\sim S, (S \longrightarrow R)^1.$$

And we furthermore say that S is in an EVEN (ODD) position of Q if S is in an EVEN (ODD) position of a subformula S' of Q which is in an EVEN position of Q, or if S is in an ODD (EVEN) position of a subformula S' of Q which is in an ODD position of Q.

We say that A occurs EVENLY in Q if each occurrence $(x \in A)$ in Q is an EVEN occurrence. Similarly we say that A occurs ODDLY in Q if each occurrence $(x \in A)$ in Q is an ODD occurrence.[2] For example, if Q is

$$\forall x\, (x \in A \longrightarrow p(x)) \wedge \exists y\, (y \in A)$$

then A occurs oddly in the first conjunct and EVENLY in the second.

[1] The only logical connectives are: $\wedge$, $\vee$, $\rightarrow$, $\sim$, $\forall$, and $\exists$.

[2] Clearly, if A occurs EVENLY (ODDLY) in P, and P is an EVEN position of Q, then A occurs EVENLY (ODDLY) in Q, and if P is in an ODD position of Q then A occurs ODDLY (EVENLY) in Q.

A set A_0 is said to be a *maximal solution* for $Q(A)$, if $Q(A_0)$ is a theorem, and for any set B,

$$(Q(B) \wedge A_0 \subseteq B \longrightarrow A_0 = B).$$

That is, A_0 is a "largest" set A which will satisfy the theorem $\exists A\ Q(A)$.

The symbol U will represent the universal set (or class). Here the only properties of U we will need are: $x \in U$, for all x; and $D \cap U = D$, for all D.

Recall the definitions of subset property, superset property, and intermediate property from Sec. 3.2.

Theorem 1. If "A" does not occur in $P(x)$, then $A_0 = \{z: P(x)\}$ is the maximal solution for $\exists A\ \forall x\ (x \in A \longrightarrow P(x))$.

Proof. It is a solution because by substituting A_0 for A we get

$$\forall x\ (P(x) \longrightarrow P(x))$$

which is true.

To show that A_0 is maximal we can show that $B \subseteq A_0$ for any solution B, that is, that

$$\forall x\ (x \in B \longrightarrow P(x)) \longrightarrow B \subseteq A_0\ ,$$

or, successively,

$$\forall x\ (x \in B \longrightarrow P(x)) \wedge z \in B \longrightarrow z \in A_0\ ,$$
$$\forall x\ (x \in B \longrightarrow P(x)) \wedge z \in B \longrightarrow P(z)\ ,$$

which follows by substituting z for x in the first hypothesis.

Theorem 2. If "A" does not occur in $P(x)$ or $f(x)$, then

$$A_0 = \{z: \forall s\ (z = f(s) \longrightarrow P(s))\}$$

is the maximal solution for $\exists A\ \forall x\ (f(x) \in A \longrightarrow P(x))$.

Proof. The proof of this is like that of Theorem 2′ below.

Theorem 2′. If "A" does not occur in $P(x,y)$ or $f(x,y)$, then

$$A_0 = \{z: \forall r\ \forall s\ (z = f(r,s) \longrightarrow P(r,s))\}$$

is the maximal solution of $\exists A\ \forall x\ \forall y\ (f(x,y) \in A \longrightarrow P(x,y))$.

Proof. It is a solution because by substituting A_0 for A we get

$$\forall x\, \forall y\, (\forall r\, \forall s\, (f(x,y) = f(r,s) \longrightarrow P(r,s)) \longrightarrow P(x,y))$$

which is true (substitute x for r and y for s).

To show that A_0 is maximal we can show that $B \subseteq A_0$, for any solution B, that is, that

$$\forall x\, \forall y\, (f(x,y) \in B \longrightarrow P(x,y)) \longrightarrow B \subseteq A_0 ,$$

or, successively,

$$\forall x\, \forall y\, (f(x,y) \in B \longrightarrow P(x,y)) \wedge z \in B \longrightarrow z \in A_0 ,$$
$$\forall x\, \forall y\, (f(x,y) \in B \longrightarrow P(x,y)) \wedge z \in B \longrightarrow \forall r \forall s\, (z = f(r,s) \longrightarrow P(r,s)),$$
$$\forall x\, \forall y\, (f(x,y) \in B \longrightarrow P(x,y)) \wedge z \in B \wedge z = f(r,s) \longrightarrow P(r,s),$$
$$\forall x\, \forall y\, (f(x,y) \in B \longrightarrow P(x,y)) \wedge f(r,s) \in B \longrightarrow P(r,s),$$

which follows by substituting r for x and s for y in the first hypothesis.

Theorem 3. If "A" does not occur in b or P then

$$A_0 = \{z\colon z = b \longrightarrow P\}$$

is the maximal solution of $(b \in A \longrightarrow P)$.

Proof. It is a solution because by substituting A_0 for A we get

$$((b = b \longrightarrow P) \longrightarrow P)$$

which is true.

To show that A_0 is maximal we can show that $B \subseteq A_0$ for any solution B, that is, that

$$(b \in B \longrightarrow P) \longrightarrow B \subseteq A_0 ,$$

or, successively,

$$(b \in B \longrightarrow P) \wedge z \in B \longrightarrow (z = b \longrightarrow P) ,$$
$$(b \in B \longrightarrow P) \wedge z \in B \wedge\ z = b \longrightarrow P ,$$
$$(b \in B \longrightarrow P) \wedge b \in B \longrightarrow P ,$$

which is true.

Theorem 4. If "A" does not occur in b, then

$$A_0 = \{z: z \neq b\}$$

is the maximal solution of $(b \notin A)$.

Proof. We must show that

$$b \notin \{z: z \neq b\}$$

which is immediate, and

$$b \notin B \longrightarrow B \subseteq A_0 \ ,$$

or $$b \notin B \wedge z \in B \longrightarrow z \neq b \ ,$$

which is immediate.

Theorem 5. If "A" does not occur in P then U is a maximal solution of P.

Proof. This is obvious.

Theorem 6. U is a maximal solution of $(t \in A)$.

Proof. U is a solution because $(x \in U)$ is true for any x. Also it is maximal since $B \subseteq U$ for any B.

Theorem 7. If every occurrence of an expression of the form $(t \in A)$ in E, is in an EVEN position of E, and "A" does not occur in E except in one of these $(t \in A)$, then U is a maximal solution for E.

Proof. Use structural induction, and Theorems 6 and 5.

Theorem 8. Each of the following has the subset property.

.1 $\forall x\,(x \in A \longrightarrow P(x))$
.2 $\forall x\,(f(x) \in A \longrightarrow P(x))$
.2′ $\forall x \forall y\,(f(x,y) \in A \longrightarrow P(x,y))$
.3 $(b \in A \longrightarrow P)$
.4 $(b \notin A)$.

Proof. In each case we must assume that B is a solution of the given formula and that $C \subseteq B$, and show that C is also a solution of that formula. For example in .1 we must show that

$$\forall x\,(x \in B \longrightarrow P(x)) \longrightarrow \forall\, z\,(z \in C \longrightarrow P(x)) \ ,$$

but this is immediate since $C \subseteq B$. Similarly

$$\forall x\, (f(x) \in B \longrightarrow P(x)) \longrightarrow \forall z\, (f(z) \in C \longrightarrow P(z)) ,$$
$$\forall x \forall y\, (f(x,y) \in B \longrightarrow P(x,y)) \longrightarrow \forall s\, \forall t\, (f(s,t) \in C \longrightarrow P(s,t)) ,$$
$$(b \in B \longrightarrow P) \longrightarrow (b \in C \longrightarrow P) ,$$

and $\quad (b \notin B \longrightarrow b \notin C)$. Q.E.D.

Theorem 9. Each of the following has the subset property.

.1 $\exists y\, \forall x\, (x \in A \longrightarrow P(x,y))$
.2 $\exists y\, \forall x\, (f(x) \in A \longrightarrow P(x,y))$
.2′ $\exists z\, \forall x \forall y\, (f(x,y) \in A \longrightarrow P(x,y,z))$
.3 $\exists y\, (b(y) \in A \longrightarrow P(y))$
.4 $\exists y\, (b(y) \notin A)$.

Proof. Similar to the proof of Theorem 8. We must show that if $C \subseteq B$ then

$$\exists y\, \forall x\, (x \in B \longrightarrow P(x,y)) \longrightarrow \exists y\, \forall x\, (x \in C \longrightarrow P(x,y)) .$$

But this is equivalent to

$$(C \subseteq B \wedge \exists y\, [\forall x\, (x \in B \longrightarrow P(x,y)) \longrightarrow \forall x\, (x \in C \longrightarrow P(x,y))]$$

which is true. Similarly for 9.2–9.4. Q.E.D.

Remark. Since $\forall x \exists y\, (x \in A \longrightarrow P(x,y))$ is equivalent to $\forall x\, (x \in A \longrightarrow \exists y\, P(x,y))$, it follows from Theorem 8.1 that $\forall x \exists y\, (x \in A \longrightarrow P(x,y))$ has the subset property. A similar result holds for $\forall x\, \exists y\, (f(x) \in A \longrightarrow P(x,y))$, and $\forall x \forall y \exists z\, (f(x,y) \in A \longrightarrow P(x,y,z))$.

Theorem 10. If "A" does not occur in t then $(t \in A)$ has the superset property.

Proof. Suppose that B is a solution of $(t \in A)$ and $B \subseteq C$, then $t \in B$ and hence $t \in C$. Q.E.D.

Theorem 11. If every occurrence of "A" in E is of the form $(t \in A)$ where $(t \in A)$ is in an EVEN position of E, and "A" does not occur in t, then E has the superset property.

Proof. Use structural induction and Theorem 10.

Theorem 12. If P and Q each have the intermediate property and "A" does not occur in H or R, then $(P \wedge Q)$, $(H \longrightarrow P \wedge Q)$, and $((R \vee P) \wedge Q)$, have the intermediate property.

Proof. This is immediate.

Theorem 13. If A_1 is the (only) maximal solution of P, and A_2 is the (only) maximal solution of Q, and P and Q have the intermediate property, then $(A_1 \cap A_2)$ is the (only) maximal solution of $(P \wedge Q)$, and of $(H \longrightarrow P \wedge Q)$, and of $((R \vee P) \wedge Q)$, provided that "A" does not occur in H or R, and provided that $(P \wedge Q)$, $(H \longrightarrow P \wedge Q)$, and $((R \vee P) \wedge Q)$ have any solution.

Proof. We will show that $(A_1 \cap A_2)$ is the maximal solution of $(P \wedge Q)$. The result for $(H \longrightarrow P \wedge Q)$ and $((R \vee P) \wedge Q)$ follows similarly.

Suppose that B is a solution of $(P \wedge Q)$. Then it is a solution of P and of Q, and since A_1 and A_2 are maximal solutions of P and Q respectively, it follows that $B \subseteq A_1$, and $B \subseteq A_2$, and hence that $B \subseteq A_1 \cap A_2$. Thus we have that B and A_1 are solutions of P and that

$$B \subseteq A_1 \cap A_2 \subseteq A_1 .$$

Thus since P has the intermediate property, it follows that $(A_1 \cap A_2)$ is a solution of P. Similarly $(A_1 \cap A_2)$ is a solution of Q, and hence $(A_1 \cap A_2)$ is a solution of $(P \wedge Q)$. It is also maximal since

$$B \subseteq A_1 \cap A_2 .$$

Theorem 14. (See Fig. 6). If $\exists A\, P(A)$ has the (only)† maximal solution

$$A_1 = \{z: p(z)\},$$

and $P(A)$ has the subset property, and $Q(A)$ is

$$\forall x\, (x \in A \wedge q(x) \longrightarrow f(x) \in A)$$

and if

$$\exists A\, (P(A) \wedge Q(A)) \tag{*}$$

has a solution, then it has the maximal solution,

$$\begin{aligned} A_2 = \{z: p(z) \wedge [&\forall n\, (n \in \omega \longrightarrow p f^n(z)) \\ &\vee \exists N\, (N \in \omega \wedge \sim q f^N(z) \wedge \forall n\, (n \in \omega \vee n \leqslant N \longrightarrow p f^n(z)))]\} \end{aligned}$$

Proof. The proof that A_2 is a solution is entirely similar to that given for Theorem 15 below.

The proof that A_2 is *maximal* will now be given.

† See footnote 5, p. 60.

To show maximality, we must show that if A_0 is any solution of (*) then $A_0 \subseteq A_2$. That is,

$$(P(A_0) \wedge Q(A_0) \longrightarrow A_0 \subseteq A_2),$$

or equivalently

$$\begin{array}{ll}
H_1 & P(A_0) \\
H_2 & \wedge \forall x(x \in A_0 \wedge q(x) \longrightarrow f(x) \in A_0) \\
H_3 & \wedge x_0 \in A_0 \\
 & \longrightarrow \\
C_1 & p(x_0) \\
C_2 & \wedge [\forall n \, (n \in \omega \longrightarrow p\, f^n(x_0)) \\
 & \vee \; \exists N \, (N \in \omega \wedge \sim q\, f^N(x_0) \wedge \forall n \, (n \in \omega \wedge n \leqslant N \longrightarrow p\, f^n(x_0)))] \, .
\end{array}$$

To prove C_1, we first recall that $A_1 = \{z: p(z)\}$ is a maximal solution of $P(A)$. So since A_0 is also a solution of $P(A)$ it follows that $A_0 \subseteq A_1$. Thus, using H_3,

$$x_0 \in A_0 \subseteq A_1 = \{z: p(z)\} \, ,$$

and hence $x_0 \in \{z: p(z)\}$, from which C_1 follows.

To prove C_2 let us suppose that $\forall\, n \, (n \in \omega \longrightarrow p\, f^n(x_0))$ is false, and let n_2 be the first member of ω for which

$$H_4 \qquad \sim p\, f^{n_2}(x_0).$$

If $n_2 = 0$, then $f^{n_2}(x_0) = f^0(x_0) = x_0$, and $\sim p\,(x_0)$ in contradiction to C_1 (which was just proved). Thus we may assume that $n_2 \geqslant 1$, and let $n_1 = n_2 - 1$. So we have $n_1 \in \omega$ and

$$H_5 \qquad \forall\, n \, (n \in \omega \wedge n \leqslant n_1 \longrightarrow p\, (f^n(x_0))).$$

Now if it were true that

$$\text{(A)} \qquad \forall\, n \, (n \in \omega \wedge n \leqslant n_1 \longrightarrow q\, (f^n(x_0)))$$

it would follow from H_2, H_3 and H_5 (using induction) that

$$f^{n_1+1}\,(x_0) \in A_0,$$

and hence, since $A_0 \subseteq A_1 \subseteq \{z: p(z)\}$, that

$$p(f^{n_1+1}\,(x_0))$$

$$\text{or} \qquad p(f^{n_2}\,(x_0))$$

in contradiction to H_4. Thus (A) is false and there is a first $N \in \omega$ for which $N \leqslant n_1$ and $\sim q f^N(x_0)$.

Since $N \leqslant n_1$, it follows from H_5 that

$$N \in \omega \wedge \sim q\, f^N(x_0) \wedge \forall n\, (n \in \omega \wedge n \leqslant N \longrightarrow p\, f^n(x_0))$$

as required for C_2.

This completes the proof of Theorem 14.

Theorem 15. (See Fig. 7). If $\exists A\, P(A)$ has the (only)† maximal solution

$$A_1 = \{z: p(z)\},$$

and $P(A)$ has the subset property, and $Q(A)$ is

$$\forall x \forall y\, ((x,y) \in A \wedge q(x,y) \longrightarrow f(x,y) \in A)$$

and if

$$\exists A (P(A) \wedge Q(A))$$

has a solution, then it has the maximal solution

$$\begin{aligned} A_2 = \{z: p(z) \wedge [&\forall n\, (n \in \omega \longrightarrow p\, f^n(z)) \\ &\vee \exists N\, (N \in \omega \wedge \sim q\, f^N(z) \wedge \forall n\, (n \in \omega \wedge n \leqslant N \longrightarrow p\, f^n(z)))]\} \end{aligned}$$

Proof. We show here that A_2 *is* a solution. The proof that it is maximal is entirely similar to the proof of maximality in Theorem 14.

We must show that $P(A_2)$ and $Q(A_2)$ are true. Since A_1 is a solution of $\exists A\, P(A)$, and $A_2 \subseteq A_1$, and since $P(A)$ has the subset property, it follows that $P(A_2)$ is true. We must now show $Q(A_2)$ is also true, that is, that

$$((x,y) \in A_2 \wedge q(x,y) \longrightarrow f(x,y) \in A_2)$$

or equivalently,

$$\begin{aligned} (*) \qquad & p(x,y) \wedge [\forall n\, (n \in \omega \longrightarrow p\, f^n(x,y)) \\ & \vee \exists N\, (N \in \omega \wedge \sim q\, f^N(x,y) \wedge \forall n\, (n \in \omega \wedge n \leqslant N \longrightarrow p\, f^n(x,y))] \\ & \wedge q(x,y) \longrightarrow p\, f(x,y) \\ & \wedge [\forall n\, (n \in \omega \longrightarrow p\, f^{n+1}(x,y)) \\ & \vee\ \exists N\, (N \in \omega \wedge \sim q\, f^N\, (f(x,y)) \wedge \forall n\, (n \in \omega \wedge n \leqslant N \longrightarrow p\, f^n(f(x,y))]. \end{aligned}$$

†See footnote 5 of the paper.

This theorem (*) is true if we can prove the two subgoals (*1) and (*2) below. (The disjunction in the hypothesis of (*) is split to help form the two subgoals (*1) and (*2).) Note also that $f^n(f(x,y)) = f^{n+1}(x,y)$.

$$\begin{array}{ll} H_1 & p(x,y) \\ H_2 & \wedge \forall n\,(n \in \omega \longrightarrow p\, f^n(x,y)) \\ H_3 & \wedge\, q(x,y) \\ & \longrightarrow \\ C_1 & pf(x,y) \\ C_2 & \wedge \forall n_0\,(n_0 \in \omega \longrightarrow p\, f^{n_0+1}(x,y)) \end{array} \qquad (*1)$$

$$\begin{array}{ll} H_1 & p(x,y) \\ H_2' & \exists N_0\,(N_0 \in \omega \wedge \sim q\, f^{N_0}(x,y) \wedge \forall n\,(n \in \omega \wedge n \leqslant N_0 \longrightarrow p\, f^n(x,y))) \\ H_3 & q(x) \\ & \longrightarrow \\ C_1 & pf(x,y) \\ C_2' & \exists N\,(N \in \omega \wedge \sim q\, f^{N+1}(x,y) \wedge \forall n_0\,(n_0 \in \omega \wedge n_0 \leqslant N \longrightarrow \\ & \qquad p\, f^{n_0+1}(x,y))). \end{array} \qquad (*2)$$

In proving Conclusion C1 of (*1) we use hypothesis H_2 with $n = 1$. (Note that $f^1(x,y)$ is the same as $f(x,y)$.)

In proving Conclusion C2 of (*1) we use hypothesis H_2 with $n = n_0 + 1$.

In these two proofs we used the facts that $1 \in \omega$, and that $n_0 + 1 \in \omega$ whenever $n_0 \in \omega$.

We now come to Conclusion C1 of (*2). Since by H_3, $q(x)$ is true, it follows from H_2' that $N_0 \neq 0$, that is, that $N_0 \geqslant 1$. So we can take $n = 1$ in H_2' to reach the desired conclusion C_1.

In proving Conclusion C_2' we again note that $N_0 \geqslant 1$. Also by H_2' we have that $N_0 \in \omega$. Thus $N_0 - 1 \in \omega$, and we can take $N = N_0 - 1$ in C_2'. With this substitution for N, we are left to prove

$$\begin{array}{ll} C_{21} & p\, f^{n_0+1}(x,y) \\ C_{22} & \wedge \sim q\, f^{N_0}(x,y) \end{array}$$

under the assumption that

$$H_4 \qquad n_0 \in \omega \wedge n_0 \leqslant N_0 - 1.$$

C_{21} and C_{22} will both follow from H_2' with $n = n_0 + 1$, after we verify, with the help of H_4, that $n_0 + 1 \in \omega$ and $n_0 \leqslant N_0 - 1$.

APPENDIX III

Further details of examples

Example 14. Verification of subgoal (2). (Continued from page 80)

We must show that

$$((x,y) \in A_2 \wedge q(x,y) \longrightarrow f(x,y) \in A_2)$$

where

$$\begin{aligned} A_2 = \{z\colon & \forall s \forall t\,(z = g(s,t) \longrightarrow P(s,t)) \\ & \wedge \forall n\,[n \in \omega \wedge q(f^n(\Pi_1(z), \Pi_2(z)) \longrightarrow \forall s \forall t\,(f^{n+1}(\Pi_1(z), \Pi_2(z)) \\ & = g(s,t) \longrightarrow P(s,t))]\} \\ = \{z\colon & \forall s \forall t\,(z = g(s,t) \longrightarrow P(s,t)) \\ & \wedge \forall n \forall s \forall t\,[n \in \omega \wedge q(f^n(\Pi_1(z), \Pi_2(z)) \wedge f^{n+1}(\Pi_1(z), \Pi_2(z)) \\ & = g(s,t) \longrightarrow P(s,t)]\} \end{aligned}$$

That, is we must show that

$$\begin{array}{ll} H_1 & \forall s \forall t\,((x,y) = g(s,t) \longrightarrow P(s,t)) \\ H_2 & \wedge \forall n \forall s \forall t\,[n \in \omega \wedge q\, f^n(x,y) \wedge f^{n+1}(x,y) = g(s,t) \longrightarrow P(s,t)] \\ H_3 & \wedge q(x,y) \\ & \longrightarrow \\ C_1 & \forall s \forall t\,(f(x,y) = g(s,t) \longrightarrow P(s,t)) \\ C_2 & \wedge \forall n \forall s \forall t\,[n \in \omega \wedge q\, f^{n+1}(x,y) \wedge f^{n+2}(x,y) = g(s,t) \longrightarrow P(s,t)]\,. \end{array}$$

To prove C_1 we assume

$$H_4 \qquad f(x,y) = g(s_0, t_0)$$

and prove

$$C_{11} \qquad P(s_0, t_0).$$

Using H_2 with $s = s_0$, $t = t_0$, and $n = 0$, we are left with the subgoal

$$0 \in \omega \wedge q\,(x,y) \wedge f\,(x,y) = g(s_0, t_0)$$

which follows from H_3 and H_4.

To prove C_2 we assume

$$\begin{array}{ll} H_5 & n_0 \in \omega \\ H_6 & \wedge q\, f^{n_0+1}(x,y) \\ H_7 & \wedge f^{n_0+2}(x,y) = g(s_0, t_0) \end{array}$$

and prove

$$C_{21} \qquad P(s_0, t_0).$$

Using H_2 with $s = s_0$, $t = t_0$, and $n = n_0 + 1$, we are left with the subgoal

$$n_0 + 1 \in \omega \wedge q\, f^{n_0+1}(x,y) \wedge f^{n_0+2}(x,y) = g(s_0, t_0)$$

which follows from H_5, H_6, H_7, and the fact that $(m \in \omega \longrightarrow m + 1 \in \omega)$. Q.E.D.

In this example, it was necessary to show that A_2 was indeed a solution because we used Rule BC2′ of Fig. 7, which is not guaranteed to produce a solution, and certainly not guaranteed to produce a *maximal* solution. Indeed A_2 is, in general, not maximal for Ex. 14, as the following counterexample will show. However, for the special case of Ex. 14 given in Ex. 15 we *do* have a maximal solution, as is shown below. Of course, Rule BC1′ of Fig. 7 would *always* give a maximal solution of Ex. 14 as is proved in Appendix II.

Counterexample. To show that the A_2 gotten here by using Rule BC2′ of Fig. 7, will not always give a *maximal* solution.

First recall that Ex. 14 is:

$$\exists A\ \forall x\ \forall y\ [(g(x,y) \in A \longrightarrow P(x,y)) \wedge ((x,y) \in A \wedge q(x,y) \longrightarrow f(x,y) \in A)].$$

We saw above that Rule BC2′ gives the solution

$$A_2 = \{z\colon \forall s\ \forall t\ (z = g(s,t) \longrightarrow P(s,t))\ \forall n\ \forall s\ \forall t\ [n \in \omega \wedge q(f^n(z)) \wedge f^{n+1}(z) = g(s,t) \longrightarrow P(s,t)]\}.$$

To see that this is not always maximal let

$$\begin{aligned} g(x,y) &\equiv (x,y) \\ P(x,y) &\equiv x \geqslant 0 \\ q(x,y) &\equiv x \neq 0 \\ f(x,y) &\equiv x - 2. \end{aligned}$$

(This in essence is Ex. 13.)

Then

$$\begin{aligned} A_2 = \{z\colon &\forall s\ \forall t\ (z = (s,t) \longrightarrow s \geqslant 0) \\ &\wedge \forall n\ \forall s_1\ \forall t_1\ [n \in \omega \wedge \text{1st term } (\lambda\, st(s-2, t)^n(z)) \neq 0 \\ &\quad \wedge (\lambda\, st(s-2, t)^{n+1}(z)) = (s_1, t_1) \longrightarrow s_1 \geqslant 0]\} \\ = \{(x,y)\colon &\forall s\ \forall t\ ((x,y) = (s,t) \longrightarrow s \geqslant 0) \\ &\wedge \forall n\ \forall s_1\ \forall t_1\ [n \in \omega \wedge x - 2n \neq 0 \\ &\quad \wedge (x-2n-2, y) = (s_1, t_1) \longrightarrow s_1 \geqslant 0]\} \\ = \{(x,y)\colon &x \geqslant 0 \wedge \forall n\ (n \in \omega \wedge x \neq 2n \longrightarrow x-2n-2 \geqslant 0)\} \\ = \{(x,y)\colon &x \geqslant 0 \wedge \forall n\ (n \in \omega \longrightarrow x = 2n \vee x \geqslant 2n + 2)\} \\ = \emptyset\ &\text{(The empty set).} \end{aligned}$$

While $A_2 = \emptyset$ is indeed a solution of this special case of Ex. 14, it is not a maximal solution, because (exactly as in Ex. 13)

$$A_2' = \{(x,y): x \geqslant 2 \wedge \exists N (N \in \omega \wedge x = 2N)\}$$

is also a solution and $A_2' \neq \emptyset$.

Incidentally, A_2' is maximal because it is produced by Rule BC1′, which always gives maximal solutions. (See Theorem 15, Appendix II.)

APPENDIX IV

Some example theorems about general inequalities

We will list here some of the theorems which appear as subgoals in the proof of Ex. 11. They are (except G1) theorems about general inequalities (i.e., where both existential and universal quantification is present).

The question we want to raise, is whether some of the methods of Presburger Arithmetic and linear programming can be extended for use on these kinds of theorems, and thereby avoid having to explicitly use the axioms for inequalities and real numbers.

These example theorems will be given in terms of LUB, LUB1, LUB2, L1 and L2, which are as follows:

LUB: $([\exists u\, \forall t(t \leqslant b \wedge f(t) \leqslant 0 \longrightarrow t \leqslant u) \wedge \exists r(r \leqslant b \wedge f(r) \leqslant 0)]$
$\longrightarrow \exists l\, [\forall x(x \leqslant b \wedge f(x) \leqslant 0 \longrightarrow x \leqslant l)$
$\wedge \forall y(\forall z(z \leqslant b \wedge f(z) \leqslant 0 \longrightarrow z \leqslant y) \longrightarrow l \leqslant y)])$

LUB1: $\forall x(x \leqslant b \wedge f(x) \leqslant 0 \longrightarrow x \leqslant l)$

LUB2: $\forall y(\forall z(z \leqslant b \wedge f(z) \leqslant 0 \longrightarrow z \leqslant y) \longrightarrow l \leqslant y)$

L1: $\forall x(a \leqslant x \leqslant b \wedge 0 < f(x) \longrightarrow \exists t(t < x \wedge \forall s(t < s \leqslant x \longrightarrow 0 < f(s))))$

L2: $\forall x(a \leqslant x \leqslant b \wedge f(x) < 0 \longrightarrow \exists t(x < t \wedge \forall s(x \leqslant s < t \longrightarrow f(s) < 0)))$

EXAMPLE Theorems

G1: $(f(l) < 0 \wedge 0 \leqslant f(b) \wedge b \leqslant l \longrightarrow b < l)$

This is a ground theorem, so the ordinary Presburger methods, with equality substitution, will suffice.

G2: $(f(l) < 0 \wedge 0 \leqslant f(b) \wedge l < t \wedge b \leqslant l \longrightarrow \exists y[(\forall z(z \leqslant b \wedge f(z) \leqslant 0$
$\longrightarrow z \leqslant y) \wedge y < l])$

G3: $(f(l) < 0 \wedge 0 \leqslant f(b) \wedge \forall s(0 \leqslant f(s) \wedge l \leqslant s \longrightarrow t \leqslant s) \wedge \text{LUB1} \wedge \text{LUB2}$
$\longrightarrow t \leqslant l)$

G4: $(a \leqslant b \wedge f(a) \leqslant 0 \wedge 0 \leqslant f(b) \wedge \text{LUB} \wedge \text{L1} \wedge \text{L2} \longrightarrow 0 \leqslant f(l))$

G5: $(a \leqslant b \wedge f(a) \leqslant 0 \wedge 0 \leqslant f(b) \wedge \text{LUB} \wedge \text{L1} \wedge \text{L2} \longrightarrow \exists x(f(x) \leqslant 0 \wedge 0$
$\leqslant f(x)).$

5

A Production System for Automatic Deduction

N. J. Nilsson
Artificial Intelligence Center
SRI International, USA

Abstract

A new predicate calculus deduction system based on production rules is proposed. The system combines several developments in Artificial Intelligence and Automatic Theorem Proving research including the use of domain-specific inference rules and separate mechanisms for forward and backward reasoning. It has a clean separation between the data base, the production rules, and the control system. Goals and subgoals are maintained in an AND/OR tree structure. We introduce here a structure that is the dual of the AND/OR tree to represent assertions. The production rules modify these structures until they "connect" in a fashion that proves the goal theorem. Unlike some previous systems that used production rules, ours is not limited to rules in Horn Clause form. Unlike previous PLANNER-like systems, ours can handle the full range of predicate calculus expressions including those with quantified variables, disjunctions, and negations.

1. BACKGROUND

Logical deduction is a basic activity in many artificial intelligence (AI) systems. Specific applications in which deduction plays a major role include question-answering, program verification, mathematical theorem-proving, and reasoning about both mundane and esoteric domains.

Of the several different approaches to deduction pursued by AI research, we might mention two extremes. In one (see for example, Hewitt, 1971), deduction procedures are based on more or less intuitive, ad hoc, and informal considerations. Such an approach derives its main advantage, namely efficiency, from the specialized, domain-dependent heuristics that can be tightly encoded in the system. The approach sometimes suffers, however, from excessive rigidity that frustrates the evolutionary development of systems. Most examples of designs based on this approach also exhibit deficient logical competence.

(See Moore, 1975, for a discussion of these deficiencies and some remedial suggestions.)

At the other extreme, deduction is based on some formal logical system such as the predicate calculus. (See for example, Chang and Lee, 1973.) This approach confers the power of a well-developed logical formalism and is compatible with the evolutionary development of systems. When deductions are based on uniform (that is, domain-independent) inference rules, however, the resulting systems are often too inefficient to be useful.

In this paper we shall propose a deduction system that enjoys most of the logical power of the formal systems without embracing their inefficient uniformity. It uses specialized, domain-dependent inference rules that are encoded as *productions*. As with most production systems, it can easily be modified and extended by adding new production rules or by modifying old ones. The system is based on a synthesis of several ideas from various authors in artificial intelligence and automatic theorem-proving. (The most immediate intellectual debts are to Bledsoe, 1977; Fikes and Hendrix, 1977; Hewitt, 1971; Kowalski, 1974a,b; Loveland and Stickel, 1973; Moore, 1975; and Sickel, 1976. Related work has been done by Nevins, 1975; Reiter, 1976; and Wilkins, 1974.)

Before describing the system in detail, we shall briefly mention some of the factors affecting its design. First we would like, in particular, to avoid the inefficiencies of resolution-based theorem-proving systems. As has been observed by several authors, the "clause form" used by resolution theorem-provers contributes to inefficiencies in two major ways: common subexpressions in goals or axioms are "multiplied-out" into several different clauses, each provoking its own separate but possibly redundant proof attempts; and conversion to clause form destroys possibly valuable heuristic information carried by the form of implicational statements among the axioms.

Second, we prefer a system in which the basic deduction steps have "common-sense" intuitive appeal. The process of resolution is, for some, difficult to relate to more familiar reasoning processes. This feature is especially important in those systems whose reasoning must be easily understood by users. Ease of understanding is also advantageous during system design and debugging. The processes of "natural deduction" more closely realize this goal than does resolution.

We want to be able to incorporate domain-specific knowledge into the system. This knowledge might consist of special inference rules and how to use them. In this regard, it is sometimes especially important, for efficiency, whether a deduction step proceeds forward (from the assertions toward goal) or backward (from the goal toward the assertions). The domain expert, who participates in the design of the system, can often indicate the most efficient direction for each inference.

We are sufficiently impressed with the advantages of production systems (Davis and King, 1977) that we would like to model our design on that paradigm. Previous production system designs for deduction systems, however, had somewhat limited logical power. (An example is the restriction to Horn Clauses in Kowalski, 1974b.) We want our system to be able to employ the full expressive power of the first-order predicate calculus, including the ability to reason with disjunctive assertions, negations, and quantification of variables. Certainly our system should be sound (that is, it should not prove invalid expressions). With regard to completeness (that is, being able to prove any theorem), we are less doctrinaire. We insist only that it behave reasonably according to criteria specific to the domain of application. Any incompletenesses that cannot be tolerated must be repairable by evolutionary changes to the system.

We also note that the production system paradigm permits a convenient separation between the "logical knowledge" embodied in the assertions and in the production rules and the use of this knowledge by a control system. Changes can be made to each component separately, depending on whether the logic or its control is to be changed. In particular we envision a more domain-specific control system than the simple, uniform interpreter used by most resolution systems.

We want the methods used by our system to be easily extendable to representations that are "richer" than the usual implementations of predicate calculus data bases. We have in mind, specifically, semantic networks (Fikes and Hendrix, 1977) and "structured-object" representations (Bobrow and Winograd, 1977) with built-in features for indexing, taxonomic reasoning, and sorting of arguments according to type.

Lastly, we attach great importance to the "aesthetic appeal" of the system. It should have a clean design, and it should itself be a clear statement of a useful synthesis of some of the best ideas in automatic theorem proving. We will gladly trade some efficiency for enhanced clarity.

2. OVERVIEW OF THE SYSTEM

The classical model of theorem-proving in the predicate calculus involves three major components. First, there is a set of axioms or assertions that express information about the domain of application. For geometry, for example, these would be the fundamental postulates plus whatever other theorems we want to start with. (It is neither necessary nor desirable to limit the assertions to some primitive or minimal set.) Second, there are domain-independent, uniform rules of inference (such as resolution, *modus ponens*) that can be used to derive new assertions from existing ones. Finally, there is a conjectured theorem, or goal, to be proved. A proof consists of a sequence of inference rule applications ending with one that produces the goal.

AI research has produced an important deviation from this approach. The assertions are divided into two distinct sets: facts and rules. Facts are specific statements about the particular problem at hand. For example, "Triangle ABC is a right triangle" would be expressed as a fact. Rules are general statements, usually involving implications or quantified variables. For example, "The base angles of an isoceles triangle are equal" would be expressed as a rule. Rules are used in combination with facts to produce derived facts. One could think of them as specialized, domain-dependent inference rules.

This distinction can be further explained by a simple example. In the classical approach, from the two assertions A and $A \Rightarrow B$ we could derive the assertion B by *modus ponens*. In the AI approach, from the fact A we could derive the fact B by using the special rule $A \Rightarrow B$. The distinction between facts and rules is an important part of our deduction system.

The rules will be used as production rules. They will be invoked by a pattern matching process. Some will be used only in a *forward* direction for converting facts to derived facts; others will be used only in a *backward* direction for converting goals to subgoals. The developing sets of facts and goals will be represented by separate tree structures. Goals will be represented in an AND/OR goal tree, and facts will be represented in a newly-proposed structure that we shall call a **fact tree**. Rules are employed until the fact tree joins the goal tree in an appropriate manner. The entire process will be under the supervision of a *control strategy* that decides which applicable rule should be employed at any stage. We shall not propose any specific control strategies in this paper but shall merely point out that the designer has the freedom to use any domain-specific information whatsoever in the control system.

Several designs of this general sort have been proposed (see, for example, Kowalski, 1974b), but most of them have had restrictions on the kinds of logical expressions that could be accommodated. Although AND/OR goal trees have been used before, the notion of a fact tree, dual to the goal tree, allows some interesting correspondences, such as that between "reasoning by cases" and dealing with conjunctive goals, for example.

We shall first explain the system by means of the propositional calculus and then indicate how we deal with quantification.

3. GOAL TREES AND FACT TREES

A. Conversion of facts and goals to standard form

In this section we shall introduce the tree structures used to represent collections of facts and goals. Facts and goals can be any expressions of the predicate calculus (propositional calculus for this section). We do convert them, though, into a standard form. Implications are changed to disjunctions by using the equivalence between $(A \Rightarrow B)$ and $(\sim A \,\&\, B)$. Negations are "moved in" by using the equivalences between $\sim(A \,\&\, B)$ and $(\sim A \vee \sim B)$ and between $\sim(A \vee B)$ and $(\sim A \,\&\, \sim B)$. Repeated negations are eliminated by using the equivalence between $\sim\sim A$ and A. Once a goal or fact expression has been converted to this standard form, it will consist of a conjuctive/disjunctive combination of literals. For example, the expression $\sim H \Rightarrow [G \,\&\, \sim(F \,\&\, \sim B)]$ would be converted to $H \vee [G \,\&\, (\sim F \vee B)]$.

Ordinarily the domain expert, who is providing us with facts and rules, would not give us any facts containing implications. These would be given as rules. Also, goal statements would not ordinarily contain implications. (The "hypotheses" of a theorem to be proved would ordinarily be represented as facts, the conclusion as a goal.) We may have disjunctive facts, however. The distinction between ~*A* ∨ *B* as a fact and *A* => *B* as a rule is simply this: as a *fact*, the domain expert is simply saying that either ~*A* or *B* is true and he doesn't know which. As a *rule*, the domain expert is saying that *A* is useful for proving *B*. The system makes quite different use of the two forms.

Also note that our conversion of facts and goals to standard form is not the same as conversion to clause form in resolution. In general, clause form involves more expressions. Our standard form is very close to the form of the original expressions.

B. AND/OR goal trees

For a goal of the form (*A*1 & ... & *An*) we must prove all of the goals *A*1 and ... and *An*. For a goal of the form (*A*1 ∨ ... ∨ *An*), it suffices to prove one of the goals *A*1 or ... or *An*. Structures called **AND/OR goal trees** (Nilsson, 1971) are used in many AI systems to represent collections of subgoals and their relation to the main goal.

Any goal expression that has been converted to our standard form can be represented by an AND/OR goal tree having single literals at its tips. For example, the expression *H* ∨ [*G* & (~*F* ∨ *B*)] would be represented by the AND/OR tree shown in Fig. 1.

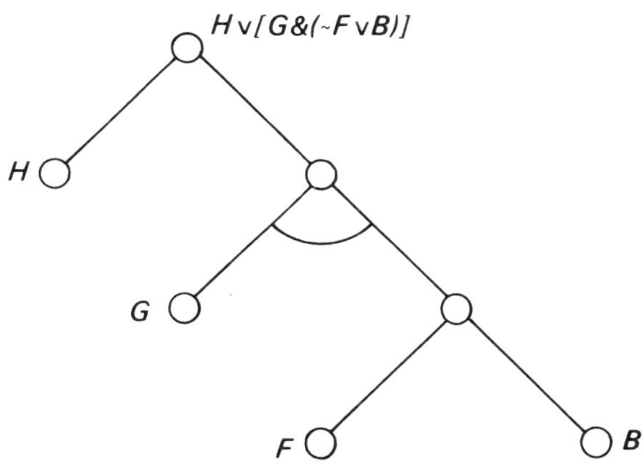

Fig. 1 – An AND/OR tree.

In AND/OR goal trees, nodes (such as node *G* in Fig. 1) whose incoming branches are connected together by an arc are called **AND nodes**. If their incoming edges are not so connected, the nodes are called **OR nodes**.

C. OR/AND fact trees

It is convenient to represent the facts to be used in a deduction by a structure that is the dual of the AND/OR goal tree. We shall call this dual structure an **OR/AND fact tree**. The notational conventions for the fact tree are the reverse of those for the goal tree. We shall represent conjunctive facts by a structure consisting of AND-nodes, thus:

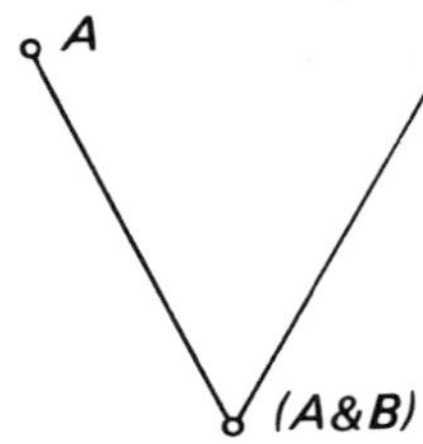

Disjunctive facts will be represented by a structure consisting of OR-nodes, thus:

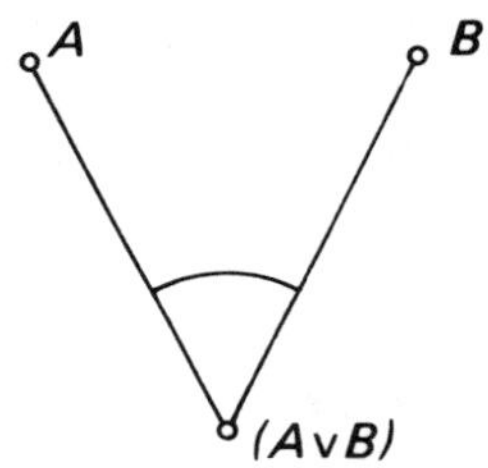

Note that for fact trees the arc connecting the branches is used with disjunctions rather than with conjunctions. Also, fact trees are drawn "upside down" compared with goal trees.

Any fact expression that has been converted to our standard form can be represented by an OR/AND fact tree having single literals at its tips. For example, the expression A & $[B \vee (C \,\&\, E)]$ & D would be represented by the OR/AND tree shown in Fig. 2.

The reason that we use opposite conventions to denote disjunctions and conjunctions in fact and in goal trees has to do with the nature of their duality. We shall see later that these opposite conventions will simplify some definitions.

(For both goals and facts we will represent repeated instances of the same literal by different nodes. This practice allows us to use trees instead of graphs.)

D. Connecting fact and goal trees: Proof termination

The problem of making a deduction is to "connect" the goal tree to the fact tree. This will be done mainly by using rules to extend the trees. We will also admit a process that allows a type of tree pruning. But before moving on to

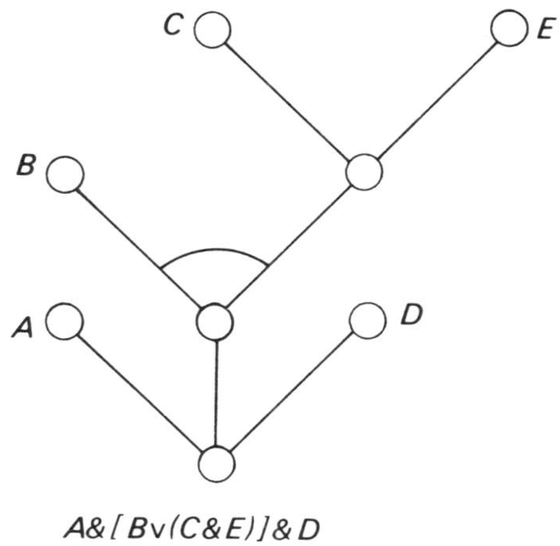

Fig. 2 – An OR/AND tree.

discuss these subjects, let us first define precisely what is meant by "connecting" a goal tree to a fact tree.

The connections between fact and goal trees are at nodes labelled by the same literal. In the original trees, such nodes must be tip nodes. After the trees are extended by rule applications, the connections might occur at any node labelled by a single literal. We shall call nodes labelled by a single literal **literal nodes**. After all such connections are made, we still have the problem of determining whether or not the expression at the root of the goal tree logically follows from the expression at the root of the fact tree. Our proof procedure will terminate when this determination can be made (or when we can conclude that it can never be made). The termination condition is a simple generalization of the condition for determining whether the root node of an AND/OR tree is "solved" (Nilsson, 1971, p. 89). The termination condition is based on a simple symmetric relationship, called **CANCEL**, between a fact node and a goal node. In the definition of CANCEL we use the phrase **arced nodes** to refer both to AND nodes in goal trees and to OR nodes in fact trees. If CANCEL holds for two nodes n and m, we shall say that n and m CANCEL each other. CANCEL is defined recursively as follows:

Two nodes n and m CANCEL each other (that is, CANCEL(n, m) holds) if one of (n, m) is a fact node and the other a goal node, and

0) if n and m are labelled by the same literal,

or 1) if n has arced successors, $\{s_i\}$, such that CANCEL(s_i, m) holds for all of them,

or 2) if n has unarced successors, $\{s_i\}$, such that CANCEL(s_i, m) holds for at least one of them.

Our definition of CANCEL supports a simple termination checking process that starts at nodes labelled by the same literal and propagates the CANCEL relation toward the roots. The proof procedure terminates successfully whenever we can show that the root of the fact tree and the root of the goal tree CANCEL each other.

Note, in particular, that our proof procedure treats conjunctive goal nodes correctly. Each conjunct must be proved before the parent is proved. Disjunctive fact nodes are treated in a dual manner. In order to use a disjunct in a proof, we must be able to prove the same result, using each of the other disjuncts in turn. This process is sometimes called "reasoning by cases".

The reader might like to establish termination for the goal-fact tree pairs of Fig. 3.

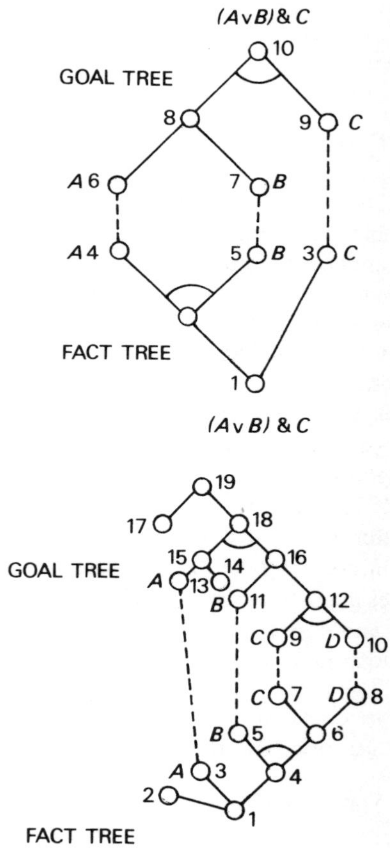

Fig. 3 – Example goal-fact tree pairs.

E. Transferring between fact and goal trees: Checking for contradictory facts and tautological goals

Being cancelled by the fact tree is only one of the ways that a goal can be satisfied. We can also show that a goal is true by reducing it to a tautology. Recognizing some tautologies in goals can be accomplished by a simple extension of the termination process just described. We shall introduce our discussion of this extension by describing how nodes could be transferred between the goal and fact trees.

Suppose from a given set, F, of facts, we must prove a disjunctive expression of the form $G1 \vee G2$, where $G1$ and $G2$ can be any expressions. In logical notation we can represent this problem by the expression:

$$F \mid\!- G1 \vee G2.$$

(The expression "$A \mid\!- B$" means "B logically follows from A".) Now we can invoke what we shall call here the **law of transfer** to convert this problem into either of the following ones:

$$(F \,\&\, {\sim}G1) \mid\!- G2$$

or

$$(F \,\&\, {\sim}G2) \mid\!- G1\ .$$

That is, one of the goal disjuncts can be negated and transferred to the fact tree, where it is conjunctively associated with the other facts. For example, the tautological goal $A \vee {\sim}A$ can be represented as a goal A and a fact A. The termination check now reveals that the two root nodes CANCEL, so we have a proof.

In a dual fashion, we could recognize contradictory facts by transferring one of the conjuncts of a fact conjunction over to the goal tree. To do so, we negate the fact tree to be transferred and disjunctively append it to the goal tree. In either case, when a tree is negated prior to transfer we need only negate the literal nodes; the reversed conventions on arced and unarced nodes automatically provide the correct interpretations when the tree is transferred.

But we really do not have to perform these transfer operations explicitly in order to deal with tautological goals and contradictory facts. Instead, we can allow oppositely signed literals of the same tree to CANCEL each other and then use the rest of the definition of CANCEL to propagate CANCELled nodes toward the roots. In this manner, the definition of CANCEL is extended to apply to nodes in the same tree. In applying the definition, we need to label the root of the goal tree and the root of the fact tree with the same identifier. Termination can now occur if the root of one tree CANCELs either itself or the root of the other.

Note that proof strategies based on proof by contradiction (refutation) involve transferring the entire negated goal tree to a conjunctive branch of the fact tree. Also in some theorem-proving systems (for example, Fikes and

Hendrix, 1977), disjunctive goals are split into alternative subproblems in which the negation of the sibling goals can be *locally* added to the fact base for each subproblem. This strategy corresponds to a local transfer process. For our purposes, with our extended definition of CANCEL, it doesn't really matter whether we leave the fact and goal trees as originally given or whether we perform explicit transfer operations.

The reader will note that computing CANCEL relations within the same tree corresponds to a type of resolution process. General resolution of facts (or goals) is not so simply accomplished, however.

The transfer operation is one way of transforming a given problem into a set of equivalent ones. Another type of transformation is used in some systems (such as that of Fikes and Hendrix, 1977) for dealing with disjunctive facts. Suppose our problem is to prove the expression G from the expression $F \& (F1 \vee F2)$, where $G, F, F1$, and $F2$ can be any expressions. We can convert this problem into either of the following pairs of problems:

$$F \vdash {\sim}F1$$

and

$$F \& F2 \vdash G$$

or

$$F \vdash {\sim}F2$$

and

$$F \& F1 \vdash G .$$

That is, we first prove one disjunct false and then use the other to prove G. But the subproblem $F \vdash {\sim}F1$ corresponds to a transfer operation that really does not need to be performed by our system with its extended definition of CANCEL. The other subproblem, $F \& F2 \vdash G$, evolves naturally in our system as a result of the recursive definition of CANCEL. There is a dual explanation that can be given for dealing with conjunctive goals.

Now that we are well equipped to recognize when our proof process can be terminated, we can begin discussing how rules are used to extend the fact and goal trees. We first discuss the form of the rules.

A. Rule forms

We allow two basic types of rules. One, called an **OPERATOR**, is used to extend the fact tree. OPERATORs permit the system to reason in a forward direction. The other type, called a **REDUCER**, is used to extend the goal tree. REDUCERs permit the system to reason in a backward direction. OPERATORs and REDUCERs are roughly analogous to the antecedent and consequent theorems, respectively, used in the PLANNER language (Hewitt, 1971). As in PLANNER, OPERATORs and REDUCERs are invoked by a pattern matching process. Each has a distinguished literal, called the **pattern**, that is used to match a corresponding literal in the fact or goal tree.

The basic form of an OPERATOR is

$$\underline{A} => EXP$$

where *EXP* is any predicate calculus expression, and where an underline beneath a literal indicates that this literal is the pattern. Thus OPERATORs are always implications whose antecedent consists of a single literal that is the pattern. If this pattern matches a literal in the fact tree, then the fact tree can be extended at this node by sprouting a descendant OR/AND tree representation of *EXP*.

The basic form of a REDUCER is

$$EXP => \underline{A}$$

where *EXP* can be any predicate calculus expression. Again, the pattern is underlined. REDUCERs are always implications whose consequent consists of a single literal that is the pattern. If this pattern matches a literal in the goal tree, then the goal tree can be extended at this node by sprouting a descendant AND/OR tree representation of *EXP*.

It is only for reasons of simplicity that we constrain our rules to have single-literal patterns. Useful variants of our system can be devised in which tree structures more complex than a literal node are used as patterns. Of course the matching process for these more complex structures would be correspondingly more tedious. Also, later, we shall discuss a technique for achieving the effect of more complex OPERATOR antecedents by allowing OPERATOR consequents to contain rules.

It has been argued by Moore (1975) that the contrapositive of a REDUCER should be expressed as an OPERATOR and vice versa. Thus if $\underline{A} => EXP$ is useful as an OPERATOR, its contrapositive form, namely $\sim(EXP) => \underline{\sim A}$, would also be useful as a REDUCER. Our system will automatically add these contrapositive forms for every rule entered into the system. (Note that after negating an expression, we must move the negation in.)

The existence of the contrapositive forms of rules means that it does not make any difference to our system whether goals and facts are kept on their own side of the line or transferred. If a goal invokes a given REDUCER, then the fact resulting from transferring that goal would invoke the corresponding OPERATOR. Thus, it is really unimportant whether we maintain goals and facts as given or whether we negate all of the goals, for example, add them to the fact base, and look for a refutation. We shall adopt the convention of maintaining goals and facts as given, mainly to ease the process of explaining the behaviour of the system to the user.

B. Use of rules

The basic cycle of operation of our deduction system can be informally described by the following steps:

(1) Initialize the goal and fact trees to the given expressions.
(2) If the termination check succeeds, exit.
(3) Use the domain-specific control strategy to select one of the literal nodes and an OPERATOR or REDUCER whose pattern matches this literal node.
(4) Apply the selected rule, extend the goal or fact tree, and go to (2).

Rule application is thus a pattern-directed process having effects on data bases (fact and goal trees). The system design can thus reasonably be described as a "production system" in the sense in which that term is generally used in AI research. In the next section we shall show how the system might work on some propositional calculus examples.

5. PROPOSITIONAL CALCULUS EXAMPLES

As a first example of how the system works, suppose we want to prove $\{H \vee [G \,\&\, (B \vee {\sim}F)]\}$ from the expression $\{A \,\&\, [B \vee (C \,\&\, E)] \,\&\, D\}$. We are given the REDUCERs

R1: $C \,\&\, E \Rightarrow {\sim}\underline{F}$
and
R2: $D \Rightarrow \underline{G}$.

From these, we construct the corresponding OPERATORs

O1: $\underline{F} \Rightarrow {\sim}C \vee {\sim}E$
and
O2: ${\sim}\underline{G} \Rightarrow {\sim}D$.

The fact and goal expressions are already in standard form. We show their tree representations in Fig. 4.

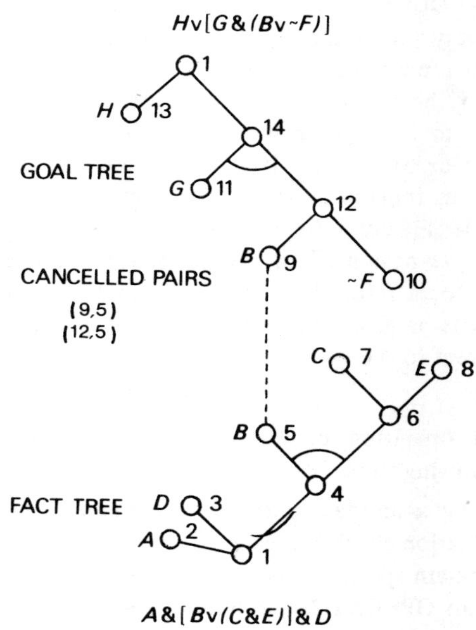

Fig. 4 – Example fact and goal trees.

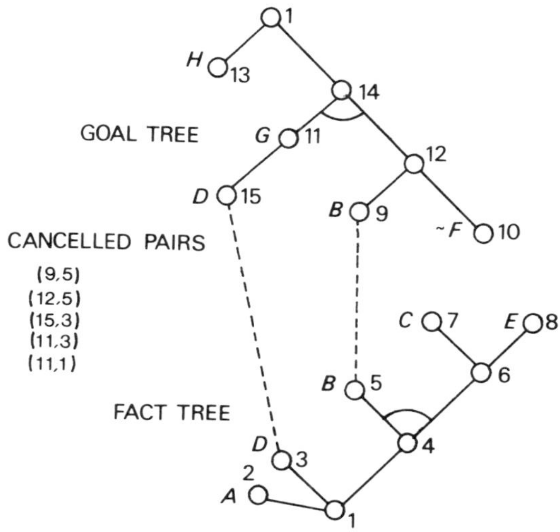

Fig. 5 – An intermediate stage of a proof.

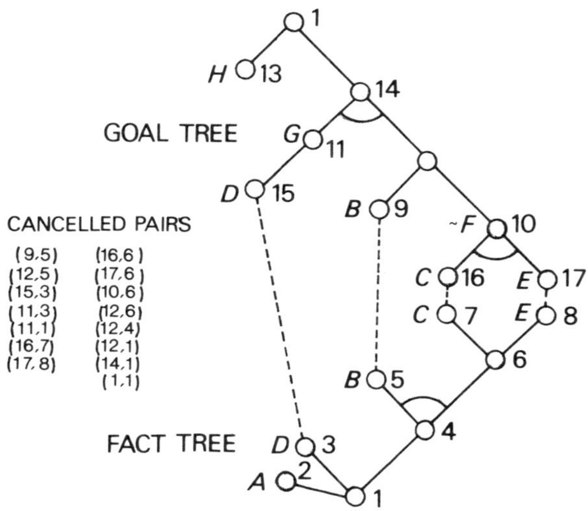

Fig. 6 – The final stage of a proof.

In Fig. 4, we use capital letters next to the tip nodes for literals, and we use numerals to label the nodes themselves for later reference. We connect matching nodes by dashed lines. From Fig. 4 we see that nodes 9 and 5 CANCEL. Using the definition of CANCEL, we note that nodes 12 and 5 CANCEL. It will be helpful to keep a list of the CANCELled pairs. This list is also shown in Fig. 4.

None of the OPERATORs is applicable, but both of the REDUCERs are. Suppose we apply R2 first, adding node 15 to the goal tree. After this cycle, the situation is as depicted in Fig. 5. We have updated the list of CANCELled pairs. At this stage we have essentially reasoned only about one case of the disjunct $B \vee (C \,\&\, E)$.

Now we apply the only remaining applicable rule, R1. The resulting trees are shown in Fig. 6. The list of CANCELled pairs includes (1,1), so we terminate successfully.

For our second example, we will illustrate how CANCELling nodes in the same tree can be used to obtain a proof. Suppose our goal is to prove $B \vee C$ and we are given the following OPERATORS:

O1: $\sim\underline{C} => D$

and

O2: $\underline{D} => B$.

We will assume we have no facts. The problem would be straightforward if we were to split $B \vee C$ into two disjunctive subgoals such that while working on subgoal B we could assume (locally) the fact $\sim C$. This fact would combine with OPERATOR O1 to produce fact D, which in turn would combine with O2 to produce B.

Our system does not make these local assumptions, but the use of contrapositive rules and CANCELling nodes within a tree accomplishes the same thing. The contrapositives of our OPERATORs are the REDUCERs

R1: $\sim D => \underline{C}$

R2: $\sim B => \sim\underline{D}$.

Now R1 can be used on subgoal C to produce subgoal $\sim D$. REDUCER R2 can be used on this subgoal to produce subgoal $\sim B$. This subgoal CANCELs the earlier subgoal B, with the ultimate result that the root CANCELs itself. (The reader may want to verify this with the help of a diagram.)

A case of special interest occurs when a rule application produces a literal node that CANCELs one of its own literal node ancestors. This corresponds to a special case of ancestor resolution. Propagation of the CANCEL relation may then ultimately result in a node CANCELling itself. For purposes of CANCEL propagation, any node that CANCELs itself can be regarded as being CANCELled by the root node of the opposite tree. (Self-CANCELing goal nodes correspond to tautologies, and self-CANCELling fact nodes correspond to contradictions.)

Another interesting case occurs when a pair of sibling nodes CANCEL each other. If the siblings are unarced, then obviously their parent CANCELs itself, and we have the previous case. If the siblings are arced, the parent node cannot possibly appear in a proof, so it is eliminated from the tree. If this parent node is itself arced, its parent is eliminated, and so on. If a root node is ever eliminated, the entire proof attempt fails.

There are some problems (even in propositional calculus) that our system cannot solve. Our tolerant attitude towards this sort of incompetence is explained as follows. We are relying on the domain expert to provide guidance about which rules are useful and in which direction they should be used. We must hope that his expertise enhances the efficiency of the system. But dependence on the expert carries a price: gaps in his expertise decrease the competence of the system. There are some simple examples that illustrate this point.

Suppose that the goal is $B \vee C$ and the OPERATORs are $\underline{A} => B$ and $\sim\underline{A} => C$. Unfortunately, these rules work in the wrong direction; if they were REDUCERs instead, the goal would be easy to prove. (The contrapositive REDUCERs of the given OPERATORs are of no help.) One way round this difficulty is to use the implict fact $A \vee \sim A$ as if it were explicitly in the fact tree. The given OPERATORs could then be used to obtain a proof. Obviously this strategy of assuming all tautologies to be explicit facts would defeat our attempts at efficient operation, because it would allow every OPERATOR to be used in every problem. Another possible approach to this problem would be to analyse the OPERATORs to look for pairs having oppositely signed patterns. The disjunction of their consequents could then be added to the fact tree. (A dual approach could be used with REDUCERs.) But this catches only first-level difficulties. The main point is that to increase efficiency we are using the rules only in a given direction, and we are not allowing the rules to interact among themselves, therefore the domain expert must pose the problem in such a way that the system can still find a solution even with these restrictions.

Another troublemaker involves the goal $A => C$ (that is, $\sim A \vee C$) and the facts $A => B$ (that is, $\sim A \vee B$) and $B => C$ (that is, $\sim B \vee C$). Suppose there are no OPERATORs and no REDUCERs. Since facts cannot interact among themselves, we cannot produce a proof. Again the domain expert has failed us in not structuring the problem correctly.

Our attitude toward these problems is to avoid the easy but inefficient approach of allowing intrafact and intrarule inferences. That is precisely what our system is trying to escape. Instead, we will exploit the inherent modularity of the system to correct inadequacies in the rule and fact base as they are discovered.

6. EXTENSION TO QUANTIFICATION

A. Overview

The system we have described for propositional calculus can be easily modified to deal with quantified variables in expressions. The modifications involve: (1) replacing certain variables by skolem functions, (2) using unification during CANCEL operations, and (3) associating a substitution with each CANCEL relation. In this section, we shall discuss these modifications and present some examples.

B. Skolemization

Fact expressions receive the same initial preparation as for the propositional calculus case; implications are eliminated, and negations are moved in. We use the equivalences between

~(EXISTS *x*) *F*(*x*) and (FORALL *x*)[~*F*(*x*)]

and between

~(FORALL *x*) *F*(*x*) and (EXISTS *x*)[~*F*(*x*)]

to move negations in through quantifiers. Next we replace all instances of existentially quantified variables by skolem functions of those universally quantified variables in whose scopes they reside. Next we drop all quantifiers and henceforward adopt the convention (for facts) that all variables are universally quantified. When a fact expression is in this form, it can be represented as an OR/AND fact tree. The literals at the tip nodes may contain variables, of course.

Goal expressions also receive the same initial treatment. Skolemization, however, is different. In goal expressions, we replace all instances of universally quantified variables by skolem functions of those existentially quantified variables in whose scopes they reside. (Recall that goals can be regarded as negated facts, and that negated existential quantifiers are equivalent to universal ones. Thus, it shouldn't be surprising that skolemization of goal expressions uses conventions dual to those of skolemization of facts. If we are able to prove some expression *F*(*a*) where *a* is a constant different from those used in the facts and rules – that is, it is a skolem constant – then we can deduce (FORALL *x*) *F*(*x*) by universal generalization. Skolemization of universally quantified variables in goals can thus be regarded as using the rule of universal generalization in reverse.)

After elimination of the universally quantified variables, we can drop all of the quantifiers and adopt the convention that all variables (in goals) are existentially quantified. When a goal expression has been thus prepared, it can be represented as an AND/OR tree.

Skolemization of variables in rules is just slightly more complicated. (We allow rules of the same general form as in the propositional calculus case; however, they can have arbitrary quantification.) Quantifier scopes in rules can be of three types: the scope can be the entire implication or limited to either the antecedent or the consequent. We skolemize any existential whose scope is either the entire implication or its consequent. We skolemize any universal whose scope is limited to the antecedent of the implication.

After skolemization, we can drop the quantifiers, and the variables will "behave correctly". That is, when an OPERATOR is used, those variables occurring in the new fact nodes will have assumed universal quantification, and similarly for REDUCERS.

C. Use of rules

When a rule is used to extend the fact or goal tree, its pattern must be unifiable with the literal at the node from which it extends. It will be convenient to represent this matching process by an explicit edge of the tree and associate the most general unifier (mgu) with this edge. Thus, when the OPERATOR $A(x, a) \Rightarrow B(z, x)$ is used to extend the fact node $A(b, y)$, we produce the following structure:

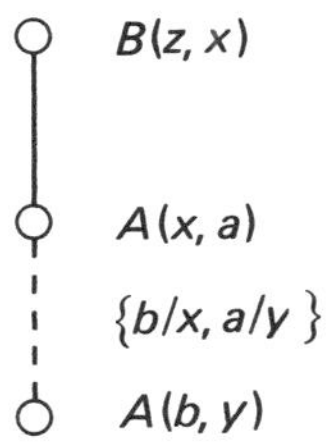

We represent "match edges" in trees by dashed lines and label them by the mgu obtained in unification. (Note that we do not apply to the rule consequent the substitution obtained by unifying with the antecedent. The equivalent of this operation will be incorporated into our new definition of CANCEL.) When a match edge is added to the tree, the node associated with the rule pattern is always an "unarced" node.

The variables that occur in the fact and goal trees should be kept **standardized apart**. This means that any variables that are common across goal disjuncts or fact conjuncts can be given different names. For example, the goal expression $A(x) \vee B(x)$ can be changed to $A(x) \vee B(y)$. The fact expression $C(x) \& D(x)$ can be changed to $C(x) \& D(y)$.

D. Extending the definition of CANCEL

We must extend the definition of CANCEL so that it takes into account the substitutions obtained during matching. For example, in propagating CANCEL relations involving arced nodes to the parent of the arced nodes, we must make sure that the substitutions for variables at these nodes are "consistent". The necessary elaboration involves associating a substitution with each CANCEL relation and modifying the definition of CANCEL to check for substitution consistency.

In the definition, we use the concept of a **unifying composition** (uc). The unifying composition of two substitutions, u_1 and u_2, is a most general substitution, u, satisfying

$$(Lu_1)u = (Lu)u_1 = Lu = (Lu_2)u = (Lu)u_2$$

for an arbitrary literal L. (The expression Lu denotes the result of applying substitution u to literal L.) If no such u exists, then the uc is undefined. The uc of a set of substitutions $\{u_1, \ldots u_n\}$ is the uc of any member, u_1, of the set with the uc of the rest of the set $\{u_2, \ldots u_n\}$. The substitutions in a set are **inconsistent** if the set has no uc.

The following are examples of unifying compositions (Sickel, 1976):

u_1	u_2	u
$\{a/x\}$	$\{b/x\}$	undefined
$\{x/y\}$	$\{y/z\}$	$\{x/y, x/z\}$
$\{f(z)/x\}$	$\{f(a)/x\}$	$\{f(a)/x, a/z\}$
$\{x/y, x/z\}$	$\{a/z\}$	$\{a/x, a/y, a/z\}$
$\{s\}$	$\{\ \}$	$\{s\}$

The new definition of CANCEL is that nodes n and m CANCEL

(1.1) If n and m are literal nodes of different trees and if the corresponding literals are unifiable. In this case, we associate the mgu with CANCEL(n, m),

or (1.2) If n and m are literal nodes of the same tree and if one of the corresponding literals unifies with the negation of the other. In this case, we associate the mgu with CANCEL(n, m),

or (2) If n has arced successors, $\{s_i\}$, such that CANCEL(s_i, m) holds for all of them, and the uc of the set of substitutions associated with the individual CANCELs exists. In this case, we associate the uc with CANCEL(n, m).

or (3) If n has unarced successors, $\{s_i\}$, such that CANCEL holds for at least one of them and the uc of the edge substitution and the substitution associated with the individual CANCEL exists. In this case, we associate the uc with CANCEL(n, m).

The consistency requirement on the individual substitutions in part 2 of our definition for CANCEL ensures proper propagation of CANCEL through arced nodes. The consistency requirement in part 3 of our definition ensures that the proper instances of matched rules are used to extend the trees. (In using part 3 of the CANCEL definition, we assume that the empty substitution is associated with nonmatch edges.)

E. An example

Several important mechanisms are implicit in our definition of CANCEL. These can best be understood by detailed examination of an example. The example is illustrated in graphical form in Fig. 7. The fact expression is shown at the bottom of the figure in OR/AND tree form; the variable "s" is assumed to have universal quantification. The goal expression is shown at the top in AND/OR tree form; the variable "x" is assumed to have existential quantification. The rules are simply shown as unconnected pieces of graph near the tip nodes where they ultimately will be used. All nodes in the graph are given a number. (In this example, it happens that the rules will be used at most once, so we prenumber their "nodes" for convenience.) Rule patterns are indicated by the usual convention. Lower-case letters near the beginning of the alphabet (for example, $a, b, c, \ldots$) denote constants, and lower-case letters near the end of the alphabet (for example, $\ldots x, y, z$) denote variables. All variables have been standardized apart. We have not shown the contrapositive forms of the given rules since they won't be used in this example.

At the outset we notice that there are several applicable rules. Since we have not yet advocated any particular control strategy, we shall trace through this example in an order that best illustrates the points we wish to make.

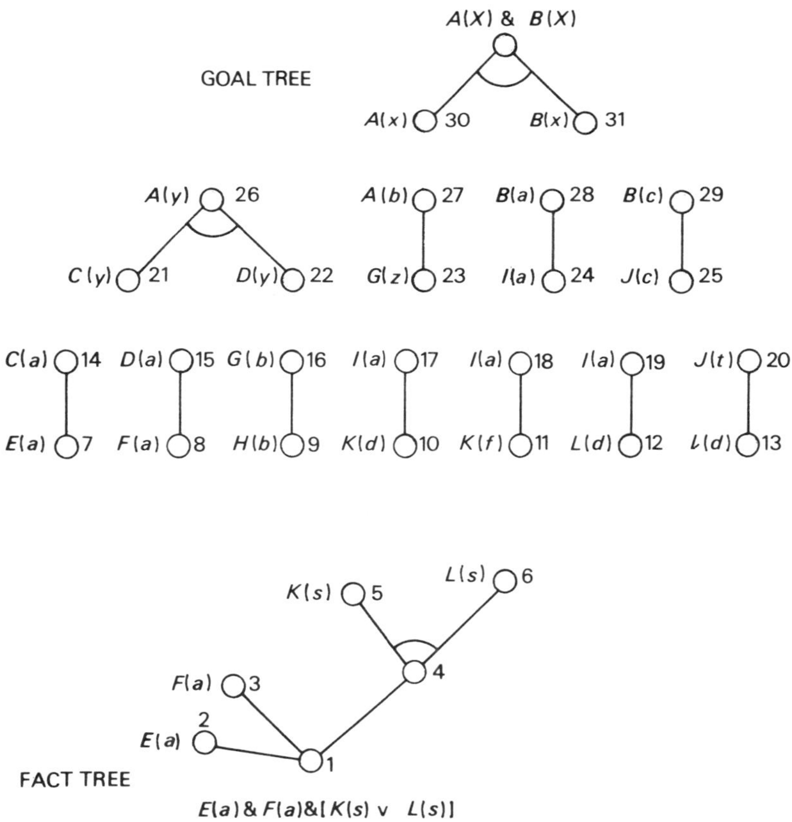

Fig. 7 – An example with variables.

First, let us match node 30 with the REDUCER node 26. The mgu is $\{y/x\}$. (When a variable is substituted for another variable, we adopt the convention of substituting the variable about to be added to the tree for the one already in the tree.) The goal tree that results after this match is shown in Fig. 8. No CANCEL relations are established yet, but we do associate $\{y/x\}$ with the match edge between nodes 26 and 30. Let's next match goal nodes against REDUCER nodes 27, 28, and 29. The goal tree will now be as shown in Fig. 9.

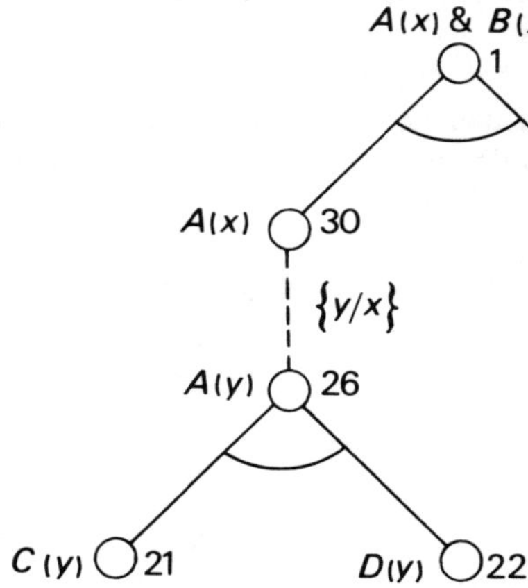

Fig. 8 – The goal tree after applying a REDUCER.

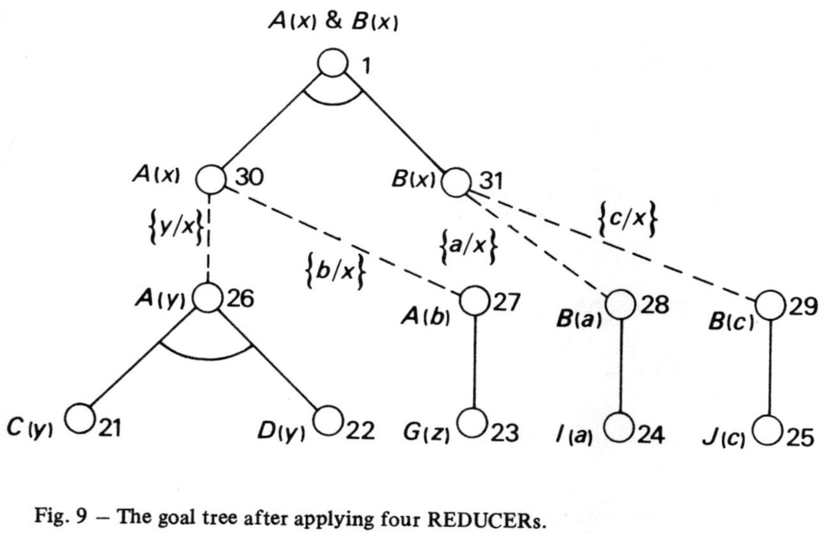

Fig. 9 – The goal tree after applying four REDUCERs.

We could continue to apply REDUCERs or OPERATORs until some nodes could be CANCELled, but already at this stage it is possible to predict that certain later attempts at CANCELling will fail. Notice in Fig. 9 that any attempt to propagate a CANCEL relation up through node 27 to node 30 will involve the substitution $\{b/x\}$. But this substitution is inconsistent with all of the substitutions shown below node 31. If we have exhausted all possible matches to node 31, then we know that the substitution $\{b/x\}$ at node 30 can never occur in a proof because only a or c can be substituted for x. Such an occurrence would correspond to a violation of **horizontal consistency** (Sickel, 1976). Thus, there can be no unifying composition of a CANCEL relation propagated up through node 27 with a substitution for any CANCEL relation in which node 31 participates. At this stage, we can prune node 27 (and, with it, node 23) from the goal tree and save ourselves the effort of attempts to prove $G(z)$. (Fishman and Minker, 1975, achieve a similar effect with their "π-representation".)

Quite analogous considerations would allow us to prune node 11 (and, with it, node 18) from the fact tree after we have matched against the OPERATOR nodes 10, 11, 12, and 13. After all of this, the fact tree is as shown in Fig. 10. (Note that *all* possible matches below a set of AND nodes must be considered before horizontal consistency violations can be detected. Practically, such consistency violations may be difficult to detect because the set of possible matches typically grows as the dual tree grows.)

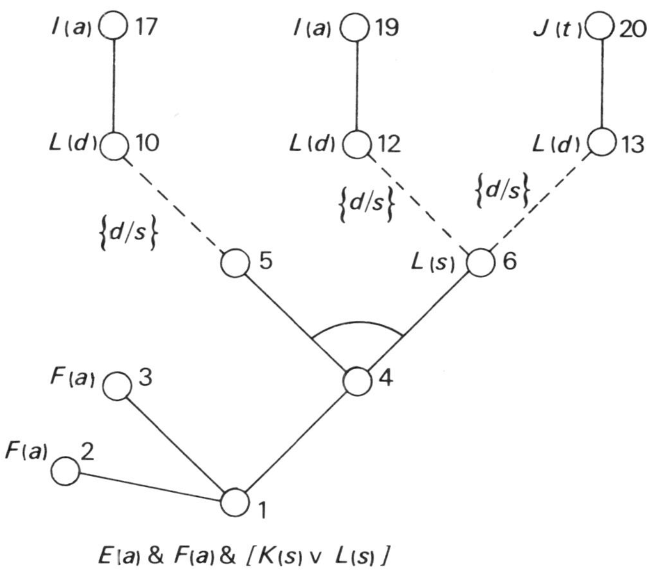

Fig. 10 – The fact tree after applying four OPERATORs.

Now, we can do some CANCELling between the literal nodes of the fact and goal trees. The following CANCELled pairs can be established:

(17, 24) { }
(19, 24) { }
and
(20, 25) {c/t} .

By using the CANCEL definition we can, for example, determine next the following CANCELled pairs:

(29, 20) {c/t}
(31, 20) {$c/x, c/t$}
(31, 13) {$c/x, c/t$}
(31, 6) {$c/x, c/t, d/s$} .

The associated substitutions are merely unifying compositions between edge substitutions and previous CANCEL substitutions. If a uc did not exist for a proposed CANCEL relation, then we could not establish this relation. Such an occurrence corresponds to a violation of **vertical consistency** (Sickel, 1976).

We can also obtain another CANCEL relation between nodes (31, 6) by a different route and thus with a different substitution, namely {d/s, a/x}. We represent both of these substitutions by repeated instances of CANCEL(31, 6).

The other CANCEL relation of interest that can be established at this stage is between the node pair (5, 31) with associated substitution {d/s, a/x}. To summarize, the CANCEL relations of interest (that is, those between nodes closest to the roots of the trees) are now:

(6, 31) {$c/x, c/t, d/s$}
(6, 31) {$d/s, a/x$}
(5, 31) {$d/s, a/x$} .

We note that the last two CANCEL relations can be combined to yield CANCEL(4, 31) with associated substitution {d/s, a/x}. This in turn yields CANCEL(1, 31), {$d/s, a/x$}.

In a straightforward manner, we can next match against the OPERATOR nodes 7 and 8 and perform matches between literal nodes to obtain:

CANCEL(2, 21) {a/y}
CANCEL(3, 22) {a/y}

These relations produce the sequence:

CANCEL(1, 21) {a/y}
CANCEL(1, 22) {a/y}
CANCEL(1, 26) {a/y} .

Proceeding through the match edge between nodes 26 and 30, we obtain:

CANCEL(1, 30) {a/x} .

Combining this relation with CANCEL(1, 31), $\{d/s, a/x\}$, we obtain finally:

$$\text{CANCEL}(1, 1)\ \{d/s, a/x\}\ .$$

Thus the goal is proved from the given facts. The relevant instance of Fact $\vdash$ Goal, useful for many information retrieval applications, can be simply obtained by applying the substitution associated with CANCEL(1, 1) to both the fact and goal expressions. This operation yields:

$$E(a)\ \&\ F(a)\ \&\ [K(d) \vee L(d)]\ \vdash\ [A(a)\ \&\ B(a)]\ .$$

7. SOME EXTENSIONS

A. Embedding new rules in operators

One way of relaxing the single-literal restriction on rule patterns is to allow rules to be embedded in the consequents of OPERATORs. Since $(\underline{A}\ \&\ \underline{B}) => C$ is equivalent to $\underline{A} => (\underline{B} => C)$, we can get the effect of the conjunctive pattern by adding the new OPERATOR $\underline{B} => C$ when A appears in the fact tree. One cannot simply add the new rule to the global rule base, however. Suppose we have the OPERATOR $\underline{A} => (\underline{B} => C)$ and the fact $A \vee D$. When $\underline{B} => C$ is added as a new OPERATOR, we must be careful not to use it on the disjunct D. The rule $\underline{B} => C$ can only be used "in the context" of A.

A simple generalization of our rule-based system supports the correct use of OPERATORs embedded in the consequents of OPERATORs. (Embedding REDUCERs in OPERATORs appears to be much more complex. Thus, we will not use REDUCER contrapositive forms of embedded OPERATORs.) The generalization involves associating each OPERATOR with a node of the fact tree. The initial set of conjunctive OPERATORs is associated with the root of the fact tree. An OPERATOR added at node n is associated with node n. The OPERATORs associated with node n can be used on facts associated with node n or its descendants.

This technique even generalizes nicely to permit "disjunctive" OPERATORs. Suppose we have an OPERATOR of the form $\underline{A} => [(\underline{B} => C) \vee (\underline{D} => E)]$. Before such a rule disjunction is associated with the fact tree at literal node A, we split node A into the disjunction $A \vee A$ and represent the disjunction by two OR node descendants of A. A different rule disjunct is then associated with each of the OR nodes. If the initial OPERATORs are in some complex logical relationship to each other, we represent this relationship by the appropriate OR/AND tree and label each of the tip nodes of this tree by the initial fact expression. This fact expression is then put in OR/AND tree form at each of the tips.

If the embedded OPERATORs contain quantified variables, these can be skolemized at the time the OPERATORs are associated with nodes in the fact tree. Care must be taken to ensure that the appropriate instance of an embedded OPERATOR is added.

B. High complexity proofs

Our system, as we have described it so far, is not able to find proofs for which any of the goal or fact expressions need to be rewritten with different variables and used a multiple number of times. (We can, of course, use the same *node* any number of times, but such usage does not rewrite any variables in the expression at the node. Also, we can use rules any number of times, each with different variables.) In analogy with a definition of proof complexity given by Sickel (1976), we shall say that the **complexity level** of a proof is precisely the number of times a fact or goal expression must be rewritten for multiple use. So far, then our system can produce only proofs of complexity level zero.

As examples of problems requiring complexity-level-one proofs, we have:

1) Goal: $A(x)$
   Fact: $A(a) \vee A(b)$

and its dual,

2) Goal: $B(a) \,\&\, B(b)$
   Fact: $B(x)$.

Straightforward attempts at proofs for these problems by our system are frustrated by horizontal consistency violations. However, if in problem 1, for example, we replace the goal by the equivalent one $A(x) \vee A(y)$, then a proof is easy to obtain.

Following Sickel, we might adopt the strategy of trying first to obtain a complexity-level-zero proof. If that attempt fails, we can look for higher complexity proofs in stages. The search for a complexity-level-one proof would involve selecting each of the goal and fact variables (in turn) and rewriting as a disjunction (for goals) or as a conjunction (for facts) the highest node in the goal or fact tree that contains that variable. Substitution consistency violations provide obvious clues about which variables should be rewritten.

To rewrite a goal node $A(x)$, for example, we produce the following tree structure:

To rewrite a goal node $A(x)$ & $B(x)$, for example, we produce the following tree structure:

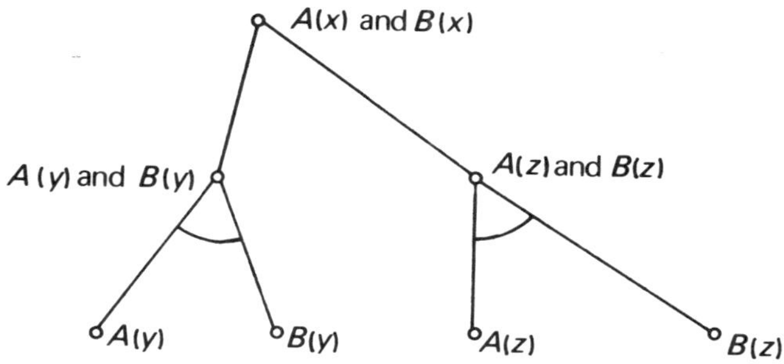

8. Conclusions

We have presented a design for a general system that uses production rules and a data base of fact and goal trees to perform deductions. The system can be regarded as a synthesis of many current and some new ideas in automatic deduction. The major innovations presented in this paper are the OR/AND fact tree and the CANCEL operation. These ideas bring a simplifying symmetry to several of the standard techniques for reasoning about facts and goals.

Logical completeness of the general system has not been a design goal. Instead, we assign responsibility for acceptable performance of any specific system to the domain expert, who provides the rules, and to the designer of the specific system, who can repair any unacceptable deficiencies in performance by adding or modifying rules or facts.

An important topic that we have not yet addressed concerns the control strategy for the system. Specialized control strategies for different domains of application (for example, deductive retrieval, theorem-proving, common-sense reasoning) will probably be necessary in order to achieve high performance. The control system must ensure that appropriate rules are used sufficiently often to prevent the usual combinatorial explosion. Separation of facts, OPERATORs, and REDUCERs should, we believe, help contain this explosion.

It is also hoped that the proposed system will serve as the beginning of a theoretical foundation for the various applications of "rule-based systems" now being developed by AI research. Many of these systems are fundamentally deduction systems even though some of them allow uncertain or probabilistic facts and rules. Extending the present system so that it could also deal with uncertain knowledge would be a valuable future project.

Acknowledgements

The author would like to thank the following people for providing helpful suggestions and criticisms and for their comments on early versions of this paper: Douglas Appelt, W. W. Bledsoe, Richard Fikes, Gary Hendrix, Robert C. Moore, and Earl Sacerdoti.

The work was supported jointly by SRI International Project 6171, Office of Naval Research Contract No. NR 049-405 and by Stanford University Heuristic Programming Project, ARPA Order No. 2494.

REFERENCES

Bledsoe, W. W. (1977). Non-resolution theorem-proving. *Artificial Intelligence* **9**, No. 1, 1–35.

Bobrow, D. and Winograd, T. (1977). An overview of KRL, a knowledge representation language. *Cognitive Science* **1** *No. 1* 31–46.

Chang, C. and Lee, R. C. (1973). *Symbolic logic and mechanical theorem-proving*. New York: Academic Press.

Davis, R. and King, J. (1977). An overview of production systems. In *Machine Intelligence 8*, pp. 300–332 (eds. Elcock, E. W. and Michie, D.). Chichester: Ellis Horwood Ltd. and New York: Wiley.

Fikes, R. and Hendrix, G. (1977). A network-based knowledge representation and its natural deduction system. *Proc 5th Int. Jnt. Conf. on Artificial Intelligence (IJCAI-77)*, pp. 235–246. Pittsburgh: Dept. of Computer Science, Carnegie-Mellon University.

Fishman, D. and Minker, J. (1975). π-representation: a clause-representation for parallel search. *Artificial Intelligence* **6** *No. 2* 103–27.

Hewitt, C. (1971). Procedural embedding of knowledge in PLANNER. *Proc 2nd Int. Jnt. Conf. on Artificial Intelligence (IJCAI-72)*, pp. 167–182. London: British Computer Society.

Kowalski, R. (1974a). A proof procedure using connection graphs. *DCL Memo No. 74.* Edinburgh: Department of Artificial Intelligence, University of Edinburgh.

Kowalski, R. (1974b). Logic for problem-solving. *DCL Memo No. 75.* Edinburgh: Department of Artificial Intelligence, University of Edinburgh.

Loveland, D. and Stickel, M. (1973). A hole in goal trees. *Proc 3rd Int. Jnt. Conf. on Artificial Intelligence (IJCAI-73)*, Stanford, pp. 153–61. Menlo Park: Stanford Research Institute.

Moore, R. C. (1975). Reasoning from incomplete knowledge in a procedural deduction system. *Memo A1-TR-347*, Cambridge, Mass: Artificial Intelligence Laboratory, Massachusetts Institute of Technology.

Nevins, A. J. (1975). A relaxation approach to splitting in an automatic theorem-prover *Artificial Intelligence* **6** *No. 2* 25–39.

Nilsson, N. J. (1971). *Problem-Solving Methods in Artificial Intelligence*. New York: McGraw Hill.

Reiter, R. (1976). A semantically guided deductive system for automatic theorem-proving *IEEE Trans on Computers* **C-25** *No. 4* 328–34.

Sickel, S. (1976). A search technique for clause interconnectivity graphs. *IEEE Trans on Computers* **C-25** *No. 8* 823–835.

Wilkins, D. (1974). A non-clausal theorem-proving system. *Proc. AISB Summer Conf. 1974*, pp. 257–267. London: British Computer Society.

REPRESENTATIONS FOR REAL-WORLD REASONING

6

First Order Theories of Individual Concepts and Propositions

J. McCarthy
Computer Science Department
Stanford University, USA

Abstract
We discuss first order theories in which *individual concepts* are admitted as mathematical objects along with the things that *reify* them. This allows very straightforward formalizations of knowledge, belief, wanting, and necessity in ordinary first order logic without modal operators. Applications are given in philosophy and in artificial intelligence. We do not treat general concepts, and we do not present any full axiomatizations but rather show how various facts can be expressed.

INTRODUCTION

"*... it seems that hardly anybody proposes to use different variables for propositions and for truth-values, or different variables for individuals and individual concepts.*" – (Carnap 1956, p. 113).

Admitting individual concepts as objects – with concept-valued constants, variables, functions and expressions – allows ordinary first order theories of necessity, knowledge, belief and wanting without modal operators or quotation marks and without the restrictions on substituting equals for equals that either device makes necessary.

In this paper we will show how various individual concepts and propositions can be expressed. We are not yet ready to present a full collection of axioms. Moreover, our purpose is not to explicate what concepts are, in a philosophical sense, but rather to develop a language of concepts for representing facts about knowledge, belief, etc. in the memory of a computer.

Frege (1892) discussed the need to distinguish direct and indirect use of words. According to one interpretation of Frege's ideas, the meaning of the phrase "*Mike's telephone number*" in the sentence "*Pat knows Mike's telephone number*" is the concept of Mike's telephone number, whereas its meaning in the sentence "*Pat dialled Mike's telephone number*" is the number itself. Thus if we also have "*Mary's telephone number = Mike's telephone number*", then "*Pat dialled Mary's telephone number*" follows, but "*Pat knows Mary's telephone number*" does not.

It was further proposed that a phrase has a *sense* which is a *concept* and is its *meaning* in *oblique contexts* like knowing and wanting, and a *denotation* which is its *meaning* in *direct contexts* like dialling. *Denotations* are the basis of the semantics of first order logic and model theory and are well understood, but *sense* has given more trouble, and the modal treatment of oblique contexts avoids the idea. On the other hand, logicians such as Carnap (1947 and 1956), Church (1951) and Montague (1974) see a need for *concepts* and have proposed formalizations. All these formalizations involve modifying the logic used; ours doesn't modify the logic and is more powerful, because it includes mappings from objects to concepts. Robert Moore's forthcoming dissertation also uses concepts in first order logic.

The problem identified by Frege – of suitably limiting the application of the substitutivity of equals for equals – arises in artificial intelligence as well as in philosophy and linguistics for any system that must represent information about beliefs, knowledge, desires, or logical necessity – regardless of whether the representation is declarative or procedural (as in PLANNER and other AI formalisms).

Our approach involves treating concepts as one kind of object in an ordinary first order theory. We shall have one term that denotes Mike's telephone number and a different term denoting the concept of Mike's telephone number instead of having a single term whose denotation is the number and whose sense is a concept of it. The relations among concepts and between concepts and other entities are expressed by formulas of first order logic. Ordinary model theory can then be used to study what spaces of concepts satisfy various sets of axioms.

We treat primarily what Carnap calls *individual concepts* like *Mike's telephone number* or *Pegasus* and not general concepts like *telephone* or *unicorn*. Extension to general concepts seems feasible, but individual concepts provide enough food for thought for the present.

This is a preliminary paper in that we don't give a comprehensive set of axioms for concepts. Instead we merely translate some English sentences into our formalism to give an idea of the possibilities.

KNOWING WHAT AND KNOWING THAT

To assert that Pat knows Mike's telephone number we write

$$true\ Know(Pat,\ Telephone\ Mike) \tag{1}$$

with the following conventions:

1. Parentheses are often omitted for one argument functions and predicates. This purely syntactic convention is not important. Another convention is to capitalize the first letter of a constant, variable, or function name

when its value is a concept. (We considered also capitalizing the last letter when the arguments are concepts, but it made the formulas ugly.)

2. *Mike* is the concept of Mike; that is, it is the *sense* of the expression "*Mike*". *mike* is Mike himself.
3. *Telephone* is a function that takes a concept of a person into a concept of his telephone number. We will also use *telephone* which takes the person himself into the telephone number itself. We do not propose to identify the function *Telephone* with the general concept of a person's telephone number.
4. If *P* is a person concept and *X* is another concept, then *Know(P, X)* is an assertion concept or *proposition* meaning that *P knows* the value of *X*. Thus in (1) *Know(Pat, Telephone Mike)* is a proposition and not a truth value. Note that we are formalizing *knowing what* rather than *knowing that* or *knowing how*. For AI and for other practical purposes, *knowing what* seems to be the most useful notion of the three. In English, *knowing what* is written *knowing whether* when the "knowand" is a proposition.
5. It is often convenient to write *know(pat, Telephone Mike)* instead of *true Know(Pat, Telephone Mike)* when we don't intend to iterate knowledge further. *know* is a predicate in the logic, so we cannot apply any knowledge operators to it. We will have

$$know(pat, Telephone\ Mike) \equiv true\ Know(Pat, Telephone\ Mike). \qquad (2)$$

6. We expect that the proposition *Know(Pat, Telephone Mike)* will be useful accompanied by axioms that allow inferring that Pat will use this knowledge under appropriate circumstances, that is, he will dial it or retell it when appropriate. There will also be axioms asserting that he will know it after being told it or looking it up in the telephone book.
7. While the sentence "*Pat knows Mike*" is in common use, it is harder to see how *Know(Pat, Mike)* is to be used and axiomatized. I suspect that new methods will be required to treat knowing a person.
8. *true Q* is the truth value, *t* or *f*, of the proposition *Q*, and we must write *true Q* in order to assert *Q*. Later we will consider formalisms in which *true* has a another argument – a *situation*, a *story*, a *possible world*, or even a *partial possible world* (a notion we suspect will eventually be found necessary).
9. The formulas are in a sorted first order logic with functions and equality. Knowledge, necessity, etc. will be discussed without extending the logic in any way – solely by the introduction of predicate and function symbols subject to suitable axioms. In the present informal treatment, we will not be explicit about sorts, but we will use different letters for variables of different sorts.

The reader may be nervous about what is meant by *concept*. He will have to remain nervous; no final commitment will be made in this paper. The formalism is compatible with many possibilities, and these can be compared by using the models of their first order theories. Actually, this paper isn't much motivated by the philosophical question of what concepts really are. The goal is more to make a formal structure that can be used to represent facts about knowledge and belief so that a computer program can reason about who has what knowledge in order to solve problems. From either the philosophical or the AI point of view, however, if (1) is to be reasonable, it must not follow from (1) and the fact that Mary's telephone number is the same as Mike's, that Pat knows Mary's telephone number.

The proposition that Joe knows *whether* Pat knows Mike's telephone number, is written

$$Know(Joe, Know(Pat, Telephone\ Mike)), \tag{3}$$

and asserting it requires writing

$$true\ Know(Joe, Know(Pat, Telephone\ Mike)), \tag{4}$$

while the proposition that Joe knows *that* Pat knows Mike's telephone number is written

$$K(Joe, Know(Pat, Telephone\ Mike)), \tag{5}$$

where $K(P, Q)$ is the proposition that P knows *that* Q. English does not treat knowing a proposition and knowing an individual concept uniformly: knowing an individual concept means knowing its value, while knowing a proposition means knowing that it has a particular value, namely t. There is no reason to impose this infirmity on robots.

We first consider systems in which corresponding to each concept X, there is a thing x of which X is a concept. Then there is a function *denot* such that

$$x = denot\ X. \tag{6}$$

Functions like *Telephone* are then related to *denot* by equations like

$$\forall P1\ P2.(denot\ P1 = denot\ P2 \supset denot\ Telephone\ P1 = denot\ Telephone\ P2). \tag{7}$$

We call *denot X* the *denotation* of the concept X, and (7) asserts that the denotation of the concept of P's telephone number depends only on the denotation of the concept P. The variables in (7) range over concepts of persons, and we regard (7) as asserting that *Telephone* is *extensional* with respect to *denot*. Note that our *denot* operates on concepts rather than on expressions; a theory of expressions will also need a denotation function. From (7) and suitable logical axioms follows the existence of a function *telephone* satisfying

$$\forall P.(denot\ Telephone\ P = telephone\ denot\ P). \tag{8}$$

Know is extensional with respect to *denot* in its first argument, and this is expressed by

$$\forall P1\ P2\ X.(denot\ P1 = denot\ P2 \supset denot\ Know(P1, X) = denot\ Know(P2, X)), \tag{9}$$

but it is not extensional in its second argument. We can therefore define a predicate $know(p, X)$ satisfying

$$\forall P\ X.(true\ Know(P, X) \equiv know(denot\ P, X)). \tag{10}$$

(Note that all these predicates and functions are entirely extensional in the underlying logic, and the notion of extensionality presented here is relative to *denot*.)

The predicate *true* and the function *denot* are related by

$$\forall Q.(true\ Q \equiv (denot\ Q = t)) \tag{11}$$

provided that truth values are in the range of *denot*, and *denot* could also be provided with a (*partial*) *possible world* argument.

When we don't assume that all concepts have denotations, we use a predicate $denotes(X, x)$ instead of a function. The extensionality of *Telephone* would then be written

$$\forall P1\ P2\ x\ u.(denotes(P1, x) \wedge denotes(P2, x) \wedge denotes(Telephone\ P1, u) \supset denotes(Telephone\ P2, u)). \tag{12}$$

We now introduce the function *Exists* satisfying

$$\forall X.(true\ Exists\ X \equiv \exists x.denotes(X, x)). \tag{13}$$

Suppose we want to assert that Pegasus is a horse without asserting that Pegasus exists. We can do this by introducing the predicate *Ishorse* and writing

$$true\ Ishorse\ Pegasus \tag{14}$$

which is related to the predicate *ishorse* by

$$\forall X\ x.(denotes(X, x) \supset (ishorse\ x \equiv true\ Ishorse\ X)). \tag{15}$$

In this way, we assert extensionality without assuming that all concepts have denotations. *Exists* is extensional in this sense, but the corresponding predicate *exists* is identically true and therefore dispensable.

To combine concepts propositionally, we need analogs of the propositional operators such as *And*, which we shall write as an infix and axiomatize by

$$\forall Q1\ Q2.(true(Q1\ And\ Q2) \equiv true\ Q1 \wedge true\ Q2). \tag{16}$$

The corresponding formulas for *Or*, *Not*, *Implies*, and *Equiv* are

$$\forall Q1\ Q2.(true(Q1\ Or\ Q2) \equiv true\ Q1 \vee true\ Q2), \tag{17}$$

$$\forall Q.(true(Not\ Q) \equiv \neg\, true\ Q), \tag{18}$$

$$\forall Q1\ Q2.(true(Q1\ Implies\ Q2) \equiv true\ Q1 \supset true\ Q2), \tag{19}$$

and

$$\forall Q1\ Q2.(true(Q1\ Equiv\ Q2) \equiv (true\ Q1 \equiv true\ Q2)). \tag{20}$$

The equality symbol "=" is part of the logic so that $X = Y$ asserts that X and Y are the same concept. To write propositions expressing equality, we introduce *Equal*(X, Y) which is a proposition that X and Y denote the same thing if anything. We shall want axioms

$$\forall X.\ true\ Equal(X, X), \tag{21}$$

$$\forall X\ Y.(true\ Equal(X, Y) \equiv true\ Equal(Y, X)), \tag{22}$$

and

$$\forall X\ Y\ Z.(true\ Equal(X, Y) \wedge true\ Equal(Y, Z) \supset true\ Equal(X, Z) \tag{23}$$

making *true Equal*(X, Y) an equivalence relation, and

$$\forall X\ Y\ x.(true\ Equal(X, Y) \wedge denotes(X, x) \supset denotes(Y, x)) \tag{24}$$

which relates it to equality in the logic. We can make the concept of equality *essentially* symmetric by replacing (22) by

$$\forall X\ Y.\ Equal(X, Y) = Equal(Y, X), \tag{25}$$

that is, making the two expressions denote the *same concept*.

The statement that Mary has the same telephone number as Mike is asserted by

$$true\ Equal(Telephone\ Mary, Telephone\ Mike), \tag{26}$$

and it obviously doesn't follow from this and (1) that

$$true\ Know(Pat, Telephone\ Mary). \tag{27}$$

To draw this conclusion we need something like

$$true\ K(Pat, Equal(Telephone\ Mary, Telephone\ Mike)) \tag{28}$$

and suitable axioms about knowledge.

If we were to adopt the convention that a proposition appearing at the outer level of a sentence is asserted and were to regard the denotation-valued function as standing for the sense-valued function when it appears as the second argument of *Know*, we would have a notation that resembles ordinary language in handling obliquity entirely by context. There is no guarantee that general statements could be expressed unambiguously without circumlocution; the fact that the principles of intensional reasoning haven't yet been stated is evidence against the suitability of ordinary language for stating them.

FUNCTIONS FROM THINGS TO CONCEPTS OF THEM

While the relation *denotes*(X, x) between concepts and things is many-one, functions going from things to certain concepts of them seem useful. Some things such as numbers can be regarded as having *standard* concepts. Suppose that *Concept*1 n gives a standard concept of the number n, so that

$$\forall n.(denot\ Concept1\ n = n). \qquad (29)$$

We can then have simultaneously

$$true\ Not\ Knew(Kepler,\ Composite\ Number\ Planets) \qquad (30)$$

and

$$true\ Knew(Kepler,\ Composite\ Concept1\ denot\ Number\ Planets). \qquad (31)$$

(We have used *Knew* instead of *Know*, because we are not now concerned with formalizing tense.)

(31) can be condensed using *Composite*1 which takes a number into the proposition that it is composite, that is,

$$Composite1\ n \doteq Composite\ Concept1\ n \qquad (32)$$

getting

$$true\ Knew(Kepler,\ Composite1\ denot\ Number\ Planets). \qquad (33)$$

A further condensation can be achieved by using *Composite*2 defined by

$$Composite2\ N = Composite\ Concept1\ denot\ N, \qquad (34)$$

letting us write

$$true\ Knew(Kepler,\ Composite2\ Number\ Planets), \qquad (35)$$

which is true even though

$$true\ Knew(Kepler,\ Composite\ Number\ Planets) \qquad (36)$$

is false. (36) is our formal expression of "*Kepler knew that the number of planets is composite*", while (31), (33), and (35) each expresses a proposition that can only be stated awkwardly in English, for example, as "*Kepler knew that a certain number is composite, where this number (perhaps unbeknownst to Kepler) is the number of planets*".

We may also want a map from things to concepts of them in order to formalize a sentence like, "*Lassie knows the location of all her puppies*". We write this

$$\forall x.(ispuppy(x, lassie) \supset$$
$$true\ Knowd(Lassie,\ Locationd\ Conceptd\ x)). \qquad (37)$$

Here *Conceptd* takes a puppy into a dog's concept of it, and *Locationd* takes a dog's concept of a puppy into a dog's concept of its location. The axioms satisfied by *Knowd*, *Locationd* and *Conceptd* can be tailored to our ideas of what dogs know.

A suitable collection of functions from things to concepts might permit a language that omitted some individual concepts like *Mike* (replacing it with *Conceptx mike*) and wrote many sentences with quantifiers over things rather than over concepts. However, it is still premature to apply Occam's razor. It may be possible to avoid concepts as objects in expressing particular facts but impossible to avoid them in stating general principles.

RELATIONS BETWEEN KNOWING WHAT AND KNOWING THAT

As mentioned before, "*Pat knows Mike's telephone number*" is written

$$true\ Know(Pat, Telephone\ Mike). \tag{38}$$

We can write "*Pat knows Mike's telephone number is* 333-3333"

$$true\ K(Pat, Equal(Telephone\ Mike, Concept1\ \text{“333-3333”})) \tag{39}$$

where $K(P, Q)$ is the proposition that $denot(P)$ knows the proposition Q and *Concept*1 ("333-3333") is some standard concept of that telephone number.

The two ways of expressing knowledge are somewhat interdefinable, since we can write

$$K(P, Q) = (Q\ And\ Know(P, Q)), \tag{40}$$

and

$$true\ Know(P, X) \equiv \exists A.(constant\ A \wedge true\ K(P, Equal(X, A))). \tag{41}$$

Here *constant A* asserts that A is a constant, that is, a concept such that we are willing to say that P knows X if he knows it equals A. This is clear enough for some domains like integers, but it is not obvious how to treat knowing a person.

Using the *standard concept* function *Concept*1, we might replace (41) by

$$true\ Know(P, X) \equiv \exists a.true\ K(P, Equal(X, Concept1\ a)) \tag{42}$$

with similar meaning.

(41) and (42) expresses a *denotational* definition of *Know* in terms of *K*. A *conceptual* definition seems to require something like

$$\begin{aligned} &\forall P\ X.(Know(P, X) = \\ &\quad Exists\ X\ And\ K(P, Equal(X, Concept2\ denot\ X))), \end{aligned} \tag{43}$$

where *Concept*2 is a suitable function from things to concepts and may not be available for all sorts of objects.

REPLACING MODAL OPERATORS BY MODAL FUNCTIONS

Using concepts we can translate the content of modal logic into ordinary logic. We need only replace the modal operators by *modal functions*. The axioms of modal logic then translate into ordinary first order axioms. In this section we will treat only *unquantified modal logic*. The arguments of the modal functions will not involve quantification, although quantification occurs in the outer logic.

Nec Q is the proposition that the proposition *Q* is necessary, and *Poss Q* is the proposition that it is possible. To assert necessity or possibility we must write *true Nec Q* or *true Poss Q*. This can be abbreviated by defining *nec Q* ≡ *true Nec Q* and *poss Q* correspondingly. However, since *nec* is a predicate in the logic with *t* and *f* as values, *nec Q* cannot be an argument of *nec* or *Nec*.

Before we even get to modal logic proper we have a decision to make – shall *Not Not Q* be considered the same proposition as *Q*, or is it merely extensionally equivalent? The first is written

$$\forall Q.\, Not\ Not\ Q = Q. \tag{44}$$

and the second

$$\forall Q.\, true\ Not\ Not\ Q \equiv true\ Q. \tag{45}$$

The second follows from the first by substitution of equals for equals.

In *Meaning and Necessity*, Carnap takes what amounts to the first alternative, regarding concepts as L-equivalence classes of expressions. This works nicely for discussing necessity, but when he wants to discuss knowledge without assuming that everyone knows Fermat's last theorem if it is true, he introduces the notion of *intensional isomorphism* and has knowledge operate on the equivalence classes of this relation.

If we choose the first alternative, then we may go on to identify any two propositions that can be transformed into each other by Boolean identities. This can be assured by a small collection of propositional identities like (44) including associative and distributive laws for conjunction and disjunction, De Morgan's law, and the laws governing the propositions *T* and *F*. In the second alternative we will want the extensional forms of the same laws. When we get to quantification a similar choice will arise, but if we choose the first alternative, it will be undecidable whether two expressions denote the same concept. I doubt that considerations of linguistic usage or usefulness in AI will unequivocally recommend one alternative, so both will have to be studied.

Actually there are more than two alternatives. Let *M* be the free algebra built up from the "atomic" concepts by the concept forming function symbols. If ≡≡ is an equivalence relation on *M* such that

$$\forall X1\ X2 \in M.((X1 \equiv\equiv X2) \supset (true\ X1 \equiv true\ X2)), \tag{46}$$

then the set of equivalence classes under ≡≡ may be taken as the set of concepts.

Similar possibilities arise in modal logic. We can choose between the *conceptual identity*

$$\forall Q.(Poss\ Q = Not\ Nec\ Not\ Q), \tag{47}$$

and the weaker extensional axiom

$$\forall Q.(true\ Poss\ Q \equiv true\ Not\ Nec\ Not\ Q). \tag{48}$$

We will write the rest of our modal axioms in extensional form.

We have

$$\forall Q.(\mathit{true\ Nec\ Q} \supset \mathit{true\ Q}), \tag{49}$$

and

$$\forall Q1\ Q2. \quad (\mathit{true\ Nec\ Q1} \wedge \mathit{true\ Nec}(Q1\ \mathit{Implies}\ Q2) \supset \mathit{true\ Nec\ Q2}). \tag{50}$$

yielding a system equivalent to von Wright's T.

S4 is given by

$$\forall Q.(\mathit{true\ Nec\ Q} \equiv \mathit{true\ Nec\ Nec\ Q}), \tag{51}$$

and S5 by

$$\forall Q.(\mathit{true\ Poss\ Q} \equiv \mathit{true\ Nec\ Poss\ Q}). \tag{52}$$

Actually, there may be no need to commit ourselves to a particular modal system. We can simultaneously have the functions *NecT*, *Nec*4 and *Nec*5, related by axioms such as

$$\forall Q.(\mathit{true\ Nec4\ Q} \supset \mathit{true\ Nec5\ Q}) \tag{53}$$

which would seem plausible if we regard S4 as corresponding to provability in some system and S5 as truth in the intended model of the system.

Presumably we shall want to relate necessity and equality by the axiom

$$\forall X.\mathit{true\ Nec\ Equal}(X, X). \tag{54}$$

Certain of Carnap's proposals translate to the stronger relation

$$\forall X\ Y.(X = Y \equiv \mathit{true\ Nec\ Equal}(X, Y)) \tag{55}$$

which asserts that two concepts are the same if and only if the equality of what they may denote is necessary.

MORE PHILOSOPHICAL EXAMPLES – MOSTLY WELL KNOWN

Some sentences that recur as examples in the philosophical literature will be expressed in our notation, so the treatments can be compared.

First we have "*The number of planets* = 9" and "*Necessarily* 9 = 9" from which one doesn't want to deduce "*Necessarily the number of planets* = 9". This example is discussed by Quine (1961) and (Kaplan 1969). Consider the sentences

$$\neg \mathit{nec\ Equal}(\mathit{Number\ Planets}, \mathit{Concept1}\ 9) \tag{56}$$

and

$$\mathit{nec\ Equal}(\mathit{Concept1\ number\ planets}, \mathit{Concept1}\ 9). \tag{57}$$

Both are true. (56) asserts that it is not necessary that the number of planets be 9, and (57) asserts that the number of planets, once determined, is the number that is necessarily equal to 9. It is a major virtue of our formalism that both meanings can be expressed and are readily distinguished. Substitutivity of equals holds in the logic but causes no trouble, because "*The number of planets* = 9" may be written

$$number(planets) = 9 \tag{58}$$

or, using concepts as

$$true\ Equal(Number\ Planets, Concepts1\ 9), \tag{59}$$

and "*Necessarily* 9=9" is written

$$nec\ Equal(Concept1\ 9, Concept1\ 9), \tag{60}$$

and these don't yield the unwanted conclusion.

Ryle used the sentences "*Baldwin is a statesman*" and "*Pickwick is a fiction*" to illustrate that parallel sentence construction does not always give parallel sense. The first can be rendered in four ways, namely *true Statesman Baldwin* or *statesman denot Baldwin* or *statesman baldwin* or *statesman*1 *Baldwin* where the last asserts that the concept of Baldwin is one of a statesman. The second can be rendered only as *true Fiction Pickwick* or *fiction*1 *Pickwick.*

Quine (1961) considers illegitimate the sentence

$$(\exists x)(Philip\ is\ unaware\ that\ x\ denounced\ Catiline) \tag{61}$$

obtained from "*Philip is unaware that Tully denounced Catiline*" by existential generalization. In the example, we are also supposing the truth of *Philip is aware that Cicero denounced Cataline*". These sentences are related to (perhaps even explicated by) several sentences in our system. *Tully* and *Cicero* are taken as distinct concepts. The person is called *tully* or *cicero* in our language, and we have

$$tully = cicero, \tag{62}$$

$$denot\ Tully = cicero \tag{63}$$

and

$$denot\ Cicero = cicero. \tag{64}$$

We can discuss Philip's concept of the person Tully by introducing a function $Concept2(p1, p2)$ giving for some persons $p1$ and $p2$, $p1$'s concept of $p2$. Such a function need not be unique or always defined, but in the present case, some of our information may be conveniently expressed by

$$Concept2(philip, tully) = Cicero, \tag{65}$$

asserting that Philip's concept of the person Cicero is *Cicero*. The basic assumptions of Quine's example also include

$$true\ K(Philip, Denounced(Cicero, Catiline)) \tag{66}$$

and

$$\neg true\ K(Philip, Denounced(Tully, Catiline)). \tag{67}$$

From (63), ... (67) we can deduce

$$\exists P.\mathit{true}\ \mathit{Denounced}(P, \mathit{Catiline})\ \mathit{And}\ \mathit{Not}\ K(\mathit{Philip}, \mathit{Denounced}(P, \mathit{Catiline})), \tag{68}$$

from (67) and others, and

$$\neg\exists p.(\mathit{denounced}(p, \mathit{catiline}) \wedge \neg\mathit{true}\ K(\mathit{Philip}, \mathit{Denounced}(\mathit{Concept}2(\mathit{philip}, p), \mathit{Catiline}))) \tag{69}$$

using the additional hypotheses

$$\forall p.(\mathit{denounced}(p, \mathit{catiline}) \supset p = \mathit{cicero}), \tag{70}$$

$$\mathit{denot}\ \mathit{Catiline} = \mathit{catiline}, \tag{71}$$

and

$$\forall P1\ P2.(\mathit{denot}\ \mathit{Denounced}(P1, P2) \equiv \mathit{denounced}(\mathit{denot}\ P1, \mathit{denot}\ P2)). \tag{72}$$

Presumably (68) is always true, because we can always construct a concept whose denotation is Cicero unbeknownst to Philip. The truth of (69) depends on Philip's knowing that someone denounced Catiline, and on the map $\mathit{Concept}2(p1, p2)$ that gives one person's concept of another. If we refrain from using a silly map that gives something like *Denouncer*(*Catiline*) as its value, we can get results that correspond to intuition.

The following sentence attributed to Russell is discussed by Kaplan: "*I thought that your yacht was longer than it is*". We can write it

$$\mathit{true}\ \mathit{Believed}(I, \mathit{Greater}(\mathit{Length}\ \mathit{Youryacht}, \mathit{Concept}1\ \mathit{denot}\ \mathit{Length}\ \mathit{Youryacht})) \tag{73}$$

where we are not analysing the pronouns or the tense, but are using *denot* to get the actual length of the yacht and *Concept*1 to get back a concept of this true length so as to end up with a proposition that the length of the yacht is greater than that number. This looks problematical, but if it is consistent, it is probably useful.

To express "*Your yacht is longer than Peter thinks it is.*" we need the expression *Denot*(*Peter*, *X*) giving a concept of what Peter thinks the value of *X* is. We now write

$$\mathit{longer}(\mathit{youryacht}, \mathit{denot}\ \mathit{Denot}(\mathit{Peter}, \mathit{Length}\ \mathit{Youryacht})), \tag{74}$$

but I am not certain this is a correct translation.

Quine (1956) discusses an example in which Ralph sees Bernard J. Ortcutt skulking about and concludes that he is a spy, and also sees him on the beach, but doesn't recognize him as the same person. The facts can be expressed in our formalism by equations

$$\mathit{true}\ \mathit{Believe}(\mathit{Ralph}, \mathit{Isspy}\ P1) \tag{75}$$

and

$$\mathit{true}\ \mathit{Believe}(\mathit{Ralph}, \mathit{Not}\ \mathit{Isspy}\ P2) \tag{76}$$

where $P1$ and $P2$ are concepts satisfying $denot\ P1 = ortcutt$ and $denot\ P2 = ortcutt$. $P1$ and $P2$ are further described by sentences relating them to the circumstances under which Ralph formed them.

We can still consider a simple sentence involving the persons as things – write it *believespy*(*ralph*, *ortcutt*), where we define

$$\forall p1\ p2.(believespy(p1, p2) \equiv \\ true\ Believe(Concept1\ p1, Isspy\ Concept7\ p2) \qquad (77)$$

using suitable mappings *Concept*1 and *Concept*7 from persons to concepts of persons. We might also choose to define *believespy* in such a way that it requires *true Believe*(*Concept*1 *p*1, *Isspy P*) for several concepts *P* of *p*2, for example, the concepts arising from all *p*1's encounters with *p*2 or his name. In this case *believespy*(*ralph*, *ortcutt*) will be false and so would a corresponding *notbelievespy*(*ralph*, *ortcutt*). However, the simple-minded predicate *believespy*, suitably defined, may be quite useful for expressing the facts necessary to predict someone's behaviour in simpler circumstances.

Regarded as an attempt to explicate the sentence "*Ralph believes Ortcutt is a spy*", the above may be considered rather tenuous. However, we are proposing it as a notation for expressing Ralph's beliefs about Ortcutt so that correct conclusions may be drawn about Ralph's future actions. For this it seems to be adequate.

PROPOSITIONS EXPRESSING QUANTIFICATION

As the examples of the previous sections have shown, admitting concepts as objects and introducing standard concept functions makes "quantifying in" rather easy. However, forming propositions and individual concepts by quantification requires new ideas and additional formalism. We are not very confident of the approach presented here.

We want to continue describing concepts within first order logic with no logical extentions. Therefore, in order to form new concepts by quantification and description, we introduce functions *All*, *Exist*, and *The* such that *All*(V, P) is (approximately) the proposition that *for all values of V P is true*, *Exist*(V, P) is the corresponding existential proposition, and *The*(V, P) is the concept of *the V such that P*.

Since *All* is to be a function, V and P must be objects in the logic. However, V is semantically a variable in the formation of *All*(V, P), *etc.*, and we will call such objects *inner variables* so as to distinguish them from variables in the logic. We will use V, sometimes with subscripts, for a logical variable ranging over inner variables. We also need some constant symbols for inner variables (got that?), and we will use doubled letters, sometimes with subscripts, for these. XX will be used for individual concepts, PP for persons, and QQ for propositions.

The second argument of *All* and friends is a "proposition with variables in it", but remember that these variables are inner variables which are constants in the logic. Got that? We won't introduce a special term for them, but will generally allow concepts to include inner variables. Thus concepts now include inner variables like *XX* and *PP*, and concept-forming functions like *Telephone* and *Know* take the generalized concepts as arguments.

Thus

$$\mathit{Child}(\mathit{Mike}, \mathit{PP})\ \mathit{Implies}\ \mathit{Equal}(\mathit{Telephone}\ \mathit{PP}, \mathit{Telephone}\ \mathit{Mike}) \tag{78}$$

is a proposition with the inner variable *PP* in it to the effect that if *PP* is a child of Mike, then his telephone number is the same as Mike's, and

$$\begin{aligned}&\mathit{All}(\mathit{PP}, \mathit{Child}(\mathit{Mike}, \mathit{PP})\\&\quad \mathit{Implies}\ \mathit{Equal}(\mathit{Telephone}\ \mathit{PP}, \mathit{Telephone}\ \mathit{Mike}))\end{aligned} \tag{79}$$

is the proposition that all Mike's children have the same telephone number as Mike. Existential propositions are formed similarly to universal ones, but the function *Exist* introduced here should not be confused with the function *Exists* applied to individual concepts introduced earlier.

In forming individual concepts by the description function *The*, it doesn't matter whether the object described exists. Thus

$$\mathit{The}(\mathit{PP}, \mathit{Child}(\mathit{Mike}, \mathit{PP})) \tag{80}$$

is the concept of Mike's only child. *Exists The*(*PP*, *Child*(*Mike*, *PP*)) is the proposition that the described child exists. We have

$$\begin{aligned}&\mathit{true}\ \mathit{Exists}\ \mathit{The}(\mathit{PP}, \mathit{Child}(\mathit{Mike}, \mathit{PP})) \equiv\\&\quad \mathit{true}(\mathit{Exist}(\mathit{PP}, \mathit{Child}(\mathit{Mike}, \mathit{PP})\\&\quad \mathit{And}\ \mathit{All}(\mathit{PP}1, \mathit{Child}(\mathit{Mike}, \mathit{PP}1)\ \mathit{Implies}\ \mathit{Equal}(\mathit{PP}, \mathit{PP}1)))),\end{aligned} \tag{81}$$

but we may want the equality of the two propositions, that is,

$$\begin{aligned}&\mathit{Exists}\ \mathit{The}(\mathit{PP}, \mathit{Child}(\mathit{Mike}, \mathit{PP})) =\\&\quad \mathit{Exist}(\mathit{PP}, \mathit{Child}(\mathit{Mike}, \mathit{PP})\\&\quad \mathit{And}\ \mathit{All}(\mathit{PP}1, \mathit{Child}(\mathit{Mike}, \mathit{PP}1)\ \mathit{Implies}\ \mathit{Equal}(\mathit{PP}, \mathit{PP}1))).\end{aligned} \tag{82}$$

This is part of general problem of when two logically equivalent concepts are to be regarded as the same.

In order to discuss the truth of propositions and the denotation of descriptions, we introduce *possible worlds* reluctantly and with an important difference from the usual treatment. We need them to give values to the inner variables, and we can also use them for axiomatizing the modal operators, knowledge, belief and tense. However, for axiomatizing quantification, we also need a function α such that

$$\pi' = \alpha(V, x, \pi) \tag{83}$$

is the possible world that is the same as the world π except that the inner variable V has the value x instead of the value it has in π. In this respect our possible worlds resemble the *state vectors* or *environments* of computer science more than the possible worlds of the Kripke treatment of modal logic. This Cartesian product structure on the space of possible worlds can also be used to treat conterfactual conditional sentences.

Let $\pi 0$ be the actual world. Let $true(P, \pi)$ mean that the proposition P is true in the possible world π. Then

$$\forall P.(true\ P \equiv true(P, \pi 0)). \tag{84}$$

Let $denotes(X, x, \pi)$ mean that X denotes x in π, and let $denot(X, \pi)$ mean the denotation of X in π when that is defined.

The truth condition for $All(V, P)$ is then given by

$$\forall \pi\ V\ P.(true(All(V, P), \pi) \equiv \forall x.true(P, \alpha(V, x, \pi)). \tag{85}$$

Here V ranges over inner variables, P ranges over propositions, and x ranges over things. There seems to be no harm in making the domain of x depend on π. Similarly

$$\forall \pi\ V\ P.(true(Exist(V, P), \pi) \equiv \exists x.true(P, \alpha(V, x, \pi)). \tag{86}$$

The meaning of $The(V, P)$ is given by

$$\forall \pi\ V\ P\ x.(true(P, \alpha(V, x, \pi)) \wedge \forall y.(true(P, \alpha(V, y, \pi)) \supset y = x) \supset denotes(The(V, P), x, \pi)) \tag{87}$$

and

$$\forall \pi\ V\ P.(\neg\exists\ x.true(P, \alpha(V, x, \pi)) \supset \neg true\ Exists\ The(V, P)). \tag{88}$$

We also have the following "syntactic" rules governing propositions involving quantification:

$$\forall \pi\ Q1\ Q2\ V.(absent(V, Q1) \wedge true(All(V, Q1\ Implies\ Q2), \pi) \supset true(Q1\ Implies\ All(V, Q2), \pi)) \tag{89}$$

and

$$\forall \pi\ V\ Q\ X.(true(All(V, Q), \pi) \supset true(Subst(X, V, Q), \pi)). \tag{90}$$

where $absent(V, X)$ means that the variable V is not present in the concept X, and $Subst(X, V, Y)$ is the concept that results from substituting the concept X for the variable V in the concept Y. *absent* and *Subst* are characterized by the following axioms:

$$\forall V1\ V2.(absent(V1, V2) \equiv V1 \neq V2), \tag{91}$$

$$\forall V\ P\ X.(absent(V, Know(P, X)) \equiv absent(V, P) \wedge absent(V, X)), \tag{92}$$

axioms similar to (92) for other conceptual functions,

$$\forall V\ Q.absent(V, All(V, Q)), \tag{93}$$

$$\forall V\ Q.absent(V, Exist(V, Q)), \tag{94}$$

$$\forall V\ Q.absent(V, The(V, Q)), \tag{95}$$

$$\forall V\ X.Subst(V, V, X) = X, \tag{96}$$

$$\forall X\ V.Subst(X, V, V) = X, \tag{97}$$

$$\forall X\ V\ P\ Y.(Subst(X, V, Know(P, Y)) = Know(Subst(X, V, P), Subst(X, V, Y))), \tag{98}$$

axioms similar to (98) for other functions,

$$\forall X\ V\ Q.(absent(V, Y) \supset Subst(X, V, Y) = Y), \tag{99}$$

$$\forall X\ V1\ V2\ Q.(V1 \neq V2 \wedge absent(V2, X) \supset Subst(X, V1, All(V2, Q)) = All(V2, Subst(X, V1, Q))), \tag{100}$$

and corresponding axioms to (100) for *Exist* and *The*.

Along with these comes the axiom that binding kills variables, that is,

$$\forall V1\ V2\ Q.(All(V1, Q) = All(V2, Subst(V2, V1, Q))). \tag{101}$$

The functions *absent* and *Subst* play a "syntactic" role in describing the rules of reasoning and don't appear in the concepts themselves. It seems likely that this is harmless until we want to form concepts of the laws of reasoning.

We used the Greek letter π for possible worlds, because we did not want to consider a possible world as a thing and introduce concepts of possible worlds. Reasoning about reasoning may require such concepts or else a formulation that doesn't use possible worlds.

Martin Davis (in conversation) pointed out the advantages of an alternative treatment avoiding possible worlds in case there is a single domain of individuals each of which has a standard concept. Then we can write

$$\forall V\ Q.(true\ All(V, Q) \equiv \forall x.true\ Subst(Concept1\ x, V, Q)). \tag{102}$$

POSSIBLE APPLICATIONS TO ARTIFICIAL INTELLIGENCE

The foregoing discussion of concepts has been mainly concerned with how to translate into a suitable formal language certain sentences of ordinary language. The sucess of the formalization is measured by the extent to which the logical consequences of these sentences in the formal system agree with our intuitions of what these consequences should be. Another goal of the formalization is to develop an idea of what concepts really are, but the possible formalizations have not been explored enough to draw even tentative conclusions about that.

For artificial intelligence, the study of concepts has yet a different motivation. Our success in making computer programs with *general intelligence* has been extremely limited, and one source of the limitation is our inability to formalize what the world is like in general. We can try to separate the problem of describing the general aspects of the world from the problem of using such a description and the facts of a situation to discover a strategy for achieving a goal. This is called separating the *epistemological* and the *heuristic* parts of the artificial intelligence problem and is discussed in McCarthy and Hayes (1969).

We see the following potential uses for facts about knowledge:

1. A computer program that wants to telephone someone must reason

about who knows the number. More generally, it must reason about what actions will obtain needed knowledge. Knowledge in books and computer files must be treated in a parallel way to knowledge held by persons.

2. A program must often determine that it does not know something or that someone else doesn't. This has been neglected in the usual formalizations of knowledge, and methods of proving possibility have been neglected in modal logic. Christopher Goad (to be published) has shown how to prove ignorance by proving the existence of possible worlds in which the sentence to be proved unknown is false. Presumably proving one's own ignorance is a stimulus to looking outside for the information. In competitive situations, it may be important to show that a certain course of action will leave competitors ignorant.
3. Prediction of the behaviour of others depends on determining what they believe and what they want.

It seems to me that AI applications will especially benefit from first order formalisms of the kind described above. First, many of the present problem solvers are based on first order logic. Morgan (1976) in discussing theorem proving in modal logic also translates modal logic into first order logic. Second, our formalisms leaves the syntax and semantics of statements not involving concepts entirely unchanged, so that if knowledge or wanting is only a small part of a problem, its presence doesn't affect the formalization of the other parts.

ABSTRACT LANGUAGES

The way we have treated concepts in this paper, especially when we put variables in them, suggests trying to indentify them with terms in some language. It seems to me that this can be done provided that we use a suitable notion of *abstract language.*

Ordinarily a language is identified with a set of strings of symbols taken from some alphabet. McCarthy (1963) introduces the idea of *abstract syntax*, the idea being that it doesn't matter whether sums are represented $a+b$ or $+ab$ or $ab+$ or by the integer 2^a3^b or by the LISP S-expression (PLUS A B), so long as there are predicates for deciding whether an expression is a sum and functions for forming sums from summands and functions for extracting the summands from the sum. In particular, abstract syntax facilitates defining the semantics of programming languages, and proving the properties of interpreters and compilers. From that point of view, one can refrain from specifying any concrete representation of the "expressions" of the language and consider it merely a collection of abstract synthetic and analytic functions and predicates for forming, discriminating and taking apart *abstract expressions.* However, the languages considered at that time always admitted representations as strings of symbols.

If we consider concepts as a free algebra on basic concepts, then we can regard them as strings of symbols on some alphabet if we want to, assuming that we don't object to a non-denumerable alphabet or infinitely long expressions if we want standard concepts for all the real numbers. However, if we want to regard *Equal*(X, Y) and *Equal*(Y, X) as the same concept, and hence as the same "expression" in our language, and we want to regard expressions related by renaming bound variables as denoting the same concept, then the algebra is no longer free, and regarding concepts as strings of symbols becomes awkward even if possible.

It seems better to accept the notion of ***abstract language*** defined by the collection of functions and predicates that form, discriminate, and extract the parts of its "expressions". In that case it would seem that concepts can be identified with expressions in an abstract language.

ACKNOWLEDGEMENTS AND BIBLIOGRAPHY

The treatment given here should be compared with that in Church (1951b) and in Morgan (1976). Church introduces what might be called a two-dimensional type structure. One dimension permits higher order functions and predicates as in the usual higher order logics. The second dimension permits concepts of concepts, etc. No examples of applications are given. It seems to me that concepts of concepts will be eventually required, but this can still be done within first order logic.

Morgan's motivation is to use first order logic theorem-proving programs to treat modal logic. He gives two approaches. The syntactic approach – which he applies only to systems without quantifiers – uses operations like our *And* to form compound propositions from elementary ones. Provability is then axiomatized in the outer logic. His semantic approach uses axiomatizations of the Kripke accessibility relation between possible worlds. It seems to me that our treatment can be used to combine both of Morgan's methods, and has two further advantages. First, concepts and individuals can be separately quantified. Second, functions from things to concepts of them permit relations between concepts of things that could not otherwise be expressed.

Although the formalism leads in almost the opposite direction, the present paper is much in the spirit of Carnap (1956). We appeal to his ontological tolerance in introducing concepts as objects, and his section on intentions for robots expresses just the attitude required for artificial intelligence applications.

We have not yet investigated the matter, but plausible axioms for necessity or knowledge expressed in terms of concepts may lead to the paradoxes discussed in Kaplan and Montague (1960) and Montague (1963). Our intention is that the paradoxes can be avoided by restricting the axioms concerning knowledge, and necessity of statements about necessity. The restrictions will be somewhat unintuitive as are the restrictions necessary to avoid the paradoxes of naive set theory.

Chee K. Yap (1977) proposes *Virtual Semantics* for intensional logics as a generalization of Carnap's individual concepts. Apart from the fact that Yap does not stay within conventional first order logic, we don't know the relation between his work and that described here.

I am indebted to Lewis Creary, Patrick Hayes, Donald Michie, Barbara Partee and Peter Suzman for discussion of a draft of this paper. Creary in particular has shown the inadequacy of the formalism for expressing all readings of the ambiguous sentence "*Pat knows that Mike knows what Joan last asserted*". There has not been time to modify the formalism to fix this inadequacy, but it seems likely that concepts of concepts are required for an adequate treatment.

REFERENCES

Carnap, R. (1956). *Meaning and Necessity*. Chicago: University of Chicago Press.

Church, A. (1951a). The need for abstract entities in semantic analysis, in "Contributions to the Analysis and Synthesis of Knowledge". *Proceedings of the American Academy of Arts and Sciences*, **80**, No. 1, 100–112. Reprinted in *The Structure of Language* (eds. Fodor, A. and Katz, J.) Prentice-Hall, 1964.

Church, A. (1951b). A formulation of the logic of sense and denotation. In *Essays in honour of Henry Sheffer* (ed. Henle, P.), pp. 3–24. New York.

Frege, G. (1892). Uber Sinn und Bedeutung. *Zeitschrift fur Philosophie und Philosphische Kritik* **100**:25–50. Translated by H. Feigl under the title "On Sense and Nominatum" in *Readings in Philosophical Analysis* (eds. Feigal, H. and Sellars, W). New York 1949. Translated by M. Black under the title "On Sense and Reference" in P. Geach and M. Black, *Translations from the Philosophical Writings of Gottlob Frege*. Oxford: 1952.

Kaplan, D. (1969). Quantifying in, from *Words and Objections: Essays on the Work of W. V. O. Quine* (eds. Davidson, D. and Hintikka, J.), pp. 178–214. Dordrecht-Holland: D. Reidel Publishing Co. Reprinted in (Linsky 1971).

Kaplan, D. and Montague, R. (1960). A paradox regained, *Notre Dame Journal of Formal Logic*, **1**, 79–90. Reprinted in (Montague 1974).

Linsky. L. (ed.) (1971). *Reference and Modality*, Oxford Readings in Philosophy. Oxford: Oxford University Press.

McCarthy, J. (1963). Towards a mathematical science of computation, in *Proceedings of IFIP Congress* 1962. Amsterdam: North-Holland Publishing Co.

McCarthy, J. and Hayes, P. J. (1969). Some philosophical problems from the standpoint of artificial intelligence. *Machine Intelligence* **4**, pp. 463–502 (eds. Meltzer, B. Michie, D.). Edinburgh: Edinburgh University Press.

Montague, R. (1963). Syntactical treatments of modality, with corollaries on reflexion principles and finite axiomatizability, *Acta Philosophica Fennica* **16**:153–167. Reprinted in (Montague 1974).

Montague, R. (1974). *Formal Philosophy*. New Haven: Yale University Press.

Morgan, C. G. (1976). Methods for automated theorem proving in nonclassical logics, *IEEE Transactions on Computers*, **C-25**, No. 8.

Quine, W. V. O. (1956). Quantifiers and propositional attitudes, *Journal of Philosophy*, **53**. Reprinted in (Linsky 1971).

Quine, W. V. O. (1963). *From a Logical Point of View*. New York: Harper and Row. First published Harvard University Press (1953).

Yap, Chee K. (1977). A Semantical Analysis of Intensional Logics, Research Report *RC* 6893 (#29538). Yorktown Heights, New York: IBM, Thomas J. Watson Research Center.

7

A Theory of Approximate Reasoning

L. A. Zadeh
Computer Science Division
University of California at Berkeley, USA

Summary

The theory of approximate reasoning outlined in this paper is concerned with the deduction of possibly imprecise conclusions from a set of imprecise premises.

The theory is based on a fuzzy logic, FL, in which the truth-values are linguistic, that is of the form *true*, *not true*, *very true*, *more or less true*, *false*, *not very false*, etc., and the rules of inference are approximate rather than exact. Furthermore, the premises are assumed to have the form of fuzzy propositions, for example, "(X is much smaller than Y) is quite true," "If X is small is possible then Y is very large is very likely," etc. By using the concept of a possibility – rather than probability – distribution, such propositions are translated into expressions in PRUF (Possibilistic Relational Universal Fuzzy), which is a meaning representation language for natural languages.

An expression in PRUF is a procedure for computing the possibility distribution which is induced by a proposition in a natural language. By applying the rules of inference in PRUF to such distributions, other distributions are obtained which upon retranslation and linguistic approximation yield the conclusions deduced from the fuzzy premises.

The principal rules of inference in fuzzy logic are the projection principle, the particularization/conjunction principle, and the entailment principle. The application of these rules to approximate reasoning is described and illustrated by examples.

1. INTRODUCTION

Informally, by *approximate* or, equivalently, **fuzzy reasoning** we mean the process or processes by which a possibly imprecise conclusion is deduced from a collection of imprecise premises. Such reasoning is, for the most part, qualitative rather than quantitative in nature, and almost all of it falls outside of the domain of applicability of classical logic. A thorough exposition of the foundations of fuzzy reasoning may be found in Gaines (1976a,b,c).

Approximate reasoning underlies the remarkable human ability to understand natural language, decipher sloppy handwriting, play games requiring mental and/or physical skill and, more generally, make rational decisions in complex and/or uncertain environments. In fact, it is the ability to reason in qualitative, imprecise terms that distinguishes human intelligence from machine intelligence. And yet, approximate reasoning has received little if any attention within psychology, philosophy, logic, artificial intelligence and other branches of cognitive sciences, largely because it is not consonant with the deeply entrenched tradition of precise reasoning in science and contravenes the widely held belief that precise, quantitative reasoning has the ability to solve the extremely complex and ill-defined problems which pervade the analysis of humanistic systems.

In earlier papers (Zadeh 1973, 1975a,b,c, 1976, 1977a,b), we have outlined a conceptual framework for approximate reasoning based on the notions of linguistic variable and fuzzy logic. In the present paper, a novel direction involving the concept of a possibility distribution will be described (see also Zadeh 1977). As will be seen in the sequel, the concept of a possibility distribution provides a natural basis for the representation of the meaning of propositions expressed in a natural language, and thereby serves as a convenient point of departure for the translation of imprecise premises into expressions in a language PRUF to which the rules of inference associated with this language can be applied.

Our exposition of approximate reasoning begins with a brief discussion of the concept of a possibility distribution and its role in the translation of fuzzy propositions expressed in a natural language. In Sec. 3, the concept of a linguistic variable is introduced as a device for an approximate characterization of the values of variables and their interrelations. In Secs. 4 and 5, we shall discuss some of the basic aspects of fuzzy logic – the logic that serves as a foundation for approximate reasoning – and introduce the concepts of semantic equivalence and semantic entailment. Finally, in Sec. 6, we formulate the basic rules of inference in fuzzy logic and illustrate their application to approximate reasoning by a number of simple examples.

2. THE CONCEPT OF A POSSIBILITY DISTRIBUTION

A basic assumption which underlies our approach to approximate reasoning is that the imprecision which is instrinsic in natural languages is, in the main, possibilistic rather than probabilistic in nature. The term **possibilistic** was coined by B. R. Gaines and L. J. Kohout in their paper on possible automata (1975).

To illustrate the point, consider the proposition $p \triangleq X$ is an integer in the interval [0,8]. The symbol $\triangleq$ stands for "is defined to be", or "denotes". Clearly, such a proposition does not associate a unique integer with X; rather, it indicates that any integer in the interval [0,8] could possibly be a value of X, and that any integer not in the interval could not be a value of X.

This obvious observation suggests the following interpretation of p. The proposition "X is an integer in the interval [0,8]" induces a possibility distribution Π_X which associates with each integer n the possibility that n could be a value of X. Thus, for the proposition in question

$$Poss\{X = n\} = 1 \quad \text{for} \quad 0 \leqslant n \leqslant 8$$

and

$$Poss\{X = n\} = 0 \quad \text{for} \quad n < 0 \quad \text{or} \quad n > 8$$

where $Poss\{X = n\}$ is an abbreviation for "The possibility that X may assume the value n". Note that the possibility distribution induced by p is *uniform* in the sense that the possibility values are equal to unity for n in [0,8] and zero elsewhere.

Next, consider the fuzzy proposition $q \triangleq X$ is a small integer, in which *small integer* is a fuzzy set defined by, say,

$$\textit{small integer} = 1/0 + 1/1 + 0.8/2 + 0.6/3 + 0.4/4 + 0.2/5 \tag{2.1}$$

in which + denotes the union rather than the arithmetic sum, and a singleton of the form 0.8/2 signifies that the grade of membership of the integer 2 in the fuzzy set *small integer* is 0.8 (see A. Kaufmann (1975), C. V. Negoita and D. Ralescu (1975), and L. A. Zadeh, K. S. Fu, K. Tanaka and M. Shimura (1975)).

As an extension of our interpretation of the nonfuzzy proposition p, we shall interpret q as follows. The proposition $q \triangleq X$ is a small integer induces a possibility distribution Π_X which equates the possibility of X taking a value n to the grade of membership of n in the fuzzy set *small integer*. Thus

$$Poss\{X = 0\} = 1$$
$$Poss\{X = 2\} = 0.8$$
$$Poss\{X = 5\} = 0.2$$

and

$$Poss\{X = 6\} = 0\,.$$

More generally, we shall say that a fuzzy proposition of the form $p \triangleq X$ is F, where X is a variable taking values in a universe of discourse U, and F is a fuzzy subset of U, *induces a* **possibility distribution** Π_X *which is equal to* F, that is,

$$\Pi_X = F\,. \tag{2.2}$$

Thus, in essence, the possibility distribution of X is a fuzzy set which serves to define the possibility that X could assume any specified value in U. Stated more concretely, if $u \in U$ and $\mu_F\colon U \to [0,1]$ is the membership function of F, then the possibility that $X = u$ given "X is F" is

$$Poss\{X = u \,|\, X \text{ is } F\} = \mu_F(u)\,, \quad u \in U\,. \tag{2.3}$$

Since the concept of a possibility distribution coincides with that of a fuzzy set, possibility distributions may be manipulated by the rules governing the manipulation of fuzzy sets and, more particularly, fuzzy restrictions. A **fuzzy restriction** is a fuzzy set which serves as an elastic constraint on the values that may be assigned to a variable. A variable which is associated with a fuzzy restriction or, equivalently, with a possibility distribution, is a **fuzzy variable**. In what follows, we shall focus our attention only on those aspects of possibility distributions which are of relevance to approximate reasoning.

Possibility versus probability

What is the difference between possibility and probability? Intuitively, possibility relates to our perception of the degree of feasibility or ease of attainment, whereas probability is associated with the degree of belief, likelihood, frequency, or proportion. Thus, what is possible may not be probable, and what is improbable need not be impossible. A more concrete statement of this relation is embodied in the *possibility/probability consistency principle* (Zadeh, 1977a). More importantly, however, the distinction between possibility and probability manifests itself in the different rules which govern their combinations, especially under the union. More specifically, if A is a nonfuzzy subset of U, and Π_X is the possibility distribution induced by the proposition "X is F", then the **possibility measure**, $\Pi(A)$, of A is defined as

$$\Pi(A) \triangleq Poss\{X \in A\} \triangleq Sup_{u \in A}\ \mu_F(u)\,. \tag{2.4}$$

The possibility measure defined by (2.4) is a special case of the more general concept of a fuzzy measure defined by Sugeno (1974) and Terano and Sugeno (1975). More generally, if A is a fuzzy subset of U, then

$$\Pi(A) \triangleq Poss\{X \text{ is } A\} \triangleq Sup_u\,[\mu_F(u) \wedge \mu_A(u)] \tag{2.5}$$

where μ_A is the membership function of A and $\wedge \triangleq min$.

From the definition of possibility measure, it follows at once that, for arbitrary subsets A and B of U, the possibility measure of the union of A and B is given by

$$\Pi(A \cup B) = \Pi(A) \vee \Pi(B) \tag{2.6}$$

where $\vee \triangleq max$. Thus, the possibility measure does not have the basic additivity property of probability measure, namely,

$$P(A \cup B) = P(A) + P(B) \quad \text{if } A \text{ and } B \text{ are disjoint} \tag{2.7}$$

where $P(A)$ and $P(B)$ denote the probability measures of A and B, respectively.

Unlike probability, the concept of possibility in no way involves the notion of repeated experimentation. Thus, the concept of possibility is nonstatistical in character and, as such, is a natural concept to use when the imprecision or uncertainty in the phenomena under study are not susceptible of statistical analysis or characterization.

Possibility assignment equations

The reason why the concept of a possibility distribution plays such an important role in approximate reasoning relates to our assumption that a proposition in a natural language may be interpreted as an assignment of a fuzzy set to a possibility distribution. More specifically, if p is a proposition in a natural language, we shall say that p *translates* into a *possibility assignment equation*:

$$p \to \Pi_{(X_1, \ldots X_n)} = F \tag{2.8}$$

where $X_1, \ldots X_n$ are variables which are explicit or implicit in p; $\Pi_{(X_1, \ldots X_n)}$ is the possibility distribution of the n-ary variable $X \triangleq (X_1, \ldots X_n)$; and F is a fuzzy relation, that is, a fuzzy subset of the cartesian product $U_1 \times \ldots \times U_n$, where U_i, $i = 1, \ldots n$, is the universe of discourse associated with X_i. In this context, the possibility assignment equation

$$\Pi_{(X_1, \ldots X_n)} = F \tag{2.9}$$

will be referred to as the **translation** of p and, conversely, p will be said to be a **retranslation** of (2.9), in which case its relation to (2.9) will be represented as

$$p \leftarrow \Pi_{(X_1, \ldots X_n)} = F\,. \tag{2.10}$$

In general, a proposition of the form $p \triangleq X$ is F, where X is the name of an object or a proposition, translates not into

$$p \to \Pi_X = F \tag{2.11}$$

but into

$$p \to \Pi_{A(X)} = F \tag{2.12}$$

where $A(X)$ is an implied attribute of X. For example,

$$\text{Joe is young} \to \Pi_{Age(Joe)} = young \tag{2.13}$$

$$\text{Maria is blond} \to \Pi_{Colour(Hair(Maria))} = blond \tag{2.14}$$

$$\text{Max is about as tall as Jim} \to \Pi_{(Height(Max), Height(Jim))} = approximately\text{-}equal \tag{2.15}$$

where *young*, *blond*, and *approximately equal* are specified fuzzy relations (unary and binary) in their respective universes of discourse. More concretely, if u is a numerical value of the age of Joe, then (2.13) implies that

$$Poss\{Age(Joe) = u\} = \mu_{young}(u)\,. \tag{2.16}$$

Similarly, if u is an identifying label for the colour of hair, then (2.14) implies that

$$Poss\{Colour(Hair(Maria)) = u\} = \mu_{blond}(u)\,, \tag{2.17}$$

while (2.15) signifies that

$$Poss\{Height(Max) = u, Height(Jim) = v\} = \mu_{approximately\ equal}(u, v) \tag{2.18}$$

where u and v are the generic values of the variables *Height*(*Max*) and *Height*(*Jim*), respectively.

Projection and particularization

Among the operations that may be performed on a possibility distribution, there are two that are of particular relevance to approximate reasoning: projection and particularization.

Let $\Pi_{(X_1,\ldots X_n)}$ denote an n-ary possibility distribution which is a fuzzy realtion in $U_1 \times \ldots \times U_n$, with the possibility distribution function of $\Pi_{(X_1,\ldots X_n)}$ (that is, the membership function of $\Pi_{(X_1,\ldots X_n)}$) denoted by $\pi_{(X_1,\ldots X_n)}$ or, more simply, as π_X.

Let $s \triangleq (i_1,\ldots i_k)$ be a subsequence of the index sequence $(1,\ldots n)$ and let s' denote the complementary subsequence $s' \triangleq (j_1,\ldots j_m)$ (for example, for $n = 5$, $s = (1,3,4)$ and $s' = (2,5)$). In terms of such sequences, a k-tuple of the form $(A_{i_1},\ldots A_{i_k})$ may be expressed in an abbreviated form as $A_{(s)}$. In particular, the variable $X_{(s)} = (X_{i_1},\ldots X_{i_k})$ will be referred to as a k-ary **subvariable** of $X \triangleq (X_1,\ldots X_n)$, with $X_{(s')} = (X_{j_1},\ldots X_{j_m})$ being a subvariable complementary to $X_{(s)}$.

The **projection** of $\Pi_{(X_1,\ldots X_n)}$ *on* $U_{(s)} \triangleq U_{i_1} \times \ldots \times U_{i_k}$ is a k-ary possibility distribution denoted by

$$\Pi_{X_{(s)}} \triangleq Proj_{U_{(s)}}\, \Pi_{(X_1,\ldots X_n)} \tag{2.19}$$

and defined by

$$\pi_{X_{(s)}}(u_{(s)}) \triangleq Sup_{u_{(s')}}\, \pi_X(u_1,\ldots u_n) \tag{2.20}$$

where $\pi_{X_{(s)}}$ is the possibility distribution function of $\Pi_{X_{(s)}}$. For example, for $n = 2$,

$$\pi_{X_1}(u_1) \triangleq Sup_{u_2}\, \pi_{(X_1,X_2)}(u_1,u_2)$$

is the expression for the possibility distribution function of the projection of $\Pi_{(X_1,X_2)}$ on U_1. By analogy with the concept of a marginal probability distribution, $\Pi_{X_{(s)}}$ will be referred to as a **marginal possibility distribution**. Note that our use of $\Pi_{X_{(s)}}$ in (2.19) to denote the projection of Π_X on $U_{(s)}$ anticipates (2.21).

The importance of the concept of a marginal possibility distribution derives from the fact that $\Pi_{X_{(s)}}$ may be regarded as the possibility distribution of the subvariable $X_{(s)}$. Thus, stated as the **projection principle** (in Sec. 6), the relation between $X_{(s)}$ and $\Pi_{X_{(s)}}$ may be expressed as follows.

From the possibility distribution, $\Pi_{(X_1,\ldots X_n)}$, of the variable $X \triangleq (X_1,\ldots X_n)$, the possibility distribution $\Pi_{X_{(s)}}$ of the subvariable $X_{(s)} \triangleq (X_{i_1},\ldots X_{i_k})$ may be inferred by projecting $\Pi_{(X_1,\ldots X_n)}$ on $U_{(s)}$, that is,

$$\Pi_{X_{(s)}} = Proj_{U_{(s)}}\, \Pi_{(X_1,\ldots X_n)}\,. \tag{2.21}$$

As a simple illustration, assume that $n = 3$, $U_1 = U_2 = U_3 = a+b$ or, more conventionally, $\{a,b\}$ and $\Pi_{(X_1,X_2,X_3)}$ is expressed as a linear form

$$\Pi_{(X_1,X_2,X_3)} = 0.8aaa + 1aab + 0.6baa + 0.2bab + 0.5bbb \tag{2.22}$$

in which a term of the form 0.6*baa* signifies that

$$Poss\{X_1 = b, X_2 = a, X_3 = a\} = 0.6 \; . \tag{2.23}$$

To derive $\Pi_{(X_1,X_2)}$ from (2.22) it is sufficient to replace the value of X_3 in each term in (2.22) by the null string Λ. This yields

$$\begin{aligned}\Pi_{(X_1,X_2)} &= 0.8aa + 1aa + 0.6ba + 0.2ba + 0.5bb \\ &= 1aa + 0.6ba + 0.5bb\end{aligned} \tag{2.24}$$

and similarly

$$\begin{aligned}\Pi_{X_1} &= 1a + 0.6b + 0.5b \\ &= 1a + 0.6b \; .\end{aligned} \tag{2.25}$$

Turning to the operation of particularization, let $\Pi_{(X_1,\ldots X_n)} = F$ denote the possibility distribution of $X = (X_1,\ldots X_n)$, and let $\Pi_{X_{(s)}} = G$ denote a specified possibility distribution (not necessarily the marginal distribution) of the subvariable $X_{(s)} = (X_{i_1}, \ldots X_{i_k})$.

Informally, by the **particularization** of $\Pi_{(X_1,\ldots X_n)}$ is meant the modification of $\Pi_{(X_1,\ldots X_n)}$ resulting from the stipulation that the possibility distribution of $\Pi_{X_{(s)}}$ is G. More specifically,

$$\Pi_{(X_1,\ldots X_n)}\,[\Pi_{X_{(s)}} = G] \triangleq F \cap \bar{G} \tag{2.26}$$

where the left-hand member places in evidence the X_i (that is, the attributes) which are particularized in $\Pi_{(X_1,\ldots X_n)}$, while the right-hand member defines the effect of particularization, with $\bar{G}$ denoting the cylindrical extension of G, that is, the cylindrical fuzzy set in $U_1 \times \ldots \times U_n$ whose projection on $U_{(s)}$ is G. Thus,

$$\begin{aligned}&\mu_{\bar{G}}(u_1,\ldots u_n) \triangleq \mu_G(u_{i_1},\ldots u_{i_k}) \,, \\ &\quad (u_1,\ldots u_n) \in U_1 \times \ldots \times U_n \,.\end{aligned} \tag{2.27}$$

As a simple illustration, consider the possibility distribution defined by (2.22) and assume that

$$\Pi_{(X_1,X_2)} = 0.4aa + 0.9ba + 0.1bb \; . \tag{2.28}$$

In this case,

$$\begin{aligned}\bar{G} &= 0.4aaa + 0.4aab + 0.9baa + 0.9bab + 0.1bba + 0.1bbb \\ F \cap \bar{G} &= 0.4aaa + 0.4aab + 0.6baa + 0.2bab + 0.1bbb\end{aligned}$$

and hence

$$\begin{aligned}&\Pi_{(X_1,X_2,X_3)}\,[\Pi_{(X_1,X_2)} = G] = \\ &\quad 0.4aaa + 0.4aab + 0.6baa + 0.2bab + 0.1bbb\end{aligned} \tag{2.29}$$

In general, some of the variables in a particularized possibility distribution (or a fuzzy relation) are assigned fixed values in their respective universes of discourse, while others are associated with possibility distributions. For example, in the case of a fuzzy relation which characterizes the fuzzy set of men who are tall, blond, and named Smith, the particularlized relation has the form

$$MAN[Name = Smith; \Pi_{Height} = TALL; \Pi_{Colour(Hair)} = BLOND] \tag{2.30}$$

(Note that the label of a relation is capitalized when it is desired to stress that it denotes a relation.) Similarly, the fuzzy set of men who have the above characteristics and, in addition, are approximately 30 years old, would be represented as

$$MAN[Name = Smith; \Pi_{Height} = TALL; \Pi_{Colour(Hair)} = BLOND; \Pi_{Age} = APPROXIMATELY\ EQUAL\ [Age = 30]] \ . \tag{2.31}$$

In this case, the possibility distribution which is associated with the variable *Age* is in itself a particularized possibility distribution.

It should be noted that the representations exemplified by (2.30) and (2.31) are somewhat similar in appearance to those that are commonly employed in semantic network and higher order predicate calculi representations of propositions in a natural language. Expositions of such representations may be found in Newell and Simon (1972), Miller and Johnson-Laird (1976), Bobrow and Collins (1975), Minsky (1975), and other books and papers listed in the bibliography. An essential difference, however, lies in the use of possibility distributions in (2.30) and (2.31) for the characterization of values of fuzzy variables, and in the concrete specification of the manner in which a possibility distribution is modified by particularization.

Meaning and information

Particularization as defined by (2.26) plays a particularly important role in PRUF – a language intended for the representation of the meaning of fuzzy propositions. A brief description of PRUF appears in Zadeh (1977b). A more detailed exposition of PRUF will be provided in a forthcoming paper.

Briefly, an expression, P, in PRUF is, in general, a procedure for computing a possibility distribution. More specifically, let U be a universe of discourse and let $\mathcal{R}$ be a set of relations in U. Then, the pair

$$D \triangleq (U, \mathcal{R}) \tag{2.32}$$

constitutes a **database**, with P defined on a subset of relations in $\mathcal{R}$. As defined here, the concept of a database is related to that of a possible world in modal logic (Hughes and Cresswell, 1968; Miller and Johnson-Laird, 1976).

If p is an expression in a natural language and P is its translation in PRUF, that is,

$$p \to P \, ,$$

then the procedure P may be viewed as defining the **meaning**, $M(p)$, of p, with the possibility distribution computed by P constituting the **information**, $I(p)$.

conveyed by p. (The procedure defined by an expression in PRUF and the possibility distribution which it yields are analogous to the intension and extension of a predicate in two-valued logic. (Cresswell, 1975.) When *meaning* is used loosely, no differentiation between $M(p)$ and $I(p)$ is made.)

As a simple illustration, consider the proposition

$$p \triangleq \text{John resides near Berkeley} \tag{2.33}$$

which in PRUF translates into

$$\begin{aligned} &RESIDENCE[Subject = John;\\ &\quad \Pi_{Location} = Proj_{\mu \times City1}\, NEAR[City2 = Berkeley]] \end{aligned} \tag{2.34}$$

where *NEAR* is a fuzzy relation with the frame $NEAR\|City1|City2|\mu|$ and the expression $Proj_{\mu \times City1}\ NEAR[City2 = Berkeley]$ represents the fuzzy set of cities which are near Berkeley. The frame of a fuzzy relation exhibits its name together with the names of its variables (that is, attributes) and μ – the grade of membership of each tuple in the relation.

The expression in PRUF represented by (2.34)) is, in effect, a procedure for computing the possibility distribution of the location of residence of John. Thus, given a relation *NEAR*, it will return a possibility distribution of the form ($\pi \triangleq$ possibility-value)

RESIDENCE	Subject	Location	π
	John	Oakland	1
	John	Palo Alto	0.6
	John	San Jose	0.2
	John	Orinda	0.8
	...	...	...

which may be regarded as the information conveyed by the proposition "John resides near Berkeley".

PRUF plays an essential role in approximate reasoning because it serves as a basis for translating the fuzzy premises expressed in a natural language into possibility assignment equations to which the rules of inference in approximate reasoning can be applied in a systematic fashion. In Sec. 4, we shall discuss in greater detail some of the basic translation rules in fuzzy logic which constitute a small subset of the translation rules in PRUF. This brief exposition of PRUF will suffice for our purposes in the present paper.

We turn next to the concept of a linguistic variable – a concept that plays a basic role in approximate reasoning, fuzzy logic, and the linguistic approach to systems analysis.

3. THE CONCEPT OF A LINGUISTIC VARIABLE

In describing the behaviour of humanistic – that is, human-centered – systems, we generally use words rather than numbers to characterize the values of variables as well as the relations between them. For example, the age of a person may be described as *very young*, intelligence as *quite high*, the relation with another person as *not very friendly*, and appearance as *quite attractive*.

Clearly, the use of words in place of numbers implies a lower degree of precision in the characterization of the values of a variable. In some instances, we elect to be imprecise because there is no need for a higher degree of precision. In most cases, however, the imprecision is forced upon by the fact that there are no units of measurement for the attributes of an object and no quantitative criteria for representing the values of such attributes as points on an anchored scale.

Viewed in this perspective, the concept of a linguistic variable may be regarded as a device for systematizing the use of words or sentences in a natural or synthetic language for the purpose of characterizing the values of variables and describing their interrelations. In this role, the concept of a linguistic variable serves a basic function in approximate reasoning both in the representation of values of variables and in the characterization of truth-values, probability-values, and possibility-values of fuzzy propositions.

In this section, we shall focus our attention only on those aspects of the concept of a linguistic variable which have a direct bearing on approximate reasoning. More detailed discussions of the concept of a linguistic variable and its applications may be found in Zadeh (1973, 1975c), Wenstop (1975, 1976), Mamdani and Assilian (1975), Procyk (1976), and other papers listed in the bibliography.

As a starting point for our discussion, it is convenient to consider a variable such as *Age*, which may be viewed both as a numerical variable ranging over, say, the interval [0,150], and as a linguistic variable which can take the values *young, not young, very young, not very young, quite young, old, not very young and not very old*, etc. Each of these values may be interpreted as a label of a fuzzy subset of the universe of discourse $U = [0,150]$, whose base variable, u, is the generic numerical value of *Age*.

Typically, the values of a linguistic variable such as *Age* are built up of one or more **primary terms** (the labels of *primary fuzzy sets* which play a role somewhat analogous to that of physical units in mechanistic systems), together with a collection of modifiers and connectives which allow a composite linguistic value to be generated from the primary terms. Usually, the number of such terms is two, with one being an antonym of the other. For example, in the case of *Age*, the primary terms are *young* and *old*.

A basic assumption underlying the concept of a linguistic variable is that the meaning of the primary terms is context-dependent, whereas the meaning of the modifiers and connectives is not. Furthermore, once the meaning of the primary terms is specified (or "calibrated") in a given context, the meaning of composite terms such as *not very young, not very young and not very old*, etc., may be computed by the application of a semantic rule.

Typically, the **term-set**, that is, the set of linguistic values of a linguistic variable, comprises the values generated from each of the primary terms together with the values generated from various combinations of the primary terms. For example, in the case of *Age*, a partial list of the linguistic values of *Age* is the following:

young	old	not young nor old
not young	not old	not very young and not very old
very young	very old	young or old
not very young	not very old	not young or not old
quite young	quite old	etc.
more or less young	more or less old	
extremely young	extremely old	
etc.	etc.	

What is important to observe is that most linguistic variables have the same basic structure as *Age*. For example, on replacing *young* with *tall* and *old* with *short*, we obtain the list of linguistic values of the linguistic variable *Height*. The same applies to the linguistic variables *Weight* (*heavy* and *light*), *Appearance* (*beautiful* and *ugly*), *Speed* (*fast* and *slow*), *Truth* (*true* and *false*), etc., with the words in parentheses representing the primary terms.

As is shown in Zadeh (1973, 1975c), a linguistic variable may be characterized by an attributed grammar (see Knuth 1968; Lewis *et al* 1974) which generates the term-set of the variable and provides a simple procedure for computing the meaning of a composite linguistic value in terms of the primary fuzzy sets which appear in its constituents.

As an illustration, consider the attributed grammar shown in which S, B, C, D, and E are nonterminals; not, and, a and b are terminals; a and b are the primary terms (and also the primary fuzzy sets); subscripted symbols are the fuzzy sets which are labelled by the corresponding nonterminals, with $L \triangleq$ left (that is, pertaining to the antecedent), $R \triangleq$ right (that is, pertaining to the consequent); and a production of the form

$$S \to S \text{ and } B \quad : \quad S_L = S_R \cap B_R \tag{3.1}$$

signifies that the fuzzy set which is the meaning of the antecedent, S, is the intersection of S_R, the fuzzy set which is the meaning of the consequent S, and B_R, the fuzzy set which is the meaning of the consequent B.

$$\begin{array}{lll} S \to B & : & S_L = B_R \\ S \to S \text{ and } B & : & S_L = S_R \cap B_R \\ B \to C & : & B_L = C_R \\ B \to \text{not } C & : & B_L = C_R' \ (\triangleq \text{complement of } C_R) \end{array} \tag{3.2}$$

$$
\begin{array}{lll}
C \to S & : & C_L = S_R \\
C \to D & : & C_L = D_R \\
C \to E & : & C_L = E_R \\
D \to \text{very } D & : & D_L = D_R^2 \ (\triangleq \text{square of } D_R) \\
E \to \text{very } E & : & D_L = E_R^2 \ (\triangleq \text{square of } E_R) \\
D \to a & : & D_L = a \\
E \to b & : & E_L = b\ .
\end{array}
$$

The grammar in question generates the linguistic values exemplified by the list:

a	*b*	*a* and *b*
not *a*	not *b*	not *a* and *b*
very *a*	very *b*	not *a* and not *b*
not very *a*	not very *b*	not very *a* and not very *b*
not very very *a*	not very very *b*	etc.
etc.	etc.	

In general, to compute the meaning of a linguistic value, ℓ, generated by the grammar, the meaning of each node of the syntax tree of ℓ is computed – by the use of equations (3.2) – in terms of the meanings of its immediate descendants. In most cases, however, this can be done by inspection – which involves a straightforward application of the translation rules which will be formulated in Sec. 4. Thus, we readily obtain, for example:

$$
\begin{array}{l}
\text{not very } a \to (a^2)' \\
\text{not very } a \text{ and not very } b \to (a^2)' \cap (b^2)'
\end{array} \tag{3.3}
$$

where a' is the complement of a and a^2 is defined by

$$\mu_{a^2}(u) = (\mu_a(u))^2, \quad u \in U\ . \tag{3.4}$$

To characterize the primary fuzzy sets a and b, it is frequently convenient to employ standardized membership functions with adjustable parameters. One such function is the S-function, $S(u;\alpha,\beta,\gamma)$, defined by

$$
\begin{aligned}
S(u;\alpha,\beta,\gamma) &= 0 && \text{for } u \leqslant \alpha \\
&= 2\left(\frac{u-\alpha}{\gamma-\alpha}\right)^2 && \text{for } \alpha \leqslant u \leqslant \beta \\
&= 1-2\left(\frac{u-\gamma}{\gamma-\alpha}\right)^2 && \text{for } \beta \leqslant u \leqslant \gamma \\
&= 1 && \text{for } u \geqslant \gamma
\end{aligned} \tag{3.5}
$$

where the parameter $\beta \triangleq \frac{\alpha+\gamma}{2}$ is the crossover point, that is, the value of u at which $S(u;\alpha,\beta,\gamma) = 0.5$. For example, if $a \triangleq$ young and $b \triangleq$ old, we may have (see Fig. 1)

$$\mu_{young} = 1 - S(20,30,40) \tag{3.6}$$

and

$$\mu_{old} = S(40,55,70) \tag{3.7}$$

in which the argument u is suppressed for simplicity. Thus, in terms of (3.6), the translation of the proposition $p \triangleq$ Joe is young (see (2.13)), may be expressed more concretely as

$$\text{Joe is young} \rightarrow \pi_{Age(Joe)} = 1 - S(20,30,40) \tag{3.8}$$

where $\pi_{Age(Joe)}$ is the possibility distribution function of the linguistic variable $Age(Joe)$. Similarly,

$$\text{Joe is not very young} \rightarrow \pi_{Age(Joe)} = 1 - [1 - S(20,30,40)]^2 . \tag{3.9}$$

An important aspect of the concept of a linguistic variable relates to the fact that, in general, the term-set of such a variable is not closed under the various operations that may be performed on fuzzy sets, for example, union, intersection, product, etc. For example, if ℓ is a linguistic value of a variable X, then, in general, ℓ^2 is not in the term-set of X.

The problem of finding a linguistic value of X whose meaning approximates to a given fuzzy subset of U is called the problem of **linguistic approximation** (Zadeh, 1975c, Wenstop, 1975; Procyk, 1976). We shall not discuss in the present paper the ways in which this nontrivial problem can be approached, but will assume that linguistic approximation is implicit in the retranslation of a possibility distribution (see (2.10)) into a proposition expressed in a natural language.

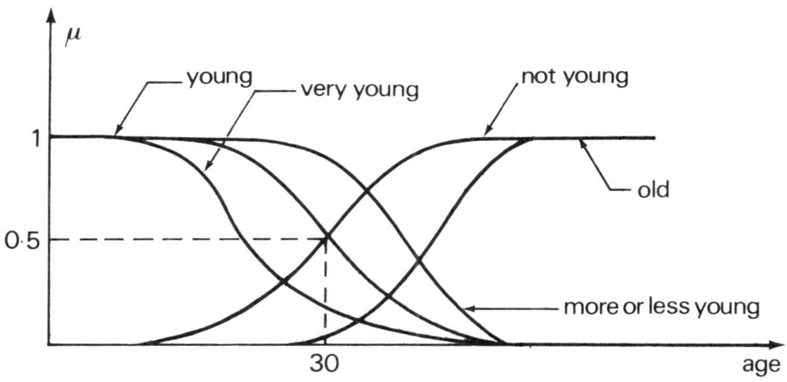

Fig. 1 – Graphical representation of linguistic values of Age.

4. FUZZY LOGIC (FL)

In a broad sense, fuzzy logic is the logic of approximate reasoning; that is, it bears the same relation to approximate reasoning that two-valued logic does to precise reasoning.

In this section, we shall focus our attention on a particular fuzzy logic, FL, whose truth-values are linguistic, that is, are expressible as the values of a linguistic variable *Truth* whose base variable takes values in the unit interval. In this sense, the base logic for FL is Lukasiewicz's L_{Aleph_1} logic whose truth-value set is the interval [0,1].

The principal constituents of FL are the following: (i) Translation rules, (ii) Valuation rules, and (iii) Inference rules.

By **translation rules** is meant a set of rules which yield the translation of a modified or composite proposition from the translations of its constituents. For example, if p and q are fuzzy propositions which translate into (see (2.8))

$$p \rightarrow \Pi_{(X_1, \ldots X_n)} = F \tag{4.1}$$

and

$$q \rightarrow \Pi_{(Y_1, \ldots Y_m)} = G \tag{4.2}$$

respectively, then the rule of conjunctive composition – which will be stated at a later point in this section – yields the translation of the composite proposition "p and q".

By **valuation rules** is meant the set of rules which yield the truth-value (or the probability-value or the possibility-value) of the modified or composite proposition from the specification of the truth-values (or probability-values or possibility-values) of its constituents. A typical example of the valuation rule is the conjunctive valuation rule which expresses the truth-value of the composite proposition "p and q" as a function of the truth-values of p and q – for example, *not very true* and *quite true*, respectively.

The principal rules of inference in FL are: (a) The projection principle, (b) The particularization/conjunction principle; and (c) The entailment principle. In combination, these rules lead to the **compositional rule of inference** which may be viewed as a generalization of the *modus ponens*.

In what follows, we shall discuss briefly only those aspects of fuzzy logic which are of direct relevance to approximate reasoning. A more detailed discussion of FL may be found in Zadeh (1975a) and Bellman and Zadeh (1976).

Translation rules

The translation rules in FL may be divided into several basic categories. Among these are:

Type I. Rules pertaining to modification.
Type II. Rules pertaining to composition.
Type III. Rules pertaining to quantification.
Type IV. Rules pertaining to qualification.

Simple examples of propositions to which the rules in question apply are the following:

Type I. X is very small.
Therese is highly intelligent.
Type II. X is small and Y is large.
If X is small then Y is large.

Type III. Most Swedes are tall.
Many men are taller than most men.
Type IV. John is tall is very true.
John is tall is not very likely.
John is tall is quite possible.

In combination, the rules in question may be applied to the translation of more complex propositions exemplified by:

If ((X is small and Y is large) is very likely) then (Z is very large is not very likely).
((Many men are taller than most men) is very true) is quite possible.

Rules of Type I

A basic rule of Type I is the **modifier rule**, which may be stated as follows.

Let X be a variable taking values in $U = \{u\}$, let F be a fuzzy subset of U, and let p be a proposition of the form "X is F". If the translation of p is expressed by

$$X \text{ is } F \to \Pi_X = F \tag{4.3}$$

then the translation of the modified proposition "X is mF", where m is a modifier such as *not, very, more or less*, etc., is given by

$$X \text{ is } mF \to \Pi_X = F^+ \tag{4.4}$$

where F^+ is a modification of F induced by m. (More detailed discussions of various types of modifiers may be found in Zadeh (1972a, 1975c), Lakoff (1973a,b), Wenstop (1975), McVicar-Whelan (1975), Hersh and Caramazza (1976), and other papers listed in the bibliography.) More specifically,

$$\text{If } m = \text{not}, \quad \text{then } F^+ = F' \triangleq \text{complement of } F \tag{4.5}$$

$$\text{If } m = \text{very}, \text{ then } F^+ = F^2 \tag{4.6}$$

where

$$F^2 = \int_U \mu_F^2(u)/u \tag{4.7}$$

The "integral" representation of a fuzzy set in the form $F = \int_U \mu_F(u)/u$ signifies that F is a union of the fuzzy singletons $\mu_F(u)/u$, $u \in U$, where μ_F is the membership function of F. Thus, (4.7) means that the membership function of F^2 is the square of that of F.

$$\text{If } m = \text{more or less}, \quad \text{then } F^+ = \sqrt{F} \tag{4.8}$$

where

$$\sqrt{F} = \int_U \sqrt{\mu_F(u)}/u \tag{4.9}$$

or,

$$F^{+} = \int_{U} \mu_F(u)K(u) \qquad (4.10)$$

where $K(u)$ is the **kernel** of more or less (Zadeh, 1972).

As a simple illustration, consider the proposition "X is small", where *small* is defined by

$$small = 1/0+1/1+0.8/2+0.6/3+0.4/4+0.2/5\ . \qquad (4.11)$$

Then

$$X \text{ is very small} \rightarrow \Pi_X = F^{+} \qquad (4.12)$$

where

$$F^{+} = F^2 = 1/0+1/1+0.64/2+0.36/3+0.16/4+0.04/5\ . \qquad (4.13)$$

It is important to note that (4.6) and (4.8) should be regarded merely as standardized default definitions which may be replaced by other definitions whenever they do not fit the desired sense of the modifier m. Another point that should be noted is that X in (4.3) need not be a unary variable. Thus, (4.3) subsumes propositions of the form "X and Y are F", as in "X and Y are close", where *CLOSE* is a fuzzy binary relation in $U \times U$. Thus, if

$$X \text{ and } Y \text{ are close} \rightarrow \Pi_{(X,Y)} = CLOSE \qquad (4.14)$$

then

$$X \text{ and } Y \text{ are very close} \rightarrow \Pi_{(X,Y)} = CLOSE^2\ . \qquad (4.15)$$

Rules of Type II

Compositional rules of Type II pertain to the translation of a proposition p which is a composite of propositions q and r. The most commonly employed modes of compositions are: conjunction, disjunction, and conditional composition (or implication). The translation rules for these modes of composition are as follows. (We are tacitly assuming that the compositions in question are noninteractive in the sense defined in Zadeh (1975c).)

Let X and Y be variables taking values in U and V, respectively, and let F and G be fuzzy subsets of U and V. If

$$X \text{ is } F \rightarrow \Pi_X = F \qquad (4.16)$$

$$Y \text{ is } G \rightarrow \Pi_Y = G \qquad (4.17)$$

then

(a) X is F and Y is $G \rightarrow \Pi_{(X,Y)} = \bar{F} \cap \bar{G} = F \times G$ (4.18)

(b) X is F or Y is $G \rightarrow \Pi_{(X,Y)} = \bar{F} + \bar{G}$ (4.19)

and (c_1) If X is F then Y is $G \rightarrow \Pi_{(X,Y)} = \bar{F}' \oplus \bar{G}$ (4.20)

or (c_2) If X is F then Y is $G \rightarrow \Pi_{(X,Y)} = F \times G + F' \times V$ (4.21) where $\Pi_{(X,Y)}$ is the possibility distribution of the binary variable (X,Y), $\overline{F}$ and $\overline{G}$ are the cylindrical extensions of F and G, respectively, that is,

$$\overline{F} = F \times V \tag{4.22}$$

$$\overline{G} = U \times G\,; \tag{4.23}$$

$F \times G$ is the Cartesian product of F and G, which may be expressed as $\overline{F} \cap \overline{G}$ and is defined by

$$\mu_{F\times G}(u,v) = \mu_F(u) \wedge \mu_G(v)\,, \quad u \in U,\ \ v \in V\,, \tag{4.24}$$

$+$ is the union, and $\oplus$ is the bounded sum, that is,

$$\mu_{\overline{F}' \oplus \overline{G}}(u,v) = 1 \wedge [1 - \mu_F(u) + \mu_G(v)] \tag{4.25}$$

where $+$ and $-$ denote the arithmetic sum and difference. Note that there are two interpretations of the conditional composition, (c_1) and (c_2). Of these, (c_1) is consistent with the definition of implication in L_{Aleph_1} logic, while (c_2) corresponds to the table

X	Y
F F'	G V

As a very simple illustration, assume that $U = V = 1 + 2 + 3$. (To be consistent with our notation for fuzzy sets, a finite nonfuzzy set $U = \{u_1, \ldots u_n\}$ may be expressed as $U = u_1 + \ldots + u_n$.)

$$F \triangleq \text{small} \triangleq 1/1+0.6/2+0.1/3 \tag{4.26}$$
$$G \triangleq \text{large} \triangleq 0.1/1+0.6/2+1/3$$

Then (4.18), (4.19), (4.20) and (4.21) yield

$$X \text{ is small and } Y \text{ is large} \rightarrow \Pi_{(X,Y)} = 0.1/(1,1) + 0.6/(1,2) + 1/(1,3) + 0.1/(2,1) + 0.6/(2,2) + 0.6/(2,3) + 0.1/(3,1) + 0.1/(3,2) + 0.1/(3,3)$$

$$X \text{ is small or } Y \text{ is large} \rightarrow \Pi_{(X,Y)} = 1/(1,1) + 1/(1,2) + 1/(1,3) + 0.6/(2,1) + 0.6/(2,2) + 1/(2,3) + 0.1/(3,1) + 0.6/(3,2) + 1/(3,3)$$

$$\text{If } X \text{ is small then } Y \text{ is large} \rightarrow \Pi_{(X,Y)} = 0.1/(1,1) + 0.6/(1,2) + 1/(1,3) + 0.5/(2,1) + 1/(2,2) + 1/(2,3) + 1/(3,1) + 1/(3,2) + 1/(3,3)$$

$$\text{If } X \text{ is small then } Y \text{ is large} \rightarrow \Pi_{(X,Y)} = 0.1/(1,1) + 0.6/(1,2) + 1/(1,3) + 0.4/(2,1) + 0.6/(2,2) + 0.6/(2,3) + 0.9/(3,1) + 0.9/(3,2) + 0.9/(3.3).$$

Rules of Type III

Quantificational rules of Type III apply to propositions of the general form

$$p \triangleq QX \text{ are } F \tag{4.27}$$

where Q is a fuzzy quantifier (*most*, *many*, *few*, *some*, *almost all*, etc.), X is a variable taking values in U, and F is a fuzzy subset of U. Simple examples of (4.27) are: "Most X's are small", "Some X's are small", "Many X's are very small". A somewhat less simple example is: "Most large X's are much smaller than α", where α is a specified number.

In general, a fuzzy quantifier is a fuzzy subset of the real line. However, when Q relates to a proportion, as is true of *most*, it may be represented as a fuzzy subset of the unit interval. Thus, the membership function of $Q \triangleq$ *most* may be represented as, say,

$$\mu_{most} = S(0.5, 0.7, 0.9) \tag{4.28}$$

where the S-function is defined by (3.5).

To be able to translate propositions of the form (4.27), it is necessary to define the cardinality of a fuzzy set, that is, the number (or the proportion) of elements of U which are in F. When U is a finite set $\{u_1, \ldots u_N\}$, a possible extension of the concept of cardinality of a nonfuzzy set – to which we shall refer as **fuzzy cardinality** – is the following. Let

$$F = \sum_{\alpha} \alpha F_{\alpha} \tag{4.29}$$

be the resolution (Zadeh, 1971) of F into its level-sets, that is,

$$F_{\alpha} \triangleq \{u \mid \mu_F(u) \geqslant \alpha\} \tag{4.30}$$

where αF_{α} is a fuzzy set defined by

$$\mu_{\alpha F_{\alpha}} = \alpha \mu_{F_{\alpha}} \tag{4.31}$$

and $\sum_{\alpha}$ denotes the union of the αF_{α} over $\alpha \in [0,1]$. Let $|F_{\alpha}|$ denote the cardinality of the nonfuzzy set F_{α}. Then, the fuzzy cardinality of F is denoted by $|F|_f$ and is defined to be the fuzzy subset of $\{0,1,2,\ldots\}$ expressed by

$$|F|_f = \sum_{\alpha} \alpha / |F_{\alpha}| . \tag{4.32}$$

As a simple example, consider the fuzzy subset *small* defined by (2.1). In this case,

$$\begin{aligned}
F_1 &= 0 + 1 , & |F_1| &= 2 \\
F_{0.8} &= 0 + 1 + 2 , & |F_{0.8}| &= 3 \\
F_{0.6} &= 0 + 1 + 2 + 3 , & |F_{0.6}| &= 4 \\
F_{0.4} &= 0 + 1 + 2 + 3 + 4 , & |F_{0.4}| &= 5 \\
F_{0.2} &= 0 + 1 + 2 + 3 + 4 + 5 , & |F_{0.2}| &= 6
\end{aligned}$$

and

$$|F|_f = 1/2 + 0.8/3 + 0.6/4 + 0.4/5 + 0.2/6 . \tag{4.33}$$

Frequently, it is convenient or necessary to express the cardinality of a fuzzy set as a nonfuzzy real number (or an integer) rather than as a fuzzy number. In such cases, the concept of the **power** of a fuzzy set (DeLuca and Termini, 1972) may be used as a **numerical summary** of the fuzzy cardinality of a fuzzy set. Thus, the power of a fuzzy subset, F, of $U = \{u_1, \ldots u_N\}$ is defined by

$$|F| \triangleq \sum_{i=1}^{N} \mu_F(u_i) \tag{4.34}$$

where $\mu_F(u_i)$ is the grade of membership of u_i in F, and $\sum$ denotes the arithmetic sum. For example, for the fuzzy set *small* defined by (2.1) we have

$$|F| = 1 + 1 + 0.8 + 0.6 + 0.4 + 0.2 = 4 .$$

For some applications, it is necessary to eliminate from the count those elements of F whose grade of membership falls below a specified threshold. This is equivalent to replacing F in (4.34) with $F \cap \Gamma$, where Γ is a fuzzy or nonfuzzy set which induces the desired threshold.

As N increases and U becomes a continuum, the concept of the power of F gives way to that of a **measure** of F (Zadeh, 1968; Sugeno, 1974), which may be regarded as a limiting form of the expression for the proportion of the elements of U which are in F. More specifically, if ρ is a density function defined on U, the measure in question is defined by

$$\|F\| \triangleq \int_U \rho(u)\mu_F(u)du \tag{4.35}$$

where μ_F is the membership function of F. For example, if $\rho(u)du$ is the proportion of men whose height lies in the interval $[u,u+du]$, then the proportion of men who are tall is given by

$$\|tall\| = \int_0^\infty \rho(u)\mu_{tall}(u)du \; . \tag{4.36}$$

Making use of the above definitions, the **quantifier rule** for propositions of the form "QX are F" may be stated as follows.

If $U = \{u_1, \ldots u_N\}$ and

$$X \text{ is } F \rightarrow \Pi_X = F \tag{4.37}$$

then

$$QX \text{ are } F \rightarrow \Pi_{|F|} = Q \tag{4.38}$$

and, if U is continuum,

$$QX \text{ are } F \rightarrow \Pi_{\|F\|} = Q \tag{4.39}$$

which implies the more explicit rule

$$QX \text{ are } F \rightarrow \pi(\rho) = \mu_Q\left[\int_U \rho(u)\mu_F(u)du\right] \tag{4.40}$$

where $\rho(u)du$ is the proportion of X's whose value lies in the interval $[u,u+du]$, $\pi(\rho)$ is the possibility of ρ, and μ_Q and μ_F are the membership functions of Q and F, respectively.

As a simple illustration, if *most* and *tall* are defined by (4.28) and $\mu_{tall} = S(160,170,180)$, respectively, then

$$\text{Most men are tall} \rightarrow \pi(\rho) =$$
$$S[\int_0^{200} \rho(u)S(u;160,170,180)du;0.5,0.7,0.9] \quad (4.41)$$

where $\rho(u)du$ is the proportion of men whose height (in cm) is in the interval $[u,u+du]$. Thus, the proposition "Most men are tall" induces a possibility distribution of the height density function ρ which is expressed by the right-hand member of (4.41).

Rules of Type IV

Among the many ways in which a proposition, p, may be qualified there are three that are of particular relevance to approximate reasoning. These are: (a) by a linguistic truth-value, as in "p is very true", (b) by a linguistic probability-value, as in "p is highly probable"; and (c) by a linguistic possibility-value, as in "p is quite possible". Of these, we shall discuss only (a) in the sequel. Discussions of (b) and (c) may be found in Zadeh (1977).

As a preliminary to the formulation of translation rules pertaining to truth qualification, it is necessary to understand the role which a truth-value plays in modifying the meaning of proposition. Thus, in FL, the truth-value of a proposition, p, is defined as the compatibility of a reference proposition, r, with p. More specifically, let

$$p \triangleq X \text{ is } F$$

where F is a subset of U, and let r be a reference proposition of the special form

$$r \triangleq X \text{ is } u \quad (4.42)$$

where u is an element of U. Then, the **compatibility** of r with p is defined as

$$Comp(X \text{ is } u/X \text{ is } F) \triangleq \mu_F(u) \quad (4.43)$$

or, equivalently (in view of (2.3)),

$$Comp(X \text{ is } u/X \text{ is } F) \triangleq Poss\{X = u \mid X \text{ is } F\} . \quad (4.44)$$

To extend (4.43) to the case where r is a fuzzy proposition of the form

$$r \triangleq X \text{ is } G\,, \quad G \subset U \quad (4.45)$$

we apply the extension principle† to the evaluation of the expression $\mu_F(G)$, yielding

$$Comp\{X \text{ is } G/X \text{ is } F\} \triangleq \mu_F(G) \qquad (4.46)$$
$$\triangleq \int_{[0,1]} \mu_G(u)/\mu_F(u)$$

in which the right-hand member is the union over the unit interval of the fuzzy singletons $\mu_G(u)/\mu_F(u)$. Thus, the compatibility of "X is G" with "X is F" is a fuzzy subset of [0,1] defined by (4.46).

In FL, the **truth-value**, τ, of the proposition $p \triangleq X$ is F relative to the reference proposition $r \triangleq X$ is G is defined as the compatibility of r with p. Thus, by definition,

$$\tau \triangleq Tr\{X \text{ is } F/X \text{ is } G\} \triangleq Comp\{X \text{ is } G/X \text{ is } F\} \qquad (4.47)$$
$$= \mu_F(G)$$
$$= \int_{[0,1]} \mu_G(u)/\mu_F(u)$$

which implies that the truth-value, τ, of the proposition "X is F" relative to "X is G" is a fuzzy subset of the unit interval defined by (4.47). In this sense, then, a linguistic truth-value may be regarded as a linguistic approximation to the fuzzy subset, τ, represented by (4.47). (See Fig. 2.)

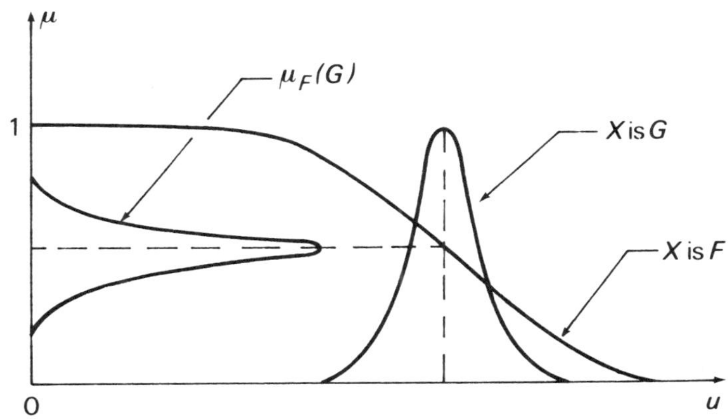

Fig. 2 – Graphical illustration of the concept of relative truth.

† The extension principle (Zadeh 1975c) serves to extend the definition of a mapping $f: U \rightarrow V$ to the set of fuzzy subsets of U. Thus, $f(F) \triangleq \int_U \mu_F(u)/f(u)$, where $f(F)$ and $f(u)$ are, respectively, the images of F and u in V.

A more explicit expression for τ which follows at once from (4.47) is the following. Let μ_τ denote the membership function of τ and let $\nu \in [0,1]$. Then

$$\mu_\tau(\nu) = Max_u\ \mu_G(u) \tag{4.48}$$

subject to

$$\mu_F(u) = \nu\ . \tag{4.49}$$

In particular, if μ_F is $1-1$, then (4.48) and (4.49) yield

$$\mu_\tau(\nu) = \mu_G(\mu_F^{-1}(\nu))\ , \quad \nu \in [0,1]\ . \tag{4.50}$$

As a simple illustration, consider the propositions (see Fig. 3)

$$p \triangleq X \text{ is } F \tag{4.51}$$
$$r \triangleq X \text{ is } G \text{ where } G = [a,b]\ .$$

In this case, it follows from (4.50) that τ is the interval given by

$$\tau = [\mu_F(b), \mu_F(a)]\ .$$

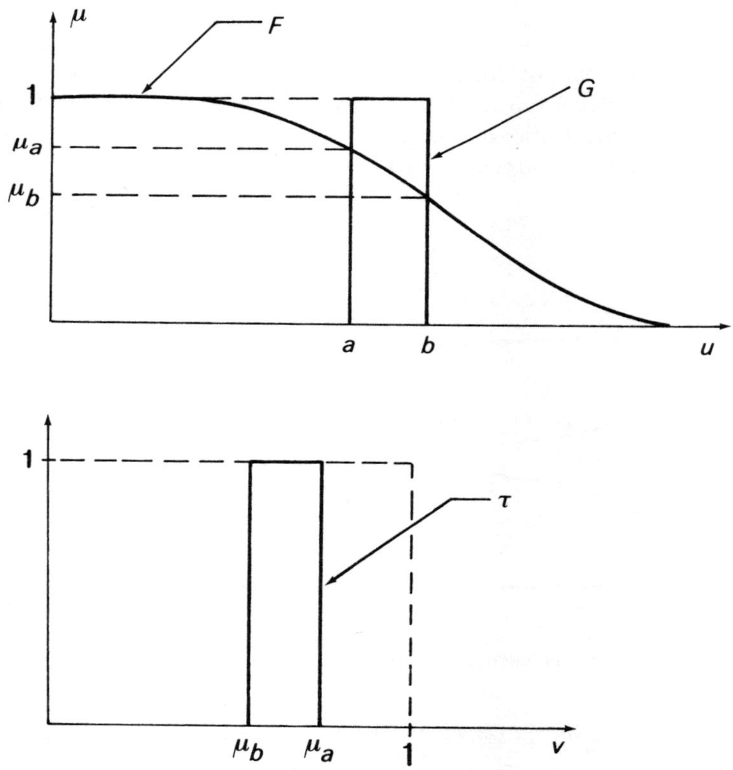

Fig. 3 – Interval-valued truth-value for an interval-valued reference proposition.

The definition of the truth-value of p as the compatibility of a reference proposition r with p provides us with a basis for the translation of truth-qualified propositions of the form "p is τ" when τ is a fuzzy subset of [0,1]. Specifically, from the relation

$$\tau = \mu_F(G) \tag{4.52}$$

which defines τ as the image of G under the mapping μ_F: $U \to [0,1]$, it follows that the membership function of G may be expressed in terms of those of τ and μ_F by (see Fig. 4)

$$\mu_G(u) = \mu_\tau(\mu_F(u)) \,. \tag{4.53}$$

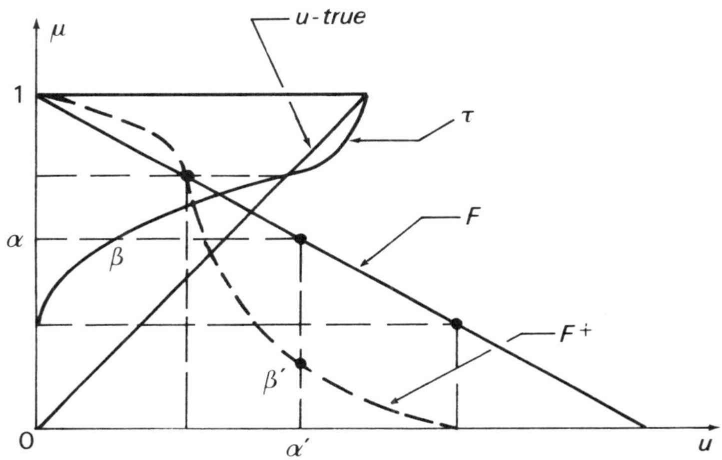

Fig. 4 – Effect of truth qualification on F. (β is mapped into β'.)

Now, if $r \triangleq X$ is G is the reference proposition for $p \triangleq X$ is F, we interpret the truth-qualified proposition

$$q \triangleq X \text{ is } F \text{ is } \tau \tag{4.45}$$

as the reference proposition $r \triangleq X$ is G. This leads us, then, to the following **rule for truth qualification**:

If

$$X \text{ is } F \to \Pi_X = F \tag{4.55}$$

then

$$X \text{ is } F \text{ is } \tau \to \Pi_X = F^+ \tag{4.56}$$

where

$$\mu_{F^+}(u) = \mu_\tau(\mu_F(u)) \,. \tag{4.57}$$

In particular, if τ is the **unitary** truth-value, that is

$$\tau \triangleq u\text{-}true \tag{4.58}$$

where

$$\mu_{u\text{-}true}(\nu) \triangleq \nu\ , \quad \nu \in [0,1] \tag{4.59}$$

then

$$X \text{ is } F \text{ is } u\text{-}true \rightarrow X \text{ is } F\ . \tag{4.60}$$

As an illustration of (4.56), consider the proposition

$$p \triangleq \text{Lucia is young is very true} \tag{4.61}$$

in which

$$\mu_{young} = 1 - S(25;35;45) \tag{4.62}$$

$$\mu_{true} = S(0.6,0.8,1.0)$$

and

$$\mu_{very\ true} = S^2(0.6,0.8,1.0)$$

On applying (4.56) to p, we obtain

$$p \rightarrow \pi_{Age(Lucia)}(u) = S^2[1 - S(u;25,35,45);0.6,0.8,1.0] \tag{4.63}$$

which may be roughly approximated by the proposition

$$p^+ \triangleq \text{Lucia is very young}\ . \tag{4.64}$$

Similarly, for the proposition

$$q \triangleq \text{Lucia is not young is very false} \tag{4.65}$$

where $false \triangleq ant\ true$, that is,

$$\mu_{false}(\nu) \triangleq \mu_{true}(1-\nu)\ , \quad \nu \in [0,1] \tag{4.66}$$
$$= 1 - S(\nu;0,0.2,0.4)$$

we obtain

$$q \rightarrow \pi_{Age(Lucia)} = \left[1 - S[S(u;25,35,45);0,0.2,0.4]\right]^2 \tag{4.67}$$

which, as can readily be verified, defines the same possibility distribution as (4.63).

The translation rules described above provide us with the necessary basis for the formulation of the rules of inference in FL and the related notions of semantic equivalence and semantic entailment. We turn to these issues in the following section.

5. SEMANTIC EQUIVALENCE AND SEMANTIC ENTAILMENT

In this section, we shall consider two related concepts in fuzzy logic that play an important role in approximate reasoning. These are the concepts of *semantic equivalence* and *semantic entailment.*

Informally, two propositions p and q are **semantically equivalent** if and only if the possibility distributions induced by p and q are equal. More specifically, if

$$p \rightarrow \Pi^{p}_{(X_1, \ldots X_n)} = F$$

and

$$q \rightarrow \Pi^{q}_{(X_1, \ldots X_n)} = G$$

where Π^p and Π^q are the possibility distributions induced by p and q, respectively, and $X_1, \ldots X_n$ are the variables that are implicit or explicit in p and q, then

$$p \leftrightarrow q \text{ iff } \Pi^{p}_{(X_1, \ldots X_n)} = \Pi^{q}_{(X_1, \ldots X_n)} \tag{5.1}$$

where $\leftrightarrow$ denotes semantic equivalence.

When (5.1) holds for all fuzzy sets in p and q that have a context-dependent meaning, the semantic equivalence will be said to be **strong**.† For example, the semantic equivalence

Adrienne is intelligent is true $\leftrightarrow$ Adrienne is not intelligent is false (5.2)

holds for all definitions of *intelligent* and *true* (*false* $\triangleq$ antonym of true) and hence is a strong equivalence. On the other hand, the semantic equivalence

Lucia is young is very true $\leftrightarrow$ Lucia is very young (5.3)

is not a strong equivalence because it holds only for some particular definitions of *young* and *true*. (See (4.64) and (4.65) *et seq.*) Usually, a semantic equivalence which is not strong is approximate in nature, as is true of (5.3).

Generally, it is clear from the context whether a semantic equivalence is or is not strong. Where it is necessary to place in evidence that a semantic equivalence is strong, it will be denoted by $s\leftrightarrow$, while approximate semantic equivalence will be denoted by $a\leftrightarrow$.

The concept of **semantic entailment** is weaker than that of semantic equivalence in that p semantically entails q (or q is *semantically entailed* by p) if and only if $\Pi^{p}_{(X_1, \ldots X_n)} \subset \Pi^{q}_{(X_1, \ldots X_n)}$. Thus, in symbols,

$$p \mapsto q \text{ iff } \Pi^{p}_{(X_1, \ldots X_n)} \subset \Pi^{q}_{(X_1, \ldots X_n)} \tag{5.4}$$

where $\mapsto$ denotes semantic entailment and $\Pi^{p}_{(X_1, \ldots X_n)}$ and $\Pi^{q}_{(X_1, \ldots X_n)}$ are the possibility distributions induced by p and q, respectively.

As in the case of semantic equivalence, semantic entailment is *strong* if (5.4) holds for all fuzzy sets in p and q that have a context-dependent meaning. As an illustration, the semantic entailment expressed by

X is very small $\mapsto$ X is small (5.5)

† The concept of strong semantic equivalence as defined here reduces to that of semantic equivalence in predicate logic (Lyndon, 1966) when p and q are nonfuzzy propositions.

is strong since it holds for all definitions of *small.* On the other hand, the validity of the semantic entailment expressed by

$$X \text{ is large} \mapsto X \text{ is not small} \tag{5.6}$$

depends on the way in which *large* and *small* are defined, and hence (5.6) is not an instance of strong semantic entailment.

In the case of propositions of the form $p \triangleq X$ is F and $q \triangleq X$ is G, it is evident that

$$X \text{ is } F \mapsto X \text{ is } G \textit{ iff } F \subset G\,. \tag{5.7}$$

From this and the definition of conditional composition (4.20), it follows at once that

$$X \text{ is } F \mapsto X \text{ is } G \;\; \textit{iff} \;\; \text{If } X \text{ is } F \text{ then } X \text{ is } G \rightarrow \Pi_X = U \tag{5.8}$$

or equivalently

$$X \text{ is } F \mapsto X \text{ is } G \;\; \textit{iff} \;\; \text{If } X \text{ is } F \text{ then } X \text{ is } G \leftrightarrow X \text{ is } U \tag{5.9}$$

where Π_X is the possibility distribution of X and U is the universe of discourse associated with X. Similarly, from the definition of conjunctive composition, it follows that

$$X \text{ is } F \mapsto X \text{ is } G \;\; \textit{iff} \;\; X \text{ is } F \text{ and } X \text{ is } G \rightarrow \Pi_X = F \tag{5.10}$$

or equivalently

$$X \text{ is } F \mapsto X \text{ is } G \;\; \textit{iff} \; X \text{ is } F \text{ and } X \text{ is } G \leftrightarrow X \text{ is } F\,. \tag{5.11}$$

An intuitively appealing interpretation of (5.11) is that p semantically entails q if the information conveyed by "p and q" is the same as the information conveyed by p alone.

As a preliminary to applying the concepts of semantic equivalence and semantic entailment to approximate reasoning – which we shall do in Sec. 6 – it will be helpful to formulate several rules pertaining to the transformation of a given proposition, p, into other propositions that have the same meaning as p, that is, are strongly semantically equivalent to p.

A general rule governing such transformations may be stated informally as follows.

If m is a modifier and p is a proposition, than mp is semantically equivalent to the proposition which results from applying m to the possibility distribution which is induced by p.

Thus, on applying this rule to the case where $m \triangleq$ not and making use of the translation rules (4.5), (4.56) and (4.40), we arrive at the following specific rules governing the negation of a proposition:

(a) $$\textit{not}(X \text{ is } F) \leftrightarrow X \text{ is not } F \tag{5.12}$$

for example,

$$\textit{not}(X \text{ is small}) \leftrightarrow X \text{ is not small}\;; \tag{5.13}$$

(b) $not(X \text{ is } F \text{ is } \tau) \leftrightarrow X \text{ is } F \text{ is not } \tau$ (5.14)

for example,

$$not(X \text{ is small is very true}) \leftrightarrow X \text{ is small is not very true} ; \quad (5.15)$$

(c) $not(QX \text{ are } F) \leftrightarrow (\text{not } Q)X \text{ are } F$ (5.16)

for example,

$$not(\text{many men are tall}) \leftrightarrow (\text{not many})\text{men are tall} . \quad (5.17)$$

Similarly, for $m \triangleq$ very, we obtain

(a) $very(X \text{ is } F) \leftrightarrow X \text{ is very } F$ (5.18)

(b) $very(X \text{ is } F \text{ is } \tau) \leftrightarrow X \text{ is } F \text{ is very } \tau$ (5.19)

(c) $very(QX \text{ are } F) \leftrightarrow (\text{very } Q)X \text{ are } F$ (5.20)

In addition, from the translation formulas (4.5), (4.40), and (4.56), it follows at once that

$$X \text{ is } F \text{ is } \tau \leftrightarrow X \text{ is not } F \text{ is ant } \tau \quad (5.21)$$

and

$$QX \text{ are } F \leftrightarrow (\text{ant } Q)X \text{ are not } F \quad (5.22)$$

where ant τ and ant Q denote the antonyms of τ and Q, respectively. (See (4.66).) Similarly, for $m =$ very, we have

$$X \text{ is } F \text{ is } \tau \leftrightarrow X \text{ is very } F \text{ is } {}^2\tau \quad (5.23)$$

where the "left-square" operation on τ is defined by

$${}^2\tau = \int_0^1 \mu_\tau(\nu)/\nu^2 , \qquad \nu \in [0,1] \quad (5.24)$$

or equivalently

$$\mu_{{}^2\tau}(\nu) = \mu_\tau(\sqrt{\nu}) \quad (5.25)$$

where μ_τ is the membership function of τ. However, as will be seen later, when F is modified to *very* F in "QX are F", we can assert only the semantic entailment – rather than the semantic equivalence – expressed by

$$QX \text{ are } F \rightarrow ({}^2Q)F \text{ are very } F \quad (5.26)$$

where

$${}^2Q = \int_0^1 \mu_Q(\nu)/\nu^2 \quad (5.27)$$

or equivalently

$$\mu_{{}^2Q}(\nu) = \mu_Q(\sqrt{\nu}) . \quad (5.28)$$

It should be noted in closing that the negation rule expressed by (5.16) appears to differ in form from the familiar negation rule in predicate calculus (Lyndon 1966), which, when F is interpreted as a nonfuzzy predicate, may be expressed as

$$\textit{not}(\text{all } X \text{ are } F) \leftrightarrow \text{some } X \text{ are not } F\,. \tag{5.29}$$

However, by the use of (5.22) it is easy to show that the right-hand member of (5.29) is semantically equivalent to that of (5.16). Specifically, from (5.22) it follows that

$$(\text{not all})X \text{ are } F \leftrightarrow (\text{ant}(\text{not all})X)\text{are not } F$$

and if *some* is defined as

$$\textit{some} \triangleq \textit{ant}(\text{not all}) \tag{5.30}$$

then

$$(\text{not all})X \text{ are } F \leftrightarrow \text{some } X \text{ are not } F \tag{5.31}$$

in agreement with (5.29).

Remark

It should be observed that most of the definitions made in this and the preceding sections – especially in regard to the semantic equivalence and semantic entailment of fuzzy propositions – are nonfuzzy and, for the most part, quite precise. What should be understood, however, is that all such definitions may be fuzzified, if necessary, by the use of the following general convention.

Let U be a universe of discourse, with u denoting a generic element of U. A concept, C, in U is a subset, A, of U (or U^n, $n > 1$) which is defined by a predicate P such that $P(u)$ is true if $u \in A$, that is, u is an instance of C, and false otherwise. Assume that $P(u)$ is of the form $P(f(u))$, where $P(f(u))$ is true if $f(u) = 0$ and false if $f(u) > 0$. Then A – and hence the concept C which is associated with it – may be fuzzified by defining the grade of membership of u in A as a monotone function of $f(u)$ which assumes the value unity when $f(u) = 0$. (The definition of such a function is, in general, application-dependent rather than universal in nature.) In this sense, any definition which has the format stated above may be viewed as providing a mechanism for a fuzzification of the concept which it serves to define.

As an illustration of this convention, consider the concept of semantic equivalence as defined by (5.1). In this case, the concept of semantic equivalence may be fuzzified by defining the degree to which p and q are semantically equivalent as a monotone function of the "distance" between Π^{p} and Π^{q}, with the distance function defined in a way that reflects the specific nature of the domain of application. It should be understood, of course, that the concept in question may also be fuzzified in other ways which do not stem directly from its nonfuzzy definition.

6. RULES OF INFERENCE AND APPROXIMATE REASONING

As in any other logic, the rules of inference in FL govern the deduction of a proposition, q, from a set of premises $\{p_1, \ldots p_n\}$. However, in FL both the premises and the conclusion are allowed to be fuzzy propositions. Furthermore, because of the use of linguistic approximation in the process of retranslation, the final conclusion drawn from the premises $p_1, \ldots p_n$ is, in general, an approximate rather than exact consequence of $p_1, \ldots p_n$.

The principal rules of inference in FL are the following.

1. Projection principle

Let p be a fuzzy proposition whose translation is expressed as

$$p \rightarrow \Pi_{(X_1, \ldots X_n)} = F .$$

Let $X_{(s)}$ denote a subvariable of the variable $X \triangleq (X_1, \ldots X_n)$, that is,

$$X_{(s)} = (X_{i_1}, \ldots X_{i_k}) \tag{6.1}$$

where the index sequence $s \triangleq (i_1, \ldots i_k)$ is a subsequence of the sequence $(1, \ldots n)$.

Let $\Pi_{X_{(s)}}$ denote the marginal possibility distribution of $X_{(s)}$; that is,

$$\Pi_{X_{(s)}} = Proj_{U_{(s)}} F \tag{6.2}$$

where $U_i, i = 1, \ldots n$ is the universe of discourse associated with X_i;

$$U_{(s)} = U_{i_1} \times \ldots \times U_{i_k} , \tag{6.3}$$

and the projection of F on $U_{(s)}$ is defined by the possibility distribution function

$$\pi_{X_{(s)}}(u_{i_1}, \ldots u_{i_k}) = Sup_{u_{j_1}, \ldots u_{j_m}} \mu_F(u_1, \ldots u_n) \tag{6.4}$$

where $s' \triangleq (j_1, \ldots j_m)$ is the index subsequence which is complementary to s, and μ_F is the membership function of F.

Let q be a retranslation of the possibility assignment equation

$$\Pi_{X_{(s)}} = Proj_{U_{(s)}} F . \tag{6.5}$$

Then, the projection principle asserts that q may be inferred from p. In a schematic form, this assertion may be expressed more transparently as

$$\begin{array}{c} p \rightarrow \Pi_{(X_1, \ldots X_n)} = F \\ \downarrow \\ q \leftarrow \Pi_{X_{(s)}} = Proj_{U_{(s)}} F . \end{array} \tag{6.6}$$

The statement of the projection principle assumes a particularly simple form for $n = 2$. In this case, writing X, Y, U, V for X_1, X_2, U_1, U_2 respectively, we have

$$p \rightarrow \Pi_{(X, Y)} = F \tag{6.7}$$

$$q \leftarrow \Pi_X = Proj_U F \tag{6.8}$$

and likewise for the projection on V.

A special case of (6.6) obtains when $\Pi_{(X,Y)}$ is the Cartesian product of normal fuzzy sets. Thus, if

$$p \to \Pi_{(X,Y)} = G \times H \tag{6.9}$$

then from p we can infer q and r, where

$$q \leftarrow \Pi_X = G \tag{6.10}$$

and

$$r \leftarrow \Pi_Y = H\,. \tag{6.11}$$

As a simple illustration, if

$p \triangleq$ John is tall and fat

then from p we can infer

$q \triangleq$ John is tall

and

$r \triangleq$ John is fat .

2. Particularization/conjunction principle

Let p be a fuzzy proposition whose translation is expressed as

$$p \to \Pi_{(X_1, \ldots X_n)} = F\,, \quad F \subset U_1 \times \ldots \times U_n\,. \tag{6.12}$$

Then from p we can infer r, where r is a retranslation of a particularization of $\Pi_{(X_1, \ldots X_n)}$, that is,

$$r \leftarrow \Pi_{(X_1, \ldots X_n)}[\Pi_{X_{(s)}} = G] = F \cap \bar{G} \tag{6.13}$$

where $X_{(s)}$ is a subvariable of X, $\bar{G}$ is a cylindrical extension of G, $G \subset U$, and $\Pi_{(X_1, \ldots X_n)}[\Pi_{X_{(s)}} = G]$ denotes an n-ary possibility distribution which results from particularizing $X_{(s)}$ to G. Equivalently, the **particularization principle** may be expressed in the schematic form

$$p \to \Pi_{(X_1, \ldots X_n)} = F \tag{6.14}$$

$$q \to \Pi_{(X_{i_1}, \ldots X_{i_k})} = G$$

$$r \leftarrow \Pi_{(X_1, \ldots X_n)} = F \cap \bar{G}\,.$$

For the special case of $n = 2$, the particularization principle may be stated more simply as:

From

$$p \triangleq (X,Y) \text{ is } F \tag{6.15}$$

and

$$q \triangleq X \text{ is } G$$

we can infer

$$r \triangleq (X,Y) \text{ is } F \cap \bar{G}\,. \tag{6.16}$$

Thus, for example, from

$$p \triangleq X \text{ and } Y \text{ are approximately equal} \tag{6.17}$$

and

$$q \triangleq X \text{ is small}$$

we can infer (without the application of linguistic approximation)

$$r \triangleq X \text{ and } Y \text{ are} (\textit{approximately equal} \cap (\textit{small} \times V)) . \tag{6.18}$$

As stated above, the particularization principle may be viewed as a special case of a somewhat more general principle which will be referred to as the **conjunction principle**. Specifically, assume that

$$p \rightarrow \Pi^p_{(Y_1, \ldots Y_k, X_{k+1}, \ldots X_n)} = F \tag{6.19}$$

$$q \rightarrow \Pi^q_{(Y_1, \ldots Y_k, Z_{k+1}, \ldots Z_m)} = G \tag{6.20}$$

where $Y_1, \ldots Y_k$ are variables which appear in both Π^p and Π^q, and U_i, V_j and W_ℓ are the universes of discourse associated with X_i, Y_j and Z_ℓ; let S be the smallest Cartesian product of the U_i, V_j, and W_ℓ which contains the Cartesian products $V_1 \times \ldots \times V_k \times U_{k+1} \times \ldots \times U_n$ and $V_1 \times \ldots \times V_k \times W_{k+1} \times \ldots \times W_m$; and let $\bar{F}$ and $\bar{G}$ be, respectively, the cylindrical extensions of F and G in S. Then, from p and q we can infer r, where (in schematic form)

$$\begin{array}{l} p \rightarrow \Pi^p_{(Y,X)} = F \\ q \rightarrow \Pi^q_{(Y,Z)} = G \\ \hline r \leftarrow \Pi_{(X,Y,Z)} = \bar{F} \cap \bar{G} \end{array} \tag{6.21}$$

and $Y \triangleq (Y_1, \ldots Y_k)$, $X \triangleq (X_{k+1}, \ldots X_n)$ and $Z \triangleq (Z_{k+1}, \ldots Z_m)$.

A particular but important case of (6.21) which we shall use at a later point results when $n = 3$, and $k = 1$. For this case, (6.21) may be expressed as

$$\begin{array}{l} p \rightarrow \Pi^p_{(X,Y)} = F \\ q \leftarrow \Pi^q_{(Y,Z)} = G \\ \hline r \leftarrow \Pi_{(X,Y,Z)} = (F \times W) \cap (U \times G) . \end{array} \tag{6.22}$$

Although the particularization principle is subsumed by the conjunction principle, it is simpler that the latter, is employed more frequently, and has a somewhat greater intuitive appeal. For this reason, we use the designation "particularization/conjunction principle" to refer to the principle which, in most applications, is the particularization principle and, in some, the conjunction principle. It should be noted that, in predicate logic (Lyndon 1966), this principle implies the generalization rule.

3. Entailment principle

Stated informally, the **entailment principle** asserts that from any fuzzy proposition p we can infer a fuzzy proposition q if the possibility distribution induced by p is contained in the possibility distribution induced by q. Thus, schematically, we have

$$\begin{array}{l} p \rightarrow \Pi_{(X_1, \ldots X_n)} = F \\ \quad\quad\downarrow \\ q \leftarrow \Pi_{(X_1, \ldots X_n)} = G \supset F\,. \end{array} \tag{6.23}$$

For example, from $p \triangleq X$ is very large we can infer $q \triangleq X$ is large.

The compositional rule of inference. In general, the inference principles stated above are used in sequence or in combination. A combination that is particularly effective involves an application of the particularization/conjunction principle followed by that of the projection principle. This combination will be referred to as the **compositional rule of inference** (Zadeh 1973). As will be seen later, the compositional rule of inference includes as a special case a generalization of the *modus ponens*.

For our purposes, it will be convenient to state the compositional rule of inference in the following schematic form

$$\begin{array}{l} p \rightarrow \Pi_{(X,Y)} = F \\ q \rightarrow \Pi_{(Y,Z)} = G \\ \hline r \leftarrow \Pi_{(X,Y)} = F \circ G \end{array} \tag{6.24}$$

where X, Y and Z take values in U, V and W, respectively; F is a fuzzy subset of $U \times V$, G is a fuzzy subset of $V \times W$, and $F \circ G$ is the composition of F and G defined by

$$\mu_{F \circ G}(u,w) = Sup_v\,[\mu_F(u,v) \wedge \mu_G(v,w)] \tag{6.25}$$

where $u \in U$, $v \in V$, $w \in W$ and μ_F and μ_G are the membership functions of F and G, respectively; and the dashed line signifies that, because of the use of linguistic approximation in retranslation, r is, in general, an approximate rather than exact consequence of p and q. It should be noted that the compositional rule of inference is analogous to the rule which yields the probability distribution of Y from the probability distribution of X and the conditional probability distribution of Y given X.

It is easy to demonstrate that the compositional rule of inference may be regarded as a result of applying the particularization/conjunction principle followed by the application of the projection principle. Specifically, on applying (6.21) to (6.24), we obtain

$$p \rightarrow \Pi_{(X,Y)} = F \qquad (6.26)$$
$$q \rightarrow \Pi_{(Y,Z)} = G$$
$$\overline{}$$
$$s \leftarrow \Pi_{(X,Y,Z)} = (F \times W) \cap (U \times G)$$

where

$$\mu_{(F \times W) \cap (U \times G)}(u,v,w) = \mu_F(u,v) \wedge \mu_G(v,w) \; . \qquad (6.27)$$

Next, on applying the projection principle to s and projecting $\Pi_{(X,Y,Z)}$ on $U \times W$, we have

$$Proj_{U \times W}[(F \times W) \cap (U \times G)] = \int_{U \times W} Sup_v \, [\mu_F(u,v) \wedge \mu_G(v,w)] \, /(u,w) \qquad (6.28)$$

which upon comparison with (6.25) shows that the resulting proposition may be expressed – in agreement with (6.24) – as

$$r \leftarrow \Pi_{(X,Z)} = F \circ G \; . \qquad (6.29)$$

An important special case of the compositional rule of inference obtains when p and q are of the form $p \triangleq X$ is F, $q \triangleq$ If X is G then Y is H. For this case, (4.20) and (6.24) yield the **compositional modus ponens**:

$$p \rightarrow \Pi_X = F \qquad (6.30)$$
$$q \rightarrow \Pi_{(X,Y)} = \bar{G}' \oplus \bar{H}$$
$$- - - - - - -$$
$$r \leftarrow F \circ (\bar{G}' \oplus \bar{H})$$

which may be regarded as a generalization of the classical *modus ponens*, with the latter corresponding to the special case of (6.30) in which F, G and H are nonfuzzy and $F = G$. For this case, (6.30) reduces to

$$p \rightarrow \Pi_{(X} = F \qquad (6.31)$$
$$q \rightarrow \Pi_{(X,Y)} = \bar{F}' \oplus \bar{H}$$
$$\overline{}$$
$$r \leftarrow \Pi_Y = F \circ (\bar{F}' \oplus \bar{H})$$

and since

$$F \circ (\bar{F}' \oplus \bar{H}) = H$$

it follows that

$$r \leftrightarrow Y \text{ is } H$$

which means that from $p \triangleq X$ is F and $q \triangleq$ If X is F then Y is H we can infer $r \triangleq Y$ is H, in agreement with the statement of the *modus ponens*.

The rules of inference presented in the foregoing discussion provide us with a basis for employing approximate reasoning for the purpose of question-answering and inference from fuzzy propositions. We shall illustrate the use of the methods based on these rules by applying them to several typical problems.

Semantic equivalence. As a simple example, assume that from the premise

$p \triangleq$ Ellen is not very tall

we wish to deduce the answer to the question "Is Ellen tall ?τ", where the symbol ?τ signifies that the answer to the question is expected to be of the form

$q \triangleq$ Ellen is tall is τ

where τ is a linguistic truth-value.

To obtain the answer to the question, we shall require that p and q be semantically equivalent, implying that the possibility distribution induced by p is equal to that induced by q.

Thus, by using the translation rules (4.5), (4.6) and (4.56), we obtain

$$\text{Ellen is not very tall} \rightarrow \pi_{Height(Ellen)}(u) = 1 - \mu^2_{tall}(u) \tag{6.32}$$

$$\text{Ellen is tall is } \tau \rightarrow \pi_{Height(Ellen)}(u) = \mu_\tau[\mu_{tall}(u)] \tag{6.33}$$

where μ_{tall}, the membership function of *tall*, is assumed to be given. From (6.32) and (6.33), then, it follows that the desired membership function μ_τ satisfies the identity

$$1 - \mu^2_{tall}(u) \equiv \mu_\tau[\mu_{tall}(u)] \ , \quad u \in [0,200] \tag{6.34}$$

from which we can conclude at once that μ_τ is given by (see Fig. 5)

$$\mu_\tau(v) = 1 - v^2 \tag{6.35}$$

to which a rough linguistic approximation may be expressed as

$$\tau \approx \text{not very true} \ . \tag{6.36}$$

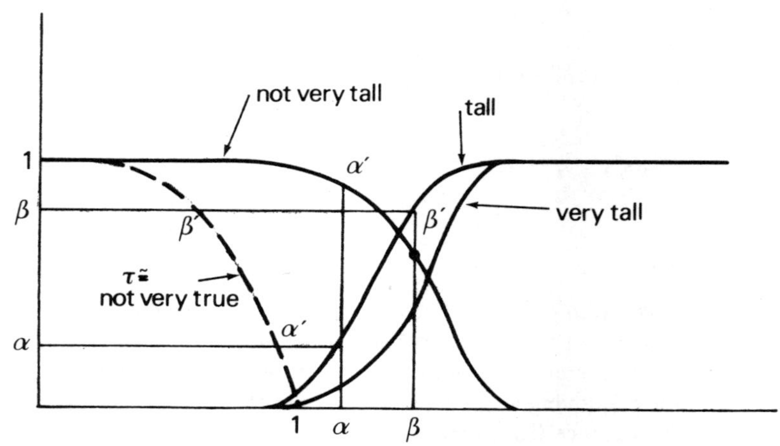

Fig. 5 – Extraction of an answer by the use of semantic equivalence.

It is instructive to obtain the same result by a succesive use of the rules governing the application of negation, truth qualification, and modification (by very). Thus, we can assert that

John is not very tall
$\leftrightarrow$ John is not very tall is *u-true* (by (4.60))

John is not very tall is *u-true*
$\leftrightarrow$ John is very tall is *ant*(*u-true*) (by (5.21))

John is very tall is *ant*(*u-true*)
$\leftrightarrow$ John is tall is $^{1/2}(ant(u\text{-}true))$ (by (5.23))

which implies that

$$\tau = {}^{1/2}(ant(u\text{-}true)) \tag{6.37}$$

that is, τ is the "left-square root" of (*ant*(*u-true*)), and since

$$\mu_{u\text{-}true}(\nu) = \nu \tag{6.38}$$

we have

$$\mu_\tau = 1 - \nu^2 \tag{6.39}$$

in agreement with (6.35).

Semantic entailment. Assume that we wish to deduce from the premise

$p \triangleq$ Most Swedes are tall

the answer to the question "How many Swedes are very tall?"

Translating p by the use of (4.40), we have

$$\text{Most Swedes are tall} \rightarrow \pi_p(\rho) = \mu_{most}[\int_0^{200} \rho(u)\mu_{tall}(u)du] \tag{6.40}$$

where $\rho(u)du$ is the proportion of Swedes whose height is in the interval $[u,u+du]$ and π_p is the possibility distribution function of ρ. (Note that height is expressed in centimetres.)

Now, by (4.30) the proportion of Swedes who are very tall is given by

$$\gamma = \int_0^{200} \rho(u)\mu_{tall}^2(u)du\ . \tag{6.41}$$

Thus, our problem is to find the possibility distribution of γ from the knowledge of the possibility distribution of ρ – which is given by the right-hand member of (6.40). In a variational formulation (which follows from (4.48)), this problem may be expressed as

$$\pi(\gamma) = Max_\rho\ \mu_{most}[\int_0^{200} \rho(u)\mu_{tall}(u)du] \tag{6.42}$$

subject to

$$\gamma = \int_0^{200} \rho(u)\mu_{tall}^2(u)du \ . \qquad (6.43)$$

The maximizing ρ for this problem is of the form (Bellman and Zadeh 1976).

$$\rho(u) = \delta(u - \alpha) \qquad (6.44)$$

where δ is a δ-function and α is a point in the interval [0,200]. The δ-function density implies that all elements of the population have the same value of the attribute in question. Thus, from (6.43) we have

$$\gamma = \mu_{tall}^2(\alpha) \qquad (6.45)$$

and hence

$$\pi(\gamma) = \mu_{most}(\mu_{tall}(\alpha)) \qquad (6.47)$$
$$= \mu_{most}(\sqrt{\gamma})$$

or equivalently (see (5.30))

$$\pi(\gamma) = \mu_{^2most}(\gamma) \qquad (6.47)$$

and hence the desired answer to the question "How many Swedes are very tall?" is (see Fig. 6)

$$q \triangleq {}^2\text{most Swedes are very tall.} \qquad (6.48)$$

To verify that p semantically entails q, we note that

$$q \rightarrow \pi_q(\rho) = \mu_{^2most}[\int_0^{200} \rho(u)\mu_{tall}^2(u)du] \qquad (6.49)$$

$$= \mu_{most}\left[\sqrt{\int_0^{200} \rho(u)\mu_{tall}^2(u)du}\right] .$$

But, by Schwarz's inequality

$$\int_0^{200} \rho(u)\mu_{tall}(u)du \leqslant \sqrt{\int_0^{200} \rho(u)\mu_{tall}^2(u)du} \ , \qquad (6.50)$$

and since μ_{most} is a monotone function, it follows that

$$\pi_p(\rho) \leqslant \pi_q(\rho) \quad \text{for all } \rho \text{ and } \mu_{tall}$$

which implies that p semantically entails q, strongly.

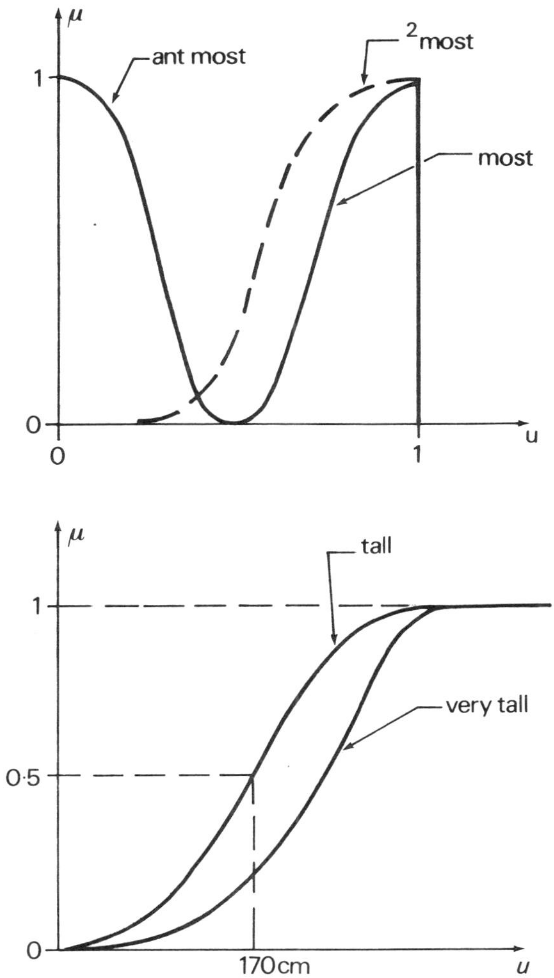

Fig. 6 – Representation of *most*, *tall* and their modifications.

Particularization and projection principles. An illustration of the application of the particularlization and projection principles is provided by the solution to the following simple problem.

Suppose that the premises are

$p \triangleq$ John is very big
$q \triangleq$ John is very tall

where big is a given fuzzy subset of $U \times V$ (that is, values of *Height* (in cms) $\times$

values of *Weight* (in kg)) and tall is a given fuzzy subset of *U*. The question is: "What is John's weight?"

Let us assume that the answer to the question is to be of the form $r \triangleq$ John is w, where w is a linguistic value of the weight of John (*heavy*, *very heavy*, *not very heavy*, etc.). Then, by employing the translation rule (4.6), the particularization principle, and the projection principle, we arrive at the retranslation relation

$$r \leftarrow Proj_{\mu \times Weight} BIG^2 [\Pi_{Height} = TALL] \qquad (6.51)$$

which expresses the answer to the posed question.

In more concrete terms, assume that the (incompletely tabulated) tables defining the fuzzy sets *BIG*, *TALL*, and *HEAVY* are of the form

BIG	Height	Weight	μ
	165	60	0.5
	170	60	0.6
	175	60	0.7
	170	65	0.75
	175	65	0.8
	180	65	0.85
	170	70	0.8
	175	70	0.85
	180	70	0.9
	170	75	0.85
	175	75	0.9
	180	75	0.95
	180	80	1

TALL	Height	μ
	165	0.7
	170	0.8
	175	0.9
	180	1
	185	1

HEAVY	Weight	μ
	60	0.7
	65	0.8
	70	0.9
	75	0.95
	80	1
	85	1

On substituting these tables in (6.51) we obtain for the attribute *Weight* a possibility distribution of the (approximate) form

$$\Pi_{Weight} = 0.5/60 + 0.7/65 + 0.8/70 + 0.9/75 + 1/80 \qquad (6.52)$$

which upon retranslation (and linguistic approximation) yields the answer

$r \triangleq$ John is very heavy .

As an additional illustration, consider the following premises

$p \triangleq$ Romy lives near a small city
$q \triangleq$ Arnold lives near Romy

from which we wish to deduce an answer to the question "Where does Arnold live?"

Assume that the relations entering in p and q have the frames shown below.

$$NEARp \parallel City1 \mid City2 \mid \mu \mid \qquad NEARq \parallel City1 \mid City2 \mid \mu \mid$$
$$SMALL\ CITY \parallel City \mid \mu \mid$$

in which $NEARp$ and $NEARq$ refer to the relations $NEAR$ in p and q, respectively. In terms of these relations, the translations of p and q may be expressed as

$$p \to \Pi_{Location\,(Residence\,(Romy))} = Proj_{\mu \times City1} NEARp\,[\Pi_{City2} = SMALL\ CITY] \tag{6.53}$$

$$q \to \Pi_{(Location\,(Residence\,(Romy)), Location\,(Residence\,(Arnold))} = NEARq\ . \tag{6.54}$$

On substituting (6.53) in (6.54) and projecting on the attribute *Location (Residence(Arnold))*, we obtain

$$r \leftarrow Proj_{\mu \times City2} NEARq\,[\Pi_{City1} = Proj_{\mu \times City1} NEARp\,[\Pi_{City2} = SMALL\ CITY]] \tag{6.55}$$

as an expression for the answer to the posed question.

Compositional rule of inference. The compositional rule of inference is particularly convenient to use when the variables involved in the premises range over finite sets or can be approximated by variables ranging over such sets.

As a simple illustration, consider the premises

$p \triangleq X$ is small
$q \triangleq X$ and Y are approximately equal

in which X and Y range over the set $U = 1 + 2 + 3 + 4$, and *small* and *approximately equal* are defined by

$$\begin{aligned} small &= 1/1 + 0.6/2 + 0.2/3 \\ approximately\ equal &= 1/[(1,1) + (2,2) + (3,3) + (4,4)] \\ &\quad + 0.5/[(1,2) + (2,1) + (2,3) + (3,2) \\ &\qquad + (3,4) + (4,3)]\ . \end{aligned}$$

In terms of these sets, the translations of p and q may be expressed as

$$\begin{aligned} p &\to \Pi_X = small \\ q &\to \Pi_{(X,Y)} = approximately\ equal \end{aligned} \tag{6.56}$$

and thus from p and q we may infer r, where

$$r \leftarrow \Pi_X \circ \Pi_{(X,Y)} = small \circ approximately\ equal\ . \tag{6.57}$$

The composition of *small* and *approximately equal* can readily be performed by computing the max-min product of the relation matrices corresponding to *small* and *approximately equal*. Thus, we obtain

$$[1 \quad 0.6 \quad 0.2 \quad 0] \circ \begin{bmatrix} 1 & 0.5 & 0 & 0 \\ 0.5 & 1 & 0.5 & 0 \\ 0 & 0.5 & 1 & 0.5 \\ 0 & 0 & 0.5 & 1 \end{bmatrix} = [1 \quad 0.6 \quad 0.5 \quad 0.2]$$

which implies that

$$\Pi_Y = \Pi_X \circ \Pi_{(X,Y)} = 1/1 + 0.6/2 + 0.5/3 + 0.2/4$$

and which upon retranslation yields the linguistic approximation

$$r \triangleq Y \text{ is more or less small} \leftarrow \Pi_Y = 1/1 + 0.6/2 + 0.5/3 + 0.2/4 \; .$$

Thus, from $p \triangleq X$ is small and $q \triangleq X$ and Y are approximately equal, we can infer, approximately, that $r \triangleq Y$ is more or less small.

As a simple illustration of the compositional *modus ponens*, assume that, as in Bellman and Zadeh (1976),

$$\begin{aligned} U &= V = 1 + 2 + 3 + 4 \\ F &= 0.2/2 + 0.6/3 + 1/4 \\ G &= 0.6/2 + 1/3 + 0.5/4 \\ H &= 1/2 + 0.6/3 + 0.2/4 \end{aligned}$$

with

$$\begin{aligned} & p \triangleq X \text{ is } F \rightarrow \Pi_X = F \\ & q \triangleq \text{If } X \text{ is } G \text{ then } Y \text{ is } H \rightarrow \Pi_{(X,Y)} = \bar{G}' \oplus \bar{H} \end{aligned} \tag{6.58}$$

and

$$r \leftarrow \Pi_Y = F \circ (\bar{G}' \oplus \bar{H}) \; .$$

In this case,

$$\bar{G}' \oplus \bar{H} = \begin{bmatrix} 1 & 1 & 1 & 1 \\ 0.4 & 1 & 1 & 0.6 \\ 0 & 1 & 0.6 & 0.6 \\ 0.5 & 1 & 1 & 0.7 \end{bmatrix}$$

and

$$\bar{F} \circ (\bar{G}' \oplus \bar{H}) = [0 \quad 0.2 \quad 0.6 \quad 1] \circ \begin{bmatrix} 1 & 1 & 1 & 1 \\ 0.4 & 1 & 1 & 0.6 \\ 0 & 1 & 0.6 & 0.6 \\ 0.5 & 1 & 1 & 0.7 \end{bmatrix}$$

$$= [0.5 \quad 1 \quad 1 \quad 0.7] \; .$$

Thus, from p and q we can infer that

$$r \triangleq Y \text{ is } 0.5/1 + 1/2 + 1/3 + 0.7/4 \; .$$

The above example is intended merely to illustrate the computations involved in the application of the compositional *modus ponens* when X and Y range over finite sets. Detailed discussions of practical applications of the compositional rule of inference in the design of so-called fuzzy logic controllers may be found in the papers by Mamdani and Assilian (1975), Mamdani (1976a,b), Kickert and van Nauta Lemke (1976), Rutherford and Bloore (1975), and others given in the References and Bibliography.

7. CONCLUDING REMARK

The theory of approximate reasoning outlined in this paper may be viewed as an attempt at an accommodation with the pervasive imprecision of the real world.

Based as it is on fuzzy logic, approximate reasoning lacks the depth and universality of precise reasoning. And yet it may well prove to be more effective than precise reasoning in coming to grips with the complexity and ill-definedness of humanistic systems, and thus may contribute to the conception and development of intelligent systems which could approach the remarkable ability of the human mind to make rational decisions in the face of uncertainty and imprecision.

Acknowledgements

This research was supported by the National Science Foundation Grant MC76-06693, the Naval Electronic Systems Command Contract N000 39-77-C-0022, and the U.S. Army Research Office Grant DAHCO4-75-G0056.

REFERENCES AND BIBLIOGRAPHY

Adams, E. W. and Levine, H. P. (1975). On the uncertainties transmitted from premises to conclusions in deductive inferences, *Synthese*, **30**, 429–460.

Aizerman, M. A. (1976). Fuzzy sets, fuzzy proofs and certain unsolved problems in the theory of automatic control, *Avtomatika i Telemehanika*, 171–177.

Bar-Hillel, Y. (1964). *Language and Information*. Reading, Mass.: Addison-Wesley.

Bellman, R. E. and Zadeh, L. A. (1976). Local and fuzzy logics, Electronics Research Laboratory *Memorandum M-584*, University of California, Berkeley. Also in *Modern Uses of Multiple-Valued Logics* (ed. D. Epstein). Dordrecht: D. Reidel.

Bezdek, J. C. (1974). Numerical taxonomy with fuzzy sets, *Journal of Mathematical Biology*, **1**, 57–71.

Bezdek, J. C. and Dunn, J. C. (1975). Optimal fuzzy partitions: a heuristic for estimating the parameters in a mixture of normal distributions, *IEEE Transactions on Computers*, **C-24**, 835–838.

Black, M. (1963). Reasoning with loose concepts, *Dialogue*, **2**, 1–12.

Bobrow, D. and Collins, A. (eds.) (1975). *Representation and Understanding*. New York: Academic Press.

Chang, S. K. and Ke, J. S. (1976), Database skeleton and its application to fuzzy query translation, *Research Memorandum*. Chicago: Department of Information Engineering, University of Illinois, Chicago Circle.

Chang, S. S. L. (1972). Fuzzy mathematics, man and his environment, *IEEE Transactions on Systems, Man and Cybernetics*, **SMC-2**, 92–93.

Cresswell, M. J. (1973), *Logics and Languages*. London: Methuen.

Damerau, F. J. (1975). On fuzzy adjectives, *Memorandum RC 5340*, Yorktown Heights, NY: IBM Research Laboratory.

Davidson, D. (1967). Truth and meaning, *Synthese*, **17**, 304–323.

DeLuca, A. and Termini, S. (1972). A definition of a nonprobabilistic entropy in the setting of fuzzy sets theory, *Information and Control*, **20**, 301–312.

Dimitrov, V. D. (1975). Efficient governing humanistic systems by fuzzy instructions, *Third International Congress of General Systems and Cybernetics*, Bucharest.

Dreyfuss, G. R., Kochen, M., Robinson, J. and Badre, A. N. (1975). On the psycholinguistic reality of fuzzy sets. *Functionalism* (eds Grossman, R. E., San, L. J. and Vance, T. J.). Chicago: University of Chicago Press.

Evans, G. and McDowell, J. (1976). *Truth and Meaning*. Oxford: Clarendon Press.

Fellinger, W. L. (1974). *Specifications for a fuzzy systems modelling language*. Ph.D. dissertation. Corvallis: Oregon State University.

Fine, K. (1975), Vagueness, truth and logic, *Synthese*, **30**, 265–300.

Fodor, J. A. and Katz, J. J. (eds) (1964). *The Structure of Language*. Englewood Cliffs, N.J.: Prentice-Hall.

Gaines, B. R. (1975). Stochastic and fuzzy logics, *Electronics Letters*, **11**, 444–445.

Gaines, B. R. (1976a), General fuzzy logics, *Proceedings of the Third European Meeting on Cybernetics and Systems Research*, Vienna.

Gaines, B. R. (1976b). Fuzzy reasoning and the logic of uncertainty, *Proceedings of the 6th International Symposium on Multiple-Valued Logic*, Utah, IEEE76CH 1111-4C, 179–188.

Gaines, B. R. (1976c). Foundations of fuzzy reasoning, *International Journal of Man-Machine Studies*, **6**, 623–668.

Gaines, B. R. and Kohout, L. J. (1975). Possible automata, *Proceedings International Symposium on Multiple-Valued Logic*, Bloomington, Indiana, 183–196.

Gaines, B. R. and Kohout, L. J. (1977). The fuzzy decade: a bibliography of fuzzy systems and closely related topics, *International Journal of Man-Machine Studies*, **9**, 1–68.

Giles, R. (1976). Lukasiewicz logic and fuzzy set theory, *International Journal of Man-Machine Studies*, **8**, 313–327.

Goguen, J. A. (1969). The logic of inexact concepts, *Synthese*, **19**, 325–373.

Goguen, J. A. (1974). Concept representation in natural and artificial languages: axioms, extension and applications for fuzzy sets, *International Journal of Man-Machine Studies*, **6**, 513–561.

Gottinger, H. W. (1973). Toward a fuzzy reasoning in the behavioral science, *Cybernetica*, **2**, 113–135.

Haack, S. (1974). *Deviant Logic*. Cambridge: Cambridge University Press.

Hamacher, H. (1976). On logical connectives of fuzzy statements and their affiliated truth functions, *Proceedings of the Third European Meeting on Cybernetics and Systems Research*, Vienna.

Harris, J. I. (1974a). Fuzzy implication – comments on a paper by Zadeh, *DOAE Research Working Paper*. Byfleet, Surrey: Ministry of Defence.

Harris, J. I. (1974b). Fuzzy sets: how to be imprecise precisely, *DOAE Research Working Paper*. Byfleet, Surrey: Ministry of Defence.

Hendrix, G. G., Thompson, C. W. and Slocum, J. (1973). Language processing via canonical verbs and semantic models, *Proceedings of the Third Joint International Conference on Artificial Intelligence*, pp. 262-269. Menlo Park, Ca.: Stanford Research Institute.

Hersh, H. M. and Caramazza, A. (1976). A fuzzy set approach to modifiers and vagueness in natural language, *Journal of Experimental Psychology*, **105**, 254–276.

Hughes, G. E. and Cresswell, M. J. (1968). *An Introduction to Modal Logic*. London: Methuen.

Inagaki, Y. and Fukumura, F. (1975). On the description of fuzzy meaning of context-free language. *Fuzzy Sets and Their Applications to Cognitive and Decision Processes*, pp. 301–328 (eds Zadeh, L. A., Fu, K. S., Tanaka, K. and Shimura, M.) New York: Academic Press.

Jouault, J. P. and Luan, P. M. (1975). Application des concepts flous a la programmation en languages quasi-naturals. *Research Memorandum.* Paris: Inst. Inf. d'Enterprise, C.N.A.M.

Kandel, A. (1974). On the minimization of incompletely specified fuzzy functions, *Information and Control*, **26**, 141–153.

Kaufmann, A. (1973). *Introduction to the Theory of Fuzzy Subsets*, Vol. 1. *Elements of Basic Theory*. Paris: Masson and Co.; (1975), Vol. 2. *Applications to Linguistics, Logic and Semantics*. Paris: Masson and Co., (1975), Vol. 3. *Applications to Classification and Pattern Recognition, Automata and Systems, and Choice of Criteria.* Paris: Masson and Co. Also English translation of Vol. 1, New York: Academic Press (1975).

Kickert, W. J. M. and van Nauta Lemke, H. R. (1976). Application of a fuzzy controller in a warm water plant, *Automatica*, **12**, 301–308.

Kling, R. (1974). Fuzzy PLANNER: reasoning with inexact concepts in a procedural problem-solving language, *Journal of Cybernetics*, **4**, 105–122.

Knuth, D. E. (1968), Semantics of context-free languages, *Mathematical Systems Theory*, **2**, 127–145.

Kochen, M. and Badre, A. N. (1974). On the precision of adjectives which denote fuzzy sets, *Journal of Cybernetics*, **4**, 49–59.

Lakoff, G. (1973a). Hedges: a study in meaning criteria and the logic of fuzzy concepts, *Journal of Philosophical Logic*, **2**, 458–508. Also paper presented at 8th Regional Meeting of Chicago Linguistic Society (1972) and *Contemporary Research in Philosophical Logic and Linguistic Semantics*, pp. 221–271 (eds Hockney, D., Harper, W. and Freed, B.). The Netherlands: D. Reidel.

Lakoff, G. (1973b). Fuzzy grammar and the performance/competence terminology game, *Proceedings of Meeting of Chicago Linguistics Society*, 271–291.

Lee, E. T. and Chang, C. L. (1971). Some properties of fuzzy logic, *Information and Control*, **19**, 417–431.

LeFaivre, R. A. (1974a). FUZZY: a programming language for fuzzy problem solving, *Technical Report 202*. Madison: Department of Computer Science, University of Wisconsin.

LeFaivre, R. A. (1974b). The representation of fuzzy knowledge, *Journal of Cybernetics*, **4**, 57–66.

Lewis, P. M., Rosenkrantz, D. J. and Stearns, R. E. (1974). Attributed translations, *Journal of Computer and System Science*, **9**, 279–307.

Lyndon, R. C. (1966). *Notes on Logic*. New York: D. Van Nostrand.

Machina, K. F. (1972). Vague predicates, *American Philosophical Quarterly*, **9**, 225–233.

MacVicar-Whelan, P. J. (1975). Fuzzy sets, the concept of height and the hedge very, *Technical Memo 1*, Allendale, Michigan: Physics Department, Grand Valley State College.

Mamdani, E. H. (1976a). Application of fuzzy logic to approximate reasoning using linguistic synthesis, *Proceedings of 6th International Symposium on Multiple-Valued Logic*, Utah, IEEE76 CH1111-4C, 196–202.

Mamdani, E. H. (1976b). Advances in the linguistic synthesis of fuzzy controllers, *International Journal of Man-Machine Studies*, **8**, 669–678.

Mamdani, E. H. and Assilian, S. (1975). An experiment in linguistic synthesis with a fuzzy logic controller, *International Journal of Man-Machine Studies*, **7**, 1–13.

Marinos, P. N. (1969). Fuzzy logic and its application to switching systems, *IEEE Transactions on Electronic Computers*, **C-18**, 343–348.

Martin, W. A. (1973). Translation of English into MAPL using Winograd's syntax, state transition networks, and a semantic case grammar, *M.I.T. APG Internal Memo 11*.

Miller, G. A. and Johnson-Laird, P. N. (1976), *Language and Perception*. Cambridge, Mass.: Harvard University Press.

Minsky, M. (1975). A framework for representing knowledge. In *The Psychology of Computer Vision* (ed. Winston, P. H.). New York: McGraw Hill.

Moisil, G. C. (1975). Lectures on the logic of fuzzy reasoning, *Scientific Editions*, Bucarest.

Montague, R. (1974). *Formal Philosophy (Selected Papers)* (ed Thomason, R. H.). New Haven: Yale University Press.

Moore, J. and Newell, A. (1973). How can MERLIN understand? Pittsburgh: Department of Computer Science, Carnegie-Mellon University.

Nahmias, S. (1976). Fuzzy variables. *Technical Report 33.* Pittsburgh: Department of Industrial Engineering, Systems Management Engineering and Operations Research, University of Pittsburgh. Presented at ORSA/TIMS Meeting, Miami.

Nalimov, V. V. (1974). *Probabilistic Model of Language.* Moscow: Moscow State University.

Negoita, C. V. and Ralescu, D. A. (1975). *Applications of Fuzzy Sets to Systems Analysis.* Basel, Stuttgart: Birkhauser Verlag.

Newell, A. and Simon, H. A. (1972). *Human Problem Solving.* Englewood Cliffs, N. J.: Prentice-Hall.

Nguyen, H. T. (1976). A note on the extension principle for fuzzy sets, *Electronics Research Laboratory Memorandum M-611.* Berkeley: University of California.

Noguchi, K., Umano, M., Mizumoto, M. and Tanaka, K. (1976). Implementation of fuzzy artificial intelligence language FLOU, *Technical Report on Automation and Language of IECE.*

Norman, D. A. and Rumelhart, D. E. (eds) (1975). *Explorations in Cognition.* San Francisco: W. H. Freeman Co.

Ostegaard, J. J. (1976). Fuzzy logic control of a heat exchanger process, *Publication No. 7601.* Lyngby: Technical University of Denmark.

Pal, S. K. and Majumdar, D. D. (1977). Fuzzy sets and decision-making approaches in vowel and speaker recognition, *IEEE Transactions of Systems, Man, and Cybernetics,* **SMC-7**, 625–629.

Procyk, T. J. (1976). Linguistic representation of fuzzy variables, *Fuzzy Logic Working Group.* London: Queen Mary College.

Putman, H. (1976). *Meaning and Truth.* Sherman Lectures. London: University College.

Rescher, N. (1969). *Many-Valued Logic.* New York: McGraw-Hill.

Rieger, B. (1976). Fuzzy structural semantics, *Proceedings of 3rd European Meeting on Cybernetics and Systems Research*, Vienna.

Rieger, C. (1976). An organization of knowledge for problem solving and language comprehension, *Artificial Intelligence*, **7**, 89–127.

Rutherford, G. and Bloore, G. C. (1975). The implication of fuzzy algorithms for control. Manchester: Control Systems Center, University of Manchester.

Sanchez, E. (1974). Fuzzy relations. Marseille: Faculty of Medicine, University of Marseille.

Sanford, D. H. (1975). Borderline logic, *American Philosophical Quarterly*, **12**, 29–39.

Schank, R. C. (1973). Identification of conceptualizations underlying natural language. *Computer Models of Thought and Language*, pp. 187–247 (eds Schank, R and Colby. M). Englewood Cliffs, N. J.: Prentice-Hall.

Schotch, P. K. (1975). Fuzzy modal logic, *Proceedings of International Symposium on Multiple-Valued Logic*, pp. 176–182. Bloomington: University of Indiana.

Shimura, M. (1975). An approach to pattern recognition and associative memories using fuzzy logic. *Fuzzy Sets and Their Applications to Cognitive and Decision Processes*, pp. 449–476 (eds Zadeh, L. A., Fu, K. S., Tanaka, K. and Shimura, M.). New York: Academic Press.

Shortliffe, E. H. and Buchanan, B. G. (1975). A model of inexact reasoning in medicine, *Mathematical Biosciences*, **23**, 351–379.

Simmons, R. F. (1973). Semantic networks, their computation and use for understanding English sentences. *Computer Models of Thought and Language*, pp. 63–113 (eds Schank, R. and Colby, K.). Englewood Cliffs, N. J.: Prentice–Hall.

Simon, H. A. and Siklossy, L. (1972). *Representation and Meaning: Experiments with Information Processing Systems*. Englewood Cliffs, N. J.: Prentice–Hall.

Siy, P. and Chen, C. S. (1974). Fuzzy logic for handwritten numerical character recognition, *IEEE Transactions on Systems, Man and Cybernetics*, **SMC-4**, 570–575.

Stalnaker, R. (1970). Probability and conditionals, *Philosophical Science*, **37**, 64–80.

Sugeno, M. (1974). *Theory of fuzzy integrals and its applications*, Ph.D. Dissertation, Tokyo: Tokyo Institute of Technology.

Suppes, P. (1974a). The axiomatic method in the empirical sciences, *Proceedings of Tarski Symposium*. Providence, Rhode Island: American Mathematical Society.

Suppes, P. (1974b). Probabilistic metaphysics, *Filofiska Studier nr. 22*. Uppsala: Uppsala University.

Tarski, A. (1956). *Logic, Semantics, Metamathematics*. Oxford: Clarendon Press.

Terano, T. and Sugeno, M. (1975). Conditional fuzzy measures and their applications. *Fuzzy Sets and Their Applications to Cognitive and Decision Processes*, pp. 151–170 (eds Zadeh, L. A., Fu, K. S., Tanaka, K. and Shimura, M.). New York: Academic Press.

Uragami, M., Mizumoto, M. and Tanaka, K. (1976). Fuzzy robot controls, *Journal of Cybernetics*, **6**, 39–64.

Wason, P. C. and Johnson-Laird, P. H. (1972). *Psychology of Reasoning Structure and Content.* Cambridge, Mass.: Harvard University Press.

Wechsler, H. (1975). Applications of fuzzy logic to medical diagnosis, *Proceedings of International Symposium on Multiple-Valued Logic*, pp. 162–174. Bloomington: University of Indiana.

Wenstop, F. (1975). *Application of linguistic variables in the analysis of organizations.* Ph.D. Dissertation. Berkeley: School of Business Administration, University of California.

Wenstop, F. (1976). Deductive verbal models of organizations, *International Journal of Man-Machine Studies*, 8, 293–311.

Zadeh, L. A. (1968). Probability measures of fuzzy events. *Journal of Mathematical Analysis and Applications*, **23**, 421–427.

Zadeh, L. A. (1971). Similarity relations and fuzzy orderings, *Information Sciences*, **3**, 177–200.

Zadeh, L. A. (1972a), A fuzzy-set-theoretic interpretation of linguistic hedges, *Journal of Cybernetics*, **2**, 4–34.

Zadeh, L. A. (1972b). Fuzzy languages and their relation to human and machine intelligence, *Proceedings of International Conference on Man and Computer*, Bordeaux, France, pp. 130–165. Basel: S. Karger.

Zadeh, L. A. (1973). Outline of a new approach to the analysis of complex systems and decision processes, *IEEE Transactions on Systems, Man and Cybernetics*, **SMC-3**, 28–44.

Zadeh, L. A. (1975a). Fuzzy logic and approximate reasoning (In memory of Grigore Moisil), *Synthese*, **30**, 407–428.

Zadeh, L. A. (1975b). Calculus of fuzzy restrictions. *Fuzzy Sets and Their Applications to Cognitive and Decision Processes*, pp. 1–39 (eds. Zadeh, L. A., Fu, K. S., Tanaka, K. Shimura, M.). New York: Academic Press.

Zadeh, L. A. (1975c). The concept of a linguistic variable and its application to approximate reasoning, Part I, *Information Sciences*, **8**, 199–249; Part II, *Information Sciences*, **8**, 301–357, Part III, *Information Sciences*, **9**, 43–80.

Zadeh, L. A. (1976). A fuzzy-algorithmic approach to the definition of complex or imprecise concepts, *International Journal of Man-Machine Studies*, **8**, 249–291.

Zadeh, L. A. (1977a). Fuzzy sets as a basis for a theory of possibility, *Electronics Research Laboratory Memorandum M77/12.* Berkeley: University of California. To appear in *Fuzzy Sets and Systems.*

Zadeh, L. A. (1977b), PRUF--a language for the representation of meaning in natural languages, *Proceedings of 5th International Joint Conference on Artificial Intelligence,* 918. Pittsburgh: Department of Computer Science, Carnegie-Mellon University.

Zadeh, L. A., Fu, K. S., Tanaka, K. and Shimura, M. (1975). *Fuzzy Sets and Their Application to Cognitive and Decision Processes.* New York: Academic Press.

Zimmermann, H. J. (1974). Optimization in fuzzy environments, Institute for Operations Research. Aachen: Technical University of Aachen.

SEARCH AND PROBLEM SOLVING

8

Application of Heuristic Problem-solving Methods in Computer Communcation Networks

S. I. Samoylenko
Council of Cybernetics
USSR Academy of Sciences, Moscow, USSR

Abstract

This paper considers heuristic procedures for deriving suboptimal solutions of complex discrete optimization problems for which no workable methods of obtaining optimal solutions are available.

The main emphasis is focused on methods for modifying heuristic search procedures in order to improve their problem solving performance in terms of selecting solutions closer to optimal ones.

The techniques discussed include fuzzy heuristics, adaptive compositions of heuristics, and suboptimal algorithms based on dynamic programming concepts. These techniques are illustrated by examples and experimental computer implementation results.

The results obtained demonstrate that the application of the above methods produces solutions superior to those derived by means of conventional heuristic procedures and brings them sufficiently close to optimal solutions.

INTRODUCTION

It is generally known that a number of complex problems of high dimensionality, especially problems with discrete variables, are not amenable to mathematical programming methods. They either fall outside the categories of problems which can be handled by conventional methods or else do not meet practical restrictions arising from the limited speed or memory of the computers used for this purpose.

Such problems are handled by the use of suboptimal solution search techniques.

The purpose of this paper is to examine methods of search for suboptimal solutions. Section 1 discusses an heuristic search method which employs several heuristics whose performance vis-a-vis a problem of a particular class is unknown. In this situation it may be an advantage to make use of a search procedure where the contributions of individual heuristics to the solution process vary in accordance with their performance at the preceding search steps.

A possible approach to handling such problems is to build the search procedure around an adaptive composition of heuristics. Sec. 1 describes this approach and pertinent experimental results in detail.

Sec. 2 deals with the concept of fuzzy heuristics. Conventional heuristic techniques usually yield one of a range of feasible solutions, and the solution thus generated cannot be improved although it may be significantly inferior to the optimal one. Fuzzy heuristics enable the researcher to derive a class of suboptimal solutions and progressively to approach a solution that may be viewed as optimal.

The idea of using fuzzy heuristics was stimulated by the general concepts of the theory of fuzzy sets and algorithms evolved by L. A. Zadeh ('A theory of approximate reasoning', pp. 149–194 of the present volume).

Sec. 3 is concerned with the techniques for generating suboptimal algorithms which are based on the ideas of dynamic programming. It has been found that dynamic programming may serve for a broad class of problems as a workable tool of optimal solution search. However, dynamic programming is often associated with a prohibitively large memory requirement for storage of intermediate results and with excessive computation time.

This paper also examines methods that may be employed to simplify dynamic programming procedures by generating a class of successively improved suboptimal solutions.

1. ADAPTIVE HEURISTIC SEARCH

In the general case the search for a feasible solution $g = (g_1, g_2, \ldots, g_n)$ may be performed in M steps.

Denote the set of coordinate numbers computed at the jth step as

$$S_j = \{j_1, j_2, \ldots, j_{m_j}\}, \; j = 1, 2, \ldots M$$

and assume that

$$\bigcup_j S_j = \{1, 2, \ldots n\}, \quad \bigcap_j S_j = \phi.$$

The subset of coordinates determined at the jth step will be defined as

$$\bar{g}_j = \{g_{j1}, g_{j2}, \ldots, g_{jm_j}\}$$

and called the jth local solution.

Step-by-step solution search may be illustrated by successive computation of the coordinates of the vector g when

$$M = n, \quad m_j = 1, \quad j = 1, 2, \ldots, M.$$

For the sake of simplicity the discussion that follows will be restricted to the above situation, although the method is extendable to a more general case.

It will be assumed that at each search step the value of g_j may be selected from a finite set G_j which contains N_j distinct solutions

$$G_j = \{g_1^j, g_2^j, \ldots g_{N_j}^j\}.$$

The set G_j will be defined as the set of local solutions at the jth step.

In the general case the set G_j may depend on the selection of solutions at the preceding steps; that is, on

$$g_1, g_2, \ldots g_{j-1}.$$

The entire set of all possible solutions $G = \bigcup_j G_j = \{g_1, g_2, \ldots, g_N\}$ will be called a generalized set of local solutions. When selecting the next local solution the current state of the system is determined by the results of the solution process at the previous steps. At the first step the system is in its initial state. At the second step the number of possible states becomes equal to N_1, as from its initial state the system may have passed into any one of the N_1 new states, associated with the set of feasible solutions G_1. At the third step the number of possible states grows to $N_1 N_2$, and in the general case at the jth step the number of possible states is defined as

$$L_j = \prod_{i=1}^{j-1} N_i \,.$$

Thus the state of the system at the jth step is the product of the entire history of the solution search process. However, the number of possible states to be examined may become excessively large, and must therefore be reduced to a certain maneagable limit.

This is achieved by using the method most appropriate for the problem to be dealt with.

Thus for the travelling salesman problem the number of possible states may be restricted to the number of the salesman's possible locations. The history of his progress to a given point is disregarded. If a more detailed description of a particular state is required the past performance of the system at one or more steps may also be reviewed.

In the general case it will be assumed that at any search step the system may be in any one of the L_0 possible states.

It will also be assumed that if the system is in the kth state, local solutions are selected by using an ensemble of hypotheses (heuristics) defined by vectors

$$\Gamma_S = (C_{S1}^k, C_{S2}^k, \ldots C_{SN}^k), k = 1, 2, \ldots L_0; S = 1, 2, \ldots Z.$$

The values of components C_{Si}^{k} indicate whether the choice of the solution g_i as suggested by this hypothesis has been appropriate, provided the system is in the kth state.

We shall suppose that the computation procedure for C_{Si}^{k} is such that $C_{Si_1}^{k} > C_{Si_2}^{k}$ if in accordance with Γ_S the solution g_{i_1} for the kth state has some advantage over g_{i_2}.

The components C_{Si}^{k} will be termed local criteria.

The impact of specific hypotheses Γ_S may vary from problem to problem depending on specific problem parameters, or from one system state to another. The adaptive procedure is intended for generating efficient compositions of heuristics for different system states, that are likely to yield suboptimal solutions. Typically, the adaptive procedure described above may be set up by varying the contributions of specific hypotheses as the procedure learns from its experience at the previous search steps.

This method may be implemented in the following manner. We shall compute local criteria C_{Si}^{k} associated with the Sth hypothesis such that

$$0 \leqslant C_{Si}^{k} \leqslant 1 ,$$

if the Sth hypothesis suggests that the ith solution in the kth state of the system is appropriate;

$$C_{Si}^{k} < 0 ,$$

if the Sth hypothesis does not suggest the ith solution;

$$C_{Si}^{k} = C^* > 1 ,$$

if the problem as formulated rules out the ith solution in the kth state.

Assume that in examining feasible local solutions, the recommendations of heuristic hypotheses at the jth search step when the system is in the kth state are presented as positive numbers $\hat{C}_{Si}^{kj}$ which satisfy $\hat{C}_{Si_1}^{kj} < \hat{C}_{Si_2}^{kj}$ if in the kth state g_{i_1} is preferable to g_{i_2}. Then particular local criteria related to the Sth hypothesis can be computed by using the relationship $C_{Si}^{kj} = \dfrac{\tilde{C}_S^{kj} - \hat{C}_{Si}^{kj}}{\tilde{C}_S^{kj}}$ if the ith solution is feasible, $C_{Si}^{kj} = C^*$ if the ith solution is not feasible where $\tilde{C}_S^{kj} = \dfrac{1}{N_{jk}} \sum_{i=1}^{N_{jk}} \hat{C}_{Si}^{kj}$ is the mean value of the Sth local criterion at the jth step in the kth state and N_{jk} is the number of feasible solutions at the jth search step. Then the generalized local criterion C_i^{kj} can be computed as the weighted sum of Z local criteria with weighting coefficients W_S^k

$$C_i^{kj} = \frac{1}{Z} \sum_{S=1}^{Z} W_S^k \cdot C_{Si}^{kj} \quad \text{if } C_{Si}^{kj} \neq C^* \quad \text{for no } S$$

$$C_i^{kj} = C^* \text{ if for at least one } S\ C_{Si}^{kj} = C^* .$$

Weighting coefficients may vary from +1 to −1 except zero. The selection at the jth is made in accordance with generalized local criteria with preference given to solutions for which C_i^{kj} is large. The selection procedure can be conveniently organized by using fuzzy heuristics which are discussed in Sec. 2. The solution derived after M steps is compared with the best of those obtained earlier, and the weighting coefficients are adjusted.

If the solution generated after M steps is an improvement on the record, the weighting vector is adjusted positively, that is, the weighting coefficients W_S^k are increased by ΔW_1 for those S and k which produced positive C_{Si}^{kj} for the i associated with a good result, or conversely are reduced by ΔW_2 if C_{Si}^{kj} was found to be negative.

The weighting coefficients may be adjusted in a similar manner but with the opposite sign if the procedure repeatedly yields results inferior in the sense that they do not improve the record. Such adjustment will be called negative. It enables the procedure to pass to another search area that fits the new composition of heuristic hypotheses.

This procedure was implemented in FORTRAN (TS program) and applied to the travelling salesman problem.†

The program was developed around two heuristic hypotheses for search path selection. Under one of the hypotheses the local criteria were the larger the smaller the distance between the travelling salesman's position and the ith point of his itinerary. The other hypothesis was selected such that its value C_{Si}^{kj} was the greater the smaller the sum of all distances not covered by the travelling salesman when he passed from a given location to point i.

When these hypotheses were examined individually the first was found to be more effective, and it tended to bring the solution closer to its optimum in less time.

Figure 1 illustrates the variation of weighting coefficients averaged over all search steps for a 25-point travelling salesman problem treated by Held and Karp (1962) [1]. This example demonstrates that the adaptation procedure enhanced the impact of the first, more effective hypothesis. Though the initial values of the mean weighting coefficients were all equal to 0.1, after several search steps they became significantly different from one another. Moreover, a more detailed examination revealed that for a number of points the coefficients of the second hypothesis were invariably larger than those for the first. It may therefore be concluded that the most efficient search procedure can best be set up by using a composition of rationally selected hypotheses.

2. FUZZY HEURISTICS

This section discusses a solution search procedure for discrete problems which relies on the use of less rigid, or fuzzy, heuristic rules [2].

The procedure is implemented through controlled expansion of the search

†The author acknowledges the assistance of E. I. Tretyakova in debugging the program and in its experimental study.

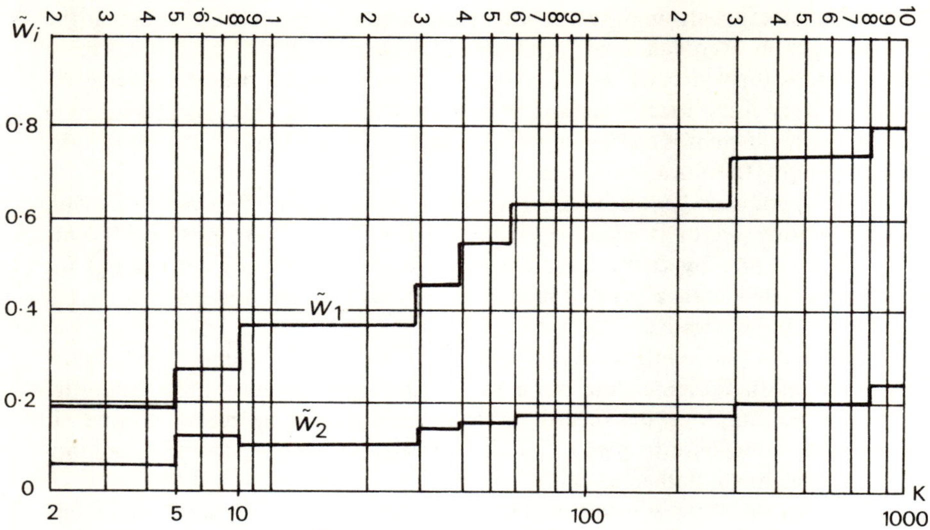

Fig. 1 – Adjustment of weighting coefficients in adaptive search: k – number of steps; $\tilde{W}_i$ – mean values of weighting coefficients.

area circumscribed by heuristics, while the extent of the fuzziness of the area may be varied to meet the search time limit or other constraints.

For further discussion we shall make use of a measure of proximity or separation between local solutions. This distance may be measured in different ways, and we shall be concerned with such separation estimates which include an assessment of the fit between local solutions derived in accordance with some heuristic.

Suppose that the local solutions at the jth step of the search procedure are defined by the generalized vector of local criteria

$$C^j = (C_1^j, C_2^j, \ldots, C_N^j)$$

Then the distance between two feasible local solutions g_i and g_k for which $C_i^j, C_k^j \neq C^*$ may be written as

$$d\,(g_i, g_k) = |\,C_i^j - C_k^j\,|.$$

The solution g_{i_0} is said to be closest if for every l for which $C_{i_l}^j \neq C^*$ the relation $C_{i_0}^j \geqslant C_{i_l}^j$ holds.

The entire ensemble of local solutions S_Δ will be referred to as a Δ neighbourhood if for all feasible local solutions $g_\Delta \in S_\Delta$ the condition $d(g_{i_0}, g_\Delta) \leqslant \Delta$ remains valid.

We shall now proceed to discuss conventional and fuzzy solution search procedures.

Unambiguous selection of local solutions

Unambiguous selection is achieved by choosing at each search step a solution g_{i_0} viewed as a local solution.

If some steps are associated with several closest local solutions one of these is selected. The above procedure is employed for conventional heuristic search. Thus when applied to the travelling salesman problem, using the heuristic hypothesis of passage to the nearest point, the procedure will produce a single solution suggested by the heuristic.

The section below discusses techniques for search area expansion.

Deterministic expansion

In this case the Δ neighbourhood at each search step is selected so that it contains a specified number of points. Search of feasible suboptimal solutions reduces to an examination of all possible alternatives, local solutions being taken from the Δ neighbourhood.

Given more time for solution search, the Δ neighbourhood may be successively expanded.

Solution search based on deterministic expansion requires an orderly procedure for examining feasible solutions and storing information about examined solutions in the computer memory. In certain situations these conditions may become unacceptable because of the prohibitively large computer memory requirement. They may be eased by using a random procedure for selecting local solutions contained in the Δ neighbourhood.

Probabilistic expansion

To select a local solution at the jth step the vector of local criteria $C^j = (C_1^j, C_2^j, \ldots C_N^j)$ is transformed into a discrete local distribution.

$$p^j = (p_1^j, p_2^j, \ldots P_N^j)$$

whose components satisfy

$$0 \leqslant p_i^j \leqslant 1, i = 1, 2, \ldots N$$

$$\sum_{i=1}^{N} p_i^j = 1.$$

A procedure for transforming C^j into p^j must meet the following conditions:

1. The closest point g_{i_0} must be associated with the largest p_{i_0}.
2. If $d(g_{i_0}, g_k) < d(g_{i_0}, g_l)$ $\quad p_k^j > p_l^j$.
3. If $d(g_{i_0}, g_k) = d(g_{i_0}, g_l)$ then $p_k^j = p_l^j$.
4. If g_m is not a feasible solution at the jth step, that is, $C_m = C^*$, then $p_m^j = 0$.

With the vector of local criteria transformed into a local distribution a local solution is selected at random such that the probability of selecting g_k is p_k^j.

Several procedures for transforming C^j into p^j meet the above conditions. By way of example we may consider the transformation procedure in accordance with the following algorithm:

$$1.\quad \tilde{p}_k^j = \begin{cases} B^{C_k^j} & \text{if} \quad C_k^j \neq C^* \\ 0 & \text{if} \quad C_k^j = C^* \end{cases}$$

$$2.\quad p_\Sigma = \sum_{k=1}^{N} \tilde{p}_k^j$$

$$3.\quad p_k^j = \tilde{p}_k^j / p_\Sigma$$

where B is the transformation base, $B \geqslant 1$.

If we take $B = 1$, all non-zero components of the local distribution will have the same value, which implies equiprobable selection of a local solution out of all feasible ones. As B grows, the neighbourhood where the selection is made contracts progressively because increasingly greater preference is accorded to solutions close to the nearest point g_{i_0}.

There may be other ways of modifying the Δ neighbourhood.

Let the local probability distribution at a certain search step have the form

$$p = (p_1, p_2, \ldots p_N).$$

Then the Δ neighbourhood may be changed by transforming distribution p into distribution $p' = (p'_1, p'_2, \ldots p'_N)$ by either of the following algorithms:

A.

$$1.\quad \tilde{p}_k = \begin{cases} p_k & \text{if} \quad p_k \geqslant p_0 \\ 0 & \text{if} \quad p_k < p_0 \end{cases}$$

$$2.\quad p_\Sigma = \sum_{k=1}^{N} \tilde{p}_k$$

$$3.\quad p'_k = \tilde{p}_k / p_\Sigma$$

where p_0 is a threshold value which restricts the Δ neighbourhood, $0 \leqslant p_0 \leqslant p_{\max}$, $p_{\max} = \max_k \{p_k\}$

B.

1. $\widetilde{p}_k = p_k^L$

2. $p_\Sigma = \sum_{k=1}^{N} \widetilde{p}_k$

3. $p'_k = \widetilde{p}_k / p_\Sigma$,

where L is the contraction factor of the Δ neighbourhood.

If the first transformation is applied, the Δ neighbourhood becomes progressively smaller with the growth of p_0, and converges to a single solution when $p_0 = p_{\max}$.

In the second case the Δ neighbourhood shrinks as L grows, and expands as L decreases. When $L = 0$ all feasible local solutions become equiprobable.

The search procedure may be performed by successively reducing L, that is, by progressively expanding the Δ neighbourhood.

It will be noted that search efficiency, that is, the rate of approaching an optimal solution, is largely dependent on the choice of heuristics. However, even for the worst possible choice this procedure is bound to yield an optimal solution in a finite number of steps. No such guarantee is provided by conventional heuristic search procedures applied to a rightly limited search area.

Several examples are considered below.

Example 1. Construction of a ring network.
The problem of setting up the shortest ring communication line running through all points of a network is identical with the classic travelling salesman problem. We shall now discuss experimental results obtained by applying the method of fuzzy heuristics to this problem.

The degree of fuzziness in the heuristic search procedure was controlled by means of probabilistic expansion of the second type with a variable parameter L.

Figure 2 illustrates the performance of the TS program for a 25-point travelling salesman problem [1]. The diagram shows search time, or the number of search steps, versus variations of the efficiency criteria, that is, path length.

The upper wavy line shows the results obtained by equiprobable random choice of paths, while the lower shaded area sets the lower limit which corresponds to the expected optimal result [1].

The broken lines demonstrate the rate of approaching the optimal result for different degrees of fuzziness defined by the parameter L.

Given large L, the heuristics significantly limit the search area, and the procedure repeatedly generates similar results (marked by little crosses).

For smaller L, that is, greater fuzziness, the initial portion of the curve slopes more slowly. However, after some time the program can yield results superior to the ones obtained for large L.

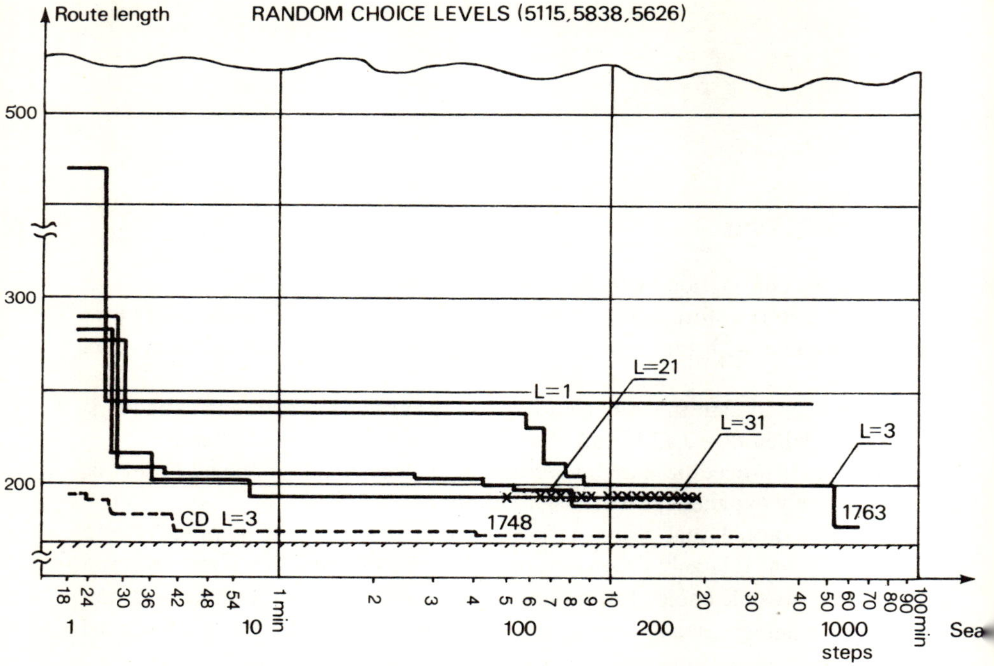

Fig. 2 – TS program performance for heuristics of variable fuzziness (L – factor of fuzziness), CD – suboptimal dynamic programming, x – repeating results.

It appears that for each period T there exists an optimal value of L which yields the best results. Thus for the example under discussion the best result for a search period of one minute is obtained by using slightly fuzzy heuristics ($L = 31$). For $T = 10$ min. and $T = 60$ min the best results are given by $L = 21$ and $L = 3$ respectively.

Example 2. Design of a computer network with multi-point communication lines.

As another example of the application of fuzzy heuristics we may consider solution search in problems associated with structural design of computer networks with multi-point communication lines and specified constraints on the number of points that may be connected to any one line.

The problem is formulated as follows.

We have the coordinates of terminal sites and of the location of a terminal concentrator. The terminals are connected to the concentrator via communication lines, and any line may pass through not more than a preassigned number of terminal sites. The designer should configure the communication lines in a way that would minimize the total length of the links which connect the terminals with the concentrator.

This problem is usually handled by means of an heuristic algorithm, for example, Prim's algorithm [5]. The connection network is successively expanded by coupling the nearest points to the initial configuration. If no constraints are placed on the number of points connected to any one line the algorithm produces a minimal length connection pattern. Conversely, in the presence of such constraints the solution may be inferior to an optimal one.

To bring the solution closer to the optimum the designer may use fuzzy heuristics for search in the neighbourhood of the solution suggested by the heuristic employed at the preceding steps.

Example 3. Heuristic routing in packet-switching networks.

In a packet-switching network node the transmission route is selected by using information on the current state of the network, and the packet is sent via the route for which the expected transmission delay is minimal at the time the routing decision is made.

If the network remained unchanged this procedure would indeed guarantee the least transmission time. However the state of the network changes continuously, and transmission via the route for which the transmission delay has been estimated to be minimal is not always the best possible choice.

In a variety of situations it is useful to have several alternative routes available for transmission of packets addressed to a particular destination.

A set of such alternative routes may be organized by means of procedures based on fuzzy heuristics, provided that the initial information on the status of the system and route distribution in terms of expected transmission delays is viewed as heuristic recommendations.

A comprehensive heuristic recommendation may be based on a composition of several specific recommendations.

1. Preference should be given to routes with the least transmission delay (a priori information).
2. Preference should be given to routes with least traffic (current information on the state of the network).

These recommendations, when combined, make it possible to identify the shortest routes with the lowest traffic loads.

3. SUBOPTIMAL DYNAMIC PROGRAMMING

Dynamic programming developed by R. Bellman is essentially based on partial successive optimization in progressively expanded solution search areas. A search area is presented as a sequence of expanded areas embedded in one another.

Although dynamic programming concepts are straightforward its practical application is associated with appreciable difficulties. Such difficulties are due not only to the absence of sufficiently general algorithms applicable to a broad spectrum of problems but also to a very rapid growth of the computer time requirement for problems of high dimensionality. The complexity of the procedure is significantly dependent on the number of problem variables and the range of the values they can assume.

Moreover, the possibilities of dynamic programming when applied to practical problems are further restricted by the high memory requirement for storing intermediate computations [3, 4].

This section discusses a method for reducing computer time and memory requirements by giving up optimal solution search in favour of a procedure that yields suboptimal solutions which may be progressively optimized as more computer time is made avialable for the search.

The procedure will be presented with the travelling salesman problem used as an illustration.

The problem is stated as follows. Consider $n + 1$ towns with the distances between them defined by the matrix

$$C = \| C_{ij} \|_{i,j}^{n} = 0.$$

The solution of the problem is the shortest closed route which passes through each town once.

We shall now consider ways of reducing computer time and memory requirements by generating a series of suboptimal solutions rather than seeking to derive an optimal one.

Assume that before the kth step we know the set of points $i_0, i_1, \ldots i_{k-1}$ and a suboptimal route of travel from the starting point i_0 to point i_{k-1} such that

$$S_{k-1}\ (i_0, i_1, i_2, \ldots i_{k-1}).$$

Let us further suppose that we can make use of a procedure for selecting the kth point included in the route at the kth step.

Then the procedure for generating the suboptimal route S_k may be defined in the following manner.

Compute

$$f_k(i_0, i_1, \ldots i_k) = \min \{[C_{i_0 i_k} + C_{i_k i_1} + Z(i_1, i_{k-1})], \\ [Z(i_0, i_1) + C_{i_1 i_k} + C_{i_k i_2} + Z(i_2, i_{k+1})], \ldots [Z(i_0, i_{k-1}) + C_{i_{k-1} i_k}]\}$$

where $Z(i_j, i_l)$ is the length of the suboptimal route $S_{k-1}\ (i_0, i_1, \ldots i_{k-1})$ from point i_j to $i_l, j < l$.

Let the minimum value of $f_k\ (i_0, i_1, \ldots i_k)$ be associated with the permutation

$$S'_k\ (i_0, i_1, \ldots i_j, i_k, i_{j+1}, \ldots i_{k-1}).$$

It is this permutation that is the result of suboptimal route selection at the kth step.

The procedure enables us to retain "good" route links found at the previous search steps, specifically between the points i_0 and i_j and the points i_{j+1} and i_{k-1}. The route thus derived may be viewed as suboptimal.

It may be further shortened by means of local optimization through permutation of some route points.

We shall estimate the computer time and memory requirements for the above procedure.

The amount of computation at the kth step required for estimating f_k for different i_k is proportional to k, that is, equal to $C_1 \cdot k$, while the number of steps is n. The amount of computation necessary for selecting a new point of the route is taken to be proportional to the number of points not yet included at a given step in the sequence of points. Thus at the kth step

$$C_2 \cdot (n - k + 1).$$

The total amount of computation is given by

$$p'_{\Sigma} = \sum_{k=1}^{n} [C_1 \cdot k + C_2 \cdot (n - k + 1)] = C(n^2 + n),$$

where $C = \dfrac{C_1 + C_2}{2}$ is a constant.

Thus the amount of computation grows approximately as $n^2 + n$, and increases with n not nearly as fast as in optimal solution search.

Practically no additional memory is required for storing intermediate results.

The procedure of search for a new suboptimal solution can be formulated as follows. If a sequence $S_{k-1}(i_0, i_1, \ldots i_{k-1})$ is considered to be suboptimal and therefore "good", it can be assumed that either of the two parts obtained by dividing S_{k-1} is also "good". If a new point i_k is included in the sequence S_{k-1}, local optimization is achieved by selecting the position of i_k between the two subsequences of S_{k-1} such as to make the total route length minimal.

We shall now examine some procedures for selecting new points. Suppose that we have at our disposal heuristics that select "good" new points for the sequence by taking advantage of an assessment of certain local criteria. One such criterion for the travelling salesman problem may be the distance between the terminal point of the route that has been travelled and each point that has not yet been passed. Here we can use as a heuristic the recommendation to pass to the nearest point. Selection of points to be included in the sequence at each step will then involve the amount of computation proportional to the number of points not yet passed.

Another illustration is the heuristic for selecting the point i_k which satisfies the relationship

$$f_k(i_0, i_1, \ldots i_k) = \min_{i_k \epsilon A} \min_{i_k} \{ Z(i_0, i_j) + C_{i_j i_k} + C_{i_k i_{j+1}} + Z(i_{j+1}, i_{k-1}) \},$$

where A is the set of all points not yet passed, and i_j is the position in the derived sequence which precedes the point i_k, $0 \leqslant j \leqslant k-1$, under examination.

The amount of computation is then proportional to the number of positions which may be occupied by the point i_k times the number of all such possible points; that is, the number of points not yet passed.

The amount of computation at the kth step is given by $Ck(n-k+1)$. The total amount of computation in this case is defined as

$$p''_{\Sigma} = \sum_{k=1}^{n} C(nk - k^2 + k) = \frac{C}{6}(n^3 + 3n^2 + 2n).$$

In summary, fuzzy heuristics may be used to generate a class of suboptimal solutions and successively approach an optimal solution. The method does not require any additional memory for intermediate computations, which is its principle advantage.

The suboptimal dynamic programming procedure described in Sec. 3 was implemented in a version of the TS program.

Each successive point of the route was selected by using fuzzy heuristics and specifically the heuristic hypotheses discussed above. Once such a point had been selected the local optimum for its position on the suboptimal route was computed.

The performance of the program is shown in Figure 2 by the dotted line. Otherwise the program was identical to the algorithm discussed in Sec. 2. It demonstrates that suboptimal dynamic programming may serve as an effective tool for handling combinatorial optimization problems.

REFERENCES

[1] M. Held and T. M. Karp (1962). A dynamic programming approach to sequencing problems. *J. Soc. Indust. and Appl. Math.* **10**, No. 1, 196–210.

[2] S. I. Samoylenko (1975). Fuzzy heuristics. Paper presented at the 4th International Conference on Artificial Intelligence (IJCAI-75). Tbilisi, USSR (in Russian).

[3] I. N. Lyashenko, E. A. Karagalova, M. B. Chernikova and N. V. Shor (1975). *Linear and Non-Linear Programming.* Kiev. (in Russian).

[4] J. F. Shamblin and C. T. Stevens (1974). *Operations Research.* New York: McGraw-Hill.

[5] R. C. Prim (1957). Shortest connection networks and some generalisations. *Bell System. Tech. J.* **36**, 1389–1401.

9

A Computational Problem-solver

E. H. Tyugu
Institute of Cybernetics, Estonian Academy of Sciences
Tallinn, USSR

Abstract
A program is discussed which is capable of solving complex computational problems. The general idea of the program is to reduce the search needed in problem solving. For this purpose the following techniques are used: (1) semantic models tailored in a special way to fit the problems to be solved, (2) procedural representation of relations in the semantic models; (3) synthesizing a particular solving algorithm for any problem to be solved. The ability of the program to solve problems is illustrated by a number of examples.

INTRODUCTION

Beginning with the early problem solvers, poor efficiency has continually restricted their useful application. Methods based on general deduction principles cease to work on practical problems because of the great amount of search needed. To reduce the search, one must either restrict the class of problems considered, or use special techniques applicable to specific problems only.

We have restricted the class of problems to computational problems, each of which can be represented by a statement of the following form: "calculate x_1, x_2, ... x_m from y_1, y_2, ... y_n, when given ⟨problem conditions⟩". We assume that problem conditions must always be presented in a natural-like language. It is the task of the solver to understand and translate the problem conditions into more formal language.

The given form of the problem statement is not as restrictive as it may look at first. Indeed, it is possible to explain in the problem conditions what is meant by any x_i and y_j. For instance, one can present a problem "calculate PROOF-OF-T from T, A_1, A_2, ... A_K when given ⟨T is a theorem, A_1, A_2, ... A_K are axioms⟩".

Though the understanding of a language is an important feature of the solver, our main interest lies in solving problems and not in understanding a language. So the linguistic part of the solver will be described in this paper only very briefly.

The implementational basis of the solver is a compiler for the problem description language UTOPIST. The compiler has been implemented on the "Minsk" and "Ryad" computers [1]. An early version of the solver was used in several computer aided design projects [2 and 3].

GENERAL DESCRIPTION

A problem can be presented to the solver in a textual form quite informally. The following is an example of an input text.

HERE ARE TANGENTIAL STRAIGHT-LINE T, CIRCLE Q AT-POINT P. LET US DENOTE K SQUARE WHICH HAS A SIDE EQUAL X-COORDINATE OF P AND AREA S. GIVEN CENTER OF Q=(Ø,Ø), A POINT OF T=(1,Ø), THE SLOPE OF T=2. CALCULATE S.

A linguistic preprocessor translates the input text into a formal problem description language, called UTOPIST. The preprocessor translates every sentence separately, first searching for delimiters and names of known notions (TANGENTIAL, STRAIGHT-LINE, etc.). These are further used as keywords for parsing and translating the sentence.

After preprocessing, the text of the given example will be as follows in UTOPIST:

```
T STRAIGHT-LINE;
Q CIRCLE;
P POINT;
TANGENTIAL
              STRAIGHT-LINE = T,
              CIRCLE = Q,
              AT-POINT = P;
K SQUARE
              SIDE = X-COORDINATE OF P,
              AREA = S;
GIVEN
              CENTER OF Q = (Ø,Ø),
              POINT OF T = (1,Ø),
              SLOPE OF T = 2;
CALCULATE S;
STOP;
```

The text in UTOPIST language is an input for a semantic processor which converts it into a semantic network and into a reduced problem statement. The semantic network is an internal representation of problem conditions which were initially given rather informally in the input text. The semantic processor uses semantic memory where the meaning of every notion such as TANGENTIAL, STRAIGHT-LINE, CIRCLES, etc. must be given.

The semantic processor builds as another output a reduced problem statement. The reduced problem statement does not contain problem conditions, as they are now represented by a semantic network. For the given example the reduced statement is:

CALCULATE S FROM CENTER OF Q, POINT OF T, SLOPE OF T.

A principal part of the solver is the planner that synthesizes an algorithm for solving the problem. At the last step the synthesized algorithm is used for calculating the results; that is, the value of the area S of the square K in the present example. The general scheme of the solver as described here is shown in Fig. 1.

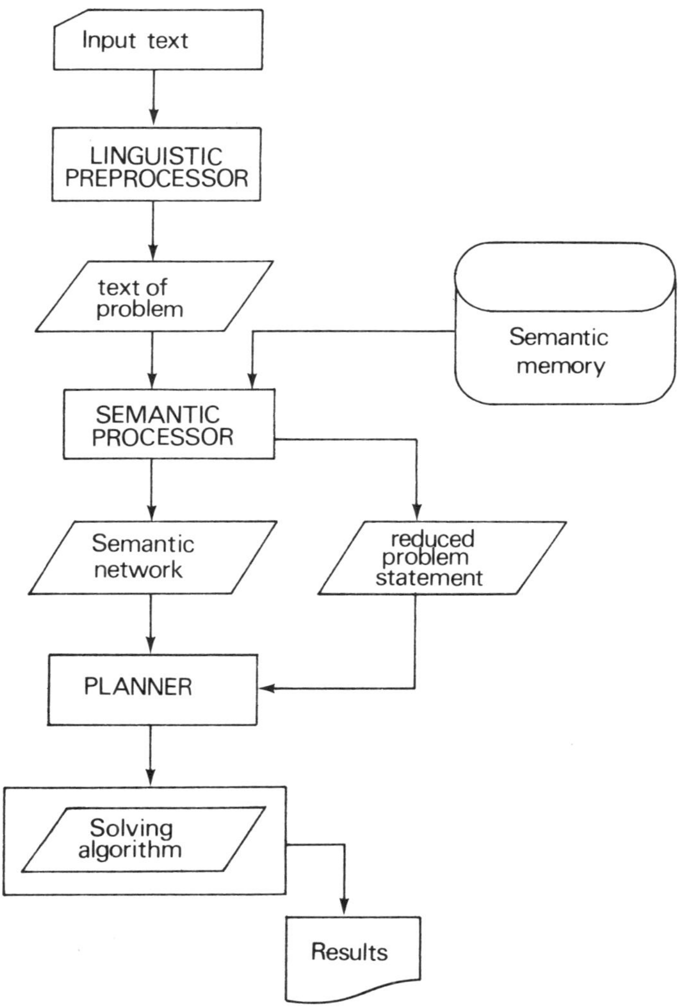

Fig. 1.

The ability of the solver to solve problems depends significantly on the contents of its semantic memory. The semantic memory is extendable, and new notions can be described to the solver in the UTOPIST language. The semantic processor is used for processing a description of a notion as shown in Fig. 2. The notion of a square that we have already used in the example can be described to the solver as follows:

```
LET SQUARE
        (SIDE, DIAGONAL, PERIMETER, AREA REAL;
         EQUATION   DIAGONAL ** 2=2 * SIDE ** 2;
         EQUATION   AREA = SIDE ** 2;
         EQUATION   PERIMETER = 4 * SIDE),
INSERT SQUARE INTO GEOMETRY:
STOP;
```

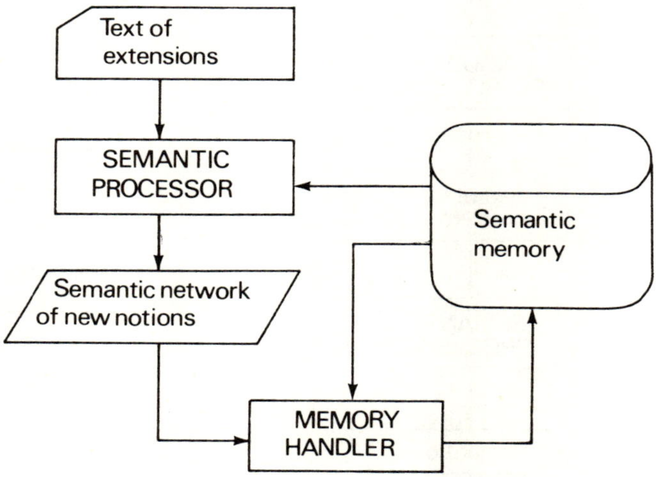

Fig. 2.

UTOPIST language

Though the solver accepts informal problem descriptions, these are immediately translated into the UTOPIST language. This language enables us to describe problem conditions as a set of objects interconnected by relations.

The main structure of UTOPIST is a declaration.

$$\langle \text{declaration} \rangle ::= \langle \text{id} \rangle \; [\; ,\langle \text{id} \rangle] \; \ldots \langle \text{type-description} \rangle$$

$$\text{type-description} ::= \left\{ \begin{array}{l} \langle \text{primary-object} \rangle \\ \langle \text{notion} \rangle \\ \left(\left\{ \begin{array}{l} \langle \text{declaration} \rangle \\ \langle \text{relation} \rangle \end{array} \right\} \; [; \left\{ \begin{array}{l} \langle \text{declaration} \rangle \\ \langle \text{relation} \rangle \end{array} \right\}] \ldots \right) \end{array} \right\}$$

The primary objects are variables of primitive types: REAL, INTEGER, LOGICAL, STRING, BINARY. So it is possible to declare:

I, J, K INTEGER,

and, using parentheses:

SQUARE (SIDE, DIAGONAL, AREA, PERIMETER REAL).

The latter is a declaration of a compound object SQUARE that consists of several components listed in parentheses.

Any declaration of a compound object contains an implicit description of a relation between the object and its components. In the present example it is the relation between SQUARE, SIDE, DIAGONAL, AREA and PERIMETER shown in Fig. 3.

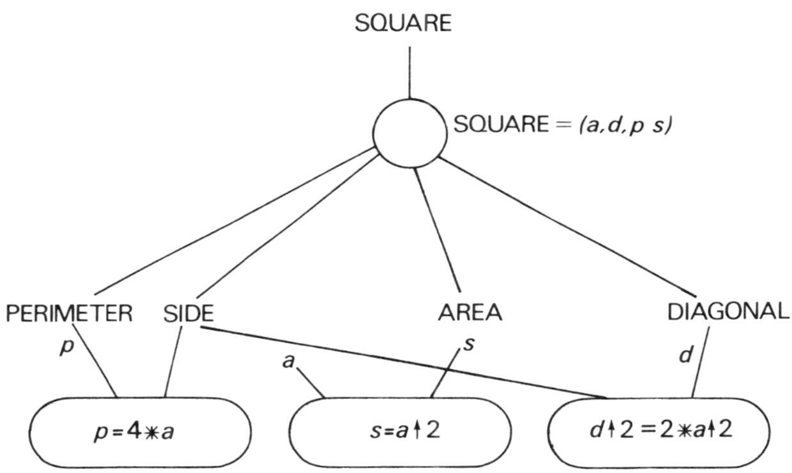

Fig. 3.

Relations may be described explicitly by using equations, as was done in the declaration of a square in the previous paragraph:

```
EQUATION  DIAGONAL ** 2=2 * SIDE ** 2;
EQUATION  AREA = SIDE ** 2;
EQUATION  PERIMETER = 4 * SIDE.
```

Finally, a relation may be described by a reference to a program. For instance, the following sentence:

PROG P   ARG X   RES Y

means that a relation between the objects X and Y is represented by the program P, and the relation can be used for calculation so that X is an argument and Y a result of the calculations.

If an object has been declared and the declaration of the object is inserted into the semantic memory, then the object becomes a notion that is known to the solver. The notion can be used as a type-declaration. When a notion is used as a type-declaration, values, identifiers, or objects can be bound with components of the notion. So we have used the notion of a square to declare a new object K in our example of a problem:

```
K SQUARE
          SIDE = X-COORDINATE OF P,
          AREA = S;
```

Here a compound name X-COORDINATE OF P denotes an object that has been defined earlier and which is bound now with the side of the square K by an equality-relation. S is a new identifier which is bound with the area of the square K and will denote the area.

There are several other statements in UTOPIST, such as the statements

```
GIVEN ...
CALCULATE ...
STOP;
```

that have been used in the example in the previous paragraph. These statements provide the means for completing the problem description.

Semantic network

As a rule, a semantic network consists of objects and relations. The semantic network of the SQUARE described in the previous paragraph is shown in Fig. 3. It contains a structural relation between the objects SQUARE, PERIMETER, SIDE, AREA, DIAGONAL. It contains three equations as well, which were given explicitly in the declaration of SQUARE. We regard all the objects as variables which may have values of some type. The main difference from other semantic networks is in the interpretation of the relations and in their representation. Often only a few types of axiomatically-described primary relations are used. Here, an extensible set of primary relation types is allowed. Nevertheless, only such relations are used which are efficiently applicable for calculations. Any relation is considered as a set of operators. For instance,

```
EQUATION AREA=SIDE ** 2
```

is regarded as a set of the operators

```
AREA: = SIDE ** 2
```

and

```
SIDE: = SQRT(AREA).
```

These operators are automatically derived by the solver from the equation.

As we have seen already, the most general way to declare a new relation is to program separately every operator that must be inserted into the relation.

This technique is analogous to declaring a procedure P(t,s) and using it in a procedure statement P(X,Y). The only significant difference is that the procedure statement P(X,Y) is an imperative prescription for calculations where the relation PROG P ARG X RES Y means that a possibility exists for calculating Y from X.

Another way of expressing a relation is to use a semantic network of a notion for this purpose. One can regard such a relation as an abbreviation for the semantic network of a notion. The semantic network of our sample problem is shown in Fig. 4. Relations of the network correspond to semantic networks of notions TANGENTIAL, CIRCLE, STRAIGHT-LINE, POINT and SQUARE.

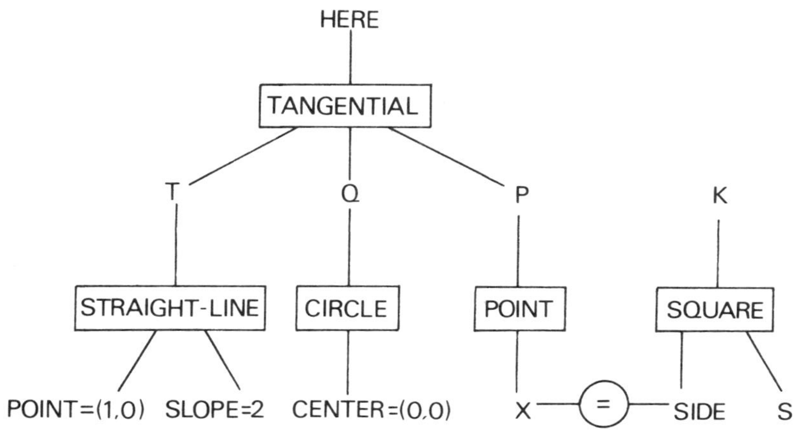

Fig. 4.

We can presume now that problem conditions which are given informally in an input text are translated into a semantic network, consisting of variables and relations which are directly applicable for calculations. Let us note once more that any relation is regarded as a set of operators. Indeed, more information than we have described is included in the semantic network in order to determine operators of any relation. This information is presented in the solver by marking the edges of the semantic network.

Solution planning

Now let us define a formal approach to the semantics of problems. We define a problem as a triple (M,U,V) of

M – problem conditions presented by a semantic network,
U – a set of input variables,
V – a set of output variables.

A semantic network M is a pair (X,A)

X – finite set of variables,
A – finite set of partial relations.

A partial relation is a finite set of operators which are not contradictory†.

An operator ϕ is a set of assignments with a set of input variables and a set of output variables. In $(\phi) = \{x_1, x_2, \ldots x_n\}$. Out $(\phi) = \{y_1, y_2, \ldots y_m\}$.

$$y_i := f_i(x_1, x_2, \ldots x_n), i = 1, 2, \ldots m.$$

If the operator is applied, all the assignments are fulfilled. We assume that In $(\phi) \cap$ Out (ϕ) is always an empty set. An operator is complete if it is applicable for any values of its input variables.

Let us call a semantic network M = (X,A) simple if the set A of its relations contains only partial relations with complete operators.

Transitive closure T(U,M) of a set of variables U on a network M is the largest set W_k for which the following sequence exists:

$$U = W_0\ \phi_1\ W_1 \ldots W_{k-1}\ \phi_k\ W_k, \qquad (*)$$

where $\text{In}(\phi_i) \subseteq W_{i-1}$, $W_i = W_{i-1} \cup \text{Out}(\phi_i)$ for $i = 1,2,\ldots k$, and each is an operator of a relation of the network. T(U,M) is the set of all these variables, values of which can be calculated from k on M.

A lot of methods exist for building transitive closure T(U,M) and the corresponding sequence of operators ϕ_1, ϕ_2, ... ϕ_k. The straightforward way of doing it is to check the operators of the network one by one and to search any operator ϕ_i for which $\text{In}(\phi_i) \subseteq W_{i-1}$ and $\text{Out}(\phi_i) \not\subseteq W_{i-1}$ on the ith step. If no such operator is available, then $T(U,M) = W_{i-1}$. The process may be broken earlier – as soon as $V \subseteq W_{i-1}$ – because then the obtained sequence of operators ϕ_1, ϕ_2, ... ϕ_k will already be a solving algorithm for the problem (M,U,V). Such straightforward solution planning is not too expensive, because the network M does not change during the solution planning (there is no need for backtracking), and the network M contains only information essential for the particular problem. Nevertheless, checking the applicability of relations instead of checking that of operators enables us to reduce the amount of search by a factor equal to the average number of operators in a relation.

The sequence of operators ϕ_1, ϕ_2, ... ϕ_k may contain superficial operators which do not perform any calculation that helps to solve the particular problem. Therefore a backward pass must be made on the sequence of operators, and for any ϕ_i, $i = k$, $_{k-1}$, ... 1 it must be checked if Needed(ϕ_i). The predicate Needed(ϕ_i) is defined in terms of sets W_{i-1} of known variables (see the sequence (*)) and sets W_i' of needed variables:

† The set of operators is not contradictory if it can be extended to a category of mappings. For instance, such is the set $x := y, y := z$, but not the set $x := y, y := 2+x$.

$$\text{Needed}(\phi_i) <=> (\text{Out}(\phi_i) \setminus W_{i-1}) \cap W'_i \neq \emptyset$$
$$W'_k = V,$$
$$W'_{i-1} = \begin{cases} W'_i, \text{if } \neg\,\text{Needed}(\phi_i) \\ (W'_i \setminus \text{Out}(\phi_i)) \cup \text{In}(\phi_i), \text{if Needed}(\phi_i). \end{cases}$$

This technique gives a minimal solving algorithm for any solvable problem (M,U,V).

It is essential that no useless calculations are made in the solver. The solution planning preceeds the calculations, and the applicability of a relation is checked by using only the structure of the semantic network that represents problem conditions.

Having some knowledge of physics, and using only the technique described above, the solver was able to solve the following problems:

IN ACCORDANCE WITH THE LAWS OF MECHANICS A LOCOMOTIVE WITH THE MASS M1 STOPPED DUE TO FRICTION FORCE F1, IN TIME-INTERVAL T1, THE VELOCITY-DIFFERENCE 33 METERS-PER-SECOND. F1 FORCE IN NEWTONS. M1 MASS IN TONS. T1 TIME IN MINUTES. GIVEN M1 = 500, T1 = 1. CALCULATE F1.

ACCORDING TO THE LAWS OF ROTATION A PILOT WHO HAS WEIGHT P FLIES WITH SPEED V AND MAKES VERTICAL LOOP WITH RADIUS R, THEREBY HE IS INFLUENCED BY CENTRIFUGAL-FORCE F. IT IS KNOWN THAT: V SPEED KM-PER-HOUR. R LENGTH METERS. P WEIGHT NEWTONS. GIVEN V = 144, R = 100, P = 800. THE FORCES ON THE PILOTS SEAT AT THE UPPER AND LOWER POINT OF THE LOOP ARE DETERMINED BY THE EQUATION XB = F − P AND THE EQUATION XH = F + P. CALCULATE F, XB, XH.

For the first problem the solver built the semantic network from the MECHANICS, MASS, TIME, VELOCITY-GAIN, and FORCE. The latter four were needed for transformation of units of physical entities. All the relations in the networks of physical phenomena were given in SI units. When other units were used, automatic transformation was needed from one measuring system into another. This was performed by using notions of physical entities.

The detailed semantic network of the first problem is shown in Fig. 5. Operators ϕ_1 ϕ_2 ϕ_3 ϕ_4 of the solving algorithm are shown there instead of these relations of the network, from which the operators were derived.

Application of theorems

The solver as described above has no automatic facilities for applying theorems, or any other assumptions containing general knowledge in the problem area. To apply a theorem for solving a problem, an explicit reference must be made to the theorem. The theorem can be included in the semantics of a notion

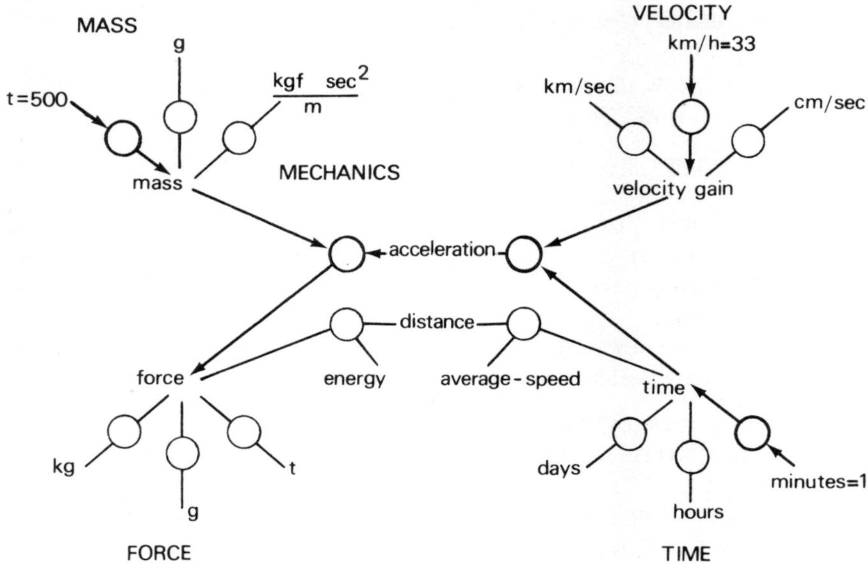

Fig. 5.

as a relation, and the notion can be explicitly mentioned in the text of a problem. Student problems are usually given without explicit references to theorems. The solver itself has to find applicable theorems and use them properly; that is, the solver must have some deductive abilities. Let us consider the example illustrated in Fig. 6:

> AC INTERVAL. APB ARC WHICH HAS LENGTH 5 AND RADIUS 3. THERE ARE TANGENTIALLY APB, AC. ROTATION OF THE INTERVAL AC AROUND THE POINT A GENERATES CAB SECTOR. CALCULATE AREA OF CAB.

To solve it, one must use the theorem: "Angle between tangent and chord from the tangential point is half of the angle of the arc". This theorem may be included in the semantics of the segment, and a segment AB may be described in the text of the problem by the sentence: APB SEGMENT OF THE CIRCLE WITH THE CENTER O AND TANGENT AC AT THE POINT A. We are interested in a more general use of theorems, as it occurs in deductive programs.

In the solver we have implemented theorems as follows. A theorem is a notion with a set of rules determining possible renaming of variables when its semantic network is copied. A theorem is applicable if and only if its variables can be renamed, so that at least two of them will have the same names as some variables in the semantic network of the problem. A set of theorems is stored in the semantic memory of the solver. When the solution planning on the semantic network of the problem fails, the solver searches for applicable theorems and adds them to the semantics. Then the solution planning is repeated on the extended network.

We have used some theorems of geometry in this way, particularly the theorems mentioned above. The following theorem also appeared useful to the solver: "If two objects are equal, then all their corresponding components are equal". The model of the theorem is the equality relation $x = y$, where x and y are the variables which can be renamed with the names of corresponding parts of equal objects. In particular, this theorem was needed for solving the geometrical problem described at the beginning of the paper.

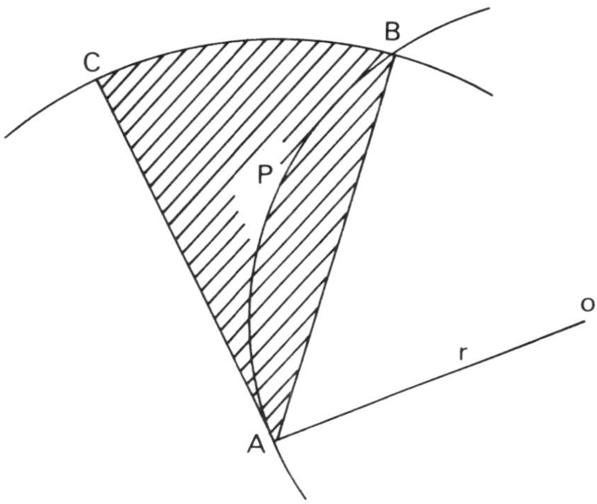

Fig. 6.

In the last sample problem we applied some well known conventions about notations for geometric objects. One letter is used for denoting a point, and the letters of characteristic points of geometric objects (arcs, triangles, etc.) are used in a fixed order for denoting these objects. We mostly implemented these conventions in the preprocessor. This is another way for using general knowledge in a problem area. The conventions on notation are used for extending the text of a problem before the problem model is built. These conventions may also be regarded as theorems. In the problem described the following deductions must be made on the basis of notations:

– interval AC has a common point A with the arc APB;
– side CA of the sector CAB is the same as the interval AC.

Improved solution planning

If the planner was able to build only linear sequences of operators, only a few of the student problems could be solved. Therefore the planner was extended, and facilities for recursive solution planning were added.

Let us consider a notion of a maximum of a function which could be expressed by the following expressions

$$m = \max_{x \in D} w$$
$$w = f(x).$$

When building the semantic network for the notation of a maximum, we can insert the following variables into the network: D – domain of the function, m – value of the maximum, x – argument of the function, w – value of the function. We have two relations as well: R1: $m: = \max_{x \in D} w$ and R2: $w: = f(x)$. Variables w and x are neither input nor output variables of the operator of the relation R1. Nevertheless, they must be used when m is calculated, and therefore we shall bind the variables with the relation R1, using the special kinds of arc shown in Fig. 7a. The function f itself can be expressed implicitly by a semantic network on which the problem "calculate w from x" is solvable, as in Fig. 7b. Now we can see that the relation R1 can be applied only if a subproblem "calculate w from x" is solvable. The solver can tackle any subproblem as an independent problem, and can perform hierarchical solution

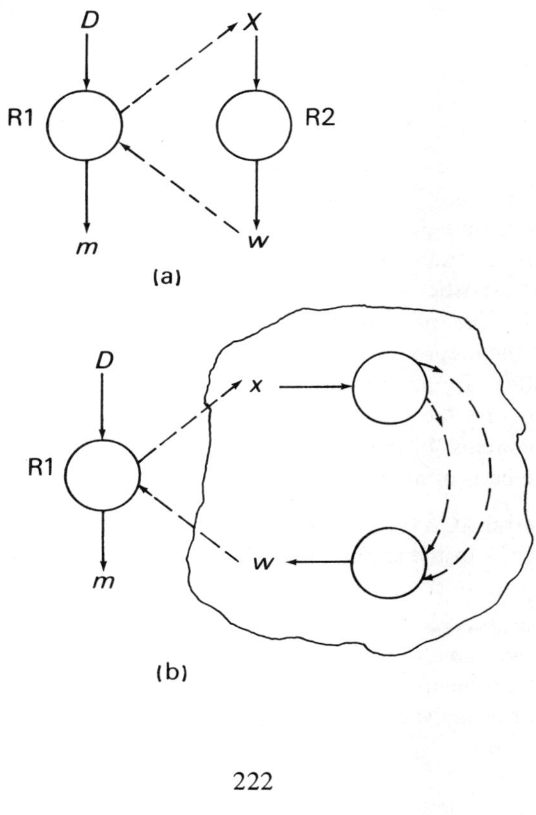

Fig. 7.

planning. Even recursion is allowed, so that the original problem itself may again appear as a subproblem in some solution planning stage. For the hierarchical solution planning and-or trees of subproblems must be used, and backtracking is needed. In the recursive solution planning a difficulty arises when termination of a solution process must be determined. It is worth mentioning that for any general recursive function f it is possible to build such a simple semantic network M that the problem "calculate ⟨value of f⟩ from ⟨values of the arguments of f⟩" is solvable on M.

Another improvement was made in the planner to enable it to solve the systems of equations which may appear when a semantic network of a problem is built from semantic networks of notions. In this case some systems of equations must be handled as new relations. But then (1) the planner must be able to find these systems, and (2) a program must be available for solving the systems numerically. Determining minimal solvable systems of equations in a large semantic network is a rather difficult problem. Some theoretical results in this direction have been presented by Karzanov and Faradjev [4]. We use a simple algorithm which can find some systems of equations and can solve them by iterating one bound variable of a system.

Using improved solution planning, the solver was able to solve the problem illustrated in Fig. 8 – probably the most complex problem solved by this solver.

A SPECTATOR IS SITTING IN THE CINEMA ON A SIDE SEAT SO THAT THE POINT P WHERE HE IS SITTING, THE NEAREST POINT B OF THE SCREEN, AND THE NEAREST POINT C OF THE PLANE OF THE SCREEN CONSTITUTE THE RIGHT-ANGLED TRIANGLE PBC. TRIANGLE ABP IS FORMED BY THE SCREEN AB AND THE POINT P. POINT B BELONGS TO THE INTERVAL AC. APB IS THE ANGLE UNDER WHICH THE SCREEN IS VISIBLE FOR THE SPECTATOR. GIVEN AB = 12, BC = 1. LET X BE MAXIMUM FOR ANGLE APB WHEN CP CHANGES. CALCULATE X.

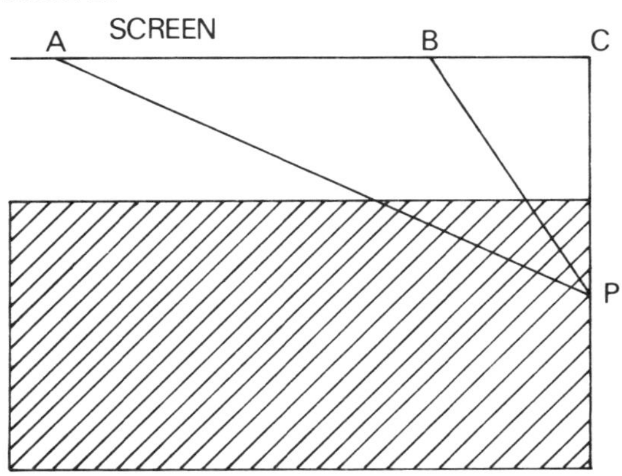

Fig. 8.

The model of the sixth statement of the problem description contains a relation for computing maximum ABP depending on CP. For determining the maximum it is necessary to compute in a cycle values of APB depending on CP. The algorithm for this computation is obtained as a result of solution planning for a subproblem, where AB, BC and CP are given and APB is requested.

SUMMARY

We have described a solver for computational problems where the algorithm for solving a problem is synthesized before computation begins. The solver described can cope with problems for senior students of secondary schools. Problems in physics and geometry have been solved as well as combined problems in these fields. Dimensions of physical entities have been taken into consideration; some theorems have been used, and simple systems of linear and nonlinear equations have been solved.

The knowledge of the solver as well as the semantics of the problems are presented by means of semantic networks, where relations are presented in a procedural way. A special semantic network is built for every problem to be solved. Only knowledge related to the particular problem is included in it. Owing to this, a large semantic memory is not used during the solution planning. This significantly reduces the amount of search.

We are not satisfied with our technique of using theorems. It seems to be restricted. We can only conclude that using theorems may significantly increase the abilities of the solver. Further investigations are needed to combine our solution planning with more advanced deductive theorem application.

Acknowledgement

I am very grateful to Miss M. Unt who performed many of the experiments and who did the greater part of programming the solver.

BIBLIOGRAPHY

[1] Kahro, M. I., Männisalu, M. A., Saan, J. P., and Tyugu, E. H. (1976). A programming system PRIZ, *Programming and computer software*, **2**, *No. 1* (in Russian).

[2] Tyugu, E. H. (1972). Data base and problem solver for computer-aided design, *Information processing 71*, North Holland.

[3] Tyugu, E. H. (1970). Problem solving on computational models, *Journal of applied mathematics and mathematical physics*, **10**, *No. 3* (in Russian).

[4] Karazanov, A. W., and Faradjev. I. A. (1975). Solution planning in problem solving on computational models, *Programming and computer software,* **1**, *No. 4* (in Russian).

INDUCTIVE PROCESSES

10

Inference of Functions with an Interactive System

J. P. Jouannaud and G. Guiho
Institute de Programmation
Paris, France

Abstract
The problem envisioned is the automatic build up of LISP functions from a finite set of examples $\{x_i \rightarrow F(x_i)\}$, x_i being a list of LISP atoms. From primitive functions and the composition rule, our system SISP is able to construct non-recursive functions from a single example $x \rightarrow F(x)$. On the other hand, SISP tries to find linear recursive functions, each with its stop condition. If it fails, new examples are requested. Then using a technique of generating new partial sub-problems, SISP may build up the recursive function by parts.

1. INTRODUCTION

In this paper, we describe the system SISP, the goal of which is the automatic inference of LISP functions from a finite set of examples $\{(x_i \rightarrow F(x_i)\}$, where x_i is a list belonging to the domain of the function F we want to infer.

The problem originates from a more general one: how to build a "Learning-Question-Answering-System" (L.Q.A.S.) using a functional method to provide an answer to any given question. The method we propose in SISP is well adapted to the L.Q.A.S. we are developing (Treuil, Jouannaud and Guiho 1976 and 1977).

Three kinds of research have dealt with the problem of "Automatic Programming from Examples". Blum and Blum (1973) using recursive function theory, developed a theoretical point of view which does not seem to open any practical result. Bierman (1972, 1973), Hardy (1975), and Green et al. (1974) developed a practical point of view, which does not seem to open any theoretical result. Recently, Summers (1977) mixed both theoretical and practical approaches which led to a very important basic work, the frame of which is summarized below:

Given a small number of well-chosen examples $\{(NIL \rightarrow F(NIL)), (x_1 \rightarrow F(x_1)), \ldots (x_k \rightarrow F(x_k))\}$ and a complete set of primitive functions:

1. Compute the predicates p_i on the inputs x_i.
2. Look for a recurrence relation between the predicates:

$$p_{i+n}(x) = p_i(b_1(x)) \qquad i \geqslant j$$

   where b_1 is computed using the primitive functions and the composition rule.
3. Compute the functions f_i which map x_i into $F(x_i)$, using the primitive functions and the composition rule.
4. Look for a recurrence relation between the functions f_i:

$$f_{i+n}(x) = a\ [f_i(b_2(x)),x] \qquad i \geqslant j$$

   where b_2 and a are computed using the primitive functions and the composition rule.
5. Define the linear approximation F_k of F as

$$\begin{aligned} F_k \leftarrow [&p_0(x) \rightarrow f_0(x) \\ &\ldots \\ &p_k(x) \rightarrow f_k(x) \\ &T \quad\ \rightarrow \omega]. \end{aligned} \qquad \text{(McCarthy conditional)}$$

6. Use an inference step by extending the domain of F_k, using the recurrence relations as follows:

   – Domain: $\{x/p_1(x) = T, \ldots p_{j+n-1}(x) = T,\ p_{i+n}(x) = p_i(b_1(x)) = T \quad \forall i \geqslant j\}$

   – Function: $\forall k > 0$, if $p_k(x) = T$ then $F(x) = f_k(x)$

7. Using the basic synthesis theorem of Summers or one of the corollaries (1977) use the recursion rule and define F as the recursive program equivalent to the limit of *Sup* (F_k) when k becomes infinite.

   Although the Summers method is very powerful, the way chosen to compute the functions f_i and the recurrence relations between the f_i and between the p_i brings out four important drawbacks.

   1. The constructed expression F is necessarily recursive:
      For instance the identity function will be inferred by

      F(x) ←[(ATOM x) → NIL
                T →(CONS(CAR x) (F(CDR x)))] .

   2. THESYS, the Summers system, needs well-chosen examples: in particular, they must contain the stop condition of the recursive function F. For instance, the synthesis of the function REVERSE requires the following set of examples:

      {(NIL → NIL);((A) → (A));((A B) → (B A)),((A B C) → (C B A))}.

3. The function to be constructed has to present only one "iterative level". For instance, THESYS fails to construct a correct function corresponding to the example

   $((P\,Q\,R\,S) \rightarrow (P\,P\,Q\,P\,Q\,R\,P\,Q\,R\,S))$.

4. When THESYS has to solve a difficult problem, it operates as if it were a simple one, and does not try to generate a partial simpler problem for which it could either find a correct solution or perhaps use knowledge previously stored in a data base by the system itself. Thus, THESYS cannot be efficently used in an L.Q.A.S. without important modifications.

The method we propose in this paper uses the frame of Summers, but is based on another way to compute the functions f_i and the recurrence relations between the f_i. It allows us to solve some of the previous drawbacks, though new ones appear:

1. Recursivity is not automatically inferred by the synthesis algorithm; for instance, using the example $((A\ B\ C) \rightarrow (A\ B\ C))$, SISP infers the function F: $F(x) = x$, for any x.
2. For some "simple" functions, SISP needs only one example $(x \rightarrow F(x))$. If a recursive expression is inferred, the stop condition is found by SISP itself. However, the list x must be long enough to be representative of the function F. For instance, REVERSE is obtained with $((A\ B\ C\ D) \rightarrow (D\ C\ B\ A))$ but is not obtained with $((A\ B\ C) \rightarrow (C\ B\ A))$.
3. When the function F is "more complex" SISP fails to construct a correct function with a single example $(x \rightarrow F(x))$ and has to ask for a second one $(x' \rightarrow F(x'))$. Then SISP generates a new partial simpler problem $(y \rightarrow G(y))$, where y is defined in terms of x and $G(y)$ is defined in terms of $F(x)$. To solve this new problem, SISP sometimes needs a new example $(x'' \rightarrow F(x''))$ which is used to deduce an example $(y' \rightarrow G(y'))$: SISP is extensible and can use a self-contained knowledge data-base.
4. At present SISP works on monadic functions. The method that we use may be extended to polyadic functions without great effort. It seems to be more difficult with the method of Summers.

In a sense SISP is more powerful than THESYS, but now only works on lists which are built with atoms, whereas THESYS is theoretically able to construct functions defined on the whole set of LISP S-expressions (in practice, it often cannot find the recurrence realtions, even if they exist).

2. FUNCTIONS, EXAMPLES, PREDICATES

2.1 The language

SISP infers LISP functions defined on character strings "$A\ B\ C\ D\ldots$" which are represented by the list $(A\ B\ C\ D\ldots)$. SISP uses the following set of six primitive functions:

LCAR: $(A\ B\ C\ D) \to (A)$ CDR: $(A\ B\ C\ D) \to (B\ C\ D)$
LRAC: $(A\ B\ C\ D) \to (D)$ RDC: $(A\ B\ C\ D) \to (A\ B\ C)$
CONC: $(A\ B\ C),(D\ E\ F\ G) \to (A\ B\ C\ D\ E\ F\ G)$
CONCT: $(A\ B\ C),(D\ E),(F\ G\ H) \to (A\ B\ C\ D\ E\ F\ G\ H)$

and a control structure with COND and NULL.

Let L_0 be the set of functions which can be obtained by the previous set of six primitive functions and the composition rule (no recursion).

Our goal is to synthesize any function in L_0 and also functions, not in L_0, the synthesis of which requires the use of the recursion rule.

2.2 Examples

Let A be an alphabet of atoms and A^* the set of finite character chains constructed on A, with the null chain. Let $^*A$ be the set $A^*\ U\{\omega\}$ where ω is the undeterminate chain.

Definition 1:

The couple $(x \to y)$ where $x \in A^*$
and $y = \mathrm{F}(x)$ is an *example* of F.

An example $(x \to y)$ is said to be *self-contained* iff:
$y \neq \omega$
Any atom in y is present in x.

An example $(x \to y)$ is said to be *non-ambiguous* iff any atom of A has at most one occurrence in x.

Definition 2: Let σ be a map from A into A. We call *alpha-substitution* of $^*A$ the applications σ_* such that:

$$\sigma_*(\omega) = \omega$$
$$\forall x \in A^*, x = a_1\ a_2 \ldots a_p, a_i \in A, i = 1, \ldots p:$$
$$\sigma_*(x) = \sigma(a_1)\,\sigma(a_2) \ldots \sigma(a_p).$$

A function F from A^* to $^*A$ is said to be Σ-*stable* iff when σ_* is an alpha-substitution of $^*A$:

$$\mathrm{F}(\sigma_*(x)) = \sigma_*(\mathrm{F}(x))$$

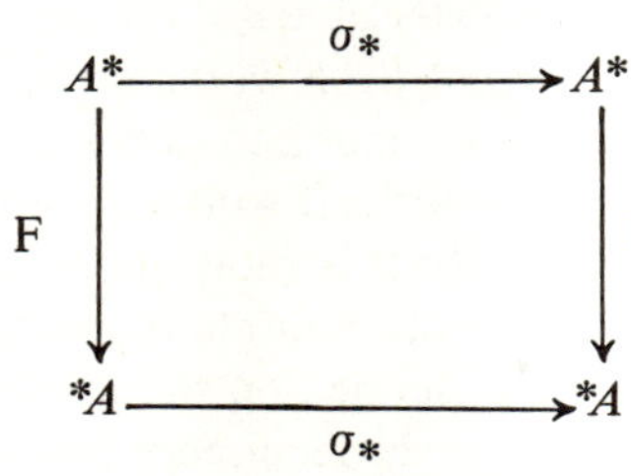

It is easy to show that any Σ-stable function has only self-contained examples. We undertake only the synthesis of Σ-stable functions using non-ambiguous examples.

2.3 The predicates

It is easy to show that if the examples $(x \to y)$ and $(x' \to y')$ may swap through alpha-substitutions, the entries x and x' have the same length. From this result it follows:

Proposition 1: Given the predicate p_i which takes the value T iff the list x has the length $|x| = i$ and given a non-ambiguous example $(x_0 \rightarrow F(x_0))$ so that $p_i(x_0) = T$, then the program:

$$[p_i(x) \rightarrow f_i(x)$$
$$T \rightarrow \omega]$$

coincides with F on the domain of the chains of length i, iff $f_i(x_0) = F(x_0)$.

Definition 3: We call *Type* any set $X = \{x / x \in A^*\}$ such that for a given i and for any x in X, $p_i(x) = T$.

- If X is a *Type* and F a function defined on X, the image F(x) is also a *Type*. In the same way, if G is a function of the image which contains X, the opposite image of X by G is also a *Type*.

From one example $(x_0 \rightarrow F(x_0))$, the proposition 1 defines a relation between the types $X = \{x / |x| = |x_0|\}$ and $Y = \{y / \exists x \in X, y = F(x)\}$. Our method is based on this important remark.

We still have to find the predicate p_i: using the primitive functions CDR and RDC, there are several ways to express p_i, as it is shown by the following relation between p_{i+1} and p_i:

$$p_{i+1}(x) = p_i(\text{CDR}(x)) = p_i(\text{RDC}(x)) \text{ for } i > 0.$$

In practice, only that relation between p_{i+k} and p_i is needed to infer the function F. Later we shall see that this relation is found naturally by our method, without having to express the predicate themselves.

3. SYNTHESIS USING ONE EXAMPLE

3.1 Segmentation pattern and approximation

Definition 4: We call a *Segmentation pattern* of the example $(x \rightarrow y)$ the following structure.

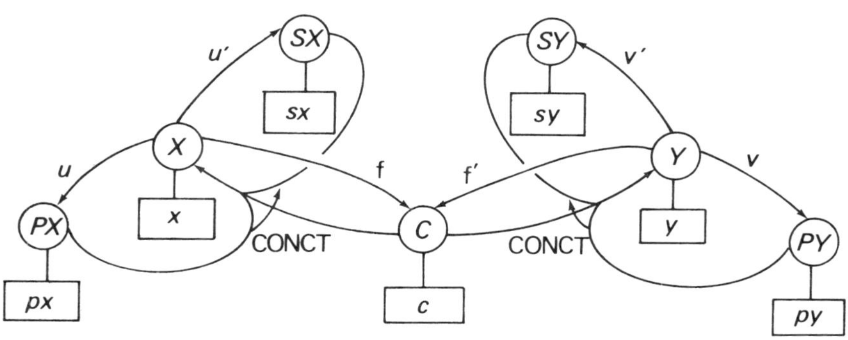

Fig. 1 – Segmentation pattern of $(x \rightarrow y)$.

- c is the common chain to x and y, of maximum length, called the pgcd of x and y (in the case of several pgcd, a systematic choice is made: for example the nearest to an extremity)
- px (resp. py) is the prefix of c in x (resp. y)
- sx (resp. sy) is the suffix of c in x (resp. y)
- the functions u, u′, v, v′, f, f′, belong to L_0. They are chosen to be of the least possible complexity.

This definition is coherent: the segmentation patterns associated with two non-ambiguous examples $(x \rightarrow y)$ and $(x' \rightarrow y')$ of the same Σ-stable function F are identical (the two pgcd c and c' swap through an alpha-substitution the same as that for x and x').

In some cases the segmentation pattern is simpler according to the following rules: when one or several chains are empty, the associated types are suppressed from the pattern; when two strings are identical, the associated types are joined together. For instance, if x and y are identical the segmentation pattern is reduced to a single type x.

Definition 5: We call *approximation of order one* associated to the example $(x \rightarrow y)$ of F, the following type of structure, extracted from the segmentation pattern of (x,y):

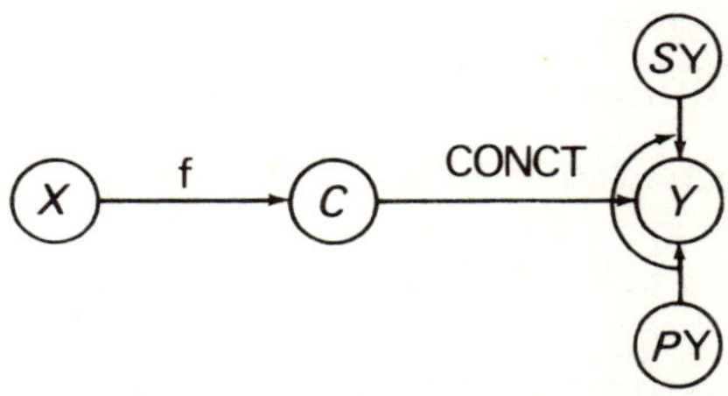

Fig. 2 – Approximation of order one associated to $(x \rightarrow y)$.

In many practical cases, one of the two chains sy and py is NIL. The approximation of order one becomes:

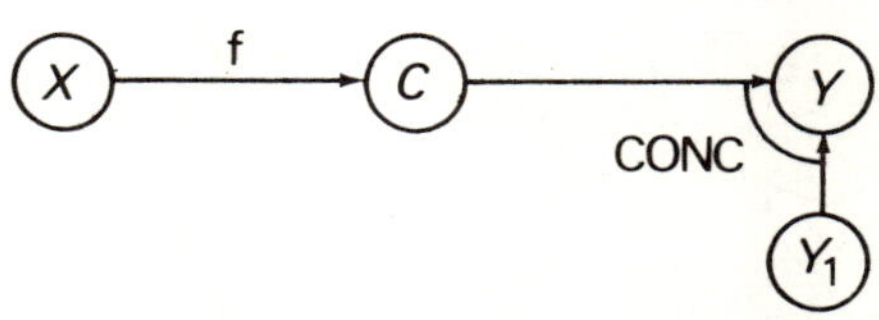

Fig. 3a – Simple case of approximation of order one associated to $(x \rightarrow y)$.

For simplicity we consider only these "simpler" cases in the following text.

Definition 6: The type Y_1 which cannot be reached from the input type X is said to be *unsatisfied.*

We call the *antecedent* of the unsatisfied type Y_1, the type X_1 taken in the set $\{X, PX, C, SX\}$ such that the example $(x_1 \to y_1)$ is self-contained, with the chain x_1 of minimal length.

Definition 7: Let us define recursively the *approximation of order n* or *n approximation* from the *n—1 approximation* and the *difference of approximation of order n—1* or *n—1 difference.*

The *n—1 difference* is defined as the *1 approximation* of the example $(x_{n-1} \to y_{n-1})$, X_{n-1} being the antecedent of the only unsatisfied type Y_{n-1} of the *n—1 approximation.*

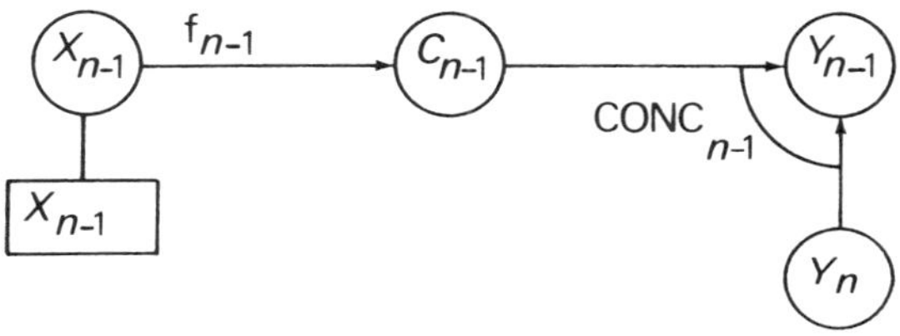

Fig. 3b — n—1 difference.

The *n approximation* is obtained by linking the *n—1 approximation* and the *n—1 difference* by the schema of Fig. 4.

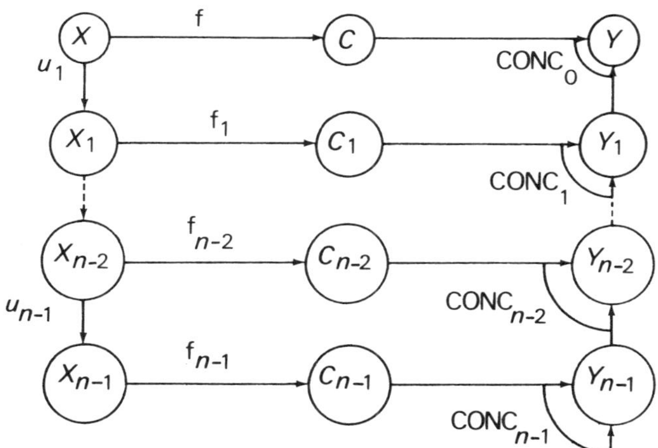

The symbol CONC$_i$ denotes a concentration of chains;
the entries order depends on the index i:
either CONC$_i$ ≡ CONC↳
or CONC$_i$ ≡ CONC↰

Fig. 4 — *n approximation* associated to $(x \to y)$.

Remarks: The approximation of order one associated to $(x \to y)$ can be considered as the approximation difference of order zero associated to $(x \to y)$

some u_i or f_i can be the identity function.

Proposition 2: There exists an integer n such that the *n approximation* of the example $(x \to y)$ contains no unsatisfied type. It is called the *approximation* associated to the example $(x \to y)$.

Proof: At each new level of approximation there are two possibilities: either the type Y_i exists in the already constructed part of the approximation and Y_i is satisfied, or Y_i is unsatisfied and the length of the chain y_i decreases strictly as i increases. As the antecedent of the unsatisfied type Y_i exists at each level, it is always possible to go further until y_i = NIL in the worst case, namely Y_{i-1} is satisfied.

Definition 7 and Proposition 2 provide a constructive algorithm for the approximation associated to the example $(x \to y)$. The approximation is nothing but the function f_i of Proposition 1, associated to the predicate p_i, with $|x| = i$.

3.2 Synthesis

Proposition 3: If the function F belongs to L_0 and if the length of x is great enough, the approximation associated to one example $(x \to F(x))$ is a correct expression of F on the set of examples.

The proof may be obtained by using two steps: first, transform the expression of f such that CAR, RAC, CDR, and RDC are never applied before CONC or CONCT; second, prove that the general form of the transformed expresssion and the approximation associated to the example $(x \to F(x))$ are similar, provided that the length of the chain x is great enough. These functions may differ only by side effects.

For this simple case the inference lies in the fact that the function f_i which maps the imput x_i into the output y_i does not depend on the index i, if $|x|$ is large enough. The only problem, simple to solve, is to compute the index j such that if $|x| \geqslant j$, the approximation associated to $(x \to y)$ is correct.

Now we study the functions F which do not belong to L_0: The recursion rule is necessary.

Definition 8a: Let us call the *(i,j) structure of approximation* denoted by SA^i_j, $i \leqslant j$, the structure of types obtained by linking together the approximation differences of order $i, i{+}1, \ldots j$. (cf. Fig. 4).

The (i,j) and $(k,1)$ structures of approximation are said to be *identical* iff $\forall h \in [i,j]$:

$i - j = k - 1$
$F_h \equiv F_{h+k-i}$
$u_{h+1} \equiv u_{h+k-i+1}$
$CONC_h \equiv CONC_{h+k-i}$.

It is clear that if F does not belong to L_0, then necessarily F is a recursive expression. When F(x) is computed, an identical sequence of operations will be called many times: The approximation associated with the non-ambiguous example ($x \rightarrow$ F(x)) has to contain a repetitive structure of approximation. Detecting such a structure is the goal of the following algorithm:

Algorithm 1:

1. $j \leftarrow 1$
2. **if** $j = n$ **then go to** step 8
   else $i \leftarrow 0$ and **go to** step 4
3. **if** $i = j - 1$ **then** $j \leftarrow j + 1$ and **go to** step 2
   else $i \leftarrow i + 1$ and **go to** step 4
4. **if** the approximation differences of order i and j are identical,
   then go to step 5
   else go to step 3
5. **if** $2j - i - 1 \geqslant n$ **then go to** step 3
   else go to step 6
6. **if** the approximation structures SA^i_{j-1} and SA^j_{2j-i-1} are not identical **then go to** step 3
   else go to step 7
7. compute the greatest integer q such that the approximation structures SA^i_{j-1} and $SA^{(q-1)(j-i)+j}_{q(j-i)+j-1}$ are identical.
   Preserve i, j and q
   and **go to** step 3.
8. **if** no i, j and q has been preserved, then let $\mathrm{F}(x) = A_n(x)$ and **stop**
   else select (i,j) with maximal q.

Definition 8b: The repetitive approximation structure SA^i_{j-1} is called the ***recursive pattern*** of F. If i is not equal to zero, the i approximation A_i associated to ($x \rightarrow y$) is called the *head* of F. The approximation structure $SA^{q(j-i)+j}_n$ is called the *tail* of F.

In practice Algorithm 1 often finds $j = i + 1 = 1$. In this case, recursivity is found readily and the function F has no head. We shall also present more complex cases.

The structures of types A_j ($j < n$) and $SA^i_j (0 \leqslant i \leqslant j < n)$ symbolize well defined diadic functions. Also A_n and $SA^j_n (0 \leqslant j \leqslant n)$ symbolize well defined monadic functions. If $j < n$, the order of the entries of A_j and SA^i_j is the same as that of the function CONC_j. For simplicity we will now suppose that $\mathrm{CONC}_j \equiv$ CONC↳, (Fig. 4).

Proposition 4: **if** $\alpha(x) = \mathrm{u}_j(\mathrm{u}_{j-1}(\ldots(\mathrm{u}_{i+1}(x)\ldots))$ is the identity function, **then** the recursive expression given in 1 belongs to F, **else** the recursive expression given in 2 belongs to F.

1. If $i = 0$ **then** the recursive expression given in 1a belongs to F **else** the recursive expression given in 1b belongs to F.

1a. $F(x) = \begin{cases} \textbf{if } x \in X_{(q+1)j} \textbf{ then } SA_n^{(q+1)j}(x) \\ \textbf{else } A_{j-1}(x, F(\alpha(x))). \end{cases}$

1b. $F(x) = A_i(x, G(\beta(x)))$

$\beta(x) = u_i(u_{i-1}(\ldots(u_1(x))\ldots))$

$G(t) = \begin{cases} \textbf{if } t \in X_{q(j-i)+j} \textbf{ then } SA_n^{q(j-i)+j}(t) \\ \textbf{else } SA_{j-1}^i(t, G(\alpha(t))). \end{cases}$

2. there exist two functions v and w in L_0 such that **if** $i = 0$, **then** the recursive expression given in 2a belongs to F. **else** the recursive expression given in 2b belongs to F.

2a. $F(x) = H(x, v(x))$

$H(x,s) = \begin{cases} \textbf{if } p_{(q+i)j}(s) \textbf{ then } SA_n^{(q+1)j}(x) \\ \textbf{else } A_{i-1}(x, h(x, w(s))). \end{cases}$

2b. $F(x) = A_i(x, G(\beta(x)))$

$\beta(x) = u_i(u_{i-1}(\ldots(u_1(x))\ldots))$

$G(t) = H(t, v(t))$

$H(t,s) = \begin{cases} \textbf{if } p_{q(j-i)+j}(s) \textbf{ then } SA_n^{q(j-i)+j}(t) \\ \textbf{else } SA_j^{i-1}(t, w(s)). \end{cases}$

The second part of Proposition 4 applies if the output y is built with a head, a tail, and a recursive pattern, which is the repetition r times of the same character chain. The problem is that r can be a constant, a linear function of $|x|$ or a non-linear one. SISP has to ask for new examples in order to solve this problem, namely compute the functions v and w: for instance, if r = $|x|$, then v $(x) = x$ and w (x) = CDR (x).

Proposition 4 can be proved by using the basic synthesis theorem of Summers or, when F has a head, by another theorem, which can be easily deducted from Summer's.

The inference step can be exhibited in the following way: given the approximation associated to the example ($x \rightarrow F(x)$) F being recursive, it is always possible to take the discovered recursive pattern out of the approximation, as many times as possible. We obtain new approximations, namely new functions f_i. But it is also possible to add, as many times as wanted, the recursive pattern in the approximation. Again we obtain new approximations. The Summers theorem is then used to obtain the least fixpoint of the set of functions.

In part 2 of Proposition 4 a fixpoint cannot be obtained on this set. The existence of a fixpoint requires the use of what Summers calls the variable addition heuristic. A second variable may be necessary for the function H. This supplementary variable is used to control the recursivity.

3.3 Detailing the stop condition

Proposition 4 does not always provide a good stop-condition: side effects often perturb the bottom of the approximation associated to the example

$(x \rightarrow y)$ giving a "bad" tail. For such cases, it is possible to substitute for the "bad" tail one or more recursive patterns with a new tail in the following way:

Assume that we have found the following stop-condition:

$$\textbf{if } t \in X_{q(j-i)+j} \textbf{ then } G(t) = SA_n^{q(j-i)+j}(t).$$

Assume that $\alpha(t)$ exists. It is possible to compute $G(t)$ by using the recursive pattern:

$$G(t) = SA_{j-1}^i(t, G(\alpha(t))) = SA_n^{q(j-i)+j}(t).$$

Because of the structure of overlapped CONC of the diadic function SA_{j-1}^i, a simple identification always allows us to compute $G(\alpha(t))$. Let now $X_{(q+1)(j-i)+j}$ be the type $\alpha(X_{q(j-i)+j})$ and $SA_n^{(q+1)(j-i)+j}$ be the approximation associated to the example $(\alpha(t) \rightarrow G(\alpha(t)))$. The new stop condition is:

$$\textbf{if } t \in X_{(q+1)(j-i)+j} \textbf{ then } G(t) = SA_n^{(q+1)(j-i)+j}(t)$$

As long as it may compute $\alpha(t)$, SISP goes on using the same method, until it gets the final stop condition after r steps. Then SISP computes the predicate which express that a chain t belongs to the type $X_{(q+r)(j-i)+j}$. The synthesis of the function F is finished.

3.4 Examples of synthesized functions

ROTATE: $(A\ B\ C\ D) \rightarrow (B\ C\ D\ A)$

The segmentation pattern associated with $(x \rightarrow y)$ is:

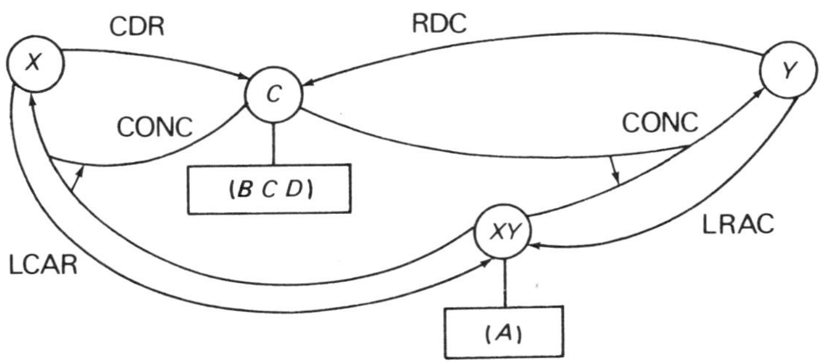

Thus, we get the following approximation associated to $(x \rightarrow y)$:

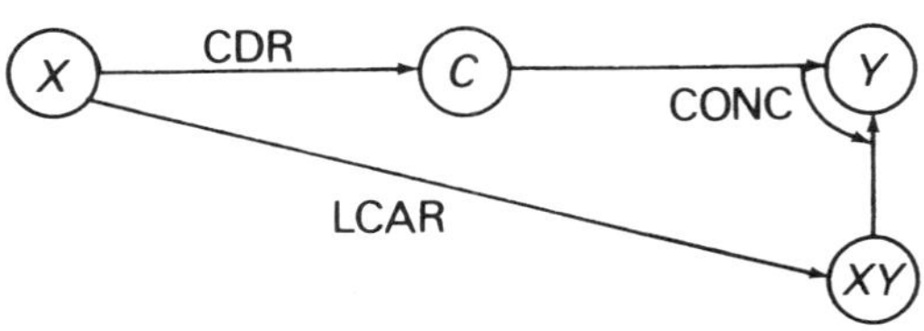

No recursivity is found: ROTATE $(x) \leftarrow$ (CONC(CDR x)(LCAR x))

(With his technique Summers finds a recursive function.)

REVERSE: $(A\ B\ C\ D) \rightarrow (D\ C\ B\ A)$

The segmentation pattern associated to $(x \rightarrow y)$ is:

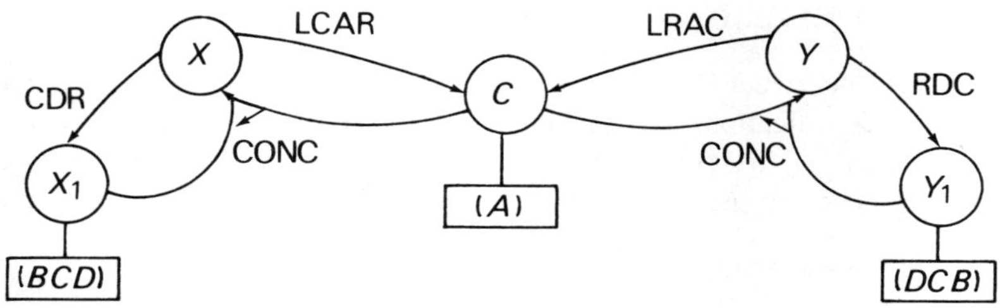

The antecedent of Y_1 is X_1. Thus, we get the following approximation associated to the example $(x \rightarrow y)$:

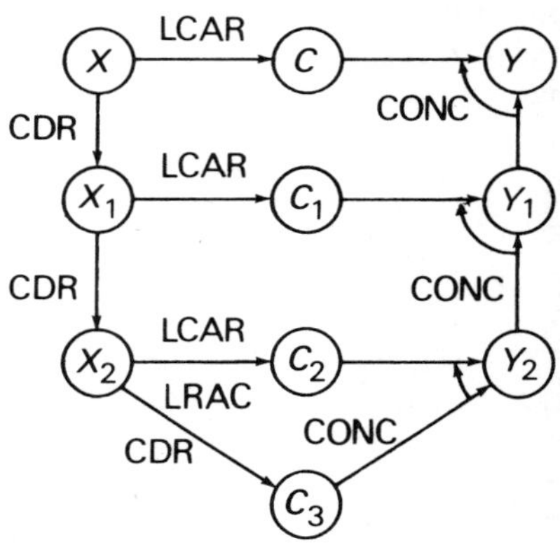

Using Algorithm 1 we find the recursivity according to $i = 0$, $j = 1$ and $q = 1$. Proposition 4 then provides the following function F:

$$F(x) = \begin{cases} \textbf{if } x \in X_2 \textbf{ then } SA_3^2(x) \\ \textbf{else } \mathrm{CONC}(F(\mathrm{CDR}(x), \mathrm{LCAR}(x)). \end{cases}$$

SISP now has to detail the stop condition:

For this apply F to the chain $x_2 = (C\ D)$:
$F(x) = SA_3^2(x) = \mathrm{CONC}(\mathrm{LRAC}(x), \mathrm{LCAR}(x)) = (D\ C)$.

Using now the recursive form of F:

$$F((C\,D)) = \mathrm{CONC}(F((D)), (C)).$$

It follows that $F((D)) = (D)$.

The stop condition is:

if $x \in \mathrm{CDR}(X_2)$ **then** x.

Then SISP tries once more:

$$F((D)) = \mathrm{CONC}(F(\mathrm{NIL}), (D)).$$

It follows that F(NIL) = NIL.

SISP cannot try once more. The following LISP function REVERSE is generated:

```
REVERSE(x) ← [(NULL x) NIL
                    T      (CONC(REVERSE(CDR x))(LCAR x))]
```

THE FUNCTION: $(P\,Q\,R\,S) \to (P\,P\,Q\,P\,Q\,R\,P\,Q\,R\,S)$

The segmentation pattern associated to $(x \to y)$ is:

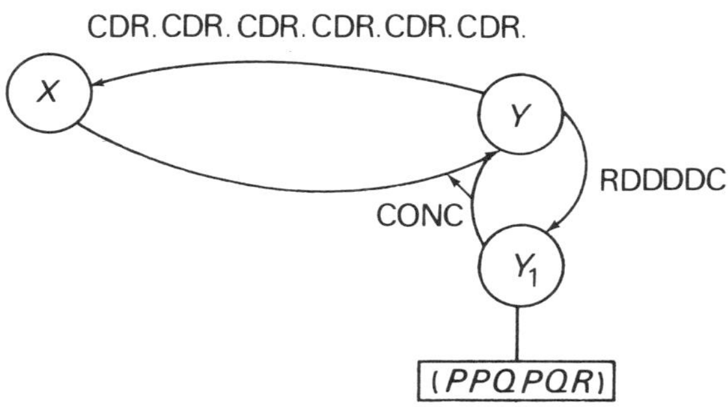

The antecedent of Y_1 is X. The segmentation pattern associated to $(x \to y_1)$ is:

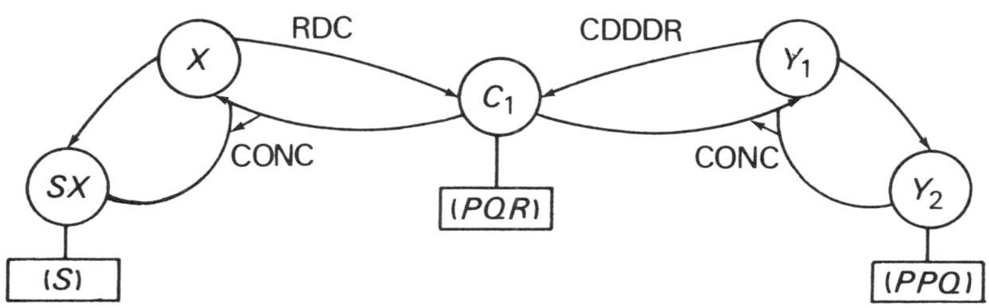

The antecedent of Y_2 is now C_1. Thus, we get the following approximation associated to $(x \rightarrow y)$:

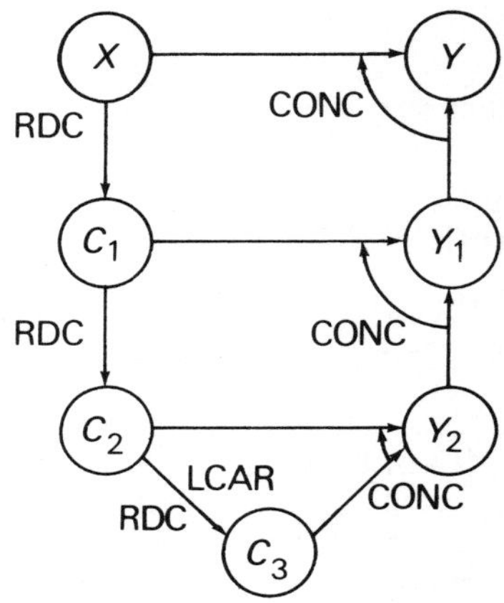

Using Algorithm 1, we find the recursivity with $i = 0, j = 1$ and $q = 1$. Proposition 4 then gives the following function F:

$$F(x) = \begin{cases} \textbf{if } x \in C_2 \textbf{ then } SA_3^2(x) \\ \textbf{else } \text{CONC}(F(\text{RDC}(x)), x). \end{cases}$$

SISP has to detail the stop condition:
It applies F to the chain $C_2 = (P\ Q)$

$$F(x) = SA_3^2(x) = \text{CONC}(\text{LCAR}(x), x) = (P\ P\ Q).$$

Using now the recursive form of F:

$$F((P\ Q)) = \text{CONC}(F((P)), (P\ Q)).$$

It follows that $F((P)) = (P)$.
The stop condition is:

$$\textbf{if } x \in \text{RDC}(C_2) \textbf{ then } x$$

SISP tries once more:

$$F((P)) = \text{CONC}(F(\text{NIL}), (P)).$$

It follows that F(NIL) = NIL.
SISP fails in the next step. Finally, it generates the following LISP function:

```
F(x) ← [(NULL x) NIL
             T          (CONC(F(RDC x)) x)]
```

THE FUNCTION: $(A\ B\ C\ D) \rightarrow (A\ A\ A\ A)$

The segmentation pattern associated to $(x \rightarrow y)$ is:

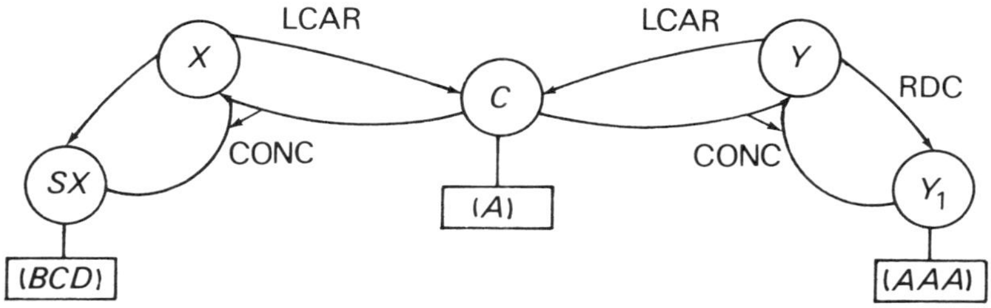

The antecedent of Y_1 is C. We get the following approximation associated to the example $(x \rightarrow y)$:

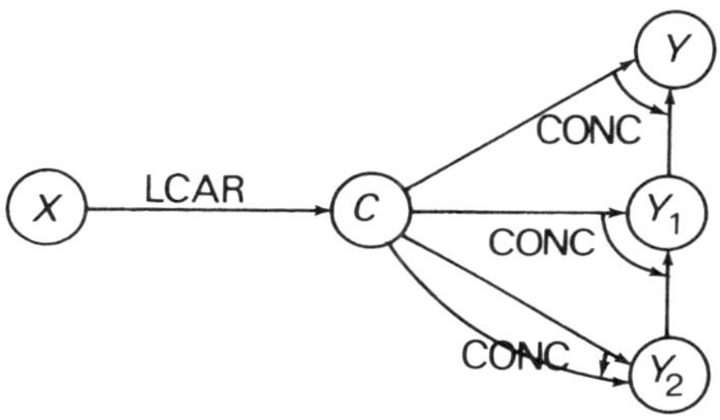

Using Algorithm 1, we find the recursivity with $i = 0$, $j = 1$ and $q = 1$. Proposition 4 provides the following function F:

$$\begin{aligned} &F(x) = H(x, v(x)) \\ &H(x,y) = \begin{cases} \textbf{if } p_2(y) \textbf{ then } SA_3^2(x) \\ \textbf{else } \mathrm{CONC}(\mathrm{LCAR}(x), H(x, w(y))) \end{cases} \end{aligned}$$

SISP has now to compute the functions v and w: it asks for a new example. Let us suppose that the professor gives the following one:

$$(A\ B\ C) \rightarrow (A\ A\ A).$$

SISP generates the approximation structure associated to this new example and verifies that this last approximation is obtained from the previous one by removing one recursive pattern. It deduces that $w(y) = \mathrm{RDC}(y)$ and then finds $v(x) = x$. The expression for F becomes:

$$\begin{aligned} &F(x) = H(x,x) \\ &H(x,y) = \begin{cases} \textbf{if } p_2(y) \textbf{ then } SA_3^2(x) \\ \textbf{else } \mathrm{CONC}(\mathrm{LCAR}(x), H(x, \mathrm{RDC}(y))). \end{cases} \end{aligned}$$

SISP has now to detail the stop condition. So it applies H to the couple of chains $x = (A\ B\ C\ D)$ and $y = (C\ D)$

$$H(x,y) = SA_3^2(x) = \mathrm{CONC}(\mathrm{LCAR}(x), \mathrm{LCAR}(x)) = (A\ A),$$

using now the recursive form of H:

$$H(x,y) = CONC((A), H(x, (D))).$$

It follows that $H(x, (D)) = (A)$. SISP tries once more:

$$H(x, (A)) = CONC((A), H(x, NIL)).$$

And $H(x, NIL) = NIL$. SISP cannot try once more. So it generates the following LISP function:

```
F(x) ← H(x,x)
H(x,y) ← [(NULL y) NIL
            T        (CONC(LCAR x) (H x(CDR y)))]
```

THE FUNCTION: $(A\ B\ C\ D\ E\ F\ G) \rightarrow (A\ A\ G\ B\ F\ C\ E\ D)$

Associated with this example, we get the following approximation:

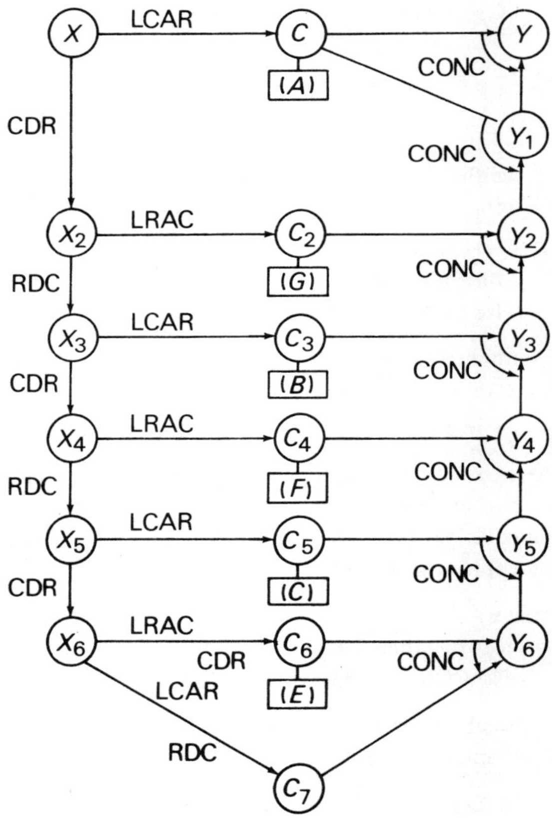

With Algorithm 1 we find the recursivity with $i = 1, j = 3, q = 1$. Now, SISP finds a head, a recursive pattern, and a tail. Proposition 4 provides the following function F:

$$\mathrm{F}(x) = \mathrm{CONC}(\mathrm{LRAC}(x), \mathrm{G}(x))$$
$$\mathrm{G}(t) = \begin{cases} \textbf{if } t \in X_5 \textbf{ then } SA_7^5(t) \\ \textbf{else } \mathrm{CONC}(\mathrm{LCAR}(t), \mathrm{CONC}(\mathrm{LRAC}(t), \mathrm{G}(\mathrm{CDR}(\mathrm{RDC}(t))))). \end{cases}$$

SISP has to detail the stop condition and after two steps finds the following one:

$$\textbf{if } \mathrm{CDR}(x) = \mathrm{NIL} \textbf{ then } x.$$

The synthesized function F is:

```
F(x) ← (CONC(LRAC x) (G x))
G(t) ← [(NULL(CDRt)) t
        T    (CONC(LCAR t) (CONC(LRAC t) (G(CDR(RDC t)))))]
```

We see that F works on the odd length lists, but does not work on the even length ones. This follows from the fact that $(j - i)$ is greater than one. The inference on the domain does not cover all the atomic lists.

4. SYNTHESIS USING SEVERAL EXAMPLES

The previous method is able to synthesize any function in L_0. In this section we are interested in recursive functions only: our goal with the following second method is to make use of a mechanism able to directly compute the recurrence relations between the functions f_i. The method lies in the comparison of two consecutive examples $(x \to y)$ and $(x' \to y')$, that is, it extracts the differences between the two examples, thus providing simpler sub-problems.

4.1 Segmentation pattern and approximation

When SISP has completed the synthesis, using one example $(x \to y)$, it asks for a second one $(x' \to y')$ to verify the correctness of the function. When the result is not correct, SISP tries to work on both examples.

Definition 9: Two examples $(x \to \mathrm{F}(x))$ and $(x' \to \mathrm{F}(x'))$ of a function F are said to be *consecutive* iff there exists no chain x'' belonging to the domain of the function F and such that $|x| < |x''| < |x'|$.

Definition 10: We call *segmentation pattern associated with the couple of consecutive examples* $\{(x \to y), (x' \to y')\}$ the following type of structure, where F is the function to be synthesized:

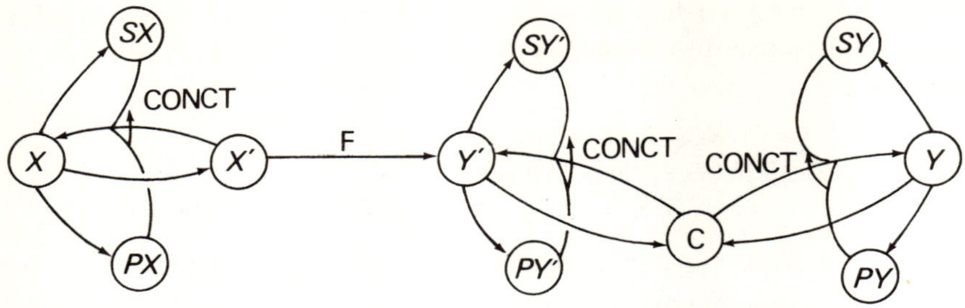

Segmentation pattern associated to $(x \rightarrow x')$ Segmentation pattern associated to $(y' \rightarrow y)$

Fig. 5 – Segmentation pattern associated to $\{(x \rightarrow y), (x' \rightarrow y')\}$.

From this segmentation pattern, it is possible to extract a path from X to Y. This path uses the following types:

$$X, X', Y', C, PY, SY, Y.$$

Sometimes, the chain y' is a part of the chain y: the types Y' and C are the same. Y' is obtained from X' by the function F. Some times Y' and C are not the same: the path $X' \rightarrow Y' \rightarrow C$ is often more complicated than the direct path $X' \rightarrow C$. Moreover the function from Y' to C may be recursive and is much more complicated than the function from X' to C.

Definition 11: We call approximation of order one associated to the couple of consecutive example $\{(x \rightarrow y), (x' \rightarrow y')\}$ of the same function F, one of the two following structures of types:

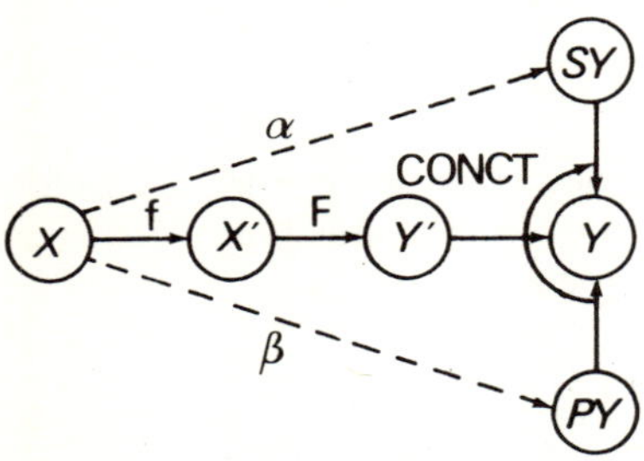

If Y' and C are identical.

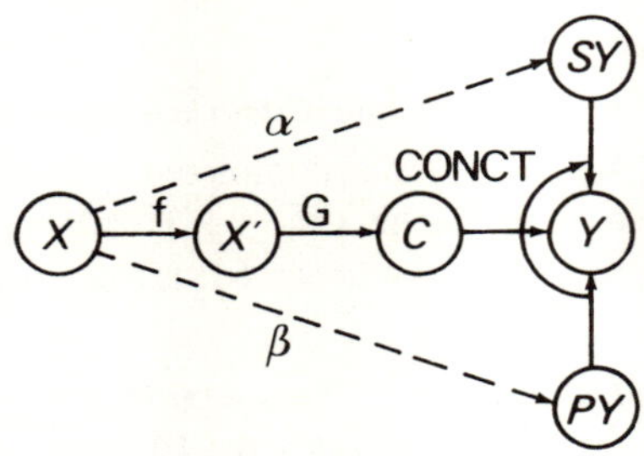

If Y' and C are not identical.

α, β and G are new functions to be built by SISP using the examples:

$(x \rightarrow sy)$ for α, $(x \rightarrow py)$ for β and $(x' \rightarrow c)$ for G.

This definition introduces the concept of the sub-problem. The functions α, β and G have to be synthesized by SISP each from one example. Thus it is able to use knowledge previously stored in a data base. If the system has no data base (such as SISP) or if it does not find the problem to be solved in the data base, then it uses the first method: it asks for a new example $(x'' \rightarrow y'')$ of the function F and uses it to deduce the examples of the functions α, β, G. Thus it may verify these functions and, if one of them gives bad results, it may try to use the second method. This possibility of using the recursion rule many times leads to a powerful technique. When all the problems are solved, each built-up function is associated with a type of structure, its approximation. Some of these approximations may present regularities which may be detected by Algorithm 1. Proposition 4 allows us to use again the recursion rule. The following is an example:

$$(A\ B\ C\ D\ E) \rightarrow (E\ D\ C\ B\ A\ E\ D\ C\ B\ A\ E\ D\ C\ B\ A\ E\ D\ C\ B\ A\ E\ D\ C\ B\ A\ D\ C\ B\ A\ D\ C\ B\ A\ D\ C\ B\ A\ D\ C\ B\ A\ C\ B\ A\ C\ B\ A\ C\ B\ A\ B\ A\ B\ A\ A)$$

We shall describe a shorter, simpler, but instructive example.

4.2 Practical use of the second technique with the following example

$$(A\ B\ C\ D\ E\ F\ G\ H) \rightarrow (D\ C\ B\ A\ H\ G\ F\ E)$$

First, SISP infers a function F from this single example, then asks for a second example $(B\ C\ D\ E\ F\ G) \rightarrow (D\ C\ B\ G\ F\ E)$ in order to control the inferred function F and finds that it is not correct. Then SISP tries to work from both examples and builds up the following approximation:

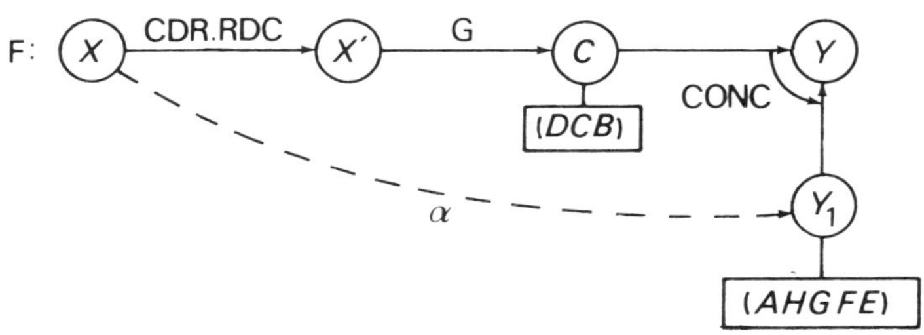

SISP now infers G and α, using the first method, asks for a third example $(C\ D\ E\ F) \rightarrow (D\ C\ F\ E)$ in order to control the inferred functions G and α:

By computing the pqcd of $(D\ C\ F\ E)$ and $(D\ C\ B\ G\ F\ E)$ SISP deduces a second example of G, that is: $(C\ D\ E\ F) \rightarrow (D\ C)$ and by computing the suffix of $(D\ C)$ in $(D\ C\ B\ G\ F\ E)$ SISP deduces a second example of α: $(B\ C\ D\ E\ F\ G) \rightarrow (B\ G\ F\ E)$. SISP notices that the inferred expressions of both G and α are not correct.

SISP now builds up the approximation associated to the couple of examples of G: {$(B\,C\,D\,E\,F\,G) \to (D\,C\,B)$ and $(C\,D\,E\,F) \to (D\,C)$}.

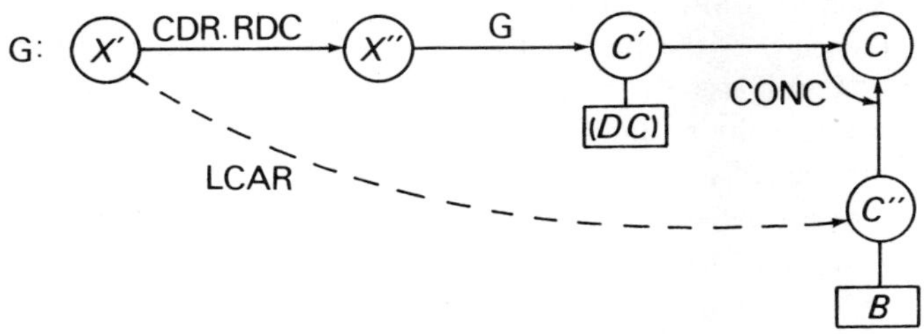

The following expression of G is obtained:

$$G(x) = \begin{cases} \textbf{if } x \in X'' \textbf{ then } c' \\ \textbf{else } \mathrm{CONC}(G(\mathrm{CDR}(\mathrm{RDC}(x))), \mathrm{LCAR}(x)). \end{cases}$$

SISP may now detail the stop condition of G:

$$G((C\,D\,E\,F)) = (D\,C) = \mathrm{CONC}(G(D\,E)), (C))$$

thus $G((D\,E)) = (D) = \mathrm{CONC}(G(\mathrm{NIL}), (D))$

thus $G(\mathrm{NIL}) = \mathrm{NIL}$

SISP may now infer the following function G:

```
G(x) ← [(NULL x) NIL
          T        (CONC(G(CDR(RDC x))) (LCAR x))]
```

SISP builds up the approximation associated with the two examples of α: $(A\,B\,C\,D\,E\,F\,G\,H) \to (A\,H\,G\,F\,E)$ and $(B\,C\,D\,E\,F\,G\,H) \to (B\,G\,F\,E)$:

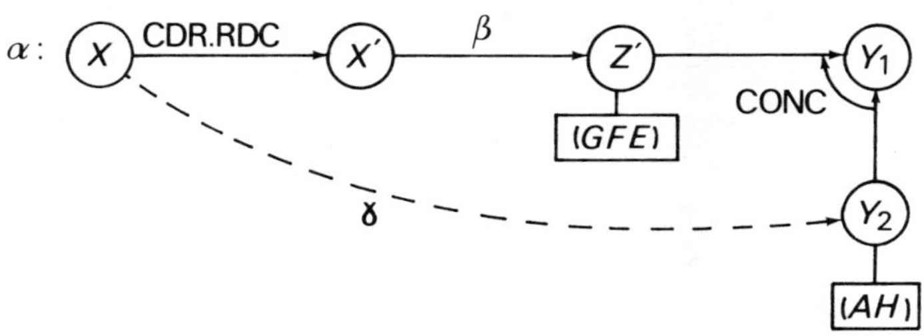

Now SISP infers β and γ, using the first method, and finds:

```
γ(x) ← (CONC(LCAR x) (LRAC x))
```

SISP asks for a fourth example $(D\,E) \to (D\,E)$ in order to control the inferred functions β and γ. SISP computes first a third example of α: $(C\,D\,E\,F)$

→ $(C\,F\,E)$ which leads to a second example of β: $(C\,D\,E\,F) \rightarrow (F\,E)$ and also to a second example of γ: $(B\,C\,D\,E\,F\,G) \rightarrow (B\,G)$.

SISP notices that the inferred expression of β is not correct whereas the inferred expression of γ is correct.

SISP builds up the approximation associated to the two examples of β $\{(B\,C\,D\,E\,F\,G) \rightarrow (G\,F\,E)$ and $(C\,D\,E\,F) \rightarrow (F\,E)\}$.

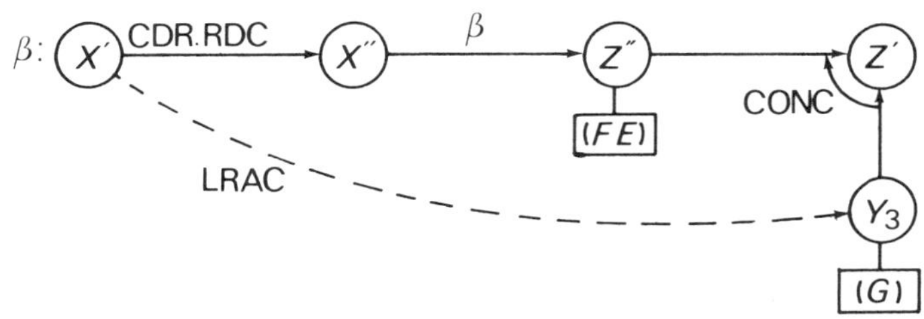

This leads to the following expression of β:

$$\beta(x) = \begin{cases} \textbf{if } x \in X'' \textbf{ then } z'' \\ \textbf{else } \mathrm{CONC(LRAC}(x), \mathrm{CDR(RDC}(x))\,). \end{cases}$$

Now SISP may detail the stop condition of β:

$$\beta((C\,D\,E\,F)) = (F\,E) = \mathrm{CONC}((F), ((D\,E)))$$

thus $\beta((D\,E)) = (E) = \mathrm{CONC}((E), \beta(\mathrm{NIL}))$

thus $\beta(\mathrm{NIL}) = \mathrm{NIL}$.

SISP infers the following function β:

```
β(x) ← [(NULL x)        NIL
         T          (CONC(LRAC x) (β(CDR(RDC x))))]
```

SISP now puts together the approximations of F and α, achieving the final approximation of F:

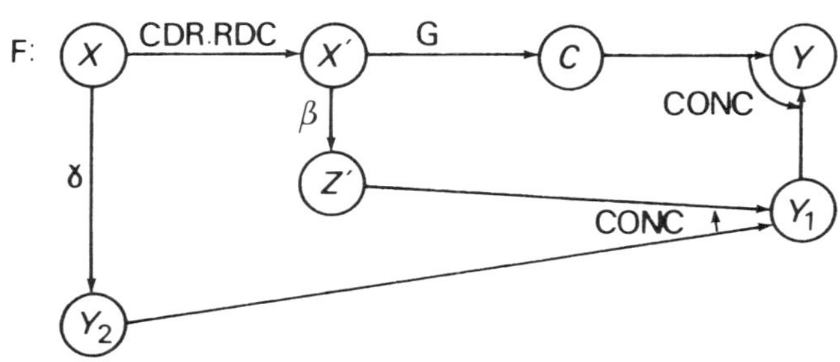

Using Algorithm 1, SISP now finds no recursivity in this approximation. The inferred expression of F is thus:

$$F(x) = \begin{cases} \textbf{if } x \in X' \textbf{ then } y' \\ \textbf{else } \mathrm{CONC}(\mathrm{G}(\mathrm{CDR}(\mathrm{RDC}(x))), \mathrm{CONC}(\gamma(x), \beta(\mathrm{CDR}(\mathrm{RDC}(x))))). \end{cases}$$

SISP details the stop of F until it finds F(NIL) = NIL. Finally SISP infers the following expression of F:

$$\boxed{\begin{array}{l} \mathrm{F}(x) \leftarrow [(\mathrm{NULL}\, x) \rightarrow \mathrm{NIL} \\ \qquad \mathrm{T} \rightarrow (\mathrm{CONC}(\mathrm{G}(\mathrm{CDR}(\mathrm{RDC}\, x)))\, (\mathrm{CONC}(\gamma x)\, (\beta(\mathrm{CDR}(\mathrm{RDC}\, x)))))] \end{array}}$$

5. LIMITS AND PROSPECTS OF THE METHOD

SISP is already able to synthesize all the functions given in Summers (1977), Hedricks (1976), Hardy (1975), and Green (1974), provided that these functions work on atomic lists. But SISP is also able to synthesize more complex functions, as shown by the last example. For instance, SISP is able to synthesize functions on the following examples:

$(A\,B\,C\,D) \rightarrow (D\,A\,B\,C)$
$(A\,B\,C\,D) \rightarrow (D\,C\,B\,A)$
$(A\,B\,C\,D) \rightarrow (A\,B\,C\,D\,C\,B\,A)$
$(A\,B\,C\,D) \rightarrow (A\,A\,B\,B\,C\,C\,D\,D)$
$(A\,B\,C\,D\,E\,F\,G) \rightarrow (A\,G\,B\,F\,C\,E\,D)$
$(A\,B\,C\,D\,E\,F\,G) \rightarrow (A\,A\,G\,B\,F\,C\,E\,D)$
$(A\,B\,C\,D\,E\,F) \rightarrow (A\,A\,F\,B\,E\,C\,D)$
$(A\,B\,C\,D\,E\,F\,G\,H\,I\,J\,K) \rightarrow (K\,B\,I\,D\,G\,F\,E\,H\,C\,J\,A)$

(given by Professor Minker)

This is done by the first technique, provided that the input list is long enough (it has to be as long as the sum of the length of the head, the length of the tail, and twice the length of recursive pattern). SISP is also able to synthesize functions on the following examples:

$(A\,B\,C\,D\,E\,F) \rightarrow (A\,B\,C)$ (HALF)
$(A\,B\,C\,D) \rightarrow (A\,B\,B\,C\,C\,C\,D\,D\,D\,D)$
$(A\,B\,C\,D) \rightarrow (D\,C\,B\,A\,D\,C\,B\,D\,C\,D)$
$(A\,B\,C\,D) \rightarrow (D\,C\,B\,A\,D\,C\,B\,D\,C\,D\,D\,C\,B\,D\,C\,D\,D\,C\,D\,D)$
$(A\,B\,C\,D\,E\,F) \rightarrow (C\,B\,A\,F\,E\,D)$
$(A\,B\,C\,D) \rightarrow (D\,C\,B\,A\,D\,C\,B\,A\,D\,C\,B\,A\,D\,C\,B\,A\,C\,B\,A\,C\,B\,A\,C\,B\,A\,B\,A\,B\,A\,A)$

This is done by the second technique, provided that the first input list is long enough and provided that the consecutive examples are the good ones, such as the following set of consecutive examples:

$(A\,B\,C\,D\,E\,F\,G\,H) \rightarrow (D\,C\,B\,A\,H\,G\,F\,E), (B\,C\,D\,E\,F\,G) \rightarrow (D\,C\,B\,G\,F\,E),$
$(C\,D\,E\,F) \rightarrow (D\,C\,F\,E), (D\,E) \rightarrow (D\,E).$

Another set, for instance:

$$(ABCDEFGH) \rightarrow (DCBAHGFE), (ABCDEF) \rightarrow (CBAFED) \ldots$$

would not have led to a correct result. This remark shows the essential importance of a clever professor. However, we hope that it would be possible to use a bad professor together with a "unification process", whose goal would be to improve the given bad examples. For instance, from the set of two examples $(ABCDEFGH) \rightarrow (DCBAHGFE)$ and $(UVWXYZ) \rightarrow (WVUZYX)$ it is possible to deduce three possible matched sets:

$$(ABCDEFGH) \rightarrow (DCBAHGFE) \text{ and } (ABCDEF) \rightarrow (CBAFED)$$
$$(ABCDEFGH) \rightarrow (DCBAHGFE) \text{ and } (BCDEFG) \rightarrow (DCBGFE)$$
$$(ABCDEFGH) \rightarrow (DCBAHGFE) \text{ and } (CDEFGH) \rightarrow (EDCHGF).$$

Only one of them leads to a correct solution. But we replaced one problem by three others which have to be performed simultaneously. This method looks good, but is not yet a part of SISP.

Future developments will tend to make SISP able to:

- define and store Σ-stable problems in its memory
- recognize that a partial sub-problem has already been encountered and solved
- improve the professor's bad examples in order to be able to solve partial problems, never met before
- infer polyadic functions using the first of the second method
- infer functions defined on the set of S-expressions.

6. CONCLUSION

If L_0 is the set of functions defined in Sec. 2.1, let us call L_1, L_2, the set of functions deduced from L_0 and necessarily using recursion once and twice respectively. We may assume that SISP is able to synthesize functions belonging to L_1 and L_2. Roughly, it seems that all functions of L_1 and some functions of L_2 may be found readily. A higher order of recursion entails a formidable complexity. On the other hand the set of primitive functions given in Sec. 2.1 is not complete; EQ is not in the set. Not all computable functions can be attained from this set.

These restrictions have restrained the complexity of computations.

It seems that the synthesized functions are often close to the functions that a LISP programmer would build up on the proposed examples. The heuristics of SISP are in fact similar to human behavior, like, for example, finding the common chains between input and output. Clearly our approach does not treat the impossible problem of synthesizing undetermined functions on a finite set of examples. Restrictions on the functions and the sequence of the techniques are essential for success.

Acknowledgement
The research presented in this paper is supported by IRIA-CESORT under contract No. 76.

REFERENCES

Bierman, A. W., Baum, R., Krishnaswany, R. and Petry, F. E. (1973). Automatic program synthesis reports. Technical Report *OSU-CISRC-TR-736*. Colombus: Computer and Information Sciences Report Center, Ohio State University.

Bierman, A. W. and Feldman, J. A. (1972). On the synthesis of finite state machines from samples of their behaviour. *IEEE Transactions on Computers* **C-21**, *No. 6*, 592–597.

Blum, L. and Blum, M. (1973). Inductive inference: a recursion theoretic approach. *Proc. of Switching and Automata Theory Symposium*, pp. 200–208. New York: IEEE Computer Society.

Green, C. C., Waldinger, R. J., Barstow, D. W., Elschager, R., Lenat, D. B., McCune, B. P., Shaw, D. E. and Steinberg, L. I. (1974). Progress report on program understanding systems. *Memo AIM-240*. Stanford: Artificial Intelligence Laboratory, Stanford University.

Hardy, S. (1975). Synthesis of LISP functions from examples. *Proc. 4th Int. Joint Conf. on Art. Int. (IJCAI-75)*, Tbilisi. pp. 240–245. Cambridge, Mass: Artificial Intelligence Laboratory, Massacusetts Institute of Technology.

Hedricks, C. L. (1976). Learning production systems from examples. *Artificial Intelligence* **7**, 21–49.

Jouannaud, J. P., Guiho, G. and Treuil, J. P. (1976). SISP; système interactif de synthèse de Programmes à partir d'exemples. Paris: L'Institut de Programmation.

Summers, P. D. (1977). A methodology for LISP program construction from examples. *J. ACM* **24**, 161–175.

Treuil, J. P., Jouannaud, J. P. and Guiho, G. (1976). Une méthode d'apprentissage de concepts. *Panorama de la Nouveauté Informatique*. Paris: Congress AFCET D'Orsay.

Treuil, J. P., Jouannaud, J. P. and Guiho, G. (1977). LQAS: un système Question-Response basé sur l'apprentissage et la synthèse de programme a partir d'examples. Paris: L'Institut de Programmation.

11

On Automated Scientific Theory Formation: A Case Study using the AM Program

D. B. Lenat†

Carnegie-Mellon University
Pittsburgh, USA

Abstract

A program called "AM" is described which carries on simple mathematics research, defining and studying new concepts under the guidance of a large body of heuristic rules. The 250 heuristics communicate via an agenda mechanism, a global priority queue of small tasks for the program to perform, and reasons why each task is plausible (for example, "Find generalizations of 'primes', because 'primes' turned out to be so useful a concept"). Each concept is represented as an active, structured knowledge module. One hundred very incomplete modules are initially supplied, each one corresponding to an elementary set-theoretic concept (for example, union). This provides a definite but immense space which AM begins to explore. In one hour, AM rediscovers hundreds of common concepts (including singleton sets, natural numbers, arithmetic) and theorems (for example, unique factorization). As AM defines concepts, and fills in their facets, it does not synthesize new heuristics for dealing effectively with those new concepts. This inability turns out to be its main limitation.

1. INTRODUCTION

1.1 Historical motivation

Scientists often face the difficult task of formulating nontrivial research problems which are soluble. In most branches of science, it is usually easier to tackle a specific given problem than to propose interesting yet manageable new questions to investigate. For example, contrast solving the Missionaries and Cannibals problem with the more ill-defined reasoning which led to inventing it. The first type of activity is formalizable and admits a deductive solution; the second is inductive and judgmental. As another example, contrast proving a given theorem and proposing it in the first place.

† Now at the Department of Computer Science, Stanford University, USA.

A wealth of AI research has been focused upon the former type of activity: deductive problem solving (see, for example, Bledsoe 1971, Nilsson 1971, Newell and Simon 1972). Approaches to inductive inference have also been made. Some researchers have tried to attack the problem in a completely domain-independent way (see, for example, Winston 1970). Other AI researchers believe that "expert knowledge" must be present if inductive reasoning is to be kept within the abilities of the human mind. Indeed, a few recent AI programs have incorporated such knowledge (in the form of judgmental rules gleaned from human experts) and successfully carried out quite complex inductive tasks: medical diagnosis (Shortliffe 1974), mass spectra identification (Feigenbaum 1971), clinical dialogue (Davis 1976), discovery of new mass spectroscopy rules (Buchanan 1975).

The next step in this progression of tasks would be that of fully automatic theory formation in some scientific field. This includes two activities: (i) discovering relationships among known concepts (for example, by formal manipulations, or by noticing regularities in empirical data), and (ii) defining new concepts for investigation. Meta-Dendral (Buchanan 1975) performs only the first of these (it doesn't develop new concepts); most domain-independent concept learning programs (Winston 1970) perform only the latter of these (while they do create new concepts, the initiative is not theirs but rather is that of a human "teacher" who already has the concepts in mind).

We are describing a computer program which defines new concepts, investigates them, notices regularities in the data about them, and conjectures relationships between them. This new information is used by the program to evaluate the newly-defined concepts, to concentrate upon the most interesting ones, and to iterate the entire process. This paper describes such a program: AM.

1.2 Choice of domain

Research in distinct fields of science and mathematics often proceeds slightly differently. Not only are the concepts different; so are most of the powerful heuristics. So it was reasonable that this first attempt should be limited to one narrow domain. Elementary mathematics was chosen, because:

1. There are no uncertainties in the raw data (arising, for example, from faulty measuring devices).
2. Reliance on experts' introspection is a powerful technique for codifying the judgmental rules needed to work effectively in a field. By choosing a familiar field, it was possible for the author to rely primarily on personal introspection for such heuristics.
3. The more formal a science is, the easier it is to automate (for example, the less one needs to use natural language to communicate information).
4. A mathematician has the freedom to explore – or to abandon – whatever he wants to. There is no specific problem to solve, no fixed "goal".
5. Unlike some fields (for example, propositional logic), elementary mathe-

matical research has an abundance (many hundreds) of powerful heuristic rules available.

6. One point of agreement between Weizenbaum and Lederberg (Buchanan *et al.*, 1976) is that AI can succeed in automating only those activities for which there exists a "strong theory" of how that activity is performed by human experts. AM is built on this kind of detailed model of mathematical research (see Sec. 1.3).

The limitations of mathematics as a domain are closely intertwined with its advantages. Having no ties to real-world data can be viewed as a liability, as can having no clear "right" or "wrong" behaviour. Since mathematics has been worked on for millenia by some of each culture's greatest minds, it is unlikely that a small effort like AM would make many startling new discoveries. Nevertheless, it was decided that the advantages outweighed the limitations, and the task domain of the program was settled.

1.3 Initial assumptions and hypotheses

The AM program got off the ground only because a number of sweeping assumptions were made about how mathematical research could be perfomed by a computer program:

1. Very little natural language processing capabilities are required. As it runs, AM is monitored by a human "user". AM keeps the user informed by instantiating English sentence templates. The user's input is rare and can be successfully stereotyped.
2. Formal reasoning (including proof) is not indispensable when doing theory formation in elementary mathematics. In the same spirit, we need not worry in advance about the occurence of contradictions.
3. Each mathematical concept can be represented as a list of facets (aspects, slots, parts, property/value pairs). For each new piece of knowledge gained, there will be no trouble in finding which facet of which concept it should be stored in.
4. The basic activity is to choose some facet of some concept, and then try to fill in new entries to store there; this will occasionally cause new concepts to be defined. The high-level decision about which facet of which concept to work on next can be handled by maintaining an ordered agenda of such mini-research tasks. The techniques for actually carrying out a task are contained within a large collection of heuristics.
5. Each heuristic has a well-defined domain of applicability, which coincides perfectly with one of AM's concepts. We can thus say the heuristic "belongs to" that concept.
6. Heuristics superimpose; they never interact strongly with each other. If one concept C1 is a specialization of concept C2, then C1's heuristics are more specific and more powerful, hence they should be tried first.
7. Each task (on the agenda of facet/concept tasks to be carried out) is

supported by a list of symbolic reasons, from which its priority is computed. We assume that the reasons always superimpose perfectly. They never change with time, and it makes no difference in what order they were noticed. It suffices to have a single, positive number for each reason, which characterizes its overall value.

8. The tasks on the agenda are completely independent. No task "wakes up" another. Only the general position (near the top, near the bottom) is of any significance (not the precise numeric value of its priority rating).
9. The set of heuristics need not grow, as new concepts are discovered. All commonsense knowledge required is assumed to be already present within the initially-given body of heuristic rules.

It is worth repeating that all the above points are merely convenient falsehoods. Their combined presence made AM do-able (by one person, in one year).

Point (4) above is a claim that a clean, simple model exists for mathematical research: a search process governed by a large collection of heuristic rules. Here is a simplified summary of that model:

1. The order in which a mathematics textbook presents a theory is almost the exact opposite of the order in which it was actually developed. In a text, definitions and lemmas are given with no motivation, and they turn out to be just the ones required for the next big theorem, whose proof magically follows. But in real life, a mathematician would (i) begin by examining some already-known concepts, (ii) try to find some regularity involving them, (iii) formulate those as conjectures to investigate further, and (iv) use them to motivate some simplifying new definitions.
2. Each of these four steps that the researcher takes involves choosing from a huge set of alternatives - that is, searching. He uses judgmental criteria (heuristics) to choose the "best" alternative. This saves his search from the combinatorial explosion.
3. Non-formal criteria (aesthetic interest, empirical induction, analogy, utility estimates) are much more important than formal methods, in the search for fruitful new definitions.
4. All such heuristics can be cast as situation/action (IF/THEN) rules. There is a common core of (a few hundred) heuristics, basic to all fields of mathematics at all levels. In addition to these, each field has several of its own rules; those are usually much more powerful than the general-purpose heuristics.
5. Nature is metaphysically pleasant: It is fair, uniform, regular. Statistical considerations are valid and valuable when trying to find regularity in mathematical data. Simplicity and synergy and symmetry abound.

1.4 Discovery in mathematics

By presenting a few examples, the preceding assumptions can, we hope, be made more plausible. We shall cite some scenarios of mathematical discoveries being made. But before discussing how to synthesize a new mathematical theory, consider briefly how to analyse one, how to construct a plausible chain of reasoning which stretches from a given discovery all the way back to well-known concepts.

1.4.1 Analysis of a discovery

One can rationalize a given discovery by working backwards, by reducing the creative act to simpler and simpler creative acts. For example, consider the concept of prime numbers. How might one be led to define such a notion, if one had never heard of it before? Notice the following plausible strategy:

> If f is a function which transforms elements of A into elements of B, and B is ordered, then consider just those members of A which are transformed into extremal elements of B. This set is an interesting subset of A. Name it and study it.

When $f(x)$ means "divisors of x", and the ordering is "by length", this heuristic says "Consider those numbers which have a minimal number of factors - that is, the primes". So this rule actually reduces our task from "how in the world did somebody first think of the concept of 'prime numbers'?" to two more elementary problems: (i) "How might 'ordering-by-length' have been discovered?" and (ii) "How in the world did anybody first think of the concept of 'divisors of a number'?". The reduction was accomplished by citing the above heuristic. Bear in mind that it's just a rule of thumb, not a rule of inference. It can't guarantee anything, the way that Modus Ponens can guarantee to preserve validity. And yet, it is cost-effective for researchers to know and apply that heuristic rule, because (as in the above case) it frequently leads to valuable new discoveries.

Now suppose we know this general rule: "If f is an interesting relation, consider its inverse f^{-1}". It reduces the task of discovering divisors-of to the simpler task of discovering multiplication. Eventually, this task reduces to the discovery of very basic notions, like substitution, set-union, and equality. To explain how a given researcher might have made a given discovery, such an analysis could be continued until that inductive task had been reduced to "discovering" notions which the researcher already knew, which were his conceptual primitives.

1.4.2 Syntheses of discoveries

Suppose a large collection of these heuristic strategies has been assembled (for example, by analysing a great many discoveries, and writing down new heuristic rules whenever necessary). Instead of using them to explain how a given idea might have evolved, one can imagine starting from a basic core of knowledge and "running" the heuristics to generate new concepts. We're talking about reversing the process described in the last subsection: not how to explain discoveries, but how to make them.

Notice that this forward search is much "bushier", much more explosive, than was the backwards analysis previously described. Instead of having fixed starting and ending concepts, we are now given only a starting point. This explains why it's much harder to actually make a discovery than to rationalize - by hindsight - how one might have made it. We have all noticed this phenomenon, the "Why-didn't-I-think-of-that-sooner!" feeling.

The forward search is quite explosive; we may hypothesize that the scientist employs some additional informal rules of thumb to constrain it. That is, he doesn't really follow rules like "Look at the inverse of each known relation f", because that would take up too much time. Rather, his heuristic rules might be more naturally stated as productions (condition/action rules) like this: "If a relation f is 1-1, and is very interesting, and Range(f) is much smaller than Domain(f), Then look at f^{-1}". Henceforth, "heuristic rule" will mean a conditional rule of thumb. In any particular situation, some subset of these rules will "trigger", and will suggest some relevant, plausible activities to perform. After following those suggestions, the situation will have changed, and the cycle will begin anew.

Such syntheses are precisely what the AM program - and perhaps what a human scientist - does. The program consists of a large corpus of primitive mathematical concepts, each with a few associated heuristics. Each such heuristic is a situation/action rule which functions as a local "plausible move generator". Some suggest tasks for the system to carry out, some suggest ways of satisfying a given task, etc. AM's activities all serve to expand AM itself, to enlarge upon a given body of mathematical knowledge. AM uses its heuristics as judgmental criteria to guide development in the most promising direction.

2. DESIGN OF THE 'AM' PROGRAM

A pure production system may be considered to consist of three components: data memory, a set of rules, and an interpreter. Since AM is more or less a rule-based system, it too can be considered as having three main design components: how it represents mathematical knowledge (its frame-like concept/facets scheme), how it enlarges its knowledge base (its collection of heuristic rules), and how it controls the firing of these rules (via the agenda mechanism). These form the subjects of the following three subsections.

2.1 Representation of concepts

The task of the AM program is to define plausible new mathematical concepts, and to investigate them. Each concept is represented internally as a bundle of slots or "facets". Each facet corresponds to some aspect of a concept, to some question we might want to ask about the concept. Since each concept is a mathematical entity, the kinds of questions one might ask are fairly constant from concept to concept. A set of 25 facets was therefore fixed once and for all. Below is that list of facets which a concept C may have. For each facet, we give a typical question about C which it answers.

Name: What shall we call C when talking with the user?
Generalizations: Which other concepts have less restrictive (that is, weaker) definitions than C?
Specializations: Which concepts satisfy C's definition plus some additional constraints?
Examples: What are some things that satisfy C's definition?
Isa's: Which concepts' definitions does C itself satisfy?
In-domain-of: Which operations can operate on C's.
In-range-of: Which operations result in C's when run?
Views: How can we view some X as if it were a C?
Intuitions: What abstract, analogic representations are known for C?
Analogies: Are there any similar concepts?
Conjec's: What are some potential theorems involving C?
Definitions: How can we tell if x is an example of C?
Algorithms: What exactly do we do to execute the operation C on a given argument?
Domain/Range: How many – and exactly what kinds of – arguments can operation C be executed on? What kinds of values will it return?
Worth: How valuable is C? (overall, aesthetic, utility, etc.)
Interest: What special features can make a C unusually interesting? Boring?

In addition, each facet F of concept C can possess a few little subfacets which contain heuristics for dealing with that facet of C's:

F.Fillin: What are some methods for finding new entries for facet F of a concept which is a C?
F.Check: How do we verify/debug potential entries for such a facet?
F.Suggest: If AM bogs down, what are some new tasks (related to facet F of concept C) to consider doing?

In the LISP implementation of AM, each concept is maintained as an atom with an attribute/value list (property list). Each facet, and its list of entries, is just a property and its associated value.

Below is a stylized rendition of the Sets concept, which intuitively corresponds to the notion of a collection of elements.

Name(s): Set, Proper Collection, Proper Class
Definitions:
    Recursive: λ (S) [S={} or Set.Definition (Remove(Any-member(S),S))]
    Recursive quick: λ (S) [S={} or Set.Definition (CDR(S))]
    Quick: λ (S) [Match S with {...}]
Specializations: Empty-set, Nonempty-set, Singleton, Doubleton
Generalizations: Unordered-Structure, Collection,
    Structure-with-no-multiple-elements-allowed
Examples:
    Typical: {{}}, {A}, {A,B}, {3}
    Barely: {}, {A, B,{C, {{{A, C, (3,3,9), ⟨4,{B},A⟩}}}}}
    Not-quite: {A,A}, (), {B,A}
    Foible: ⟨4,1,A,1⟩
Conjectures: All unordered-structures are sets.
Intuitions: Geometric: Venn diagram.
Analogies: {set, set operations}≡{list, list operations}
Worth: 600 [on a scale of 0–1000]
View:
    Predicate: λ(P) {x∈Domain(P) | P(x)}
    Structure: λ (S) Enclose-in-braces(Sort(Remove-multiple-elements(S)))
Suggest: If P is an interesting predicate over X,
    Then consider {x∈X | P(x)}.
In-domain-of: Union, Intersection, Set-difference, Subset, Member,
    Cartesian-product, Set-equality
In-range-of: Union, Intersect, Set-difference, Satisfying

To decipher the Definitions facet, there are a few things you must know. Facet F of concept C will occasionally be abbreviated as C.F. In those cases where F is "executable", the notion C.F will refer to applying the corresponding function. So the first entry in the Definitions facet is recursive because it contains an embedded call on the function Set.Definition. Notice that we are implying that the name of the lambda expression itself is "Set.Definition". Since there are three separate but equivalent definitions, AM may choose whichever one it wants when it recurs. AM can pick one via a random selection scheme, or always try to recur into the same definition as it was just in, or perhaps suit its choice to the form of the argument at the moment.

All concepts possess executable definitions (LISP predicates), though not necessarily effective ones. When given an argument x, Set.definition will return "True", "False", or will eventually be interrupted by a timer (indicating that no conclusion was reached about whether or not x is a set).

The "Views", "Intuitions", and "Analogies" facets must be distinguished from each other. "**Views**" is concerned with transformations between instances of two specific concepts (for example, how to view any predicate as a set, and vice versa). An entry on the "**Analogies**" facet is a mapping from a set of concepts (for example, between {bags, bag-union, bag-intersection, ...} and {numbers, addition, minimum, ...}; or between {primes, factoring, numbers, ...} and {simple groups, factoring into subgroups, groups ...}). "**Intuitions**" deals with transformations between a bunch of concepts and one of a few large, standard scenarios (for example, intuit the relation "$\geq$" as playing on a see-saw; intuit a set by drawing a Venn diagram). Intuitions are characterized by being (i) opaque (AM cannot introspect on them, delve into their code), (ii) occasionally fallible, (iii) very quick, and (iv) carefully handcrafted in advance (since AM cannot pick up new intuitions via metaphors to the real world, as we humans can).

Since "Sets" is a static concept, it had no Algorithms facet (as did, for example, "Set-union"). The algorithms facet of a concept contains a list of entries, a list of equivalent algorithms. Each algorithm must have three separate parts:

1. Descriptors: Recursive, Linear, or Iterative? Quick or Slow? Opaque (difficult to analyse statically) or Transparent (cleanly coded)? Destructive or non-destructive?
2. Relators: Is this just a special case of some other concept's algorithm? Which others does this one call on? Is this similar to any other algorithms for any other concepts?
3. Program: A small, executable piece of LISP code. It may be used for actually "running" the algorithm; it may also be inspected, copied, reasoned about, etc.

There are multiple algorithms for the same concept because different ones have different properties: some are very quick in some cases, some are always slow but are very cleanly written and hence are easier to reason about, etc.

Another facet possessed only by active concepts is "**Domain/Range**". It is a list of entries, each of the form $<D_1\ D_2 \ldots D_i \rightarrow R>$, which means that the concept takes a list of arguments, the first one being an example of concept D_1, the second of D_2, ..., the last argument being an example of concept D_i, and if the algorithm (any entry on the Algorithms facet) is run on this argument list, then the value it returns will be an example of concept R. We may say that the Domain of the concept is the Cartesian product $D_1 \times D_2 \times \ldots \times D_i$, and that the Range of the concept is R. For example, the Domain/Range of Set-union is <Sets Sets → Sets>; Set-union takes a pair of sets as its argument list, and returns a set as its value.

Several other facets were considered from time to time, including "Uninterestingness", "Justification", "Recognition", etc. They were all dropped eventually, because of their insignificant contribution to the performance of the AM program. The Intuitions facet was eventually dropped, because it never led to any discoveries which had not been foreseen by the author.

Once the representation of knowledge is settled, there remains the actual choice of what knowledge to put into the program initially. One hundred elementary concepts were selected, corresponding roughly to what Piaget might have called "prenumerical knowledge". Appendix 1 presents a graph of these concepts, showing their interrelationships of Generalization/Specialization and Examples/Isa's. There is much static structural knowledge (sets, truth-values, conjectures ...) and much knowledge about simple activities (boolean relations, composition of relations, set operations, ...). Notice that there is no notion of proof, of formal reasoning, or of numbers or arithmetic.

2.2 Top-level control: the agenda

AM's basic activity is to find new entries for some facet of some concept. But which particular one should it choose to develop next? Initially, there are over one hundred concepts, each with about twenty blank facets; thus the "space" from which to choose is of size two thousand. As more concepts are defined, this number increases. It's worth having AM spend some time deciding which basic task (facet/concept) to work on next, for two reasons: most of the tasks will never be explored, and only a few of the tasks will appear (to the human user) rational things to work on at the moment.

Much informal expert knowledge is required to constrain the search, to quickly zero in on one of these few very good tasks to tackle next. This is done in two stages:

1. A list of plausible facet/concept pairs is maintained. No task can get onto this "agenda" unless there is some reason why working on that facet of that concept would be worthwhile.
2. Each task on this agenda is assigned a priority rating, based on the number (and strengths) of reasons supporting it. This allows the entire agenda to be kept ordered by plausibility.

The first of these constraints is much like replacing a legal move generator with a plausible move generator, in a heuristic search program. The second kind of constraint is akin to using a heuristic evaluation function to select the best move from among the good ones. Here is a typical entry on the agenda, a task:

Activity:	Fill in some entries
Facet:	for the GENERALIZATIONS facet
Concept:	of the PRIMES concept
Reasons:	because
	(1) There is only 1 known gen'l. of Primes, so far.
	(2) The worth rating of Primes is now very high.
	(3) Focus of attention: AM just worked on Primes.
	(4) Very few numbers are primes; a slightly more plentiful concept may be more interesting.
Priority:	350 [on a scale of 0–1000]

The actual top-level control policy is to pluck the top task (highest priority rating) from the agenda, and then execute it. While a task executes, some new tasks may be proposed (and merged into the agenda), some new concepts may get created, and (one hopes) some entries for the specified facet of the specified concept will be found and filled in. Once a task is chosen, the priority rating of that task then serves a new function: it is taken as an estimate of how much computational resource to devote to working on this task. The task above, in the box, might be allotted 35 cpu seconds and 350 list cells, because its rating was 350. When either resource is exhausted, work on the task halts. The task is removed from the agenda, and the cycle begins anew (AM starts working on whichever task is now at the top of the agenda).

2.3 Low-level control: the heuristics

After a task is selected from the agenda, how is it "executed"? A concise answer would be: AM selects relevant heuristics and executes them; they satisfy the task via side-effects. This really just splits our original question into two new ones: How are relevant heuristics located? What does it mean for a heuristic to be executed and to achieve something?

2.3.1 How relevant heuristics are located

Each heuristic is represented as a condition/action rule. The condition or left-hand side of a rule tests to see whether the rule is applicable to the task on hand. The action or right-hand side of the rule consists of a list of actions to perform if the rule is applicable. Below is a typical heuristic:

IF the current task is to check examples of a concept X,
  and (Forsome Y) Y is a generalization of X,
  and Y has at least 10 known examples
  and all examples of Y are also examples of X,

THEN conjecture: X is really no more specialized than Y,
    and add that conjecture as a new entry on the
        Examples facet of the Conjecs concept,
    and add the following task to the agenda:
        "Check examples of Y"
        for this reason: Y may analogously turn out to be
            equal to one of its supposed generalizations.

It is the heuristics' right-hand (THEN-) sides which actually accomplish the selected task; that process will be described in the next subsection. The left-hand (IF-) sides are the relevancy checkers, and will be focused on now:

Syntactically, the left side must be a predicate, a LISP function which returns True or False depending upon the situation at that moment. It must be a conjunction $P_1 \wedge P_2 \wedge P_3 \wedge \ldots$ of smaller predicates P_i, each of which must be quick and must have no side effects. Here are five typical conjuncts which might appear within rules' left-hand sides:

Over half of the current task's time allotment is used up;
There are some known examples of Structures;
Some known generalization of the current concept (the concept mentioned as part of the current task) has a completely empty Examples facet;
A task recently worked on had the form "Fill in facet F of C", for any F, where C is the current concept;
The user has used this program at least once before;

It turned out that the laxity of constraints on the form of the heuristic rules proved excessive: it made it very difficult for AM to analyse and modify its own heuristics.

From a "pure production system" viewpoint, we have answered the question of locating relevant heuristics. Namely, we evaluate the left sides of all the rules, and see which ones respond "True". But AM contains hundreds of heuristics, and to repeatedly evaluate each one's condition would use up tremendous amounts of time. AM is able quickly to select a set of potentially relevant rules, rules whose left sides are then evaluated to test for true relevance. The secret is that each rule is stored somewhere a propos to its "domain of applicability". The proper place to store the rule is determined by the first conjunct on its left-hand side. Consider this heuristic:

IF the current task is to find examples of activity F,
    and a fast algorithm A for computing F is known,
THEN one way to get examples of F is to run A on
    randomly chosen examples of the Domain of F.

The very first conjunct of a rule's left side is always special. It specifies the domain of applicability (potential relevance) of the heuristic, by naming a particular facet of a particular concept to which this rule is relevant (in the above rule, the domain of relevance is therefore the Examples facet of the Activity concept). AM uses such first conjuncts as pre-preconditions: Each potentially relevant rule can be located by its first conjunct alone. Then, its left-hand side is fully evaluated, to indicate whether it's truly relevant. Here are a few typical expressions which could be first conjuncts:

The current task (the one just selected from the agenda) is of the form "Check the Domain/range facet of concept X", where X is some surjective function;
The current task matches "Fill in boundary examples of X", where X is an operation on pairs of sets;
The current task is "Fill in examples of Primes";

The key observation is that a heuristic typically applies to all examples of a particular concept C. The rule above has C = Activity; it's relevant to each individual activity. For example, it can be used to find examples of Set-union, since Set-union is an activity.

When a task is chosen, it specifies which concept C and which facet F are to be worked on. AM then "ripples upward" to gather potentially relevant rules: it looks on facet F of concept C to see if any rules are tacked on there, it looks on facet F of each generalization of C, on each of their generalizations, etc. If the current task were "Check the Domain/range or Union-∘-Union",† then AM would ripple upward from Union-∘-Union, along the Generalization facet entries, gathering heuristics as it went. The program would ascertain which concepts claim Union-∘-Union as one of their examples. These concepts happen to include Compose-with-self, Compose, Operation, Active, Any-concept, Anything. AM would collect heuristics that tell how to check the Domain/range of any composition, how to check the Domain/range facet of any concept, etc. Of course, the further out it ripples, the more general (and hence weaker) the heuristics tend to be. Here is one heuristic, tacked onto the Domain/range facet of Operation, which would be garnered if the selected task were "Check Domain/range of Union-∘-Union":

IF the current task is "Check the Domain/range of F", for some Activity F,
and an entry on that facet has the form ⟨D D... D → R⟩,
and concept R is a generalization of concept D,
THEN it is worth spending time checking whether or not
the range of F might be simply D, instead of R.

Suppose that one entry on Union-∘-Union's Domain/range facet was "<Nonempty-sets Nonempty-sets Nonempty-sets → Sets>". Then the above heuristic would be truly relevant (all three conjuncts on its left-hand side would be satisfied), and it would pose the question: Is the union of three nonempty sets always nonempty? Empirical evidence would eventually confirm this, and the Domain/range facet of Union-∘-Union would then contain that fact. AM would ask the same question for the operation Intersect. Although the answer in that case is negative, it is nonetheless a rational idea to investigate whether or not the intersection of two nonempty sets is always nonempty.

Here is another way to look at the heuristic-gathering process. All the concepts known to AM are arranged in a big hierarchy, via subset-of links (Specializations and Generalizations) and element-of links (Isa's and Examples) as diagrammed in Appendix 1. Since each heuristic is associated with one individual concept (its domain of applicability), there is a hierarchy induced

†This operation is the result of composing set-union with itself. It performs $\lambda\,(x,y,z)\; x \cup (y \cup z)$.

upon the set of heuristics. Heritability properties hold: a heuristic tacked onto concept C is applicable to working on all "lower" (more specialized) concepts. This allows us efficiently to analogically access the potentially relevant heuristics simply by chasing upward links in the hierarchy. Note that the task selected from the agenda provides an explicit pointer to the "lowest" - most specific - concept; AM ripples upward from it. Thus concepts are gathered in order of increasing generality; hence so are the heuristics.

Below are summarized the three main points that comprise AM's scheme for finding relevant heuristics in a "natural" way and then using them:

1. Each heuristic is tacked onto the most general concept for which it applies: it is given as large a domain of applicability as possible. This will maximize its generality, while leaving its power untouched, hence bringing it as close as possible to the ideal tradeoff between generality and power.
2. When the current task deals with concept C, AM ripples upward from C, tracing along Generalization and Isa links, to quickly find all concepts which claim C as one of their examples. Heuristics attached to all such concepts are potentially relevant.
3. All heuristics are represented as condition/action rules. As the potentially relevant rules are located (in step 2), AM evaluates each's left-hand side, in order of increasing generality. The rippling process automatically gathers the heuristics in this order. Whenever a rule's left side returns True, the rule is known to be truly relevant, and its right side is immediately executed.

2.3.2 What happens when heuristics are executed

When a rule is recognized as relevant, its right side is executed. Precisely how does this accomplish the chosen task?

The right side, by contrast to the left, may take a great deal of time, have many side effects, and return a value which is simply ignored. The right side of a rule is a series of little LISP functions, each of which is called an *action.* Semantically, each action performs some processing which is appropriate in some way to the kinds of situation in which the rule's left side would have been satisfied (returned True). The only constraint which each action must satisfy is that it have one of the following three kinds of side-effects, and no other kinds:

1. It suggests a new task to add to the agenda.
2. it dictates how some new concept is to be defined.
3. It adds some entry to some facet of some concept.

Bear in mind that the right side of a single rule is a list of such actions. Let's now treat these three kinds of actions:

2.3.2.1 Heuristics suggest new tasks

The left side of a rule triggers. Scattered among the list of "things to do" on its right side are some suggestions for future tasks. These new tasks are then simply added to the agenda. The suggestion for the task includes enough information about the task to make it easy for AM to assemble its parts, to find reasons for it, numerically to evaluate those reasons, etc. For example, here is a typical rule which proposes a new task. It says to generalize a predicate if it appears to be returning "True" very rarely:

IF the current task was "Fill in examples of X", for some predicate X,
    and over 100 items are known in the domain of X,
    and at least 10 cpu secs. have been spent so far on this task,
    and X has returned True at least once,
    and X returned False over 20 times as often as True,
THEN add the following task to the agenda:
    "Fill in generalizations of X"
    for the following reason:
    "X is rarely satisfied; a slightly less restrictive
        predicate might be much more interesting"
    This reason has a rating which is the False/True results ratio

Let's see one instance where this rule was used. AM worked on the task "Fill in examples of List-Equality". One heuristic (displayed in Sec. 2.3.1, and again in detail in Sec. 2.3.2.3) said: randomly pick elements from that predicate's domain and simply run the predicate. Thus AM repeatedly plucked random pairs of lists, and tested whether or not they were equal. Needless to say, not a high percentage returned True (in practice, 2 out of 242). This rule's left side was satisfied, and it executed. Its right side caused a new task to be formulated: "Fill in generalizations of List-Equality". The reason was as stated above in the rule, and that reason got a numeric rating of 240/2 = 120. That task was then assigned an overall rating (in this case, just 120) and merged into the agenda. It sandwiched in between a task with a rating of 128 and one with a 104 priority rating. Incidentally, when this task was finally selected, it led to the creation of several interesting concepts, including the predicate which we might call "Same-length".

2.3.2.2 Heuristics create new concepts

One of the three kinds of allowable actions on the right side of a heuristic rule is to create a specific new concept. For each such creation, the heuristic must specify how the new concept is to be constructed. The heuristic states the Definition facet entries for the new concept, plus usually a few other facets' contents. After this action terminates, the new concept will "exist". A few of its facets will be filled in, and many others will be blank. Some new tasks may be added to the agenda at concept-time, tasks which indicate that AM ought to spend some time filling in some of those blank facets in the near future. Here is a heuristic rule which results in a new concept being created:

IF the current rask was "Fill in examples of F"
        for an operation F, say from domain A into range B,
    and more than 100 items are known examples of A,
    and more than 10 range items (examples of B) were
        found by applying F to these domain elements,

and at least one of these range items 'b' is a distinguished
member (especially, an extremum) of B,
THEN for each such 'b'∈B, create the following kind of concept:

NAME: F^{-1}-of-b
DEFINITION: λ (a) F(a) is a 'b'
GENERALIZATIONS: A
WORTH: Average(Worth(A), Worth(B), Worth(b), Worth(F), ||Examples(B)||)
INTEREST: Any conjec. involving this concept and either F or F^{-1}

and the reason for this creation is:
"It's worth investigating A's which have unusual F-values"
and add five new tasks to the agenda,
each of the form "Fill in facet x of F^{-1}-of-b"
where x is Conjectures, Gereralizations, Specializations, Examples, Isa's;
each for the following reason:
"This concept was newly synthesized; it is crucial
to find where it 'fits in' to the hierarchy"
The reason's rating is computed as:
Worth(F^{-1}-of-b) = Arg(Worth(F), Worth(b)).

One use of this heuristic was when the current task was "Fill in examples of Divisors-of". The heuristic's left side was satisfied because: Divisors-of is an operation (from Numbers to Sets of numbers), and far more than the required 100 different numbers are known, and more than 10 different sets of factors were located altogether, and some of them were in fact distinguished by being extreme kinds of sets (for example, singletons, empty sets, doubletons, tripletons, ...). After its left side triggered, the right side of the rule was executed. Four new concepts were created immediately. Here is one of them:

NAME: Divisors-of^{-1}-of-Doubleton
DEFINITION: λ (a) Divisors-of(a) is a Doubleton
GENERALIZATIONS: Numbers
WORTH: 100
INTEREST: Any conjec. involving this concept and either Divisors-of or Times

This is a concept representing a certain class of numbers, in fact the numbers we call "primes". The heuristic rule is of course applicable to any kind of operation, not just numeric ones. As another instance of its use, consider what happened when the current task was "Fill in examples of Set-intersect". This rule caused AM to notice that some pairs of sets were mapping over into the most extreme of all sets: the empty set. The rule then had AM define the new concept we would call "disjointness": pairs of sets having empty intersection. Similarly, "subset" arose as the relation that holds between sets A and B iff Set-difference$(A,B)=\{\}$. So we see how the above heuristic rule led to the discovery of many well-known concepts.

Here is just a tiny bit of "theory" behind how these concept-creating rules were designed: A facet of a neonatal concept is filled in immediately at birth iff both (i) it's trivial to fill in at creation-time, and (ii) it would be very difficult to fill in later on. The following facets are typically filled in right away: Definitions, Algorithms, Domain/range, Worth, plus a pointer to a "parent" concept (for example, the trivially-computed entry "Numbers" for the Generalizations facet of the Primes concept). Each other facet is either left unmentioned by the rule, or else is explicitly made the subject of a new task which gets added to the agenda. For instance, the heuristic rule above would propose five new tasks at the moment that the Primes concept was created, including "Fill in conjectures about Primes", "Fill in specializations of Primes", "Fill in examples of Primes", etc.

2.3.2.3 Heuristics fill in entries for a specific facet

If the task plucked from the agenda were "Fill in examples of Set-union", it would not be too much to hope for that by the time all the heuristic rules had finished executing, some examples of that operation would indeed exist on the Examples facet of the Set-union concept. Let's see how this can happen.

AM starts by rippling upward from Set-union, looking for heuristics which are relevant to finding examples of Set-union (there are no such rules), relevant to finding examples of Set-operations, of Operations, of any Activity, of any Concept, of Anything. Here is one rule garnered in the search, a rule which is tacked onto (hence assumed applicable to) the Examples facet of Activity:

IF the current task is to fill in examples of activity F,
    and there is a fast known algorithm for F,
THEN one way to get examples of F is to run F's algorithm
    on randomly chosen examples of the domain of F.

Of course, in the LISP implementation, this situation-action rule is not coded quite so neatly. It would be more faithfully translated as follows:

IF CURR-TASK matches (FILLIN EXAMPLES F←any-activity),
    and the Algorithms facet of F contains an entry with descriptor "Quick",
THEN carry out the following procedure:

1. Find the domain of F, and call it D;
2. Find examples of D, and call them E;
3. Find a fast algorithm to compute F; call it A;
4. Repeatedly:
    - 4a. Choose any member of E, and call it E1.
    - 4b. Run A on E1, and call the result X.
    - 4c. Check whether ⟨E1,X⟩ satisfies the definition of F.
    - 4d. If so, then add ⟨E1 → X⟩ to the Examples facet of F.
    - 4e. If not, then add ⟨E1 → X⟩ to the Non-examples facet of F.

Let's see exactly how this rule found examples of Set-union. Step (1) says to locate the domain of Set-union. The facet labelled Domain/range, on the Set-union concept, contains the entry (SET SET → SET), which indicates that the domain is a pair of sets. That is, Set-union is an operation which accepts (as its arguments) two sets.

Since the domain elements are sets, step (2) says to locate examples of sets. The facet labelled Examples, on the Sets concept, points to a list of about 30 different sets. This includes $\{Z\}$, $\{A,B,C,D,E\}$, $\{\}$, $\{A,\{\{B\}\}\}$,...

Step (3) involves nothing more than accessing some entry tagged with the descriptor "Quick" on the Algorithms facet of Set-union. One such entry is a recursive LISP function of two arguments, which halts, when the first argument is the empty set, and otherwise pulls an element out of that set, Set-inserts it into the second argument, and then recurs on the new values of the two sets. For convenience, we'll refer to this algorithm as UNION.

We then enter the loop of Step (4). Step(a) has us choose one pair of our examples of sets, say the first two $\{Z\}$ and $\{A,B,C,D,E\}$. Step (4b) has us run UNION on these two sets. The result is $\{A,B,C,D,E,Z\}$. Step (4c) has us grab an entry from the Definitions facet of Set-union, and run it. A typical definition is this formal one:

(λ ($S1$ $S2$ $S3$)
    (AND
        (For all x in $S1$, x is in $S3$)
        (For all x in $S2$, x is in $S3$)
        (For all x in $S3$, x is in $S1$ or x is in $S2$)))).

It is run on the three arguments $S1=\{Z\}$, $S2=\{A,B,C,D,E\}$, $S3=\{A,B,C,D,E,Z\}$. Since it returns "True", we proceed to Step (4d). The construct $\langle\{Z\}, \{A,B,C,D,E\} \rightarrow \{A,B,C,D,E,Z\}\rangle$ is added to the Examples facet of Set-union.

At this stage, control returns to the beginning of the Step (4) loop. A new pair of sets is chosen, and so on.

But when would this loop stop? Recall that as soon as a task is selected from the agenda, it is assigned a time and a space allotment (based on its priority value). If there are many different rules all claiming to be relevant to the current task, then each one is allocated a small fraction of those time/space quanta. When either of these resources is exhausted, AM would break away at a "clean" point (just after finishing a cycle of the Step (4) loop) and would move on to a new heuristic rule for filling in examples of Set-union.

3. RESULTS

3.1 Excerpt of the AM program running

Repeatedly, the top task is plucked from the agenda, and heuristics are executed in an attempt to satisfy it. AM has a modest facility that prints out a description of these activities as they occur. Below is a tiny excerpt of this self-trace monologue, in which AM discovers prime numbers. In Appendix 3, the reader may observe (in much more condensed form) summaries of the tasks which preceded these, tasks in which elementary set theory was explored, cardinality was discovered, and arithmetic was developed.

** *TASK CHOSEN:* ** Fill in Examples of the concept "Divisors-of".
3 Reasons:
(1) No known examples of Divisors-of yet.
(2) Times (related to Divisors-of) is now very interesting.
(3) Focus of attention: AM just defined Divisors-of.
26 examples found, in 9 secs. e.g., Divisors-of(6)={1,2,3,6}

** *TASK CHOSEN:* ** Consider numbers having small sets of Divisors-of.
2 Reasons:
(1) Worthwhile to look for extreme cases.
(2) Focus of attention: AM just worked on Divisors-of.
Filling in examples of numbers with 0 divisors.
0 examples found, in 4.0 seconds.
Conjecture: no numbers have precisely 0 divisors.
Filling in examples of numbers with 1 divisors.
1 examples found, in 4 secs. e.g., Divisors-of(1)={1}.
Conjecture: 1 is the only number with exactly 1 divisor.
Filling in examples of numbers with 2 divisors.
24 examples found, in 4 secs. e.g., Divisors-of(13)={1,13}.
No obvious conjecture. May merit more study.
Creating a new concept: "Numbers-with-2-divisors".
Filling in examples of numbers with 3 divisors.
11 examples found, in 4 secs. Divisors-of(49)={1,7,49}.
All numbers with 3 divisors are also Perfect Squares. Unexpected!.
The chance of coincidence is below acceptable limits.
Creating a new concept: "Numbers-with-3-divisors".

** *TASK CHOSEN:* ** Consider square-roots of Numbers-with-3-divisors.
2 Reasons:
(1) All known Numbers-with-3-divisors unexpectedly turned out to all be Perfect Squares as well.
(2) Focus of attention: AM just defined Numbers-with-3-divisors.
All square-roots of Numbers-with-3-divisors seem to be Numbers-with-2-divisors.
E.g., Divisors(169) = Divisors(13) = {1,13}.
Even the converse of this seems empirically to be true.
I.e., the square of each Number-with-2-divisors seems to be a Number-with-3-divisors.
The chance of coincidence is below acceptable limits.
Boosting the Worth rating of both concepts.

** *TASK CHOSEN:* ** Consider the squares of Numbers-with-3-divisors.
3 Reasons:
(1) Squares of Numbers-with-2-divisors were very interesting.
(2) Square-roots of Numbers-with-3-divisors were interesting.
(3) Focus of attention: AM just worked on Numbers-with-3-divisors.

The last task goes nowhere, and is a good place to terminate this excerpt and this subsection.

3.2 Overall performance

AM began its investigations with scanty knowledge of a hundred elementary concepts of finite set theory (Appendix 1). Most of the obvious finite set-theoretic concepts and relationships were quickly found (for example, de Morgan's laws; singletons), but no sophisticated set theory was ever done (for example, diagonalization).

Rather, AM decided that "equality" was worth generalizing, and thereby discovered the relation "same-size-as". "Natural numbers" were based on this, and soon most simple arithmetic operations were defined (as analogs to set-theoretic operations; for example, "subtract" is the analog of "Set-difference"). See Appendix 2.

Since addition arose as an analog to union, and multiplication as a repeated substitution, it came as quite a surprise to AM when it noticed that they were related (namely, $N+N=2\times N$). AM later rediscovered multiplication in three other ways: as repeated addition, as the numeric analog of the Cartesian product of sets, and by studying the cardinality of power sets. These operations were defined in different ways, so it was an unexpected (to AM) discovery when they all turned out to be equivallent. These surprises caused AM to give the concept 'Times' quite a high Worth rating. Exponentiation was defined as repeated multiplication. Unfortunately, AM never found any obvious properties of exponentiation, hence lost all interest in it.

Soon after defining multiplication, AM investigated the process of multiplying a number by itself: squaring. The inverse of this turned out to be interesting, and led to the definition of square-root. AM remained content to play around with the concept of integer-square-root. Although it isolated the set of numbers which had no square root, AM was never close to discovering negative numbers, let alone irrationals. No notion of "closure" was provided to - or discovered by - AM.

Raising to fourth-powers, and fourth-rooting, were discovered at this time. Perfect squares and perfect fourth-powers were isolated. Many other numeric operations and kinds of numbers were found to be of interest: Odds, Evens, Doubling, Halving, etc. Primitive notions of numeric inequality were defined, but AM never even discovered Trichotomy.

The associativity and commutativity of multiplication indicated that it could accept a Bag of numbers as its argument. When AM defined the inverse relation corresponding to Times, this property allowed the definition to be: "λ (x) any bag of numbers (each >1) whose product is x". This was just the notion of factoring a number x. Minimally-factorable numbers turned out to be what we call primes. Maximally-factorable numbers were also thought to be interesting, and this motivated some new results in number theory (see Lenat 1976, Appendix 4).

Prime pairs were discovered in a bizarre way - by restricting the domain and range of addition to primes (that is, solutions of $p+q=r$ in primes).

AM conjectured the fundamental theorem of arithmetic (unique factorization into primes) and Goldbach's conjecture (every even number >2 is the sum of two primes) in a surprisingly symmetric way. The unary representation of numbers gave way to a representation as a bag of primes (based on unique factorization), but AM never thought of exponential notation. Diophantine equations were isolated, but not developed very far.

Since the key concepts of remainder, greater-than, gcd, and exponentiation were never mastered, progress in number theory was arrested. Other crucial concepts which were never uncovered include: infinity, proof, rationals, residues, etc. Most of these "omissions", could have been discovered by the existing heuristic rules in AM. The paths which would have resulted in their definition were simply never rated high enough (by AM, by itself) to warrant exploration.

All the discoveries mentioned (including all those in Appendix 2) were made in a run lasting one cpu hour (Interlisp+100K, Sumex PDP-10 K1). Two hundred jobs in toto were selected from the agenda and executed; many of these are summarized (in order) in Appendix 3. On the average, a job was granted 30 cpu seconds, but actually used only 18 seconds (by which time all the truly relevant heuristics had finished executing). For a typical job, about 35 rules were located as potentially relevant, and about a dozen actually fired (were executed). AM began with 115 concepts and ended up with three times that many. Of the synthesized concepts, half were technically termed "losers" (both by the author and by AM; for example, "Subtract-*x*-from-itself" was a real zero), and half the other new concepts were only marginal (for example, "Numbers which are uniquely representable as the sum of two primes"). Two hundred and fifty heuristic rules were present during this run of the program.

Although AM fared well according to several different measures of performance (see Sec. 3.4), its limitations have considerable significance. As AM ran longer and longer, the concepts it defined were further and further from the primitives it began with. For example, "prime-pairs" were defined using "primes" and "addition", the former of which was defined from "divisors-of", which in turn came from "multiplication", which arose from "addition", which was defined as a restriction of "union", which (finally!) was a primitive concept that we had supplied (with heuristics) to AM initially. When AM subsequently needed help with prime pairs, it was forced to rely on rules of thumb supplied originally about unioning. Although the heritability property of heuristics did ensure that those rules were still valid, the trouble was that they were too general, too weak to deal effectively with the specialized notions of primes and arithmetic.

For instance, one general rule indicated that $A \cup B$ would be interesting if it possessed properties absent both from A and from B. This translated into the prime-pair case as "If $p+q=r$, and p,q,r are primes, Then r is interesting if it has properties not possessed by p or by q". The search for categories of such interesting primes r was of course barren. It showed a fundamental lack of understanding about numbers, addition, odd/even-ness, and primes. As another example, AM didn't recognize a priori that the UFT (unique factorization theorem) was more significant than Goldbach's conjecture.

The key deficiency was the lack of adequate meta-rules (Davis 1976): heuristics which reason about heuristics: keep track of their performance, modify them, create new ones, etc. Here is one such rule, which would have taken care of the "Goldbach vs UFT" problem:

> After applying the "look at the inverse of extrema" heuristic, and thereby defining a new concept C (as f^{-1} of b), where C is a new specialization of concept A,
> Synthesize a heuristic which indicates that conjectures involving C and f (or f^{-1}) are very significant and natural, whereas those involving C and unrelated operations are probably anomalies,
> and synthesize another heuristic which indicates that C is a good kind of A upon which to test conjectures involving f or f^{-1}.

How would this meta-rule be used? When primes are defined as the inverse image of doubletons, under the operation "divisors-of", the meta-rule would trigger, and two brand new rules would be synthesized. The first of those new heuristics would say that conjectures about primes were natural iff they involved multiplication or division. Thus the UFT would be rated as important, and Goldbach's conjecture as cute but useless. The second new rule would say that Primes are a useful kind of Number upon which to test out conjectures involving multiplication or division; this, too is quite a powerful piece of informal knowledge.

Aside from the preceding major limitation, most of the other problems pertain to missing knowledge: Many concepts one might consider basic to discovery in mathematics are absent from AM; analogies were under-utilized; physical intuition was hand-crafted only; the interface to the user was far from ideal; etc.

3.3 Experiments with AM

One valuable aspect of AM is that it is amenable to many kinds of experiment. Although AM is too ad hoc for numeric results to have much significance, the qualitative results of such experiments may have some valid implications for mathematical research, for automating mathematical research, and for designing "scientist assistant" programs.

3.3.1 Must the Worth numbers be finely tuned?

To signify its overall worth, each of the 115 initial concepts had a rating number (0–1000) supplied by the author. The worth ratings affect the overall priority values of tasks on the agenda. Just how sensitive is AM's behaviour to the initial settings of the Worth numbers?

To test this, a simple experiment was performed. All the concepts' Worth facets were set to 200 initially. By and large, the same discoveries were made as before. But there were now long periods of blind wandering (especially near the beginning of the run). Once AM hooked into a line of productive developments, it advanced at the old rate. During such chains of discoveries, AM was guided by massive quantities of symbolic reasons for the tasks it chose, not by nuances in numeric ratings. As these spurts of development died out, AM would wander around again until the next one started.

3.3.2 How finely tuned is the agenda?

The top few tasks on the agenda almost always appear to be reasonable things to do at the time. But what if, instead of picking the top-rated task, AM is always made to select one randomly from the top 20 tasks on the agenda? In that case, AM's rate of discovery is slowed only by about a factor of 3. But the apparent "rationality" of the program (as perceived by a human onlooker) disintegrates.

3.3.3 How valuable is the presence of symbolic 'reasons'?

One effect of note was observed: When a task is proposed which already exists on the agenda, then it matters very much whether the task is being suggested for a new reason or not. If the reason is an old, already-known one, then the priority of the task on the agenda shouldn't rise very much. But if it is a brand new reason, then the task's rating should be boosted tremendously. The importance of this effect argues strongly in favour of having symbolic justification of the rank of each task on a priority queue, not just "summarizing" each task's set of reasons by a single number.

3.3.4 What if certain concepts are excised?

As expected, eliminating certain concepts did seal off whole sets of discoveries to the system. For example, excising Equality prevented AM from discovering Cardinality. One surprising result was that many common concepts get discovered in several ways. For instance, multiplication arose in no fewer than four separate chains of discoveries.

3.3.5 Can AM work in the new domain of plane geometry?

One demonstration of AM's generality (for example, that its "Activity" heuristics really do apply to any activity) would be to choose some new mathematical field, add some concepts from that domain, and then let AM loose to discover new things. Only one experiment of this type was actually carried out on the AM program.

Twenty concepts from elementary plane geometry were defined for AM (including Point, Line, Angel, Triangle, Equality of points/lines/angles/triangles). No new heuristics were added to AM.

AM was able to find examples of all the supplied concepts, and to use the character of such empirical data to determine reasonable directions to proceed in its search. AM derived the concepts of congruence and similarity of triangles, plus many other well-known concepts. An unusual result was the repeated derivation of the concept of "timberline": this is a predicate on two triangles, which is true iff they share a common vertex and angle, and if their opposite sides are parallel. AM also came up with a cute geometric interpretation of Goldbach's conjecture: Any angle (0–180°) can be approximated to within 1° as the sum of two angles each of a prime number of degrees. But lacking a geometry "model" (an analogic representation of Euclidean space, for example, the kind that Gelernter (1963) employed,) AM was doomed to propose many implausible geometric conjectures.

More and more drastic changes to the knowledge base of AM would be required if its task domain were to be shifted further and further from simple finite set theory. For example, to work reasonably well in analysis, AM would need the additional concepts of continuity, infinity, limits, measure, etc. To work in a non-formalized field (such as mass spectroscopy), AM would have to be spoon-fed data, the way that Meta-Dendral is, or else be connected directly to physical sensing devices to that it could gather its own empirical data. One other alternative would be to provide AM with a formal model of some real-world phenomenon (for example, gravitation). But in such a case, AM could never do more than reformulate the model, could never discover any "real" effects which were not taken into account by the model. If fed a model of a Newtonian world, AM might discover Lagrangian mechanics, but it could never observe any relativistic effects. The impracticality of all these alternatives seems to indicate that AM-like programs are best suited to theory formation in fully formalizable fields (mathematics, programming, games, etc.).

3.4 Evaluating the AM program

We may wish to evaluate AM by using various criteria. Some obvious ones, with capsule results, appear below:

1. *By AM's ultimate achievements.* Besides discovering many well-known useful concepts, AM discovered some which aren't widely known: maximally-divisible numbers, numbers which can be uniquely represented as the sum of two primes, timberline. The first of these is related to Ramanujan's "highly composite numbers", and represents a real (albeit miniscule) contribution to number theory.

2. *By the character of the differences between initial and final states.* AM moved all the way from finite set theory to divisibility theory, from sets to numbers to interesting kinds of numbers, from skeletal concepts (none of which had any Examples filled in) to completed concepts, from one hundred concepts to three hundred.

3. *By the quality of the route AM took to accomplish this mass of results.* Only about half of AM's forays were dead-ends, and most of those looked promising initially.

4. *By the character of the human-machine interactions.* AM was never pushed far along this dimension. The human "user" is really little more than an observer, a monitor; he occasionally interrupts AM to ask one of a few possible questions, or to rename some common concept, etc.

5. *By its informal reasoning abilities.* AM was able quickly to "guess" the truth value of its conjectures, to estimate the overall worth of each new concept, to zero in on plausible things to do each cycle, and to notice glaring analogies (sometimes).

6. *By the results of experiments – and the fact that experiments could be performed at all on AM.* See Sec. 3.3.

7. *By future implications of this project.* Only time will tell whether this kind of work will impact on how mathematics is taught (for example, explicit teaching of heuristics?), on how empirical research is carried out by scientists, on our understanding of such phenomena as discovery, learning, and creativity, etc.

8. *By comparisons with other, similar systems.* Some of the techniques AM uses were pioneered earlier: for example, prototypical models (Gelernter 1963), and analogy (Evans 1968 and Kling 1971). There have been many attempts to incorporate heuristic knowledge into a theorem prover (Wang 1960, Guard 1969, Bledsoe 1971, Brotz 1974, Boyer and Moore 1975). Most of the apparent differences between them and AM vanish upon close examination: The goal-driven control structure of these systems is a compiled form of AM's rudimentary "focus of attention" mechanism. The fact that their overall activity is typically labelled as deductive is a misnomer (since constructing a difficult proof is usually in practice quite inductive). Even the character of the inference processes are analogous: The provers typically contain a couple of binary inference rules, like Modus Ponens, which are relatively risky to apply but can yield big results: AM's few "binary" operators have the same characteristics: Compose, Canonize, Logically-combine (disjoin and conjoin). The deep distinctions between AM and the "heuristic theorem provers" are these: the underlying motivations (heuristic modelling *vs* building tools for problem solving), the richness of the knowledge base (hundreds of heuristics *vs* only a few), and the amount of emphasis on formal methods.

Theory formation systems in any field have been few. Meta-Dendral (Buchanan 1975) represents perhaps the best of these. But even that program is given a fixed set of templates for the bond-breaking rules which it wishes to find, and a fixed vocabulary of mass spectral concepts to plug into those hypothesis templates; whereas AM selectively enlarges its vocabulary of mathematical concepts.†

There has been very little published thought about "discovery" from an algorithmic point of view; even clear thinkers like Polya (1954) and Poincaré (1929) treat mathematical ability as a sacred, almost mystic quality, tied to the unconscious. The writings of philosophers and psychologists invariably attempt to examine human performance and belief, which are far more manageable than creativity *in vitro*.†

Amarel (1967) notes that it may be possible to learn from "theorem finding" programs how to tackle the general task of automating scientific research. AM has been one of the first attempts to construct such a program.

† Also note that unlike Meta-Dendral, AM must gather its own data. On the other hand, this is mich easier in mathematics than in organic chemistry.

† It is not clear how to design a null hypothesis experiment, one with a control group, for tasks in which real scientists are performing real research. Hence psychologists simply don't study such human activities. This is the danger Kuhn (1970) warns us against, of becoming "paradigm-locked".

3.5 Final conclusions

- AM is a demonstration that a few hundred general heuristic rules suffice to guide an automated mathematics researcher as it explores and expands a large but incomplete knowledge base of mathematical concepts. Results indicate that some aspects of creative research can be effectively modelled as heuristic search.
- This work has also introduced a control structure based upon an ordered agenda of small research tasks, each with a list of supporting reasons attached.
- The main limitations of AM was its inability to synthesize powerful new heuristics for the new concepts it defined.
- The main successes were the few novel ideas it came up with, the ease with which a new task domain was fed to the system, and the overall rational sequences of behaviour AM exhibited.

Acknowledgements

This research was initiated as my PhD thesis at Stanford University (Lenat 1976), and I wish to deeply thank my advisers and committee members: Bruce Buchanan, Paul Cohen, Edward Feigenbaum, Cordell Green, Donald Knuth, and Allen Newell. In addition, I gladly acknowledge the ideas received in discussions with Avra Cohn and with Herbert Simon.

This work was supported in part by the National Science Foundation (MCS77-0440) and in part by the Defense Advanced Research Projects Agency (F44620-73-C-0074).

REFERENCES

Amarel, S. (1967). On representations and modelling in problem solving and on future directions for intelligent systems. *RCA Labs Scientific Report No. 2,* Princeton: Princeton University.

Bledsoe, W. W. (1971). Splitting and reduction heuristics in automatic theorem proving. *Artificial Intelligence* **2,** 55–77.

Boyer, R. S and Moore, J. S. (1975). Proving theorems about LISP functions. *J. ACM* **22,** No. 1, 129–144.

Brotz, D. K. (1974). Embedding heuristic problem solving methods in a mechanical theorem-prover. *STAN-CS-74-443.* Stanford: Dept. of Computer Science, Stanford University.

Buchanan, B. G. (1975). Applications of Artificial Intelligence to Scientific Reasoning. *Proc. USA–Japan Computer Conference (AFIPS and IPSJ),* Tokyo, pp. 189–194. New Jersey: American Federation of Information Processing Societies.

Buchanan, B. G., Lederberg, J. and McCarthy, J. (1976). Three Reviews of J. Weizenbaum's "Computer Power and Human Reason". *SAIL AIM-291,* Stanford: Artificial Intelligence Laboratory, Stanford University.

Davis, R. (1976). Applications of meta-level knowledge to the construction, maintenance and use of large knowledge bases. *SAIL AIM-291,* Stanford: Artificial Intelligence Laboratory, Stanford University.

Evans, T. G. (1968). Program for the solution of geometric-analogy intelligence test questions, *Semantic Information Processing,* pp. 271–353. (ed. Minsky, M. L.). Cambridge, Mass.: MIT Press.

Feigenbaum, E. A., Buchanan, B. G. and Lederberg, J. (1971). On generality and problem-solving: a case study using the DENDRAL program. *Machine Intelligence 6,* pp. 165–190, (eds Meltzer, B. and Michie, D.). Edinburgh: Edinburgh University Press.

Gelernter, H. (1963). Realization of a geometry-theorem proving machine. *Computers and Thought,* pp. 134–152, (eds Feigenbaum, E. A. and Feldman, J.) New York: McGraw Hill.

Guard, R., et al (1969). Semi-automated mathematics. *J. ACM* **16,** 49–62.

Kling, R. E. (1971). Reasoning by analogy with applications to heuristic problem-solving: a case study. *AI Memo AIM-147,* Stanford: Artificial Intelligence Laboratory, Stanford University.

Kuhn, T. S. (1970). *The Structure of Scientific Revolutions,* 2nd ed. Chicago: Chicago University Press.

Lenat, D. B. (1976). AM; an artificial intelligence approach to discovery in mathematics as heuristic search. *SAIL AIM-286.* Stanford: Artificial Intelligence Laboratory, Stanford University.

Newell, A. and Simon, H. (1972). *Human Problem Solving.* New Jersey: Prentice Hall.

Nilsson, N. J. (1971). *Problem Solving Methods in Artificial Intelligence.* New York: McGraw Hill.

Poincaré, H. (1929). *The Foundations of Science: science and hypothesis; the value of science; science and method.* New York: The Science Press.

Polya, G. (1954). *Mathematics and Plausible Reasoning.* Princeton: Princeton University Press.

Shortliffe, E. H. (1974). MYCIN – a rule-based computer program for advising physicians regarding antimicrobial therapy selection. *SAIL AIM-251*: Stanford: Artificial Intelligence Laboratory, Stanford University.

Wang, H. (1960). Towards mechanical mathematics. *IBM Journal of Research and Development* **4,** *No. 1,* 2–22.

Winston, P. H. (1970). Learning structural descriptions from examples. *TR-231.* Cambridge, Mass.: Artificial Intelligence Laboratory, Massachusetts Institute of Technology.

APPENDIX I

Concepts initially given to AM

Below is a graph of the concepts which were present in AM at the beginning of its run. Single lines denote Generalization/Specialization links, and triple lines denote Examples/Isa links.

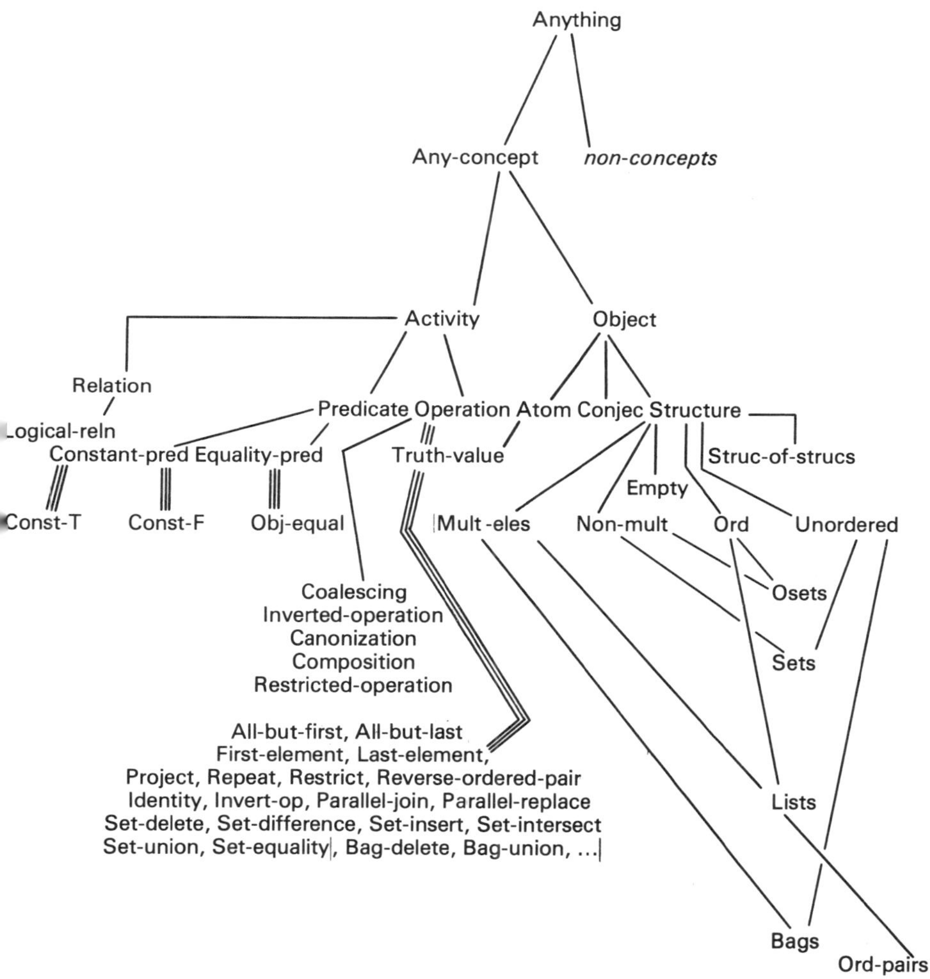

APPENDIX II

Concepts discovered by AM

The list below is meant to suggest the range of AM's creations; it is far from complete, and many of the omissions were real losers. The concepts are listed in order in which they were defined. In place of the (usually awkward) name chosen by AM, I have given either the standard mathematics/English name for the concept, or else a short description of what it is.

Sets with less than 2 elements (singletons and empty sets).
Sets with no atomic elements (nests of braces).
Bags containing (any number of copies of) just one kind of element.
Superset (contains).
Doubleton bags and sets.
Set-membership.
Disjoint bags.
Subset.
Disjoint sets.
Same-length.
Same first element.
Count (Length).
Numbers (in unary).
Add.
Minimum.
SUB1 (λ (x) x–1).
Subtract (except: if $x<y$, then x–y results in zero).
Less than or equal to.
Times.
Compose a given operation F with itself (form F–○–F).
Insert structure S into itself.
Try to delete structure S from itself (a loser).
Double (add 'x' to itself).
Subtract 'x' from itself (as an operation, this is a real zero).
Square (λ (x) Times(x,x)).
Coalesced-join: (λ (S F) append together F(s,s), for each $s \in S$).
Coalesced-replace: replace each element s of S by F(s,s).
Coa-repeat2: create a new op which takes a struc S, op F,
    and repeats F(s,t,S) all along S.
Compose three operations: λ(F,G,H) F–○–(G–○–H).
Compose three operations: λ(F,G,H) (F–○–G)–○–H.
Add^{-1} (x): all ways to repr. x as the sum of nonzero nos.
G–○–H, s.t. H(G(H(x))) is always defined (wherever H is).
Insert–○–Delete; Delete–○–Insert.
Size–○–Add^{-1}. (λ (n) The number of ways to partition n).
Cubing.
Exponentiation.
Halving (in natural numbers only; thus Halving(15)=7).
Even numbers.
Integer square-root.
Perfect squares.
Divisors-of.
Numbers-with-0-divisors; Numbers-with-1-divisor.
Primes (Numbers-with-2-divisors).
Squares of primes (Numbers-with-3-divisors).
Squares of squares of primes.
Square-roots of primes (a loser).
Times^{-1} (x): all ways of repr. x as the product of nos. (>1).

All ways of representing x as the product of primes.
All ways of representing x as the sum of primes.
All ways of representing x as the sum of two primes.
Numbers uniquely representable as the sum of two primes.
Products of squares.
Multiplication by 1; by 0; by 2.
Addition of 1; of 0; of 2.
Product of even numbers.
Sum of squares.
Sum of even numbers.
Pairs of squares whose sum is also a square ($x^2+y^2=z^2$).
Prime pairs ($\{(p,q,r) \mid p,q,r$ are primes $\wedge\ p+q=r\}$).

APPENDIX III

A brief, task-by-task trace

1. Fill in examples of Compose. Failed, but suggested next task:
2. Fill in examples of Set-union. Also failed, but suggested:
3. Fill in examples of Sets. Many found (e.g., by instantiating Set.Defn) and then more derived from those examples (e.g., by running Union.Alg).
4. Fill in specializations of Sets (because it was very easy to find examples of Sets). Creation of new concepts. One, INT-Sets, is related to "Singletons". Another, "BI-Sets", is all nests of braces (no atomic elements).
5. Fill in examples of INT-Sets. This indirectly led to a rise in the worth of Equal.
6. Check all examples of INT-Sets. All were confirmed. AM defines the set of Nonempty INT-Sets; this is renamed "Singletons" by the user.
7. Fill in examples of Bags.
8. Check examples of Bags. Defined INT-Bags and BI-Bags.
9. Fill in examples of All-but-first.
10. Fill in examples of All-but-last.
11. Fill in specializations of All-but-last. Failed.
12. Fill in examples of List-union.
13. Fill in examples of Projl.
14. Check examples of All-but-first.
15. Fill in examples of Empty-structures. 4 found.
16. Fill in generalizations of Empty-structures. Failed.
17. Fill in examples of Set-union.
18. Check examples of Set-union. Define λ (x,y) $x \cup y = x$, later called Superset.
19. Fill in examples of Bag-insert.
20. Check examples of Bag-insert. Range is really Nonempty bags. Isolate the results of insertion restricted to Singletons: call them Doubleton-bags.
21. Fill in examples of Bag-intersect.
22. Fill in examples of Set-insert.
23. Check examples of Set-insert. Range is always Nonempty sets. Define λ (x,S) Set-insert(x,S)=S; i.e., set membership. Define Doubleton sets.
24. Fill in examples of Bag-delete.
25. Fill in examples of Bag-difference.
26. Check examples of Bag-intersect. Define λ (x,y) $x \cap y = ()$; i.e. disjoint bags.
27. Fill in examples of Set-intersect.
28. Check examples of Set-intersect. Define λ (x,y) $x \cap y = x$; i.e., subset. Also define disjoint sets: λ (x,y) $x \cap y = \{\}$.
29. Fill in examples of Equal. Very difficult to find examples; this led to:
30. Fill in generalizations of Equal. Define "Same-size", "Equal-CARs", and some losers.
31. Fill in examples of Same-size.

32. Apply an Algorithm for Canonize to the args Same-size and Equal. AM eventually synthesizes the canonizing function "Size". AM defines the set of canonical structures: bags of T's; this later gets renamed as "Numbers".
33. Restrict the domain/range of Bag-union. A new operation is defined, Number-union, with domain/range entry ⟨Number Number → Bag⟩.
34. Fill in examples of Number-union. Many found.
35. Check the domain/range of Number-union. Range is 'Number'. This operation is renamed "Add2"; it adds any two natural numbers.
36. Restrict the domain/range of Bag-intersect to Numbers. Renamed "Minimum".
37. Restrict the domain/range of Bag-delete to Numbers. Renamed "SUB1".
38. Restrict the domain/range of Bag-insert to Numbers. AM calls the new operation "Number-insert". Its domain/range entry is ⟨Anything Number → Bag⟩.
39. Check the domain/range of Number-insert. This doesn't lead anywhere.
40. Restrict the domain/range of Bag-difference to Numbers. This becomes "Subtract".
41. Fill in examples of Subtract. This leads to defining the relation LEQ (≤).
42. Fill in examples of LEQ. Many found.
43. Check examples of LEQ.
44. Apply algorithm of Coalesce to LEQ. Conjecture: LEQ(x,x) is Constant-True.
45. Fill in examples of Parallel-join2. Included is Parallel-join2(Bags,Bags'Proj2), which is renamed "TIMES", and Parallel-join2(Structures,Structures,-Prolj1), a generalized Union operation renamed "G-Union", and a bunch of losers.
46. Fill in and check examples of the operations just created (really several tasks).
47. Fill in examples of Coalesce. Created: Self-Compose, Self-Insert, Self-Delete, Self-Add, Self-Times, Self-Union, etc. Also: Coa-repeat2, Coa-join2, etc.
48. Fill in examples of Self-Delete. Many found.
49. Check examples of Self-Delete. Self-Delete is just Identity-op.
50. Fill in examples of Self-Member. No positive examples found.
51. Check examples of Self-Member. Self-Member is just Constant-False.
52. Fill in examples of Self-Add. Many found. User renames this "Doubling".
53. Check examples of Coalesce. Confirmed.
54. Check examples of Add2. Confirmed.
55. Fill in examples of Self-Times. Many found. Renamed "Squaring" by the user.
56. Fill in examples of Self-Compose. Defined Squaring-○-Squaring. Created Add-○-Add (two versions: Add21 which is λ (x,y,z) (x+y)+z, and Add22 which is x+(y+z)). Similarly, two versions of Times-○-Times and of Compose-○-Compose.
57. Fill in examples of Add21. (x+y)+z. Many are found.
58. Fill in examples of Add22. x+(y+z). Again many are found.
59. Check examples of Squaring. Confirmed.
60. Check examples of Add22. Add21 and Add22 appear equivalent. But first:

61. Check examples of Add21. Add21 and Add22 still appear equivalent. Merge them. So the proper argument for a generalized "Add" operation is a Bag.
62. Apply algorithm for Invert to argument 'Add'. Define Inv-add(x) as the set of all bags of numbers (>0) whose sum is x. Also denoted Add-1-(x).
63. Fill in examples of TIMES21. (xy)z. Many are found.
64. Fill in examples of TIMES22. x(yz). Again many are found.
65. Check examples of TIMES22. TIMES21 and TIMES22 may be equivalent.
66. Check examples of TIMES21. TIMES21 and TIMES22 still appear equivalent. Merge them. So the proper argument for a generalized "TIMES" operation is a Bag. Set up an analogy between TIMES and ADD, because of this fact.
67. Apply algorithm for Invert to argument 'TIMES'. Define Inv-TIMES(x) as the set of all bags of numbers (>1) whose product is x. Analogic to Inv-Add.
68. Fill in examples of Parallel-replace2. Included are Parallel-replace2(Bags, Bags,Proj2) (called MR2-BBP2), and many losers.
69. Fill in an check examples of the operations just created.
70. Fill in examples of Compose. So easy that AM creates Int-Compose.
71. Fill in examples of Int-Compose. The two chosen operations G,H must be such that ran(H)^dom(G), and ran(G)^dom(H); both G and H must be interesting. Create G-Union-∘-MR2-BBP2, Insert-∘-Delete, Times-∘-Squaring, etc.
72. Fill in and check examples of the compositions just created. Notice that G-Union-∘-MR2-BBP2 is just TIMES.
73. Fill in examples of Coa-repeat2. Among them: Coa-repeat2(Bags-of-Numbers, Add2) [multiplication again!], Coa-repeat2(Bags-of-Numbers, Times) [exponentiation], Coa-repeat2(Structures, Proj1) [CAR], Coa-repeat2-(Structures, Proj2) [Last-element-of], etc.
74. Check the examples of Coa-repeat2. All confirmed.
75. Apply algorithms for Invert to 'Doubling'. The result is called "Halving" by the user. AM then defines "Evens", and also "Odds".
76. Fill in examples of Self-Insert.
77. Check examples of Self-Insert. Nothing special found.
78. Fill in examples of Coa-repeat2-Add2.
79. Check examples of Coa-repeat2-Add2. It's the same as TIMES.
80. Apply algorithm for Invert to argument 'Squaring'. Define "Square-root".
81. Fill in examples of Square-root. Some found, but very inefficiently.
82. Fill in new algorithms for Square-root. Had to ask user for a good one.
83. Check examples of Square-root. Define the set of numbers "Perfect-squares".
84. Fill in examples of Coa-repeat2-Times. This is exponentiation.
85. Check examples of Coa-repeat2-Times. Nothing special noticed, unfortunately.
86. Fill in examples of Inv-TIMES. Many found, but inefficiently.
87. Fill in new algorithms for Inv-TIMES. Obtained opaquely from the user.
88. Check examples of Inv-TIMES. This task suggests the next one:

89. Compose G-Union with Inv-TIMES. Good domain/range. Renamed "Divisors-of".
90. Fill in examples of Perfect-squares. Many found.
91. Fill in examples of Divisors-of.

This is where the excerpt presented in Sec. 3.1 begins: primes are defined, and AM soon discovers some unexpected (and hence, interesting) relationships involving them, which makes the Worth rating of Primes increase greatly.

PERCEPTION AND WORLD MODELS

12

Local Organizing Processes and Motion Schemas in Visual Perception

M. A. Arbib

Center for Systems Neuroscience and Department of Computer and Information Science
University of Massachusetts at Amherst, USA

Abstract

We examine models of low-level visual circuitry: "choice circuitry" in the frog tectum, and circuitry in mammilian visual cortex for segmentation on depth. We then examine some logical properties of schemas which represent visual input and sketch experiments which suggest approaches to schemas which represent dynamic states.

INTRODUCTION

Fig. 1 gives an overview of a number of subsystems which seem to be part of the overall design of a visual system [1], be it that of an animal or a general purpose robot. The visual input, light intensity maps varying over space and time, goes through a family of interacting transformations (hinted at by the multi-directionality of arrows in the figure) until a high-level interpretation is achieved which can provide a satisfactory basis for planning, learning, and action.

The low-level systems can be thought of as "preceding" interpretation, though in much processing the interpretation of one part of an image will guide the low-level processing of other parts. Low-level neural systems can be explored by single-cell neurophysiology; and can be implemented by multi-layer computational systems where each layer is made up of identical components (for example, the VISIONS system described in [37]. Feature extraction over windows local in space and time is followed by simple operations which allow local organizing processes to remove spurious activity due to such things as noise in the data, blurred gradients, overlap of windows, and false disparity cues. At the next level, processes for aggregating local edges and areas into boundaries and regions are applied.

We have characterized the output of the aggregation procedures as being "symbolic", but we cannot yet give neurophysiological correlations to the names and lists of descriptive attributes for shape, motion, texture, etc., that we assign to boundaries and regions in a computer visual system. But, presumably, such symbolic descriptors must play a role in activating the schemas which represent the various objects or domains of interaction which occasion the visual input.

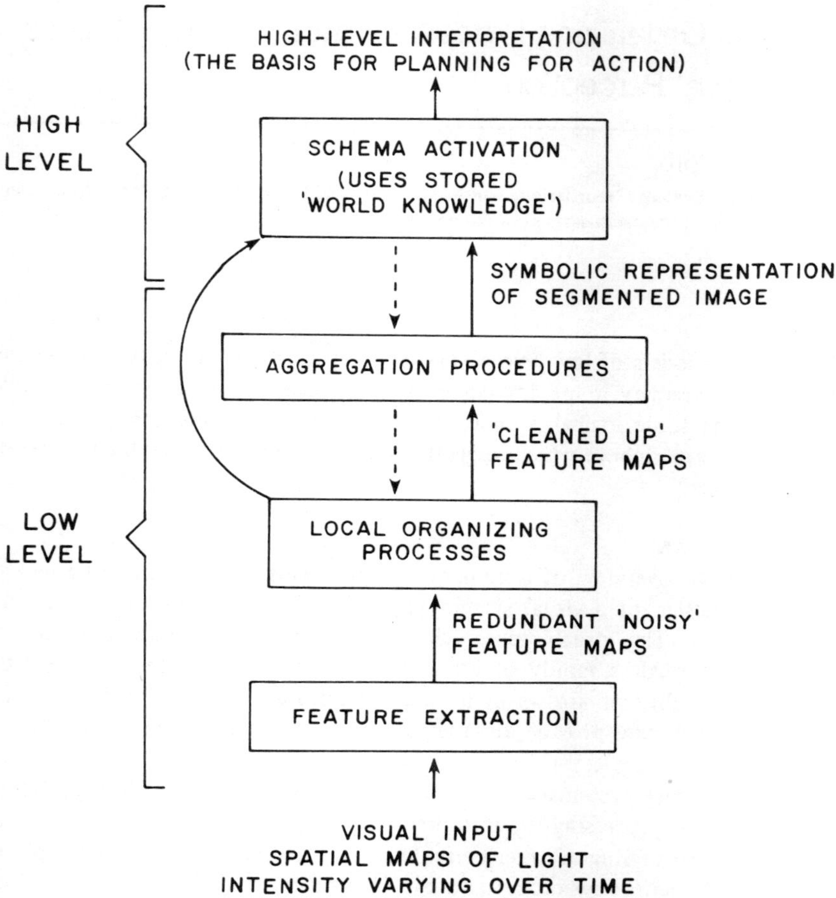

Fig. 1 – Overall design of a generalized vision system in terms of a number of subsystems.

In Secs. 2 and 3 we examine models of low-level visual circuitry: "choice circuitry" in the frog tectum, and circuitry in mammalian visual cortex for segmentation on depth. In Sec. 4 we examine some logical properties of schemas which represent (visual) input, while Sec. 5 sketches experiments which suggest approaches to schemas which represent dynamic states.

2. CHOICE CIRCUITRY IN THE FROG TECTUM

The ganglion cells of the frog retina send four or more "maps" in spatial register to the visual midbrain system, the tectum [2]. One of these maps may be called a "bugness" map – peaks of activity are spatially correlated with the position of wiggling fly-like stimuli in the visual field. When confronted with more than one fly, a frog may snap at one of the flies, snap at neither, or exhibit more complicated behaviour which need not concern us here [3,4]. The fact that the frog may not respond to multiple stimuli each of which is potent enough to trigger a snapping response when presented in isolation, suggests that there is a process of competition between their representatives. Didday [5,6] offered a model which made plausible use of the neurophysiology known before 1970 – "sameness" cells would turn down local activity if there was much activity elsewhere in the "bugness map", thus providing the competition mechanism; while "newness" cells would "alert" the circuitry to novel input. (For a recent survey of behavioural and physiological studies of the, related, toad visual system, and a modelling approach to the prey-enemy recognition system, see Ewert [7].)

New insight into Didday's computer simulation model is offered by a recent mathematical analysis [8]. Here, the "bugness map" is represented by a sequence $(s_1, \ldots s_n)$ of input values (Fig. 2(a)) feeding a bank of identical excitatory neurons whose membrane potential u_j yields the "firing rate" $f(u)$ via the nonlinear transformation f. Competitive interaction is mediated via a single inhibitory interneuron, whose firing rate is a monotone function of its membrane potential, so long as the latter is positive.

Once plausible restrictions are placed on the coefficients, mathematical analysis of the equations

$$\dot{u}_i = -u_i + w_1 f(u_i) - w_2 g(v) - h_1 + s_i \qquad i = 1, \ldots n$$

$$\tau \dot{v} = -v + \sum_{i=1}^{n} f(u_i) - h_2$$

yields results such as the following:

(i) At most, one element can be excited in an equilibrium.
(ii) If all u_i's are initially the same, and the element remains excited in the equilibrium, it is the one receiving the maximum stimulus. Fig. 2(b) shows, however, that other elements may fire prior to equilibrium.
(iii) The network exhibits hysteresis. A tempory change in the threshold h_i can be used (cf. "newness" cells) to "release" a "blocked" response to a new maximal stimulus.

3. CIRCUITRY FOR SEGMENTATION ON DEPTH

Mammalian visual cortex contains "line detectors" which are tuned not only for spatial direction but also for disparity [9,10]. Presumably, a random dot stereogram excites many "spurious" disparity pairs, and interest thus focuses on "cooperative phenomena" which suppress "false" correlations to allow perception of an image cleanly segmented in depth [11]. A nonlinear neural model [12] proposed by P. Dev and others achieved this on the principle "nearby cells of the same disparity cooperate to signal surface; while nearby cells of differing

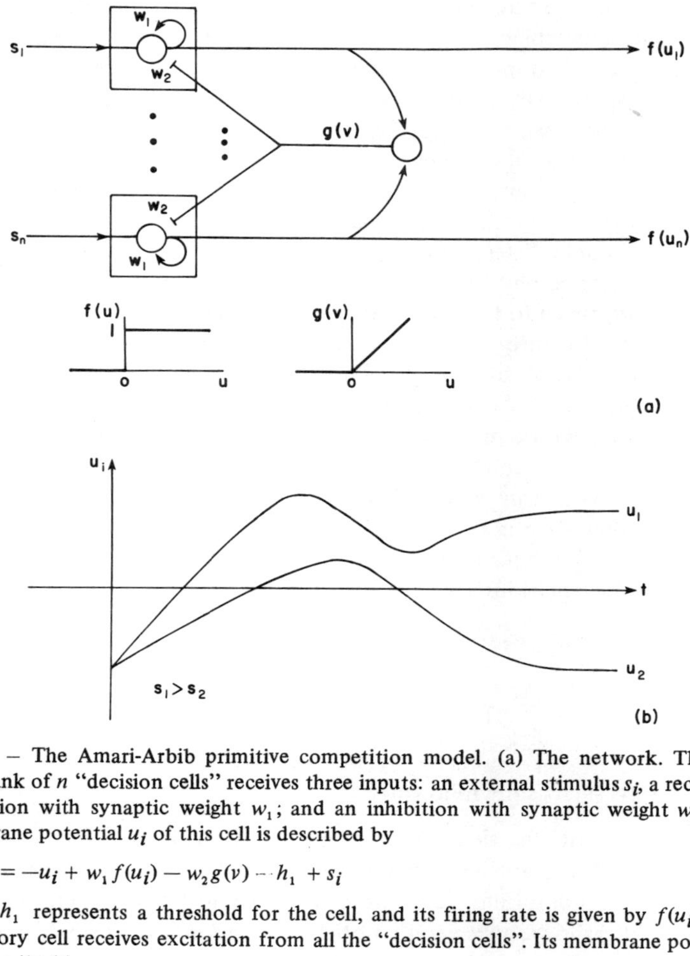

Fig. 2 – The Amari-Arbib primitive competition model. (a) The network. The i-th of a bank of n "decision cells" receives three inputs: an external stimulus s_i, a recurrent excitation with synaptic weight w_1; and an inhibition with synaptic weight w_2. The membrane potential u_i of this cell is described by

$$\dot{u}_i = -u_i + w_1 f(u_i) - w_2 g(v) - h_1 + s_i$$

where h_1 represents a threshold for the cell, and its firing rate is given by $f(u_i)$. The inhibitory cell receives excitation from all the "decision cells". Its membrane potential v is described by

$$\tau \dot{v} = -v + \sum_{i=1}^{n} f(u_i) - h_2$$

where h_2 represents a threshold, and τ is its time constant (on a time scale which assigns a unit time constant to the "decision cells").
(b) The response curves for two "decision cells" of the network showing the time course of initially equal membrane potentials u_1 and u_2 for constant external stimuli $s_1 > s_2$.

disparity compete to avoid multiple surfaces in a given direction". The model, in the form shown in Fig. 3, has been mathematically analysed [8], using the equations:

$$\frac{\partial u_d(x,t)}{\partial t} = -u_d(x,t) + \int_{-\infty}^{\infty} w_1(x-\xi)\, f(u_d(\xi,t))\, d\xi - \int_{-\infty}^{\infty} w_2(x-\xi)\, g(v(\xi,t))\, d\xi - h_1 + S_d(x,t)$$

$$\frac{\partial v(x,t)}{\partial t} = -v(x,t) - h_2 + \sum_d f(u_d(x,t))$$

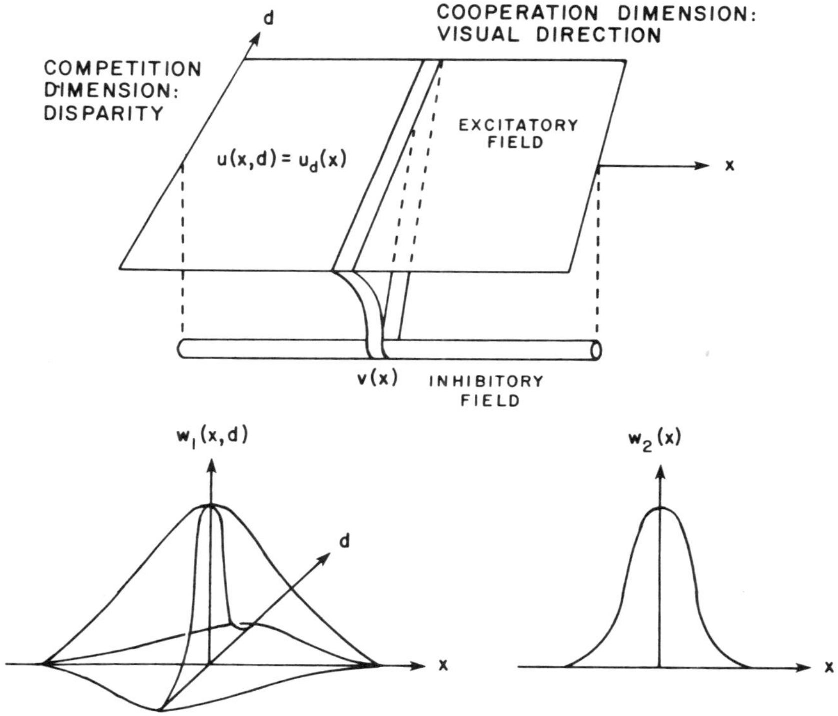

Fig. 3 – The full Amari-Arbib model. Excitatory cells are arranged along two coordinates – the cooperation dimension x corresponds to visual direction in a stereopsis model, while the competition dimension d corresponds to disparity in such a model. The net result of the excitatory effects via the weighting function w_1 and the inhibitory effects via the summing of excitation on the inhibitory layer with weighting function w_2 is that cells of nearby visual direction "cooperate" (are mutually excitatory) if their disparity agrees, but "compete" (are mutually inhibitory) if their disparity differs by more than some critical amount. Such competition and cooperation leads to segmentation as described in the text.

where d indexes "disparity layers" in the excitatory field, and $S_d(x,t)$ is the stimulus array at time t. (Unfortunately, the first detailed analysis of the Dev model [13] did not use the f nonlinearity, thus losing the crucial multistability). Typical results include

(i) When a single-peaked stimulus is applied to a single d-layer, there is a critical coherence length – dependent on the intensity of the stimulation – and no excitation occurs unless the stimulus is wider than that length.

(ii) It is impossible for two or more layers of the full model to be excited at the same spatial positions, except for a small overlap at the boundaries of excited regions.

Computer simulations developing the Dev model not only use nonlinearity but also involve a careful analysis of the geometry of the projection field [14, 15].

4. SCHEMAS

We have argued that low-level systems segment the visual image, and that these segments activate schemas which represent objects or domains of interaction. (For other approaches to "internal representation" see, for example, Minsky [16], Bartlett [17] and Schank and Abelson [18].) In our theory [19,20] a schema is viewed as a system with 3 components:

(i) Input-matching routines which test for evidence that that which the schema represents is indeed present in the environment.

(ii) Action routines – whose parameters may be tuned by parameter-fitting in the input-matching routines.

(iii) Competition and cooperation routines which, for example, use context (activation levels and spatial relations of other schemas) to lower or raise the schema's activation level.

Rather than repeat earlier observations [19,20], we adduce evidence (supplied in part by Burt [21]) that an episode is represented by a spatially tagged array of activated parametrized schema instantiations. (The treatment is brief, and omits many subtleties.) The Jastrow duck-rabbit shown in Fig. 4(a), can be seen as either duck or rabbit, but not as part of each or as both simultaneously. This initially suggests that schemas are interconnected via mutual inhibition, as in Fig 4(b), so that only one of the schemas can be above the threshold level of excitation (compare Sec. 2). However, the fact that we can see a duck and a rabbit side by side suggests the modification shown in Fig. 4(c) in which inhibition is not at the schema level. (However, we still posit schema-level cross excitation [19,20] embodying real world knowledge – so that increased activity of an ice-cream schema augments activity of a cone schema for an appropriate spatial relation.) We now posit, Fig. 4(c), that schemas compete for lower-level features, and that as a feature contributes to the raised activation of a schema, so does the schema to some extent "cover" the lower level features. For the duck-rabbit input, increasing activity of one schema goes with increasing coverage of lower level features – taking them from the other schema and thus effectively inhibiting it. But if the input has duck and rabbit separate, then duck schema and rabbit schema can be activated without covering features required to activate the other schema.

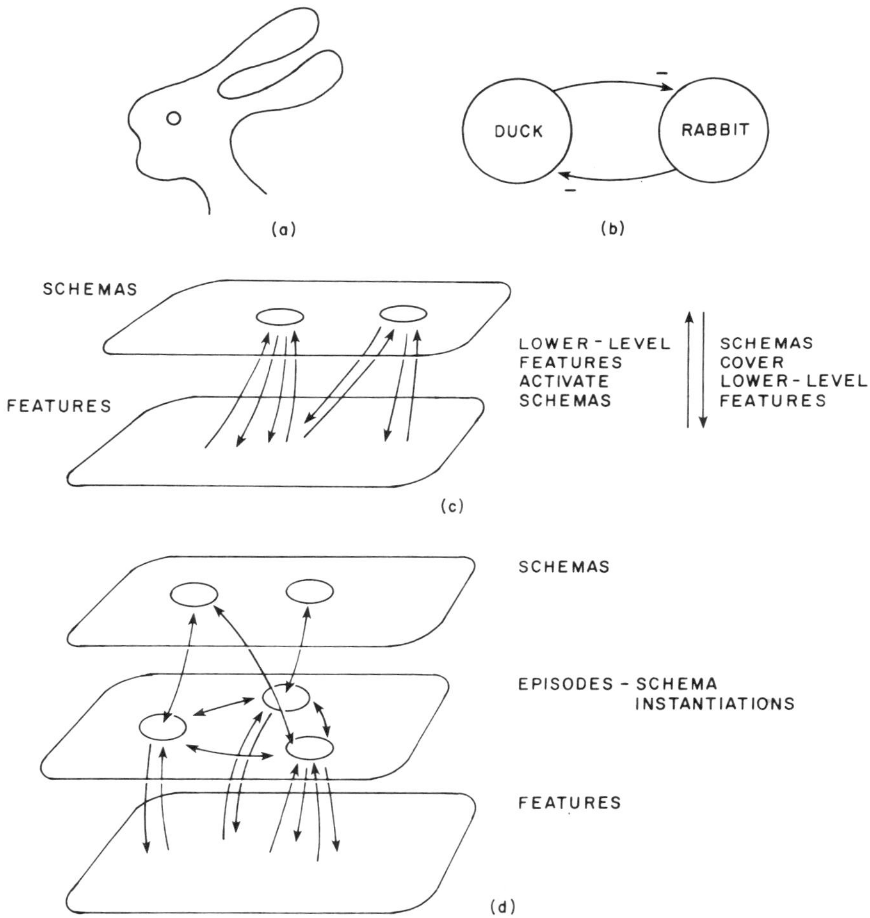

Fig. 4 – From schema to episode. The duck-rabbit (a) suggests that mutual inhibition between the schemas (internal representations) of duck and rabbit are mutually inhibitory (b) so that only one schema can be above a threshold level of excitation. However, the fact that we can see a scene containing both a duck and rabbit suggests that this inhibition is not "wired-in", but is rather mediated by the competition for low-level features (c). Finally, our ability to see a scene with several ducks, say, argues that perception does not so much activate a set of particular schemas as it activates a schema-assemblage consisting of instantiations of schemas (d).

We trace one more step in the logic of schemas. The fact that we can recognize a scene containing, say, two ducks and a rabbit argues that the internal representation of a scene is not the activation of schemas per se, but rather the activation of a pattern of schema instantiations – parametrized and spatially tagged to cover lower-level features in terms of input-matching routines of higher-level schemas. These "episodes" – the patterns of schema instantiations of Fig. 4(d) – can then be "stored" both for episodic memory and as building blocks for new schemata. However, rather than elaborate Fig. 4(d) further in this article, we now turn to motion schemas.

5. MOTION SCHEMAS

Our theory of schemas grew out of concern with action-oriented perception [24]. If an animal or a robot perceives in order to guide its interactions with a dynamic world, then the schemas which embody its perceptions will often represent dynamic rather than static states of the environment – it may be more important to distinguish whether a man is approaching to shake your hand or to hit you than it is to classify his facial structure.

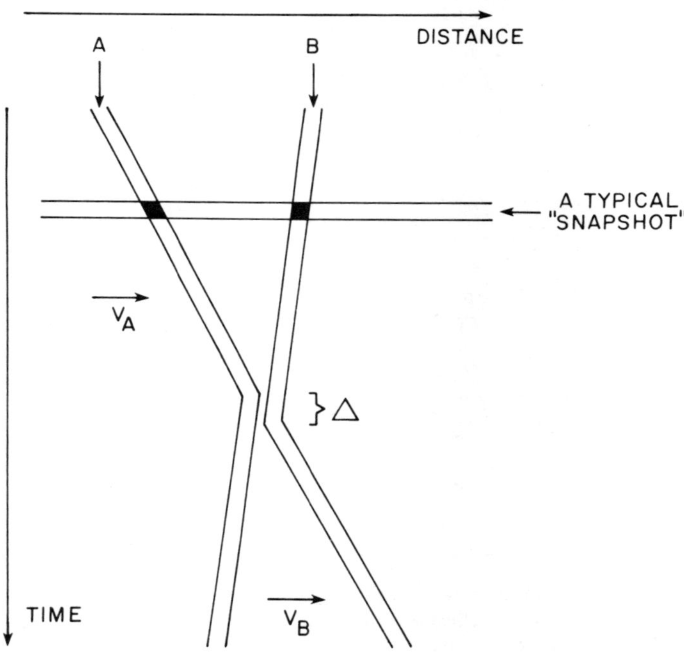

Fig. 5 – The set-up for a number of Michotte's experiments on the perception of causality. The subject sees a portion of tracks *A* and *B* revealed as they are moved behind a slit – the effect the view of particle *A* moving toward *B*, the two particles "sticking" for time Δ, and then *B* moving away from *A*.

One encouraging initial attempt [25] to place motion schemas in a formal artificial intelligence framework models the finding of Michotte's studies [26] of the perception of causality, such as those exemplified in Fig. 5. The typical "snapshot" indicates what a human observer is shown at any time – a pair of squares. The two "tracks" *A* and *B* indicate how the positions of the squares vary with time. If the "contact time" Δ is small, and the apparent velocities v_A and v_B are similar, a subject instructed to fixate the square *B* will say that "*A* bumps into *B* and pushes it", while a subject fixating away from *B* will simply see *A* pass through a stationary object. If Δ exceeds 0.2 seconds, the subject sees two successive independent movements. If $v_B > 1.8v_A$, the subject no longer sees *A* as pushing *B* – rather "it is as if *A*'s approach frightened *B*, and *B* ran away" or "as if *A* triggered a mechanism in *B*." Weir [25] is the first attempt to posit control structures which will appropriately activate the various "causality schemas" under varying input conditions.

Important studies of dynamic aspects of low-level visual processing include the analysis of use of texture flow information to guide locomotion [27,28], and texture-motion neurons in the pons [29] may provide the bridge to a neural-net theory which could tie up with our earlier model [30] of how the cerebellum and related brainstem nuclei [31] might tune the parameters of

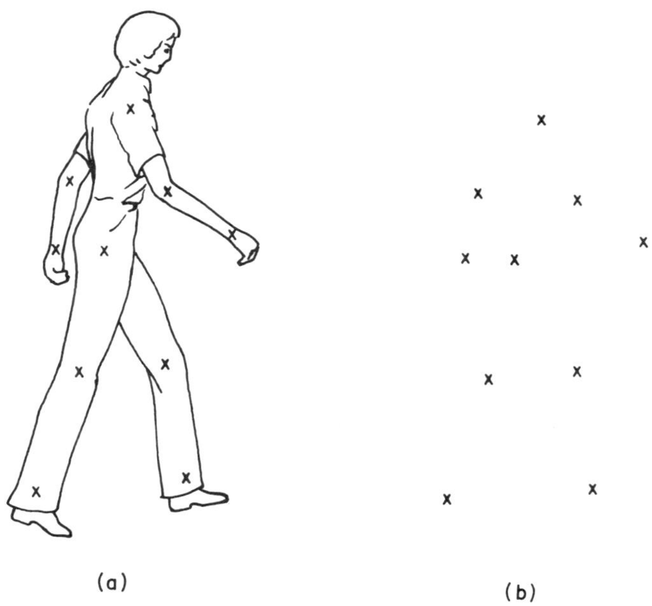

Fig. 6 – Joint pattern (b) of a walking man (a). Johansson observed that a static such pattern is hard to recognize, but that a movie of such joint patterns gives a compelling impression of walking.

synergies [32,33] during locomotion. We close with a description of experiments on perception of locomotion (rather than for locomotion) which suggest a high-level schematic description of locomotion which could play a role in the generation, and not only the perception, of movement. Johansson [34] found, that a pattern of dots such as that of Fig. 6(b) has no compelling perceptual effect. However, a motion picture showing such dots as taken, for example, with high-contrast videotaping, of a walking man yields a compelling perception of human locomotion. This shows that simple motion cues may activate schemas without benefit of shape recognition. This suggests two questions for the modeller: How are points in successive frames matched up [35], and what bears the "locomotion information" in the trajectories? Low-level matching processes in motion perception are analogous [21] to those we studied for disparity matching in Sec. 3. Hoenkamp [36] analysed curves such as that shown by a sawtooth and the knee motion by a sinusoid as shown in Fig. 7(b). He found that CRT displays of dots – for example, for hip, 2 knees, and 2 ankles – generated according to these time courses still yielded compelling perceptual effects. He could vary the observed style of progression simply by altering α – from skating ($\alpha \sim 0.4$) to walking ($\alpha \sim 0.6$) to running ($\alpha \sim 0.8$). This is a strikingly pure representation of a motion schema.

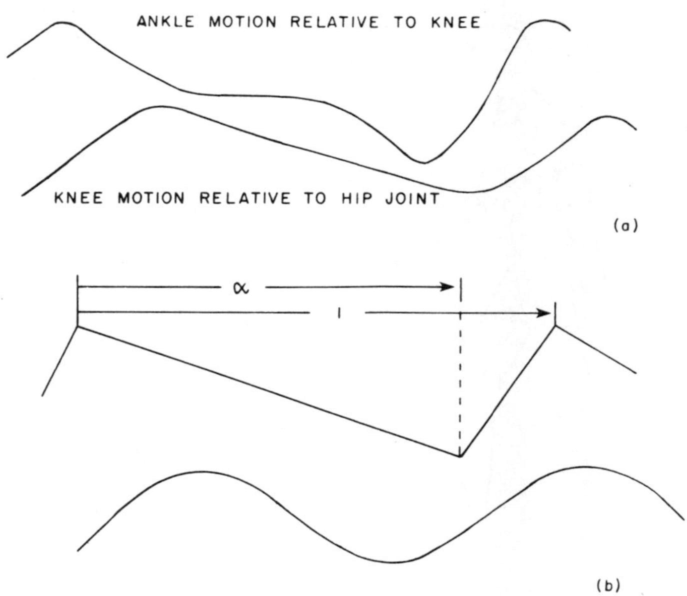

Fig. 7 – Hoenkamp's crude approximations of ankle and knee motions by sawtooth and sinusoidal curves respectively preserved the perceptual effect, but variations of the parameter x induced the perception of different forms of progression – skating, walking, and running.

Acknowledgements

Research reported in this article was supported in part by NIH under Grant No. NS 09755-COM of NINCDS.

REFERENCES

[1] Arbib, M. A. and Riseman, E. M. (1976). Computational Techniques in visual systems. Part I. The overall design. Technical Report. Amherst: Computer and Information Science, University of Massachusetts at Amherst.
[2] Lettvin, J. Y., Maturana, H. R., McCulloch, W. S. and Pitts, W. H. (1959). What the frog's eye tells the frog's brain. *Proc. IRE*, **47**, 1940–1951.
[3] Ingle, D. (1968). Visual releasers of prey-catching behaviour in frogs and toads. *Brain Behav. Evol.*, **1.**, 500–518.
[4] Ingle, D. (1973). Selective choice between double prey objects by frogs, *Brain Behav. Evol.*, 7, 127–144.
[5] Didday, R. L. (1970). The simulation and modelling of distributed information processing in the frog visual system. *Tech. Rep. 6112-2*, Stanford: Info. Syst. Lab., Stanford University.
[6] Didday, R. L. (1976). A model of visuomotor mechanisms in the frog tectum, *Math. Biosci.*, **30**, 169–180.
[7] Ewert, J. P. (1976). The visual system of the toad: Behavioural and physiological studies on a pattern recognition system. *The Amphibian Visual System, a Multidisciplinary Approach*, pp. 141–202, (ed. Fite, K. V.). New York: Academic Press.
[8] Amari, S. and Arbib, M. A. (1977). Competition and co-operation in neural nets. *Systems Neuroscience*, pp. 119–165. (ed. Metzler, J.) New York: Academic Press.
[9] Barlow, H. B., Blakemore, C. and Pettigrew, J. D. (1967). The neural mechanism of depth discrimination, *J. Physiol.*, **133**, 327–342.
[10] Pettigrew, J. D., Nikara, T., and Bishop, P. O. (1968). Binocular interaction on single units in cat striate cortex, *Exp. Brain. Res*, **6**, 391–410.
[11] Julesz, B. (1970). *Foundations of Cyclopean Perception*, Chicago: Chicago University Press.
[12] Arbib, M. A., Boylls, C. C. and Dev. P. (1974). Neural models of spatial perception and the control of movement. *Kybernetik and Bionik/ Cybernetics and Bionics*, pp. 216–231 (eds. Keidel, W. D., Handler, W. and Spreng, M.). Munchen: Oldenbourg.
[13] Dev. P. (1975). Computer simulation of a dynamic visual perception model, *Int. J. Man-Machine Studies*, 7, 547–569.
[14] Marr, D. and Poggio, T. (1976). Co-operative computation of stereo disparity, *Science*, **194**, 283–287.
[15] Burt, P. (1976). A model for stereopsis. Stimulus Organizing Processes in Stereopsis and Motion Perception, *COINS Technical Report 76-15*, Amherst: University of Massachusetts at Amherst.
[16] Minsky, M. L. (1975). A framework for representing knowledge. *The Psychology of Computer Vision*, pp. 211–277. (ed. Winston, P. H.) New York: McGraw Hill.
[17] Bartlett, F. C. (1932). *Remembering*, Cambridge: Cambridge University Press.
[18] Schank, R. C. and Abelson, R. P. (1975). Scripts, plans and knowledge. *Advance Papers 4th Int. Joint Conf. on Art. Int. (IJCAI-75)*. Tbilisi. pp. 151–157. Cambridge, Mass. Artificial Intelligence Laboratory, Massachusetts Institute of Technology.
[19] Arbib, M. A. (1975). Artificial intelligence and brain theory: unities and diversities, *Ann. Biomed. Eng.* **3**, 238–274.
[20] Arbib, M. A. (1978). Segmentation, schemas and co-operative computation. *Studies in Biomathematics*, pp. 118–155 (ed. Levin, S.). Mathematical Association of America.
[21] Burt, P. (1976). Stimulus organizing processes, in Ref. 15.
[22] Jastrow, J. (1899). The mind's eye, *Pop. Sci. Monthly*, **54**, 299–312.

[23] Wittgenstein, L. (1953). *Philosophical Investigations* (G. E. M. Anscome, Trans). Oxford: Pergamon Press.

[24] Arbib, M. A. (1972). *The Metaphorical Brain*. New York: Wiley Interscience.

[25] Weir, S. (1974). Action perception. *Bionics Research Report No. 21*. Edinburgh: School of Artificial Intelligence, Edinburgh University.

[26] Michotte, A. (1963). The Perception of Causality. (T. Miles and E. Miles, Trans.). London: Methuen.

[27] Gibson, J. J. (1958). Visually controlled locomotion and visual orientation in animals, *Brit. J. Psychol*, **49**, 182–194.

[28] Lee, D. N. (1974). Visual information during locomotion, *Perception Essays in Honour of J. J. Gibson*, pp. 250–267 (eds. McLeod, R. B. and Pick Jnr., H. L.). Cornell: Cornell University Press.

[29] Glickstein, M. and Gibson, A. R. (1976). Visual cells in the pons of the brain. *Sci. Amer.* **235**, 90–98.

[30] Boylls, C. C. (1973). A theory of cerebellar function with applications to locomotion. II. The relation of exterior lobe climbing fiber function to locomotor behaviour in the cat. *Technical Report 76-1*, Amherst: Computer and Information Science, University of Massachusetts at Amherst.

[31] Orlovsky, G. N. (1972). The effect of different descending systems on flexor and extensor activity during locomotion, *Brain Research* **40**, 359–371.

[32] Bernstein, N. A. (1967). *The co-ordination and regulation of movements,* Oxford: Pergamon Press. (trs. from Russian).

[33] Greene, P. H. (1972). Problems of organization of motor systems, *Progr. Theor. Biol.* **2**, 303–308.

[34] Johansson, G. (1973). Visual perception of biological motion and a model for its analysis, *Perception and Psychophysics*, **14**, 201–211.

[35] Clocksin, W. (1976). Inference of gadgets from examples of their motion. *Technical Report*, Edinburgh: Department of Artificial Intelligence, Edinburgh University.

[36] Hoenkamp, E. (1977). Psychology Laboratory, Catholic University, Nijmegen. Technical Report.

[37] Hanson, A. R. and Riseman, E. M. (eds.) (1978). *Computer Vision Systems*. New York: Academic Press.

13

Formation of the World Model in Artifical Intelligence Systems

V. P. Gladun and Z. L. Rabinovich
Institute of Cybernetics
Ukranian Academy of Sciences, Kiev, USSR

Abstract
The problem of automatic formation of a world model in artificial intelligence systems is discussed. It is considered as a complex process which combines the processes of classification, generalization and concept formation. Realization of the suggested principles is described using a special (pyramidal) semantic network.

INTRODUCTION

We know that a model of the real world is one of the most important elements of artificial intelligence systems in determining the processes of decision-making [1]. There is a common concept of the world model as a semantic network. We should like to concentrate on a subject which has received little attention so far, but which is of paramount importance; that is, how the model is formed. Automation of the process of model formation is necessary in adaptive systems of artificial intelligence if they are to be capable of mastering new classes of problem in new environments.

Information enters the world model by two channels: (1) inputs to the system and (2) outputs from the system. Information introduced into the model from outputs contains the results of information processing within the system, for example, problem solutions. This information is necessary to "fix" experience. In the process of inserting information into the model, the fragments of the model representing generalized knowledge of object classes, situations, and reactions should be formed. It is this generalized knowledge which provides the system with its ability for adaptation. It is useful to fix the experience of the system in the form of generalized knowledge because only in this case can it be used to solve new problems. Therefore, the insertion of any information into the model must be accompanied by the processes of classification, generalization, and concept formation, including modification of concepts already existing in the system. When inserting information, an associative proximity of descriptions of individual objects, situations and reactions should be established automatically. The algorithm for construction of the world model is in this case simultaneously the algorithm for classification, etc. and for establishing the associative proximity of objects.

Naturally, such information processing is possible only by using structures which exist already in the system memory, that is, on the basis of the existing world model. Thus, on the one hand, the model is the result of the processes of classification, generalization, and so on, while on the other hand, it is the means of realization of these processes.

So, we draw the following conclusion: in a developed adaptive system of artificial intelligence, it is necessary to consider the world model in active interaction with a complex of facilities for its formation. The question of what the world model should be must not be separated from the question of how the world model should be formed automatically, in the process of the interactions which take place between the system and the environment.

Let us point out some features of the world model which are important for the processes of decision-making:

1. Several levels of knowledge generalization should exist in the world model, that is, the model should be *hierarchical.*
2. Information retrieval should be possible in the world model by tracing associative links among individual fragments of knowledge, without the revision of the whole memory, that is, the model should be *associative.*

The important consequence of these features is the changeover from the purely informational representation of the world model as a sum of knowledge, to the understanding of the importance of the organization of the information in the model, that is, the changeover to representation of the model as a structure. Such structural features eliminate the necessity of scanning the whole memory when the system is functioning. The complex engineering problem of eliminating memory scanning (which disappears completely when problems are considered at a theoretical level) is at present one of the main problems when organizing the effective functioning of artificial intelligence systems which operate with large amounts of data. Thus constructing a world model is the process of forming the structures which constitute the model. We believe that more developed forms of organization are called for than those usually put forward in the context of semantic networks.

We shall now describe the complex of facilities which are used in our construction of models of this type. A special data structure, called a pyramidal network (PN), is the element which combines the mechanisms described below.

After the definition of a pyramidal network we shall describe the algorithm of input which executes its construction, and the algorithm of concept formation. In the last section, problems of the employment of pyramidal networks in the artificial intelligence systems ANALAYSER, PPR-1, and PPR-2 are discussed.

PYRAMIDAL NETWORKS

Organization of memory in the form of a pyramidal network serves for the storage of information about objects represented by sets of values of attributes. The concept "object" in any given case is to be understood broadly. Articles, sets of data characterizing a process or phenomenon, situations of the environment or the internal state of the system in which the pyramidal network is used, can all be objects.

Input elements of the network through which signals associated with values of attributes are received will be called *receptors*. Each receptor corresponds to one value of the attribute. Apart from receptors there are *associative elements*, with several inputs and one output. The associative element generates an output signal if, during a definite interval of time, signals come to all its inputs.

A network consisting of receptors and associative elements can be illustrated with a directed graph whose vertices correspond to the network elements. Links among elements are designated by arrows directed towards inputs of the elements.

Definition 1

A set of elements of the network incorporating the element a and all the elements from which there are paths to the element on the network graph is called a subset of the element a.

Definition 2

The pyramidal network (PN) is the network consisting of receptors and associative elements which are connected among themselves provided that the following conditions hold:

(a) output of any element of the network must not be connected with inputs of the elements composing its subset,
(b) inputs of the receptors must not have links with other elements.

Examples of PN graphs are given in Figs. 1 and 2.

Definition 3

A set of the network elements towards which there are paths from the element a on the network graph is called a superset of the element a.

Definition 4

Elements from the subset of the element a, connected with it directly, form the O-subset of the element a.

Definition 5

Elements from the superset of the element a, connected with it directly, form the O-superset of the element a.

Definitions 1 to 5 define a class of pyramidal networks. With the help of subsequent definitions supplementary restrictions are introduced, typical of the PN variety which is used in our developments. It will be called α-PN. α-PN serves to store the information about objects by non-ordered sets of values of attributes.

Definition 6

By an *active input* of the element of α-PN is denoted the input connected with the output of another element.

Definition 7

By an α-associative element is denoted the associative element which generates the output signal when there are signals at all its active inputs.

Definition 8

The input of an α-associative element which is not connected with other elements is called a *passive input.*

Definition 9

The state of the element of α-PN at which it generates the output signal is called the *state of excitation*, and the time of existence of the input signal is the *period of excitation.*

Before insertion of the information about objects, the network consists only of receptors. The input algorithm is, in principle, the algorithm for constructing the network from the elements which are in reserve. Inserting the information about the object into the network or, as it will be called, the *perception of the object*, is carried out by simultaneous application of external signals to the inputs of receptors corresponding to values of attributes of the given object. The time interval between two successive perceptions is more than the period of network excitation, therefore up to the moment of perception of the next object there are no excited elements in the network.

The α-PN can be constructed with the help of various input algorithms. One of them, the most popular, is given below. The time of executing each of the steps of the given algorithm is small in comparison with the period of excitation. The algorithm is started when perceiving each object.

THE INPUT ALGORITHM OF α-PN

1. If, when perceiving the object, the subset $\mathcal{F}$ of O-subset of α-associative element a, containing no less than two elements, is excited, the links of the element a with the elements of the set $\mathcal{F}$ are eliminated and a new α-associative element is added to the network whose inputs are connected with outputs of all elements of the set $\mathcal{F}$, and the output is connected with one of the passive outputs of the element a. The new element is in excited state immediately after insertion into the network.

The execution of step 1 is illustrated by Fig. 1(a),(b).

After inserting the new element into all sections of the network where the condition of step 1 is satisfied, step 2 is executed.

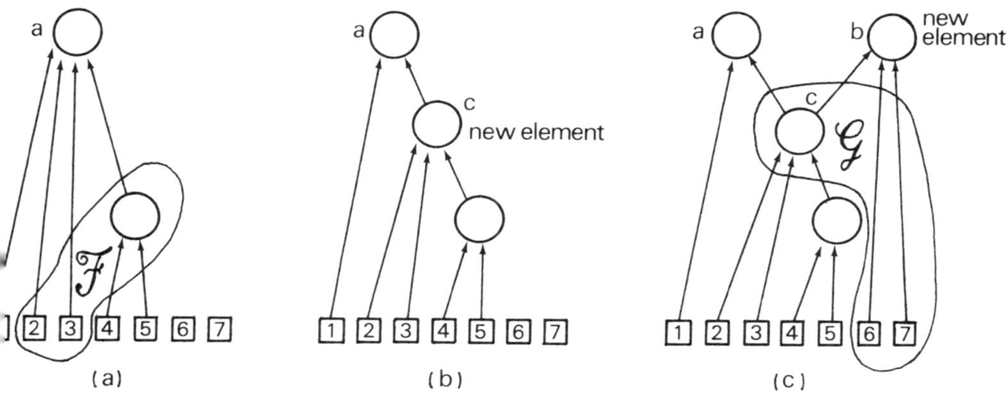

Fig. 1 – (b) is the network after excitation of receptors 2,3,4,5 in situation (a).
(c) is the network after excitation of receptors 2,3,4,5,6,7 in situation (b).

2. Let $\mathcal{G}$ be a set of excited elements of the network having no other excited elements in their O-superset. If $\mathcal{G}$ contains no less than two elements, a new α-associative element adds to the network whose inputs are connected with outputs of all elements from the set $\mathcal{G}$. The new element is in the excited state immediately after insertion into the network.

The execution of step 2 is illustrated by Fig. 1(b),(c).

When perceiving the first object the condition which is presented in step 1 is not satisfied, because in the network there are no associative elements. The execution of step 2 leads to the appearance of a simple pyramidal structure of data with one associative element. After inserting many objects a complex network arises.

Pyramids of the elements, construction of which is completed with the execution of step 2 of the input algorithms, correspond to individual objects. Pyramids being formed when executing step 1 correspond to combinations of values of attributes belonging to several objects. For example, the pyramid of the element c (Fig. 1) serves to store a combination of values of attributes perceptible by receptors 2,3,4,5 which belongs to the objects represented in the network by pyramids of the elements a and b.

CONCEPT FORMATION ON THE BASIS OF PYRAMIDAL NETWORKS

Let a set of attributes be specified each of which has a set of values.

A concept is generalized information about a set of objects represented by collections of values of attributes which

(a) represent logical relations among individual values of attributes, typical for the set, and
(b) are sufficient to distinguish, with the help of a recognition rule, between objects belonging to the set and objects which do not belong to it.

The word "generalized" means, in the given case, that the concept includes only essential values of attributes which characterize a set of objects as a whole and does not contain some particular values of attributes which individualize separate objects.

A set of objects to which the concept corresponds is called the *volume* of the concept. Depending on whether the object enters or does not enter into the volume of certain concept it will be called a *positive* or *negative* object of this concept.

Let us define the problem of inductive concept formation for a given set of objects $\mathfrak{V}$.

Let $\mathcal{L}$ be a set of objects such that $\mathcal{L} \cap \mathfrak{V} = \phi$ and $\mathfrak{V} \not\subset \mathcal{L}$. For each $a \in \mathcal{L}$ there is an indication of the type $a \in \mathfrak{V}$ (positive object) or $a \notin \mathfrak{V}$ (negative object). It is necessary to construct, by the analysis of set $\mathcal{L}$, a concept which discriminates between its positive and negative objects (that is, notions on the basis of which it is possible, applying a certain recognition rule, to recognize correctly all positive and negative objects of the set $\mathcal{L}$ of a learning sample).

The algorithm of inductive concept formation on the basis of α-PN is started after the construction of α-PN for all objects of the learning sample. The operation of the algorithm of concept formation after the execution of the input algorithm is described by the three rules given below. The time taken for the execution of all these operations is considerably smaller than the period of excitation of network elements.

Two numbers m and k are then placed into correspondence with each element of the network. m is the number of excitatations of this element when perceiving all positive objects of the learning sample, and k is the number of receptors in the subset of elements. In the process of learning, special elements are singled out in the network with the help of which the objects from the concept volume should be recognized. We shall call them *positive* or *negative checking elements* of the given concept.

Rule 1

If, when perceiving a positive object of the concept $\mathcal{R}$, there are no checking elements of the concept $\mathcal{R}$ in its pyramid, the element having the largest k of all elements of the pyramid with the largest m is marked as a positive checking element of the concept $\mathcal{R}$.

This statement of the rule takes into account the possibility of existence, among the excited elements, of several elements with the same m exceeding the m of all other excited elements. If in the group of elements having the largest

m, the values of k of all elements are equal, any one of them can be marked as a checking element of the concept $\mathcal{R}$.

Rule 2

If, when perceiving the negative object of the concept $\mathcal{R}$, there are positive checking elements of the concept $\mathcal{R}$ in its pyramid which do not contain in their supersets $U_1, U_2, \ldots U_l$ other excited checking elements of the concept $\mathcal{R}$, in each of the sets $U_1, U_2, \ldots U_l$ the element having the smallest k among all excited elements is marked as a negative checking element of the concept $\mathcal{R}$.

According to this rule the excitation of the pyramid of element 2 (Fig. 2(a)), on condition that the pyramid represents the negative object of the concept $\mathcal{R}$, leads to singling out elements 4 and 5 (Fig. 2(b)) as negative checking elements of the concept $\mathcal{R}$.

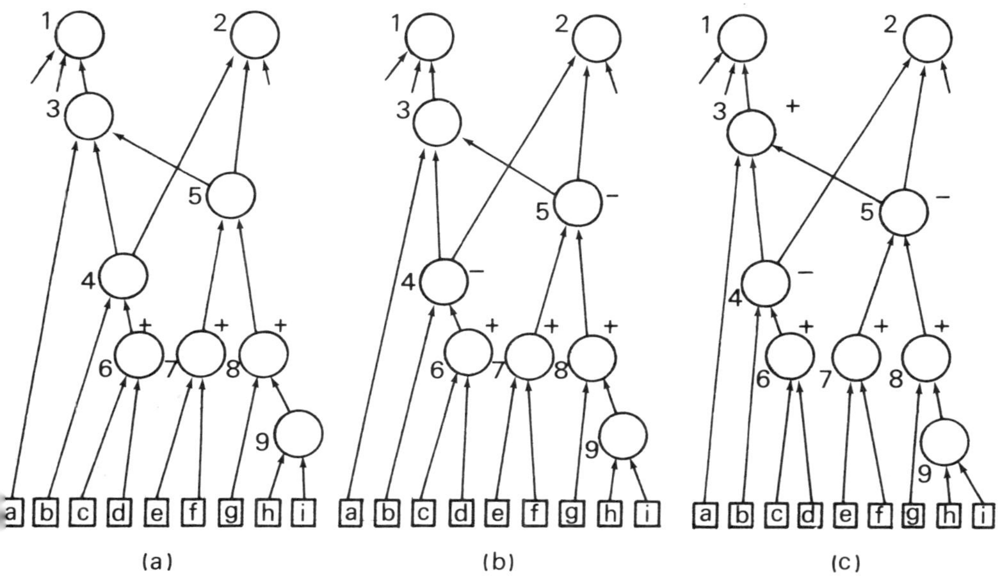

Fig. 2.

Rule 3

If, when perceiving the positive object of the concept $\mathcal{R}$, there are negative checking elements of the concept $\mathcal{R}$ in its pyramid which do not contain in their supersets $U_1, U_2, \ldots U_l$ other excited checking elements of the concept $\mathcal{R}$ in each of sets $U_1, U_2, \ldots U_l$ the element having the smallest k among all excited elements is marked as a positive checking element of the concept $\mathcal{R}$.

According to this rule the excitation of the pyramid of element 1 (Fig. 2(b)), on condition that the pyramid represents the positive object of the concept $\mathcal{R}$, leads to singling out element 3 (Fig. 2(c)) as the positive checking element of the concept $\mathcal{R}$.

With the help of positive checking elements the most typical (having the largest m) combinations of values of attributes belonging to the objects from the concept volume are singled out. For example, singling out element 8 (Fig. 2(a)) as the positive checking element means singling out combinations of volumes of attributes perceptible by receptors g, h, i. With the help of negative checking elements the combinations of values of attributes of negative objects are singled out. Note that such combinations are singled out only in cases when in perceiving the negative objects the positive checking elements are excited, that is, when perceiving those objects which are negative even if they incorporate the singled-out attributes of positive objects.

If at the revision of all objects of the learning sample at least one new checking element appears, that is, the conditions contained in rules 1,2,3 have been fulfilled at least once, a new revision of all objects of the learning sample is carried out. The algorithm operation is completed if at the next revision of the learning sample no new checking element appears.

After the learning the following *recognition rule* can be used.

An object enters into the volume of the concept $\mathcal{R}$ if in its pyramid there are the excited checking elements of the concept $\mathcal{R}$, and among them there is not a single negative checking element of the concept $\mathcal{R}$ the superset of which is free from the excited checking elements of the concept $\mathcal{R}$.

An object does not enter into the volume of the concept $\mathcal{R}$ if in its pyramid there is not a single excited positive checking element of the concept $\mathcal{R}$ the superset of which is free from the excited checking elements of the concept $\mathcal{R}$.

If none of the conditions of this rule is fulfilled the object is considered to be undefined.

Thus, in the process of executing the defined algorithm a data structure arises in which, with the help of checking elements, the generalized information about a set of positive objects is singled out which permits discrimination between positive and negative objects. The distribution of checking elements in the constructed structure reflects logical relations between values of attributes, typical of the set of positive objects. For example, the ensemble of checking elements of the network fragment shown in Fig. 2(b) is described by the logical expression

$$(c \wedge d) \wedge \neg b \vee (e \wedge f) \wedge \neg (g \wedge h \wedge i) \vee (g \wedge h \wedge i) \wedge \neg (e \wedge f),$$

in which designations of attributes associated with receptors serve as variables (the algorithm for constructing the logical expression based on the analysis of distribution of checking elements of PN has been demonstrated [3,7]. Thus, in accordance with the definition of the concept when executing the algorithm described above the *concept of a set of positive objects* is constructed.

The following two important statements which characterize the algorithm of concept formation on the basis of α-PN have been proved [3,7].

1. The algorithm provides for singling out the concept, discriminating

between positive and negative objects of an arbitrary complex learning sample.

2. The algorithm realizes a piece-wise linear separation of distribution areas of positive and negative objects of the learning sample in the space of attributes.

After the process of learning is completed it is not necessary to retain the network elements outside the pyramid of checking since they are not used for recognition.

PYRAMIDAL NETWORKS IN ARTIFICIAL INTELLIGENCE

Let us consider the features of PN.

The network is suitable for executing various operations of associative search. For example, it is possible to select all objects incorporating a given combination of attributes, tracing the output links of the element which corresponds to this combination. To select all objects associatively connected with the given one it is sufficient to trace output links of the elements entering into its pyramid. The pyramidal structure fixes the hierarchy of combinations of attributes by length and thus makes it possible to look through combinations belonging to one object in order of changing lengths. The algorithm of the network construction provides automatic establishment of associative proximity of objects with common combinations of values of attributes. The domain of search in the realization of algorithms of input and concept formation incorporates only elements of the pyramid of the perceivable object, and those of the excited elements which are directly connected with this pyramid.

Associative elements of the network correspond to combinations of values of attributes which determine conjunctive classes of objects. More complex definitions (concepts) of classes are represented by ensembles of checking elements. Through the inclusion of the excited elements into the pyramid of the perceivable object the object is tied up with classes whose definitions are represented by these elements. Thus the perceivable objects are classified.

In the inductive formation of complex concepts the main difficulties are connected with the problem of reducing the scannings of great amounts of data. Using the PN for concept formation enables us considerably to reduce scannings in comparison with other methods. When examining the algorithm of concept formation on the basis of α-PN, 3 to 5 scannings of the learning sample are sufficient to construct concepts of any complexity; this is fewer than the number of scannings in the program CLS [2] by an order of magnitude.

Apart from the aforesaid, the advantage of the PN consists in the economical expenditure of memory elements, owing to the fact that the same combinations of values of attributes of several objects are represented by one common pyramid.

In the PN the information is stored by way of its representation in the memory structure. Information about objects and classes of objects is represented by ensembles of memory elements distributed over the whole network.

The introduction of new information into such a memory leads to redistribution of links among memory elements; that is, to the change of the memory structure.

Two methods of realization of PN are possible: physical and programmed. The first method entails the creation of physical media having the features of PN, the second a computer simulation of pyramidal networks. Physical realization is hampered by the fact that the network structure must reflect the information being stored and, therefore, must change when new information is introduced. In program realization, the cells of a computer main memory correspond to the elements and links of the network. Cells of the output links of each element form an associative list whose head is the cell corresponding to the element. Cells of the links contain addresses of the elements to which these links lead. To form new elements and links, free memory cells are used which are integrated into an associative list-stack. Naturally, the advantages of PN must fully manifest themselves in a physical realization admitting parallel distribution of signals. PNs are used in a number of systems developed at the Institute of Cybernetics of the Ukrainian Academy of Sciences. In the scientific research automation system ANALYSER [3,4,7], the algorithm for concept formation on the basis of α-PN is used with the purpose of singling out regularities when performing scientific researches. Concepts formed by ANALYSER when solving complex problems in the field of chemistry, economics, astronomy, and medicine are far in excess of concepts synthesized by the human brain, in the number of attributes taken into account and in logical complexity.

In systems of search for solutions of transformation problems and planning actions of robots PPR-1 [5,6] and PPR-2 [7] the algorithms described are at the root of processes forming the world model. The world model in these systems contains the information about situations, goals, operations, generalized plans of

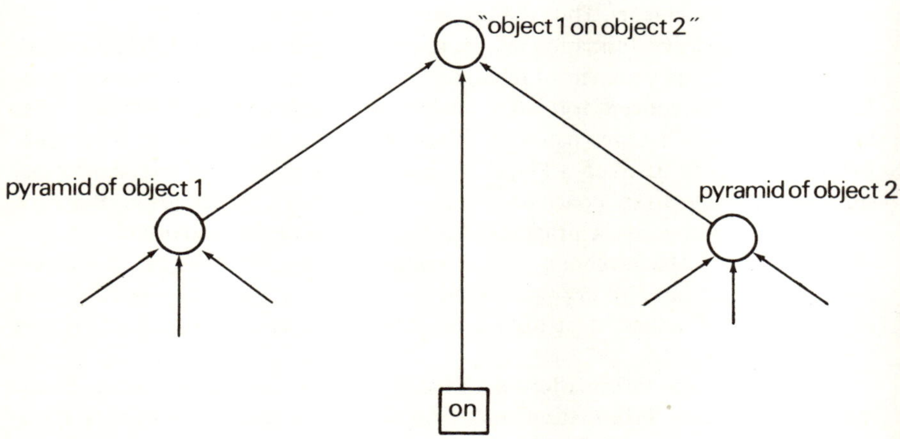

Fig. 3.

search for solutions, classes of situations and problems. All information is represented in the form of PNs. Apart from α-PN, pyramidal networks β-PN are used intended to store the information about objects represented by ordering sets of values of attributes (texts, programs, plans). Attributes in descriptions of situations are characteristics, states of the objects, and relations among objects. Fig. 3 shows the network fragment representing the relation "object 1 on object 2". Individual receptors correspond to names of relations.

The structural features of PN make it possible successfully to overcome the difficulties which arise in searching for problem solutions; in particular, the problems of planning a robot's behaviour, in a complex multicomponent environment. With the help of the operations of associative search in PN the selection of information related to the problem being solved (the information field of problems), and the choice of the applicable operator are carried out comparatively simply. The algorithm for concept formation based on the α-PN is used for the formation of definitions of classes of situations corresponding to generalized plans of searching solutions.

As a whole, the process of constructing a solution can be interpreted as the "routeing" among network fragments, representing the initial and objective situations, through a number of intermediate situations. Here the network is complemented by new concepts defining new situations, classes of situation, the obtained solutions, and generalized plans of searching solutions.

The PN in which relations among objects are represented is, in principle, a semantic network. The structural features of the PN, considered above, are convenient for performing semantic analysis of the information represented in the network. It is very important for performing operations of semantic analysis that in PN, the associative links of a complex structure, corresponding to combinations of properties of objects or relations among objects, are represented with the help of associative elements.

REFERENCES

[1] Pospelov, D. A. and Puskin, V. N. (1972). Thought and Automata. Sovetskoe Radio. Moscow (in Russian).

[2] Hunt, E., Marin, J. and Stone, P. (1966). *Experiments in Induction.* New York: Academic Press.

[3] Gladun, V. P. (1974). Computer description of classes of objects. *Cybernetics*, 824–832 (Trans. from Russian: (1972), *Kibernetika* **5**, 109–117).

[4] Gladun, V. P. and Vashenko, N. D. (1976). Methods of forming concepts with a computer. *Cybernetics*, 295–301 (Trans. from Russian: (1975), *Kibernetika* **2**, 107–112).

[5] Gladun, V. P., Galagan, N. I. and Sasina, S. P. (1976). A certain strategy for search for the solution of transformation problems. *Cybernetics*, 898–906 (Trans. from Russian: (1974), *Kibernetika* **10**, *No. 6*, 134–141).

[6] Gladun, V. P. and Galagan, N. I. (1977). An approach to the classification and comparison of methods of solution search in transformation problems. *Cybernetics*, 295–301 (Trans. from Russian: (1975), *Kibernetika* **12**, *No. 5*, 131–134).

[7] Gladun, V. P. (1977). Heuristic search in a complex environment. *Naukova Dumka* (in Russian).

ROBOT AND CONTROL SYSTEMS

14

Integrated Walking Robot

D. E. Okhotsimski
Institute of Applied Mathematics, USSR Academy of Sciences, Moscow, USSR

V. S. Gurfinkel
Institute for Transmission Problems, USSR Academy of Sciences, Moscow, USSR

E. A. Devyanin
Institute of Mathematics, Moscow State University, USSR

A. K. Platonov
Institute of Applied Mathematics, USSR Academy of Sciences, Moscow, USSR

INTRODUCTION

A robot in developed form is an automatic machine with a certain degree of autonomy, designed for active interaction with the environment. It integrates systems for perception of the environment, decision taking, and the formation and execution of plans. All these systems co-function.

The robot's activities can be complex and diverse, including as they do movements associated with the execution of working operations, the robot's own movement, and movements which provide active perception of the environment.

Organization of the robot's movement should be hierarchical. Plans formed at the upper level are then instructions for the lower levels, and are used by them as the initial data for planning. As a rule, the sequential acts of planning take place at the upper levels, with greater time intervals than at the lower ones. In planning at each level conditions for plan realizability at the lower levels are taken into account, using simplified models of the lower level functioning. In principle, a hierarchical structure for motion planning is not obligatory, and planning can be effected directly by taking account of all the peculiarities of the movement. However, a hierarchical organization is preferable for complex problems.

GENERAL DESIGN PRINCIPLES

Designing an efficient robot is an informal problem in large-system design. One of its aims must be to decrease the information flow.

One problem is the need to create simultaneously both the robot itself and its "world", that is, the environment in which the robot operates and which it interacts. The world of a "walker", designed exclusively for locomotion, may be regarded as comparatively simple, in that only the mechanical properties of the world have to be considered.

The characterisitic size of the robot body can be used as the natural linear unit for all kinds of measurements in its environment and the same unit is used for measuring the region of leg movement relative to the body.

It seems reasonable to take the value of 10 × body size as the maximum for the robot's world. The complexıty of motion tasks is not likely to be much increased in an enlarged environment when the speed is moderate. We suggest the minimal size should be from 0.1 to 0.01 of the robot's body. It characterizes the world's lowest level of detail and defines the amount of information and the accuracy of the required measurements.

As the walker solves only one problem, namely that of locomotion, the relief of the supporting surface is the most important geometrical characteristic.

The locomotion goals solved by the walker in his world are prescribed from outside.

All movements should be made up from a set of standardized actions, developed beforehand and stored in the robot's memory. Planning involves arranging the sequence of these standard actions modified by changes in a small number of free parameters. Such a method, applied at all the levels of planning, secures a great variety of movements and requires only moderate computer resources.

A similar approach is advisable in solving the problems of perception of the environment. The robot's current environment can be described by using a set of standard situations. Perception is then reduced to recognizing these situations and determining the values of the characterisitic parameters. The term "situation" includes the robot's state and its position in the environment. The situations are described by signs reflecting the properties of the environment which are essential for the robot's functioning. For each different level of perception, an appropriate set of standard situations should be developed. The scope of environment perception and the depth of analysis are different for different levels of perception. This multilevel analysis makes for efficient perception of the properties of the environment, and is in good agreement with the multilevel organization of motion planning.

It is expedient to organize the descision-making process so as to include a "situation-action" dictionary that establishes correspondence between the results of perception analysis and the movement actions, or other actions that should be performed. "Situation-action" dictionaries should be designed in the form of separate, specific modules of the algorithm. This simplifyies the logical structure of the algorithm, and any subsequent modification and extension of the decision-making rules.

For adequate functioning in the environment, the robot should be supplied with a model of the world which includes some *a priori* information on the environment and on the eventual results of the robot-environment interaction. The perception, decision-making and motion-design systems contain this information, which in this case may be treated as the robot's *a priori* knowledge. It seems reasonable to consider robots with stored knowledge as a specific class of robots.

It is possible to imagine a more intelligent automatic device which is able to modify and extend the stored knowledge by itself, using an appropriate algorithmic complex. However, a more complicated self-modifiable system of this nature is worth developing only when it promises a marked increase in efficiency. There are reasons to suppose that a stored knowledge system, well organized, would provide the building blocks for knowledge modifications at higher system levels.

Organization of the robot's movements requires an information feedback channel from the environment. This channel should provide motion correction capability for which it is primarily necessary to determine the geometrical characterisitcs of the environment. Direct location measurements of distances from the robot to the points of its environment are therefore convenient.

SIMULATION STUDIES

Properties of environment location measurements were studied for the automatic walker's motion organization [1,2], and a method of active scanning of the environment was used that decreased the load on the control computer.

The rules of active scanning provide information on the environment in the direction of the robot's planned motion.

In the standard situation, the centre of the scanning sector follows a point which moves along the planned route, some distance ahead. If the information obtained is poor, the motion design system lifts the scanning sector.

If the required information can be received by rescanning the relief elements previously screened, the scanning sector is lowered or removed to the point of the uncertainty region which is nearest to the robot. Then the scanning sector returns to the initial position. If the distance is found to be too great, the scanning plane is lowered.

If the robot discovers an insurmountable obstacle in its path, the scanning sector turns from an extreme right position to an extreme left one to determine obstacle boundaries, etc.

The perception and motion-planning algorithms are essentially dependent on the rate and extension of the environment scanning, and on the robot's velocity.

Let us turn now to the design of the walker's movements.

Motor control problems can be considered as the reverse of pattern recognition problems. In the latter the aim is to create a generalized image reflecting only essential characteristics of the real object. For motor control, detailed real movements must be designed given the most general instructions.

The control of mechanical systems with many degrees of freedom is an unusual task in engineering. In studies of motor activity in men and animals, N. A. Bernstein [3] has formulated the simple hypothesis that the basic problem of movement coordination is concerned with overcoming a large number of degrees of freedom; in other words, in lowering the number of independent variables controlling movement. This result can be achieved in two ways:

1. By the fixation (switching off) of some degrees of freedom by permanent muscle tension. This method is usually used at the first stage of forming a new motor skill. It helps to implement motor control but greatly restricts the whole system.
2. The second way (more often found at the next stage of motor skill learning) is to form motor synergies. For each synergy specific connections are imposed on certain muscle groups, all the muscles participating in a movement being subdivided into a small number of connected groups. Thus, in order to make a movement, it is enough to control a few independent parameters, although the number of muscles participating in the movement can be large.

These ideas can be used for designing the control system of the walker. A simple synergy can be organized for the regular gait. Each leg of the walker is controlled by only one generator of programmed kinematics. A system of interlimb interaction is used for the coordination of the movements of all the legs [4,5]. The generator controls the switching of locomotion phases, that is, lifting, swinging, placing, and stance. The system of interlimb coordination is responsible for the switching sequence of the programmed kinematic generator, which is itself dependent on the type of the gait and on the movement feedback signals.

The mechanism of synergy is, of course, only one way of simplifying the problem of movement control. A six-legged walker needs a multilevel algorithm able to control the body's motion and plan the walker's forces for some distance ahead [8,9,10]. This problem also includes the choice of gait, footholds, and step schedule. The motion design system uses the environment information which the perception system accumulates in the information field. It should be stressed again that well-developed methods of collecting and processing information about the environment and the robot's state are of the utmost importance for integrated walking robots. We believe that it is helpful to consider biological prototypes in this context, and that these robots must possess some technical counterparts of the sensory system.

When speaking about technical analogues of sensory systems, it should be remembered that, though the receptors of different animal species are complex in structure and function, the organization of afferent processes is much more so. Morpho-functional analysis has shown that the main factor stimulating the development of the central part of the sensory systems is not the processing of the sensory information of different modalities but the formation of sensory complexes [3]. We should like to point out that the sensory system of an adult individual is affected not only by genetically controlled structural-functional organization but by the subject's past experience. Even the structure of the sensory system may thus be influenced. It is essential that this experience be gained during an inter-sensory and sensory-motor interaction. Motor activity serves as a school for sensory systems.

We took as our point of departure the notion that the perception of the external world is not an end in itself, but serves to perform definite actions.

Let us discuss some problems of the dynamics of the walking robot. These arise mainly in the motion execution phase and also in the motion planning phase when the robot has a small stability margin.

Thus, the six-legged robot has no fewer than 24 degrees of freedom: 18 in the legs, and 6 in the body. To test the efficiency of the motion control algorithms, a complete dynamic scheme has to be used [11,12], though in special cases the dynamic scheme may be simplified, for example by taking no account of the inertia of the legs [10,13].

It is a statically indeterminate system. For the walker as a whole, six equations of statics or kinetostatics have to balance 9 to 18 components of support reaction forces in the leg tips. This gives rise to force balancing problems.

Force distribution in the leg reactions has to be considered [10,13,14]. A reasonable approach is to apply some optimization criteria, for example, minimizing the maximum value of the vertical reaction components in the supporting legs, in order to decrease the load on the ground; the horizontal components should be chosen so as to minimize the maximum value of the angles between the reaction force vector and the axis of the friction cone in the point supporting the leg. The last criterion proves to be efficient in the case of motion over a surface with a small friction coefficient [10,14].

A reasonable force distribution makes it possible to avoid antagonism in the leg actuators, and decreases the load and energy consumption. Force balancing should be ensured in the leg motion control [10,14].

Some problems of dynamics also arise in designing the servo-systems controlling the leg actuators and in testing their performance.

Our investigations with integrated walking robot systems include computer simulation and laboratory models in hardware.

When using computer simulation the control algorithms should be implemented as software complexes. The walker itself and its environment must be simulated as well as measurement data collection and processing. Our simulation results were presented on a computer graphics display in the form of a moving image of the robot walking over the terrain.

The early stages of computer simulation [15,16] were devoted (1) to the development of the motion design algoithms, and (2) to the analysis of gaits and the investigation of kinematic potentialities.

A special algorithmic complex was developed to analyse the problem of interaction of the walking robot with a human operator. The complex operated in real time [17]. Two coupled computers were used. The main calculation was carried out in a BESM-6 computer. The second computer, supplied with a built-in graphics display, played the role of a terminal and was used for the input of the operator commands and visualization of the robot's walking. By moving the two-degrees-of-freedom joystick the human operator could prescribe both the velocity and the direction of the walker. As to the terrain, a plane surface was used, complicated by "pits", that is, areas impossible for leg tip placement.

The first programs developed were for movement along a rectilinear route over a terrain with prismatic obstacles (Fig. 1). The active-perception principle was used, with a controllable distance-measuring beam. This made it possible for the robot to climb over complicated obstacles near the margin of feasibility [1,18]. Fig. 2 shows the movement phase when the robot is stepping over one pit and scanning the bottom of a second and larger one. This cannot be stepped over, and the robot will have to climb over by moving down to the pit bottom and up again on the other side. The rectangle with a dot inside it which is seen in the top of Fig. 2, shows the centre of gravity inside the supporting polygon, which is used for estimating the static stability margin of the moving walker. Fig. 3 shows two phases of the robot climbing over "very difficult" obstacles.

The problem of walking in a 3-D world is much more complicated. While solving the motion design problem the algorithms were synthesized which controlled the capacity to walk along a prescribed curved route, under the contraint that footholds should be chosen only inside small areas irregularly placed on the supporting plane (Fig. 4). Heuristics were provided for selecting foothold points and scheduling which would maximize the walker's static stability margin.

Fig. 5 represents the walker moving over terrain with "pits" arbitrarily placed on the supporting plane. The route is rectilinear. Information about the terrain relief is delivered by processing the distance measurement data. The measuring beam oscillates inside some sector shown as a triangle in Fig. 5. The walker uses a "free" gait [9,19,20]. The footholds and walking schedule are produced by a control algorithm which makes decisions depending on the shape of the obstacles under the constraint of maintaining a large static stability margin.

To test the algorithms in the case of the walker's motion on terrain with more complicated relief, a special terrain model was constructed, based on the use of the square grid. Three object scale levels (Fig. 6a) and several standard object types made it possible to design a complex terrain relief, while saving the computer resources needed for storing the 3-D terrain model, transforming it into a CRT picture, and solving the hidden-line problem [21]. As the specific

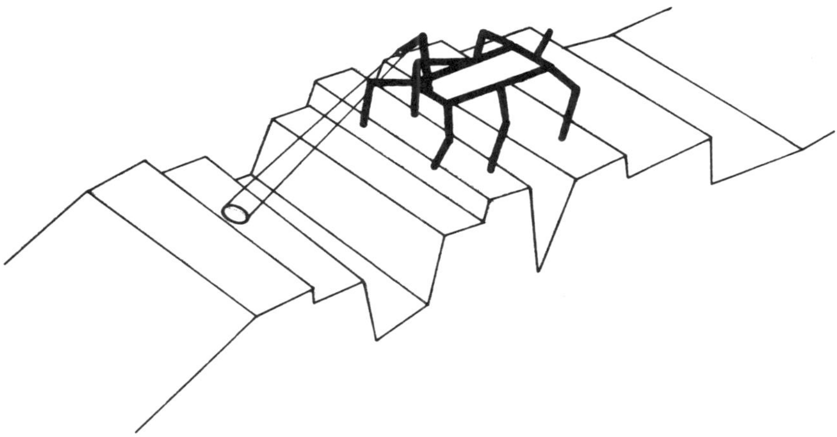

Fig. 1.

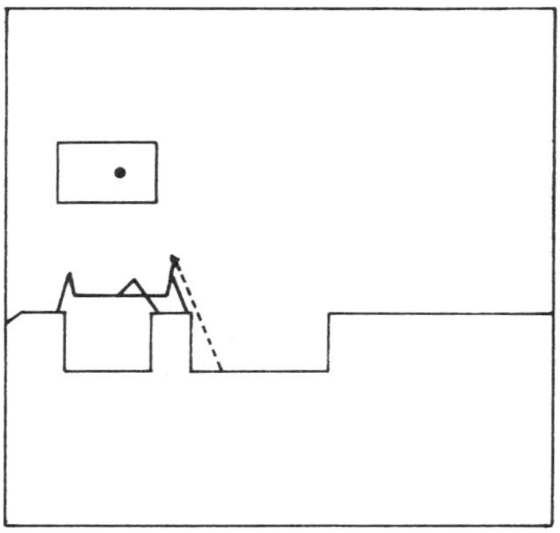

Fig. 2.

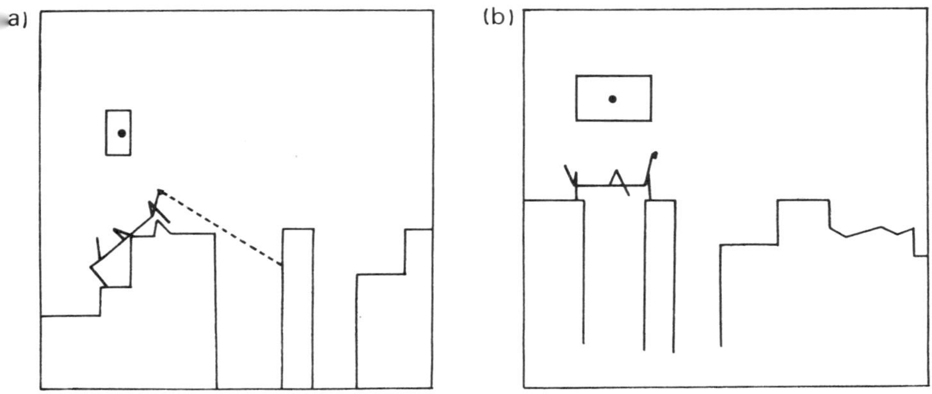

Fig. 3.

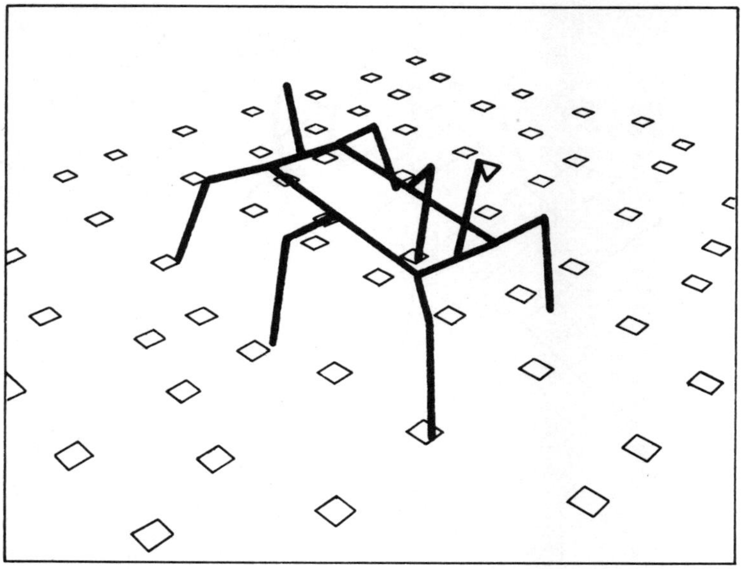

Fig. 4.

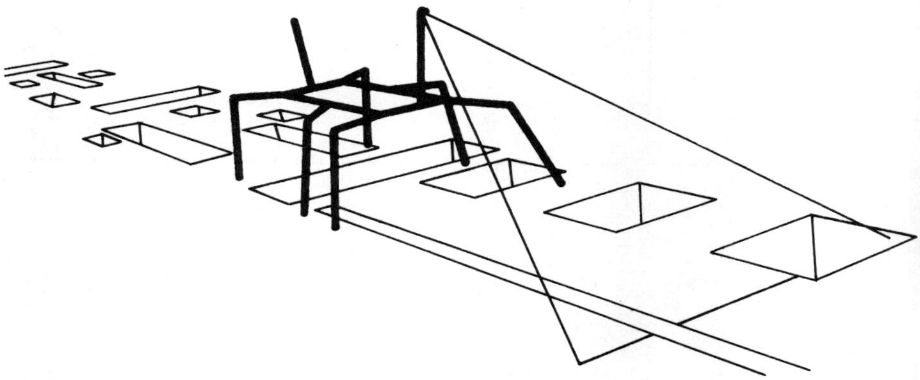

Fig. 5.

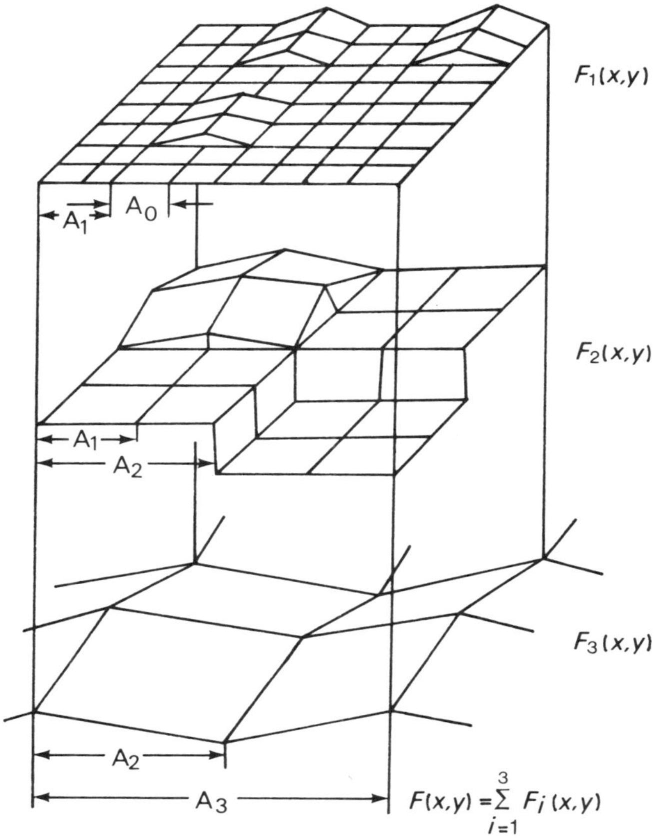

Fig. 6a.

properties of the terrain model are not used when testing the motion control algorithms, it is reasonable to assume that the algorithm's efficiency is thus severely tested. Fig. 6b and Fig. 7 present examples of relief with "pits" and "boulders".

Specific modules of the algorithm were designed for simulating the perception of the terrain relief, the walker's motion along both rectilinear and curved route, and the route selection to avoid collisions and to by-pass large-scale obstacles.

Tests made it clear that for the motion along a slightly curved route, the same logic of relief measurement can be used as for a rectilinear route. The central line of the scanning sector should at all times be in the vertical plane of symmetry of the walker's body. If the route has significant curvature or contains break points with considerable change of route direction, a scanning plane manoeuvre should be used. Here the scanning plane turns from side to

Fig. 6b.

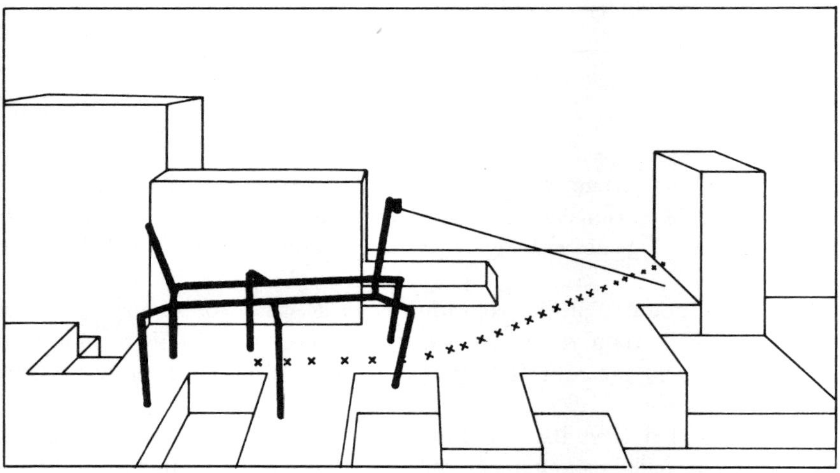

Fig. 7.

side around the vertical axis, so as to investigate in advance the relief area round the bend of the route.

Route replanning contains the following operations. When the robot discovers an obstacle, the scanning sector expands its width and elevates its central line of vision. The right or left path round the obstacle is selected on the criterion of minimal route perturbation. After making the decision and modifying the route, the scanning sector returns to its regular mode of operation. The dotted line in Fig. 7 shows the walker's route in the process of replanning.

The above-mentioned control algorithms for the integrated walking robot cover levels from the collecting and processing of measurement information about terrain relief up to planning the kinematics of the robot's body and legs. For the execution of the planned movement, the problems of robot stabilization and reasonable force distribution in a statically indeterminate system must be solved. Appropriate algorithms and some test results using computer simulation are presented in [10,14,22]. The approach used was briefly described above, in the discussion of dynamic problems.

HARDWARE MODELS

Fig. 8 shows one of the first models designed for developing methods of low-level leg motion control and interleg coordination [5,23]. The vehicle could walk along both the rectilinear and curved route. Direction and velocity of walking were prescribed by a human operator. Some of the model's design principles were taken from physiology, and components of a quasineuron type were used in the control system.

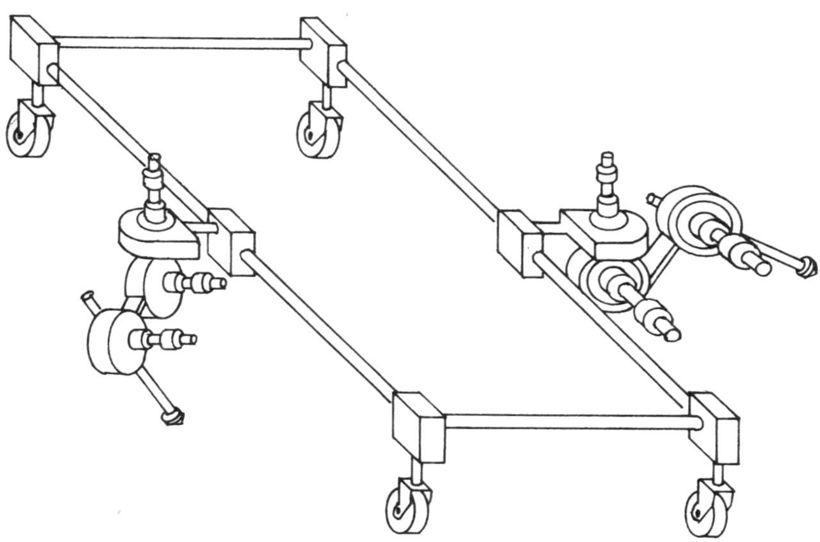

Fig. 8.

Fig. 9 shows the first attempt to implement the execution part of the six-legged walking robot [6]. Methods of generating regular gaits of different types – for example, "tripod gait", "wave gait", and others – were investigated.

A new model, RICKSHA, was designed for elaborating the logic of leg motion control [24,25,26]. Each of two legs had three degrees of freedom. The tips of both legs were supplied with contact sensors to monitor contact with the supporting surface. The angles in the joints were measured by potentiometers, and angular velocity by tachometers. The control system was implemented by using an analog computer. The model was supplied with an elementary capability for terrain profile adaptation and was able to move autonomously over an uneven surface with small-scale obstacles while maintaining smooth body motion. The investigations carried out with RICKSHA resulted in a method of generating a flexible step cycle and an efficient method with simple hardware for transforming the leg-tip Cartesian coordinates into joint angles. The results obtained achieved an economy in computer hardware and in specially designed electronic circuits.

RICKSHA was further developed in two ways. First, an improved suspension system was designed which made it possible to test the motion

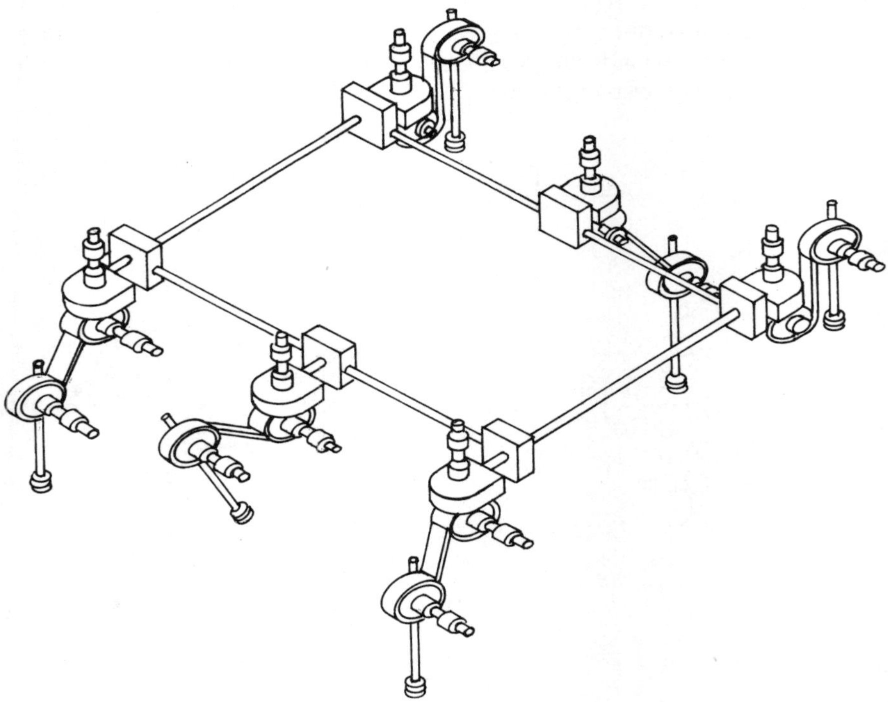

Fig. 9.

control methods in a greater range of movements. RICKSHA was able to climb over larger and higher obstacles, using a body-tilting and clearance manoeuvre. Secondly, some distance-sensing elements were used, in the form of a two-link lever system supplied with a contact sensor at its tip and potentiometers in the joints. When following the obstacle profile, the lever system delivered the measurement information which was used (1) for estimating the size and shape of the obstacles, and (2) for planning the foothold points and scheduling the leg motion. It should be noted that the measurement information delivered by the lever system is, in some sense, similar to the information obtained by the system with the distance-measuring beam. Thus the robot equipped with the coupled-lever measurement system may be considered as a prototype of the the robot with a distance-measuring system.

The next step in modelling the walking robots was in designing a robot with more powerful legs. Fig. 10 shows a pair of such legs being tested in the same way as the modified RICKSHA. Each leg has a "free orienting" foot with three degrees of freedom and a contact sensor. Successful results made it possible to design and test the whole six-legged walker shown as Fig. 11. At present, the six-legged model is controlled by an analog computer.

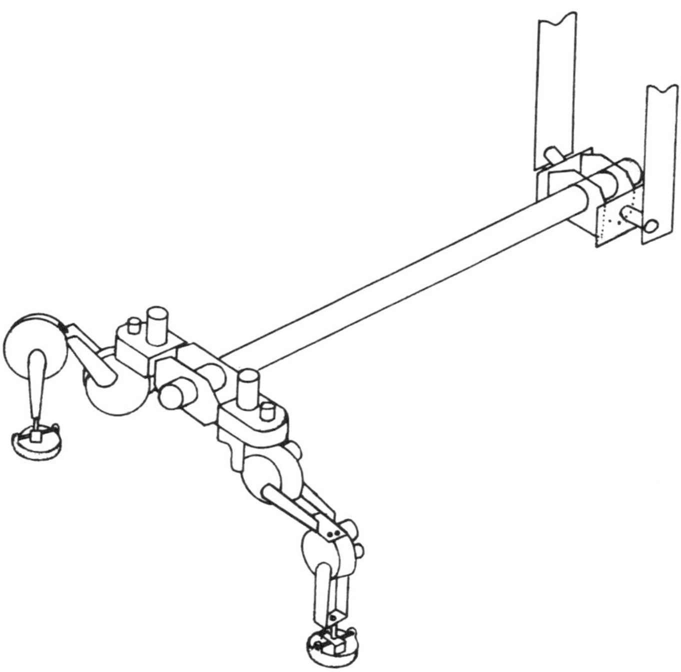

Fig. 10.

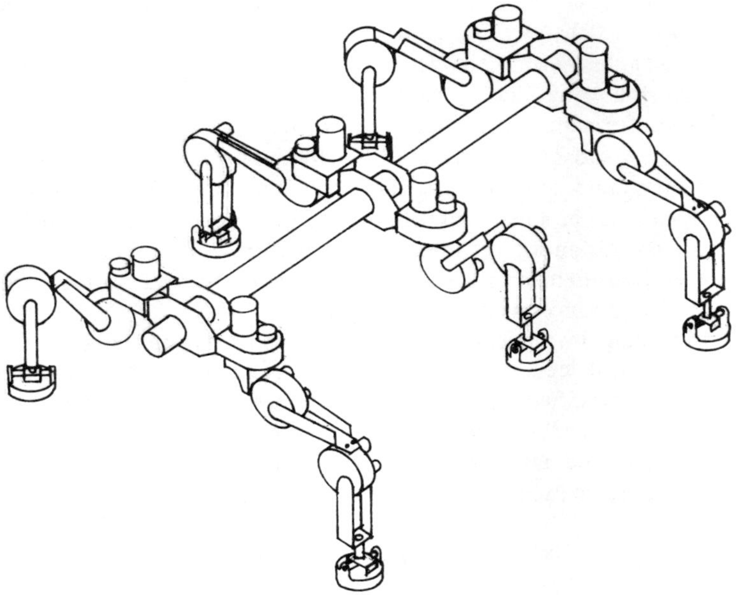

Fig. 11.

Fig. 12 shows another model supplied with a scanning distance-measuring system [27]. When connected to a computer the model will make use of the previously designed motion control algorithms for simulating autonomous walking over rough terrain.

Along with autonomous walking robots capable of operating in new and complex environments, it is reasonable to consider the development of walking vehicles controlled by a human operator (driver) [7,28,29,30] who is responsible for the long-range planning, route selection and mode of operation. Such a walking vehicle could be implemented in the form of a "proprioceptive" robot, supplied only with tactile perception of the environment or in the form of a robot with restricted tele-receptors oriented only towards problems of short-scale planning. In the latter case, when walking over complicated terrain, the robot might be restricted to selecting foothold points, scheduling leg movements, and planning body motion.

The development of integrated walking robots is a wide and challenging field of investigation. We believe that progress will lead to the successful integration of results obtained in many different branches of artificial intelligence.

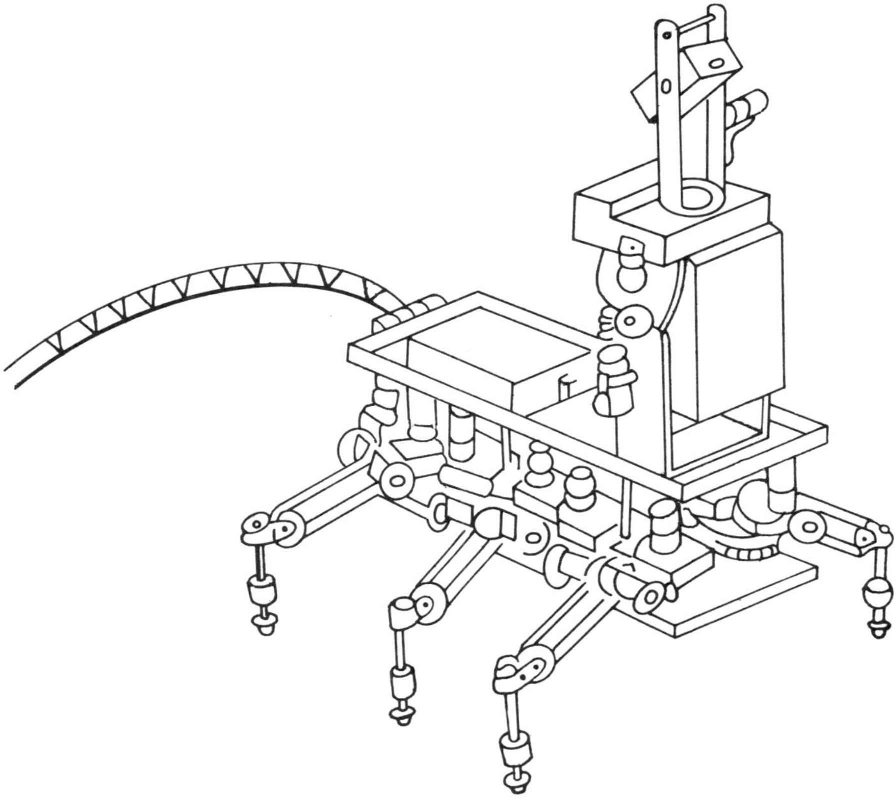

Fig. 12.

REFERENCES

[1] Okhotsimski, D. E., Platonov, A. K., Borovin, G. K., Karpov, I. I., Kugushev, E. I., Lasutin, Yu. M., Pavlovski, V. E. and Yaroshevsky, V. S. (1974). Control of an integrated locomotive robot, *Proc. 4th IFAC Symposium on Automatic Control in Space*, Tsakhadzor, Armenian SSR.

[2] Okhotsimski, D. E. and Platonov, A. K. (1975). The perceptive robot moving in a 3-D world. *Proc. 4th Int. Joint Conf. on Artif. Int. (IJCAI-75)*, Tbilisi.

[3] Bernstein, N. A. (1947). *On the Construction of Motion.* Med. Gov. Pub. House. Also as *The Co-ordination and Regulation of Movements*, Oxford: Pergamon Press (1967).

[4] Okhotsimski, D. E., Platonov, A. K., Gurfinkel, V. S. and Devyanin, E. A. (1973). Modelling of locomotion systems, *Proc. 4th All-Union Conf. on Bionics* **1** (in Russian).

[5] Gurfinkel, V. S., Schneider, A. Yu., Kanaev, E. M. and Ostapchuk, V. G. (1973). A model of a walking apparatus with autonomous control, *Bionika* **6** (in Russian).

[6] Gurfinkel, V. S., Devyanin, E. A., Gurfinkel, E. V., Zhikharev, D. N., Kanaev, E. M., Lenskii, A. V., Ostapchuk, K. G., Schneider, A. Yu. and Shtil'man, L. G. (1974). Organization of the locomotive cycles of a walking apparatus, *Proc. of 4th All-Union Meeting on Problems of Control*, Moscow: Nauka Pub. (in Russian).

[7] Devyanin, E. A., Lenskii, A. V. and Samsonov, V. A. (1975). The problem of controlling a walking apparatus, *Biomechanics* **13** (in Russian).

[8] McGhee, R. B. et al. (1974). On the problem of selecting a gait for a legged vehicle, *Trans. 4th IFAC Symposium*, Erivan, USSR (in Russian).

[9] Kugushev, E. I. and Yaroshevsky, V. S. (1975). Problems of selecting a gait. *Proc. 4th Int. Joint Conf. on Artif. Int. (IJCAI-75)*.

[10] Okhotsimski, D. E., Golubev, Yu. F. and Alekseeva, L. A. (1974). Control of a dynamic model of a walking apparatus. *Preprint: Institute of Applied Mathematics Academy of Sciences USSR, No. 20* (in Russian).

[11] Alekseeva, L. A. and Golubev, Yu. F. (1975). A model of the dynamics of a walking apparatus, *Izvestia USSR Academy of Sciences*, and *Technical Cybernetics, No. 5* (in Russian).

[12] Alekseeva, L. A. and Golubev, Yu. F. (1976). Adaptive algorithms for the stabilization of an automatic walking apparatus. *Izvestia, USSR Academy of Sciences*, and *Technical Cybernetics, No. 5* (in Russian).

[13] Okhotsimski, D. E., Golubev, Yu. F. and Alekseeva, L. A. (1974). A stabilization algorithm for an automatic walking machine. *Proc. of 4th IFAC Symposium on Automatic Control in Space*, Tsakhadzor, Armenian SSR.

[14] Golubev, Yu. F. and Alekseeva, L. A. (1974). Stabilization of the motion of a walking machine in the presence of disturbance. *Thesis of lectures*, Moscow (in Russian).

[15] Okhotsimski, D. E., Platonov, A. K., Borovin, G. K. and Karpov, I. I. (1971). Computer modellling of the motion of a walking machine. *Preprint: Institute of Applied Mathematics, Academy of Sciences. Izvestia, USSR Academy of Sciences, Technical Cybernetics, No. 3* (1972).

[16] Okhotsimski, D. E., Platonov, A. K., Borovin, G. K., Karpov, I. I., Lazutin, Yu. M., Pavlovsky, V. E. and Yaroshevsky, V. S. (1972). Algorithms for controlling the motion of a walking machine. *Preprint: Institute of Applied Mathematics, USSR Academy of Sciences, No. 63* (in Russian).

[17] Okhotsimski, D. E., Platonov, A. K., Kugushev, E. I., Lazutin, Yu. M. and Yaroshevsky, V. S. (1974). Problems of constructing and modelling a walking machine controlled by an operator. *Preprint: Institute of Applied Mathematics, USSR Academy of Sciences, No. 125* (in Russian).

[18] Okhotsimski, D. E. and Platonov, A. K. (1973). Control algorithms for a walker climbing over obstacles. *Proc. 3rd Int. Joint Conf. on Artif. Int. (IJCAI-73)*, Stanford. pp. 317–323. Menlo Park; Stanford Research Institute.

[19] Okhotsimski, D. E. and Platonov, A. K. (1976). On the problems and principles of robot motion, *Proc. 14th IUTAM Congress*, Delft.

[20] Okhotsimski, D. E. and Platonov, A. K. (1976). Motion control of a walking machine, *Proc. 2nd CISM-IFTOMM Symposium, "ROMANSKY"*, Warsaw.

[21] Platonov, A. K. and Pyranichnikov, V. E. (1977). Modelling the external environment of a locomotive robot. *Preprint: Institute of Applied Mathematics, USSR Academy of Sciences, No. 84* (in Russian).

[22] Alekseeva, L. A. (1976). Modelling the dynamics and motion control of a walking machine. *Izvestia, USSR Academy of Sciences, No. 5* (in Russian).

[23] Schneider, A. Yu., Gurfinkel, E. B., Kanaev, E. M. and Ostapchuk, V. G. (1974). Control system for an artificial limb for a walking machine, *Trudy, MFTI, No. 5* (in Russian).

[24] Devyanin, E. V., Lavrovskii, Z. K., Lenskii, A. V., Samsonov, V. A., Chistyakov, A. I. and Shtil'man, L. G. (1973). A prototype of the control of a walking machine, *Bionics* **1** (in Russian).

[25] Vasenev, V. A., Devyanin, E. A., Zhikharev, D. N., Lavrovskii, Z. K., Lenskii, A. V. and Samsonov, V. A. (1974). A prototype of a walking machine and its system of control. *Izvestia, USSR Academy of Sciences, Technical Cybernetics, No. 6* (in Russian).

[26] Devyanin, E. A., Lenskii, A. V., Samsonov, V. A. and Shtil'man, L. G. (1975). Development of prototype walking machine and its control system, *Nauka* (in Russian).

[27] Gerkhen-Gubanov, G. B. and Kuzvetsov. V. G. (1976). A range-finder scanning system for the recognition of three-dimensional objects, *Sektsiya* **40** (in Russian).

[28] Bessonov, A. P. and Umnov, N. V. (1975). *Mashinovedenie* **6** (in Russian).

[29] Davydov, O. I. and Platonov, A. K. (1972). Computer modelling of the motion of an operator-controlled four-legged walking machine. *Preprint: Institute of Applied Mathematics, USSR Academy of Sciences, No. 73* (in Russian).

[30] Orin, D. E., McGhee, R. B. and Jaswa, V. C. (1976). Interactive computer-control of a six-legged robot vehicle with optimization of stability, terrain adaptability and energy, *Proc. IEEE Conf. on Decision and Control*, pp. 382–391.

15

Influence of Artificial Intelligence Methods on the Solution of Traditional Control Problems

G. S. Pospelov and D. A. Pospelov

Computer Centre, USSR Academy of Sciences, Moscow, USSR

Abstract

The paper demonstrates how methods of knowledge representation and solution search characteristic of artificial intelligence theory influence the solution of control problems for discrete processes which have a combinational field of allowable solutions.

INTRODUCTION

When a new view on old problems opens and new problem presentation languages are developed, with solution methods based on them, one naturally wants to estimate the influence of these new ideas on progress in the solution of traditional problems. In this publication we try to estimate the effect of description and representation methods and languages on the development of methods for solution of combinational problems that are characterized by the "dimensionality curse"; that is, by combinatorial growth of the number of operations required to solve a problem with linear increase of problem dimensionality. Such problems may be exemplified by allocation of limited resources within an integrated operational schedule, graph cutting into a prescribed number of minimally connected components, processing of parts on a set of machines, search for a path of a given type over a network, and numerous others. There is an exact method for solution of all of these problems that lies in complete enumeration of variants, but the size of these problems in practice prevents implementation even on modern computers.

A standard way to solve such problems is to use various heuristic methods satisfying "local success criteria" [1-6]. But the informality of heuristics and the impossibility of estimating their effectiveness are the shortcomings of this approach.

We hope that progress in the field of artificial intelligence may open a way to the development of purposeful methods for the solution of combinatorial control problems. In this connection, two of the results obtained by artificial intelligence theory are of interest to us, namely methods for construction of compact hierarchical models of knowledge useful in the determination of solution plans, and those for the design of interactive systems providing man-computer dialogue in the course of solution.

Before discussing the influence of these methods on the solution of control problems, we shall describe the principal difficulties that discourage application of the classical automatic control methods. Over recent decades, classical control theory has gone through a certain crisis. The theory used to deal with plants whose structure and functioning could be formally described, for instance, by some type of differential equations. The control goals and criteria were also easy to describe. Control theory, thus, was developing as a purely mathematical science, dealing solely with formal models and exact methods. The control engineer could even do without knowing the actual plant for which he studied a control model. He ought only to be confident that the model was adequate, but that was the headache of a specialist operating the plant. The plants and control techniques could thus be standardized.

In the early fifties, however, control engineers became aware of plants having essentially new features. Firstly, describing the structure and functioning of these in terms of customary formal models as a certain (albeit very complicated) set of equations (logical, algebraic, differential, etc.) was out of the question. Secondly, these plants were active themselves, varied in time and had "free will". Thirdly the goals and control criteria were not formalizable and also changed with time. One example is a city, the problem of whose management was posed almost simultaneously in several countries. Above all, the purpose of its existence is not clearly defined. What is a city for? This question has no ready-made answer and is unlikely to have one. As a result, no exact formulation of the city-management criterion can be given. The city's evolution, in the course of which it can grow, expand, and die, changes the basic functions of its existence and renders construction of any closed city-management model impossible. A city is by no means the sole example. A large enterprise, an industry or service (for example, the care of public health), an economic region, etc. exemplify other control plants of this sort.

Inapplicability of the classical control techniques is evident here. One might assume that since no formal description is possible, no statement of the problem is possible either. But the experience of people who control such plants, well or not-so-well, is that the control problem can still be stated and solved.

Psychological analysis of the behaviour of people sharing in control or management of such plants [7] reveals that, in learning to control, people develop a mental model of the plant, the processes therein, and the transformations of these processes to make decisions on control. In that model, structural situational relations between components of the plant and inputs into the plant are the core. In our paper we shall take this for granted because it has been sufficiently well justified [8]. Some necessary additional considerations leading to more precise description of models developed by the operator have also been given [9].

The psychological analyses enable us to formulate two hypotheses which will underlie the further discussion:

> Whatever the operator has to know to exercise control may be expressed as a set of texts in a conventional language. In other words, all data on the plant, its purpose, control criteria, and the set of possible decisions may be supplied to the control system as a sequence of phrases in a natural language.
>
> The control system required for the kind of plants, in principle, cannot be closed-loop. It is an essentially open-loop system, and its learning process is never completed by development of a final formalized model.

These two hypotheses give rise to the above-mentioned interest in methods for constructing models of knowledge about plants and their operation, and also in dialogue systems.

An illustrative example

Consider a well-known example from the computer system theory problem of program allocation [10].

A computer system has n processors or computers (not necessarily of a single type), and at most m various tasks may be simultaneously presented at the system input.

Denote by t_{ij} the time required by the computer j to execute task i. Introduce binary values defined as follows

$$x_{ij} = \begin{cases} 1 \text{ if } i\text{th task is handled by } j\text{th computer,} \\ 0 \text{ otherwise} \end{cases}$$

Now the problem of optimal allocation of m tasks between n processors/computers may be presented as an $n \times m$ matrix $\| t_i^j \|$ whose binary entries x_{ij} should be determined so that

$$\sum_{j=1}^{m} x_j i_j > 1 \qquad \text{for } i = 1, 2, \ldots n;$$

$$\sum_{i=1}^{n} x_i i_j = 1 \qquad \text{for } j = 1, 2, \ldots m;$$

and

$$f = \sum_{i=1}^{n} \sum_{j=1}^{m} x_{ij}\, t_i^j$$

reaches minimum.

This is a standard Boolean programming problem that may be solved by numerous methods [11]. Nevertheless, none of them is applicable to task allocation in an actual computer system. This is easily explained by the fact that the time required for optimal task allocation completely overlaps the time saved by the optimal allocation. This situation is reminiscent of short-term weather forecasting where, according to an expert, "We are already able to forecast tomorrow's weather, but it would take a month of computer time".

That is why designers of computer operating systems prefer to use allocation procedures based on some heuristic considerations rather than on exact methods. It is important to note that the screening of heuristic considerations might itself take much time, but it should result in an approximate method which requires little time and prevents combinational growth of the number of operations with problem dimensionality; that is, the number of computers in a system and the number of executed tasks. We shall describe below a procedure for construction of heuristic allocation rules as proposed by D. Boev [12]; examples are taken from the same publication.

At each step of allocation there is a matrix. Allocation depends on both matrix entries and relations between them. The gist of Boer's approach is to construct allocation decision rules in the form of logical functions of t_i and relations between them. This approach is based on a recognition method described by Bongard [13].

Linearly ordered sets of elements of $\|t_i^j\|$ tabulated as below are used as source situation descriptions:

Table 1.

g_1	g_2	g_3	g_4	g_5	g_6	g_7	g_8
3	7	9	5	11	8	6	13
5	7	13	12	4	6	14	9
4	3	9	2	7	4	1	11

Numbers in the first row of Table 1 may represent the following situation: there are two computers; four terminals have received tasks, the first task may be executed by the first processor in 3 time units (g_1), and by the second one in 7 units (g_2); the second task is executed by the processors, respectively, in 9(g_3) and 5(g_4) time units. In each table of this sort all given situations that require, in an expert's opinion, a similar type of allocation are summarised. Description of a situation class (generalized situation) should contain all the peculiar features of the individual situations involved in the table for a given class. To generate such descriptions, the following special operators are used:

(a) if $g_i > g_j$, then $L_{ij} = 1$
otherwise $L_{ij} = 0$.

(b) if $g_1 = max[min(\ldots g_i \ldots g_j), min(\ldots g_k \ldots g_s) \; min(\ldots g_s \ldots g_t)]$
then $L_{ij} = 1$
otherwise $L_{ij} = 0$.

Four logic functions are used: $a \vee b, \bar{a} \vee b, a \vee \bar{b}$ and $\bar{a} \vee \bar{b}$.

Now introduce a notion of a characteristic that is constructed as follows: two arbitrary logic operators are applied to each row resulting in two logic variables ξ_1 and ξ_2; next, one of the four above functions is applied to them:

$$\phi_m(\xi_1,\xi_2) = \xi_m \, [L_i(g_1,g_2 \ldots g_k)s, L_j(g_1,g_2 \ldots g_k)s] \, ,$$

and its result is a characteristic of the row.

A logic product of the characteristics of all the rows constituting a table is a table characteristic.

The next stage is separation of the so-called useful characteristics. For each class of situations there are two tables, working and checking ones. Charac-eristics are computed for both tables. The major requirement for the useful characteristic is that it should be the same for the working and checking tables of a class.

The second requirement for the useful characteristic is that is should allow decomposition of a set of objects (tables) used for learning; that is, the charac-teristic should never be the same (0 or 1) for all the tables.

Now the process proceeds by separation of the so-called minimal charac-teristic basis. A set of characteristics is referred to as a minimal basis of some class of tables (situations) if a product of the characteristics constituting the minimal basis of class i is "1" for this class, and "0" otherwise.

The minimal basis of characteristics for some class is identified with a generalized situation (situation-solution) for this class. A meaningful writing of the characteristics involved in the minimal basis points to those relations between elements of a situation t_i^j that are essential in terms of classification.

Consider a particular example of allocation of two tasks to two computers whose throughputs are not multiples.

There are two situation-solutions:

– the first task is assigned to the first computer, and the second one to the second computer;
– the first task is assigned to the second computer, and the second one to the first computer.

The learning situations are summarized in the tables below, using a similar construction to that in Table 1.

Table 2.

	g_1	g_2	g_3	g_4
Working table	26	6	7	6
	4	1	5	2
	3	9	2	1
	4	6	5	3
Checking table	5	6	3	4
	7	9	6	8
	9	3	11	6
	8	4	10	7

	g_1	g_2	g_3	g_4
Working table	2	5	1	6
	5	3	4	2
	7	5	4	8
	3	4	5	6
Checking table	1	2	3	4
	9	1	2	8
	10	8	4	7
	5	3	8	9

Here

g_1 is the time (in conventional units) for execution of the first task on the first computer, denote it by t_1^1;

g_2 is the time taken by the second computer to execute the first task, t_1^2.

g_3 is t_2^1, and

g_4 is t_2^2.

The following logic operators are utilized:

L_1 : if $g_1 > g_2$, then $\xi(i) = 1$; otherwise $\xi(i) = 0$.

: if $g_1 > g_3$, then $\xi(i) = 1$; otherwise $\xi(i) = 0$; etc.

Characteristics of situation classes were selected by computer, and a table was compiled for this example.

Table 3.

L_I	L_J	F	T_1	T_2	E_1	E_2
1	5	7	1	0	1	1
3	5	7	1	0	1	0
1	3	8	1	0	1	0
2	4	8	1	0	1	0
1	3	9	0	1	0	1
1	5	9	0	1	0	1
2	3	9	0	1	0	1
2	6	9	0	1	0	1
3	5	9	0	1	1	1
5	6	9	0	1	1	1
1	2	10	1	0	1	0
1	4	10	1	0	1	1
1	5	10	1	0	1	1
2	6	10	0	1	0	1
5	6	10	0	1	1	1

where L_T is the number of the first logic operator; L_J is that of the second operator, F is the number of logic function (No. 7 – $a \vee b$; No. 8 – $\bar{a} \vee b$; No. 9 – $a \vee \bar{b}$ and No. 10 – $\bar{a} \vee \bar{b}$). Totality of the first three columns of the table makes up a logic characteristic that will be denoted as $(L_I\, L_J\, F)$ for the sake of brevity. Columns T_1 and T_2 contain values of the characteristics for the first and second classes of the table, respectively. Columns E_1 and E_2 have values of characteristics for two examination situations

$$E_1(5,11,8,3) \text{ and } E_2(4,2,3,5).$$

As can be seen from the table, even application of a simple concordance procedure classifies situations E_1 and E_2 as belonging, respectively, to the first and second classes of situations-solutions.

To find out minimal characteristic bases, values are required of characteristics of all the rows of learning tables, that is, of all situations. Tabulated below are the results of calculations.

Table 4.

L_I	L_J	F	T_1	T_2
1	5	7	1 1 1 1 1 1 1 1	0 1 1 0 0 1 1 1
3	5	7	1 1 1 1 1 1 1 1	0 1 0 0 0 1 1 0
1	3	8	1 1 1 1 1 1 1 1	1 1 0 1 1 1 1 0
2	4	8	1 1 1 1 1 1 1 1	1 0 1 1 1 0 1 1
2	5	8	1 1 1 1 1 1 1 1	0 1 0 1 1 0 1 1
1	3	9	1 1 0 0 0 1 1 1	1 1 1 1 1 1 1 1
1	5	9	0 1 0 0 0 0 1 1	1 1 1 1 1 1 1 1
2	3	9	1 0 1 0 1 1 0 0	1 1 1 1 1 1 1 1
2	6	9	0 0 1 0 1 1 0 0	1 1 1 1 1 1 1 1
3	5	0	0 1 1 1 1 0 1 1	1 1 1 1 1 1 1 1
5	6	9	1 0 1 1 1 1 0 0	1 1 1 1 1 1 1 1
1	2	10	1 1 1 1 1 1 1 1	1 0 0 1 1 0 0 1
1	4	10	1 1 1 1 1 1 1 1	1 1 0 1 1 1 0 1
1	5	10	1 1 1 1 1 1 1 1	1 0 1 1 1 1 0 1
2	6	10	0 0 1 0 1 1 0 0	1 1 1 1 1 1 1 1
5	6	10	1 0 1 1 1 1 0 0	1 1 1 1 1 1 1 1

Characteristics (3, 5, 7) and (1, 2, 10) may be taken as minimal bases for the first class of situations-solutions. As may be seen from Table 4, product of these characteristics is "1" for class T_1 and "0" for all the situations in T_2.

Meaningfully, a statement for the minimal basis for T_1 is as follows:

$$\begin{aligned} f_1 = {} & [(g_1 > g_4) \vee (g_2 > g_4)] \cdot [(g_1 > g_2) \vee (g_1 > g_3)] = \\ & [(t_2^2 < t_1^1) \vee (t_2^2 < t_1^2)] \cdot [(t_1^1 \leqslant t_1^2) \vee (t_1^1 \leqslant t_2^1)] = \\ & (t_2^2 < t_1^1)(t_1^1 \leqslant t_1^2) \vee (t_2^2 < t_1^1)(t_1^1 \leqslant t_2^1) \vee \\ & (t_2^2 < t_1^2)(t_1^1 \leqslant t_1^2) \vee (t_2^2 < t_1^2)(t_1^1 \leqslant t_2^1). \end{aligned}$$

A minimal basis for T_2 is determined in a similar manner (for instance, characteristics (1, 5, 9) and (2, 6, 9)).

$$\begin{aligned} f_2 = {} & [(g_1 > g_2) \vee \overline{(g_2 > g_4)}] \cdot [(g_1 > g_3) \vee \overline{(g_3 > g_4)}] = \\ & [(t_1^2 < t_1^1) \vee (t_1^2 \leqslant t_2^2)] \cdot [(t_2^1 < t_1^1) \vee (t_2^1 < t_2^2)]. \end{aligned}$$

Physically, the above expressions mean that the first task is allocated to the second computer and the second task to the first one if the first task is better executed by the second computer (in less time) than by the first one, or the first task is executed by the second computer no worse that the second one on the second computer; and at the same time the second task is better executed by the first computer than the first one by the first computer, or the second task is executed by the first computer no worse than by the second one.

Being derived, expressions for f_1 and f_2 are stored in the operating system memory as heuristic rules for dynamic scheduling of a flow of tasks in the computer system. The rules, of course, do not ensure one hundred percent infallibility of situation classification. Note that the above-mentioned minimax operators lead to more effective classification rules for this problem:

L_1: if $g_1 = MX$, then $\xi = 1$,
otherwise $\xi = 0$,

. . . .

L_4: if $g_4 = MX$, then $\xi = 1$,
otherwise $\xi = 0$;

where

$$\begin{aligned} MX = max\,[&min\,(g_1,g_2), min\,(g_1,g_3), \\ &min\,(g_3,g_4), min\,(g_2,g_4)]. \end{aligned}$$

The following generalized situations result in this case:

$$\begin{aligned} f_1^1 = {} & [(g_1 = MX) \vee (g_4 = MX)] = \{[(g_1 < g_2) \vee (g_1 < g_3)] \ \& \\ & (g_1 > g_4) \vee [(g_4 < g_3) \vee (g_4 < g_2)](g_4 > g_1)\} = \\ & \{[(t_1^1 < t_1^2) \vee (t_1^1 < t_1^3)] \cdot (t_1^1 > t_2^2) \vee \\ & [(t_2^2 < t_1^2) \vee (t_2^2 < t_1^3)] \cdot (t_2^2 > t_1^1)\} = \\ & (t_1^1 < t_1^2) \cdot (t_2^2 < t_1^1) \vee (t_1^1 < t_2^1) \cdot (t_2^2 < t_1^1) \vee \\ & (t_2^2 < t_1^2) \cdot (t_1^1 < t_2^2) \vee (t_2^2 < t_2^1) \cdot (t_1^1 < t_2^2). \end{aligned}$$

$$\begin{aligned} f_2^1 = {} & [(g_2 = MX) \vee (g_3 = MX)] = \{[(t_1^2 < t_1^1) \vee (t_1^2 < t_2^2)] \ \& \\ & (t_1^2 > t_2^1) \vee [(t_2^1 < t_1^1) \vee (t_2^1 < t_2^2)] \ (t_2^1 > t_1^2)\}. \end{aligned}$$

These decision rules give essentially fewer classification errors as compared with those above.

With increase of problem dimensionality, the number of operations required to verify decision rules (but not the number of operations for determining them!) grows with the same rate as dimensionality [12].

The detailed illustrative example above demonstrates a way that may be followed by the theory of complex-system control, making use of the advances of artificial intelligence theory. Below we shall describe a fragment of this theory known as "situational control" [9,14,15].

Method of situational control

The idea of the method is simple. Assume that at each time we can have an informal description of the current situation including the state of a control system and its current objectives and tasks. Denote that description as $S(t)$. The data contained in $S(t)$ with that already stored in the control system memory are sufficient to make a control decision which is generated by means of a specified set of elementary decisions $\{P_i\}$. The decision is regarded as a certain chain consisting of elementary decisions, or a tree the path through which is defined by a set of situations occurring at the input of the control system. Then, for each time t one can consider an elementary problem of determining that decision P_j out of $\{P_i\}$ which has to be made at this time in a situation $S(t)$. This implies that in the course of learning a covering of the set $\{S_i(t)\}$ should be found such that each class in the covering corresponds to a certain elementary decision P_j. On the face of it, the formulated problem is remiscent of statements characteristic of pattern recognition theory, but the classification problem in situational control needs not only to ascertain the presence or absence of the classification characteristics in $S(t)$ but also the additional data introduced into the system during learning. These data are not explicitly contained in the descriptions $S(t)$ and cannot be extracted from them. Besides, the classifying functions which are either statistical or analytical in pattern recognition are in our case replaced by informal text-classification rules derived from operations with texts written in a natural language. Two more remarks are in order. In constructing a classifier, it is not the decomposition of the set $\{S_i(t)\}$ but its cover that is sought. In actual problems with informal descriptions $S(t)$ this is impossible. Control engineers use different classifications among which preferences cannot be strictly set. The boundaries between classes of situations are fuzzy, and the classes are a remarkable example of what L. Zadeh calls fuzzy sets [16]. The second remark concerns the fundamental multi-level nature of the classifier. The situations are generalized into classes gradually and the utility of each intermediate generalization is tested as a result of making decisions on that generalization. In addition to the vertical connections between the strata of the classifier, the horizontal ones corresponding to relations that may be established between elements of generalized situations have an important role to play.

Let us now describe the process of decision making in situational control. Two stages that are always present in the process may be isolated: classifier updating and, most important, decision making. Let us take them separately. In situational control, the situations are described in a special micro-description language [5]. Without going into details of that language [6] let us note two features useful for comprehending the essence of classifier updating. The texts of the micro-description language use five fundamental sets: basic concepts $A = \{a_1, a_2, \ldots a_n\}$, basic relations $R = \{r_1, r_2, \ldots r_m\}$, basic names $I = \{i_1, i_2, \ldots i_e\}$, elementary decisions $P = \{P_1, P_2, \ldots P_w\}$, and estimates $O = \{O_1, O_2, \ldots O_5\}$. Elements of these sets are assembled into texts describing input situations $S(t)$. The set of basic concepts consists of physical concepts and concept-classes. The physical concept is specified as a set of values of characteristics defining that concept (for example, a set of readings of some instruments installed in the control plant). Denote that set as $\langle \Pi_1, \Pi_2, \ldots, \Pi_\nu \rangle$. The concept-classes are simply totalities of physical concepts homogenous from some point of view, for example "machine tool", "workshop", "part", etc. Associating a physical concept with a concept-class is for a situational control system an external function, and no rules for that association are formulated. Names serve to personify elements of a certain concept-class. Relations established binary connections between elements of A, I and P. Consequently, the situation description $S(t)$ is a certain structure. Let us give an example. A part No. 2754 is on the conveyor belt and approaches a machine tool No. 12. In the language of micro-descriptions that text will be represented as follows:

$$S(t) = (((a_2\, r_1\, i_1)r_3\, a_3)r_2((a_2\, r_1\, i_1)\\ r_4(a_1\, r_1\, i_2)))$$

where a_1 denotes the concept-class "machine tool", a_2 the concept-class "part", a_3 the concept-class of conveyor belt, i_1 and i_2 are names 2754 and 12; the relations r_i denote: r_1 "to have name", r_2 "simultaneously", r_3 "to be on", and r_4 "to approach". To link the description of that situation with certain decisions on control, a correlation rule is developed in the form $\alpha \Rightarrow \beta$ which essentially denotes that in the presence of α one should do β. In particular, if the decision P_1 signifies "start machine tool", then for our example the correlation rule may be written in the form $S'(t) \Rightarrow (p_1\, r_1\, i_2)$. Elements of P may be directly included into the situation description, for example $S^*(t) = (S'(t)r_5\ (p_1\, r_1\, i_2))$ which signifies (with r_5 denoting precedence): "once the situation $S'(t)$ had arisen, the machine tool No. 12 was started". Formulate now a very important hypothesis which is the core of all studies in situational control and concerns the power of the set R. For any developed natural language, the set of basic relations is finite and contains about 200 elements. It has been proved [3,5] that all other relations can be obtained from the basic set by combining the basic ones. Once accepted, this hypothesis enables development of a universal set of rules for transformation and generalization of situation micro-descriptions.

Now let us take up the description of situations. If there existed a practically observable set of situations $S(t)$, then one could hope to develop a finite set of correlation rules whose left-hand parts would enumerate all possible descriptions, and the right-hand parts would list the necessary elementary control actions. It is quite obvious, however, that in cases of practical interest the cardinality of the set $\{S(t)\}$ is so high that development of a set of correlation rules is out of the question. The only way to reduce the number of these rules is to use generalized descriptions in their left-hand parts. This is the reason why generalization of situation descriptions is the key problem of situational control.

The existing systems of situational control use three types of situation generalizations. The simplest are generalizations by names whereby one class includes all those situations which differ only in names put in certain sites and which require the same type of decisions when they arise. One example is the situation $S''(t)$ obtained from a situation of the type

$$S'(t) : S''(t) = (((a_2\, r_1\, x_1) r_3\, a_3) r_2\, ((a_2\, r_1\, x_1) r_4\, (a_1\, r_1\, i_2))).$$

Here x_1 denotes "arbitrary name". The generalized correlations rule for that case is of the form $S''(t) \Rightarrow (p_1, r_1, i_2)$. Performing one more generalization by name and obtaining a description of the situation in the form

$$S'''(t) = (((a_2\, r_1\, x_1) r_3\, a_3) r_2\, ((a_2\, r_1\, x_1) r_4\, (a_1\, r_1\, x_2)))$$

where x_1 and x_2 denote "arbitrary names", the generalized correlation rule takes the form

$$S'''(t) \Rightarrow (p_1\, r_1\, x_2).$$

Another type of generalization rules are those used in forming the function of belonging to a class of situations through the values of the characteristics Π_i pertaining to the physical concepts involved in the description of $S(t)$. These functions are, as a rule, of the form of certain Boolean functions of binary-encoded values of Π_i or predicates of these values.

A third type of generalization rules are those related to generalization of situations in terms of the structure of relations which describe them [9,14,15]. Essentially, in the situations associated with a class these rules isolate a certain frame (standard structure) whose presence is sufficient to relate a particular current situation to that generalized class. In situational control, generalization by frame has proved most productive and effective. It should be noted that in the theory of robots this method of description generalization is also the key point in the generalization problem.

An important point is estimating the quality of a generalization. The system of generalization may be viewed as a puff-pastry with links between the layers to indicate transition from lower-level descriptions to descriptions in broader terms. In the process of search for a generalization, weights are assigned to these vertical links via estimates O_i whose values are selected during the learning. The arrangements for the learning process have been described in D. A. Pospelov [14]. It should only be noted that, as already stated, the object of learning is the search for the covering of the set $\{S_i(t)\}$ rather than for its decomposition into a set of situations. This signifies that in a trained system there may be correlation rules of the form $\alpha \Rightarrow \beta$ and simultaneously rules of the form $\alpha \Rightarrow \gamma$ where the recommendations β and γ are different. To make a decision, estimates of applicability should be formulated for these rules. The estimates are made of the same set O and are semantic rather than numerical ("nearly always useful", "needed in nearly half of the cases", "occasionally useful", etc.).

The overall structure of situational control at the functioning state after completion of the first stage is like this: the system receives the current situation which is classified into a certain class by the classifier, the decision making unit uses the name of that class to select the necessary rule, from among the correlation rules and implements that rule. The results of implementation, together with the decision made, serve further (never ceasing!) learning. If the system comes across a non-typical situation which cannot be classified, then it either turns to an expert teacher or tries various decisions by simulating the process dynamics. Gorbatov [6] describes and analyses the structure of this system and its functioning as used for situational control in artificial intelligence problems.

Applications of situational control

Over recent years, situational control methods have been widely applied in various control systems. In this paper we concentrate on three examples. Other applications have also been described and have, in addition bibliographies on situational control.

The first example will be prompt control of batch production. In such plants the accurately computed long-term production schedule (which is usually the outcome of employment of mathematical programming techniques) undergoes large fluctuations over short periods such as shifts or days. All possible disturbances cannot be taken into consideration in advance over these intervals because they are due to human factors, specific technological facilities and other non-typifiable factors. Therefore, no accurate mathematical models can be expected for this kind of prompt control. An instrumentation factory control system has been described [19,20] that proved cost effective by improving the rhythm of schedule fulfilment. In industrial information and control systems, situational control will evidently be especially effective at that level.

The second example is situational management in non-typical situations. Normally, operation of many industrial processes can be controlled through simple and formal models. But intermittent deviations from the setpoint require the making of prompt decisions which are outside the scope of standard models. In such cases situational control can be of certain help. For instance, a control system has been studied for clinker cement roasting [21,22] where this approach proved highly effective.

Situational control is also useful in those problems where an accurate model is feasible but too cumbersome to be practicable. Situational control methods can reduce the dimensionality of the model, and isolate only that subset of versions which contains the best variant, which then is sought with some formal method. This approach has been used, for instance, to develop an effective chess end-game program [23]. This approach also helped to reduce the dimensionality of the transport problem in management of automotive transport deployment in an oil field [24].

Finally, we would like to discuss the influence on the control theory of today of dialogue systems using languages close to natural ones.

Dialogue systems for control

To make our conclusions more obvious, we now discuss the structure and operation of a system of this type that is under development in the Computer Center of the USSR Academy of Sciences and is called DILOS (Dialogue Information and Logical System) [25]. The system is oriented to computational, informational, and logic tasks and to man-computer dialogue in a language as close to natural language as possible. Therefore, DILOS has five special-purpose processors: linguistic, information, logic, computational, and one for system learning and specification. Each of the above processors has its own data banks organized according to processor specificity.

User's data presented at the system input in the form of typed text in Russian (or any other language) are sent to the linguistic processor whose task is to translate the source message into an interval system language (ϕ-language). Translation is necessary because the natural language is not a formal system, it may be ambiguous and very redundant, and the system can operate only with strictly formally represented facts, directions and questions. The ϕ-language is such a stringent analogue of the natural language.

Messages in the ϕ-language are first classified into several types, the most important of them being facts for checking (and possibly storing) rules, requests and direction. Depending on message type, it is sent by the analyser to an appropriate processor (information, logic, or computational).

Facts to be stored are sent to the information processor, which is a factographic data-retrieval system. The processor executes procedures for storing a fact in the data bank.

For checking, the fact is sent by the analyser to the logic processor that verifies its truth and consistency in terms of the world model. The logic processor is a set of facilities enabling theorem-proving, inductive inference, data classification, and generalization. The processor can also enrich the input message by new facts that may be inferred from the input data. If necessary, the checked and enriched fact may be sent through the information processor to the data bank.

A message concerning the world model and classified as a rule is sent to the logic processor. As a result of its processing, the world model may be updated.

A request is first sent to the information processor. If the data bank has a ready answer, it is sent to the analyser and then to the user in the form of either a synthesized oral answer, or printed or displayed text. If there is no direct answer to the request, it is sent to the logic processor which attempts to obtain an answer by adding new facts to the data bank so as to satisfy the request (in DILOS a special request-generated logic inference is realized). Possibly some computations (of new facts) are required to generate an answer. In this case the logic processor generates a direction to the computational processor.

Directions thus come to the computational processor from both the logic processor and the analyser. Directions are compiled by the computational processor into a program consisting of applied program modules stored either in this computer, or in other computers connected to this one through an information network. Computation results are either sent to the logic processor for further handling, or to the user through the analyzer.

Thus, each type of message in the ϕ-language has a certain addressee, which is one of the DILOS executive processors. DILOS also includes a system processor that is a set of facilities enabling DILOS' dialogue with the system programmer. This processor performs initial filling of data bank, world model, and memories with standard computational modules. The system processor is also used for system debugging and for updating operational algorithms of other processors.

Now we shall describe in more detail what DILOS gives to the user:

1. A factographic structured data bank, enabling (by means of the information processor) storage and retrieval of data on the basis of a system of "superconcepts – individual objects". Such an organization permits answers to be formed to non-standard requests (with respect to any system of superconcepts or relations).

   Particular filling of the bank and assignment of this or that system of structuring superconcepts or relations is performed by the system analyst through special system facilities without any changes in operation of the information processor. The information processor may operate as a descriptor data-retrieval system, if necessary.

2. Reduction of information requests in conventional Russian to a standard form. Only those concepts and relations should be used in requests that are embedded in the system.

3. Generation of answers to complicated questions which do not have a direct answer in the data bank. Generation of answers to such questions requires computations, logic inferences, and data handling. In DILOS, these additional programs are generated ad hoc by the system itself through request analysis.

4. Generation of complicated computer programs from a set of standard modules is also performed automatically in terms of a request for computation formulated in a conventional natural language by means of an established set of concepts and relations.

5. Updating of the data base and the set of realizable functions through direct user-system dialogue. To put it differently, the system may be taught either to execute new programs, or to make new logic inferences based on the world model.

Thus, DILOS is able to perform various functions whose automation was not feasible until very recently.

In actual applications, various versions of DILOS may be employed:

(a) The natural-language based data-retrieval system. In this case only the linguistic and informational processors are used along with the data bank. In contrast to the conventional data retrieval systems, this version of DILOS can accept requests in a natural language in typed or oral form. One can organize the data retrieval system either as the descriptor type, or as a type where search is done through a set of object characteristics.

(b) The factographic data-retrieval system. This makes use of a simplified logic processor performing factographic search in the data base in terms of a given set of relations. The world model is not used. This version may include all the facilities of (a).

Such a data-retrieval system supplies the user with answers to any question provided that the data bank has information to be actuated by the question.

(c) A computer system using a natural language as a task presentation language. This system involves only linguistic and computational processors and applied program modules as well. The user presents his tasks in his habitual professional language. The computational processor complies by means of a built-in semantic network complex computation program consisting of computational modules.†

(d) An Intelligent Data Bank (IDB) which makes use of all the facilities of version (a) plus logic processor and the world model. The IDB opens up essentially new possibilities to the user as compared with data retrieval systems.

The world model and logic processor enable the IDB to answer questions for which the data base has no direct answer. Missing information will be inferred by the logic processor from the content of the data bank by means of the laws (logics) of the environment.

(e) The IDB with computations contains, in addition to the above version, a computational processor deriving new data from the source one, if necessary. Such an IDB is most comprehensive in terms of the possibilities offered to the user. This version may be regarded as a logic and computational system using a natural language as the input one.

† Outside the scope of DILOS, an operable system of this type (PRIZ) has been designed at the Institute of Cybernetics of the Estonian Academy of Sciences (Tallinn) [26, 27].

In addition to the above versions of DILOS, other modifications are possible where system facilities may be used in different combinations.

The possibility of making various modifications is due to a special structural feature of DILOS where all the processors can operate idependently. For the information, logic, and computational processors, the ϕ-language is the input one. This enables a sufficiently simple combination of the processors resulting in the system most convenient for a particular user.

Besides the problems solved by the advent of DILOS, there is one more problem of control automation whose solution is impossible without interactive man-computer systems.

An essential component of managerial activity is the formulation of objectives and tasks for people and organizations that have a specific aim. A clear-cut formulation of an objective or task is rather difficult except in the simplest cases (stabilization of technological parameters, robot motion control, etc.). But at the higher level of national economy or scientific activity it is reasonable to ask whether this or that objective is necessary and whether this particular result is desirable. Apart from this, two more questions arise: what higher purposes would be served by attainment of a particular objective, and what are its consequences (including also undesirable spin-offs)? If it turns out that the objective was defined correctly, one may proceed to decompose it into a hierachical set of particular objectives and tasks, concerning subordinate persons and organizations; that is, in essence, one begins to plan, to make preliminary decisions about assignment of partial tasks and resource allocation.

Thus, mathematical decision-making models are required that can be adjusted to operate in dialogue mode, and are capable of being embedded into the organizational structure of planning and management agencies and are compatible with their functions. This aspect of the dialogue problem is discussed in more detail in the monograph by Pospelov and Irikov [5].

CONCLUSION

In our paper we have treated only a segment of the spectrum of questions involved in the estimation of the effects of artificial intelligence theory on the theory and practice of complex plant control. We have not discussed such important areas as design automation and control robotization. Nevertheless, we can confidently assert that the influence of artificial intelligence methods in this field is very significant and, before long, will become of still greater weight.

REFERENCES

[1] Newell, A. and Simon, H. A. (1961). GPS, a program that simulates human thought (ed. Billing, H.). *Lernende Automaten*, Müchen: Oldenbourg.

[2] Shtein, M. E. and Shtein, B. E. (1973). *Methods of computer-aided design of digital intrumentation*, Moscow: Sovetskoe Radio Publ. (in Russian).

[3] Polovinkin, A. I. (ed.) (1976). *Design optimization algorithms*, Moscow: Energiya Publ. (in Russian).
[4] Tanaev, V. S. and Shkurba, V. V. (1975). *Introduction to scheduling theory*, Moscow: Nauka Publ. (in Russian).
[5] Pospelov, G. S. and Irikov, V. A. (1976). *Program and objective-oriented planning and control*, Moscow: Sovetskoe Radio Publ. (in Russian).
[6] Gorbatov, V. A. (1976). *A theory of partially-ordered systems*, Moscow: Sovetskoe Radio Publ. (in Russian).
[7] Pushkin, V. N. (1965). *Prompt thinking in large systems*, Moscow; Energiya Publ. (in Russian).
[8] Pushkin, V. N. (1971). *Psychology and cybernetics*, Moscow: Pedagogika Publ. (in Russian).
[9] Pospelov, D. A. and Pushkin, V. N. (1972). *Thinking and automata*, Moscow: Sovetskoe Radio (in Russian).
[10] Pospelov, D. A. (1972). *Introduction to the theory of computer systems*, Moscow, Sovetskoe Radio (in Russian).
[11] Korbut, A. A. and Finkel'shtein, Yu. Yu. (1969). *Discrete programming*, Moscow: Nauka Publ. (in Russian).
[12] Boev, D. (1975). Application of situational control to scheduling in multi-computer systems, *Method of situational control*, Moscow: publication of the Scientific Council for Cybernetics, USSR Academy of Sciences (in Russian).
[13] Bongard, M. M. (1967). *The Recognition problem*. Moscow: Nauka Publ. (in Russian).
[14] Pospelov, D. A. (1975). Large systems (situational control). Moscow: Znanie Publ. (in Russian).
[15] Klykov, Yu. I. (1974). Situational control of large systems, Moscow: Energiya Publ. in Russian).
[16] Kaufmann, A. (1972). Theory of fuzzy sets. Paris: Masson. See also Zadeh, L., this volume.
[17] Pospelov, D. A. and Klykov, Yu. I. (eds.) (1974). *Problems in cybernetics, No. 13, Situational control, Theory and practice, Part 1*, Moscow: Scientific Council for Cybernetics, USSR Academy of Sciences (in Russian).
[18] Pospelov, D. A. and Efimov, E. I. (eds.) (1975). *Problems in cybernetics, No. 4, Situational control. Theory and practice. Part 2.* Moscow: Scientific Council for Cybernetics, USSR Academy of Sciences (in Russian).
[19] Leviatov, A. Yu. (1975). A system for situational control of operative technological planning. Thesis, Moscow, Institute of Physical Engineering (in Russian).
[20] Leviatov, A. Yu. and Aizikovich, A. A. (1973). A situational system of enterprise control, *Izvestia AN USSR, Technical cybernetics*, **3**, (in Russian).
[21] Selyugin, A. A. (1975). Situational computerized control of clinker cement roasting, Thesis, Frunze (in Russian).
[22] Kopytin, V. S. and Selyugin, A. A. (1973). A structure of information and control system for clinker cement roasting in rotary furnaces, *Information and control systems for cement production*. Frunze: Ilim Publ. (in Russian).
[23] Gadzhiev, R. (1975). An experimental study of human decision making and its simulation by means of situational control (as exemplified by a chess end-game). *Proc. of the Fourth International Joint Conference on Artificial Intelligence* (IJCAI-75), **10**, Moscow: Scientific council for Cybernetics, USSR Academy of Sciences, in Russian).
[24] Afonin, L. A. et al. (1974). Prompt control of special-purpose automotive transport, *Information and control system for borings*, Groznyi (in Russian).
[25] Briabrin, V. M. and Pospelov, D. A. (1975). DILOS-dialogue system for information retrieval, *Computation and Logical Inference, Conf. on Artificial Intelligence: QA Systems*, Laxenburg: IIASA.

[26] Tyugu, E. H. (1972). Data base and problem solver for computer-aided design, *Information Processing, 71*, Amsterdam: North Holland.

[27] Tyugu, E. and Unt, M. (1975). Experiments with a computational problem solver, Delivered but not published *4th Int. Joint Conf. on Artif. Int.* Tbilisi, (IJCAI-75). Text available from authors, Institute of Cybernetics, Estonian Academy of Sciences, Tallinn.

MACHINE ANALYSIS OF CHESS

16

CHEOPS: A Chess-oriented Processing System

J. Moussouris†, J. Holloway, and R. Greenblatt
Massachusetts Institute of Technology, USA

Abstract
A chess-oriented processing system was built, capable of extremely rapid search in the game-tree. This report describes the special hardware designed for the system. There is also a brief summary of some software developed to make this facility easier to use, and to integrate it into existing AI-oriented programs.

INTRODUCTION

Computer chess was one of the first areas of research into machine intelligence. Some of the founding fathers of computer science lavished their attention on the problem [1, 2]. But after a few decades of development, the best chess programs are still no match for the best human players. In this paper we describe a chess-oriented processing system (CHEOPS) which we hope will boost the rate of progress in this area.

Ever since Claude Shannon wrote his classic paper on computer chess in 1950, debate has raged on the potential strength of his methods. By the early sixties, his fundamental ideas of minimax search and the later addition of alpha-beta cutoff were fairly well understood. These ideas have formed the basis of most chess programs, and virtually all strong ones, to the present day.

As computer chess developed during the 1960s, there became apparent a dichotomy in approaches to the search algorithm. Brute-force programs played surprisingly well, using algorithms which incorporated relatively little chess-specific knowledge, but concentrated on attaining the highest possible searching speed. On the other hand, much effort was expended on programs which greatly reduce the size of the search tree by using heuristic methods, which mimic some of the complexities of human techniques of play.

† Present address: IBM Thomas J. Watson Research Laboratories, Yorktown Heights, New York State, USA.

The strength of brute-force programs derives both from speed and from simplicity. The search strategy used is very straightforward; for example:

Examine all moves for a certain number of plies (called the basic depth), and all capture chains to indefinite depth beyond that. Search by a simple recursive depth-first enumeration. After the basic depth, update the current best-so-far (minimax) scores alpha or beta when necessary, using the material balance as a static evaluation function (sometimes simple positional terms are added in as well). Pop from a given node when there are no more successors to that position, or when one of the successors has already been shown to be an adequate rejoinder to the previous move (alpha-beta cutoff).

In the course of this search, the effectiveness of cutoffs is improved by generating moves at each node in a specific order: for example, captures of high-valued pieces by pawns first, then captures by pieces, then non-capturing moves by pawns, etc. Only modest amounts of memory are required to hold state information during the search. With sufficient static ordering (as in the example given), the algorithm requires only a push-down list containing the ancestors of the current node together with the corresponding alpha-beta values found so far at each level. (A more complex ordering might require the push-down list to hold the set of legal moves possible at ancestors of the current node, still a modest amount of memory).

Brute-force programs are usually rather small and simple. Furthermore, they are quite easy to debug. On the other hand, a moderately strong human chess player can learn to predict at a glance what variations the program will and will not see with given settings of the parameters (modulo 'oversights' on his part, of course).

The CHEOPS system is capable of executing brute-force chess programs at speeds considerably faster than any of the general purpose machines commonly available for chess research – for example, more than a hundred times faster than a Digital Equipment Corporation PDP10-KA10. Such a speed increase corresponds to an exhaustive search 6 to 8 plies ahead in about two minutes, as compared to 4 or 5 plies for current programs. One of the aims of the CHEOPS project is to determine just how quickly the standard of play improves with increased depth of lookahead in brute-force programs, as measured by ratings in play with human competition.

As an alternative to the brute-force approach, a variety of heuristic or knowledge-based programs have been developed [3]. These also incorporate the basic search algorithm described by Shannon, but the trees searched are very much smaller: perhaps 100 to 1000 nodes are examined in the course of making a move instead of several hundreds of thousands of nodes. Two basic heuristic methods are used to achieve this reduction in tree size:

i) Instead of examining all moves from a given position, the program attempts to identify the interesting ones and examines those only.

ii) Instead of having a relatively fixed basic depth, the program attempts to adjust the search depth to the types of positions encountered, proceeding deeper only if necessary to clarify the situation.

Although these methods are clearly right in that they correspond closely to what human masters do, in practice certain difficulties have been encountered in attempting to apply these ideas. Consider, for example heuristic (i), which reduces to writing a program which tests a move for being interesting. How many different criteria are there for determining whether a given move could possibly be interesting? Let us assume a moderate number, for example 50. Suppose at a given time we have procedures for checking for 49 of these criteria coded and debugged, but have not yet programmed the fiftieth one. We find that our forty-nine fiftieths completed program plays very weak chess! Every time a move good for the fiftieth reason comes up, the program overlooks it, and hence may produce arbitrarily gross blunders, perhaps permitting checkmate in a few moves. More commonly the loss occasioned will be smaller but in tournament chess even a single blunder which loses a piece without compensation usually results in eventual loss of the game.

In chess, only within a context supplied by very nearly perfect tactics can anything called strategy or positional play exist. To arrive at this state of affairs the program must be nearly finished: in its earlier stages of development, a supposedly sophisticated program will be unable to beat even rank beginners. One can imagine that this is very discouraging for the developers of the program.

One of the aims of the CHEOPS system is to develop ways to combine brute-force lookahead with the knowledge-based approach, so that they support each other in their complementary characteristics. In the simplest case, a brute-force program running in CHEOPS can serve as a backstop to preserve the morale of the developers by assuring a respectable level of play. It also gives them an opportunity to obtain badly needed feedback before their program is completed, and it is too late to introduce major changes.

Sophisticated chess programs tend to be very large and complicated, and difficult to debug adequately. This in itself can largely explain their poor performance in computer chess championships. If a sophisticated program is designed with the knowledge that CHEOPS will be available, the size and complexity of the program can be much reduced. By supplying tactical support to the heuristic methods mentioned above, CHEOPS frees the high-level program to deal with strategic issues of play.

1. HARDWARE

1.1 The anatomy of the CHEOPS processor

The core of the CHEOPS system is a high-speed microprogrammable processor which is specially designed to execute chess-oriented algorithms. This processor incorporates all the major data paths of general purpose machines (see left side of Fig. 1). In particular, it has a 16-bit arithmetic logic unit (ALU) which accepts operands selected from an ABUS and from a set of 16 accumulators (ACC), and produces a result on the output bus (OBUS). The ABUS selects data from a variety of sources – including accumulators, a 1024-word push-down list (PDL), and various flags and interfacing registers.

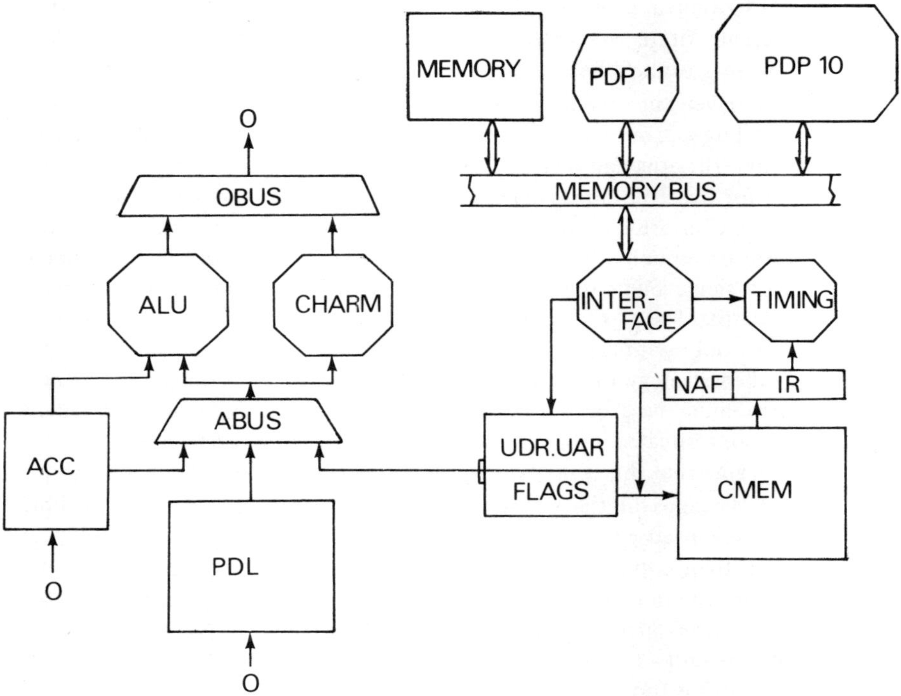

Fig. 1 – CHEOPS Block Diagram.

In addition to the ALU, however, the CHEOPS processor possesses a powerful chess array module (CHARM), which contains most of the chess-specific logic of the system. Like the ALU, this module takes its inputs from the ABUS, and outputs results into the OBUS, whence they may be written into any of the internal memories of the machine. The role of CHARM, however, is to perform the basic non-numeric operations which are required by all chess-playing algorithms. For example, CHARM can accept a record from the PDL of the last move tried from a given position, and generate the next possible move in a specified order. It can also detect conditions such as king-in-check and raise the appropriate flag, all in a single cycle. Thus CHARM acts as a powerful "combinatorial engine" that reduces most fundamental chess operations and decisions to the execution of a single CHEOPS micro-instruction.

1.2 The chess arrays

The chess-specific power of CHARM derives from an 8 × 8 hardware chess array, whose design was originally suggested by Prof. Edward Fredkin. The purpose of this array is to find a specified subset of legal board moves. Each of the 64 squares retains information about the colour and type of piece (if any) occupying it. The basic operation of the board array is as follows: first a signal indicating side-to-move is applied; then an individual square is designated as destination-square. The output from the array consists of 64 lines which specify which of the 64 squares contain pieces of the moving colour which can capture or move to this destination. Alternatively, a square can be designated as the originating-area, in which case the 64 lines assert possible destinations for moves from this square. Special control bits can cause the array function to be more specific: for example, it can discriminate captures from non-capturing moves, or pawn from noble captures. Also, one control bit causes the entire board to be designated as originating or destination area, so that such general questions as "any captures possible?" can be answered in a single operation.

The logic which drives the 64 square lines is a purely combinational 8 × 8 array, containing about a dozen TTL DIPs in each cell. For example, an OR-gate (actually, a NAND-gate in inverted logic) senses whether any of the 8 squares immediately adjacent to a given square has been designated as a destination; and if the given square contains a King as well, it asserts "King origin here" signal. Similarly, other OR-gates detect the presence of possible destinations for pawn and knight moves from the given square. Sliding pieces are handled differently: for example, a signal asserting "destination to Northeast" trickles through squares in each NE-SW diagonal until it encounters an occupied cell, which then asserts "Queen origin" or "Bishop origin" if the corresponding piece exists. (Since the selectors through which these sliding piece signals trickle form the longest signal path in the arrays, they are implemented in Schottky TTL). All the various kinds of origin signals are gathered together and selectively enabled by control function bits (that is, depending on whether we are currently generating pawn or noble moves) to drive the 64 corresponding square lines which form the final output of the array.

Design and construction of the chess array was greatly facilitated by use of the Stanford Drawing System. A "template" drawing was prepared for the logic required in an individual square of the array, with the signal names indexed by rank and file. Then macros were written which repeated this circuit 64 times, replacing the indices with the successive square locations. Other macros took care of edge connections and actual location of the DIPs on Augat boards. Finally, the program generated a wire list deck which was used to drive automatic wire-wrapping machines. This system not only obviated manual construction of the machine, but thanks to its error messages and file-sharing capabilities, greatly economized on the design process itself, and automatically produced a standardized set of documentation. With the help of this automated design aid, the entire design and construction of the CHEOPS hardware was completed with about one and a half man-years of effort.

1.3 The array module

The inner structure of the array module itself (see Fig. 2) is dictated by the need to drive the array at a rate approaching design capacity. Most of this structure amounts to a hardwired implementation of the inner DO loops which scan pieces and squares for the next move or capture. In particular, a square scanner (S-SCAN) is provided which looks at the 64 square lines, and given a last square number (LS) generates the number of the next active square line (in raster order). Similarly, a piece scanner (P-SCAN) takes as input the piece existence register (PXR). The PXR contains a bit for each piece, which is set for each piece that currently exists on the board. Given a last piece number and the PXR, P-SCAN produces the next one, in order of the value of the pieces.

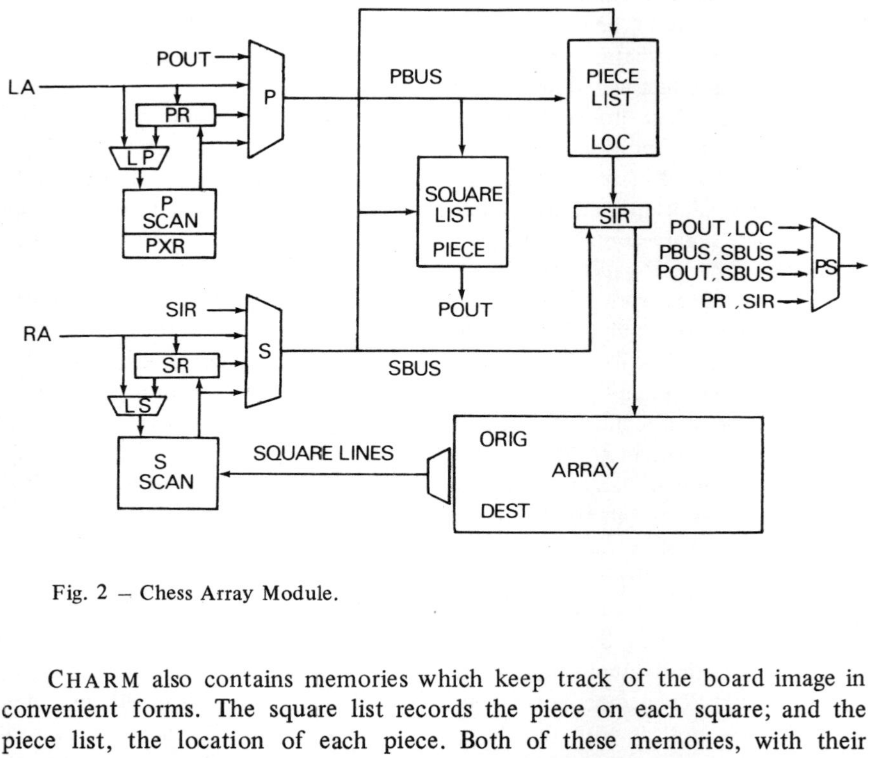

Fig. 2 – Chess Array Module.

CHARM also contains memories which keep track of the board image in convenient forms. The square list records the piece on each square; and the piece list, the location of each piece. Both of these memories, with their corresponding scanners, are driven by data paths organized into two busses: the piece bus (PBUS) and the square bus (SBUS). (Note that in Fig. 2, input enters the tops of memory boxes, addresses enter the sides, and data is output from the bottom).

These 8-bit busses are entirely internal to CHARM. When the 16-bit input to CHARM arrives from the ABUS, it is divided into a left byte and a right byte, which enter the PBUS and SBUS respectively. In this piece-square format, a chess move can be coded within the machine as two words: the first describing the piece moved and origin square, and the second, the piece captured (if any) and destination square. Selectors within CHARM allow such data to be routed very flexibly. It can either be fed directly into the scanners, or be buffered in the piece and square registers (PR, SR), or loaded into the board memories. The output of CHARM (which goes into the OBUS – see Fig. 1) also maintains the piece-square format. These two halves of the output word are selected by the piece-square bus (PSBUS) from a variety of alternative sources within the module – for example PBUS, SBUS or POUT, SBUS or POUT, LOC or PR, SIR (see Fig. 2, right side).

Some basic operations of the chess array module are as follows. A move is *made* (rather than generated) in two CHARM cycles: first the origin square is cleared, then the moving piece is deposited on the destination square. A capture takes three cycles, an additional one to clear out the captured piece. (Although the captured piece would get properly overwritten on the board, the extra cycle is required to update the piece existence register (PXR). Each of these cycles involves routing the desired square to the SBUS and the desired new contents of that square to the PBUS. Once this is done, activating a single control line will cause the piece-list, square-list, and piece-existence-register to get updated simultaneously. Unmaking a move is similarly accomplished by restoring the piece moved to the origin and then the piece captured to the destination on the board.

During this unmaking process, the PR can be loaded with the piece moved, the SIR (designated square input to the arrays) with the origin, and the SR with the destination. Then CHARM is immediately ready to generate a next move by scanning the array lines to find the next square to which the same origin piece can move. If there are no more moves by this piece, the next existing piece is produced by P-SCAN, its location is loaded into the SIR, and S-SCAN outputs the first possible destination for this piece. There is no need to enumerate all the legal moves on the PDL. Instead, only the most recently searched move (the one in fact played in the current variation) is retained there. Later, when that move is reverted, CHARM will concurrently be generating the next move to look at, should it be decided to do so.

CHARM and the ALU work in close coordination during the search process. In a typical case, the blocks that are pushed and popped on the PDL for each node searched consist of four words. The first two describe the corresponding move to CHARM, the third is an alpha or beta value which the ALU checks for minimaxing and alpha-beta cutoffs, and the fourth records such special conditions as castling rights, ghosts for *en passant* captures, promotion, etc. Just as the ALU makes available Overflow and Carry-out bits to the branching control logic of the processor, so does CHARM generate a variety of flags which influence the flow of control in the machine – for example, ANYMORE-PIECES (from P-SCAN), ANYMORE-SQUARES (from S-SCAN), KING-IN-CHECK and CASTLING-POSSIBLE (from special logic on the array). The coordination of CHARM and the ALU is thus facilitated by their parallel roles not only in the data paths but also in the control logic of the CHEOPS processor.

1.4 Microcontrol

The sequence of operations in CHEOPS is determined by a large (1K by 64 bit) RAM control memory (CMEM on right of Fig. 1). Each micro-instruction consists of four 16-bit words. At the beginning of a machine cycle, all four of these words are loaded from the current microaddress into the instruction register (IR), from which the bits are routed to the various function control, selector, and write enable bits in the machine. The first word of each instruction includes a next address field (NAF), and a conditions field, which specify a set of four flag bits to be IOR-ed with the four lower-order bits in the NAF to produce the next microaddress. Hence every micro-instruction is potentially a 16-way branch. There is also an OP-code bit which determines whether the rest of the instruction should be decoded as an ALU or array operation. In the ALU case, the remaining words specify ALU function, A source, accumulator source, OBUS destination, etc. In the array operation case, they specify array function, bus select and write enable for memories internal to CHARM, and the A source and O destination for communication between CHARM and the rest of the processor.

The first word of an array instruction (specifying array function and internal bus select) is latched in a separate array instruction register (IRA) during ALU operations, so that arithmetic can be done during array operations that take longer than one cycle to settle. Thanks to this technique, the cycle time of the machine is about 180 nanoseconds. In other respects, the timing is completely straightforward. The IR is latched at the beginning of each cycle, setting up addresses for the sources and all the data path selectors, and specifying the function control bits for the ALU and CHARM. During the middle of the cycle, the data trickles through CHARM and the ALU and settles on the OBUS. At the end of the cycle, the destination is clocked and a new IR is strobed in. Slightly higher speed might have been achieved by attempting to overlap the RAM writes, but the resulting complexity would have made it more difficult for the user to microprogram the special-purpose machine.

The remainder of the CHEOPS system consists of a PDP-11 and a time-shared PDP-10 which communicate with the special processor through a special bus interface (see upper right part of Fig. 1). In the crudest mode of interaction, the general purpose machines can stop CHEOPS, read and write directly into memories and microstore, and restart at an arbitrary address. Without stopping the processor, the machines can effect CHEOPS through flag bits, and can read the contents of a status register. Finally, CHEOPS itself can initiate data transfers or interrupts on the UNIBUS. These various facilities provide a basis for efficient communication between algorithms running on the CHEOPS processor and high-level programs running on other computers.

2. SOFTWARE

2.1 Utility programs

A series of utility programs were written to make CHEOPS accessible to the user from video terminals on the time-shared PDP-10 system. A chess micro-assembler (CHASM) accepts mnemonic specifications of fields for CHEOPS microcode. It also resolves address labels and efficiently allocates blocks for branch destinations. A CONSOLE program provides all of the usual facilities of a console to the special processor – for example, start, stop, and single-step, examine and deposit registers, load microcode, etc. In addition it automatically translates data into alphanumeric or other implicit data types, recalls the CHASM labels corresponding to micro-addresses, displays square lines and board image, examines the stack of moves in the current game, and executes rapid store and restore of the state of the entire machine from disc file. Finally, it implements a variety of debugging features that facilitate the finding of speed-dependent errors, as well as other less subtle problems with CHASM code.

2.2 Baisleys's TECH II program

Alan Baisley of the MIT Artificial Intelligence Laboratory has developed a number of brute-force oriented programs, the simplest of them resembling Gillogly's TECH Program in many respects [4]. The moves from the top level position are ordered according to plausibility by a program on the PDP-10, using a variety of measures, such as pawn structure, control of centre, and king safety. The resulting positions are shipped over to the CHEOPS processor, where an alpha-beta minimax search with material balance as an evaluator is performed, returning a principal variation. This search contains a few refinements, such as a weighted depth parameter, which is incremented by 1 for normal moves and by 0 for replies to check. Out of the positions which receive the highest evaluation from CHEOPS, the first (hence presumably most plausible) is actually played. Special high-level routines deal with endgame situations.

2.3 The Greenblatt program

The Greenblatt MACHACK Program [5] is also being integrated into the CHEOPS system. The CHEOPS processor plays two kinds of roles in this context. First, as a background task, it does a Baisley-type brute-force search from the top position, the result of which is used for comparison with the final choice made by the heuristic program. Second, as a foreground task, it does short searches (that is, 3 plies exhaustive, plus capture chains) from nodes within the game-tree searched by MACHACK, to provide a tactical backstop for the two kinds of heuristics mentioned in the introduction.

In particular, CHEOPS performs these mini-searches to rectify the action of the plausible move generator, alerting the high-level program to possible material gains for either side that might otherwise be missed. Finally, a mini-search is also initiated during static evaluation of a terminal node. If the result does not agree with the heuristic evaluation, or if CHEOPS indicates future material exchange in an apparently stable position. MACHACK will proceed deeper to clarify the situation.

Acknowledgments

This research was carried on jointly at the Laboratory for Computer Science and at the Artificial Intelligence Laboratory of the Massachusetts Institute of Technology. Professor Edward Fredkin was instrumental in the original conception and design of CHEOPS. The special processor was developed in parallel with Thomas Knight's CONS special processor for the LISP machine. P. Jarvis and R. Lebel helped in the use of the Stanford Drawing System; W. Freeman designed the interface to the PDP-10 and PDP-11; and C. Waldrop aided in the main-frame construction. A. Baisley provided his expertise in brute-force oriented chess algorithms. We would also like to thank J. Cocke for his encouragement and interest in this work.

REFERENCES

[1] Turing, A. M. (1950). Computing machinery and intelligence. *Mind* **59**, 433–460.

[2] Shannon, C. E. (1950). Programming a computer for playing chess. *Phil. Mag. (London), 7th ser.* **41**, 256–75.

[3] Levy, D. N. L. (1976). *Chess and Computers.* London: Batsford.

[4] Gillogly, J. J. (1972). The Technology Chess Program. *Artificial Intelligence* **3**, 145–164.

[5] Greenblatt, R. D., Eastlake, D. E. and Crocker, S. D. (1967). The Greenblatt Chess Program. *Proceedings of the FJCC* **31**, 801–810.

17

Computer Analysis of a Rook End-game

V. L. Arlazarov and A. L. Futer
Institute of Control Sciences, Moscow, USSR

Abstract
This paper describes an algorithm for dividing the set of positions in a single-pawn Rook end-game into winning ones for White and drawing. Data arrangement and processing methods are described whereby within reasonable computer time, large (up to about 1500-million bits) data arrays can be studied; a number of procedures are put forward, such as search for problem symmetry, levels of data arrangement, data restructuring, batch processing of data, and others.

1. INTRODUCTION

In programming a computer for chess, the end-game is of special significance. The reason is that there are approximately as many alternative moves in an end-game position as in the middle game, namely several dozen. For playing, however, strategies many moves deeper are needed, and so the methods of tree search to a limited depth [1,2] do not work very well in end-games.

On the other hand, full analysis of certain end-games with a few pieces seems a promising idea. This implies that for each position the result of the game and strategies of the players are determined. A substantial step forward in this direction was the analysis of a single-Pawn Queen end-game (the King, the Queen, and a Pawn against the King and the Queen) with a White Pawn on g7 [3].

This paper will discuss a single-Pawn Rook end-game with the Pawn in an arbitrary position.

There, a set of positions is taken up where White has the King, a Pawn, and a Rook agains Black's King and Rook (KPR-KR). For each position (of four pieces, a Pawn, and the move) it is required to determine whether it is a win for White, and indicate the best possible move.

Note that the size of such a set of positions is about 1500-million ($64^4 \times 48 \times 2$). If each position takes one bit, then practically all the resources of one of today's large computers will be used up. And each computer operation for one position takes up to one hour (with the computation rate of 500 thousand operations per second). Therefore if the previous algorithm [3] were simply transferred into this problem it would require about one thousand hours of computer time.

This paper will propose a general procedure of end-game study. Then an algorithm is described whereby the set of positions in a KPR–KR end-game is divided into winning and drawing ones. For each winning position we determined the number of moves to win the position, so that the best move is indicated for each position. The data structuring and processing methods and procedures, which may be of special interest, are described.

2. A STUDY PROCEDURE

Any arbitrary end-game is studied in two stages. First positions are defined which incorporate successful moves leading to another end-game. Then positions are written in sequence that are reducible to the desired one in one move, two moves, etc.

Let us give a more detailed explanation of each stage. White has, for instance, the following moves to other end-games. The pawn can become a Queen or a Rook, or the Black Rook can be captured, possibly together with promotion. If any of these moves is successful, or leads to a winning position, the original position is assumed won for White in zero steps and is included into the class W_o (zero rank). If there are no such moves in a position or if none leads to a victory, the position is ranked as *NW*, nonranked White.

In a similar way, Black can take the Pawn or Rook and secure a draw (or a victory, which will not be discussed hereafter). Thus a set B_o is obtained. Positions without such a move are the *NB*, non-ranked Black, class. Now let us take up a set of positions from *NB* which has no moves in *NW*. These are positions all moves from which lead to the complement of *NW*, or they are Black's games lost in one move. These positions will be referred to as the set of the first Black rank, RB_1.

Remove RB_1 from *NB* and take up RW_1 (the first White rank), or those positions of *NW* from which there is a move into RB_1. These are White's wins in one move. Remove them from *NC*, etc. Fig. 1 illustrates this ranking procedure. (Here A^{-1} denotes the class of positions which may have at least one move in to the set *A* and the symbol \ denotes set-subtraction).

The procedure ends when the set of positions of the next rank, RB_i or RW_i, is empty. The sets *NB* and *NW* at that time are draws with moves of Black or White, respectively. This ranking is consistent with Zermelo's approach [4] if the end positions are those of the sets W_o and B_o.

Let us apply this procedure to all the end-games obtained from KPR–KR (referred to as *junior*). The end-games will be taken successively upward, starting with the simplest ones. In this way the positions inferior to the current ones will have been studied. Fig. 2 shows the graph of end-games.

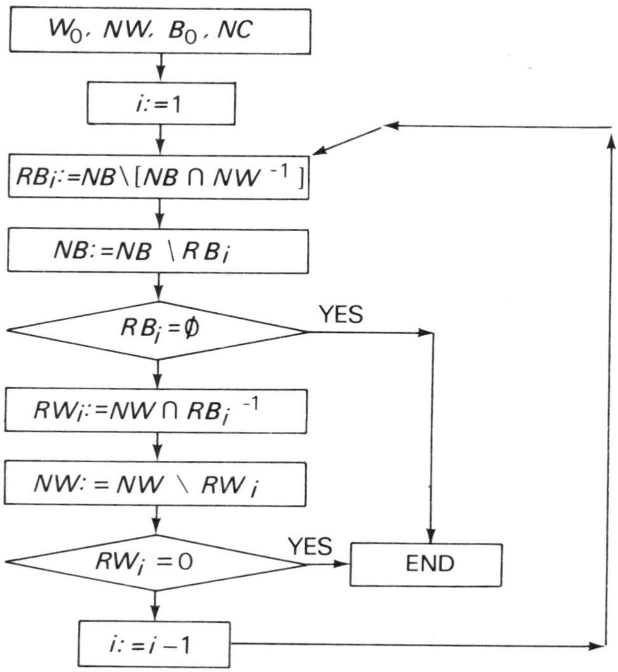
W_0, NW, B_0, NC
$i := 1$
$RB_i := NB \setminus [NB \cap NW^{-1}]$
$NB := NB \setminus RB_i$
$RB_i = \emptyset$
YES
$RW_i := NW \cap RB_i^{-1}$
$NW := NW \setminus RW_i$
$RW_i = 0$
YES
END
$i := i - 1$

Fig. 1.

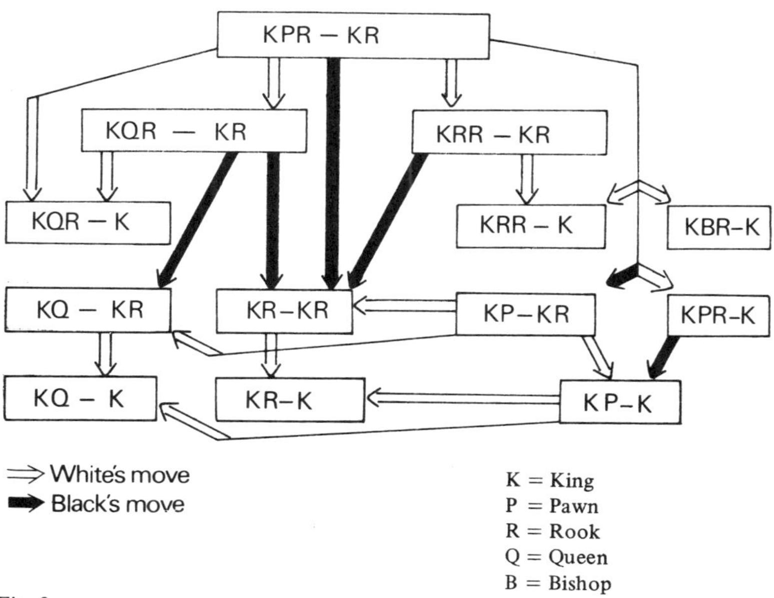
KPR – KR
KQR – KR
KRR – KR
KQR – K
KRR – K
KBR–K
KQ – KR
KR–KR
KP–KR
KPR–K
KQ – K
KR–K
KP–K
White's move
Black's move
K = King
P = Pawn
R = Rook
Q = Queen
B = Bishop

Fig. 2

Each of the junior end-games was studied separately and in different ways. None of them is of interest to chess players. For our problem, however, we needed complete sets of winning positions or drawing positions or both for each of them.

3. REDUCING A KPR–KR END-GAME TO A FOUR-PIECE ONE

Because of the vertical symmetry of the chessboard the KPR–KR ending can be studied only for one half of possible Pawn positions. Besides this, the Pawn can move to another column only by capturing, which would result in another end-game. For these reasons the whole study is four independent analyses of the a, b, c, and d column.

Now let us show that one column can be studied in steps the size of a square, in other words, the problem is reducible to study of a four-piece end-game with the Pawn fixed.

This reduction can be performed by a method analogous to the junior end-game procedure with a move by the Pawn regarded as obtaining a new end-game. In other words, in studying positions with the Pawn at the jth row an array can be obtained of P_j losing positions with Black's move. Then, in studying a square of $(j\text{-}1)^{\text{th}}$ row, White's positions having a Pawn move into that array are included in the zero rank set.

In this approach, however, the position ranking becomes artificial because the position rank denotes the minimal number of moves until the Pawn is advanced rather than the minimal number of moves to a victory. This kind of ranking is an incentive for White to advance the Pawn even at the risk of heading into a difficult, albeit winning, position. In real games the advance of the Pawn should often be stalled; the larger pieces should secure good positions and then win the game quickly.

To obtain a natural ranking in studying a square of the jth row we store the array P_j as a merger of sets of successive Black ranks $P_j = \bigcup_i P_j^i$ where $P_j = RB_i$ are sets of positions with a Black's move lost in i moves (with the Pawn at the jth row). Now in processing a square of the $(j\text{-}1)^{\text{th}}$ row, positions with White's move of the Pawn in P_j^i are assigned to RW_i, the ith White rank; Blacks's losses are entered in the array $P_{j-1} = \bigcup_i P_{i-1}^i$ etc.

This procedure significantly reduces the data storage for one problem to $64^4 \times 2$, 32 million positions, which with one bit allocated per position means about four million bytes.

4. METHODS OF DATA PROCESSING AND STRUCTURING

Data arrays of the size of about a million bytes can be stored only in magnetic media. As follows from section 2 these arrays need to be repeatedly processed to go through the ranking procedure.

This is why economical access to media is an urgent requirement. We will enumerate the basic methods and procedures whereby this, essentially an exchange problem, can be solved at a practically possible processor rate. A reasonable time of program operation was needed, a mere 60 computer hours.

4.1 The data structure

This requires three levels: distribution of data components into blocks (a block being an exchange unit), the location of units in the array, and allocation of arrays among shelf media. Thanks to the existence and interaction of the first and second levels, the number of accesses to the magnetic media is not high. The third level requires, in particular, the use of different kinds of media, sequential and random access.

The number of the latter is usually limited in each computer configuration, we needed them for performing the data *re-ordering* algorithms. Thus in the program for creating a set of positions of a subsequent rank, transposition algorithms for 4096 × 4096 square matrices were needed. (When a Black rank is obtained, Black chessmen retreat and White chessmen are fixed, and the reverse is true). To reduce the output arrays of the program to a format convenient for computer playing of a Rook end-game, a transposition algorithm was developed for a rectangular matrix of 60 × 16 million. Thanks to transposition, each unit of the arrays was processed the first time it was accessed.

4.2 Formats of data arrays

As is often the case, in our problem two conflicting requirements had to be met, reduction of the amount of the data stored and ease of its use. To resolve this conflict, two chief formats were used, unpacked and packed. In the former the address of a four-piece end-game position in the data array is defined as a linear function of the position of these pieces. In the latter the positions are stored as a list.

4.3 Buffering

In all parts of the program the processor and the exchange channels operated in parallel. When a new rank was constructed, three buffer spaces were used. At each instant a block of the array, for example *NW*, was read into one of them, another was accessed by the processor, and in the third the renewed state of the array was written into the medium. Once an operating cycle was completed, the regions changed their function by circulation. The program itself needed appropriate restructuring because all its commands were adjusted for using the appropriate part of the store.

4.4 Development of improved exchange software

Convenient macro-operations were developed for array opening and closure. Also, for compatibility with the multi-buffer configuration and for making the exchange periods approach the potential of the media, the macro-operations of exchange with the tape and the disc had to be improved.

5. PROGRAM IMPLEMENTATION OF THE ALGORITHM

5.1 Batch processing of positions

In analysis of end-games the positions were handled individually in almost no part of the program. The argument and the operation result are position sets: a *document* of 4096 bits (positions of two chessmen change), a *board* of 64 bits (the position of one chessman is variable) or still smaller sets of bits.

The method proved especially effective in transposition algorithms for unpacked arrays (Sec. 5.2) and back-up (Sec. 5.3).

5.2 Transposition

A square matrix of unpacked format is transposed in two stages. First each row of the original matrix is divided into equal parts. Parts of different rows belonging to the same groups of columns are assembled and written into the medium. This is performed repeatedly (twice in our case) until the set of columns of the original matrix can be stored in the core memory in its entirety. Then in the memory the transposition is completed by the method put forward by M. M. Bongard, involving permutations and conjunctions of sets of bits.

The algorithm takes somewhat less than a minute for a 4096 × 4096 matrix.

A square matrix in packed format is transposed in a similar way. The matrix is divided several times. Each of its squares is covered by some part denoted by the ordinal number of the column. The transposition time for a packed array is proportional to its size and is the same as the unpacked transposition time for about 500,000 nonempty elements.

The ouput of the ranking program was a totality of arrays P_j^i (see Sec. 3). To facilitate computer playing of Rook end-games, this totality should be recorded. For each jth position of the Pawn a rectangular $a \times 2^{24}$ matrix should be tranposed where the number of ranks a varies for different j from 20 to 60. Originally, this matrix was represented as rows, or as successive subarrays, each represented in a packed format. In transposition each block of these subarrays was transferred to a disc, a random access medium. Concurrently, an inquiry file $\tilde{S}$ is made in main memory, where for each block B of the disc the disc address of that block and the number of the column of the matrix for the first element in B are entered.

Then the inquiry file S is ordered in terms of the numbers of the columns; an $\tilde{S}$ file is obtained. Now the processor memory successively calls block of the disc in compliance with the movement in $\tilde{S}$. Elements of similar columns are grouped and entered into the medium.

This routine takes 20 to 30 minutes for each j.

5.3 Backing moves

The argument and the result of the operation *MRK*, that is, backward moves by the Rook and the King, is a document of unpacked format, $64^2 = 4096$ bits.

Let the White pawn be in square p; the document D assumes positions m and n of the Rook and the King of the colour and inside the values k and l of squares of the same pieces of the other colour. Let us refer to pieces taking the squares p, m and n as external (for the document D) and those taking k and l as internal. Also, let us define the position of the Rook in terms of the coordinates m and k and that of the King, n and l; in other words, the Rook is assumed senior to the King.

A document is required, $D = MRK(D)$ whose unit bits will be associated with positions with at least one move by internal pieces into some position recorded in D.

The operation MRK is represented as a merger of two operations, MR, moves of the Rook, and MK, moves of the King: $MRK = MR \cup MK$; in other words, we will have two intermediate documents, $D_R = MR(D)$ and $D_K = MK(D)$ which will be merged later: $MRK(D) = D_R \cup D_K$.

The document $D_R = MR(D)$ is obtained as a totality of boards $D_R(q)$, $0 \leqslant q \leqslant 63$ where $D_R(q)$ denotes a portion of the document D_R, namely 64 successive bits associated with the position of the Rook at the square q.

Let the internal Rook be at the square q_c. Then there are fourteen squares, $q_1, q_2, \ldots q_2$, within its range in an empty board. Remove from this set those squares that are shielded by external chessmen. The remaining squares make a set $Q = \{q_i\}$.

Let us take up a totality of positions recorded in the board $D(q_i)$ of the original document D, $q_i \in Q$. From this totality remove positions associated with the positions of the internal King between the squares q_i and q_c. Then for each of the remaining positions there is a move of the internal Rook from the square q_i to the field q_c. Therefore to implement this move, first, the board $D(q_i)$ should be moved to $D_R(q_c)$ and, second, to make the bits associated with the fields between q_i and q_c zero. Perform this operation for all q_i from K and unite the results in $D_R(q_c)$.

To save computer time, for each square of the chessboard a separate program without cycles was written which implements the moves of the Rook to that field (with the chessboard empty). The program was not written manually; instead, a sentence of its commands (approximately 64×50 long) was developed by another program. The resulting back-up program was corrected for each set of positions of external chessmen which shielded certain squares from the internal Rook.

The operations of MK (moves of the King) over the document D are performed separately for each board $D(q)$, $0 \leqslant q \leqslant 63$. The board $D(q)$ leads to the board $MK(D(q))$ where one's are in the bits of those squares from which there is at least one move of the King to the unity bit of the board $D(q)$. The MK operation for one board takes several logical commands of the computer.

The entire MRK operation over a document of 64^2 bits took five to six thousand computer commands, or about a minute of computer time for each rank.

6. COMPUTER RESULTS

In program operation, obtaining first ranks of each square took a few minutes and for subsequent ranks, 30 to 45 seconds. Each column took about 15 computer hours.

Computations revealed that in the seventh row the number of ranks varied from 20 to 23 (for different columns). This number increased with decreasing ordinal number of the row and amounted to 50 by 60 by the second row. The number of positions won by White with the move of White varied from square to square within 1.5 to 4.5 million and with Black's move from 0.5 to 5.5 million.

Only these positions, or losses of Black, were retained in the program output, which required, depending of the position of the Pawn, from two to eight million bytes. The overall size of this set of positions for all the squares was about 60 million and their storage required about 120 million bytes.

After classification of all the positions into winning for White and drawing, the same procedure was used to classify the drawing positions into enforced and positional draws. Enforced draws are those achieved by capture of the White Rook or Pawn in several moves in positions of the KPR–KR type. For human players the outcome in such positions is a foregone conclusion; the fraction of such positions, especially for the last rows, is tremendous. Thus, for the square d7 there are about 2 million draws, achieved with a move by Black, and among those only 35,000 are positional.

In positions which take White the longest to win (60 moves) the white Pawn is on the field b2. These positions are shown in Figs. 3–6 (Black's move):

Fig. 3 – w: K c3, R c4, P b2; b: K e4, R d1.

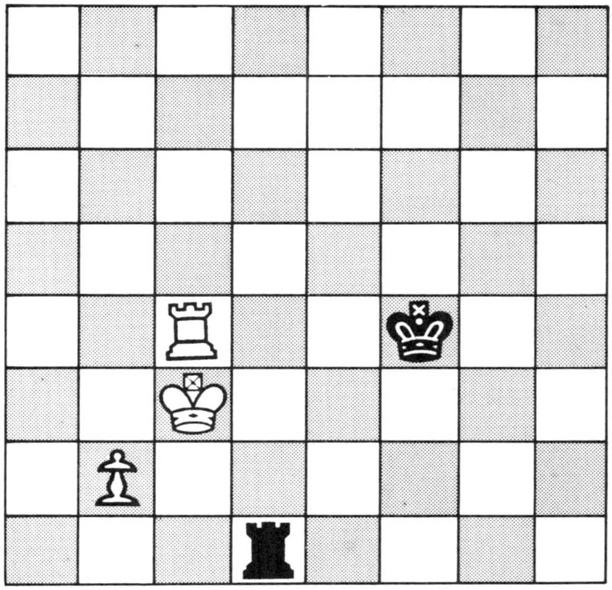

Fig. 4 – w: K c3, R c4, P b2; b: K f4, R d1.

Fig. 5 – w: K d1, R d6, P b2; b: K h6, Ra8.

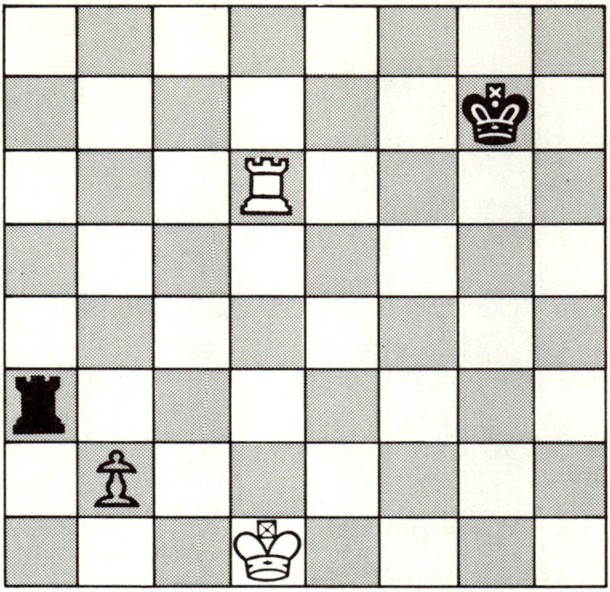

Fig. 6 – w: K d1, R d6, P b2; b: K g7, R a3.

What follows is the optimal way to victory from the position of Fig. 3 (1):

	White	Black		White	Black
1.	...	Ke5	20.	Kd5	Rd8+
2.	Rc5+	Kd6	21.	Kc4	Rc8+
3.	Kb4	Rb1	22.	Kd3	Rd8+
4.	Rc2	Rf1	23.	Kc2	Rc8+
5.	Kb5	Rf5+	24.	Kb1	Rb8
6.	Kb6	Rf8	25.	Re3	Rd8
7.	Rd2+	Ke5	26.	Kc2	Rc8+
8.	Kc7	Rf4	27.	Kd3	Rb8
9.	Kc6	Rc4+	28.	Kc3	Rc8+
10.	Kb5	Rc8	29.	Kd4	Rd8+
11.	Rh2	Rb8+	30.	Kc5	Rc8+
12.	Kc6	Ke6	31.	Kd6	Rb8
13.	Rh6+	Kf7	32.	b3	Rb5
14.	Rh7+	Ke6	33.	Kc6	Rb8
15.	Rh2	Ke7	34.	Rd3	Kf8
16.	Kc7	Rb3	35.	Kc5	Ke7
17.	Re2+	Kf7	36.	b4	Rc8+
18.	Kc6	Rb8	37.	Kb5	Rb8+
19.	Kc5	Rc8+	38.	Ka4	Ra8+

	White	Black		White	Black
39.	Kb3	Rb8	50.	Ka6	Re7
40.	Rd4	Ke6	51.	b6	Re3
41.	Kc4	Ke5	52.	Ka7	Kc6
42.	Rd5+	Ke6	53.	Rg6+	Kb5
43.	b5	Rc8+	54.	Rd6	Rf3
44.	Rc5	Rb8	55.	b7	Ra3+
45.	Kb4	Ke7	56.	Kb8	Rc3
46.	Ka5	Kd6	57.	Rd2	Kc6
47.	Rg5	Rc8	58.	Ra2	Rb3
48.	Kb6	Rd8	59.	Kc8	Re3
49.	Kb7	Rd7+	60.	Rc2+	Kd6
			61.	b8=Q+	

White easily wins in the resultant position.

Acknowledgements

The authors are indebted to A. R. Bitman, Master of Sports in Chess, for valuable consultations. They would also like to thank the following colleagues in the Institute who helped in programming the algorithms: A. G. Aleksandrov, A. M. Baraev, V. N. Deza, I. A. Faradzhev, Ya. Yu. Gol'fand, T. P. Il'ina, E. A. Komissarchik, and A. V. Uskov.

Editors' note

The reader should be aware that not all possible derived sub-games are covered in the authors' Fig. 2. Some of these (e.g. KN–KR) would require further computations for subdivision according to the "won-drawn-lost" criterion.

REFERENCES

[1] Arlazarov, V. L., Adelson-Velsky, G., Bitman, A., Zhivotovsky, A. and Uskov, A. (1970). O Programmirovanii Igry Vychiclitelnoy Mashiny v shahmaty. *Uspehi Mat. Nauk*, **15**, No. 2 (152), 221–261.

[2] Donskoy, M. V. (1974). Programme, Igrayushchey v shahmaty, *Problemy Kybernet*, **29**, 169–200.

[3] Komissarchik, E. and Futer, A. (1974). Ob Analize Ferzevogo Endshpilia pri Pomoshchi EVM. *Problemy Kybernet*, **29**, 211–220.

[4] Zermelo, E. (1913). Uber eine Anwendung der Mengenlehre auf die Theorie des Schachspiels, *Proceedings of the Fifth International Congress of Mathematicians (Cambridge, 1912)*, pp. 501–504. Cambridge: Cambridge University Press.

18

Algorithms of Adaptive Search

G. M. Adelson-Velsky, V. L. Arlazarov, and M. V. Donskoy
Institute of Control Sciences, Moscow, USSR

Abstract
Adaptive search algorithms are considered, built around the KAISSA chess program. Adaptation of the program to a given search problem consists of building, treating, and using information contained in a so-called "Reference Book". The information consists of a number of elements describing the duration and results of searches of various subtrees. So in the program local search rules are built and used. These rules advise or forbid certain moves in the search. This paper contains both a formal and an informal description of the adaptive search algorithms. A number of chess illustrations of the program's working are given. On the basis of the chess program, algorithms can be written that use human chess experience.

INTRODUCTION

This paper describes algorithms of adaptive search that act as a superstructure of the chess program KAISSA. A detailed description of the basic program algorithms and their theoretical substantiation can be found in the reference which also gives precise definitions of notions used in this paper.

Program adaptation to a specified search is data generation, processing, and use in a so-called Reference Book. This consists of element lists describing the results of the search of various subtrees. In this way rules banning or advising moves in the search are generated, corrected, deleted, or applied to the program search. In comparison with the global rules for search reduction used in all chess programs these rules have two advantages: (a) high frequency of applicability and simplicity of applicability check, and (b) absolute accuracy of applicability, in that application does not change the search results obtained without using this rule.

The paper consists of seven parts. The first updates and explains the definition of "influence" [1] which is the basic linguistic tool for the algorithms of adaptive search.

The second part contains a general description of the algorithms.

The third part describes the Reference Book format, contents, data structures, and links between elements of these data.

The fourth part gives a detailed description of algorithms for data generation and processing in the Reference Book.

The fifth part describes the Reference Book algorithms for search reduction and improvement of move ordering.

The sixth part illustrates elements of both the notion of influence and the algorithms of adaptive search.

The seventh part discusses results, the problems facing further advances along these lines, and approaches to their solution.

1. THE INFLUENCE RELATION

Let $L = (p,q)$ be a pair of plies from the position U to the position V. Define the boards of this pair.

p^0, q^0 are *squares-from* for the ply p and the ply q respectively.

p^1, q^1 are *squares-to* of the respective plies.

$\bar{L}^0$ – are squares of the line along which the move p was made, excluding the initial p^0 and the final p^1 fields of the move p;

$\bar{L}^1$ – if in the position V the q-King (of the player who made the move q) is not checked, then $\bar{L}^1$ is empty; otherwise these are check lines including squares where the q-King and the checking piece are;

$\bar{L}^2$ – if in the position V there are no pinned q-pieces, then $\bar{L}^2$ is empty; otherwise for each pinned q-piece $\bar{L}^2$ contains a pinning line starting with the square where the pinner is and ending with a square where the q-King is, both these square inclusive;

$\bar{L} = \bar{L}^0 \cup \bar{L}^1 \cup \bar{L}^2$ – are paths of the pair L.

L^+ – are positive lines of the pair L or sets of squares for which there is a q-piece attacking this square in the position V and not attacking it in the position U. The square q^0 is not included in L^+.

$L^\oplus$ – are positive long-range lines, or sets of squares for which there is a long-range q-piece (a Bishop, a Rook, or a Queen) attacking this square in the position V and not attacking in the position U. The square q^0 is not included in $L^\oplus$.

L^- – are negative lines of the pair L, or squares for which there is a p-piece which attacks this square in the position U and does not in the position V.

$\widetilde{L}^+$ – are new checking potential, or a set of squares for which there exists a piece type so that a q-piece of that type can check from that square in the position V and cannot do so in the position U.

L^* – blocking the q-King. If in the position V the q-King was not checked the set L^* is empty; otherwise it contains squares where the q-King cannot move because they are occupied by its own pieces;

$L^{\circledast}$ – if in the position V the q-King is not checked, then $L^{\circledast}$ is empty; otherwise it contains squares where the q-King cannot move because these squares are under attack by the opponent's pieces.

The boards of the set of pairs are defined as logical sums of associated boards of each pair. The set of pairs L_1 "influences" the set of pairs L_2 if one of the following intersections is nonempty.

$$(q_1^0 \cup p_1^0 \cup p_1^1) \cap (p_2^0 \cup p_2^1 \cup L_2^+ \cup q_2^1)$$
$$(p_1^0 \cup p_1^1 \cup q_1^0 \cup q_1^1) \cap \bar{L}_2$$
$$(p_1^0 \cup q_1^0) \cap (\widetilde{L}_2^+ \cup L_2^*)$$
$$\widetilde{L}_1^+ \cap (p_2^0 \cup q_2^0 \cup L_2^+)$$
$$\bar{L}_1 \cap (p_2^0 \cup p_2^1 \cup q_2^0 \cup q_2^1)$$
$$L_1^+ \cap (\widetilde{L}_2^+ \cup p_2^1 \cup \bar{L}_2^+)$$
$$L_1^- \cap L_2^{\circledast}$$
$$(p_1^1 \cup q_1^1 \cup L_1^{\oplus}) \cap (p_2^0 \cup q_2^0)$$

In chess terms, "influence" implies the following:

If the variation L_2 lost and the moves L_1 include those that can affect the results of the variation L_2 (either by generating new possibilities for the losing q-player or hindering best moves of the p-player), this will necessarily be felt in the influence of L_1 on L_2 by the formula. The reverse is not true, the formula may speak of the influence of L_1 on L_2 although this is not the case.

Notes on the notion of influence

(1) $p_1^0 \cap p_2^0$ – the same piece acts in both variations. In particular, this intersection is nonempty in overloading.

(2) $p_1^1 \cap p_2^1$ – a square where the opponent moves in one variation, is taken in another. This intersection may indicate decoying.

(3) $p_1^0 \cap p_2^1$ and $p_1^1 \cap p_2^0$ – occur only with other intersections.

(4) $q_1^0 \cap p_2^1$ – a piece which was captured in one variation leaves the dangerous square in the other.

(5) $q_1^0 \cap p_2^0$ – occurs only simultaneously with other intersections.

(6) $p_1^1 \cap L_2^+$ – in one variation a piece moves to the square on which, in the other variation, there is a new attack.

(7) $(q_1^0 \cup p_1^0) \cap L_2^+$ – in one variation a piece which was under attack in the other has moved. This may indicate opening up a line for another attack.

(8) $(q_1^0 \cup p_1^0) \cap q_2^1$ – occurs only simultaneously with other intersections.

(9) $p_1^1 \cup q_2^1$ – in one variation an opponents's piece has moved to a square to which, in another variation, one's own piece has moved.

(10) $(p_1^1 \cup q_1^1) \cap \bar{L}_2$ – in one variation a piece moves to the path of a move in the other variation. Then the latter may either become impossible or ceases to be a check. This intersection may also be cutting a pin.

(11) $q_1^0 \cap \bar{L}_2$ – in one variation the q-King made a move and in the other it was checked. Now the latter may cease to be a check.

(12) $p_1^0 \cap \bar{L}_2$ – in one variation a piece has made a move which pins a piece in another. Now the pin may cease to exist.

(13) $(p_1^0 \cup q_1^0) \cap \tilde{L}_2^+$ – in one variation the piece has moved from the square through which checks could be made in the other. May indicate a new check.

(14) $p_1^0 \cap L_2^*$ – can occur only with other intersections.

(15) $q_1^0 \cap L_2^*$ – in one variation a piece leaves which blocked the q-King in the other. Indicates a new check evasion.

(16) $\tilde{L}_1^+ \cap (p_2^0 \cup q_2^0)$ – see (12).

(17) $\tilde{L}_1^+ \cap L_2^+$ – there is a square from which a check can be made in one variation; simultaneously, it belongs to positive lines of the other. Indicates the possibility of a new check.

(18) $\bar{L}_1 \cap (p_2^2 \cap q_2^1)$ – see (10).

(19) $\bar{L}_1 \cap (p_2^0 \cup q_2^0)$ – see (11) and (12).

(20) $L_1^+ \cap \tilde{L}_2^+$ – see (17).

(21) $L_1^+ \cap p_2^1$ – see (6).

(22) $L_1^+ \cap \bar{L}_2^1$ – in one variation the check path of the other variation is intercepted. Indicates a new response to a check.

(23) $\bar{L}_1 \cap L_2^{\circledast}$ – in one variation the attack is removed on a square where the q-King could not go because of the opponent's attack. May indicate a new evasion of a check.

(24) $p_1^1 \cap q_2^0$ – see (5).

(25) $p_1^1 \cap p_2^0$ – see (3).

(26) $q_1^1 \cap p_2^0$ – in one variation an opponent's piece is captured that made a move in the other. The opponent's move becomes impossible.

(27) $q_1^1 \cap q_2^0$ – see (8).

(28) $L_1^{\circledast} \cap (q_2^0 \cup p_2^0)$ – in one variation a long-range piece has attacked a square left by a piece in the other version. May indicate discovered attack.

2. THE GENERAL ALGORITHM

At any time the Reference Book contains elements of data associated with positions of the current branch (sequences of moves leading from the initial position of the search into the one treated at this particular time). Each element contains data on certain moves; these data represent, generally speaking, the course and result of searching a variation beginning from that move in the position associated with this element. These data include the refutation of the opponent to that move, the material loss from this variation (this loss may be negative; instead of the contention "the move loses at least a Pawn", the contention "the move gains no more than a Knight" is true) and boards of that variation.

At the time when the move generator proposes some move into the search, the program verifies whether there are elements which contain data on that move in the Reference Book. Then for each element tests are made (using the influence formula) also whether the variation described by that element holds and whether we can afford the material gain specified in the element. If there is an element for which the loss is large enough and the variation holds, the search of the move is delayed.

When the search of all non-delayed moves from the position has been completed, for each delayed move the influence of the version described in the boards of the associated element on the minimax subtree of a variation from that position is tested. If there is no such influence, then the move is cut off because the move loses by virtue of the condition of the preceding paragraph, by itself and, by virtue of the latter condition, in combination with others.

Special attention should be given to elements containing data on an "empty" move. They describe material loss if they are in a position to let the opponent make a move without moving on the board, and are thus referred to as "threats".

In each position it is established, even before move generation, whether there is a threat whose variation holds in this position with a large enough material gain.

If there is such a threat and the other side is not poised for a new attack, the search is stopped because this threat can be carried through and a gain be obtained.

The Reference Book elements are constructed in moving upwards along the tree. When the search from position V is completed, for each element assigned to this position the program first decides whether the data which is contained in that element is valid in the position U of the current branch one level higher. If it is, the element is assigned without change to the position U.

If this is not the case, or if in point of fact the variation at hand has been provoked by the move, *p*, along which backing up is made, it is checked whether this element was generated at the minimax subtree from the position *V*. If this is not so, the element is simply deleted from the Reference Book. If this *is* so, the data contained in that element will be merged into the data of the new element describing the move *p*.

If the move *p* wins in the sense of the minimax procedure, then the resultant element is a threat; if it does not, it is an ordinary element.

3. THE REFERENCE BOOK FORMAT

The Reference Book is structured as a number of lists. Two lists are pushed up through each element: the list of elements of a specified level and the list of elements associated with a specific move described by a "piece-square-to" couple. For each level there is a heading of the list of elements at a given level, containing the address of the first element of the level, and each element has a reference to the subsequent element of the same level.

Also, for each square of the board there is a heading of the piece list on whose moves to this square at least one element in the Reference Book is available. This list is made of references. The list of pieces is made by heading elements of the list of elements with a fixed "piece-square" couple. Simultaneously, they contain data on a certain variation of that move.

Thanks to this structure two basic operations take little time: access to all elements of a specified level, and access to each element for a specified move.

In addition to these four references a Reference Book element contains the refutation, the amount of material loss, and boards of the variation.

4. ALGORITHMS OF REFERENCE BOOK USE

Once a certain move defined by the "piece-square-to" couple has been generated, the program looks for elements in the Reference Book that would contain data on that move. When the first such element is found, the program verifies whether the material difference brought about by the variation of this element is sufficient for α-β pruning. If it is not, the program proceeds to the next element. If it *is*, the program constructs boards of the branch which leads from the position to which the element is assigned to the current position. Then these boards and the variation boards contained in this element are used to verify the influence of the branch on the variation. If this exists, the program proceeds to the next element. If not, the search of the move is delayed and the element which causes this delay is stored.

If none of the elements causes a postponement, in the beginning of the "piece-square" list a special element is written which prevents the move verification on the knowledge of the already existing elements in the entire subtree of the current node.

After dealing with the nondelayed moves, the program takes up the delayed ones and verifies whether the variation element causing a delay influences the minimax subtree of the current node. If it does not, the move is kept delayed.

When such influence is present, the next element of this move is taken up, and both the influence of a branch which leads from the position associated with this element toward the current position on the variation of this element and the influence on the same variation of the minimax variation from the current vertex are verified.

If an element is found with neither of these influences, the move is delayed again. The address of the element causing a new delay is memorized.

Moves with influence for all the elements are included in the search. Upon completion of searching these moves the program again verifies the influence of the minimax variation which is naturally broader, on the corresponding variations of elements.

The procedure terminates in one of two cases – either all the moves are included in a complete search, or none of the delayed moves is included in it. In both cases the search from the current node terminates. In the other case a part of the moves is cut off.

Testing threats is much more complicated. Apart from the influence on threat boards of the branch leading to the current position from the one with which this threat is associated, one has to check whether the opponent can make new attacks or has any threats of his own.

The latter case is most unpleasant since there are no means of testing whether the threat grows (an influence is just a means to test whether the threat weakens); to say nothing of the difficulties in determining, with the use of these two threats, the result of their interaction.

In this case, the present program does not stop the search, because the information available is insufficient for a satisfactory prediction of the search result from this position.

The Reference Book is finally used for improving the order of the moves in the position. The threats which were found by tests to be futile are included in the search before other moves, together with the profitable captures. This is substantiated by the relative redundancy of the influence formula [1].

Often, even if influence exists, the threat wins. On the other hand the complete search of threats which are not now winning, costs little, and mistakes are not crucial, because the search ceases very rapidly.

For the same reason, before allowing the inclusion of a move whose elements the Reference Book contains, the program at first responds by searching the moves written down in these elements as refutations.

5. THE REFERENCE BOOK UPDATE ALGORITHM

Going back up the tree with each element associated with positions where the search is completed, the program carries out the following procedure.

Depending on the side which runs the variation described by this element the boards for one backward ply are built (to be more exact, the pairs "empty move–backward move" or "backward move–empty move" depending on the side which made this move). Then these boards are used to verify the influence of this ply upon the element version. With no influence the program adds this element to the position from which this ply was made. If influence exists, the program verifies whether this element is taken from the minimax tree of the current vertex. If it is not, the element is simply deleted from all the lists, otherwise it is included in one of the two special lists (for each player) of elements associated with the current ply.

Thus after processing all the elements associated with the current position, some of these elements will be associated with the previous position of the current branch, some deleted, and the remaining ones associated with the current ply.

The program then starts processing the current ply. If its estimate does not go as high as the upper bound, an element is generated which describes this move. Its boards comprise logical sums of the squares of the entire ply and those of all the elements associated with the current element of the same side.

If the estimate of the current ply exceeds the lower boundary, a threat is generated, along with an element holding the information on an empty move. Then the current ply is recorded in this element as the refutation. The threat squares are logical sums of squares of the "empty move – current ply" pair and of all the elements of the other player associated with this element. The material difference as a result of the threat is that of the "empty move – current ply" pair plus the minimum of the material differences of all the elements of the other player (not the one which has made the current ply).

A single exception to this scheme is made when the threat is not transferred over the move by the same player. In this case a current ply will substitute for an empty move in the element, and its boards and material difference will be added to those of a threat.

Thus a number of elements may be generated for a move when the position of this ply is associated with several threats of the other side which influence this move.

6. CHESS ILLUSTRATIONS

In the position given at Fig. 1 let us take up a variation where the Bishop from QB2 captures a Pawn on QR4. This capture is refuted by a Knight K5 check with subsequent capture of the Rook on KN3. The tree of variations of Fig. 2 results.

Construction of the boards of this variation starts with backing up through the move N × KN6 after the move K–K2. A threat N × KN6 is generated with a material difference equal to (R–N). In returning through the move K–K2 it is found that the threat N × KN6 arises because of K–K2, and the move is replaced by an empty move in the threat element N × KN6.

Fig. 1 – Example chess position (see text).

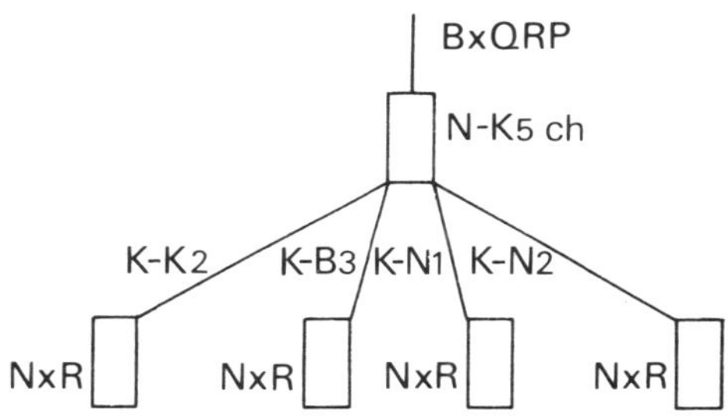

Fig. 2 – Tree of variations.

An element is obtained on the move K–K2 with N × KN6 as the best response and a material difference of (R–N). In the same way elements are obtained on the moves K–B3, KN1, KN2. In backing up through the move N–K5, the program assigns all these elements to the move N–K5 and generates a threat N–K5 with a material difference of (R–N) and boards containing boards of all these elements and also of the move N–K5. In returning through B × RP the program finds that this move has provoked the threat N–K5 (having removed the attack from the square K5), and therefore the move B × RP replaces the empty move in the threat. An element is thus obtained on the move B × RP with the best response N–K5 and material difference (R–N–P). Let us write down its boards:

$$
\begin{aligned}
\Sigma q^0 &= \{\text{QB2, KB2}\};\\
\Sigma q^1 &= \{\text{QR4, K2, KB3, KN1, KN2}\},\\
\Sigma p^0 &= \{\text{Q3, K5}\};\\
\Sigma p^1 &= \{\text{K5, KN6}\};\\
\Sigma \bar{L}^0 &= \{\emptyset\};\\
\Sigma \bar{L}^1 &= \{\text{KB2}\};\\
\Sigma \bar{L}^2 &= \{\emptyset\};\\
\Sigma \tilde{L}^{2+} &= \{\text{QB6}\};\\
\Sigma L^* &= \{\text{K1, K3, KB1, KN3}\},\\
\Sigma L^{\circledast} &= \{\text{KN3}\};\\
\Sigma L^+ &= \{\text{QN5, QB6, Q1, Q2, Q3, K4, KB4, KN4, KR1, KR2, KR3}\};\\
\Sigma L^{\oplus} &= \{\text{QN5, QB6}\};
\end{aligned}
$$

Assume that in the position in Fig. 1 two moves have been made. Does the variation of Fig. 2 remain valid? We will build now different branches from the two moves and try to answer.

1. P-KR3, R-QN4: intersection (6) = {QN5}. The move B × R4 should be searched again ($p_1^1 \cap L_2^+$).
2. P-KR3, P-KR3: all intersections are empty. The move B × R4 should be cut off.
3. P-KR3, P-QN4: intersection (7) is QN6 ($p_1^0 \cap L_2^+$)
4. P-KR3, N-QN4: intersection (1) is Q6 ($p_1^0 \cap p_2^0$)
5. P-KR3, P-K5: intersection (2) is K4 ($p_1^1 \cap p_2^1$)
6. P-KR3, P-KR4: intersection (4) is KN3 ($q_1^0 \cap p_2^1$)
7. B-QR3, P-KN4, B × N, K × B: intersection (26) is Q6 ($q_1^1 \cap p_2^0$)
8. P-QB4, P × P: intersection (13) is Q5 ($p_1^0 \cap \tilde{L}_2^+$)
9. R-Q1, P-KN4: intersection (20) is Q5 ($L_1^+ \cap \tilde{L}_2^+$)
10. K-KN1, P-KN4: intersection (11) is KB2 ($q_1^0 \cap \bar{L}_2$)
11. N-Q2, P-KN4: intersection (21) is K4 ($L_1^+ \cap p_2^1$)

Several examples illustrating influence redundancy are given below.

1. R-K2, P-KN4: intersection (15) is K1 ($q_1^0 \cap L_2^*$)
2. B-QR3, P-KN4: intersection (18) is Q6 ($L_1^+ \cap p_2^0$)
3. P-QB4, P-Q5: intersection (13) is Q5 ($p_1^0 \cap \tilde{L}_2^+$)

Another example will be the variation R × Q6, RB8 in the position in Fig. 3.

Branches permitting search of the capture R × Q6 are as follows:

1. N-Q3, P-QN4: intersection (10) is Q3 ($q_1^1 \cap \bar{L}_2$)
2. P-KB3, P-QN4: intersection (15) is KB2 ($q_1^0 \cap L_2^*$)
3. P-QN3, N-KB3: intersection (23) is KR2 ($L_1^- \cap L_2^{\circledast}$)
4. N-QN3, P-QN4: intersection (22) is KB1 ($L_1^+ \cap \bar{L}_2^1$)
5. K-KB1, P-QN4: intersection (11) is KN1 ($q_1^0 \cap \bar{L}_2$)

The final example is the variation R × Q4, K × Q5 in the position in Fig. 4.

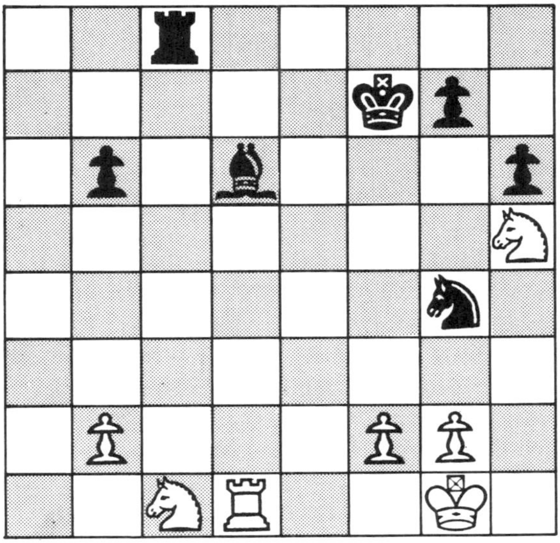

Fig. 3.

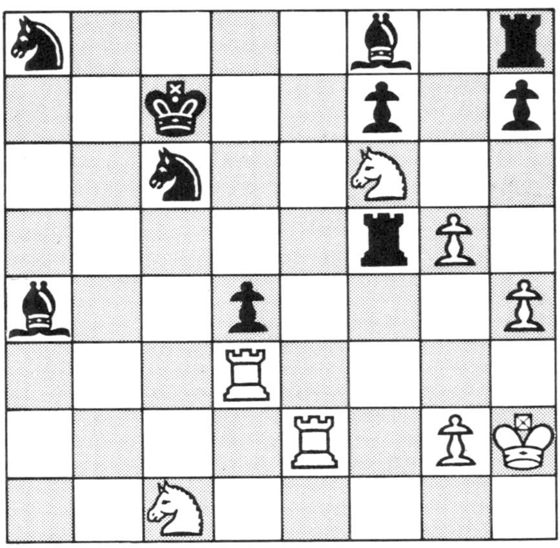

Fig. 4.

The branches permitting search of this variation are as follows:

1. P-KN3, K-Q3: intersection (16) is QB6 ($\widetilde{L}_2^+ \cap p_2^0$)
2. P-KN3, K-QB1: intersection (17) is Q7 ($\widetilde{L}_1^+ \cap L_2^+$)
3. N-QN3, K-QN1, N × P, N × N: intersection (9) is Q4 ($p_1^1 \cap q_2^1$)
4. R-QB2, R-KN1: intersection (28) is QB6 ($L_1^{\oplus} \cap p_2^0$)

7. CONCLUSIONS

Adaptive search algorithms have been implemented as a superstructure over the chess program KAISSA. They reduced the search by a factor of 4 while the time for studying one position was increased by a factor of 1.5.

A side effect of introducing these algorithms was accurate posing of the problem of interaction of the plans and strategies in terms of threat interaction. The algorithm employs little human chess experience, but nevertheless difficulties arise which are typical of algorithms which make more use of this experience. We believe that this fact indicates the possibility of solving these difficulties without introducing the complex and often poorly-formulated chess notions of a human.

In this respect we intend to use formal plans where the notion of the purpose of a variation is formally defined in the same influence language.

Included in the search after a certain move of White are either the moves influenced by this move of White, or by Black's response, or by "globally acting" moves. Without the implementation of this idea it is not plain how a program built round this principle would play: nevertheless, the results of adaptive search algorithms show that influence language is reliable for determining the deep-rooted links between moves.

Another direction in which these algorithms could develop is in making a Reference Book structure more sophisticated, so that it could represent more complex search elements. For instance, once an element has been associated with the previous move, the existing algorithms lose it altogether. After the same move is made on a different search branch, all the elements are constructed anew. A more sophisticated structure would avoid reconstructing these elements.

The work carried out has shown the potential of the chess program KAISSA as a test-bench for algorithms which need only little infacing with search algorithms. In particular, routines using human chess experience can be developed over these algorithms.

REFERENCE

[1] Adelson-Velsky, G. M., Arlazarov, V. L. and Donskoy, M. V. (1975). Some methods of controlling the tree-search in chess programs. *Artificial Intelligence*, **6**, 361–71.

19

A Bibliography of Computer Chess

T. A. Marsland

Computing Science Department
University of Alberta

The following is a fairly comprehensive list of English language articles on computer chess. Although works about related games like checkers and GO have been excluded, it would be wrong not to refer here to A. L. Samuel's early masterpiece "Some studies in machine learning using the game of checkers" In *IBM J. Res. Dev.*, **3**, (1959) 210-229, also in *Computers and Thought* (eds. E. A. Feigenbaum and J. Feldman) McGraw-Hill 1963, pp. 71-105 and *IBM J. Res. Dev.*, **11**, 601-617, and to the follow-up papers by A. K. Griffiths, "A new machine learning technique applied to the game of checkers" *AI Memo 94*, Project MAC, Cambridge, USA: Mass. Inst. Techn. (1966), and "A comparison and evaluation of three machine learning procedures as applied to the game of checkers" *Artificial Intelligence*, **5**, 1974, 137-148. In addition, a few chess books have been listed which are known to contain useful data or ideas for programmers, along with a number of papers on general mechanisms and theoretical foundations. It is probably not possible to account for all the articles which have been written on the subject of computer chess. In particular, 'popular press' items have in general been neglected, as also have reviews of books or papers.

This bibliography is available in machine-readable form. Its generation was simplified through the use of a program developed by Ken J. McDonell, whose general assistance was much appreciated. Many people reviewed and commented upon early drafts, the comments and observations by Max Bramer and Hartmut Tanke being especially valuable. Readers may also be interested in the excellent annotated bibliography by Harald Reksten [259], whose reviews include not only quotations and paraphrased abstracts, but interesting observations. For computer chess works in other languages, especially German and Russian, a revised version of the bibliography by Egbert Meissenberg "Schach liche leistungen von computer", Deutsche Schachblaetter (1968), 1-4, is reputed to be the most correct.

BIBLIOGRAPHY

1. Adelson-Velsky, G. M., Arlazarov, V. L., Bitman, A. R., Zhivotovskii, A. A., and Uskov, A. V. (1969). Programming a computer to play chess. *Proc. 1st summer school Math. Prog.*, 2, 216-252. Also (Russian) *Math. Surveys*, **25**, Mar-Apr 1970, 221-262.
2. Adelson-Velsky, G. M., Arlazarov, V. L., and Donskoy, M. V. (1974). More commentary of the Cichelli heuristics. *Sigart Newsletter*, **45**, 12.
3. Adelson-Velsky, G. M., Arlazarov, V. L., and Donskoy, M. V. (1975). On the structure of an important class of exhaustive problems and on ways of search reduction for them. Advance Papers *4th Int. Joint Conf.* on *A.I.*, Tbilisi, 304-308. Also in *Advances in Computer Chess 1*, pp. 1-6 (ed. M. R. B. Clarke). Edinburgh: Edinburgh University Press.
4. Adelson-Velsky, G. M., Arlazarov, V. L., and Donskoy, M. V. (1975). Some methods of controlling the tree search in chess programs. *Artificial Intelligence*, **6**, 361-371.
5. Adelson-Velsky, G. M., Arlazarov, V. L., and Donskoy, M. V. (1979). Algorithms of adaptive search. *Machine Intelligence 9* (eds. J. E. Hayes, D. Michie, and L. I. Mikulich). Chichester: Ellis Horwood and New York: John Wiley (Halsted Press) (this volume).
6. Akl, S. G., and Newborn, M. M. (1977). The principal continuation and the killer heuristic. *Proc. ACM77*, Seattle, 466-473.
7. Alekhine, A. *The New York International Tournament 1924* (ed. H. Helms). Dover reprint 1961.
8. Alekseev, V. E. (1969). Compilation of chess problems on a computer. *Technical translation FSTC-HT-23-124-69*, US Army, NTIS AD 689470 (*Problemy Kibernetiki*, **19**, 1967).
9. Arlazarov, V. L., and Futer, A. V. (1979). Computer analysis of a Rook end-game. *Machine Intelligence 9*, (eds. J. E. Hayes, D. Michie, and L. I. Mikulich). Chichester: Ellis Horwood and New York: John Wiley (Halsted Press) (this volume).
10. Arnold, G. and Newborn, M. M. (1972). A chess playing program: the OSTRICH. *ACM72 Computer chess notes*. Boston, 10-14.
11. Ashby, W. R. (1952). Can a mechanical chess player outplay its designer? *British Journal of Philosophy of Science*, **3**.
12. Atkin, L. R. (1975). *Chess 3.6: A chess playing computer program*. Master's thesis. Evanston: Northwestern University.
13. Atkin, R. H. (1972). Multi-dimensional structure on the game of chess. *Int. J. of Man-Machine Studies*, **4**, 341-362.
14. Atkin, R. H. (1977). Positional play in chess by computer. *Advances in Computer Chess 1*, pp. 60-73 (ed. M. R. B. Clarke). Edinburgh: Edinburgh University Press.
15. Atkin, L. R., Gorlen, K., and Slate, D. J. (1971). *Chess 3.0 – An Experiment in Heuristic Programming*. Privately circulated, Northwestern Univ.

16. Atkin, R. H., Hartston, W., and Whitten, I. H. (1976). Fred CHAMP, positional-chess analyst. *Int. J. Man-Machine Studies*, **8**, 517-529.
17. Atkin, R. H., and Witten, I. H. (1975). A multidimensional approach to positional chess. *Int. J. Man-Machine Studies*, **7**, 727-750. Also in *Computer Chess*, pp. 37-79 (ed. A. G. Bell). Chilton: SRC Atlas Laboratory.
18. Banerji, R. B. (1969). *An overview of game playing programs.* Tech. Report. Cleveland: Case Western Reserve University.
19. Banerji, R. B. (1971). Similarities in games and their use in strategy construction. *Computers and Automata: Proc. 21st Brooklyn Polytechnic Symposium*, 337-357.
20. Banjeri, R. B., and Ernst, G. W. (1971). Changes in representation which preserve strategies in games. *Proc. 2nd Int. Conf. on AI*, pp. 651-658. London: British Computer Society (longer version available in a technical report of same name. Cleveland: Case Western Reserve University).
21. Barker, R. (1971). *Report on human game-playing as illustrated by the game of halma.* M.Sc. thesis. London: Computer Science Department, Queen Mary College.
22. Barnes, C. (1976). *Computer chess techniques.* Report for CS H198. Berkley: Comp. Sci. and Elec. Eng. Dept., University of California.
23. Baudet, G. M. (1978). On the branching factor of the alpha-beta pruning algorithm. *Artificial Intelligence*, **10**, 173-199.
24. Baylor, G. W. (1965). *Report on a mating combinations program.* SDC Paper SP-2150.
25. Baylor, G. W. (1966). A computer model of checkmating behaviour in chess. *Heuristic Processes in Thinking* (eds. A. D. De Groot and W. R. Reitman). Moscow: Nauka.
26. Baylor, G. W., and Simon, H. A. (1966). A chess mating combinations program. *SJCC*, 431-447.
27. Beal, D. (1977). *Discriminating wins from draws in King + Pawn versus King chess endgames*. Privately circulated. London: Queen Mary College.
28. Beal, D. F. (1979). Staged search in minimax trees. *Advances in Computer Chess 2* (ed. M. R. B. Clarke). Edinburgh: Edinburgh University Press (in press).
29. Beal, D. F., and Clarke, M. R. B. (1979). Economical and provably correct algorithms for King and Pawn against King. *Advances in Computer Chess 2* (ed. M. R. B. Clarke). Edinburgh: Edinburgh University Press (in press).
30. Bell, A. G. (ed.) (1973). *Computer Chess. Proc. May 73 Meeting on Chess Playing by Computer.* Chilton. SRC Atlas Laboratory, Oct. 1973.
31. Bell, A. G. (1968). Kalah on Atlas. *Machine Intelligence 3*, pp. 181-194 (ed. D. Michie). Edinburgh: Edinburgh University Press.
32. Bell, A. G. (1970). Algorithm 50: how to program a computer to play legal chess. *Computer Journal*, **13**, 208-219.
33. Bell, A. G. (1972). *Games Playing with Computers.* London: Allen and Unwin.

34. Bell, A. G. (1973). Computer chess experiments. *Computer Chess*, pp. 1-14 (ed. A. G. Bell). Chilton: SRC Atlas Laboratory.

35. Bell, A. G., Hallowell, P. J., and Long, D. H. (1973). A university benchmark. *Software Practice and Experience*, **3**, 355-357.

36. Bellman, R. (1965). On the application of dynamic programming to the determination of optimal play in chess and checkers. *Proc. Nat. Acad. Sci.*, **53**, 244-247.

37. Bellman, R. (1968). Stratification and control of large systems with applications to chess and checkers. *Information Sciences*, **1**, 7-21.

38. Berliner, H. J. (1969). Chess playing programs, **17**, 19-20. *Sigart Newsletter*, **17**, 19-20.

39. Berliner, H. J. (1970). Experiences gained in constructing and testing a chess program. *IEEE Symp. Sys. Sci. and Cyb*., pp. 216-223. Pittsburgh.

40. Berliner, H. J. (1973). Some necessary conditions for a master chess program. *Proc. 3rd Int. Joint Conf. on AI*, pp. 77-85. Menlo Park: Stanford Research Institute.

41. Berliner, H. J. (1974). *Chess as problem solving: the development of a tactics analyzer*. Ph.D. thesis. Pittsburgh: Carnegie-Mellon University.

42. Berliner, H. J. (1974). A comment on improvement of chess playing programs. *Sigart Newsletter*, **48**, 16.

43. Berliner, H. J. (1975). A new sub-field of computer chess, *Sigart Newsletter*, **53**, 20-21.

44. Berliner, H. J. (1975). Computer chess. *Sigart Newsletter*, **55**, 14-15.

45. Berliner, H. J. (1976). Outstanding performance by CHESS 4.5 against human competition. *Sigart Newsletter*, **60**, 12-13.

46. Berliner, H. J. (1976). Man against machine 1974. *Firbush News 6*, pp. 63-70. Edinburgh: Machine Intelligence Research Unit.

47. Berliner, H. J. (1977). A representation and some mechanisms for a problem solving chess program. *Advances in Computer Chess 1*, pp. 7-29 (ed. M. R. B. Clarke). Edinburgh: Edinburgh University Press.

48. Berliner, H. (1977). Two games from the Minnesota Open. *Sigart Newsletter*, **62**, 9-10.

49. Berliner, H. (1977). CHESS 4.5 vs. Levy. *Sigart Newsletter*, **62**, 11.

50. Berliner, H. J. (1977). On the use of domain-independent descriptions in tree searching. *Perspectives in Computer Science*, 10th Aniv. of C.S. at C.M.U., (ed. Jones). New York: Academic Press.

51. Berliner, H. L. (1977). Search and knowledge. *Proc. Fifth Int. Joint Conf. on AI*, 975-979.

52. Berliner, H. J. (1978). A chronology of computer chess and its literature. *Artificial Intelligence*, **10**, 201-204.

53. Berliner, H. J. (1978). Computer chess. *Nature*, **274**, 745-748.

54. Bernstein, A. and Roberts, M. de V. (1958). Computer vs chess player. *Scientific American*, **198**, 96-105.

55. Bernstein, A., Roberts, M. de V., Arbuckle, T., and Belsky, M. A. (1958). A chess playing program for the IBM 704. *Western Joint Computer Conference*, 157-159.

56. Binet, A. (1893). Mnemonic virtuosity: a study of chess players. *Genetic Psych. Monog.*, **74**, 1966, 127-162. (Translation of 1893 paper in *Revue des Deux Mondes*, **117**).

57. Birmingham, J. A., and Kent, P. (1977). Tree-searching and tree-pruning techniques. *Advances in Computer Chess 1*, pp. 89-107 (ed. M. R. B. Clarke). Edinburgh: Edinburgh University Press.

58. Birmingham, J. A. and Kent, P. (1979). Mate at a glance. *Advances in Computer Chess 2* (ed. M. R. B. Clarke). Edinburgh: Edinburgh University Press (in press).

59. Bond, A. H. (1973). Psychology and computer chess, *Computer Chess*, pp. 29-36 (ed. A. G. Bell). Chilton: SRC Atlas Laboratory.

60. Bond, A. H. (1973). Descriptor Index. *Computer Chess*, pp. 95-112 (ed. A. G. Bell). Chilton: SRC Atlas Laboratory.

61. Boos, G., Cooper, D. W., Gillogly, J. J., Levy, D. N. L., Raymond, H., Slate, D. J., Smith, R. C., and Mittman, B. Computer chess programs (panel). *Proc. 1971 Annual ACM Conference*, **25**, 97-102.

62. Boos, G. (1972). The VIKING: *ACM72 Computer chess notes*, Boston 41-42.

63. Botvinnik, M. M. (1970). *Computers, Chess amd Long-Range Planning.* New York: Springer Verlag.

64. Botvinnik, M. M. (1975). Will computers get self-respect? *Sovietsky Sport.*

65. Bramer, M. A. (1975). *Representation of knowledge for chess endgames.* Technical Report. Milton Keynes: Open University.

66. Bramer, M. A. (1976). Computer chess: the knowledge approach. *Chess*, **41**, 347-349.

67. Bramer, M. A. (1977). *King and Pawn against King: some quantitative data.* Techincal Report. Milton Keynes: Open University.

68. Bramer, M. A. (1977). *King and Pawn against King: using effective distance.* Technical Report. Milton Keynes: Open University.

69. Bramer, M. A. (1977). *Representation of knowledge for chess endgames: towards a self-improving system.* Ph.D. thesis. Milton Keynes: Open University.

70. Bramer, M. A. (1978). *Computer-generated databases for the endgame in chess.* Technical Report. Milton Keynes: Open University.

71. Bramer, M. A. (1979). An optimal algorithm for king and pawn against king. *Advances in Computer Chess 2* (ed. M. R. B. Clarke). Edinburgh: Edinburgh University Press (in press).

72. Bratko, I. (1978). Proving correctness of strategies in the AL1 assertional language. *Information Processing Letters*, **7**, 223-230.

73. Bratko, I., Kopec, D., and Michie, D. (1978). Pattern-based representation of chess end-game knowledge. *Computer Journal*, **21**, 149-153.
74. Bratko, I., and Michie, D. (1978). Advice table representations of chess endgame knowledge. *Proc. 3rd AISB/GI Conf. on AI*, (ed. D. Sleeman), 194-200.
75. Bratko, I., and Michie, D. (1979). A representation for pattern-knowledge in chess end-games. *Advances in Computer Chess 2* (ed. M. R. B. Clarke). Edinburgh: Edinburgh University Press.
76. Bratko, I., and Tancig, P. (1975). On the role of strategy in computer chess. *3rd Int. Conf. on Cyb. and Gen. Syst.* Bucharest: Abacus Press, Int. Scol. Book Serv.
77. Bratko, I., Tancig, P., and Tancig, S. (1976). Some new aspects of chess board reconstruction experiments. *3rd European meeting on Cyb. and Sys. Res.*, Vienna.
78. Brundo, A. L. (1968). Bounds and valuations for shortening the scanning of variations. *Probl. Kibernetiki*, **10**, 141-150.
79. Buckholtz, T. J., and Wetherell, C. S. (1975). A program to referee kriegspiel and chess. *Computer Journal*, **18**, 177-183.
80. Burger, J. F. (1967). UMPIRE: and automatic kriegspiel referee for a time-shared computer. *Proc. 22nd Nat. Conf., ACM*, 187-193.
81. Cahlander, D. (1977). *Tournament games of a chess playing computer.* Minneapolis: Control Data Corporation.
82. Callon, R., and Willoner, R. (1975). *A chess-problem solver.* Class note for course CS502. University of British Columbia.
83. Carley, G. (1962). *A program to play contract bridge.* M.Sc. thesis. Cambridge, USA: Dept. of Elec. Eng., Mass. Inst. of Technology.
84. Cerf, V., and Kline, C. (1969). *The Greenblatt chess program*. Unpublished term paper at UCLA.
85. Charness, N. (1974). *Memory for chess positions: the effects of inference and input modality*. Doctoral dissertation. Pittsburgh: Carnegie-Mellon University.
86. Charness, N. (1977). Human chess skill. *Chess Skill in Man and Machine* pp. 34-53 (ed. P. J. Frey). New York: Springer-Verlag.
87. Chase, W. G., and Simon, H. A. (1973). Perception in chess. *Cog. Psych.*, **4**, 55-81.
88. Church, R. M., and Church, K. W. (1977). Plans, goals, and search strategies for the selection of a move in chess. *Chess Skill in Man and Machine*, pp. 131-156 (ed. P. J. Frey). New York: Springer-Verlag.
89. Cichelli, R. J. (1973). Research progress report in computer chess. *Sigart Newsletter*, **41**, 32-36.
90. Cichelli, R. J. (1973). Preliminary testing of the effectivenesss of the Cichelli depth-2 and refutation heuristics. *Sigart Newsletter*, **42**, 49-52.
91. Cichelli, R. J. (1973). Reader commentary on the Cichelli heuristics, *Sigart Newsletter*, **43**, 27-28.

92. Citrenbaum, R. L. (1970). *Efficient representation of optimal solutions for a class of games.* Thesis. Technical Report SRC-69-5. Cleveland: Case Western Reserve University.
93. Clarke, M. R. B. (1977). A quantitative study of King and Pawn against King. *Advances in Computer Chess 1*, pp. 108-118 (ed. M. R. B. Clarke). Edinburgh: Edinburgh University Press.
94. Clarke, M. R. B. (1973). Some ideas for a chess compiler. *Artificial and Human Thinking*, pp. 189-198 (eds. A. Elithorn and D. Jones). Amsterdam: Elsevier.
95. Clarke, M. R. B. (ed.) (1977/1979). *Advances in Computer Chess 1 and 2.* Edinburgh: Edinburgh University Press.
96. Clarke, M. R. B. (1979). Kings and pawns: the theory of co-ordinate squares. *Advances in Computer Chess 2* (ed. M. R. B. Clarke). Edinburgh: Edinburgh University Press (in press).
97. Cooper, D. W., and Kozdrowicki, E. W. (1973). *COKO User Manual.* Privately circulated.
98. Cooper, D. W. (1972). *Heuristic tree searching in the game of chess.* Privately circulated.
99. Cooper, R., and Elithorn, A. (1973). The organization of search procedures. *Artificial and Human Thinking*, pp. 199-213 (eds. A. Elithorn, and D. Jones). Amsterdam: Elsevier.
100. Coriat, I. H. (1941). The unconscious motives of interest in chess. *Psychoanalytic Review*, **28**, 30-36.
101. Courtois, G. (1975). *Etaoin Shrdlu Documentation.* Privately circulated, Boulder, University.
102. Daly, W. (1961). *Computer strategies for the game of Qubic.* M.Sc. thesis. Cambridge, USA: Electrical Engineering, Mass Inst. of Techn.
103. De Groot, A. D. (1964). Chess playing programs. *Proc. Kononkl Nedrlands Akad. Wentensch.*, Amsterdam, ser A-67, 385-398.
104. De Groot, A. D. (1965). *Thought and Choice in Chess.* The Hague: Mouton.
105. De Groot, A. D. (1966). Perception and memory versus thought: some old ideas and recent findings. *Problem Solving* (ed. B. Kleinmuntz). New York: John Wiley.
106. Douglas, J. R. (1978). GM Walter Browne vs. CHESS 4.6. *Chess Life and Review*, **33**, 363-364.
107. Dunning, C. A., Ko, H. M., and Banerji, R. B. (1969). *Some results on graph interpretable games.* Technical Report. Cleveland: Case Western Reserve University.
108. Edwards, D. J. and Hart, T. P. (1963). The alpha-beta algorithm. *MIT AI Memo, 30.* Cambridge, USA: Mass. Inst. Techn.
109. Eisenstadt, M. and Kareev, Y. (1973). Towards a model of human game playing. *Proc. 3rd Int. Joint Conf. on AI*, pp. 458-463. Menlo Park. Stanford Research Institute.

110. Elithorn, A. and Jagoe, R. (1969). The computer analysis of human problem solving behaviour: the choice of problem. *Proc. NATO Symp. on the Computer Simulation of Human Behaviour*, Paris.

111. Elithorn, A. and Telford, A. (1969). Computer analysis of intellectual skills. *Int. J. Man-Machine Studies*, **1**, 189-209.

112. Elithorn, A. and Telford, A. (1970). Game and problem structure in relation to the study of human and artificial intelligence. *Nature*, **227**, 1205-1210.

113. Euwe, M. (1970). Computers and chess. *The Encyclopedia of Chess*, pp. 78-88 (ed. A. Sunnucks). London: St. Martin's Press.

114. Findler, N. V. Computer experiments on the formation and optimization of heuristic rules. *Artificial and Human Thinking*, pp. 117-188 (eds. A. Elithorn and D. Jones). Amsterdam: Elsevier.

115. Fine, R. (1941). *Basic Chess Endings*. New York: David McKay Co. Inc.

116. Frey, P. J. (ed.) (1977). *Chess Skill in Man and Machine*. New York: Springer-Verlag.

117. Frey, P. J. (1977). An introduction to computer chess. *Chess Skill in Man and Machine*, pp. 54-81, 210-205 (ed. P. J. Frey). New York. Springer-Verlag.

118. Fuller, S. H., Gasching, J. G., and Gillogly, J. J. (1973). *Analysis of the alpha-beta pruning algorithm*. Technical Report. Pittsburgh: Carnegie-Mellon Univ.

119. Garst, B. (1976). *A report on the validation of AQVAL's King-can-take-Pawn expressions*. Project for CS397. Urbann-Champaign Dept. of Computer Science, Univ. of Illinois.

120. Gillogly. J. J. (1970). *Max: a Fortran chess player*. Technical Report. P-4428. Santa Monica. Rand Corporation.

121. Gillogly, J. J. (1972). The technology chess program. *Artificial Intelligence*, **3**, 145-163.

122. Gillogly, J. J. (1977). Games. *Encyclopedia of Computer Science and Technology*, Vol. 8, 392-408.

123. Gillogly, J. J. (1978). *Performance analysis of the Technology chess program*. Technical Report CMU-CS-78-189. Pittsburgh: Computer Science Dept., Carnegie-Mellon Univ.

124. Good, I. J. (1968). A five year plan for automatic chess. *Machine Intelligence 2*, pp. 89-118. (eds. E. Dale and D. Michie). Edinburgh: Edinburgh University Press.

125. Good, I. J. (1969). Analysis of the machine chess game J. Scott (White), ICL-1900 versus R. D. Greenblatt, PDP-10. *Machine Intelligence 4*, pp. 267-269 (eds. B. Meltzer and D. Michie). Edinburgh: Edinburgh University Press.

126. Good, I. J. (1976). Dynamic probability, computer chess, and the mesurement of knowledge. *Firbush News 6*, 43-62. Edinburgh: Machine Intelli-

gence Research Unit. Also in *Machine Intelligence 8,* pp. 139–150 (eds. E. W. Elcock and D. Michie). Edinburgh. Edinburgh University Press.

127. Greenblatt, R. D., Eastlake, D. E., and Crocker, S. D. (1967). The Greenblatt chess program. *Proceedings of the FJCC,* **31**, 801–810.

128. Greene, P. (1961). Networks which realise a model for information representation. *Trans. Univ. Illinois Symp. Self Org.*

129. Griffith, A. K. (1976). Empirical exploration of the performance of the alpha-beta tree search heuristic. *IEEE Trans. on Computers,* 6–10.

130. Hadiev, R. E. (1975). Experimental studies of human decision-making etc. (on the basis of a chess endgame). Advance Papers of the *4th Int. Joint Conf. on AI,* Tbilisi, pp. 912–916. Cambridge, Mass.: Mass. Inst. Tech.

131. Haldane, J. B. S. (1952). The mechanical chess-player. *British Journal of Philosophy of Science,* **3**, 189–191.

132. Hansen, R. (1977). *TREEFROG: a chess program.* Master of Math. essay, Computer Science, Univ. of Waterloo, Canada.

133. Harkness, K. and Battell, J. S. (1947). This made chess history. *Chess Review.* Feb.–Nov.

134. Harris, L. R. (1972). *A model for adaptive problem solving applied to natural language acquisition.* Technical Report TR72-133. Ithaca: Cornell University.

135. Harris, L. R. (1973). The bandwidth heuristic search. *Proc. 3rd Int. Joint. Conf. on AI,* Stanford, 23–29. Menlo Park: Stanford Research Institute.

136. Harris, L. R. (1974). The heuristic search under conditions of error, and plan oriented play. *Artificial Intelligence,* **5**, 217–239.

137. Harris, L. R. (1975). The heuristic search and the game of chess: a study of quiescence sacrifices, and plan oriented play. Advance Papers *4th Int. Joint Conf. on AI,* Tbilisi, pp. 334–339. Cambridge, Mass.: Mass. Inst. Techn.

138. Harris, L. R. (1977). The heuristic search: an alternative to the alpha-beta minimax procedure. *Chess Skill in Man and Machine,* pp. 157–166 (ed. P. J. Frey). New York: Springer-Verlag.

139. Hayes, J. E. and Levy, D. N. L. (1976). *The World Computer Chess Championship,* Edinburgh: Edinburgh Univ. Press.

140. Hearst, E. (1977). Man and machine: chess achievements and chess thinking. *Chess Skill in Man and Machine,* pp. 167–200 (ed. P. J. Frey). New York: Springer-Verlag.

141. Horning, J. J. (1972). *Outline of a strategy for a chess playing program.* Unpublished. Toronto: Dept. of Computer Science, Univ. of Toronto.

142. Horowitz, I. A. and Mott-Smith, G. (1973). *Point Count Chess.* London: Allen & Unwin.

143. Huberman, B. J. (1968). *A program to play chess end games.* Ph.D. thesis. Technical Memo CS 106. Stanford: Computer Science Department, Stanford University.

144. Hyatt, R. M. (1977). *BLITZ V, a computer chess program.* Privately circulated.

145. Jackson, P. C. (1974). *Introduction to Artificial Intelligence.* Petrocelli/ Charter.

146. Jennings, P. R. (1978). The second world computer chess championship. *BYTE magazine*, 108–118.

147. Jones, R. D. (1971). *The design and implementation of a chess playing program for the IBM 360.* M.Sc. thesis. Univ. of Toronto.

148. Kalme, C. I. (1974). *Teaching chess at the human and machine level.* Psychology Program Report. Dept. of Mathematics, University of Indiana.

149. Kalme, C. I. (1974). *The basic search routine for the move in chess.* Psychology Program Report. Dept. of Mathematics, University of Indiana.

150. Kent, P. A simple working model. *Computer Chess*, pp. 15–27 (ed. A. G. Bell). Chilton: SRC Atlas Laboratory.

151. Kent, P. and Birmingham, J. A. (1979). Structural description of MASTER. *Advances in Computer Chess 2* (ed. M. R. B. Clarke). Edinburgh: Edinburgh University Press (in press).

152. King, P. F. (1971). *A computer program for positional games.* Report 1107. Pittsburgh: Jennings Computer Centre, Case Western Reserve University.

153. Kister, J., Stein, P., Ulam, S., Walden, W., and Wells, M. (1957). Experiments in chess. *Jour. Assoc. Comp. Mach.*, **4**, 174–177.

154. Kitov, A. I. and Krinitsky, N. A. (1962). The solution of chess problems: programme controlled computers playing chess. *Electronic Computers*, pp. 106–108. Oxford: Pergamon.

155. Kmoch, H. (1969). *Pawn Power in Chess.* McKay.

156. Knuth, D. E. and Moore, R. (1975). An analysis of alpha-beta pruning. *Artificial Intelligence*, **6**, 293–326.

157. Koffman, E. B. (1967). *Learning through pattern recognition applied to a class of games.* Systems Research Centre Report SRC 107-1-67-45. Cleveland: Case Institute of Technology.

158. Koniver, D. (1963). *Computer heuristics for five-in-a-row.* M.Sc. thesis, Mathematics, Mass. Inst. of Techn.

159. Kopec, D. (1977). Recent developments in computer chess. *Firbush News 7*, 28–36. Edinburgh: Machine Intelligence Research Unit.

160. Kopec, D. and Niblett, T. (1979). How hard is the play of the King & Rook v. King & Knight ending? *Advances in Computer Chess 2* (ed. M. R. B. Clarke). Edinburgh: Edinburgh University Press (in press).

161. Kotok, A. (1962). *A chess playing program for the IBM 7090.* B.S. thesis, AI Project Memo 41. Cambridge, USA: Computation Center, Mass. Inst. Techn.

162. Kotov, A. (1971). *Think Like a Grandmaster.* Dallas: Chess Digest.

163. Kozdrowicki, E. W. (1967). *An adaptive tree pruning system: a language*

for programming heuristic tree searches. Defense Documentation Center, No. AD663750.

164. Kozdrowicki, E. W. (1968). A practical application of machine learning: use of learning in an interpreter for a tree searching language. *Proc. IEEE Systems Science and Cybernetics Conf.*, San Francisco, Ca., 250-257.
165. Kozdrowicki, E. W. (1968). An adaptive tree pruning system: a language for programming heuristic tree searches. *Proc. ACM National Conference*, 725-735.
166. Kozdrowicki, E. W. (1969). The complexity of chess algorithms: the limitations of machines when compared with human thought. *Proc. 3 Princeton Conf. on Inf. Sci. and Sys.*, 92-96.
167. Kozdrowicki, E. W. and Cooper, D. W. (1973). COKO III. The Cooper-Koz chess program. *Comm. Ass. Comp. Mach.*, **16**, 411-427.
168. Kozdrowicki, E. W. and Cooper, D. W. (1974). COKO III: The Cooper-Kozdrowicki chess program. *Int. Jour. Man-machine studies*, **6**,627-699.
169. Kozdrowicki, E. W. and Cooper, D. W. (1974). COKO III and the future of inter-snap judgement communication. *Proc. ACM73*, Atlanta, 213-218.
170. Kozdrowicki, E. W., Licwinko, J. S., and Cooper, D. W. (1971). Algorithms for a minimal chess player: a blitz player. *Int. Jour. Man-machine Studies*, **3**, 141-165.
171. Levy, D. N. L. (1968). *A measure of the performance of evaluation functions*. Privately circulated.
172. Levy, D. N. L. (1969). Computerised chess: prospects. *Chess*, April 22, 242-245 + 245-251.
173. Levy, D. N. L. (1971). Computer chess – a case study on the CDC 6600. *Machine Intelligence 6*, pp. 151-163 (eds. B. Meltzer and D. Michie). Edinburgh: Edinburgh University Press.
174. Levy, D. N. L. (1973). Computer chess – past, present and future, *Chess Life and Review*, **28**, December, 723-726.
175. Levy, D. N. L. (1976). *1975 U.S. Computer Chess Championship*. Woodland Hills, California: Computer Science Press.
176. Levy, D. N. L. (1976). The robots are coming: or are they? *Chess Life and Review*, May, 250-260.
177. Levy, D. N. L. (1976). *Chess and Computers*. London: Batsford.
178. Levy, D. (1977). Invasion from cyberland. *Chess Life and Review*, **32**, 312-313.
179. Levy, D. N. L. (1977). *1976 U.S. Computer Chess Championship*. Woodland Hills, California. Computer Science Press.
180. Levy, D. N. L. (1978). *Computer Chess 1977: World computer chess championship, US computer chess championship*. Woodland Hills, California: Computer Science Press.
181. Levy, D. N. L. (1978). *Can computer programs play real chess?* Presented at the Third Jerusalem Conf. on Info. Technology (JCIT), August.

182. London, R. L. and Salako, A. *Game playing by computer: a selected bibliography*. Comp. Sci. Dept., Univ. Wisconsin.

183. Malik, R. (1973). Observations. *Computer Chess*, pp. 89-94 (ed. A. G. Bell). Chilton: SRC Atlas Lab.

184. Manning, J. R. (1971). White to move and mate in N moves. *Computer Journal*, **14**, Algorithm 68, 209-213.

185. Marino, L. R. (1966). *Winning and non-losing strategies in games and control*. Technical Report SRC 91-A-66-36. Cleveland: Case Western Reserve University.

186. Marsland, T. A. (1972). *WITA, a selective search chess program in Algol W.* Privately circulated.

187. Marsland, T. A. (1974). *Users guide to WITA, a chess playing program.* Technical Report TR74-2. Edmonton: Comp. Sci. Dept., Univ. Alberta.

188. Marsland, T. A. (1977). 1976 Canadian computer chess workshop. *Firbush News* 7, 37-40. Edinburgh: Machine Intelligence Research Unit.

189. Marsland, T. A. and Rushton, P. G. (1973). A study of techniques for game-playing programs. *J. I. Computer Science*, **4**, No. 2, 26-30. Also *Advances in Cyb. & Systems*, **1**, 1974, 363-371.

190. Marsland, T. A. and Rushton, P. G. (1973). Mechanisms for comparing chess programs. *Proc. 1973 ACM Annual Conference*, 202-205.

191. Matanovic, A. (1971). Chess Informant – Classification of chess openings.

192. Maynard-Smith, J. and Michie, D. (1961). Machines that play games. *New Scientist*, November, 367-369.

193. McCarthy, J. (1968). Programs with common sense. *Semantic Information Processing*, pp. 403-418 (ed. M. Minsky) MIT Press. Reprinted from *Mechanisation of Thought Processes*. London: HMSO, 1957.

194. Michalski, R. and Negri, P. (1977). An experiment on inductive learning in chess end games. *Machine Intelligence 8*, pp. 175-192 (eds. E. W. Elcock and D. Michie). Chichester: Ellis Horwood Ltd., and New York: John Wiley (Halsted Press).

195. Michie, D. (1965). Game playing and game learning automata. *Programming and Non-numerical Computation*, pp. 183-200 (ed. L. Fox). Oxford: Pergamon Press.

196. Michie, D. (1972). Programmer's gambit. *New Scientist*, **56**, Aug. 329-332. Also in *On Machine Intelligence*. Edinburgh: Edinburgh University Press, 1974.

197. Michie, D. (1973). Knowledge Engineering. *Kybernetics, International Journal of Cybernetics and General Systems*, 2, 197-200. Also in *On Machine Intelligence*. Edinburgh: Edinburgh University Press, 1974.

198. Michie, D. (1974). *A theory of evaluative comments in chess*. Research Memorandum MIP-R-105. Edinburgh: Machine Intelligence Research Unit.

199. Michie, D. (1974). *On Machine Intelligence*, pp. 31-49, 135-142, 186--192. Edinburgh: Edinburgh University Press.

200. Michie, D. (1976). An advice taking system for computer chess. *Computer Bulletin*, December, 12-14.
201. Michie, D. (1976). AL1: A package for generating strategies from tables. *Sigart Newsletter*, **59**, 12-14.
202. Michie, D. (1976). *Measuring the knowledge content of programs*. Technical Report UIUCDCS-R-76-786. Comp. Sci. Dept., Univ. Illinois.
203. Michie, D. (1977). King and Rook against King: historical background and a problem on the infinite board. *Advances in Computer Chess 1*, pp. 30-59 (ed. M. R. B. Clarke). Edinburgh: Edinburgh University Press.
204. Michie, D. (1977). A theory of Advice. *Machine Intelligence 8*, pp. 151-168 (eds. E. W. Elcock and D. Michie). Chichester: Ellis Horwood Ltd., and New York: John Wiley (Halsted Press).
205. Michie, D. (1977). David Levy challenge game, 1 April 1977. *Sigart Newsletter*, **62**, 10-11.
206. Michie, D. (1979). Chess with computers. *Interdisciplinary Science Reviews* (in press).
207. Michie, D. (1979). A prototype knowledge refinery. *Advances in Computer Chess 2* (ed. M. R. B. Clarke). Edinburgh: Edinburgh University Press (in press).
208. Michie, D. and Bratko, I. (1978). Advice table representations of chess end-game knowledge. *Proc. 3rd AISB Summer Conference on Artif. Int. 1978*, (ed. D. Sleeman), 194-200.
209. Michie, D. (1979). Machine models of perceptual and intellectual skills. In *Scientific Models and Man*. The 1976 Heibat Spencer Lectures (ed. H. Harris). Oxford: Oxford University Press.
210. Michie, J. E. (ed.). *Firbush Chess Supplements* **5**, **6**, **7**, **8** (1974, 76, 77, 78). Edinburgh: Machine Intelligence Research Unit, University of Edinburgh.
211. Minker, J. (1975). A review of COKO III. *ACM Computing Reviews*, No. 28820, **16**, 369-370.
212. Mittman, B. (1973). Can a computer beat Bobby Fischer? *Datamation*, **19**, June, 84-87.
213. Mittman, B. (1974). First World Computer Chess Championship at IFIP Congress, Stockholm, August 1974. *Comm. of the ACM*, **17**, 604.
214. Mittman, B. (1977). A brief history of computer chess tournaments: 1970-1975. *Chess Skill in Man and Machine*, pp. 1-33 (ed. P. J. Frey). New York: Springer-Verlag.
215. Morrison, M. E. (1976). 4th annual Paul Masson American Class Championship, *Chess Life and Review*, **31**, 553.
216. Moullen, F. L. (1968). Chess and the computer. *Datamation*, **14**, April, 65-68.
217. Moussouris, J., Holloway, J., and Greenblatt, R. (1979). CHEOPS: a chess-oriented processing system. *Machine Intelligence 9* (eds. J. E. Hayes, D. Michie, and L. I. Mikulich). Chichester: Ellis Horwood, and New York: John Wiley (Halsted Press) (this volume).

218. Myron, M. S. and May, W. H. (1963). A note on serendipity, aesthetics and problem solving. *Behavioral Science*, **8**, 242–243.

219. Negri, P. (1977). Inductive learning in a hierarchical model for representing knowledge in chess end games. *Machine Intelligence 8*, pp. 193–204 (eds. E. W. Elcock and D. Michie). Chichester: Ellis Horwood, and New York: John Wiley (Halsted Press).

220. Nemes, T. N. (1969). *Cybernetic Machines* (translated by I. Foldes from 1962 Hungarian edition), Iliffe Books.

221. Newborn, M. M. (1972). A review of the 1st and 2nd US Computer Championships and an analysis of recent developments in computer chess. *ACM72 Computer chess notes*, Boston 1972, 1–9.

222. Newborn, M. M. (1975). *Computer Chess*. New York: Academic Press.

223. Newborn, M. M. (1977). PEASANT: An endgame program for Kings and Pawns. *Chess Skill in Man and Machine*, pp. 119–130 (ed. P. J. Frey). New York: Springer-Verlag.

224. Newborn, M. M. (1977). The efficiency of the alpha-beta search on trees with branch-dependent terminal node scores. *Artificial Intelligence* 8, 137–153.

225. Newborn, M. M. (1978). *Computer chess: recent progress and future expectations*. Presented at the Third Jerusalem Conf. on Info. Technology (JCIT), August.

226. Newborn, M. M. (1979). Recent progress in computer chess. *Advances in Computers*, (M. Yovits editor). New York: Academic Press.

227. Newell, A. (1955). The Chess Machine: an example of dealing with a complex task by adaptation. *Western Joint Comp. Conf.*, 101–108.

228. Newell, A. (1966). On the representations of problems. *Computer Science Research Report*. Pittsburgh: Carnegie-Mellon University.

229. Newell, A. and Prasad, N. S. (1963). IPL-V chess position program. *Internal Memo No. 63*, CS Dept., Carnegie-Mellon University.

230. Newell, A. and Simon, H. A. (1961). Computer simulation of human thinking. *Science*, **134**, 2011–2017.

231. Newell, A., Shaw, J. C., and Simon, H. A. (1962). The processes of creative thinking. *Contemporary Approaches to Creative Thinking*, Gruber, H. E. *et al*;

232. Newell, A., Shaw, J. C., and Simon, H. A. (1963). Chess playing programs and the problem of complexity. *Computers and Thought*, pp. 39–70 (eds. E. A. Feigenbaum and Feldman). New York: McGraw-Hill.

233. Newell, A, and Simon, H. A. (1965). An example of human chess play in the light of chess playing programs. *Progress in B10-Cybernetics, Vol. 2*, pp. 19–75 (eds. N. Weiner and J. P. Shade). Amsterdam: Elsevier.

234. Newell, A. and Simon, H. A. (1972). *Human Problem Solving*. Prentice-Hall.

235. Newman, C. and Uhr, L. (1965). Bogart: a discovery and induction program for games. *Proc. ACM Conf. 65*, 176–186.

236. Nievergelt, J. and Farrar, J. C. (1972). What machines can and cannot do. *Computing Surveys*, **4**, June, 81-96.
237. Nievergelt, J. (1977). Information content of chess positions – information for chess-specific knowledge of chess players. *Sigart Newsletter*, **62**, April, 13-15.
238. Nilsson, N. J. (1968). Searching problem solving and game-playing trees for minimal cost solutions. *Information Processing*, **68**, North Holland, 1556-1562.
239. Nilsson, N. J. (1971). *Problem Solving Methods in Artificial Intelligence.* New York: McGraw-Hill.
240. Parry, J. (1974). Computer chess. *Chess Federation of Canada Bulletin*, Sept.-Oct., 11-13.
241. Parry, J. (1974). *The Ribbit Papers*. Privately circulated from the University of Waterloo.
242. Penrod, D. and Shershow, H. (editor). Computer Chess Newsletter. *Personal Computing*, 1978 onward.
243. Penrose, J. (1965). The psychology of chess. *New Society*, **29**, 967-968.
244. Perdue, C. and Berliner, H. J. (1977). EG – a case study in problem solving with King and Pawn endings. *Proc. 5th Int. Joint Conf. on AI*, pp. 421-427. Pittsburgh: Carnegie-Mellon University.
245. Piasetski, L. (1976). An evaluation function for simple King and Pawn endings. M.Sc. thesis, McGill Univ., Montreal.
246. Pitrat, J. (1968). Realization of a general game-playing program. *Proc. IFIP*, **68**, 1570-1574.
247. Pitrat, J. (1971). A general game-playing program. *Artificial Intelligence and Heuristic Programming* (eds. N. V. Findler, and B. Meltzer). Edinburgh: Edinburgh University Press.
248 Pitrat, J. (1974). Realization of a program learning to find combinations in chess. *Computer oriented learning processes*, NATO Advanced Study Inst. proceedings.
249. Pitrat, J. (1976). A program for learning to play chess. *Pattern recognition and artificial intelligence* (ed. C. H. Chen), 399-419. New York: Academic Press.
250. Pitrat, J. (1977). A chess combination program which uses plans. *Artificial Intelligence*, **8**, 275-321.
251. Pitrat, J. (1977). Using plans in a chess playing program. *Proc. 5th Int. Joint Conf. on AI*, pp. 979-982. Pittsburgh: Carnegie-Mellon University.
252. Pitrat, J. (1979). The behaviour of a chess combinations program using plans. *Advances in Computer Chess 2* (ed. M. R. B. Clarke). Edinburgh: Edinburgh University Press (in press).
253. Pohl, I. (1973). Avoidance of (relative) catastrophies, heuristic competence, genuine dynamic weighting and computational issues in heuristic problem solving. *Proc. 3rd Int. Joint Conf. AI*, pp. 12-17. Menlo Park: Stanford Research Institute.

254. Popplestone, R. J. (1969). An experiment in automatic induction. *Machine Intelligence 5*, pp. 203-218 (ed. B. Meltzer and D. Michie). Edinburgh: Edinburgh University Press.
255. Prinz, D. G. (1952). Robot chess. *Research,* **5**, 261-266.
256. Proskurowski, W. (1974). Ordering method to accelerate the solution of mate-in-two chess problems by computer. *Computer Journal,* **17**, 80-81.
257. Puskin, V. A. and Shershnev (1972). On different modes of acquiring information in a person solving discrete combinatorial problems. *Problems of Heuristics* (ed. V. N. Puskin). Israel Program for Scientific Translations, Jerusalem.
258. Reksten, H. (1978). *An annotated bibliography on computer chess.* Wilmington: Computer Science Dept., Univ. of Delaware.
259. Richards, P. I. (1952). On game learning machines. *Scientific Monthly*, **74**, April.
260. Richter, H. (1976). *A chess program based on principles of human thought processes on playing chess.* Technical Report, Institut fur Informatik, Hamburg, Oct.
261. Richter, H. (1976). The first German computer chess championship at Dortmund. *Sigart Newsletter,* **56**, 2.
262. Rollason, J. (1977). *MERLIN a chess playing program.* Privately circulated, Westfield College London.
263. Ruben, I., Swartz, F., Winograd, J., Berman, V., and Toikka, W. (1973). *Chaos.* Privately circulated from Sperry Univac, Cinaminson, New Jersey.
264. Rubin, E. (1972). Time consumption in master chess. *American Statistician,* April, 34-36.
265. Rushton, P. (1972). *A critique of programming techniques for playing chess*. M.Sc. thesis, University of Alberta.
266. Rushton, P. G. and Marsland, T. A. (1973). Current chess programs: a summary of their potential and limitations. *INFOR*, **11**, 13-20.
267. Russell, R. (1964). Kalah: The game and the program. *AI Memo No. 22*, Stanford: Computer Science Dept.
268. Samuel, A. L. (1959). Machine learning. *Technol. Review,* **62**, 42-45.
269. Samuel, A. L. (1960). Programming computers to play games. *Advances in Computers*, **1**, 165-192.
270. Scott, J. J. (1969). A chess-playing program. *Machine Intelligence 4*, pp. 255-265 (eds. B. Meltzer and D. Michie). Edinburgh: Edinburgh University
271. Scott, J. J. (1969). Lancaster vs. MAC HACK. *Sigart Newsletter,* **16**, 9-11.
272. Scurrah, M. J. and Wagner, D. A. (1970). Cognitive model of problem-solving in chess. *Science*, **169**, July, 209-211.
273. Selfridge, O. (1965). Reasoning in game playing by machine. *Symposium on Computer Augmentation of Human Reasoning* (eds. M. A. Sass and W. D. Wilkinson). Washington: Spartan Books.
274. Shannon, C. E. (1950). A chess-playing machine. *Scientific American,* **182**, February, 48-51.

275. Shannon, C. E. (1950). Programming a computer for playing chess. *Philosophical Mag.*, **41**, 256-275.
276. Simon, H. (1974). How big is a chunk? *Science*, **183**, 482-488.
277. Simon, H. A. and Barenfield, M. (1969). Information-processing analysis of perceptual processes in problem solving. *Psych. Rev.* **76**, 473-483.
278. Simon, H. A. and Chase, W. G. (1972). The mind's eye in chess. *Visual Information Processing* (ed. W. G. Chase) (Proc. 8th Annual Carnegie Psychology Symposium). New York: Academic Press.
279. Simon, H. A. and Chase, W. G. (1973). Skill in chess. *American Scientist*, **61**, No. 4.
280. Simon, H. A. and Chase, W. G. (1973). Perception in chess. *Cognitive Psychology*, **4**, 55-81.
281. Simon, H. A. and Gilmartin, K. (1974). A simulation of memory for chess positions. *Cognitive Psychology*, **5**, 29-46.
282. Simon, H. A. and Siklossy, L. (1972). *Representation and Meaning*. Prentice-Hall.
283. Simon, H. A. and Simon, P. A. (1962). Trial and error search in solving difficult problems: evidence from the game of chess. *Behavioral Sci.*, **7**, 425-429.
284. Slagle, J. R. (1963). *Game trees, M & N minimaxing, and the M & N alpha-beta procedure*. Artificial Intelligence Group Report 3, University of California.
285. Slagle, J. R. (1971). *Artificial Intelligence: The Heuristic Programming Approach*. New York: McGraw-Hill.
286. Slagle, J. R. and Bursky, P. (1968). Experiments with a multi-purpose theorem-proving heuristic program. *Journal of the ACM*, **15**, 85-99.
287. Slagle, J. R. and Dixon, J. K. (1969). Experiments with some programs which search game trees. *J. Ass. Comp. Mach.*, **16**, 189-207.
288. Slagle, J. R. and Dixon, J. K. (1970). Experiments with the M & N Tree Searching Program. *Comm. Assoc. Comp. Mach.*, **13**, 147-154 + 159.
289. Slagle, J. R. and Koniver, D. (1970). *Finding resolution proofs and using duplicate goals in AND-OR trees*. Bethesda, Md: Heuristics Lab., Div. of Computer Research and Technology, National Institute of Health.
290. Slate, D. J. (1977). Chess 4.5. *Sigart Newsletter*, **63**, June, 84-85.
291. Slate, D. J. and Atkin, L. R. (1970). *CDC File Printout from ULCC*. London: Westfield College.
292. Slate, D. J. and Atkin, L. R. (1977). CHESS 4.5 – The Northwestern University chess program. *Chess Skill in Man and Machine*, pp. 82-118 (ed. P. J. Frey). New York: Springer-Verlag.
293. Slate, D. J., Atkin, L. and Gorlen, K. (1972). Chess 3.5. *ACM72 Computer chess notes*, Boston, 15-21.
294. Slate, D. J. and Mittman, B. (1978). CHESS 4.6 – where do we go from here. *Third Jerusalem Conf. on Info. Technology*.

295. Slater, E. (1950). Statistics for the chess computer and the factor of mobility. *Symposium on Information Theory*, 150-152. London: Ministry of Supply.

296. Smith, R. C. (1969). The Schach chess program. *Sigart Newsletter*, **15**, 8-12.

297. Smith, R. C. and Ceruti, F. D. (1972). SCHACH. *ACM72 Computer chess notes*, Boston, 37-40.

298. Soule, S. and Marsland, T. A. (1975). Canadian computer-chess tournament. *Sigart Newsletter*, **54**, Oct., 12-13.

299. Stein, P. and Ulam, S. (1957). Experiments in chess on electronic computing machines. *Computers and Automation*, **6**.

300. Strachey, C. S. (1952). Logical or non-mathematical programmes. *Proc. ACM Conf.*, 46-49.

301. Sugar, L. (1975). *An experimental evaluation of chess playing heuristics*. Technical Report CSRG-63, Univ. Toronto.

302. Swets, B. (1978). *Second world computer chess championship*. Privately circulated translation of Wereldkampionschap Computerschacken, *de ingenier*, No. 8, 23 Feb., 167-173.

303. Tan, S. T. (1973). A knowledge based program to play chess endgames. *Computer Chess*, pp. 81-88 (ed. A. Bell). Chilton: SRC Atlas Laboratory.

304. Tan, S. T. (1972). *Representation of knowledge for very simple Pawn endings in chess*. Research Memorandum MIP-R-98. Edinburgh: Department of Machine Intelligence.

305. Tan, S. T. (1974). The winning program. *Firbush News 5* (chess supplement), 38-45. Edinburgh: Machine Intelligence Research Unit.

306. Tan, S. T. (1974). *Kings, Pawn and Bishop*. Research Memorandum MIP-R-108. Edinburgh: Department of Machine Intelligence.

307. Tan, S. T. (1977). Describing Pawn structures. *Advances in Computer Chess 1*, pp. 74-88 (ed. M. R. B. Clarke). Edinburgh: Edinburgh University Press.

308. Taube, M. (1961). *Computers and common sense, the myth of thinking machines*. Columbia University Press.

309. Thompson, K. (1973). *Tinker Belle, a 'C' language chess program under UNIX*. Privately circulated, Bell Telephone Laboratories, Murray Hill, N.J.

310. Tikhomirov, O. K. and Poznyanskaya, E. D. (1966). An investigation of visual search as a means of analyzing heuristics. *Soviet Psych.*, **5**, 2-15 (translated from *Voprosy Psikhologii*, **12**, 39-53).

311. Tikhomirov, O. K. and Vinogradov, Y. E. (1970). Emotions in the heuristic function. *Soviet Psychology*, **8**, 198-223.

312. Turing, A. M. (1953). Digital computers applied to games. *Faster than Thought*, pp. 286-310 (ed. V. Bowden). London: Pitman.

313. Valenti, F. M. (1974). *CHUTE1, An easily modifiable chess playing program*. M.A.Sc. thesis, University of Toronto.

314. Valenti, F. M. and Vranesic, Z. G. (1977). Experiences with CHUTE. *Proc. ACM77*, Seattle, 474-478.

315. Vigneron, H. (1914). Robots. (Translation of Les Automates, *La Nature*, 1914, 56-61.) *Computers and Chess*, (ed. D. N. L. Levy), 14-23.

316. Von Neuman, J. and Morgenstern, O. (1947). Application to Chess. *Theory of Games and Economic Behavior*, Princeton University Press.

317. Wagner, D. A. and Scurrah, M. J. (1971). Some characteristics of human problem-solving in chess. *Cognitive Psychology 2*, 454-478.

318. Waterman, D. (1970). Generalization learning techniques for automating the learning of heuristics. *Artificial Intelligence*, **1**, 121-170.

319. Wason, P. (1972). The psychology of chess. *New Scientist*, 134-137, July 20.

320. Weizenbaum, J. (1962). How to make a computer appear intelligent: five-in-a-row offers no guarantee. *Datamation*, 24-26.

321. Weizenbaum, J. and Shepherdson, R. C. (1962). Gamesmanship. *Datamation*, **10**.

322. Wetherell, C. S., Buckholtz, T. J. and Booth, K. S. (1972). A director for kriegspiel: a variant of chess. *Computer Journal*, **15**, 66-70.

323. Williams, T. G. (1965). *Some studies in game playing with a digital computer.* Thesis. Pittsburgh: Carnegie-Mellon University.

324. Wolf, G. (1973). Implementation of a dynamic tree searching algorithm in a chess program. *Proc. ACM73*, Atlanta, 206-208.

325. Zermelo, E. (1912). An application of set theory to the theory of chess-playing. English translation of (German) paper at *5th Int. Cong. of Math.* 1912, in *Firbush News 6*, 1976, 37-42. Edinburgh: Machine Intelligence Research Unit.

326. Zielinski, G. (1975). *Heuristics for computer chess*. Applied Math. and Physics Dept., Warsaw Tech. Univ.

327. Zielinski, G. (1976). Arrays for programming chess. *Kybernetes*, **5**, 91-96.

328. Zobrist, A. L. (1969). *A hashing method with applications for game playing.* Technical Report 88. Madison: Computer Sciences Dept., University of Wisconsin.

329. Zobrist, A. L. and Carlson, F. R. (1973). An advice-taking chess computer. *Scientific American*, June, 92-105.

330. Zobrist, A. L. and Carlson, F. R. (1973). The USC chess program. *Proc. ACM73*, Atlanta, 209-212.

331. Zuidema, C. (1974). Chess: how to program the exceptions? *Afdeling Informatica*, 1W21/74. Amsterdam: Math. Centrum.

332. Zuse, K. (1945). Chess Programs (translation of *Plankalkül*, 1945), Rept. No. 106, Geselschaft für Mathematik und Datenverarbeitung, Bonn, 1976, 201-204.

KNOWLEDGE ENGINEERING

20

Issues of Representation in Conveying the Scope and Limitations of Intelligent Assistant Programs

B. G. Buchanan

Department of Computer Science
Stanford University, USA

1. INTRODUCTION

Success of a knowledge-based program depends on both competence and acceptability. It must perform well for it to be worth using, but is must be acceptable to users for it to be used. There are many dimensions to developing competent and acceptable knowledge based systems which can serve as "intelligent assistants" for problem solvers in science (see Shortliffe and Davis, 1975). One of these is the old AI problem of representation of knowledge. Since most previous work on representation has stressed its importance for problem-solving (e.g. Amarel, 1971), we will concentrate here on the importance of representation in acquiring knowledge for a reasoning program and in making the program acceptable to users.

In the past, computer assistance in science was limited to numerical calculation. Beyond numerical help, however, the computer can provide more assistance if given combinatorial and inferential abilities. That is, the problem-solving assistant should be a problem solver for the non-numeric, as well as numeric, subproblems the scientist finds tedious. For example, manipulating graph structures systematically enters into routine problems of chemistry and molecular biology: and finding the consequences of prescribing different combinations of drugs frequently enters into medical practice.

As computer programs become more complex and powerful, new problems of program design and use become apparent. Simple programs need only simple introductions. Their use is straightforward, and their output is easily interpreted. For example, a procedure that computes mean and standard deviation from a set of data requires little explanation. The most complicated step is formatting the input data. By contrast, using a complex reasoning program such as CONGEN (discussed below) requires a substantial investment of time to understand the program's scope and limitations as well as its input and output conventions. For these purposes, the choice of representation of the program's knowledge becomes as important for communicating with users as for solving problems in the first place.

This point is illustrated in this paper by three of the DENDRAL programs, described in the next section. We briefly discuss some aspects of these programs that are relevant for the representation issues. Then in the following sections we look at two ways, in addition to problem solving, that the representation of knowledge is important for designing intelligent assistants. Communicating the scope and limits of programs is especially critical at times when a user is either augmenting the knowledge base or requesting assistance. Thus our examples focus on these two aspects. It is not necessary that the reader fully understand the details of the examples, and it is suggested that the discussion of the DENDRAL programs in the next section be skimmed on first reading.

In order to use a program intelligently, a user needs to understand the program's scope and limits. The scope, roughly, is the broad class of problems which it is designed to solve and the context in which solutions will be found. The limitations include the idiosyncrasies that must be remembered to obtain reliable solutions, but which are less fundamental to the whole procedure. For example, enumerating polymeric structures is outside the scope of CONGEN, while its working definition of aromaticity is a limitation that is more easily changed. Operationally, the scope is the broad definition of the problem which can be changed only at the cost of writing an entirely new procedure. The limitations are the explicit and implicit items in the problem definition that are added to make the problem solvable but that may be changed or removed more readily. It is not a sharp distinction; the point is that a scientist needs to understand the assistant's interpretation of the problem before the program (assistant) can be used responsibly and confidently.

2. DENDRAL PROGRAMS

The Heuristic Programming Project at Stanford University has developed a family of computer programs, collectively known as DENDRAL, which are designed to provide assistance to chemists with structure elucidation problems. In this section three of these programs are described: CONGEN, the DENDRAL Planner, and Meta-DENDRAL. The tasks that they perform are complex, even for chemists. And the depth of knowledge required for high performance forced early confrontations with problems of knowledge representation.

Many of the examples are difficult to read, and to this extent constitute negative examples to the point that input and output conventions ought to be transparent. However, we are concerned here with the more fundamental issue of conveying enough information so that the programs' reasoning framework and abilities are transparent.

2.1 CONGEN

CONGEN (see Carhart, Smith, Brown and Djerassi, 1975) is a generator of molecular structures that are consistent with constraints inferred from chemical and spectroscopic data. (The name of the program stands for "constrained generator".) CONGEN produces a list of all plausible structural descriptions for an unknown compound with a guarantee that none has been ommitted and that there are no duplicates. The criteria of plausibility, the constraints, come from the chemist or another program called the DENDRAL Planner. CONGEN provides assistance by generating chemical graphs, displaying them, and testing them for the chemist.

CONGEN is valuable for structure elucidation problems because it provides the chemist with all and only structures that are consistent with the interpretations. The empirical formula (that is, the numbers of atoms of each type in the unknown) is a necessary piece of information; the other constraints inferred from the data are all optional. The kinds of constraints one can give to CONGEN are shown in Table 14. This list describes features of chemical molecules that can be represented as features of graphs, and thus helps delimit the scope of CONGEN.

Table 1 – Types of constraints accepted by CONGEN.

Composition:	
(a) SUPERATOMS	– Inferred polyatomic structural fragments with one or more potential bonding sites (free valences).
(b) ATOMS	– Any remaining atoms of any type, e.g., C, N, O.
Constraints:	
(c) BADLIST	– Forbidden structural features.
(d) GOODLIST	– Required structural features.
(e) BADRINGS	– Forbidden ring sizes.
(f) GOODRINGS	– Required ring sizes.
(g) PROTON	– Desired protons and their environments.
(h) ISOPRENE	– Desired isoprene units and their linkages.
(i) HRANGE	– Allowed numbers of hydrogens on specific atoms.

A convenient substructure definition language (EDITSTRUC) allows easy construction and modification of superatoms and other structural subunits the chemist wants to mention in the problem statement. An example of its use (to define a superatom named "parabridges") is shown in Fig. 1. This substructure used on BADLIST will disallow structures possessing an aromatic ring with a bridge of fewer than eight atoms between atoms that are opposite ("para" to) one another. Although this language is not self-documenting and requires brief instruction, the commands are easily understood and remembered by chemists. They are designed to be terse enough to be fast; for example, repeated calls to the same command can be avoided by typing additional sets of arguments into the first call.

```
  [editstruc]
NAME:[parabridges]
(NEW STRUCTURE)
>[ring 6]
        ; Start with a six membered ring.
>[bord 1 2 any 2 3 any 3 4 any 4 5 any 5 6 any 6 1 any]
        ; Allow any bond order between atoms 1&2, 2&3, 3&4, etc.
>[artype 1 a 2 a 3 a 4 a 5 a 6 a]
        ; Require all atoms to be aromatic.
>[link 1 4 1]
        ; Link atoms 1 & 4 with a new atom.
>[lnode 7 1 7]
        ; Allow the new linking atom (7) to be a chain of one to
         seven atoms.
>[atname 7 x]
        ; Let atom 7 be any atom type (x).
>[adraw]

PARABRIDGES: (AROMATIC ATOMS AND "ANY" BONDS NOT
INDICATED)
LNODES ARE INDICATED BY AN ATTACHED @
```

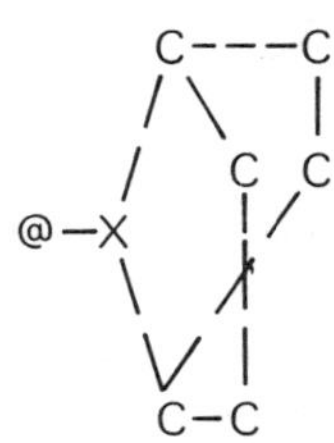

[A chemist would reconstruct this as:

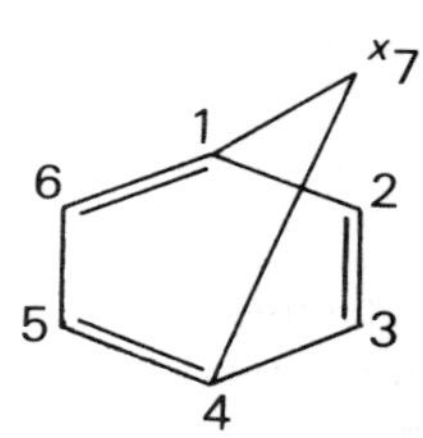

where node 7 (*X*) stands for a bridge containing 1–7 atoms.]

Fig. 1 – Definition of a superatom for CONGEN with the structure editing language EDITSTRUC. [Bracketed characters typed by use. Annotations follow a semi-colon.]

The more constraints there are, naturally, the smaller the list of structures will be. For example, the program will produce 284 structural isomers with the composition C6H13N, but will generate only 4 if the program is told there is one six-membered ring and one methyl group. More complex examples of CONGEN problems are given by Carhart *et al.* The size and complexity of problems that CONGEN can handle are limited more by the number of structural units (superatoms plus remaining atoms) than by the total number of atoms in the empirical formula. Thus CONGEN can help with structural problems of real interest when the chemist is able to infer some structural features from available data.

2.2 DENDRAL Planner

The DENDRAL Planner (see Smith *et al.*, 1972) is a program designed to aid in the interpretation of mass spectra. It is not "automatic" in the sense of producing structural interpretations of an unknown mass spectrum with no intervention from the chemist. Instead, it uses the chemist's relevant knowledge of mass spectrometry and applies it systematically to the spectrum of an unknown. That is, using the chemist's definitions of the structural skeleton of the molecule and the relevant fragmentation rules, the program does the bookkeeping of associating peaks with fragments and the combinatorics of finding consistent ways of placing substituents around the skeleton.

Fig. 2 shows the structure of the common skeleton (defined with EDITSTRUC) for a class of compounds called capnellanes. For purposes of illustration, three major fragmentations were defined, which are shown schematically in Fig. 2, overdrawn on the computer's drawing of the skeleton. It is possible to specify other definitions of the context in which the chemist wants the interpretation to be made, such as the intensity threshold for noise peaks.

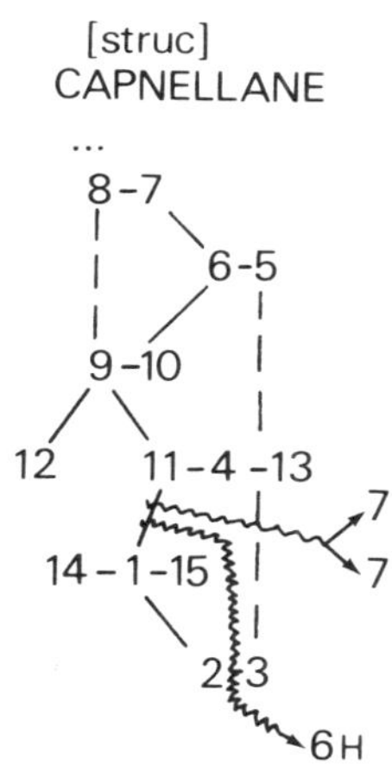

Fig. 2 – A structural skeleton defined for the DENDRAL Planner. Fragmentations were manually drawn on the computer's output. [Bracketed characters typed by user.]

From the information about the skeleton and fragmentations for the general class, the program begins interpreting the mass spectrum as shown in Figs. 3 and 4. First the empirical formula (or "molecular ion") is determined (see Dromey, Buchanan, Lederberg, and Djerassi, 1975). Then it finds data points (peaks) in the spectrum that could plausibly be associated with the defined fragmentations, with and without combinations of substituents. (The range of possible substituents is determined by subtracting the composition of the skeleton from the empirical formula for the determined molecular ion.)

```
   [plan]
  (COMPUTING MOLECULAR ION(S))

  MOLECULAR IONS
  (234. 1609 100 (C . 15) (H . 22) (0 . 2))

      ;Only one plausible molecular ion peak is found for this
      problem, at mass 234.1609 and intensity 100.
      ;From the exact mass 234. 1609 only one empircal formula is
      plausible, viz, C15 H22 O2.
```

Fig. 3 – Start of planning: molecular ion determination. Annotations follow semicolons.

```
(STARTING ANALYSIS PART)
BREAK : SUBSTITUENTS ON CHARGED FRAGMENT : EVIDENCE (M/E)
6H    ((DOT . 4) (C . 0) (O . 1))      161.0975
      ((DOT . 2) (C . 0) (O . 1))      163.1136
      ((DOT . 4) (C . 0) (O . 2))      178.0993

;The format is not clear as it should be. There are three sets of alternative
substituents on the fragment resulting from Break 6H (see Fig. 2).
These are (a) 2 double bonds or rings (4 "dots") and one oxygen,
(b) 1 double bond or ring and one oxygen, or (c) 2 double bonds or rings
and two oxygens.
Each has supporting evidence in the data at the masses shown,
------------------------------
7H    ((DOT . 4) (C . 0))              133.1009
      ((DOT . 2) (C . 0))              133.1009
      ((DOT . 4) (C . 0) (O. 1))       150.1038  149.0951  148.088
                                       147.0811
      ((DOT . 2) (C . 0) (O . 1))      150.1038  149.0951
      ((DOT . 4) (C . 0) (O . 2))      163.0758
------------------------------
7L    ((DOT . 4) (C . 0))              65.03971
      ((DOT . 2) (C . 0))              67.05513
      ((DOT . 0) (C . 0))              69.07053
      ((DOT . 0) (C . 0) (O . 1))      85.06461
------------------------------
```

Fig. 4 – Intermediate planning results: likely assignments of special peaks to fragmentations. Fragmentations 6H, 7H, and 7L are shown in Fig. 2. Annotations follow semicolons.

The output from the Planner is a list of structure descriptions with as much detail filled in as the data and defined fragmentations will allow. Because there are limits to the degree of refinement allowed by mass spectrometry alone, sets of atoms are assigned to sets of skeletal nodes. Thus the task of fleshing out the plan – specifying possible structures assigned to specific skeletal nodes – is left to CONGEN. Figure 5 shows the program's output for the capnellane example: there is only one structure, and it has one oxygen and two double bonds (or extra rings) within nodes C4–C13, with one oxygen on node C3. (Most probably, these are a keto [C=O] group and carbon-carbon double bond somewhere within C4–C13 and hydroxyl [OH] on C3.) This partial description of the unknown can be used by CONGEN, together with other constraints, to produce a list of complete structures.

```
        BEGIN SYNTHESIS OF MOLECULAR ION = 234.1609
STRUCTURE 1
(((DOT . 4) (O . 1)) C4 C5 C6 C7 C8 C9 C10 C11 C12 C13)
(((O . 1)) C3)

      ;The evidence shown in Figures 4 can be consistently
      combined in only one way.

      ;I.e., two double bonds or rings (four "dots")
      and one oxygen atom can be placed within nodes 4-13 of
      the skeleton, and one oxygen is on node 3.

EVIDENCE USED TO BUILD STRUCTURE:
(6H (DOT . 4) (O . 2))
(7H (DOT . 4) (O . 1))
(7L (O . 1))

      ;The parens and dotted pairs are not helpful,
       but the information helps the chemist relate
       final conclusions to the intermediate reasoning.

DONE
```

Fig. 5 – Results of DENDRAL Planner: description of structure(s) consistent with the data. Annotations follow semicolons.

2.3 Meta-DENDRAL

The Meta-DENDRAL program (Buchanan *et al.*, 1976) is designed to provide assistance to mass spectroscopists who are formulating new fragmentation rules to explain the behaviour of a new set of compounds. It begins with a collection of known structure-spectrum pairs. From these data, together with the chemist's defined criteria of plausibility, the program finds plausible fragmentations and rearrangements that account for many of the most significant peaks in the spectra. For example, rules 6H, 7H, and 7L used in the example above (Figs. 2 to 5) can result from the program's examination of a training set of capnellane structures and their known mass spectra.

The mass spectrometry rules are written in terms of a topological description of a piece of a molecule (a subgraph) and a corresponding fragmentation or rearrangement process. For example, rule M-6 in Fig. 6 says that in the presence of a keto group we would see evidence for fragmentation of the bonds opposite and adjacent to that group. The subgraphs are described in "ball and stick" terms, with no stereochemistry. The corresponding processes are defined in terms of bond cleavage(s), net transfer(s) of hydrogen, or neutral species such as water, and charge placement. Because the program writes new rules in terms of an existing vocabulary (and does not invent new terms) it is extending an existing theory but not developing a new one.

Two rules produced by the program are shown in Fig. 6 along with a summary of the evidential support for them in the training set. These are taken from a results table of a paper (see Buchanan *et al.*, 1976) describing the program's help in formulating mass spectrometry rules for three classes of compounds not previously codified in this way (the mono-, di-, and triketoandrostanes).

Name	Subgraph	Positive Evidence Any	Positive Evidence Unique	Negative Evidence	Average Intensity Percent
	. . .				
M-4	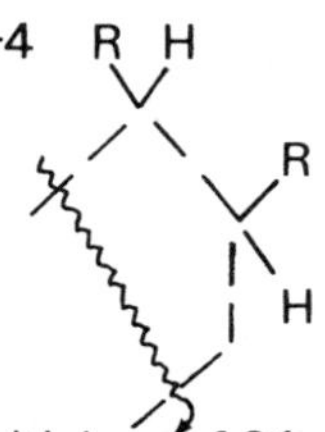 (with loss of 0,1, or 2 H's)	21	0	1	3.71
M-6	 (with loss of one H)	8	4	0	3.29

Fig. 6 – Two general fragmentation rules found by Meta-DENDRAL. (The positive evidence is the number of data points correctly predicted by the rule: it is unique if no other rules also predict the same data point.
Negative evidence is the number of peaks predicted by the rule but not found in the data.

The rules are formed in three distinct stages: (1) data interpretation and summary, (2) rule generation, and (3) rule modification. Each depends on the chemist's definitions of the context in which rules will be formed. For example, the context includes whether the program should consider cleavage of aromatic ring bonds and multiple bonds, the numbers of hydrogens to consider in rearrangements, the types and numbers of neutral fragments (such as water) to be lost, and the complexity of the processes that can count as explanations of peaks. A sample of the interaction specifying the context is shown in Fig. 7.

```
specify fragmentation process constraints? Y/N. : [Y]

prompt for all constraint values? Y/N. : [Y]
forbid cleavage of more than one bond
      to the same atom? Y/N. : [Y]
forbid cleavage of aromatic ring bonds? Y/N. : [N]
allow default definition of aromatic rings? Y/N. : [Y]
forbid cleavage of double and triple bonds? Y/N. : [Y]
minimum number of carbons in a fragment? : [2]
allowed hydrogen transfers? : [2 1 0 -1 -2]
maximum number of bonds allowed to cleave
      in a single step process? : [2]
maximum number of steps in a fragmentation process? : [2]
maximum number of bonds allowed to cleave
      in a multiple-step process? : [2]
maximum number of rings allowed to fragment
      in a multiple-step process? : [1]
allowed neutral transfers (other than H)?
      : [CO -1]
any other constraints? Y/N. : [N]
```

Fig. 7 – A sample of the context definition for Meta-DENDRAL. [Bracketed characters were typed by user.]

The rule formulation procedure is not modelled after human procedures, but is perhaps more systematic and thorough than the creative methods of scientists. At bottom, it is a systematic exploration of the space of more and more specific rules that can explain the interpreted data. This is followed by a final "fine tuning" of the rules to make them more general, when possible, or more specific (if this helps reduce the negative evidence), or to merge similar rules into a common form (see Buchanan *et al.*, 1976, for details).

3. REPRESENTATION PROBLEMS IN KNOWLEDGE ACQUISITION AND VERIFICATION

Accumulating knowledge of a domain in a form that a program can interpret and use is essential for the program to assist with problems of reasoning. This is one of the central themes of all the work at the Stanford Heuristic Programming Project. We have experimented with various ways of adding scientific and medical knowledge to programs. The three main methods that we have used we call handcrafting, interactive dialog, and automatic rule formation. The work has been performed by several persons at Stanford in the context of work on DENDRAL and other programs.

In each case we are concerned with giving the program the same kind of knowledge that an expert in the domain uses for problem solving. We do not pretend to be able to make the problem-solving assistant as sophisticated as an expert in all respects. But we want to transfer enough knowledge into the program to make it a useful assistant.

3.1 Functional components

In order to build a high performance reasoning program four logically separable systems must interact. These are

(1) an expert,
(2) a transfer agent,
(3) a reasoning program,
(4) a verifier.

In most instances, AI programs are built by single individuals who act as expert, transfer agent and verifier, very often in domains that require no more formal source of knowledge than common sense. Many interesting specialized systems have recently been developed which rely on much more than common sense. Some programs are constructed by persons who are first and foremost domain experts (for example, Colby in psychiatry, Berliner in chess); others are constructed by programmers who become experts in a specialized area of science (for example, Reddy in speech understanding). However, even in cases where an individual fills the role of two or more of the four systems, it is instructive to separate the activities of the component parts.

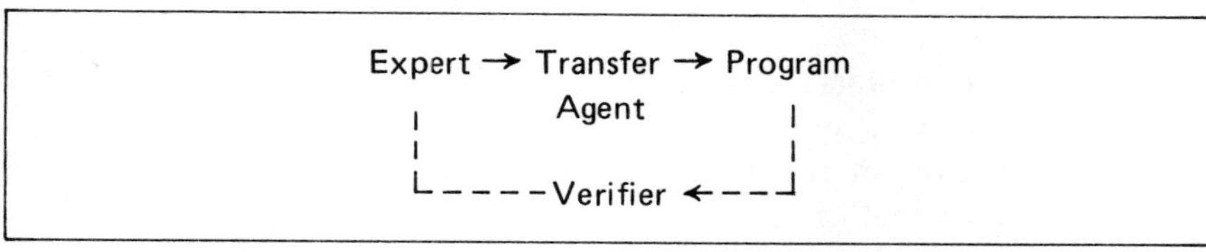

Fig. 8 – Functional components for building an expert system.

3.1.1 *Expert*

For most system building activities we think of the expert as a human being. In this decade, a person is far more effective in this role than a program would be, because of the breadth and depth of knowledge required for teaching complex tasks. (See Waterman, 1970, for comparisons of both a human and a program as expert.) Representation problems become critical in knowledge acquisition and in verification, since the expert is expected to match what the program can and cannot do.

Although we often think of the domain expert as the ultimate source of expertise for AI programs, we can also consider the origin of that individual's expertise as a source of knowledge. In science there is one ultimate source – observations, or empirical data. Experts also learn from textbooks and papers written by others who have codified and explained empirical observations.

3.1.2 *Transfer Agent*

There is no reason to expect the expert to know the details of the programming language and the implementation of the reasoning program. Perhaps it is more accurate to say that the expert's own codification of knowledge is not executable as a program without some translation. The expert sometimes serves as translator, but usually this task is given to someone closer to the program itself.

Transfer can also be accomplished by a program. See Davis, 1976, for a fuller discussion of interactive knowledge transfer issues and methods for aiding the transfer. Meta-DENDRAL avoids the link with the expert by formulating rules directly from the original data and transferring them to the performance program.

3.1.3 *Program*

There are many examples of expert systems which illustrate the kind of performance we expect from a program built under the supervision of an expert. DENDRAL and Meta-DENDRAL are two of these.

For the cost of eliciting knowledge from experts, we expect the resulting program to be superior to one developed without the aid of an expert. Primarily this means that we expect superior performance. In addition, however, we want the program to be easier to understand, easier to justify, and easier to modify.

3.1.4 *Verifier*

In addition to the performance program, we, as system builders, need mechanisms for determining the program's level of expertise. Programmers are used for correcting syntactic errors and verifying that the program meets performance requirements on test cases. If we were translating algorithms into programs, almost all of the verification could be done this way. However, in a knowledge-based AI program there may be errors in the knowledge base that are impossible for anyone but an expert to detect and correct. For this reason the feedback is shown to the expert in Fig. 8, not to the transfer agent. For this reason also, the output of the reasoning program and its intermediate conclusions must be easily understood by the expert.

3.2 Representation issues

The choice of representation for the expert's knowledge must be a compromise between what is natural and easy for the expert and what is natural and easy for the programmer (transfer agent). The choice of concepts and relations must certainly come from the expert, but the means of encoding them be partly chosen by the programmer. For example, the DENDRAL representation of chemical molecules as two-dimensional connected graphs was chosen by Professor J. Lederberg as an appropriate representation for mass spectrometry problems. The actual implementation of graph theoretic concepts and operations in LISP lists, and operations on lists, was based more on programming convenience than on chemical considerations.

However, there is no reason to believe that the expert's first conceptualization is complete or correct. The expert will begin with classical textbook statements that are reasonably certain and well accepted. But in domains like mass spectrometry and medicine there is still a gap between what the textbooks say and what is needed for expert performance. The differences can show up in many ways. For example, the textbooks may lack statements of relations that are less than certain but are used in practice; they may fail to make distinctions that are useful in practice, and they may state facts at a theoretical level not used in practice. In addition, as the field grows, the textbooks lose their claim to completeness.

Similarly, there is no reason to believe that the programmer's first implementation is correct and appropriate. There is tremendous potential for misinterpreteing what the expert says when the programmer has little understanding of the domain. A more serious problem is that the internal representation chosen by the programmer, on the basis of initial conversations with the expert, will be inappropriate for ideas to be incorporated later.

Overcoming this communication barrier is a major hurdle in constructing a knowledge-based system. Both the expert and the programmer are simultaneously developing representations of the domain that they believe are appropriate for the task and for the program that performs that task. Thus it is not surprising that new applications programs often need to be completely rewritten after their initial implementations.

Figs. 1 and 2 show parts of the knowledge acquisition processes for DENDRAL programs. These have been designed with an experienced user in mind – one who has read the documentation, but not necessarily one who understands the details of the program. The knowledge built up in these ways can be saved and used in other problems. The TEIRESIAS system (Davis, 1976) emphasizes interaction with naive users much more than DENDRAL's knowledge acquisition procedures. The main point is still the same: limits on what the program can represent are limits on what knowledge it can acquire.

The programs' conceptualization of the domain of chemistry was moulded by chemists. It does not include everything chemists know about molecular structures or mass spectrometry, but it meshes well with a subset of their knowledge. The most significant difficulties come from mismatches between how chemists think about part of a problem and how the program represents that part. For example, CONGEN treats double bonds as rings of size two, for reasons of efficiency and completeness, yet chemists often make a clear distinction between rings and double bonds, for chemical reasons. Thus CONGEN has been modified in many places to recognize the distinction even though it is not necessary for problem solving. Without mapping the program steps into the chemist's conceptual framework, there would be great difficulty in verifying and augmenting the knowledge base.

4. REPRESENTATION ISSUES IN USE AND ACCEPTANCE

For a high-performance computer program to capture the sustained, widespread attention of working scientists, it must contain a large number of features that make it easy and pleasant to use. These features are commonly termed "human engineering aspects" of a program. In very rare instances, a program will be so useful that it will be widely adopted even without proper attention to human engineering. But the general principle seems to be that programs that are only understandable to programmers are used only by programmers, if at all.

Just as the expert creating the program must feel that the representation of knowledge is appropriate for the task, the user of the system must also feel comfortable with it. This is an indispensable element of acceptability: problem solutions must be presented to the user in a familiar vocabulary. A common error we make is to present solutions in the vocabulary of the programmer, using the concepts of the program instead of those of the domain practitioners and experts. (Even though the output shown in Fig. 5, for example, could be improved with respect to notation and readability, the concepts are the right ones to convey.) Occasionally one might find cases where the expert's conceptualization is not fully shared by the users, in which cases some further translation is also required for the users.

Because an AI program can be a powerful tool it also has the potential of powerful misuse. Paraphrasing a message by J. Weizenbaum (1976) (to teachers of computer science), the designers of intelligent programs have a responsibility to teach users the limitations of their tools as well as their power. A most important set of limitations stems from the choice of representation of knowledge about the problem domain. Whatever representation is chosen, it will have its own set of limitations and peculiarities that can mislead and confuse the users of the program. For example, users who expect DENDRAL to give them information about bond lengths and angles in its drawings of molecular structures are going to misinterpret those drawings.

4.1 Documentation and assistance

A designer usually leaves to the user the task of understanding a program's scope and limitations by telling him that he must read and understand the program documentation before beginning. But documentation usually does not discuss appropriate uses of a program or the program's limitations. (Unfortunately, the more complex a program is and the more a user needs full documentation of its scope and limits, the less willing programmers are to create the document).

While it is tempting to think of intelligent use of a program in terms of understanding its documentation, the program itself can aid considerably. One of the exciting possibilities of the future is creating intelligent assistants that carry an awareness of their own problem-solving abilities and can explain them to users.

Documentation is the most obvious way of conveying the scope and limitations of a program. We are beginning to work with some of the easier steps of learning about a program and to shift some of the burden from documentation to interactive aids built into the program. For example, the programs themselves can be asked what to do next, what the available commands are, what a prompt means, what the effect of a parameter is. Some of these features are illustrated in the context of the DENDRAL Planner. Fig. 9 shows the program's response to a request for a summary of available commands. Fig. 10 shows the program's descriptions of two critical parameters.

```
  [menu]
  *** MENU OF AVAILABLE COMMANDS ***
COMMAND              WHEN-APPLICABLE          PURPOSE
?                        ANYTIME       TO GET MORE INFORMATION
CNTRL-E                  ANYTIME       TO CANCEL COMMAND
GET                      AFTER >       TO GET PARAMETERS FROM A
                                       CLASS FILE
<PARAMETERNAME>          AFTER >       TO DEFINE NEW VALUE FOR
                                       PARAMETER
<PARAMETER>?             AFTER >       TO SEE THE VALUE OF A PARAMETER
READ                     AFTER >       TO READ A MASS SPECTRUM FROM A
                                       FILE
PLAN                     AFTER >       TO RUN THE PLANNER PROGRAM
SAVE                     AFTER >       TO SAVE THE DEFINED PARAMETERS
DESCRIBE <COMMAND>       AFTER >       TO SEE A DESCRIPTION OF THE
                                       COMMAND
LIST                     AFTER >       TO SEE IMPORTANT PARAMETER
                                       NAMES
DESCRIBE <PARAM>         AFTER >       TO DESCRIBE THE NAMED
                                       PARAMETER
DONE                     AFTER >       TO EXIT FROM THE PROGRAM
```

Fig. 9 – The DENDRAL Planner's description of commands. [Bracketed characters were typed by user.]

Through documentation or otherwise, it is necessary to convey to the chemist what the program knows about the current problem. This is harder as more knowledge is put into the program. We have tried to keep the judgmental knowledge used by DENDRAL programs separate from the coded procedures that depend on that knowledge. In this way we can, in principle, explain what each program knows. In CONGEN, for example, we give the chemist control over (almost) all the specifications of the structure elucidation problem. The constraints are defined and modified by the person with the immediate problem, as illustrated in Fig. 1. The whole set of constraints can be examined on-line in the course of problem solving, as shown in Fig. 11.

```
    [list]
       *** ESSENTIAL PARAMETERS ***
>>> STRUC
"STRUC (PARAMETER) IS THE STRUCTURE OF THE BASIC SKELETON OF
THIS CLASS. IT MAY BE EDITED BY USING THE FOLLOWING COMMAND:
    EDIT STRUC
THIS COMMAND INVOKES THE STRUCTURE EDITING PROGRAMS USED
IN CONGEN AND OTHER DENDRAL PROGRAMS."

>>> BREAKS
"BREAKS (PARAMETER) IS THE SET OF FRAGMENTATION RULES FOR
THE SKELETON; EACH BREAK DESCRIBES THE BONDS BROKEN AND
THE HYDROGENS TRANSFERRED"
```

Fig. 10 – Example of program's description of its parameters. [Bracketed characters were typed by user.] Programs with the same names as the parameters are available to aid in defining new values.

```
    [contraints?]
------
BADLIST CONSTRAINTS
    NAME
PARABRIDGES
------
GOODLIST CONSTRAINTS
    NAME  MIN MAX
CH-3        1   1
------
```

Fig. 11 – CONGEN's response to request for description of current constraints. Parabridges is shown in Fig. 1; other superatoms would be defined similarly.

There remains much subtle knowledge of chemistry embedded in the programs that we are not able to display, except through hard-copy documentation. For example, Meta-DENDRAL uses "built in" criteria to decide when an emerging rule is good enough or when one rule is better than another. And CONGEN cannot explain to the chemist how subproblems are ranked to determine their order of solution, or how problem size is estimated. Perhaps the closest we have come to this is in the DENDRAL Planner, where the user can see and change the complex conditions under which the program assigns evidence to fragmentations as shown in Fig. 12.

```
[controlrules]
USE ONLY THE STRONGEST EVIDENCE FOR SOME BREAKS (Y/N)?[y]
APPLICABLE BREAKS: [6h]
PASSES: [1]
USE EVIDENCE THRESHOLD FOR SOME BREAKS (Y/N)?[y]
APPLICABLE BREAKS: [7h 7l]
APPLY ON PASSES: [1]

PERCENT OF MAXIMUM INTENSITY (DEFAULT = 33): [?]

WHAT THRESHOLD DO YOU WANT AS A CUTOFF – GIVE A NUMBER THAT
WILL BE USED AS PERCENT OF MAXIMUM INTENSITY TO THROW AWAY
(RELATIVELY) SMALL INTENSITY PIECES OF EVIDENCE.
PERCENT: [33]

; This requires the chemist to understand that different
  criteria can be applied to the evidence in successive attempts
  ("passes") to find structures consistent with the evidence.
  Only the strongest evidence for Break 6H, and only evidence
  above 33 percent of the maximum intensity for 7H and 7L, will be
  used on the first pass, in this example.
```

Fig. 12 – Example of user control over the DENDRAL Planner's procedure that selects evidence for fragmentations (see Fig. 2 for drawings of 6H, 7H and 7L). [Bracketed characters were typed by user.]

4.2 Laboratory notebook

With a simple program, there is little point in asking for a detailed record of progress: between problem specification and solution there is little to note. As soon as a program is expected to behave as a problem-solving assistant on complex subproblems, however, progress notes printed by the program take on the importance of a laboratory notebook.

There are three different kinds of notes we expect the DENDRAL programs to provide:

(a) a record of initial conditions, intermediate conclusions, and final results;
(b) a complete record of the interaction between chemist and program (including false starts and typing mistakes);
(c) a trace of the program's reasoning steps.

Each of these is important for a different reason. The final results, of course, are the *sine qua non* of the assistant's work. The record of initial conditions and major intermediate conclusions gives the chemist at a glance the context in which the problem was solved and the major steps in its solution. This serves as a useful reminder of scope and limits; in addition, disagreement on initial conditions or intermediate conclusions would be sufficient reason to request the assistant to start over. Meta-DENDRAL, for instance, immediately precedes its stored and printed results with a summary of the context specified by the chemist. Because they are together there is less chance that the results will be interpreted without proper regard for the context.

The record of the chemist's interaction with the program is a detailed account of what the investigator requests of the assistant. Failure to find a solution to a problem can often be attributed to ill-specified requests, so it is helpful to review the complete record of specifications made by the investigator. The requests for help and the program's response illustrated in the previous section are important entries in the experimental record.

Finally, the trace of the assistant's reasoning steps is helpful whenever the investigator wants to keep track of the inferential steps of an assistant. In any case it is often useful to have a record in order to justify moving from one point to the next. For example, before the DENDRAL Planner prints the results shown in Fig. 5 above, it prints the plausible molecular ions it inferred from the data (Fig. 3) and the data it associates with each of the separate fragmentations (Fig. 4).

In all cases, the entries in the laboratory notebook must be easily interpreted by the investigator for them to be useful. We have much to learn in this respect. The examples above are still cryptic and hard for outsiders to understand. But within each entry there is much information of value to a chemist about the program's problem solving procedure.

4.3 Multiple representations

One thing that we can do to help the chemist discover the scope and limits of the program's problem-solving abilities is to present information to the chemist in more than one way. Our representation of chemical structures is very limited. We do not know how to convey its limitations adequately, although we do present structures in several ways in order to give the chemist as good a feeling for the limits of the representation as we can. The documentation is explicit in these matters: the programs themselves are usually not as explicit. In CONGEN we present structures as pictures of graphs, as connection matrices, as descriptions of graphs with node properties listed. From the collection of these representations we hope that a chemist will be able to see accurately what the program assumes about molecular structures, even if he avoids reading the documentation. Fig. 1 above showed the definition of a superatom and the program's rough drawing of it. Another description of the superatom (for experienced users) is shown in Fig. 13.

The scope of Meta-DENDRAL is conveyed in similar ways. For example, the program works with mass spectrometry fragmentaion rules with possible hydrogen migration and loss of neutral species. By describing those processes in different ways, we expect the chemist to see, for example, that the program knows only about net losses.

```
>[show]
NAME=PARABRIDGES
ATOM TYPE ARTYPE NEIGHBORS  LNODE
  1      C     AROM       7  6  2
  2      C     AROM       1  3
  3      C     AROM       2  4
  4      C     AROM       7  3  5
  5      C     AROM       4  6
  6      C     AROM       5  1
  7      X     NON-AR     1  4        1-7
BONDS 6-1, 5-6, 4-5, 3-4, 2-3 AND 1-2 ARE OF TYPE "ANY"
>[done]
```

Fig. 13 – Another description of the superatom in Fig. 1.

4.4 Description of context

The context in which problem solving proceeds is essential information for interpreting the solutions. The more an assistant can make explicit the assumptions and initial conditions of a problem, the easier it is for an investigator to understand the answers. This has always been true, but the emergence of computer programs as assistants brings the problem clearly into focus.

In a program the assumptions are often completely hidden. As computer programs become able to convey many of their own assumptions and limitations, however, the users will be able to delegate significant parts of their problems with confidence they will be solved as the user wants them solved.

The only step we have made along these lines with DENDRAL programs is to keep a good laboratory notebook, as described above. One of the items we try to make explicit at the time problem solutions are printed is the set of assumptions under which the program arrived at those solutions. Much more remains to be done.

5. CONCLUSION

We do not want to inflate our expectations of future programs to the point that we are bound to be disappointed. On the other hand we cannot remain content with computer programs in which the whole burden of intelligent use is placed on the user. Computer programs will have to contain much more knowledge of the domain and of their own procedures in order to make significant differences in the practice of science.

It is essential to find representations of the knowledge contained in programs that are appropriate for the persons using them and for the experts who help build them. Clever representations for expert problem solving are only half the story of creating intelligent assistants that aid working scientists. Equally important are the representations commonly used in human practice that allow users to determine the scope and limitations of what their assistants can do.

Acknowledgements

These ideas were developed in collaboration with numerous members of the Heuristic Programming Project at Stanford University. I am particularly grateful to Drs. Dennis Smith, Randy Davis, Robert Engelmore, and Tom Mitchell for their help. This work was supported, in part, by the National Institutes of Health (Grant RR-00612) and the Advanced Research Projects Agency (ARPA Order DAHC 15-73-C-0435).

REFERENCES

Amarel, S. (1971). Representation and modelling in problems of program formation, *Machine Intelligence 6*, pp. 165–190 (eds. Meltzer, B. and Michie, D.). Edinburgh: Edinburgh University Press.

Buchanan, B. G., Smith, D. H., White, W. C., Gritter, R., Feigenbaum, E. A., Lederberg, J. and Djerassi, C. (1976). Applications of artificial intelligence for chemical inference XXII. Automatic rule formation in mass spectrometry by means of the Meta-DENDRAL program. *Journal of the American Chemical Society*, **98**, 6168–6178.

Carhart, R. E., Smith, D. H. Brown, H. and Djerassi, C. (1975). Applications of artificial intelligence for chemical inference XVII. An approach to computer-assisted elucidation of molecular structure. *Journal of the American Chemical Society*, **97**, 5755–5762.

Davis, R. (1976). Applications of Meta-Level Knowledge to the Construction, Maintenance and Use of Large Knowledge Bases, Ph.D. thesis in Computer Science, Stanford University.

Dromey, R. G., Buchanan, B. G., Lederberg, J. and Djerassi, C. (1975). Applications of artificial intelligence for chemical inference XIV. A general method for predicting molecular ions mass spectra. *Journal of Organic Chemistry*, **40**, 770–774.

Shortliffe, E. H., Davis, R. (1975). Some considerations for the implementation of knowledge-based expert systems, *SIGART Newsletter*, **55**, 9–12.

Smith, D. H., Buchanan, B. G., Engelmore, R. S., Duffield, A. M., Yoe, A., Feigenbaum, E. A. Lederberg, J. and Djerassi, C., (1972). Applications of artificial intelligence for chemical inference VIII. An approach to the computer interpretation of the high resolution mass spectra of complex molecules. Structure elucidation of estrogenic steroids, *Journal of the American Chemical Society*, **94**, 5962–5971.

Waterman, D. A. (1970). Generalization techniques for automating the learning of heuristics, *Artificial Intelligence*, **1**, 121–70.

Weizenbaum, J. (1976). *Computer Power and Human Reason*. San Francisco: Freeman.

21

The Dialogue Information Logical System

V. M. Briabrin

Computer Centre, USSR Academy of Sciences
Moscow, USSR

Abstract

The general structure and functional features of the Dialogue Information Logical System (DILOS) are considered. The system provides the user with the possibility of natural language communication with the computer. It is intended for the control of typical computational processes: information retrieval, logical analysis, calculation planning and realization. The system is developed at the Computing Center of the Academy of Sciences of the USSR on the basis of the LISP programming language, and transferred to the other computer systems with appropriate adaptation for different LISP versions and input/output environment.

1. INTRODUCTION

During the last 10 to 15 years programming methods have been developed very intensively, and at the present they constitute the relatively stable field of "computer science". The main developments of this science include the theory of formal grammars and translation systems, computer networks and data-bases, the packages of application programs and problem-oriented languages for interaction with them. Different methods have been developed, and many practical systems have been implemented; however there are few ideas now in the air which imply revolutionary changes in the traditional practice of computer utilization.

Science fiction writers, at the very beginning of the computer era created the image of the "supercomputer", capable of speech understanding, and familiar with the general laws of human behaviour, and able to solve almost any problem which is based on logically correct premisses. We are still rather far from the possibility of having a conversation with such a supercomputer, but many scientific laboratories around the world are producing results in this direction.

At the Software Systems Laboratory at the Computing Center of the Academy of Sciences, Moscow, we are engaged in the development of a dialogue system which *understands* written natural language expressions; it *knows* the the basic facts and laws that characterize the area of research; it also *knows how* to analyze and solve specific problems in that area. We would like to stress that the approach described does not ask for another programming language but for another programming style. This style implies that the user provides the system with a verbal description of the initial prerequisites and then poses the problem in question, including a description of the desirable goals. However, it is not necessary to specify an algorithm for the system's behaviour, impelling it to analyse the state of the world, together with the given task description, and to find the solution. The user plays an active role in the process of problem solving. He provides the system with the necessary remarks, interpretations, and preferences, by means of natural language dialogue through a terminal.

We do not expect to attain perfect results immediately. The first goal consists of the development of a practical system using a small number of highly qualified people. The system's structure and the basic software must allow for natural extension, and the attainment of more ambitious results in the future.

2. THE GENERAL CHARACTERISTIC OF THE SYSTEM

The Dialogue Information Logical System (DILOS) is intended to be a mediator between the end-users, such as translators, application programs, data management systems, network interface processors etc, and traditional means of computation. The system consists of a set of programs written in LISP. It controls the following basic operations:

–creation of, and associative search in, the "model data base" which contains the system's "knowledge" about the external world and problem areas (PA);
–initiation of application programs, extraction, and storage of data in application data sets;
–logical analysis of the PA models, development of plans for the calculation
–of specific results, consistency checking when new facts are considered for storage in the model data base etc.

We are trying to make a clear distinction between the process of *specification*, performed by the systems analysts, and the process of *utilization*, performed by the end users. The specification stage when the model data base (MDB) with relevant information about the PA is constructed, is time- and knowledge-consuming; on the other hand, the utilization stage tends to become a rapid and simple method of planning, or getting advice on how to solve the given problem.

DILOS facilities are enhanced by the special linguistic processor which accepts natural language phrases (NL-phrases) at the input and translates them into the formal interface expressions (ϕ-expressions) which control further operations.

The system's "intelligence" is embodied on the one hand in DILOS procedures performing linguistic transformations, information retrieval, logical analysis and calculation planning. On the other hand it is based on the system's "knowledge" about the PAs, represented by the contents of the MDB.

Dialogue communication between the human and the system is the basic idea propagated through all the system's operations. Each processor – linguistic, logical, information-retrieval, or computational – appeals to the user's terminal each time some ambiguity arises, or one of alternative paths has to be chosen. This leads to greater efficiency in the problem-solving process and creates psychological comfort for the user, who is able to understand what is going on.

3. PROBLEM CLASSIFICATION

The system can be applied to different PAs. It is useful to distinguish the following problem classes, which have obvious practical interpretation.

(1) **Model modification**: the process that utilizes information extracted from the input phrases, and transforms it into new knowledge about the world (Fig. 1a). This process is governed by the current MDB contents and could be called the system's "learning", as it results in filling the MDB with the new pieces of knowledge.

(2) **Question-answering**: based on logical analysis and information retrieval from the MDB (Fig. 1b). New knowledge usually does not appear in the MDB during this process. Linguistic and logical analysis are the basic stages in the process of question-answering.

(3) **Calculation planning**: an important part of users' interaction with the system. Given the initial data and a description of desirable results, the system tries to build up an activation sequence of applied programs (Fig. 1c). Such a sequence constitutes an algorithm for solving the specific problem which was not envisaged in advance.

(4) **Action planning**: similar in a sense to calculation planning. Given initial and goal situation descriptions, the system develops a plan of actions by means of which the object of interest could change its position (state) in the desirable direction (Fig. 1d). This process could be called "situation control".

All these processes are intermingled in real problem solving in the sense that they work on the same MDB, and each of them utilizes the same set of general DILOS procedures.

Different research groups concentrate usually on one of the above mentioned processes. For example R. Schank, C. Rieger, C. Riesbek, N. Goldman and S. Veber have developed a "general theory of language understanding", but their systems [1,2] are intended first of all for adequate interpretation of the input text in terms of existing world models. In our classification this corresponds in part to the system's learning and in part to question-answering processes. A similar idea underlies the research of the Soviet school of mathematical linguistic investigating the transformations "meaning" ⇔ "text" [3,4,5].

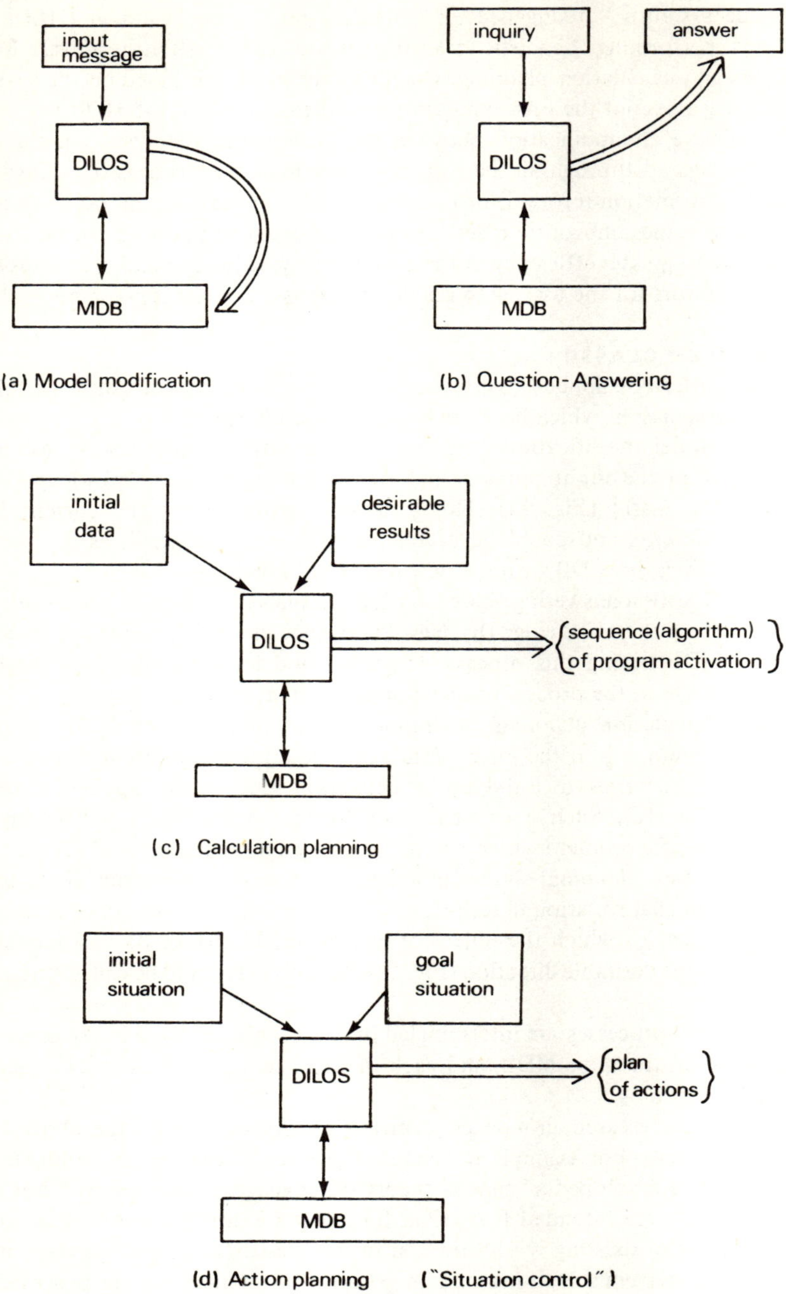

Fig. 1 – Problem classification.

Question-answering systems are being developed successfully by many researchers in the USA (T. Winograd, E. Charniak, G. Hendrix, F. Thompson et al), USSR (Y. Bukchshtav, M. Malkovsky, G. Senin), Japan (H. Nishino, M. Nagao), German Democratic Republic (E. Lehmann), Federal Republic of Germany (H. Lehmann), and other countries [6,7,8]. Most really operational QA's are based on limited lexicons and simple procedures of logical inference. However, complex systems are now at the door.

From our point of view the most interesting prototype of our calculation-planning system is being developed by E. Tyugu and his colleagues in Tallinn [9,10]. Other researchers working in the same field are providing interesting ideas on automatic program synthesis [11,12].

Situation control systems are being developed in the USSR by D. Pospelov, Y. Klykov, L. Zagadskaya and their followers. Their work is now supported by developed theory and a number of practical systems [13,14,15,16].

Thus the principles underlying DILOS rely on the successful research of many different groups in many countries.

We have no intention of reproducing all the useful functions of other systems; rather, we wish to develop the basic procedures and representations which would allow creation of adequate world models and provide solutions to the practical problems of the problem classes mentioned above.

4. SYSTEM COMPONENTS

The general system structure from the end-user's point of view is shown in Fig. 2.

The **Principal Data Base** (PDB) contains the sets of application programs, data files, translators, and other conventional computer instrumentation.

The **Model Data Base** (MDB) is a medium for representation of the system's knowledge about the world. It consists of different divisions each containing a set of objects. An MDB object serves as a carrier for an elementary unit of knowledge. It possesses properties with values; the properties may obtain terminal values or they are used as descriptors for other objects' properties. A particular group of MDB objects is utilized for description of the PDB contents: for example, each application program residing in the PDB has its "representative" in the MDB, the latter carrying all the necessary information about program arguments, results, location in the file system etc.

DILOS is a set of LISP programs, which receives users' messages and interprets them on the basis of MDB contents.

DILOS can modify MDB, generate answers to the user's terminal, initiate application programs etc. Application programs in their turn can produce changes in the PDB, print texts or numbers on the line printers or draw pictures on the plotters; however all such actions are considered to be a side effect of the operation of DILOS.

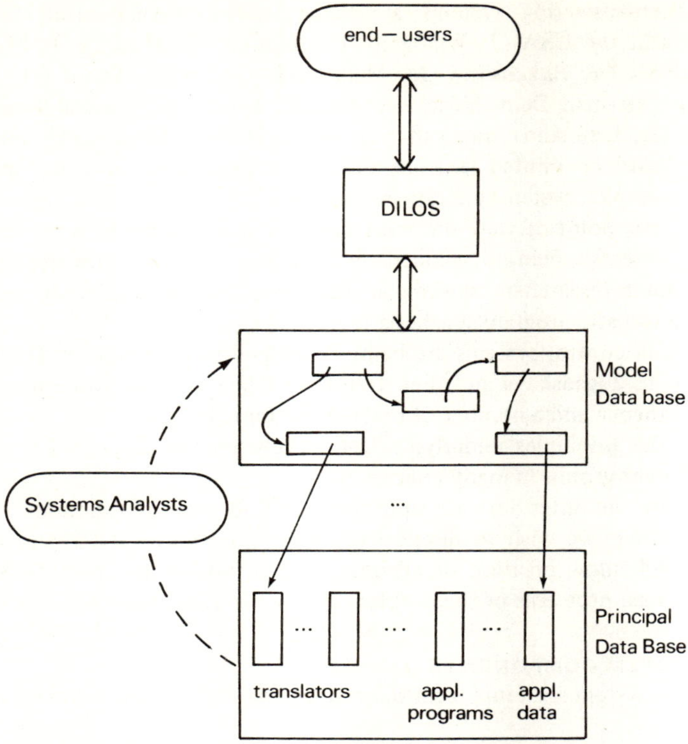

Fig. 2 – System components.

Hence, the computing system has three basic components from the user's point of view: DILOS, MDB, and PDB. With respect to this structure we can consider the process of system specification. The systems analyst has to fill MDB with appropriate objects representing his view of PA. In addition, the corresponding application programs and data should be stored in PDB while the corresponding descriptors find their places in MDB.

MDB specification may be performed in two ways:

(1) by conventional computer methods, such as reading texts from cards, editing from the terminal etc.;

(2) by means of special DILOS functions, providing for the creation and amendment of MDB objects.

The first method is used when a considerable number of homogeneous objects have to fill MDB. The second way is more appropriate for "individualized" storage and modification of MDB objects, such as particular vocabulary entries created by the linguistic processor.

The procedures for automatic learning have not yet been implemented. The procedures will rely on various inductive inference and learning-by-analogy mechanisms.

5. DILOS CONFIGURATION AND FUNCTIONING

All DILOS operations are performed by sets of functions grouped into four basic units called "processors" (Fig. 3):

(1) The **Linguistic Processor** (LingP) transforms input natural language phrases (NL-phrases) into formal inference expressions (ϕ-expressions) that are directed to the other, "executive", processors;

(2) The **Information Retrieval Processor** (InfP) provides object creation, modification, and associative search in MDB, each object possessing a unique name and set of properties which reflect the object's semantics or serve the purposes of the internal system.

(3) The **Computational Processor** (ComP) is for establishing links between MDB and PDB, in particular for the activation of application programs, computation control, and the organization of program interaction through the flow of their results/arguments, and the extraction and storage of application-oriented data sets etc;

(4) The **Logical Processor** (LogP) is the basic part of the system, controlling the logical analysis and modification of the world model. It performs the planning of actions (computations) that lead to the achievement of a desired goal or the calculation of specific results. LogP usually interacts with the other executive processors and could be considered as a complement to LingP in the process of natural language "understanding".

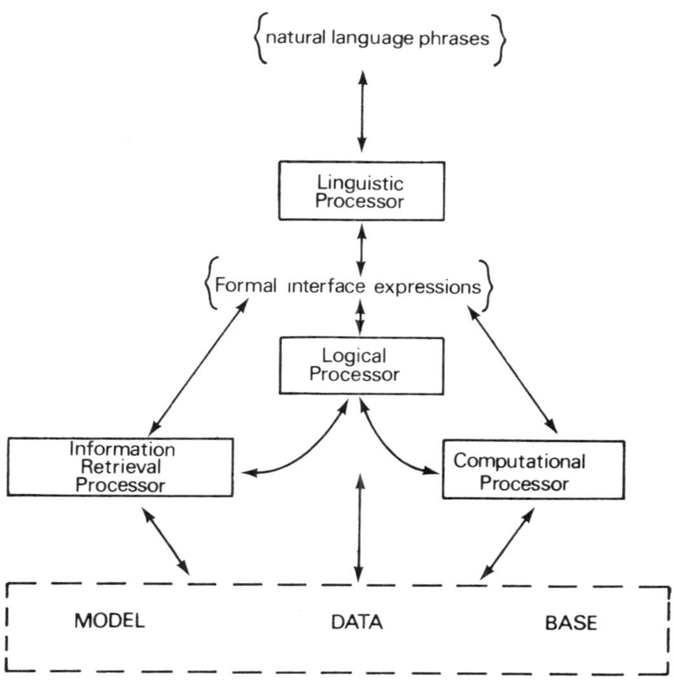

Fig. 3 – DILOS configuration.

The language of the formal interface (ϕ-language), being an input for InfP, ComP and LogP, is essentially a set of top-level LISP-functions. Function calls are generated within program evaluation† thus allowing all DILOS processors to interact with each other as desired.

The end-users (or systems analysts) can also directly access executive processors by simply typing in appropriate function calls instead of NL-phrases, thus bypassing the LingP. This fact is widely used in the process of debugging and MDB specification, when a quick response is essential.

6. KNOWLEDGE REPRESENTATION IN THE MDB

Any problem-oriented world model can be represented in MDB by a set of objects which may appropriately be divided into the following categories:

(1) **Concept classes** (CC) describe abstract sets of objects possessing similar properties. Some CCs serve as "superconcepts" with respect to others – "subconcepts". The basic properties of the superconcepts are projected over the lower-level subconcepts and individual objects, although the latter can possess additional properties.

Examples of CC: "city"; "aircraft"; "polygon"; "clothes",

(2) **Individual objects** (IO) are particular representatives of specific CCs, in the sense that they obtain terminal values for the properties described in a general way within the corresponding CCs. IOs can never be considered as superconcepts, that is, they occupy the lowest level in the hierarchy of super-sub-concepts.

Examples of IO; "Leningrad"; "TU-144"; "triangle ABC"; "my hat".

(3) **Relation descriptors** (RD) characterize semantic relations by means of which CCs, IOs and terminal values can be combined in such a way as to represent a state of a problem-oriented world model. Some RDs can be considered as basic "super-relations" with respect to others – "sub-relations". RDs may also be used in DILOS for the purpose of "theorem" activation considered below. By contrast to the CCs properties which represent the inherent semantics of the problem-oriented model, RDs specify the dynamic, time-dependent links between different objects and values.

Examples of RD: "to exceed"; "to obtain the numerical values"; "to move", "to be allocated in".

(4) **Facts** (F) constitute "knowledge units" constructed on the basis of appropriate RDs. Different objects, values, and other facts may be connected by semantic relations specified by appropriate RDs. Facts usually represent different actions, events, and states of the world.

Examples of facts: "The speed of our airplane exceeds 800 km/hour"; "The parameter D obtains the numerical value V"; "Robot R moves box $B1$ into room $N3$"; "John's house is situated on the outskirts of London".

† A peculiarity of LISP is used in this process: programs are indistinguishable from data and can be generated within other programs for later evaluation.

(5) **Regularities** (R) or theorems† describe the general rules of static and dynamic behaviour of the objects under investigation. A typical regularity could be verbally expressed as the following:
"If a sequence of actions $A_1, A_2 \ldots A_m$ is performed in the presence of facts constructed from relations $R_1, R_2, \ldots R_k$, then another set of facts constructed from relations $Q_1, Q_2, \ldots Q_n$ appear in MDB". We can represent this kind of regularity by the following formula:

$$\{R_1, R_2, \ldots R_k\} \xRightarrow[A_1, A_2, \ldots A_m]{} \{Q_1, Q_2, \ldots Q_n\}.$$

If the actions $A_1, A_2, \ldots A_m$ are omitted from this formula then it corresponds to the ordinary cause-effect relation; other combinations of $\{R\}$, $\{A\}$ and $\{Q\}$ have appropriate semantic interpretations. It is possible, for example, to indicate by means of an appropiate regularity that a combination of "primary" relations $R_1, \ldots R_k$ can produce a "derivative" relation Q.

Examples of regularities: "After the aircraft has landed the unloading procedures commence"; "If in the triangle θ two angles X, Y and the side W opposite Y obtain numerical values then by application of formula $V = W.\dfrac{\sin X}{\sin Y}$ the numerical values for the side V opposite X can be calculated"; "If John doesn't have a whisky at 6 p.m. he loses his sense of humour till the end of the party".

Other researchers introduce different classifications for the objects constituting the world models. For example, in Schank et al (1975), the objects are classified into: (1) general concepts and tokens; (2) events, including actions and states; (3) characteristic features of general concepts and tokens; (4) conceptual modifiers represented by adverbial constructions in natural language; (5) conceptual patterns describing typical events; (6) time relations; (7) inference molecules representing cause-effect relations between events.

Careful analysis reveals that the latter categorization is similar to the one exploited in DILOS, and this is an encouraging factor. It is worth noting that the adequacy of a particular categorization is completely defined by the availability of appropriate mechanisms by means of which the programming system handles the objects of each category.

A fragment of a semantic model is illustrated in Fig. 4. The simplified picture corresponds to a phrase:

"FLIGHT 2172 LANDED AT LENINGRAD AT 19:40".

The various elements of this scheme fall into different categories. For example "means-of-transportation" and "flights" are concept-classes, while "flight-2172" is an individual object in the class "flights". It has properties "type", "pass", and "speed" with appropriate values, the assumption being that these values match the descriptions given in the object "flights".

† The term "theorem" has stuck to our notation owing to the influence of PLANNER.

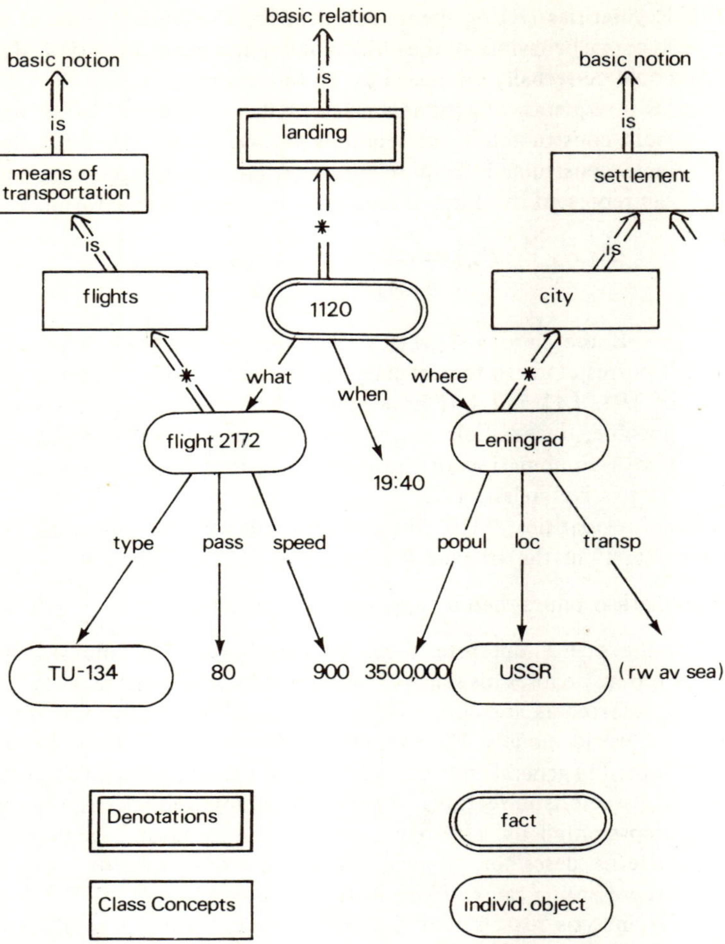

Fig. 4 – A fragment of a semantic model corresponding to the phrase "FLIGHT 2172 LANDED AT LENINGRAD AT 19:40".

A similar chain of concept classes and individual object is represented by "settlement", "city", and "Leningrad". These two chains correspond to the "static" knowledge about the world, and they are bound dynamically by the fact "1120" which is a concrete representative of the "landing" relation. The arguments of this relation "what", "when", and "where" (presumably defined in general form within the "landing" relation description) have actual values "flight-2172", "19:40", and "Leningrad". Thus the essence of this fact is that two individual objects referring to different class concepts, and a terminal value with the meaning day-time are connected by the relation "landing"; the whole thing now corresponds to the specific event described in the input phrase.

Note that the property values of individual objects as well as the argument values of the facts can be represented by *terminal values* (80, 19:40, . . .), *individual object names* (TU-134, Leningrad, USSR, . . .), *fact names* (1120, . . .). The terminal values in DILOS in their turn can be represented by:

–simple numerical or character string values;
–special values designating day-time, calendar time etc.;
–set-values designating enumerable groups of objects;
–range values designating upper and lower limits of numerical values;
–executable values assuming the evaluation of an arbitrary expression which is legitimate in the given system.

The above example illustrates that relation descriptors and concept classes play equal roles in constructing fragments of the semantic model. Similarly, individual objects look externally the same as facts except that they play different roles in representing "static" and "dynamic" knowledge about the world. Moreover, "theorems" in DILOS are also represented in the form of similar MDB objects possessing names and sets of properties, which allow them to be manipulated like ordinary individual objects.

This uniformity of representation is deliberately introduced in DILOS with the purpose of unifying the basic processing functions, and facilitating system portability and maintenance.

7. ϕ-LANGUAGE

According to the DILOS general configuration (Fig. 3) the formal interface language has the following functions:

–it plays the role of the formal output representation in the process of the natural language analysis performed by LingP;
–it serves as a medium of intercommunication between the executive processors LogP, InfP, and ComP;
–it allows end-users to access the executive processors directly, bypassing the linguistic analysis stage.

The above functions require that ϕ-language should be characterized by a number of features including the following:

(1) The expressive means of ϕ-language must ensure sufficient *power* for its usage as a bearer of meaning of the NL-phrases in the process of NL→ϕ transformation. In this role ϕ-language has to be comparable with predicative and relational formalisms [16,17,18].

(2) The ϕ-expressions must be *operational* in a sense that they must comply as much as possible with the actions performed by executive processors over the MDB and PDB contents. This means that the syntax of ϕ-language should be tightly correlated with its pragmatics, namely with the necessity of controlling the various processes in computer system.

(3) The syntax of ϕ-language should be also *concise*, *unambiguous* and *comfortable* for a human accessing the executive processors directly,

without NL→ϕ transformation. Besides that, the end-user has to be able to read and understand ϕ-expressions which are generated dynamically by the system so that the user may verify the correctness of the system's behaviour.

7.1 Relations

Each executive processor has its own set of ϕ-expressions (top-level LISP functions) evaluated in an appropriate way. The most frequently generated expressions are likely to be directed to LogP. The general form of such ϕ-expressions is:

(ADDR ⟨relation⟩)
(DELR ⟨relation⟩) (1)
(CHECK ⟨relation⟩).

The ADDR function tries to enter new facts into MDB, DELR provides deletion, and CHECK performs the search of appropriate facts. However, each of these functions could invoke any other ϕ-expression depending on the actual contents of ⟨relation⟩.

The general syntax of ⟨relation⟩ is as follows:

(prefix : arg0 rel argl ... argk) (2)

⟨prefix⟩ specified the range of a given function, that is, the name of the division of MDB where the action starts†. It could be omitted from (2), in which case the system considers the previously established division as the current one. The rest of ⟨relation⟩ is a generalization of elementary "syntagmatic formulae" which is utilized in the relational RX-language [16]. The meaning of such an expression could be formulated verbally as follows:

An object corresponding to the main argument ⟨arg0⟩ falls into relation ⟨rel⟩ with the objects (values) corresponding to the arguments ⟨argl⟩...⟨argk⟩.

In contrast with the *RX*-language [16] where only binary relations are considered, this system can work with *n*-ary relations, each of arguments ⟨argl⟩, ⟨arg2⟩, . . . usually corresponding to adverbial modifiers in NL-phrases.

Example of relation corresponding to the NL-phrase considered earlier:

```
(*AEROFLOT : flight-2172 landing Leningrad 19:40)
    ↑              ↑         ↑        ↑       ↑
 ⟨prefix⟩       ⟨arg0⟩     ⟨rel⟩    ⟨argl⟩  ⟨arg2⟩
```

Each of the relation arguments could be represented by a terminal value, object name, or another relation thus allowing an arbitrary nesting of relations.

Any relation name ⟨rel⟩ can be connected in MDB with a set of theorems, invoked by appropriate patterns during the evaluation of the ADDR, DELR, and

† During the evaluation process, the system can skip from one MDB division to another.

CHECK functions. Theorem activation can produce different side-effects including the prohibition of the initially requested action. This is implemented through a special "filtering" mechanism which is a part of ⟨relation⟩ processing.

7.2 Semantic Expressions

Another set of ϕ-expressions is processed by InfP. The general form of appropriate functions is as follows:

(ADD	⟨semex⟩)	
(DEL	⟨semex⟩)	
(CHANGE	⟨semex⟩)	(3)
(ADDNEW	⟨semex⟩)	
(FIND	⟨semex⟩).	

The basic difference between ⟨relation⟩ and ⟨semex⟩ is that the latter tends to describe the inherent ("static") semantics of the appropriate objects. The general syntax of ⟨semex⟩ is:

(prefix : property1 ; property2 . . .). (4)

The prefix part plays the same role here as in ⟨relation⟩, but it can include also pattern variables and a list of particular object names which are subject to modification or search operation.

The ⟨property1⟩ ; ⟨property2⟩ . . . part of the semantic expression describes particular properties of the objects which have to be ADDed, DELeted, CHANGEd or are subject to ADDNEW and FIND operations.

Each property consists normally of a pair {⟨indicator⟩ ⟨prop-value⟩} which means that the corresponding object has to possess a given property value under the given indicator. However, when the FIND operation is involved the property can consist also of a single ⟨indicator⟩ or an ⟨indicator⟩ followed by pattern-variables.

Example of FIND expression:

$$\underbrace{\text{(FIND (*CITIES} = W}_{\langle\text{prefix}\rangle}\ :\ \underbrace{\text{loc USSR}}_{\langle\text{property1}\rangle}\ ;\ \underbrace{\text{popul (: 1000000 \$)}}_{\langle\text{property2}\rangle}\ ;\ \underbrace{\text{transp} = Y))}_{\langle\text{property3}\rangle}$$

This expression corresponds to the question "What means of transportation have USSR cities with a population of more than 1,000,000?" The prefix part here contains pattern-variable $=W$ which will obtain the list of city names after completion of the FIND operation. The ⟨property1⟩ and ⟨property2⟩ parts work as the search restrictions, whereas ⟨property3⟩ indicates that we are interested in the values of "transp" property. The pattern variable $=Y$ will be bound to the list of appropriate values after completion of the FIND operation.

7.3 Calculation Planning and Realization

Finally, there is a special set of ϕ-expression directed to ComP. The purpose of the appropriate functions lies in initiating the process for creating sequences of actions (calculations) which lead to achievement of the desired goals.

Two basic functions are used for this purpose:

(ATTAIN ⟨pattern⟩) (5)
(CALC ⟨pattern⟩).

The argument ⟨pattern⟩ usually contains references to a problem area, a description of the initial data and a description of desired results, in the form of a binary relation:

```
(prefix : initial-descr  probl-area  result-descr)      (6)
               ↑              ↑            ↑
              arg0           rel          arg1
```

Thus, an example of the ATTAIN function call, referring to "robot moving boxes", could be the following:

(ATTAIN
(*ROBOTICS:
(, (robot at X) (box-1 at X) (box-2 at Y))
robot-move-boxes
(, (box-2 at Z) (box-1 on box-2)))).

Line 1 here contains function name, while line 2 establishes ROBOTICS as the current MDB division name. Line 3 contains ⟨arg0⟩ represented by a set of three relations which describe the initial situation concerning the position of two boxes and a robot on some surface. Line 4 contains the atom "ROBOT-MOVE-BOXES" which serves as an indicator of ⟨probl-area⟩. Finally, line 5 contains the description of the resulting situation represented by a set of two relations that show the new positions of BOX-1 and BOX-2.

Thus the above example illustrates a formal representation of a particular task to be solved by the system, also the use of nested relations. In the process of executing ATTAIN, the system generates appropriate function calls† and builds up a sequence of actions to be executed later. This sequence is inspected and possibly modified by the end-user, and finally becomes a plan for attaining a desirable goal. The plan is identified by a special ⟨process-identifier⟩.

The constructed plan usually comprises a sequence of special function calls of which the following could be mentioned:

(EX	⟨process-identifier⟩)	
(INIT	⟨appl-progr-descr⟩)	(7)
(RUN	⟨appl-progr-descr⟩)	
(FINISH	⟨appl-progr-descr⟩)	

† Relations constituting ⟨initial-desc⟩ become arguments of CHECK operations, while relations constituting ⟨result-descr⟩ finally become arguments of the operation ADDR.

The first function starts the execution of a computational process identified by ⟨process-identifier⟩. Within this process several different things can happen – for example, brief conversations with the user's terminal about the values of some control variables, extraction of data from MDB/PDB etc.

In particular, functions INIT, RUN, and FINISH provide initialization, execution, and finalization of the appropriate applied program(s) identified by ⟨appl-progr-descr⟩. The latter functions can also be used in stand-alone mode, that is, called directly from the user's terminal or from some other place in the system.

Thus ϕ-language is determined by the set of functions (1), (3), (5), and (7), each group of functions reflecting appropriate pragmatics, that is, actions performed by the corresponding executive processor.

8. IMPLEMENTATION

The system is implemented at the Computing Center of the Academy of Sciences of the USSR on the basis of a LISP translator for the BESM-6 computer [19,20]. The choice of this powerful and elegant programming tool allows us to modify and extend the system's facilities relatively easily. In addition it makes the system portable, as was demonstrated when a sub-version of DILOS was installed on the PDP 11/45 computer at the International Institute of Applied System Analysis (IIASA) in Laxenburg, Austria [21,22].

In Moscow DILOS is exploited under the control of the BESM-6 multi-access system. All application-oriented programs† and data sets are accessed by means of the general operating system utilities, which can themselves be considered as parts of the principal data base. The Model Data Base is also implemented by means of a general file system accessed by built-in LISP functions. The possibility of using a distributed data base is being considered, where some programs and data sets are stored and processed on different computers connected through a network. In such a case copies of DILOS and the corresponding MDBs could be located at the node computers, each "local" MDB containing particular knowledge corresponding to the interests of the owners of that node.

Up to the present (January 1977) the system has been used in an experimental environment for tasks connected with administrative management, new industrial regions development, and computer automated design.

We believe that natural language dialogue in connection with the logical analysis of problem-oriented models and advanced methods of information retrieval and calculation planning will become a widespread instrument of systems analysis and other computer-assisted research.

† Most of the application programs are written either in ALGOL-60, FORTRAN, or PASCAL.

REFERENCES

[1] R. C. Schank (1975). *Conceptual Information Processing.* Amsterdam: North Holland.

[2] Rieger, C. (1975). A mechanism for the interpretation of sentence meaning in context. *Advance Papers, 4th Int. Joint Conf. on Artif. Int (IJCAI-75),* Tbilisi, pp. 143–150. Cambridge Mass; Artificial Intelligence Laboratory, Massachusetts Institute of Technology.

[3] I. Melchuk (1974). *A Theory of Linguistic Models: meaning text.* Moscow: Nauka (in Russian).

[4] E. Paducheva (1974). *On the Semantics of Syntax.* Moscow: Nauka.

[5] T. Korelskaya (1975). *On the Formal Description of Semantical Synonymy.* Moscow: Nauka.

[6] *Proc. of Int. Conf on Artif. Int: QA Systems,* (1975). *CP-76-6* Laxenburg: IIASA.

[7] V. M. Briabrin (1977). Intelligent data-base management system in LISP. *Symbol Information Processing,* **4**, Moscow: Computing Center of the Academy of Sciences.

[8] A. P. Ershov, I. A. Melchuk and A. S. Narin, jari (1975). RITA – an experimental man-computer system on a natural language basis. *Advance Papers 4th Int. Joint Conf. on Artif. Int. (IJCAI-75)* Tbilisi, pp. 387–396. Cambridge, Mass: Artificial Intelligence Laboratory, Massachusetts Institute of Technology.

[9] E. H. Tyugu and M. Unt (1975). Experiments with the computational problem-solver. Delivered but not published, *4th Int. Joint Conf. on Artif. Int. (IJCAI-75)* Tbilisi. Text available from authors, Institute of Cybernetics, Estonian Academy of Sciences, Tallin.

[10] E. H. Tyugu (1970). Problem solving with computational models. *Journal of Computer Mathematics and Mathematical Physics,* **10**, *No. 3.*

[11] Z. Manna and R. Waldinger (1975). Knowledge and reasoning in program synthesis. *Advance Papers 4th Int. Joint Conf. on Artif. Int. (IJCAI-75),* Tbilisi, pp. 288–295. Cambridge, Mass: Artificial Intelligence Laboratory, Massachusetts Institute of Technology.

[12] L. Siklossy and D. Sykes (1975). Automatic program synthesis from example problems. *Advance Papers of 4th Int. Joint. Conf on Artif. Int. (IJCAI–75),* Tblisi, pp 268–273. Cambridge, Mass. Artificial Intelligence Laboratory, Massachusetts Institute of Technology.

[13] Yu. Klykov (1974). *Situation Control in Big Systems.* Moscow: Energiya Pub.

[14] Yu. Klykov and D. Pospelov (eds). Situation Control: theory and practice. *Proc. 1st All-Union Conf on Situation on Situation Control, Voprosy Kybernetika, 13.*

[15] D. Pospelov (1975). Semantic models in Artificial Intelligence, *Advance Papers 4th Int Joint Conf on Artif. Int (IJCAI-75)* Tbilisi, pp. 65–70. Cambridge, Mass: Artificial Intelligence Laboratory, Massachusetts Institute of Technology.

[16] D. A. Pospelov (1975). *Big Systems: Situation Control.* Moscow: Znanie Pub.

[17] J. Tou (ed.) (1972). *Information Systems. 4th Computer Information Science Symposium.* Plenum Press.

[18] E. Sandewall (1972). PCF-2. a first-order calculus for expressing conceptual information. *Computer Science Report.* Uppsala: Computer Sciences Department, Uppsala University.

[19] V. Yufa (1973). Improvements in LISP-BESM-6, *Symbol Information Processing,* **1**, Moscow: Computing Centre of the Academy of Sciences.

[20] V. M. Briabrin and G. V. Senin (1977). Natural language processing within a restricted context, *International Workshop on Natural Language for Interaction with Data Bases.* Laxenburg: IIASA.

[21] V. M. Briabrin (1976). DILOS Reference Manual, *RM-76–52.* Laxenburg: IIASA.

[22] V. M. Briabrin (1977). Natural language access to a model data base, *IIASA Internal Publication.* Laxenburg: IIASA.

[23] V. M. Briabrin et al. (1970). PULT – BESM-6 multiple access system, *Trans. on Computer Mathematics,* **6**, Moscow: Computer Centre of the Academy of Sciences.

NATURAL LANGUAGE

22

Natural Language for Interaction with a Database

G. V. Senin

Computing Center, USSR Academy of Sciences, and
Department of Numerical Mathematics and Cybernetics
Moscow State University, USSR

INTRODUCTION

The Dialogue Information Logical System (DILOS) has been developed for the purpose of serving as an "intelligent" mediator between the user and the set of applied programs and data modules [1]. The system is written in LISP, and it could be divided functionally into several parts called "processors". Three executive processers are activated by the "formal interface expressions" (ϕ-expressions), and they perform logical inference, information retrieval, and calculation planning/realization. Thus ϕ-language constitutes one possible medium for users' communication with the system.

The special Linguistic Processor (LingP) is a front-end part of the system intended for the transformation of the input natural language phrases (NL – phrases) into the corresponding ϕ-expressions. We present here a short description of LingP operation and its underlying principles.

RESTRICTED CONTEXT

The problem of natural language (NL) understanding has always been considered a difficult one because it was believed that a processing system should operate successfully in a practically infinite context and handle a gigantic variety of individual lexicons. However, we accept the hypothesis that natural language communication with a computing system, which is intended for specific problem-solving, involves rather restricted lexicon and context, and this frame is sufficient for creating an NL processor by comparatively simple means.

In fact, any system that "understands" NL, is characterized by the context in which it "places" the user. If we put some restrictions, lexical or grammatical, on the input language, then the latter ceases to be "natural".†

† Therefore, NL understanding either implies complete knowledge of grammar, or is semantic-oriented, that is, it is determined by world knowledge, not linguistic.

We distinguish between the following kinds of context:

(a) The *general context* is defined by the purposes and possibilities of the whole system; part of that is NL recognition. In our case the context is connected with the pragmatics of data base (DB) management and with the data representation. It means each input phrase tends to be converted into a meaningful ϕ-expression, leading to some operation on the data base contents.

(b) The *local context* is specified by the particular knowledge of the given problem area (PA), that is, by a restricted world model. Such context is represented by the set of class concepts, relations, and inference rules as well as by individual objects and facts, which reside in the current data base division (file).

(c) Finally, the *current context* emerges as the "story" of the user's communication with the system and includes the previous user's phrases and their interpretation by the system; in particular, concrete individuals, facts, "situations", described by the user and as a rule kept temporarily in the DB.

Thus, the system's reaction would be relevant only if inputs are pragmatic, problem-oriented, and correctly refer to each other.

While using ϕ-language as an input one, this means the correctness of the ϕ-inputs syntax and semantics.

While using NL, the context is appealed to indirectly, through a vocabulary that expresses knowledge of language in terms of the above mentioned context.† So the amendment of vocabulary can be considered as teaching the system the language in the given context frame.

VOCABULARIES

Thus, LingP operates in the restricted environment defined by the general, current, and some specific local contexts.

Any two vocabularies, first of all, can differ in the latter, that is, they can be adjusted to a different PA. Besides that, a vocabulary (VOC) is characterized by the language of communication (English, Russian etc.) as well as by the user, which "starts" the VOC and works with it (naturally, each user has his own style of conversation, lexicon, and so on).

Hence, vocabulary may be considered as a function of three parameters: $V(A,L,U)$, where A is a specific problem area, L – an NL, U – a user. All the information in vocabularies is segmented "along" these parameters, and in each session the LingP is to be adjusted to some PA, language, and user.

Such an approach permits:

(a) Restriction of the lexicon of each vocabulary, and, therefore, a reduction in the time of word retrieval.

† Of course, a vocabulary should contain also some linguistic (grammatical) knowledge.

(b) Simplified description of the sense of some words.
(c) Avoidance or reduction of homonymy.

The defects of this organization are (1) that much memory is expended and (2) that the LingP is scarcely able to adjust itself to some individual VOCs.

So it is reasonable to unify several VOCs with similar contents.†

It is not expedient to unify two VOCs with different A or L, because in this case the above mentioned requirements (a), (b), (c) are not satisfied.

On the contrary, it is convenient to unify "by users", since lexicon and style of conversation of several users, working within the same PA, almost coincide.

It is worth noting that, generally speaking, the hierarchy of the vocabularies is as necessary as their segmentation; that is, drawing the common lexicon out of several specially-oriented VOCs.

In DILOS the formal mechanisms for that is a division-subdivision structure.

THE GENERAL PRINCIPLES OF NL → ϕ TRANSFORMATION

Let us consider LingP interaction with an Information Retrieval Processor (IRP). The general syntax of a ϕ-expression directed to IRP looks as follows [3]:

$$\Big(\langle\text{func-name}\rangle\,\langle\text{div-name}\rangle\begin{Bmatrix}\langle\text{obj-names}\rangle\\ \langle\text{var}\rangle\end{Bmatrix}:\begin{Bmatrix}\langle\text{restriction}\rangle\\ \langle\text{prescription}\rangle\end{Bmatrix};\ldots\Big) \tag{1}$$

⟨func-name⟩ defines the type of operation (FIND, ADD, DEL, ...). ⟨div-name⟩ sets up the scope of operation to be performed; that is, it establishes a current data base division name; ⟨obj-names⟩ put further restrictions on the scope of operation requiring that it should be applied only to the objects with the given names. If ⟨var⟩ is used instead of the ⟨obj-names⟩ then all objects of the current division participate in the operation.

⟨restriction⟩ is represented usually by the pair ⟨ind⟩⟨val⟩ implying that a required object should possess the given value ⟨val⟩ under the given indicator ⟨ind⟩. ⟨prescription⟩ is represented by the pair ⟨ind⟩⟨var⟩ impelling the system to extract the value of ⟨ind⟩ property from a given object and assign it to the variable ⟨var⟩. ⟨ind⟩ could be represented by an atom or a list;

⟨val⟩ – by an atom, a list, a number, an interval, or a set of values.
⟨var⟩ is a pattern variable designated by = ⟨identifier⟩.

Example:

$$(\text{FIND}\ \underbrace{\text{CITIES}}_{\text{div-name}}\ \underbrace{= X}_{\text{var}} :\ \underbrace{\text{LOC USSR}}_{\text{restr 1}}\ ;\underbrace{\text{POPUL 1.0}}_{\text{restr 2}}\ ;\underbrace{\text{INDUST} = Y}_{\text{prescr}})$$

† For the LingP implementation in DILOS (see the next section) the operation of vocabulary unification has a simple formal definition: if $V_1 = V(A_1, L_1, U_1)$ and $V_2 = V(A_2, L_2, U_2)$, then $V_3 = V_1 \cup V_2$ has a lexicon, unifying as sets lexicons of V_1 and V_2, and each entry contains under the corresponding indicators (S-type and code) homonymic unification of the indicator values from the entry in V_1 and V_2 (see in DILOS [3] value type "set" of the form (, ...)).

In the process of NL $\rightarrow \phi$ transformation an attempt is made to tackle each word from the input string in such a way that is would help to fill an appropriate position in the ϕ-expression which becomes an output of LingP.

Thus a phrase "what industries have the USSR cities with population 1M?" has to be transformed into a ϕ-expression as in the above example. For this purpose a problem-oriented vocabulary (which is a part of the data base) should contain appropriate entries for the words from the input phrase. Each word has among other properties two that are most essential:

(a) *Internal code*, substituting the given word in the constructed ϕ-expression; this property often refers to a local context.
(b) *Semantic type* (S-type) usually designates the role played by the given word in the general context (compare [2]).

The analysis is directed by the augmented transition network (ATN) where each node contains *preconditions* allowing transitions from one state to another and *predictions* about the likely S-types of the words which can occur in the current state.

Preconditions could be connected with:

(1) features (properties) of the current input symbol, particularly its S-type;
(2) contents of the "registers" (variables) reflecting the history of input phrase processing.

Of course, an input phrase could contain "unknown" words which are not found in the vocabulary. A special arrangement is made for dealing with such words, and we shall discuss it later.

ATOMIC S-TYPES AND THEIR COMBINATIONS

Each word possibly has one of the following elementary (or atomic) S-types:

i – plays the role of ⟨ind⟩ in ϕ-expression;
v – plays the role of ⟨val⟩;
q – designates interrogative word; impels to introduce the ⟨var⟩ in ϕ-expression;
p – punctuation mark; such a word or character usually serves for transition to another state (changing expectations);
or – separator of alternatives;
leq, greq – substitutors for the words, designating "$\leqslant$" and "$\geqslant$" relations;
fn – plays the role of ⟨func-name⟩;
fl – plays the role of ⟨div-name⟩;
n – plays the role of ⟨obj-name⟩;
c – designates a "superconcept" of an object;
aa – designates an additional action (for example, calculation of minimum, maximum, average, etc.);
last – marks the end of the text.

Generally speaking, S-type does not depend directly on the syntactic properties of a word or its "ordinary" semantics, but it is entirely defined by the above-mentioned contexts. For example, if we consider a local context describing the employees of an institution, then LingP possibly has to deal with the following words and their S-types:

S-type ("get") = S-type ("salary") = i
S-type ("sit") = S-type ("room") = i
S-type ("earlier") = S-type ("before") = leq.

There exists an approximate correspondence between the words and their senses (reflected in S-types). This could be one-to-one correspondence, that is, "i word → i sense2", but three other cases could also emerge:

(1) *Auxiliaries*, that is, words with "less than atomic" sense are processed during the pre-editing stage (see below).
(2) *Composites*, that is, words with "more than atomic" sense are assigned sequences of atomic S-types (in the form of LISP-lists). When encountering such a word the input string processing is suspended until all atomic senses constituting the composite sense are tackled in a proper way. Afterwards the input string processing is resumed.

Examples:

oldest = most + age → aa + I
who = what + person → q + c
woman = person + sex + female → c + i + v

(3) *Homonyms*, that is, words with multiple (alternative) senses s1, s2, ... are represented by the lists which have the form: (, S1 S2 ...). We shall call it "a list of alternative senses" (LAS).

Each homonym creates a branch point (BP) in the input string processing. All the necessary information is stored in BP; then the first (the next) element from LAS is extracted and treated as a possible S-type of the current word. If the following processing becomes upset for some reason, then the analysis backtracks to the BP, restores all the necessary information, and tries to handle the next alternative from LAS.

Besides the three above-mentioned cases, some words may be declared as "unimportant", they are assigned "null" S-type, and LingP ignores them in the process of input string analysis (for example, articles, some prepositions etc.).

PROCESSING OF UNKNOWN WORDS

The system can deal with the unkown words in two modes.

(a) In "*careful*" mode, the system interrogates the user about each unknown word, stores the information received in the vocabulary (if the user encourages the system to do it), and proceeds with normal analysis.

(b) In "*careless*" mode, all the unknown words are assigned "null" S-type, impelling the system to ignore them at the first scan. But the analysis proceeds from this moment exactly as in the case of homonyms, except that the LAS content emerges not from the vocabulary but from the ATN state in which the corresponding unknown word was encountered. As mentioned above, each ATN state contains predictions about S-types, which are "acceptable" in this state, and these predictions become a source of LAS contents.

Thus in careless mode each unknown word creates a new BP leading the system to backtrack to this point if the analysis fails in the future.

When all the alternative LAS are exhausted and there is still no success (LingP or the user is unhappy with the constructed ϕ-expression) then we have two possibilities:

– to cease processing at the current BP (that is, backtracking allows only 1 level back, not more, to be jumped);
– to backtrack along the entire tree of alternatives with an attempt to consider all the possibilities created by homonyms and unknown words.

The first decision seems to be more applicable when an input phrase contains a small portion of homonyms and unknown words, because "verification" of alternatives produced by one BP usually takes place before the next BP will be established.

The user can help the system deal with unknown words in careless mode by defining some of them. In this case both modes are adjoined into one.

NL – SENTENCE → ϕ-EXPRESSIONS CORRESPONDENCE

In this version LingP receives the input text from the user by portions, and in each input there can be many phrases, which are to be processed one by one. One of the previously-established symbols serves as end-marker for each phrase.

Each NL-phrase is mapped into exactly one output ϕ-expression except the following cases:

(a) "*Preliminaries*": Execution of the "basic" expression is possible only after some preliminary actions.
Example: Who gets more than Brown?
Preliminary: How much does Brown get?
Basic: Whose salary is more than the one just found?

(b) "*Additions*": After execution of the basic expression some additional actions are necessary.
Example: What is the average salary of RDD laboratory employees?
Basic: What are the salaries of RDD laboratory employees?
Addition: Compute the average of the numbers found.

When the situations relating to (a) and (b) are recognized, the corresponding

ϕ-expressions are generated and pushed into the special stores ("preliminary" store and "addition" store). After terminating the analysis, all preliminaries are executed first, then the basic expression is processed and after that all additions are executed.

After the ϕ-interpretation of the current portion and the corresponding operations on the DB, LingP is ready to take another portion.

PRE-EDITING STAGE

Words, marked in the vocabulary as "auxiliaries", are processed before the principal block of translator starts operation. In the vocabulary the following information is connected with such words:

(a) What is the "master" of the given word, to which it "adds" its sense?
(b) What is the "summary" sense of the two words?

As a rule, auxiliaries are predicates and syntactically govern its master. The master is usually represented at the entry by means of its syntactic and possibly semantic properties.

If the master is found in the sentence it acquires the "total" sense. The aux-word in this case is excluded from the input string and does not participate in further considerations.

The following NL word classes can be considered as auxiliaries.

– prepositions and postpositions,
– articles;
– elements which are used within analytical forms of verbs, adverbs and adjectives;
– possibly, some adverbs, adjectives, etc.

It is worthy of note here that marking a word as an auxiliary is guided by consideration of convenience and uniformity of further analysis rather than by linguistics, and on the whole is determined by the pragmatic purposes of the system.

CONCLUSION

Two basic features are inherent in DILOS:

– the uniformity of internal data representation,
– the independence of basic procedures from data base contents.

Relating to LingP processing, it means, that all VOC's are stored apart from the programs, which do not explicitly use the VOCs' contents. This allows the system to translate from one language to another by its adjustment to corresponding VOC.

Furthermore, the ATN is also kept as one of the DILOS divisions, being written uniformly. Hence, LingP is rather flexible, because of the possibility of being adapted for special purposes by slight ATN amendment without changing the basic programs.

We have performed the first tests of the system in Russian and English, and the results encourage us to develop it further.

REFERENCES

[1] Briabrin, V. M. and Pospelov, D. A. (1975). DILOS: dialogue system for information retrieval, computation and logical inference. *Proc. Int. Conf. on Art. Int.: QA Systems.* Laxenburg: IIASA.

[2] Codd, E. F. (1974). Seven steps to rendezvous with casual users. *Data-base Management* (eds. J. W. Klimbie and K. L. Koffeman), Amsterdam: North Holland.

[3] Briabrin, V. M. (1976). DILOS Reference Manual. *IIASA R.M.-76-52.* Laxenburg: IIASA.

23

AI Work in the Computer Centre of the Siberian branch of the USSR Academy of Sciences

A. S. Narin'jani

Computer Center, Siberian Branch USSR Academy of Sciences
Novosibirsk, USSR

Abstract

AI research in Novosibirsk Computer Center is limited to two main subjects:

(1) Non-deterministic model of behaviour control (for movement of a stepping robot).
(2) Natural language for human-computer interaction. This includes:
   (i) Development of a structured multi-level formal model of natural language syntax.
   (ii) Formal means for presentation of semantic information. Software support for this.
   (iii) Application systems for analysis of natural language interrogation of a simple data base.

INTRODUCTION

The activity of our AI group includes first the use of natural language for man-machine interaction, and second a non-determinisitic approach to robot control in complex environments. It is a small three-man project and for the last four years our work has centred on the construction of simple models of walking robots on complex surfaces.

THE ROBOT PROJECT

Stepping over pits with maximal non-determinism.

This model has three principal levels of control, as follows:

(a) The *bottom level* is a behaviour generator; that is a directed graph, in which the vertices correspond to different states of the robot (individual points of the discrete space of the states or some generalized states), and each arc from the state S_i to the state S_j corresponds to some elementary act of control which is possible for the robot in the state S_i and transfers it into the state S_j. The bahaviour generator has only those arcs and vertices which are incorporated either in cycles or in the paths entering the cycles. All other states are excluded, thus guaranteeing absence of a priori deadlocks.

Each non-terminating path in the generator corresponds to some line of behaviour in ideal conditions without any obstacles. In general, such a behaviour line is irregular and does not correspond to that which we usually call "a gait", although of course every gait is a particular case of cyclic path in the graph.

(b) The *middle level* is a look-ahead mechanism, its task being to mark out a "corridor" of allowed behaviour for the bottom level. This corridor is planned for several steps ahead and takes into account all main details of the surface at the given distance, plus the values of some external parameters of control (speed, the height of the platform, "the co-efficient of caution", etc.). The corridor must be as wide as possible, yet guarantee the absence of "dynamic" deadlocks due to particularities.

(c) The *top level* is for planning the route. It is not connected directly with the stepping feature or with the non-determinism of the lower levels, and it was included in the model only for the sake of completeness for demonstrations.

Progress so far is as follows:

(a) The behaviour generator: we have tried three different approaches to control a sufficiently general method which could be synthesized for comparatively complex models.

- Direct presentation of the discrete space of the states. In fact it is reduced to the general problem of compact presentation of a multi-dimensional function, which in our case is the space of all possible states.
- Description of that function with some system of predicates. Such a system turns out to be most unwieldly, even for simple models.
- Reduction version, whose main component is some base set of representative states, chosen so that each (or almost each) permissible state could be traced to one of the base states with a simple procedure. So far, the generators obtained were too reduced to give sufficient non-determinism.

(b) Look-ahead: our attempts to find a method to define "the corridor" in precise form were successful only for the simplest cases, so we were forced to look for some heuristic approach. Now we use a simple mechanism, which can be described in brief as a set of several behaviour lines which are realized simultaneously and are ahead of the real position of the robot. If some of the lines come to a deadlock, another grows a new "branch" from a point several states back, and the "dead branch" is pruned.

These look-ahead lines fill the corridor and are used as a support for the control to define a way for moving along the corridor.

(c) Planning the route: in the beginning we used Bellman's algorithm for a defined optimal route for a "black-white" map of the range. Planning was therefore on the basis of complete information. Now it is not so simple: the range is presented with a three-dimension map, and the robot knows only what it has seen or can see at the particular moment. It defines some subgoal and moves to it to see more, and then defines the next subgoal.

THE NATURAL LANGUAGE PROJECT

Our natural language project (NL) covers three main fields of interest:

(i) Syntax: linguistic model of natural language, formal means suitable for description, formal model for the syntax of Russian.
(ii) Semantics: formal means to shape semantic information and to work with it.
(iii) Application systems (AS): this direction makes it possible for us to be active in the wide gap between the syntax and semantics fields, to probe and use practical concrete results from (i) and (ii).

AS development is planned as a sequence of AS versions with NL input at first and dialogue capabilities in the future.

We began with a simple data base which understood NL queries. The simple data base here is merely a list of objects with a standard set of attribute values, that is, personnel files, catalogues of goods or industrial shipment, etc.

A user may use "min", "max", "average", $>$, $\geqslant$, $<$, $\leqslant$, $=$, $\neq$, "number of", "sum" without syntax or vocabulary limitations on queries. So he is able to ask a question such as: "How many holders of Ph.D.'s older than average and earning less than $10,000 work in the computer science department?"

A toy system which can answer queries of that type with the attributes "name", "wages", "position", "subdivision", "year of birth" was worked out, programmed, and debugged by the author and our chief programmer D. Levin. The process took no more than two weeks, owing to the following:

(a) As an implementation language we used SETL, an ultra-high-level language designed by Prof. Schwartz of N.Y. University, on our BESM-6 computer.

(b) The object-world of our data base is so primitive that it allows the system to understand queries using only the semantic information and the order of words in input sentences. The system needs no syntactic analysis to understand most of the queries, even rather cumbersome ones. When processing a query the system takes into account only semantically significant words and completely ignores the rest. After the substitution of significant words with corresponding semantic symbols and the exclusion of non-significant words, the system (with the help of a simple two-stack mechanism) constructs a formula defining the program to compute an answer for the given query.

This experiment brought us to the idea of a "bottom up" style of analysis, under which a system tries at first to understand a query with the help of pure semantics, and only if more than one variant is produced the system turns to syntactic analysis in order to choose among them.

The syntactic analysis has to be as local structurally as possible, because its function is to prove (or to refute) that each of the variants obtained corresponds to the syntactic structure of the sentence. If at some stage only one variant remains unrefuted, the system regards it as the meaning of the given query and stops troubling itself with further syntactic details.

We based our work preceding the experiment on the positional "surface down" scheme of syntactic analysis which is the traditional approach to automatic translation. So the idea of the "reversed" analysis was a real revelation for us as we could see at least three reasons to prefer it to the "standard" way:

(i) It is much more effective: the gain is more noticeable when the object world of the system is smaller.
(ii) It makes it possible to produce a good application system without waiting for a good formal model of NL syntax.
(iii) It makes it possible for a computer to understand a text in "an incorrect form", even "broken" language, if the text is non-ambiguous from the semantic point of view.

Of course, the more complex and wide the object world is, the more complete and detailed syntactic analysis the system needs. If the object-world is complex enough, it needs all the syntax information to resolve the ambiguity of the semantic analysis, or to prove that the input sentence is really ambiguous.

Before the experiment with the toy system our project had only investigated the first domains out of the three enumerated above, and our idea of text processing was formed by the nature of the previous model of syntax. It was a level-to-level position process directed from surface to deep structure under analysis and backward under synthesis.

After the three-year experience, we decided to change our syntax philosophy and to begin at the same time on the third domain; that is, the application systems.

It now seems to us that the analysis ought to be realized by some mixed strategy under which the process is developed simultaneously from the surface inwards and from the semantic level towards the surface with the primacy of the second direction.

Such a process requires that the formal syntactical model is well structured not only in the "horizontal" levels of representation but also in the hierarchy of constituents of a phrase. It allows analysis as a synchronous interaction of concurrent processes of analysis of individual constituents.

This has not yet been achieved, but we have launched a project which we hope will result in a sequence of versions of successively increasing power.

Our recent (second) version took much more time to implement than the first one. It is a transitional version, not as "toy" as the previous one, but without the complete scheme of "backward" analysis, and its object world corresponds to the original simple data base.

The analysis in this version has two levels. The first one carries out preliminary processing: it recognizes word-complexes with the elementary meanings for this data base (such as "greater-than-or-equal-to", "twenty-three-point-five", or "project-leader"). The second level combines semantic and partial syntactic analysis. Both levels are realized by the same program mechanism, using two different sets of rules. Each of the sets is a binary context-dependent grammar of constituents where the context is limited to the elementary constituents for this level.

All "lines" of the analysis are carried out simultaneously by a process which can be defined as "parallel" and "non-deterministic". As in the toy version, every ultimate constituent obtained as one of the results of the analysis corresponds to a formula which can be translated into a program to compute the answer to the query. If the system obtains no ultimate constituents it answers that it does not understand the query, and when the analysis gives two or more different formulas the query is recognized as ambiguous. Only in the case of a single result does the system assume that the query has only one meaning and that this meaning corresponds to the obtained formula. This second version is almost finished and corresponds in its recent form to the scheme shown as Fig. 1.

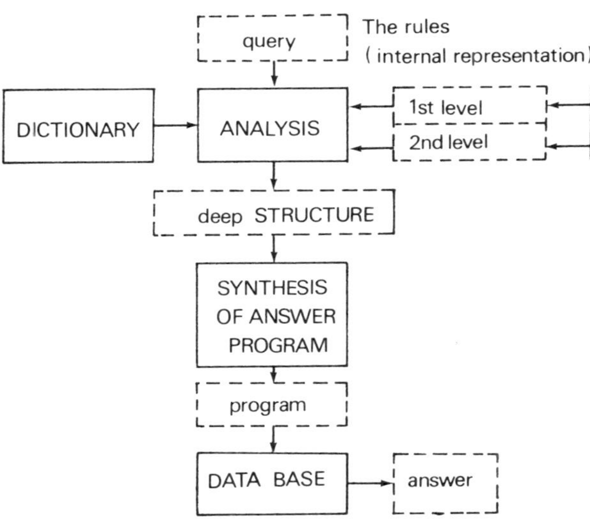

Fig. 1.

This is an experimental system: we intend to use it for two main purposes: to probe and perfect the program mechanism and to debug the linguistic model, that is, the complex of rules.

To make the second task easier, the system is provided with a preprocessor-editor which permits work with the rules in their external "natural" form while the program uses them in their internal representation. The deep structure here is a tree of constituents including all the semantically significant lexemes.

As stated above, this recent version is a transitional one: we regard it as the next version in embryo.

(a) The grammar it uses, that is, the binary context-dependent grammar of constituents, is too low-level to be convenient for a linguistic model. We believe that it would not be high-level enough even with an arbitrary context and constituents with a gap allowed. We think that a grammar combining the constituent structure with a dependency tree would be more adequate, and we hope to have a corresponding mechanism in the next version.

(b) The recent version does not use semantic and syntactic analysis as two separate processes to realize the "reversed" scheme. More exactly, it permits the use of the scheme, but the methods of the semantic analysis are too weak and eclectic in this version to regard it as an autonomous stage.

For the next version we plan a separate and more powerful semantic analysis module which will include a special data base and an inference mechanism for the description of the object world, and active use of this information for the analysis. This will help to make it more universal and will facilitate its orientation for a particular object world. We hope that it will be possible to use this data base for the recognition of the equivalence of deep structures.

(c) We plan that the next, that is, the third, version will be ready in two years, during which time the linguistic group will consider some comparatively simple variants of the syntax model and attempt at the same time, in cooperation with mathematicians, to find a complex of formal constructions which would be high-level enough to permit "natural" and compact formalization of the model.

24

Purposive Understanding

R. C. Schank and G. DeJong

Computer Science Department
Yale University, USA

1. INTRODUCTION

For the past ten years we have been working on the problem of getting a computer to understand natural language. In the beginning, work centred on the problem of parsing. We built an early version of a parser that mapped from English into a language-free representation of the meaning of input sentences (Schank and Tesler, 1969). Simultaneously we worked on the meaning representation itself. We developed Conceptual Dependency which represents meaning as a network of concepts independent of the actual words that might be used to express those concepts (Schank, 1969).

Over the years the parser and the representation evolved as we began to understand the complexity of the problem with which we were dealing. Conceptual Dependency began to rely more on underlying primitives for the representation of the similarities in meaning that transcend the particular words of a language (Schank, 1975). Similarly, our parser developed into a program that relied less on syntactic information to aid it than on predictions that could be obtained by exploiting the properties of the conceptual representation into which we were mapping (Riesbeck, 1975).

We began at this point to worry about the possible use of the conceptual parse that we were producing. We built an inference program (Schank and Rieger, 1974) that exploited the properties of the primitive concepts uncovered by the parser and derived new information from them. These inferences then added information to the conceptual content extracted by the parser. One problem with the inferencer was that it was hard to control. It made inferences without regard for their need. This was part of Rieger's (1975) theory of inferences, but its effect on our programs was to make them rather purposeless and slow.

At this point we developed a theory of understanding of connected text. Part of the problem that we had with controlling inference was due to the fact that we had been working on sentences taken out of context. Sentences considered in the context of the rest of the text in which they were contained in a sense pointed the way towards the appropriate and necessary inferences. Thus, an inference was considered to be crucial if it helped to tie together the sentences of a text. The end product of such an inference procedure was a connected causal chain of events that represented the implicit and explicit information in a text (Schank, 1974).

At this point we began to program a computer understanding system that would attempt to process input texts. An item crucial to our ability to accomplish this task was what we called a script. A script is a frequently repeated causal chain of events that describes a standard situation. In understanding, when it is possible to notice that one of these standard event chains has been initiated, then it is possible to understand predictively. That is, if we know we are in a restaurant then we can understand where an "order" fits with what we just heard, who might be ordering what from whom, what preconditions (menu, sitting down) might have preceded the "order", and what is likely to happen next. All this information comes from the restaurant script.

The method of processing text outlined above is analgous to that used in parsing. Once we have a well-defined idea of what belongs in the conceptual representation we can determine what is missing and go back into the text to look for it. Thus in both parsing and script application, processing is bottom up until enough information is available to allow the switch to top down.

The program we built to understand texts by the use of scripts is called SAM and is described in Schank et al. (1975), Schank and Abelson (1977) and Cullingford (1977). The program works on the domain of newspaper stories. It does a tremendous amount of detailed processing including inferencing, reference specification, disambiguation, and memory simulation. The program can produce summaries, long paraphrases, translations into other languages as well as answer questions about the input story.

SAM is a very complicated program. It attempts to understand exhaustively and completely. Because of this SAM has two major problems: First, it is rather slow. Although there are ways in which it could be speeded up, it is not at this point the kind of program one would want to have running all the time on one's system. Second, it is a bad simulation of how people actually read newspapers. We built SAM to test out our ideas about how people read as well as to attempt to get a program to read. Obviously there are many kinds of texts besides newspapers, but there is a common basis to reading that transcends what you read. However, we began to wonder if there wasn't something special about newspaper reading that we could exploit so as to build a faster and thus more useful program.

One obvious thing is that people tend to read newspapers with a purpose. They do not read every article nor do they read every word of the articles that they choose to read. People skim until they decide to read in detail.

It seemed reasonable to us to attempt to model this skimming process, using what we had learned about the process of understanding in general. In other words we set out to build a program that would be an extremely top down system. It would know what it wanted to know or what it was interested in and go out and look for it. Finding what it wanted would cause it to generate new goals to find related information that would amplify what it had found. This purposive understanding program we named FRUMP for Fast Reading and Understanding Memory program.

UNDERSTANDING WITH A PURPOSE

Although there undoubtedly are people who read every word in their daily newspaper, most people do not. The usual procedure is to scan the paper for items of interest, perhaps by starting in a relevant section of the paper, or else by starting randomly. When an interesting headline is found then the reader begins to read. He may read in several modes:

(1) If the story is a completely new one, he may read every word until he becomes tired or the article is finished.
(2) If the story is an update of a currently running story, he may scan for the new information present in the story.
(3) If the story is of a generally continuing nature, he may go quickly through it, looking for items relevant to his particular interests.
(4) If the story is in the reader's domain of special interest, he may read every word and make all possible inferences.

These four modes of reading exemplify four very different processes. Completely new stories occur somewhat less frequently than the others. Examples might be earthquake reports, plane crashes, assassinations, the introduction of a new bill in the legislature, a special announcement by a political figure. Mode 1 stories have usually a "one-time-only" nature, or else they are the beginning of a continuing story.

Mode 2 stories usually contain little if any new information for someone who has kept up to date on the story. Newspapers are written in such a fashion that people who have not kept up can still figure out what was going on. Thus, for example, recent long-running stories in the news such as the Patty Hearst kidnapping or the Philadelphia Legionaires' disease, continually retell the initial setup of the story in each subsequent report. Readers who already know these facts skim them to search for new developments. Often these developments are told in the headline and lead paragraph, and readers will stop there.

Mode 3 stories are probably the most common type of newspaper story. Continuing situations such as the Middle East situation or the energy shortage are problems about which there are usually one or two new developments per week in peak periods, drifting down to a few items a month in slower periods. Some of these kinds of updates occur only once or twice a year in a situation that is very long-term, for example, stories about high taxes and socialism in Sweden.

To read a mode 3 story, a reader must have an interest in the situation in general, along with one or more specific interests related to the situation. Thus a businessman might be interested in the possibilities for trade with Israel and nothing else about the Middle East. Similarly, a socialist might want to read only about the successes of the government in Sweden and care little about party infighting, for example. Such a goal-oriented reader is easier to simulate than a more passive reader. If we know what we are looking for, we can go in and find it. We need not be disturbed by the complications involved in reading where we have no interest. An obvious advantage for computers here is that we also need not put in all possible knowledge for a situation, where situation is defined very broadly. Rather, by limiting our domains of reading ability to those that coincide with what we are interested in, we solve both the problem of too broad domains causing unbounded amounts of knowledge to be needed and the problem of having to do a lot of useless work to read stories or parts of stories in which we have no interest.

Mode 4 corresponds most to what we normally assume to be the process of reading. However, as we have been arguing, this "normal" reading mode may not occur all that often in newspaper reading. It might occur for reading columnists, or reports of a game in which a favourite team is playing, or other special interest kinds of things.

The four modes correspond to our programs as follows:

mode 1 – this is what SAM does
mode 2 – this is what FRUMP does in update mode
mode 3 – this is what we are designing FRUMP to do
mode 4 – this is what the ultimate reading program would do.

An important point here is that there is a class of stories that we described as being mode 1 that are best read by a FRUMP-type program rather than by a SAM-type program. That is, new events such as car accidents or earthquakes need not always be read for all the detail they contain. Thus, we decided that FRUMP's first task would be in the area of mode 1 stories. Next we worked on updating those stories by quick skimming (mode 2). We are aiming eventually for mode 3 ability in FRUMP.

THE GENERAL STRATEGY

We will assume that a reader should approach a newspaper story as follows:

1. Reading headlines

We have four options here:

(a) quit and forget
(b) quit and remember
(c) go on in a careful detailed manner
(d) go on and skim.

2. Skimming

(a) old story recognized: fill in and update information

(b) new story: scan for concepts predicted by the domain of the story
(c) any story: scan for key concepts of special interest.

3. Updates

(a) look for the continuation of a previously instantiated script
(b) look for unfulfilled expectations from the last reading
(c) look for update-specific problems (for example, the death toll mounts in an earthquake each day).

4. Special interest concepts

(a) instantiate scripts specific to special interest
(b) begin reading carefully when a key concept is found.

A FRUMP RUN

With the above in mind we began to build FRUMP. FRUMP was designed to work on mode 1 and mode 2 kinds of news stories. In theory, when it becomes interested is something it could send control to SAM; however, we have not actually tried to implement this.

To demonstrate its understanding, FRUMP produces summaries of what it has read. Since its basis is language-free Conceptual Dependency type scripts, its summaries can come out in any language, thus Russian and Spanish summaries are produced in addition to English ones. FRUMP's scanning ability is based on abstracting out the principles behind SAM. It is by no means a key-word parser. Its parser is connected to the scripts that it has which describe news situations. It only looks at what it is interested in, ignoring the rest. It is thus a very fast program. FRUMP can understand and produce a brief summary of a 150-word news article taken directly from a newspaper in about 5 seconds of CPU time on a DEC KA10 processor.

To give an idea of FRUMP's capabilities we will now show an example of a run of FRUMP:

Sample run of FRUMP

INPUT:

10–11 CHIHUAHUA, MEXICO, – A PASSENGER TRAIN CARRYING TOURISTS, INCLUDING SOME AMERICANS, COLLIDED WITH A FREIGHT TRAIN IN THE RUGGED SIERRA MADRE OF NORTHERN MEXICO, KILLING AT LEAST SEVENTEEN PERSONS AND INJURING 45, THE POLICE REPORTED TODAY.

THEY SAID THAT AT LEAST FIVE OF THE INJURED WERE AMERICANS, AND THERE WERE UNOFFICIAL REPORTS THAT ONE OF THE DEAD WAS FROM NEW YORK CITY.

SOME OF THE PASSENGERS WERE TRAVEL AGENTS, MOST FROM MEXICO CITY, MAKING THE TRIP AS PART OF A TOURISM PROMOTION, THE POLICE SAID.

THE AMERICAN SOCIETY OF TRAVEL AGENTS HAD BEEN MEETING IN GUADALAJARA, THOUGH IT WAS NOT KNOWN WHETHER ANY OF THE GROUP WERE ABOARD THE TRAIN.

ONE OBSERVATION CAR ON THE RAILROAD TO THE PACIFIC TUMBLED INTO A 45 FOOT CANYON WHEN THE PASSENGER TRAIN SMASHED INTO THE FREIGHT YESTERDAY AFTERNOON NEAR THE VILLAGE OF PITTORREAL ABOUT 20 MILES WEST OF CHIHUAHUA CITY AND 200 MILES SOUTH OF THE UNITED STATES BORDER, THE POLICE SAID.

THEY SAID THAT RESCUE WORKERS WERE STILL TRYING TO PRY APART THE CAR'S WRECKAGE TO REACH PASSENGERS TRAPPED INSIDE. THE RESCUE SQUADS COULD NOT USE CUTTING TORCHES ON THE WRECKAGE BECAUSE SPILLED DIESEL FUEL MIGHT IGNITE, THE POLICE REPORTED.

```
SELECTED SKETCHY SCRIPT $VEHACCIDENT

DONE PROCESSING
SATISFIED REQUESTS:

((<=> ($DATELINE LOC &DLOC MONTH &MON DAY &DAY)))
&DLOC
          CLASS          (#LOCATION)
          LOCALE         (*MEXICO*)
          SATISFIED      ((10) (11))
&MON
          NUMBER         (10)
          SATISFIED      (NIL (11))
          CLASS          (#NUMBER)
&DAY
          NUMBER         (11)
          SATISFIED      (NIL NIL)
          CLASS          (#NUMBER)

((<=> ($VEHACCIDENT VEH &VEH OBJ &OBJ LOC &LOC)))
&VEH
          CLASS          (#PHYSOBJ)
          TYPE           (*VEHICLE*)
          SROLE          (&TRAIN)
          SCRIPT         ($TRAIN)
          SATISFIED      ((10) (11))
&OBJ
          CLASS          (#PHYSOBJ)
          TYPE           (*VEHICLE*)
          SROLE          (&TRAIN)
          SCRIPT         ($TRAIN)
          SATISFIED      ((10) (11))
```

```
&LOC
        CLASS         (#LOCATION)
        LOCALE        (*MEXICO*)
        SATISFIED     ((10) (11))

((ACTOR &DEADGRP TOWARD (*HEALTH* VAL (-10))))
&DEADGRP
        NUMBER        (17)
        SATISFIED     ((10) (11))
        CLASS         (#PERSON)

((ACTOR &HURTGRP TOWARD (*HEALTH* VAL (-LT10))))
&HURTGRP
        NUMBER        (45)
        SATISFIED     ((10) (11))
        CLASS         (#PERSON)

CPU TIME = 7.522 SECONDS

SUMMARY:
17 PEOPLE WERE KILLED AND 45 WERE INJURED WHEN A TRAIN
CRASHED INTO A TRAIN IN MEXICO.
```

HOW FRUMP WORKS

The basis of FRUMP is the script. However, rather than using a script like SAM's, FRUMP uses what we call a sketchy script. The crucial difference is that sketchy scripts have far fewer conceptual dependency representation (only those corresponding to the most important events in SAM's scripts) and more often than not, the causal connections between conceptualizations are not included. The result is that FRUMP understands most of what is important to understand in news articles and works very much faster than SAM. The article of several paragraphs that takes SAM a quarter of an hour to understand can be processed by FRUMP in under ten CPU seconds.

When FRUMP begins to read a newspaper story, it already knows what facts it wants to find. For each type of newspaper story, FRUMP has a list of expected facts that it wants to see. These expectations are called "requests". The collection of all the requests for one type of story makes up the "sketchy script" for that story type. In the remainder of the paper, when we refer to a script we will mean FRUMP's sketchy scripts, not SAM's scripts unless otherwise noted.

In understanding an article, FRUMP must select a script and then try to find occurrences in the article of the facts represented by the requests. Requests are in Conceptual Dependency format and contain unfilled slots. These slots are called "script variables". Understanding an article consists of finding the information corresponding to a request in the text and filling in the slots (binding the script variables) in that request. When an instance of one of the requests is found in the text and the script variables have been bound, that request is said to be satisfied. The process of satisfying the requests of a script is called instantiating that script. The number of requests in each script is small. The requests correspond to the most important information in a particular type of story. For example, the vehicle accident script used in the sample run above contains four requests. The first request in the vehicle accident script will be satisfied when FRUMP finds the type of vehicle in the accident, the object that the vehicle collided with, and the location of the accident. FRUMP can satisfy the second request by finding the number of people killed; the third by the number injured, and the fourth by who was at fault in the accident. When all of these requests are satisfied by a story. FRUMP knows all that it wants to know about that news event. The rest of the article will be ignored.

When FRUMP is given a new article to understand it skims the first paragraph for identifying information. This information is used to find the appropriate script to use to understand the article. Once the script is identified, FRUMP begins skimming the article.

FRUMP is composed of two conceptually different parts: a parser and a script applier. The parser FRUMP employs was inspired by Becker's phrasal lexicon (Becker, 1975) which was presented at the TINLAP conference in 1975 but unfortunately was not actively pursued by him after that. The parser parses phrases from the text into Conceptual Dependency representations. The script applier then matches these conceptual representations against the requests in the script. When a match is found, the fillers in the parser representation are used to bind the script variables occurring in the request.

FRUMP uses the same language-free system of representation as is used by Riesbeck's parser (Riesbeck, 1974) which is used in SAM. Yet FRUMP's parser is very different from the parser in the SAM system. The Riesbeck parser parses an entire sentence at a time. There is very little communication allowed with the script applier of SAM during parsing; FRUMP's parser is concerned only with parsing parts of a sentence. In SAM the parser and script applier are very distinct. As a result, each does its thing with little influence over the other. FRUMP, however, is much more integrated. The parser and script applier do different tasks, but the precise division between the two is fuzzy. The advantage of the fuzziness is that the two modules can communicate with each other freely. This allows the script applier to control parsing to an extent not possible in SAM. FRUMP's script applier can tell the parser which of several interpretations is correct or even to stop trying to parse the current input text.

THE CONCEPTUAL FRAGMENT PARSER

FRUMP's parser is very top down. It is driven by the high-level requests of the sketchy scripts and works very closely with the script applier. The parsing strategy is to find conceptual fragments from the input text being skimmed that will satisfy all or part of some script request. Important properties of the actual conceptual referents in the text are then copied to variables in the conceptual representation from FRUMP's dictionary. Finally, this conceptual representation of the meaning of the input text is returned as the parse. Dictionary entries for each word are made up of a list of meaning fragments in conceptual dependency format. For each different meaning there is a series of context tests that must be satisfied before this meaning can be realized as the parse. There are also instructions on how to bind variable role fillers in the conceptual dependency representation. FRUMP has two dictionaries: one is the conceptual fragment dictionary described below; the other contains information about objects and forms and tenses of entries in the other dictionary.

The following is the conceptual fragment dictionary entry for "strike".

```
( (BKWRDS (M1 (TYPE (*VEHICLE*))))
  (FRWRDS (M2 (CLASS (#PHYSOBJ))))
  ((MERGE P1 M1) (MERGE P2 M2))
  ((<=> ($VEHACCIDENT VEH P1 OBJ P2))) )
```

The context tests are arranged in two lists which search backward and forward respectively from the entry word for words that will satisfy the context tests. If a context test is a single word, that word must be present in the input text. If the context test is a list, it is satisfied by finding a word in the input text that has all the properties specified, and copying them to a temporary variable. For example, the first line in the above dictionary entry searches backward from a form of the word "strike" for a vehicle. If it finds one, all the properties of that vehicle are copied to the temporary variable M1, and the forward tests are evaluated. The forward tests require that the word "strike" be followed by a physical object. If all the context tests are satisfied, the properties of the temporary variables are copied to the role fillers in the conceptual representation. This representation is then returned as the parse.

The output of FRUMP's parser is not modified English as it is in Colby's system (Parkinson, Colby, and Faught, 1976), but a language-free conceptual representation. The advantage of a language-free representation is that different phrases with the same meaning will be parsed into the same representation. This in turn means that the test to see if a request is satisfied by a parse is very efficient. It also makes generating summaries in different languages no harder than generating the summary in English.

EXAMPLE OF A SKETCHY SCRIPT

One of the scripts that FRUMP has is a vehicle accident script. All vehicle accidents, whether they are train wrecks, boat collisions, plane crashes etc., have many things in common. In a vehicle accident story there is always a vehicle and there is always an object that it collides with. There is always the possibility that a number of people are killed or injured. In addition, in newspaper stories, the cause of the collision is often reported. These are the important points of a vehicle accident, and these are what FRUMP tries to find out when reading a vehicle accident article. There are, of course, many other things that can happen in a collision. For example, the injured people are often taken to a hospital, for auto crashes there is often a policeman called to the scene etc. These are less important facts, and unless there is some special reason for noticing them, a human skimming the article will usually miss them. FRUMP also ignores these lesser points. The vehicle accident script currently consists of four requests at three important levels.

```
Request R1
  value:  (((<=> ($VEHACCIDENT VEH &VEH OBJ &OBJ LOC &LOC)))
           ((EQU (<=>) $VEHACCIDENT))
           (PROP (<=> VEH) *VEHICLE* TYPE)
           (PROP (<=> OBJ) #PHYSOBJ CLASS)
           (PROP (<=> LOC) #LOCATION CLASS))
  importance: 0

Request R2
  value:  (((ACTOR &DEADGRP TOWARD (*HEALTH* VAL (-10))))
           ((EQU (TOWARD) *HEALTH*)
            (EQU (TOWARD VAL) -10))
           (PROP (ACTOR) #PERSON CLASS))
  importance: 1

Request R3
  value:  (((ACTOR &HURTGRP TOWARD (*HEALTH* VAL (-LT10))))
           ((EQU (TOWARD) *HEALTH*)
            (EQU (TOWARD VAL) -LT10))
           (PROP (ACTOR) #PERSON CLASS))
  importance: 1

Request R4
  value:  (((<=> ($FAULT ACTOR &ACTOR)))
           ((EQU (<=>) $FAULT))
           (PROP (<=> ACTOR) #PERSON CLASS))
  importance: 2
```

Before FRUMP's processing can be understood in detail, one must understand the requests of its sketchy scripts. As a typical example of FRUMP's requests consider request R2 above. The first line of the request is the Conceptual Dependency representation of the request. &DEADGRP is one of variables of the vehicle accident script. (*HEALTH* VAL (−10)) is the Conceptual Dependency representation for dead. When the variable &DEADGRP is bound to something, the meaning of this Conceptual Dependency representation is that the something it gets bound to is dead. The next three lines are constraint tests that are applied to the output of FRUMP's parser. If the parser yields a representation that passes all of these tests, the script variables contained in the request are bound to the corresponding conceptual role fillers in the parser representation, and the request is satisfied. The first test in the example request checks that the filler of the TOWARD role in the parser representation is *HEALTH*. The second test checks that the filler of the VAL slot in the filler of the TOWARD slot is —10. The third test checks that the filler of the ACTOR slot (that is the thing that the parser proposes should be bound to &DEADGRP in the request) is of conceptual type PERSON. This means that the only thing that can be bound to &DEADGRP is a person or group of people. In fact the parser is set up so that only groups will be generated in this slot. One of the important properties of groups is the number of things in them. When &DEADGRP is bound to something, all of its properties are copied over to the script variable &DEADGRP. Therefore one of the pieces of information available from this request after it is satisfied (and indeed the most important datum of this request) is the number of people who were killed. The observant reader will have realized that the first two tests in the request are set off from the third one by parentheses. This is to group the tests by whether or not they involve one of the script variables. The first two tests in the example do; the third does not. The grouping makes the understanding process more efficient. This will become clear in the next section.

HOW FRUMP UNDERSTANDS

Once FRUMP has the correct script to use, it starts to scan the article, looking for conceptual fragment words. When it finds one, it retrieves the dictionary entry for that word. Recall that the dictionary entry consists of a list, each element of which contains context tests and a representation that corresponds to one meaning. FRUMP tries to realize each meaning one at a time until all the context tests are satisfied or the dictionary list is exhausted.

The processing of each dictionary word sense or possible meaning consists of first making a list of all the outstanding requests the conceptual representation of this meaning might satisfy. This is done to avoid evaluating all of the context tests of a word sense that has no chance of satisfying a request, and to limit the number of requests that the parse needs to be matched against. A request is included in the list only if all of the first group of role-filler tests of this request are satisfied. Remember that the first group role-filler tests are all tests that do not reference one of the script variables. Therefore these tests can be made before the script variables or the variables in the context tests are bound. For example, if while processing a vehicle accident story, the parser found a word that indicated ((ACTOR P1 TOWARD (*HEALTH* VAL (—10)))) might be a parse, the list of possible requests would be just (R2). The tests that do not look at script variables require that the <=> filler for R1 be $VEHACCIDENT, the filler of the VAL slot in the TOWARD slot must be —LT10 for R3, and the <=> slot in R4 must be filled with $FAULT. Thus the only request that might be satisfied is R2. If the list is empty, there is no need to evaluate any of the context tests; it cannot satisfy a high-level request. At this point, none of the context tests have been evaluated, so that this word sense might not be correct. However, the list is very cheap to create and usually cuts down on processing later. This is the reason for separating the request tests that reference script variables from those that do not. If the list contains at least one element, the context tests for this meaning are evaluated one at a time. If there is at least one context test that fails, this sense is not a proper reading of the text. If all the word sense fail, the word that was found was a false alarm, and FRUMP reverts to the original scan. If all the context tests are satisfied, the conceptual representation is filled out with the variables bound while evaluating the context tests. This representation is then matched against elements of the list of potentially satisfiable requests made earlier. If one matches, the script variables in that request are bound to the role fillers of the representation, the request is marked with the date of the article, and it is marked as satisfied. At this point, FRUMP can dynamically modify the sketchy script. Associated with each script variable can be a set of demons which are checked when the script variable is satisfied. They can make arbitrary tests and load or delete requests. Thus, it is possible, for example, to have FRUMP look for aid to a country if it is hit by a severe earthquake but not if it was a mild quake. This amounts to high-level inferencing and makes FRUMP much more efficient by eliminating the need to process large numbers of very specialized requests, the specialized requests are not loaded until they are needed. After processing the satisfied request, FRUMP continues its scan for conceptual fragment words. If no request fulfils the detailed match, FRUMP reverts to the original text scan. Notice that there were three ways in which parsing can be discontinued; in these cases FRUMP does just enough work to realize it is working on a bad parse. This is in a large way responsible for FRUMP's efficiency in processing and is directly attributable to the broad communication between the parser and the control structure that makes up the script applier.

When FRUMP has finished processing an article, some requests will have been satisfied but, very likely, others will not. The script has been partly instantiated. This partly instantiated script is then stored on a disk file. If FRUMP should later come across an article updating this news event, it can then retrieve this partly instantiated script and continue satisfying requests where it left off.

DECIDING ON A SCRIPT

Presented with an article FRUMP chooses one of three following ways to process it. First, it can decide that the article is an update of a news event that it has previously processed and select the partly instantiated script from that article to understand with. Second, it can decide that it is the first article of a news event and select the appropriate virgin script. Third, it can fail to recognize the article as one of the types of events for which there exists a script, in which case it will ignore the entire article. The choice is made from information gleaned from a preliminary scan of the article's first paragraph. This scan is made with a special set of active requests.

There is for each script one key request which, if satisfied in the text, strongly indicates that its script is appropriate to understand the article. For example, the key request for the vehicle accident script is ((<=> ($VEHACCIDENT VEH &VEH OBJ &OBJ LOC &LOC))): here &VEH, &OBJ, and &LOC are script variables which get bound to the vehicle, the object collided with, and the location of the accident respectively. Furthermore, owing to the style of newspaper writers, this request seems always to be satisfied in the first paragraph (and usually the first sentence). The special set of requests is therefore composed of the key request from each virgin script that FRUMP has.

The first paragraph is skimmed until one key request is satisfied. FRUMP now knows which script type the story is and also some information about the story. In the case of the vehicle accident it knows what the vehicle and object are and where the accident occurred. This information is used to decide if the current article refers to a previous news event or a new one. After a sketchy script is partly instantiated by the first article of an event, it is stored away. The type of script it is and the key information about the event are stored specially. After a new article's first paragraph is skimmed, the key information gained is matched against all stored scripts of the same type. If a stored, partly-instantiated script is found that matches, it is brought into core and used to understand the new article. If no previous script is matched, a virgin script with no requests satisfied is used to understand the story. When it is finished, FRUMP writes this partly instantiated script out on the disk file so that any update articles that it finds will have access to it.

UPDATING STORIES

There are three main types of update that FRUMP must handle. These types correspond to pieces of information and not to articles, so that an update article can cause more than one type of update to be made. The update types differ from one another by how the new information is added to the partly instantiated sketchy script.

In the first kind of update, information is only added to a sketchy script. That is, a new article is found to refer to the same news event as previous articles and it supplies information that satisfies a request that was never before satisfied. This is the simplest type of update and is handled as follows: After FRUMP finishes an article, the sketchy script is written out to a file with the key identifying information discussed above. Some of the requests will have been satisfied and some will not. All the requests, whether satisfied or not, are written on the file. When this partly instantiated script is read back into core, the unsatisfied requests are, of course, still active. On reading the update article then, this type of update is treated exactly as if it were a virgin script. When a previously unsatisfied request is satisfied, it is marked as satisfied and tagged with the date of the newspaper.

In the second type of update, the information in the update article replaces the information in an already satisfied request. In this type, generally only one request is changed at a time, and the change is a direct modification of one or more role-fillers of the request. All requests, whether satisfied or not, are processed during understanding as if they are not. When the role-fillers of a request are to be bound, the date that they were last bound is compared to the date of the current article. If the current article is later, the fillers are updated. If not, the information from the current article is thrown away.

The third type of update is the most complicated. There are many news event types where an arbitrary number of similar sub-events can occur. These sub-events themselves may be rather complex. For example, an earthquake may be followed by any number of aftershocks. Each aftershock may cause death and injury. The recent fighting in Lebanon was made up of a number of individual clashes. Oil from a leaking tanker can wash ashore in several places at different times, each causing different kinds and varying degrees of damage to the shoreline. There are three things to notice about such updates. First, they add new rather than replace old information. Therefore, they must be processed by as yet unsatisfied requests. Second, the structure of each sub-event can be complex so that it cannot be represented by one request alone. Third, since the initial requests for each sub-event must be the same, there is the possibility for any number of copies of the same request to exist in a script each satisfied by a different sub-event. For example, an earthquake and two of its aftershocks may all cause people to be killed. In this earthquake script, then, there will be three copies of the request ((ACTOR &DEADGRP <=> (*HEALTH* VAL (–10)))) each satisfied with a different &DEADGRP.

The solution to these problems of the third update type is to organize the requests corresponding to sub-events into bundles. The script will always have one fresh copy of the bundle active and completely uninstantiated. When a bundle is about to be partly instantiated (that is, when at least one of its requests is to be satisfied) a copy of the uninstantiated bundle is made and these new requests are added to the script. Then FRUMP continues instantiating the bundle. This enables FRUMP to understand any number of the sub-events. Of course, an article could update an update article (for example, revising the death toll caused by an aftershock of an earthquake). If one of the requests in a particular bundle has to be changed, FRUMP must first identify the bundle. After that the update can be handled exactly as the type two updates above.

Bundles are subsections or scenes of scripts. They are very similar to scripts in many ways. In particular, they can always be differentiated by key information. This key information is often simply the date or location of the sub-event. For example, a newspaper report might update the death toll from last Thursday's aftershock of the earthquake that struck Eastern Turkey five days ago. Five days ago, Eastern Turkey, and the fact that it is an earthquake, are used to find the original script. Within this script, FRUMP then finds the bundle of requests for the proper aftershock by matching the date of each to the date last Thursday. When it finds the correct bundle, FRUMP finds the request corresponding to the number of people killed and updates the proper script variable.

More FRUMP output

The following news stories were taken directly from the *New York Times* and the *New Haven Register*. The Spanish summarizer was written by Jaime Carbonell and the Russian summarizer by Anatole Gershman.

```
INPUT:
     2 - 4 ITALY - - A SEVERE EARTHQUAKE STRUCK
NORTHEASTERN ITALY LAST NIGHT, COLLAPSING ENTIRE
SECTIONS OF TOWNS NORTHEAST OF VENICE NEAR THE
YUGOSLAV BORDER, KILLING AT LEAST 95 PERSONS AND
INJURING AT LEAST 1000, THE ITALIAN INTERIOR MINISTRY
REPORTED.
     IN THE CITY OF UDINE ALONE, A GOVERNMENT SPOKESMAN
SAID THEY FEARED AT LEAST 200 DEAD UNDER THE DEBRIS.
THE CITY, ON THE MAIN RAILROAD BETWEEN ROME AND VIENNA,
HAS A POPULATION OF ABOUT 90000.
     THE SPOKESMAN FOR THE CARIBINIERI, THE PARAMILITARY
NATIONAL POLICE FORCE, SAID THERE HAD BEEN REPORTS OF
SEVERE DAMAGE FROM HALF A DOZEN TOWNS IN THE
FOOTHILLS OF THE ALPS, WITH WHOLE FAMILIES BURIED IN
BUILDING COLLAPSES. COMMUNICATIONS WITH A NUMBER OF
POINTS IN THE AREA WERE STILL OUT.
     THE EARTHQUAKE WAS RECORDED AT 6.3 ON THE RICHTER
SCALE, WHICH MEASURES GROUND MOTION. IN POPULATED
AREAS, A QUAKE REGISTERING 4 ON THAT SCALE CAN CAUSE
MODERATE DAMAGE, A READING OF 6 CAN BE SEVERE AND A
READING OF 7 INDICATES A MAJOR EARTHQUAKE.

SELECTED SKETCHY SCRIPT $EARTHQUAKE

DONE PROCESSING
SATISFIED REQUESTS:

((<=> ($DATELINE LOC &DLOC MONTH &MON DAY &DAY)))
&DLOC
          CLASS          (#LOCATION)
          LOCALE         (*ITALY*)
          SATISFIED      ((2) (4))
&MON
          NUMBER         (2)
          SATISFIED      (NIL (4))
          CLASS          (#NUMBER)
&DAY
          NUMBER         (4)
          SATISFIED      (NIL NIL)
          CLASS          (#NUMBER)
```

```
((<=> ($EARTHQUAKE LOC & LOC SEVERITY &RIC)))
&LOC
        CLASS          (#LOCATION)
        LOCALE         (*ITALY*)
        SATISFIED      ((2) (4))
&RIC
        NUMBER         (6.3)
        SATISFIED      ((2) (4))
        CLASS          (#NUMBER)

((ACTOR &DEADGRP TOWARD (*HEALTH* VAL (–10))))
&DEADGRP
        NUMBER         (95)
        SATISFIED      ((2) (4))
        CLASS          (#PERSON)

((ACTOR &HURTGRP TOWARD (*HEALTH*) VAL (–LT10))))
&HURTGRP
        NUMBER         (1000)
        SATISFIED      ((2) (4))
        CLASS          (#PERSON)

CPU TIME = 9.440 SECONDS
```

RUSSIAN SUMMARY:
ZEMLETRYASENIE SREDNEI SILY PROIZOSHLO V ITALII. CILA ZEMLETRYASENIYA OPREDELENA V 6.3 BALLA PO SHKALE RIKHTERA. PRI ZEMLETRYASENII 95 CHELOVEK BYLO UBITO I 1000 RANENO.

SPANISH SUMMARY:
HUBO 95 MUERTOS Y 1000 HERIDOS EN UN TERREMOTO FUERTE EN ITALIA. EL TERREMOTO MIDIO 6.3 EN LA ESCALA RICHTER.

ENGLISH SUMMARY:
95 PEOPLE WERE KILLED AND 1000 WERE INJURED IN A SEVERE EARTHQUAKE THAT STRUCK ITALY. THE QUAKE REGISTERED 6.3 ON THE RICHTER SCALE.

INPUT:

11 – 29 KATHEKANI, KENYA, – AT LEAST 12 PEOPLE WERE REPORTED KILLED EARLY TODAY WHEN AN EXPRESS TRAIN RAN ONTO A FLOODED BRIDGE WHOSE RAILS HAD BEEN SWEPT AWAY, CRASHED THROUGH IT AND PLUNGED INTO A RIVER IN KENYA.

THE OFFICIAL PRESS AGENCY REPORTED THAT THE DEATH TOLL WAS AT LEAST 12 AND THAT 70 WERE INJURED IN WHAT RAILROAD OFFICIALS CALLED THE WORST PASSENGER TRAIN DISASTER IN EAST AFRICAN HISTORY.

```
SELECTED SKETCHY SCRIPT $VEHACCIDENT

DONE PROCESSING
SATISFIED REQUESTS:

((<=> ($DATELINE LOC &DLOC MONTH &MON DAY &DAY)))
&DLOC
        CLASS        (#LOCATION)
        LOCALE       (*KENYA*)
        SATISFIED    ((11) (29))
&MON
        NUMBER       (11)
        SATISFIED    (NIL (29))
        CLASS        (#NUMBER)
&DAY
        NUMBER       (29)
        SATISFIED    (NIL NIL)
        CLASS        (#NUMBER)

((<=> ($VEHACCIDENT VEH &VEH OBJ &OBJ LOC &LOC)))
&VEH
        CLASS        (#PHYSOBJ)
        TYPE         (*VEHICLE*)
        SROLE        (&TRAIN)
        SCRIPT       ($TRAIN)
        SATISFIED    ((11) (29))
&OBJ
        CLASS        (#PHYSOBJ)
        CONENT       (*RIVER*)
        CPRPS        (*WATER*)
        SATISFIED    ((11) (29))
&LOC
        CLASS        (#LOCATION)
        LOCALE       (*KENYA*)
        SATISFIED    ((11) (29))

((ACTOR &DEADGRP TOWARD (*HEALTH* VAL (-10))))
&DEADGRP
        NUMBER       (12)
        SATISFIED    ((11) (29))
        CLASS        (#PERSON)

((ACTOR &HURTGRP TOWARD (*HEALTH* VAL (-LT10))))
&HURTGRP
        NUMBER       (70)
        SATISFIED    ((11) (29))
        CLASS        (#PERSON)
```

CPU TIME = 9.539 SECONDS

RUSSIAN SUMMARY:
V ZHELEZNODOROZHNOI KATASTROFE V KENII 12 CHELOVEK BYLO UBITO I 70 RANENO.

SPANISH SUMMARY:
HUBO UN ACCIDENTE DE FERROCARRIL EN KENYA QUE RESULTO EN 12 MUERTOS Y 70 HERIDOS.

ENGLISH SUMMARY:
A TRAIN CRASH CLAIMED 12 LIVES AND INJURED 70 IN KENYA.

INPUT:

3 – 4 PISA, ITALY – OFFICIALS TODAY SEARCHED FOR THE BLACK BOX FLIGHT RECORDER ABOARD AN ITALIAN AIR FORCE TRANSPORT PLANE TO DETERMINE WHY THE CRAFT CRASHED INTO A MOUNTAINSIDE KILLING 44 PERSONS.

THEY SAID THE WEATHER WAS CALM AND CLEAR, EXCEPT FOR SOME GROUND LEVEL FOG, WHEN THE US MADE HERCULES C130 TRANSPORT PLANE HIT MT. SERRA MOMENTS AFTER TAKEOFF THURSDAY.

THE PILOT, DESCRIBED AS ONE OF THE COUNTRY'S MOST EXPERIENCED, DID NOT REPORT ANY TROUBLE IN A BRIEF RADIO CONVERSATION BEFORE THE CRASH.

SELECTED SKETCHY SCRIPT $VEHACCIDENT

DONE PROCESSING
SATISFIED REQUESTS:

```
((<=> ($DATELINE LOC &DLOC MONTH &MON DAY &DAY)))
&DLOC
        CLASS         (#LOCATION)
        LOCALE        (*ITALY*)
        SATISFIED     ((3) (4))
&MON
        NUMBER        (3)
        SATISFIED     (NIL (4))
        CLASS         (#NUMBER)
&DAY
        NUMBER        (4)
        SATISFIED     (NIL NIL)
        CLASS         (#NUMBER)

((<=> ($VEHACCIDENT VEH &VEH OBJ &OBJ LOC &LOC)))
```

```
&VEH
        CLASS         (#PHYSOBJ)
        TYPE          (*VEHICLE*)
        SROLE         (&AIRPLANE)
        SCRIPT        ($AIRPLANE)
        SATISFIED     ((3) (4))
&OBJ
        CLASS         (#PHYSOBJ)
        CONENT        (*MOUNTAIN*)
        SATISFIED     ((3) (4))
&LOC
        SATISFIED     ((3) (4))
        CLASS         #LOCATION
        LOCALE        (*ITALY*)

((ACTOR &DEADGRP TOWARD (*HEALTH*) VAL (—10))))
&DEADGRP
        NUMBER        (44)
        SATISFIED     ((3) (4))
        CLASS         (#PERSON)

CPU TIME = 6.778 SECONDS

RUSSIAN SUMMARY:
V AVIATSIONNOI KATASTROFE V ITALII 44 CHELOVEK BYLO
UBITO.

SPANISH SUMMARY:
HUBO 44 MUERTOS CUANDO UN AVION CHOCO CONTRA UN
MONTANA EN ITALIA.

ENGLISH SUMMARY:
44 PEOPLE WERE KILLED WHEN AN AIRPLANE CRASHED INTO A
MOUNTAIN IN ITALY.
```

CONCLUSION

We are now hooking up FRUMP to the United Press International wire service. We intend to produce a system that will know about the interests of the users logged in to it and will provide them with summaries of events that they care about as soon as they happen.

Our intention is to produce a practical working Artificial Intelligence program. We do not see FRUMP as the solution to all the complexities of language understanding. It is certainly not a replacement for SAM in anything except an immediate practical sense. However, it does have some theoretical validity of its own. When people skim they use some but not all of the reading techniques available to them. FRUMP, in a sense, has abstracted out the essence of SAM. Viewed in that way it is analogous to how skimming abstracts out the essence of reading. That is, FRUMP both works and tests out a theory. We view it as a success.

Acknowledgements

The research described in this paper was supported by the Advanced Projects Agency of the Department of Defence and monitored by the Office of Naval Research under Contract N0014-75-C-1111.

REFERENCES

Becker, J. (1975). The phrasal lexicon. *Proc. Theoretical Issues in Natural Language Processing Workshop*, pp. 70–73. Cambridge, Mass.: Bolt, Beranek and Newman.

Cullingford, R. E. (1977). Organizing World Knowledge for Story Understanding by Computer. Ph.D. thesis. Department of Engineering and Applied Science, Yale University.

Parkinson, R., Colby, M., and Faught, W. (1976). Conversational Language Comprehension Using Integrated Pattern-Matching and Limited Parsing. *Technical Report*, UCLA Psychiatry Department, Los Angles, California.

Rieger, C. J. (1975). Conceptual memory and inference. *Conceptual Information Processing*, pp.157–268 (ed. R. C. Schank). Amsterdam: North Holland Publishing Company.

Rieger, C. K. (1975). Conceptual analysis. In *Conceptual Information Processing*, pp. 83–155 (ed. Schank, R. C.). Amsterdam: North Holland Publishing Company.

Riesbeck, C. K. (1974). Computational Understanding: Analysis of Sentences and Context Ph.D. thesis. Stanford University. Also *AI Memo AIM-238*. Stanford: Artificial Intelligence Laboratory, Stanford University.

Schank, R. C. and Abelson, R. P. (1977). *Scripts, Plans, Goals and Understanding: An Inquiry into Human Knowledge Structures.* Hillsdale, New Jersey: Lawrence Erlbaum Associates.

Schank, R. C. and Yale, A. I. (1975). Project. SAM – A Story Understander. *Research Report 43*, Computer Science Department, Yale University.

Schank, R. C. (1975). *Conceptual Information Processing*. Amsterdam: North Holland Publishing Company.

Schank, R. C. (1974). Understanding Paragraphs. Technical Report. Castagnola, Switzerland: Instituto per gli studi Semantici e Cognitivi.

Schank, R. C. and Tesler, L. (1969). A conceptual parser for natural language. *Proceedings of the International Joint Conference on Artificial Intelligence*, Washington D.C., pp. 569–578 (eds. D. E. Walker and L. M. Norton). Bedford, Mass.: The Mitre Corporation.

Schank, R. C. (1969). A Conceptual Dependency Representation for a Computer-oriented Semantics. Ph.D. thesis. University of Texas.

Schank, R. C. and Rieger, C. K. (1974). Inference and the computer understanding of natural language. *Artificial Intelligence*, Vol. 5, pp. 373–412.

AUTHOR INDEX

References are to text of chapters, not to the bodies of bibliographies.

SUBJECT INDEX

THE MACHINE INTELLIGENCE SERIES . . .

The Machine Intelligence Series occupies a unique and universally recognised position in the world literature. The books have evolved from the unbroken sequence of now-famous Workshops conducted by the editor-in-chief Donald Michie, each planned to its own theme and organised as a carefully structured and cohesive source book.

No rigid demarcations are imposed between new results and tutorial overviews, which two elements are so blended as to stimulate and at the same time to instruct.

Novel discoveries and trends are set into a solid background of exposition, and related to previous knowledge in such a way as to serve an advanced tutorial function. No work can be a classic at the time of its publication, but some of the contributions are classics in the making.

The combined bibliographies put into the reader's hands the keys to virtually everything which is yet known in this subject.

MACHINE INTELLIGENCE

Editor-in-chief: Professor Donald Michie, Professor of Machine Intelligence, University of Edinburgh

Volumes 1–7 published by Edinburgh University Press, and in the USA by Halsted Press (a division of John Wiley and Sons, Inc.).

Volume 8 onwards published by Ellis Horwood Limited, Chichester, and in the USA by Halsted Press (a division of John Wiley and Sons, Inc.).

MACHINE INTELLIGENCE 1 (1967)

Contents: Abstract Foundations
Theorem Proving
Machine Learning and Heuristic Programming
Cognitive Processes: Methods and Models
Pattern Recognition
Problem-Oriented Languages

MACHINE INTELLIGENCE 2 (1968)

Contents: Abstract Foundations
Mechanised Mathematics
Machine Learning and Heuristic Programming
Cognitive Processes: Methods and Models
Problem-Oriented Languages

MACHINE INTELLIGENCE 3 (1968)

Contents: Mathematical Foundations
Theorem Proving
Machine Learning and Heuristic Programming
Man-Machine Interaction
Cognitive Processes: Methods and Models
Pattern Recognition
Problem-Oriented Langauges

MACHINE INTELLIGENCE 4 (1969)

Contents: Mathematical Foundations
Theorem Proving
Deductive Information Retrieval
Machine Learning and Heuristic Programming
Cognitive Processes: Methods and Models
Pattern Recognition
Problem-Oriented Languages
Principles for Designing Intelligent Robots

MACHINE INTELLIGENCE 5 (1970)

Contents: Prologue
Mathematical Foundations
Mechanised Reasoning
Machine Learning and Heuristic Search
Man-Machine Interaction
Cognitive Processes: Methods and Models
Pattern Recognition
Principles for Designing Intelligent Robots
Appendix

MACHINE INTELLIGENCE 6 (1971)

Contents. Perspective
Program Proof and Manipulation
Mechanised Reasoning
Heuristic Paradigms and Case Studies
Cognitive and Linguistic Models
Approaches for Picture Analysis
Problem-Solving Languages and Systems
Principles for Designing Intelligent Robots

MACHINE INTELLIGENCE 7 (1972)

Contents: Prehistory
Program Proof and Manipulation
Computational Logic
Inferential and Heuristic Search
Perceptual and Linguistic Models
Problem-Solving Automata

MACHINE INTELLIGENCE 8: Machine Representations of Knowledge (1977)

Contents: Knowledge and Mathematical Reasoning
Problem-Solving and Deduction
Measurement of Knowledge
Inductive Acquisition of Knowledge
Programming Tools for Knowledge-Representation
Dialogue-Transfer of Knowledge to Machines
Dialogue-Transfer of Knowledge to Humans
Case Studies in Empirical Knowledge
Perceptual Knowledge
World-Knowledge for Language-Understanding

MACHINE INTELLIGENCE 8:

Machine Representations of Knowledge

Edited by: Professor E. W. Elcock, Department of Computer Science, University of Western Ontario
and
Professor Donald Michie, Director, Machine Intelligence Research Unit, University of Edinburgh

A compact account of recent advances by leading investigators, concerning the important problem of representing human knowledge in formal schemes, so that it can be assimilated, manipulated and 'understood' by machines.

No previous book gathers together into a single compass such a range of studies on the unitary theme of knowledge-representation in its bearing on machine intelligence.

"a good survey . . . if your library users are seriously interested in machine intelligence, then you should have this volume."

– *Choice* (USA)

"a widely-based collection . . . readers who are commonly and principally concerned with machine intelligence would be well advised to purchase MI8 for themselves"

– Godfrey Harrison in *British Journal of Psychology*

"it can be recommended . . . unlikely to date"

– Brian Meek in *Quantitative Society Newsletter*

Readership: Professional and Research Workers, and Advanced Students in:

Computer and Information Science
Artificial Intelligence
Psychology
Psycholinguistics
Linguistics
Philosophy
Bio-mathematics
Neurology
Bio- and Brain Science

ISBN 085312 058 7

COMPUTERS AND THEIR APPLICATIONS

Series Editor: Brian Meek, Director, Computer Unit,
Queen Elizabeth College, University of London

Aims to provide up-to-date and readable texts on the theory and practice of computing, with particular (though not exclusive) emphasis on computer applications. Preference is given in planning the series to new or developing areas, or to new approaches in established areas.

The books will usually be at the level of introductory or advanced undergraduate courses, suitable as course texts, and written wherever possible for industrial and commercial workers. Together they will provide a valuable nucleus for a computing science library.

INTRODUCTORY ALGOL 68 PROGRAMMING

D. F. Brailsford and A. N. Walker, Department of Mathematics, University of Nottingham.

Teaches the elements of computers through the use of Algol 68. Develops programming style and skill in the context of real-life problems.

SOFTWARE ENGINEERING

K. Gewald, G. Haake and W. Pfadler, Siemens AG, Munich

Introduces a new engineering discipline based on an industrial research project aimed at widening knowledge on methods and equipment in the field.

FUNDAMENTALS OF COMPUTER LOGIC

D. Hutchinson, Department of Computer Science, University of Strathclyde

Helps the reader analyse logic circuits with insight into their design. Worked design examples with complete circuit diagrams related to computer parts.

INTERACTIVE COMPUTER GRAPHICS IN SCIENCE TEACHING

Editors: J. McKenzie, Dept. of Physics & Astronomy, University College London
L. Elton, Head, Institute of Technology, University of Surrey
R. Lewis, Head of Educational Computing, Chelsea College, London

Records experience of National Development Programme CAL project, presenting interdisciplinary teaching packages as subject-specific material for physics, chemistry and biology. Covers technical matters of computers.

SYSTEMS ANALYSIS AND DESIGN FOR COMPUTER APPLICATION

D. Millington, Department of Computer Science, University of Strathclyde

Sets out foundations of systems developed and follows through the task to be performed. Discusses tools and techniques. A sound introduction.

GUIDE TO PROGRAMMING PRACTICE

Edited by: Brain Meek, Director, Computer Unit, Queen Elizabeth College
Patricia Heath, Plymouth Polytechnic

A compact guide to all aspects of a programmer's work. Discusses problems, guides on choice of facilities, program documentation, maintenance. Specially recommended for trainee programmers.

RECURSIVE FUNCTIONS IN COMPUTER SCIENCE

R. Peter, formerly Professor of Mathematics, University of Budapest

Relates the theory as it exists in the fundamental mathematical theory of computation to actual uses of recursive constructs found in programming language.

AUTOREGRESSIVE ALGORITHMS

L. J. Slater, Department of Applied Economics, University of Cambridge, and
H. M. Pesaran, Trinity College, Cambridge

A statistical background with numerical examples of such calculations for teaching and study. Lists and describes 4 Fortran programs developed for such study.

CLUSTER ANALYSIS ALGORITHMS

Helmut Späth, Professor of Mathematics, Oldenbourg University

A useful unification of the problems involved in application. Interspersed with discussion of techniques, adequately documented FORTRAN programmes, 21 sub-routines and examples.

Of related interest . . .

COMPUTATION GEOMETRY FOR DESIGN AND MANUFACTURE

I. D. Faux and M. J. Pratt, Cranfield Institute of Technology

Outlines mathematical techniques available for the representation, analysis and synthesis of shape information by a computer.

COMPUTER AIDED DESIGN AND MANUFACTURE

C. B. Besant, Imperial College of Science and Technology, University of London

Introduces CAD and CAM from basics of computers to applications in real engineering draughting design and manufacture. Describes both hard- and software.

The 9th Machine Intelligence Workshop. The proceedings of which are recorded here, was made possible by the generosity of A.I. Council of the U.S.S.R. Academy of Sciences, the Leningrad Academy of Sciences and the Edward Fredkin Foundation.